R. I. Payton

KENT HISTORY PROJECT

1

TRAFFIC AND POLITICS

The Construction and Management of
Rochester Bridge, AD 43–1993

KENT HISTORY PROJECT

ISSN 1352–805X

Volumes in progress

Kent to AD 800, ed. Alec P. Detsicas

Kent 800–1220, ed. Richard Eales

Kent 1220–1540, ed. Nigel Ramsay

Kent 1540–1640, ed. Michael Zell

The Government of Kent 1640–1914, ed. H.C.F. Lansberry

The Economy of Kent 1640–1914, ed. Alan Armstrong

Religion and Society in Kent 1640–1914, ed. Nigel Yates

Kent since 1914, ed. Alan Armstrong and Nigel Yates

A History of Rochester Cathedral, ed. Paul A. Welsby and Nigel Yates

TRAFFIC AND POLITICS

The Construction and Management of Rochester Bridge, AD 43–1993

EDITED BY

NIGEL YATES AND JAMES M. GIBSON

THE BOYDELL PRESS

ROCHESTER BRIDGE TRUST

First published 1994
The Boydell Press, Woodbridge, and
Rochester Bridge Trust

ISBN 0 85115 356 9

The Boydell Press is an imprint of Boydell & Brewer Ltd
PO Box 9, Woodbridge, Suffolk IP12 3DF, UK
and of Boydell & Brewer Inc.
PO Box 41026, Rochester, NY 14604-4126, USA

British Library Cataloguing-in-Publication Data
Traffic and Politics:Construction and Management of
Rochester Bridge, AD 43–1993. – (Kent History Project;No.1)
I. Yates, Nigel   II. Gibson, James M.   III. Series
942.2323
ISBN 0–85115–356–9

Library of Congress Cataloging-in-Publication Data
Traffic and politics : the construction and management of Rochester
Bridge, AD 43–1993 / edited by Nigel Yates and James M. Gibson.
p.   cm. – (Kent history project, ISSN 1352–805X ; 1)
Includes bibliographical references and index.
ISBN 0–85115–356–9
1. Rochester Bridge (Rochester, England)   2. Bridges – England
– Kent – Medway River – History.   3. Rochester (Kent, England)
– Buildings, structures, etc.   4. Rochester (Kent, England) – History.
I. Yates, Nigel.   II. Gibson, James M. (James Melvin), 1948–   .
III. Series.
TG58.R63T73   1994
388.1'32'09422323 – dc20   93–50852

This publication is printed on acid-free paper

Printed in Great Britain by
St Edmundsbury Press Ltd, Bury St Edmunds, Suffolk

Contents

List of Tables   vii
List of Figures   viii
List of Plates   x
Preface   xiii
Introduction   xv
Notes on the Contributors   xvii

Rochester Bridge, AD 43–1381   *by Nicholas P. Brooks*   1
    Origins   3
    Sub-Roman and Early Anglo-Saxon Times   12
    Later Anglo-Saxon Times   16
    Reconstruction of the late Anglo-Saxon Bridge   21
    The Territory of the late Anglo-Saxon Bridge   26
    The Bridge from 1066 to the 1380s   35

Rochester Bridge, 1381–1530   *by R.H. Britnell*   41
    The New Bridge   43
    Maintenance and Rebuilding   60
    Income   76
    Administration   92

Rochester Bridge, 1530–1660   *by James M. Gibson*   107
    Decline of the Medieval System   109
    The Elizabethan Commissions   118
    The Elizabethan Statutes   130
    The Civil War and Commonwealth   156

Rochester Bridge, 1660–1825   *by David Ormrod*   161
    The Trade and Navigation of the Medway Valley   163
    The Management and Control of Bridge Affairs   172
    Maintenance, Repairs and Projects   183

[handwritten annotations:] put in Bibliography? — he is one of the Editors so ? not nec.?

Rochester Bridge, 1825–1950   *by James Preston*   221
   Planning the New Bridge   223
   Building the New Bridge   237
   Maintaining and Modifying the New Bridge   246
   Supporting the Bridge: Finance and the Estate   257

Rochester Bridge, 1950–1993: An Epilogue   275
   by P.F. Cooper and Glyn C. Jones

Appendices   287
   A: Wardens and Assistants of Rochester Bridge   289
   B: Rochester Bridge Accounts, 1391–1914   311
   C: The Rochester Bridgework List   362

Index   371

List of Tables

1. The dimensions of some large medieval English bridges.   48
2. The plan of Sir John de Cobham and Sir Robert Knolles for allocating responsibility for the new bridge, 1391.   51
3. Alms received from parishes and landowners in 1398–9.   52
4. Rents paid to Rochester Bridge in 1407–8.   56
5. Elms bought and used for piles, 1436–1446.   63
6. Chalk acquired for Rochester Bridge.   65
7. Average annual receipts of the Wardens of Rochester Bridge for each decade, 1390–1529.   76
8. Properties belonging to Rochester Bridge in 1443–4, listed in order of the dates when they first yielded rent.   78
9. Properties rented by Rochester Bridge in 1478–9 and 1556–7.   81
10. Average annual net income from the property of Rochester Bridge for each decade, 1390–1479.   83
11. Annual rents from land in documented periods, 1500–1528.   83
12. Recorded donations to Rochester Bridge of £10 and more, 1398–1479.   88
13. Henry Hunte's travels on bridge business in 1449–50.   94
14. The bridge establishment, 1449–50 and 1522–4.   105
15. Mid-sixteenth-century leases.   114
16. Rochester Bridge toll charges, 1557–1561.   116
17. Toll proceeds, 1557–1561.   117
18. Revenue from the Fifteenth levied August 1561.   124
19. Rochester Bridge Wardens and Assistants in Parliament, 1555–1660.   139
20. Increase in selected rents.   145
21. Rent increases on selected properties, 1575–1650.   146
22. Population of the Medway Towns, 1676 and 1801.   164
23. Shipping tonnage registered in Kentish ports, 1709–82.   168
24. The trade of the Medway: bulk cargoes imported into the port of Rochester, annual averages, 1694–1825.   169
25. MPs sitting for Rochester who also served as Bridge Wardens.   177
26. Rochester Bridge accounts, 1660–1825.   178
27. Daniel Alexander's report on the state of the Bridge funds, 1812.   182
28. Daniel Alexander's analysis of bridge maintenance, 1788–1796.   201

List of Figures

1. The site of the Roman and Anglo-Saxon town and bridge at Rochester, showing the course of the River Medway and the location of the mud-flats on the North East and South West of the town.   4

2. Early Anglo-Saxon Kent showing the principal physical regions or *pays* and the Roman roads and towns.   6

3. Reconstruction of pier, timber roadway and coffer dam of the second Roman bridge at Trier, c. AD 140.   7

   Pier and foundation of oak piles and rubble from the first bridge at Trier, c. AD 75.

   Reproduced by permission from H. Cuppers, *Die Trierer Römerbrücken*, 1969

4. Alternative reconstructions (A and B) of the Anglo-Saxon bridge at Rochester, showing the nine piers and the beams of the timber superstructure, their allocation to lords and estates, and the measurements in rods and perches.   23

5. Map of the estates owing bridgework at Rochester, showing their relationship to the lathe of Aylesford.   28

6. The territories assigned to the repair of the nine piers of Rochester Bridge.   32

7. Conjectural reconstruction of the original pier-territories of Rochester Bridge as they may have existed in the seventh or eighth century.   32

8. Family ties between the Fanes, Nevilles and Brookes.   137

9. Rental income on all properties, 1575–1650.   147

10. Percentage increase of rental income and costs, 1575–1650.   148

11. Average annual surplus, 1585–1660.   152

12. Rochester Bridge estates: rental income, 1660–1825.   180

13. Rochester Bridge estates: rents and arrears, 1660–1825.   180

14. Rochester Bridge maintenance, 1660–1825.   187

15. Drawing of a pile-driver used at Rochester Bridge in the early eighteenth century.   189

16. Plan showing a staddle or dense mass of piles upon which each pier was raised, surrounded by a starling for protection.   190

17. Cross-section of pier and staddle, with plan of staddle and pile heads below, showing the sides of the staddles and starlings enclosed by rows of interlocking piles known as stoppers and binders.   191

18. Sagging arches: sketch by John Price illustrating problems created by the defective arch, c.1730.   194

19. Collapsing parapets: sketch from an unsigned memorandum of 1730 in   195
    the Thorpe Mss in the Society of Antiquaries' Library.
20. Bridge widening plan and design for timber centre by John Gorham,   203
    1780.
21. Advertisement for timber to repair the starlings in 1812.   204
22. Handbill opposing the construction of a new bridge circulated during   227
    the contested election of 1832.
23. Rival slate of wardens and assistants proposed by the Rochester faction   230
    of the Commonalty opposed to the swing bridge during the contested
    election of 1846.
24. Plan of the Medway Tunnel downstream from Rochester Bridge.   282

Figures 16–20 have been redrawn from the originals by Michael Carter.

List of Plates

Plates 1–4 appear between pages 46 and 47

1. Brass in Cobham church of Sir John de Cobham who died in 1407.

2. Estate Map drawn in 1659 of the Manor of Langdon given to the Bridge Wardens in 1399.

3. Royal Grant from Henry VI to the Bridge Wardens for support of the Bridge Chapel in 1442.

4. Account roll of Bridge Wardens Robert Rowe and John Wolcy, 1399–1400.

Plates 5–8 appear between pages 110 and 111

5. (a) Monument in Cobham church to Sir George Brooke, Lord Cobham (1497–1558), his wife Anne, and their ten sons and four daughters, including Sir William Brooke, Lord Cobham (1527–1597)
   (b) The Wardens Roll begun in 1585 by William Lambarde and Sir Roger Manwood.

6. (a) Plan and elevation of the medieval bridge showing the staddles and the riverbed.
   (b) Print of Rochester Bridge showing boat with lowered mast passing under the drawbridge (from an original in the private collection of Michael Lewis).

7. (a) View of the Medway Towns inscribed to Bridge Warden Sir Thomas Palmer, Bart, published in John Harris, *History of Kent*, 1719.
   (b) View of Rochester Bridge showing the 'great rush of water' at the arches, published in John Harris, *History of Kent*, 1719.

8. (a) Plan of Rochester showing the bridge properties in 1717.
   (b) Plan of Rochester by R. Sale published in *The History and Antiquities of Rochester and its Environs*, 1817.

Plates 9–12 appear between pages 174 and 175

9. John Thorpe, MD (1682–1750). Engraving by J. Bayly from a portrait by Wollaston published in *Registrum Roffense*, 1769.

10. Engraving showing the horse-powered pile-driver used at Westminster Bridge in 1738 (reproduced by kind permission from an original in the British Library).

after p 110

11. (a) Daniel Alexander's plan for the construction of the great central arch, 1817.
    (b) Nineteenth century painting of Rochester Bridge showing the enlarged central arch.
12. (a) Daniel Alexander's design for a new stone bridge of five arches, 1818.
    (b) William Cubitt's design for the proposed suspension bridge, 1844.

Plates 13–16 appear between pages 238 and 239

13. (a) Plan and elevation of William Cubitt's cast iron bridge showing its position downstream from the old bridge.
    (b) Demolition of the medieval stone bridge by the Royal Engineers from *Illustrated Times*, 24 January 1857.
14. (a) The Bridge Chamber (right) built in 1879 and Chapel (left) restored in 1937.
    (b) Damage to the central arch of Rochester Bridge by the lighter *Diamond* in 1896.
15. (a) Slow-moving traffic across the River Medway during the reconstruction of the cast iron bridge in 1912.
    (b) Removing the arches after the reconstruction of Rochester Bridge in 1913.
16. (a) Aerial view of Traffic crossing the duplicated Rochester Bridge in 1977.
    (b) Aerial view of Rochester Bridge and the Frindsbury peninsula before the latter's development as an industrial estate.

Preface

As I stand down today, after holding office for three memorable years as a Warden of Rochester Bridge, it is exciting to have the privilege of launching into the world this first volume of the Kent History Project – exciting because the Rochester Bridge Trust uniquely 'bridges' the past, the present and the future. Rochester Bridge has always been inexorably entwined with the threads of history. It is not surprising that in the past the Rochester Bridge Trust should have attracted to its membership a number of leading Kentish historians. William Lambarde, who wrote one of the first histories of Kent, was a member of the Court from 1585 to 1601; John Thorpe, the great Rochester historian was a member from 1731 to 1750, as was the best known of all Kentish historians, Edward Hasted, from 1761 to 1771. And now the Trust has gathered together a group of historians to write its own history for future generations to read.

My own parish of Wormshill, although some sixteen miles distant from the Bridge, was bound to provide oak planking for the sixth pier from at least the beginning of the eleventh century and was still theoretically so liable until the passing of the Rochester Bridge Act 1908. Nicholas Brooks tells us that the concept of maintaining a bridge in this way from contributory lands was a Roman concept, and I like to imagine that Wormshill was providing planking for the first Roman Bridge and that the office of Warden to oversee the maintenance of the Bridge goes back to the Roman period, making it the oldest office in the country. Wormshill no longer provides the planking, but I represent on Maidstone Borough Council the parishes of Hollingbourne, Bicknor, Frinsted, Hucking and Wormshill, which were all amongst the contributory lands. In turn, Maidstone has appointed me to serve on the Rochester Bridge Trust – yet another 'bridging' of the past and present. As I write this at home, I think too of a previous owner, the poet and dramatist Sir Charles Sedley, Senior Warden in 1683, 1690 and 1697; and I look up at the portraits hanging on my wall of Francis Barrell, Junior Warden in 1678, and his son Francis, who served on the Court of Wardens and Assistants from 1690 to 1720.

The Bridge Chapel was an important part of the medieval foundation, and although it fell into a shocking state of disrepair, even losing its roof during the nineteenth century, I am happy that during my term I was able to arrange for the first service held there since the Reformation. On All Souls Day, 2nd November 1990, the Dean of Rochester celebrated a Requiem Mass sung in Latin as a Commemoration Service for our founders and benefactors. The presence in the Chapel of the carved and painted Arms of Richard II and his uncles suggests that they may have attended such a service shortly after the Chapel was built. The Commemoration Service was repeated in 1991 and is to take place on All Souls

Day again this year, becoming I hope another permament tradition bridging the past, present and future of this unique institution.

The Rochester Bridge Trust is fortunate in having such an unbroken series of records in its own muniment room kept by its own archivist James Gibson, who with Nigel Yates has so ably put together this volume. There can be few institutions that can boast a series of annual balance sheets from 1576 to 1908 all on one large vellum roll. Having so much material together in one place has clearly assisted in the preparation of this history.

Turning from the past to the future, I have been fortunate to be associated with the promotion of the Medway Tunnel Act 1990 and the complicated arrangements and negotiations that flowed from it for the construction of the tunnel. I wish to record how fortunate we have been to have had the support of senior politicians like Geoffrey Howe, Cecil Parkinson and Malcolm Rifkind, as well as our local Members of Parliament, Peggy Fenner, Andrew Rowe and James Couchman, and the tireless energy of our present Bridge Clerk, Glyn Jones, without whom I do not believe the tunnel, as a project of the Rochester Bridge Trust, would have been possible.

James Preston has pointed to the debate during the past 150 years, both amongst members of the Court and the Charity Commission, about the use of surplus financial resources. Should it all be used for bridge works? Does this mean only crossings at Rochester or all bridges across the Medway? To what extent might surplus funds be used for other good works? On the whole a catholic outlook seems to have prevailed: several distant bridges over the Medway have been assisted, a number of important schools founded and churches built or repaired over the past hundred years. Our co-founder, Sir John de Cobham, does not seem to have been worried by this problem. Without fear that it would deprive the Bridge of precious resources, he built our fine chapel to be served, not by one, but by three chaplains. He also founded with great munificence the charity of Cobham College, which his kinsman, Sir William Brooke, caused to be closely linked with Rochester Bridge by ensuring that from 1598 the Wardens were to be *ex officio* Presidents of the New College of Cobham, as they still are today. I am happy that in my own time on the Court a permanent Grants Fund has been established and, although small at present, as it grows will be available for all time as a common good fund bridging the past, present and the future of the Rochester Bridge Trust – Publica Privatis!

Wormshill Court   Michael Nightingale of Cromarty
4 June 1992   Senior Warden

Introduction

The preparation of a history of Rochester Bridge was first mooted in 1973, but not until 1979 was the 'preparation of a definitive history of the Trust' approved in principle by the Wardens and Assistants. Felix Hull, then County Archivist, was approached about the possibility of writing the history, but he declined due to previous research commitments, and the project fell into abeyance. In June 1983 the Bridge Clerk was again ordered to make enquiries to find a qualified person 'to undertake the writing of a definitive history of the Trust', and though he was urged to continue his enquiries in October 1983, no author was forthcoming. In December 1986 the Wardens and Assistants once again ordered that 'various historical bodies be contacted to seek advice on historians who might be willing to undertake a definitive history of the Trust.' This time Assistant Warden Michael Nightingale approached the County Archivist, Nigel Yates, who agreed to co-ordinate the project and act as editor. During 1987 Richard Britnell was recruited to write the medieval chapter and David Ormrod to write the Restoration, eighteenth-century and early nineteenth-century chapter. James Gibson was engaged as archivist to catalogue the Trust's archives, to assist in the research of the history, and to write the sixteenth- and early seventeenth-century chapter. In 1990 Nicholas Brooks was invited to write the Roman and Anglo-Saxon chapter, and in 1991 James Preston agreed to write the nineteenth- and early twentieth-century chapter. The epilogue, covering the construction of the 1970 road bridge and the new Medway Tunnel, was written by former Bridge Clerk Frederick Cooper and present Bridge Clerk Glyn Jones.

In June 1989 the Wardens and Assistants agreed to participate in the Kent History Project, the principal aim of which is to produce the first authoritative history of Kent since the late eighteenth century. This project was commissioned by the Kent County Council in 1989 to celebrate its centenary. It will include eight volumes covering the history of the county from earliest times to the present day, together with a number of specialist monographs. Thus far the editorial board has approved volumes on the history of Rochester Bridge and the history of Rochester Cathedral.

The editors are most grateful to their contributors, who have met all their deadlines and requirements, and to the Court of Wardens and Assistants of Rochester Bridge for the interest they have taken in the publication of the history of the Rochester Bridge Trust. They are also grateful to Michael Lewis for the loan of prints of Rochester Bridge from his private collection, to James Derriman for research carried out at the Public Record Office, to Bernard Snell of Fine Arts Studio for the photography, and to Terry Schofield for patiently typing many drafts of parts of this book.

Nigel Yates
James M. Gibson

Notes on the Contributors

R.H. BRITNELL graduated from Cambridge in 1964 and took his doctorate in 1970. Since 1966 he has taught at Durham University. He has written *Growth and Decline in Colchester, 1300–1525* (Cambridge, 1986) and *The Commercialisation of English Society, 1000–1500* (Cambridge, 1993) as well as articles concerning agriculture and local trade in the Middle Ages. He is currently writing *The Closing of the Middle Ages, 1471–1529*, a book commissioned by Basil Blackwell for the series *A History of Medieval Britain*.

NICHOLAS P. BROOKS received his BA in Modern History from the University of Oxford in 1962 and his D.Phil. in 1969. He was Lecturer in Medieval History in the University of St Andrews from 1964 and Senior Lecturer from 1978, until his appointment as Professor and Head of the Department of Medieval History at the University of Birmingham in 1985, where he is currently Dean of the Faculty of Arts. He is a Fellow of the British Academy, the Royal Historical Society and the Society of Antiquaries. He is author of *The Early History of the Church of Canterbury*, editor of *Latin and the Vernacular in the Early Middle Ages* and general editor of Leicester University Press's 'Studies in the Early History of Britain'. He is chairman of the joint BA/RHS research project on Anglo-Saxon Charters, and is currently editing a volume for the Millennium of St Oswald of Worcester. He is also researching widely into the history and technology of medieval bridges throughout Europe.

PHILIP FREDERICK COOPER worked for many years as management accountant for the Electricity Board and served as Councillor and Alderman of Gillingham Borough Council from 1951 to 1967, where he was twice elected Deputy Mayor in 1957 and 1961 and Mayor in 1962. From 1964 to 1974 he represented Gillingham as an Assistant Warden of the Rochester Bridge Trust, serving as Junior Warden 1971–72 and Senior Warden 1972–74. He was appointed Bridge Clerk in 1974 with the brief to update the administration and maximise the income after the construction of the 1970 bridge, and during his tenure he led the reclamation of Frindsbury Peninsula and the redevelopment of the Dartford Industrial Estate. Since his retirement in 1980, he has lectured on the history of the Trust to schools and local history societies.

JAMES M. GIBSON received his Ph.D. in English from the University of Pennsylvania in 1976 and lectured on writing and literature at Houghton College in New York for nine years before coming to Kent in 1984. Employed since 1987 as Archivist for the Rochester Bridge Trust, he is author of *The Philadelphia Shakespeare Story: Horace Howard Furness and the New Variorum Shakespeare* and has edited the East Kent records for the Records of Early English Drama (REED). He lives in Maidstone where he is currently editing the West Kent records for REED and has recently been appointed Associate Editor for the New Variorum Shakespeare *The Merry Wives of Windsor*.

GLYN C. JONES, LL.B. qualified as a solicitor in 1948, being awarded the Travers-Smith Scholarship of the Law Society, and entered upon a career in local government in the course of which he was Deputy Town Clerk of Chatham 1952–57 and Town Clerk of Gillingham 1966–86, adding the title and function of Chief Executive for the period 1974–86. He became Clerk to the Rochester Bridge Trust in 1987 after retiring from Gillingham and has been particularly closely concerned with the Medway Tunnel Project from its inception in 1981.

DAVID ORMROD studied at the London School of Economics before completing a doctorate at Christ's College, Cambridge. He has taught economic and social history at the University of Kent since 1970, and is the author of *English Grain Exports and Agrarian Capitalism*, as well as numerous essays and articles on English commercial history and the social history of religion. He is currently working in the Centre for Metropolitan History at the University of London's Institute of Historical Research, on the community of immigrant Dutch and Flemish artists in London in the period 1550–1750, and their place within the expanding skilled workforce of the metropolis.

JAMES PRESTON was a senior lecturer in History at Mid-Kent College and since 1988 has been involved with curriculum development in further education. He is author of *Industrial Medway, Aveling and Porter Ltd, A Short History* and with Malcolm Moulton *A Brief History of Rochester Airport*. Under the North Kent Books imprint he has published works of Kent military and aviation interest, and he helped originate the *Bygone Kent* magazine. He is one of the founder trustees of the Fort Amherst and Lines Trust and is active in the Lower Medway Archaeological Research Group and the Medway Industrial Archaeology Group.

NIGEL YATES is the General Editor of the Kent History Project of which this volume is a part. He holds the degrees of MA in History and Ph.D. in Theology from the University of Hull. He was City Archivist of Portsmouth 1975–80 and County Archivist of Kent 1980–90, and is currently Consultant Historian to Kent County Council and Visiting Senior Research Fellow in Economic and Social History at the University of Kent. Elected a Fellow of the Royal Historical society in 1974, he has written *Kent and The Oxford Movement* (1983), *The Later Kentish Seaside* (with Felicity Stafford 1985), and *Buildings, Faith and Worship: The Liturgical Arrangement of Anglican Churches 1600–1900*, published by Oxford University Press in 1991.

PATRICK YATES, an undergraduate in the History Department at St David's University College, Lampeter, served as a research assistant for the Rochester Bridge Trust and is primarily responsible for the list of Wardens and Assistants.

ROCHESTER BRIDGE
AD 43–1381

Origins

We do not know exactly when the estuary of the Medway was first bridged at Rochester. In prehistoric times the principal east-west routes in Kent were the ancient trackways, now known as the 'Pilgrims' Way' and the neighbouring 'Greenway', which crossed the river by fords at Lower Halling and Aylesford.[1] We can be certain that a bridge already existed at Rochester in the Roman era, for the name of the Romano-British town, *Durobrivae* or *Durobrivas* is British and means 'the fort by the bridges'.[2] The plural form of the suffix may derive from a time when an early timber bridge and its stone replacement were both visible at Rochester; but it more probably reflects the fact that a bridge over the Medway at Rochester required many arches and could not, in contrast with the Stour at Canterbury or with other Kentish rivers, be bridged by a single span between land-abutments. Rochester is situated at the point where the Medway breaks through the northern dip slope of the North Downs and on the inside bank of an acute-angled meander in its course within the river's gravel terrace and alluvial flood-plain. The Roman walled town, built at the end of the chalk ridge on the east bank of the river, was therefore superbly situated in conjunction with the bridge to control river-traffic (Fig. 1). On present evidence the primary earthwork defences of the town date from the late second century, so the British name referring to the 'fort' (*duro-*) may be no older than that.[3]

The fact that the name of the city is British in origin rather than Latin carries no implication that a timber bridge had already been constructed on or near this site in the pre-Roman iron age. Indeed if Cassius Dio is (as is usually supposed) referring to the Medway when he describes the Britons assuming in AD 43 that the Roman armies would be unable to cross the river,[4] then it is clear that there was no pre-Roman bridge at the time of the conquest. The engineering problems of

---

[1] *Victoria County History of the Counties of England: Kent*, I, London 1908, 332–4; A. Everitt, *Continuity and Colonization: the evolution of Kentish Society*, Leicester 1986, passim.

[2] A.L.F. Rivet and C. Smith, *The Place-Names of Roman Britain*, London 1979, 346–7.

[3] T.F.C. Blagg, 'Roman Kent', in *Archaeology in Kent to AD 1500*, ed. P. Leach, Council for British Archaeology, Research Reports xlviii, London 1982, 51–63 (at 54). We do not know whether there had been a conquest-period Roman fort at Rochester. For the giving of Celtic names to new Roman forts and settlements, see A.L.F. Rivet, 'Celtic names and Roman places', *Britannia*, xi (1980), 1–19. For the geology, see H.G. Dines et al., *Geology of the Country around Chatham*, Memoirs of the Geological Survey of Great Britain (for Sheet 272), 2nd edn, London 1971.

[4] *Historiae Romanae*, lx, 20.2. See D.R. Dudley and G. Webster, *The Roman Conquest of Britain, AD 43–57*, London 1965, 65–7, and P. Thornhill, 'A lower Thames ford and the campaigns of 54 BC and AD 43', *Archaeologia Cantiana*, xcii (1976), 119–28.

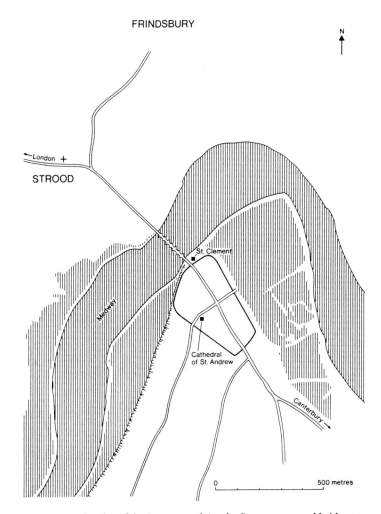

Figure 1. The site of the Roman and Anglo-Saxon town and bridge at Rochester, showing the course of the River Medway and the location of the mud-flats on the North East and South West of the town.

bridging the river at Rochester are indeed so severe as to suggest that the first bridge must have been Roman. A crossing at Rochester had to be about five hundred feet long and the piers had to withstand the pressures of the tides in the estuary, though the mean water level and the river-bed were then some 12–15 feet lower than today. The daily difference in the levels of high and low tides at the bridge now varies from about 14½ feet in winter to about 17½ feet in summer. The force of the water eroding the piers of any timber bridge would have required a continuous and massive programme of timber replacement if they were not to be quickly washed away. Indeed we know that after 1391 the timber and chalk foundations (or 'starlings') of the 'new', medieval stone bridge required between one and two hundred elm piles to be added to the foundations every year.[5] It seems unlikely that before the advent of the Romans there was the necessary engineering expertise to construct the bridge-piers in such a depth of running and tidal water or to maintain them when built.

Rochester bridge would have been one of the more important river estuary crossings in Roman Britain: shorter than the bridge over the Thames at London (approx. 1,000 feet) or the *Pons Aelius* over the Tyne at Newcastle (approx. 700 feet), but rather longer than the bridge over the Dee at Chester (540 feet, but including the approaches) and considerably greater than that over the Ouse at York (210 feet). In the Roman period such major bridges were built and maintained by the state.[6] They were indeed an essential and integral part of the communications system formed by the network of Roman roads. Like the principal roads, bridges were normally first built by the army. Watling Street, the great east-west road linking the richest agricultural land of south-eastern Britain and running from Dover to Canterbury, Rochester and London is likely to have been among the first Roman roads surveyed and built in Britain (Fig. 2). It may, indeed, have been *the* first.[7] We should certainly expect that a bridge had been planned at Rochester from the earliest months of the Roman conquest and that the first bridge would have been built well before the end of the first century AD. We should perhaps envisage a timber bridge constructed by the army as part of the conquest campaign and its replacement by a bridge with stone piers later in the same century.

---

5 See Britnell, below 63–4. It remains, of course, uncertain to what extent the reclamation and embankment of parts of the Medway marshes and mudflats in medieval and modern times may have increased the tidal flow at Rochester. The figures for the difference between the high and low tide levels relate to Chatham Lock Approach, some two miles downstream from the bridge.

6 For the measurements, see M. Rhodes, 'Roman coinage from London Bridge', *Britannia*, xxii (1991), 179–90 and fig. 1; D.P. Dymond, 'Roman bridges on Dere Street, Co. Durham', *Archaeological Journal*, cxviii (1961), 136–64; R.J. Stewart-Brown, 'Bridgework at Chester', *English Historical Review*, liv (1939), 83–7 (at 85 n. 3); *Inventory of the Historical monuments in the City of York*, I, *Eburacum*, Royal Commission on Historical Monuments, London, 1962, 3–5. For the state's responsibility for bridge construction and maintenance, see B. Ward-Perkins, *From Classical Antiquity to the Middle Ages: Urban Public Building in Northern and Central Italy, AD 300–850*, Oxford 1984, 186–91.

7 I.D. Margary, *Roman Roads in Britain*, London 1955, ii, 224. Cf. Caesar's campaign bridge over the Rhine: *De bello Gallico*, iv, 17.

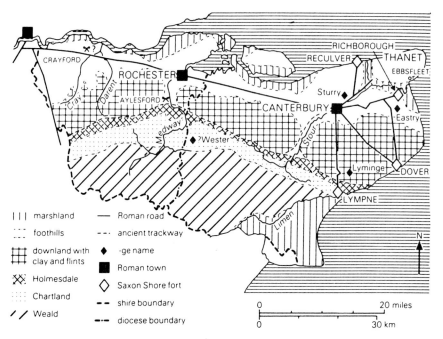

Figure 2. Early Anglo-Saxon Kent showing the principal physical regions or *pays* and the Roman roads and towns.

Figure 3. *(above)* Reconstruction of pier, timber roadway and coffer dam of the second Roman bridge at Trier, c. AD 140.

(below) Pier and foundation of oak piles and rubble from the first bridge at Trier, c. AD 75.

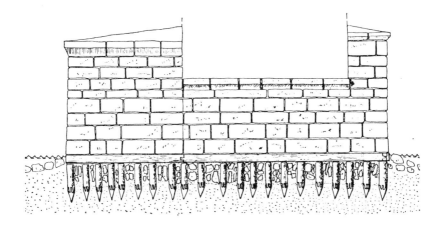

Many Roman bridges (like those over the Tiber in Rome) and bridge-like structures (such as the famous Pont-du-Gard at Nîmes) still survive today in the Mediterranean world.[8] Roman engineers had mastered the techniques of constructing substantial arched structures in stone, when they could either found them on dry ground or when they needed only to keep out the shallow water of a river whose flow was reduced in the summer months and where the (Mediterranean) tides were slight. In northern Europe, however, where the main rivers have a substantial flow throughout the year and tides are far larger, the engineering problems of constructing a bridge across a major estuary or in its alluvial flood-plain are infinitely greater.

It therefore remains uncertain, and to some extent controversial, how common it was for the larger Roman bridges in the north to be built with stone arches or whether the norm was for Roman bridges to have a timber superstructure resting upon stone piers, like Trajan's bridge over the Danube.[9] Reconstruction of the form of a bridge from surviving foundations visible in the riverbed and a small number of dressed stones recovered from the river (as at Chesters in Northumberland), is of necessity a conjectural exercise. A more helpful comparison for Rochester may be found in the only major Roman bridge in northern Europe that remains largely intact and in use today, namely the second-century bridge over the Mosel at Trier. Not only its structure and foundations, but also those of its first-century predecessor, have been the subject of detailed architectural and archaeological investigation.[10] The Mosel crossing of approx. 450 feet (137 metres) is closely comparable to that at Rochester, but the river is not, of course, tidal. Trier, however, was always a very much larger city and a more important governmental centre than was Rochester. It is therefore of interest that even the larger second-century Roman bridge at Trier only had a timber superstructure (Fig. 3). It was not arched in stone until the eighteenth century.

The piers of both Roman bridges at Trier provide an even more instructive parallel for Rochester. They had required the construction of a series of elaborate coffer-dams on the riverbed, within which a shaft could be excavated and each pier then be built on a firm foundation. The second bridge was an extremely ambitious construction involving the excavation of some four metres of alluvium and subsoil within each coffer to allow the ashlar piers to be built directly onto the bedrock. The earlier bridge had followed what German archaeologists now recognise as

---

[8] P. Gazzola, *Ponti Romani*, Florence 1963; *Reallexikon der germanischen Altertumskunde*, iii, 19, s.v. Brücke, 578ff; E. Nash, *Pictorial Dictionary of Ancient Rome*, London 1962, ii, passim; J. Le Gall, *Le Tibre, fleuve de Rome de l'antiquité*, Paris 1953; R. Chevallier, *Roads in the Roman Empire*, London 1976, 93–104.

[9] R.G. Collingwood and I. Richmond, *The Archaeology of Roman Britain*, London 1969, 2–3; *Reallexikon d. g. Altertumskunde*, iii, 578ff; P.T. Bidwell and N. Holbrook, *Hadrian's Wall Bridges*, London 1989, 34–40, 66–71; G. de la Bédoyère, *The Buildings of Roman Britain*, London 1991, 211–15.

[10] H. Cuppers, *Die Trierer Römerbrücken*, Trierer Grabungen und Forschungen v, Rheinisches Landesmuseum Trier, Mainz 1969. Subsequent dendrochronological analysis of the piles of the earlier bridge suggests that construction began in AD 71. See E. Hollstein, *Mitteleuropäische Eichendendrochronologie*, Trierer Grabungen und Forschungen xi, Mainz 1980, 135ff.

standard Roman practice in northern Europe: seven coffer-dams had been constructed in the stream of the river within which, once the water had been removed, excavation through the alluvium of the riverbed had proceeded until they reached the gravel terrace; massive piles of oak, up to 50 centimetres in diameter and shod in iron, were then driven into the gravel subsoil and a rubble foundation of ballast had then been tipped in and rammed down around the piles to form a secure rubble foundation on which the limestone masonry piers could be built (Fig. 3).[11] This is exactly the form of construction for which we have evidence at Rochester.

In 1851 during the construction of the Strood (i.e. the western) pier of the modern cast-iron bridge at Rochester the builders encountered, only a few inches beneath the riverbed of that time, the remains of a pier built of Kentish ragstone, belonging to an earlier bridge that had stood on the same site. Because the 1850s engineers were using a novel 'pneumatic' method of sinking the cylindrical piles for the new bridge, it was necessary to remove the earlier stonework in its entirety. The ancient stone pier-foundation comprised:

> a mass of Kentish ragstone, of the nature of rubble without mortar, [*which*] is found for a depth varying from 13 feet to 25 feet below the present bed of the river. Pieces of timber of considerable dimensions, and which had been used as piles, or framing, occurred in this bed of rubble stone, penetrating a foot or two into the gravel, which proved to be 6 or 8 feet thick. This timber is oak, elm and beech, – all except the last perfectly sound and tough (a few pieces had evidently been burnt); the beech was saturated with water, and was in the condition of a soft pulp. Some fragments of iron proved that the piles had been shod with that material.[12]

Written by the engineer in charge at a time when very little was known of Roman bridge-building techniques, this account is describing a construction system closely comparable to that used for the first bridge at Trier and for other Roman bridges on the continent. Rochester Bridge had been constructed on a foundation of piles, mainly of oak, driven into the gravel that overlies the chalk bedrock and packed around with ragstone rubble to a depth of at least thirteen feet. Some of this

---

11 Cuppers, *Trierer Römerbrücken*, 42–51, 176–202; D. Gündel, 'Die römischen Mainbrücke bei Frankfurt', *Germania*, vi (1922), 68–77; L. Blondel, 'Le pont romain de Genève', *Bullétin de la Société historique et archéologique de Genève*, v (1925–34), 128–40. For an account of the construction of this form of coffer-dam for marine piers, see Vitruvius, *De Architectura*, v. 12 (ed. F. Granger, London 1931, i, 314–16).

12 J. Hughes, 'On the pneumatic method adopted in constructing the foundations of the new bridge across the Medway', *Minutes of Proceedings of the Institution of Civil Engineers*, x (1850–1), 353–67 (at 365). This paper was delivered on 13 May 1851. On p. 356 Hughes indicated that the top of the ragstone was encountered very close to the 1850 river-bed. For information drawn from the 'overseer of the works' that most of the timber extracted was oak, see H.G. Adams, 'On Rochester Bridge', *Journal of the British Archaeological Association*, ix (1854), 348–58. The elm and beech recovered may have had specialist functions or have represented medieval repairs. For subsequent disagreements about the form of the first bridge, see A.A. Arnold, 'The earliest Rochester bridge: was it built by the Romans?', *Archaeologia Cantiana*, xxxv (1921), 127–38; J.J. Robson, 'Rochester bridge: the Roman bridge in masonry', ibid., 139–44.

rubble may have comprised the core of the pier from which masonry facing had been subsequently robbed. But most of it must have been the foundation that the Romans had constructed beneath the bed of the river. The 'timber framing', can be interpreted on the basis of parallels at Trier, Geneva and Mainz as part of the coffer dam which served both to allow the foundations of the piers to be built and as their subsequent protection.

It is unfortunate that only one of the three piers of the nineteenth-century bridge at Rochester coincided with those of its Roman predecessor and that no drawings or more detailed accounts of what was then found appear to survive. On present knowledge it is therefore impossible to reconstruct the Roman bridge,[13] but the discoveries of 1851 at least prove that the Roman bridge was located, as might have been expected, between the principal street of the small Roman town and the nearest point on the western (Strood) bank (Fig. 1). They also established the astonishing depth – at least thirteen and perhaps up to twenty-five feet (almost eight metres) – of the pier-foundations that the Romans had excavated beneath the Roman riverbed at Rochester in order to reach a geological stratum to which their pier-foundations could be fixed by driven piles. We need to envisage an oak framework on top of the rubble foundation, fixed both to the piles beneath and to the ashlar masonry of the piers above. The masonry piers were alone exposed to the flow of the river and tides. Their good stonework will doubtless have been robbed, after the final collapse of the bridge in the late Middle Ages, for the benefit of its successor or of other buildings reachable by water transport. Thus only the rubble foundation beneath the Roman river-bed and perhaps some part of the rubble core of the pier remained to be discovered in 1851.

In the future the prospects for recovering further details of the Roman foundations are good. The other Roman pier-foundations await detection beneath the river bed between the nineteenth-century piers. Excavation underwater in a busy tidal estuary at that depth beneath the modern riverbed would be a prohibitively expensive and dangerous procedure. But the prospects for detection by remote sensing devices are promising, though still difficult. Systematic probing of the riverbed by the author and Mr A.J. Clark in the autumn of 1990 established that beneath the bridge the bottom does not consist of the thick alluvial mud that is general in the Medway estuary, but has a compacted hard surface of stone or brick probably representing material deposited when the bridge was built in the 1850s or else during its reconstruction of 1908–11.[14] It seems unlikely that the present generation of 'subbottom profilers', which use radar to penetrate and depict the gravel, sand or mud that normally form river- and sea-beds, would be able to pierce what is likely to be several feet of compacted stone overlying the nineteenth-century

[13] But see Fig. 4 and pp. 22–5 below, for an attempt to reconstruct the late Anglo-Saxon bridge from documentary evidence and for the suggestion that this still used the Roman piers.

[14] Thanks are due to Mr Clark, the foremost British authority on archaeological remote sensing devices, for his experiments and advice on the suitability of resistivity and other prospecting techniques; to Mr B. Carey, the bridge caretaker, for making an extendable aluminium probe to our specification, and to the Medway Ports Authority for providing a motor launch for the Bridge Trust, which made this preliminary probing possible.

riverbed, and to distinguish those areas where the rubble of the Roman pier-foundation lies beneath.[15] Technology moves rapidly in these matters, however, and it may not be long before it will be possible to secure a complete computer-generated picture of the piers of the Roman bridge at Rochester.

[15] The assistance of Mr D. Hampshire of Ferranti ORE Ltd in providing technical advice is gratefully acknowledged. The contrast in the nature of the bottom with that of the surrounding estuary suggests that a considerable thickness of bottoming was laid down to protect the foundation of the nineteenth-century bridge.

The Bridge in Sub-Roman and
Early Anglo-Saxon Times

It must remain in doubt how long the Roman bridge at Rochester remained usable. In the last quarter of the fourth century legal responsibility for the maintenance of such major bridges lay upon the leading landowners of the *civitas*-territory, whilst all men of status and all officials, and churches and churchmen were exempted from the actual menial work in a series of imperial enactments preserved in the Theodosian code and belonging to the years 370, 382 and 390.[16] At least from that time, therefore, we must expect that the landed aristocracy of the *civitas* of *Durobrivae* under the aegis of the town council would have been responsible through their agents for organizing work-parties from their estates for the upkeep of the bridge. We have no direct evidence of how they fulfilled that responsibility, nor of what happened to their obligation when political authority in West Kent was transferred to British and then to pagan Anglo-Saxon hands in the course of the fifth century.[17] Scholars are today more willing to concede than hitherto that major Roman monuments (and also Roman or pre-Roman field-systems) remained in use in the Anglo-Saxon period and even beyond; it is even possible that some Roman sites had a continuous history as seats of political authority or of Christian cult from the fourth century.[18] Nonetheless the dramatic collapse of the Romano-British economy in the fourth and fifth centuries, and in particular of the villa-system and of anything resembling urban life,[19] would make most hesitate to suppose that

---

[16] *Theodosiani libri XVI cum constitutionibus Sirmondianis et leges novellae ad Theodosianum pertinentes*, I, i, ed. T. Mommsen and P.H. Meyer, Berlin 1905, xi. 10. 2 (370) for Italy, xi. 16. 15 (382) and xi. 16. 18 (390) for the whole of the empire.

[17] N.P. Brooks, 'The creation and early structure of the kingdom of Kent', in *The Origins of Anglo-Saxon Kingdoms*, ed. S.R. Bassett, Leicester 1989, 55–74.

[18] For the survival of Roman and iron-age field-systems in neighbouring Essex, see T. Williamson, 'Settlement chronology and regional landscapes: the evidence from the claylands of East Anglia and Essex', in *Anglo-Saxon Settlements*, ed. D. Hooke, Oxford 1988, 153–75; and for a prescient study of a small part of Kent, see M.D. Nightingale, 'A Roman land settlement near Rochester', *Archaeologia Cantiana*, lxv (1952), 150–9; for the continuing role of the Roman theatre in Anglo-Saxon Canterbury, see N.P. Brooks, *The Early History of the Church of Canterbury*, Leicester 1984, 24–5; for similar continuities in London, see M. Biddle, 'A city in transition', in *British Atlas of Historic Towns*, ed. M.D. Lobel, iii, *The City of London*, Oxford 1989, 23–4, and for the continental background, see C. Brühl, *Palatium und Civitas*, 3 vols, Köln 1975–81; for the continuities implied by the place-name Eccles and by the sites of holy wells, see Everitt, *Continuity and Colonisation*, 93–116, 296–300.

[19] S. Esmonde-Cleary, *The End of Roman Britain*, London 1990, passim; T.W.T. Tatton-Brown, 'Canterbury's urban topography: some recent work', in *The Medieval Town in Britain*, ed. P. Riden, Gregynog Seminars in Local History, i (1980), 85–98; id., 'The towns of Kent', in *Anglo-Saxon Towns in Southern England*, ed. J. Haslam, Chichester 1984, 1–36.

arrangements for the maintenance of Rochester Bridge by estates in the city's territory could have continued in operation throughout the Dark Ages. Moreover the structure of the bridge itself may have been threatened by the inexorable rise in sea- and river-levels in relation to the land in south-eastern England between the fifth and ninth centuries.[20] The piers and the roadway of the bridge may have had to be raised, even supposing that the piers remained intact.

Thus the choice of Rochester as the site for the second English see in 604 need not imply that the Medway bridge was then still in use. If one or more of the bridge spans had collapsed, a boat could have served as a ferry. Bishop Justus, the first bishop, and his tiny community could have crossed in that way when attending to the pastoral needs of the diocese. Nonetheless the Roman missionaries and their Frankish assistants would have been familiar at home, either in Rome or in Merovingian Gaul, with Roman bridges and with the advantages of keeping them in repair. Gregory of Tours has an instructive story of a fugitive breaking his leg when he caught his foot in a gap between two planks of the *Grand pont* over the Seine at Paris.[21] In Paris, as at Trier, the Roman bridge had a timber superstructure which required (even if it did not always receive) periodic maintenance. It remains uncertain to what extent in Frankish Gaul, or even in Italy, the late-Roman arrangements for bridge repair continued to be enforced. We hear of bridges in historical narratives or in saints' *Lives* only when they were damaged by fires or floods or when their condition gave rise to accidents and occasions for miracles. It seems, however, that it was city-based bishops in the sixth and seventh centuries who had most to gain from the maintenance of the old Roman obligations. Here, as in so much else, the work of preserving *romanitas* fell to the bishops.

At Rochester the bishops and cathedral community acquired control of an increasing proportion of the land within the Roman walls until by the mid-ninth century they owned the whole city.[22] It was they, therefore, who had the prime interest in persuading the rulers of Kent that the exaction of labour for the repair of bridges from estates throughout the kingdom was part of the 'public' rights or obligations involved in kingship. Already in the year 732 King Æthelberht II of Kent insisted that he was entitled to exact 'royal right' (*ius regium*) from an estate that he was granting to a Kentish monastery on the grounds that such a right was

[20] J.H. Evans, 'Archaeological horizons in the North Kent Marshes', *Archaeologia Cantiana*, lxvi (1953), 103–46. For medieval and Roman levels on the Strood bank, see P. Thornhill, 'Second thoughts on Strood's causeway', *Archaeologia Cantiana*, xciv (1978), 249–55.

[21] *Libri Historiarum X*, vi. 32, Monumenta Germaniae Historica, Scriptores rer. Merovingicarum, i, ed. B. Krusch and W. Levison, 1937–51, 303; for the interpretation and for the general development of bridges in the Frankish world, see W.N. Boyer, *Medieval French Bridges: a History*, Medieval Academy of America, Cambridge Mass., 1976, 17–18.

[22] *Anglo-Saxon Charters*, I, *Charters of Rochester*, ed. A. Campbell, London 1973, nos. 1, 5, 7, 11, 13, 23, 24, 26 (P.H. Sawyer, *Anglo-Saxon Charters: an annotated list and bibliography*, London 1968 [hereafter cited as S], nos. 1, 32, 34, 266, 131, 315, 327, 339). For the interpretation of the bounds (despite his misunderstanding of charter references to the Medway) see G. Ward, 'A note on the Mead Way, the street and Doddinghyrnan in Rochester', *Archaeologia Cantiana*, lxii (1949), 37–44.

'general in all the ecclesiastical lands that are known to be in Kent'.[23] It is likely that bridgework formed part of that right. Certainly from the middle of the eighth century Mercian kings began to insist, when granting away immunities in their own kingdom, that bridgework should continue to be obligatory; from the last decade of the eighth and the first of the ninth century similar clauses began to appear in Kentish charters. Thereafter they increasingly became a matter of set form.[24] We can be sure, therefore, that at least from the 790s, very probably from the 730s and possibly as far back as the days of Justus, Augustine and Æthelberht I of Kent, there was a system by which all lands in the kingdom were obliged to contribute men to build or repair bridges.

The insistence that ecclesiastical lands (like the imperial fisc and like men of rank and status) were not exempt from this public obligation also has its roots in the Theodosian code, but the key enactments of 423 and 441,'which assert that work on bridges was not one of the *sordida munera* and that there were therefore no immunities, were probably too late to have been enforced in sub-Roman Britain.[25] It is instructive that the English evidence for such Roman ideas of the state in the 730s and 750s shortly precedes the evidence for their assertion by Carolingian Frankish rulers in capitularies, charters and chronicles. Not until the 780s do we find Carolingian rulers insisting that the repair of bridges was obligatory on great lords, churches and ecclesiastics and that 'according to ancient custom' no immunity could be invoked to claim exemption. Here, as in other fields,[26] the route of transmission appears to go from late sixth-century Rome and early Merovingian Gaul to England and then back to Carolingian Frankia. That may well be an accident of the survival of evidence. It is certainly possible that the Roman *munera* or labour services had continued to be enforced by local counts and aristocrats in parts of Merovingian Frankia. It is even conceivable that they had been exacted in Britain without major break by British and then by Anglo-Saxon kings. Both the south-west Midlands and Kent, where bridgework may first be detected in the Anglo-Saxon royal diplomas, are areas where some transfer of Romano-British

---

[23] W. de G. Birch, *Cartularium Saxonicum*, 3 vols, London 1885–93 [hereafter cited as BCS, followed by the charter no.], no. 148 (S 23).

[24] N.P. Brooks, 'The development of military obligations in 8th and 9th century England', in *England Before the Conquest: Studies Presented to D. Whitelock*, ed. P. Clemoes and K. Hughes, Cambridge 1971, 69–84.

[25] *Theodosiani Libri XVI*, i, edd. Mommsen and Meyer, xv.3.6 (423); ibid., ii, Nov. Val. 10 (441); *Corpus Iuris Civilis*, ii, *Codex Iustinianus*, ed. P. Krüger, Berlin 1954, i. 2. 7 (citing *Theod.* xv.3.6 of 423). These enactments reversed *Theod.* xi.16.15 (382) and xi.16.18 (390) which had equated road- and bridge-work with the *sordida munera* from which men of rank and privileged institutions were exempt.

[26] For Carolingian insistance that ecclesiastical immunities did not provide exemption from bridge-work, see *Pippini Italiae regis capitulare* (782–7), c.4 and *Cap. Mantuanum secundum* (813), c.7 (both in *Monumenta Germaniae Historica, Capitularia*, i, 192, 197); *Gesta Karolini*, i.30 (ed.); and the diploma of 772 to the church of Metz (*MGH, Diplomata Karol.*, no. 91, p. 132). For the transmission of concepts of ecclesiastical hierarchy and for liturgy, see Brooks, *Church of Canterbury*, 66–7, 84–5, 91–3, 314–15; for the origins of the diplomatic of early Anglo-Saxon royal charters, see P. Wormald, *Bede and the Conversion of England: the Charter Evidence*, Jarrow Lecture 1984, 1–19.

social institutions may be posited on other grounds.[27] But it is more likely that Roman ideas of public obligation and the late antique notion that church estates were not immune were reintroduced to Kent and to other English kingdoms, either through Frankish secular contacts or by churchmen. The Roman missionaries in the early seventh century or Theodore and Hadrian in the latter half, may have brought the Roman legal attitudes to such 'public' works. With some confidence we may conclude that the levying of bridgework in Kent from all estates, even church lands, is likely to have been imposed by one of the Kentish kings between c.600 and c.730; pushing conjecture very hard we might suggest from the universality of the obligation in the southern English kingdoms, that it may have been a measure that the church had encouraged Æthelberht I to consider worthy of his *imperium* at the beginning of the seventh century. Be that as it may, the repair (and any necessary reconstruction) of Rochester Bridge must have been the most important single aim of the application of such a system of bridgework in Kent.

[27] For the south-west Midlands, see P. Sims-Williams, *Religion and Learning in Western England, 600–800*, Cambridge 1990, 54–86 and S.R. Bassett, 'Churches in Worcester before and after the conversion of the Anglo-Saxons', *Antiquaries Journal*, lxix (1989), 225–56, and id., 'The Roman and medieval landscape of Wroxeter', in *From Roman Viriconium to Medieval Wroxeter*, ed. P.A. Barker, Worcester 1990, 10–13; for Kent J.E.A. Jolliffe, *Pre-feudal England: the Jutes*, Oxford 1933 has to be reassessed in the light of his own 'Northumbrian Institutions', *English Historical Review*, xxxv (1926), 161–99 and G.W.S. Barrow, 'Pre-feudal Scotland: shires and thegns', in *The Kingdom of the Scots*, London 1973, 7–68.

The Bridge in Later Anglo-Saxon Times

In the ninth, tenth and early eleventh centuries the charters of English kings continue to require the service of bridgework (*pontis instructio, pontis restauratio* etc.) as a matter of course. If bridgework had been as effectively levied as it was regularly specified in royal diplomas, then Rochester Bridge is likely to have been maintained throughout these centuries. It is only from the early eleventh century, however, that we have specific information about the bridge and about how it was supported. A document of that period, known as the 'Rochester bridgework list', records the estates that were responsible for the upkeep of each of the piers of the bridge and specifies the quantities of beams and planking that they had to provide. It provides precious information both about the form of the bridge at Rochester and about the territory that supported it. The bridgework list governed the manner in which repairs to the bridge were in fact carried out and paid for over several centuries until the final collapse of the bridge in the 1380s. Moreover, long after that time it continued to determine the ultimate legal responsibility for the Medway crossing at Rochester and therefore to affect the constitution of the Rochester Bridge Trust. In any history of Rochester Bridge the bridgework list therefore has a central place.

The text of the list is first recorded in the *Textus Roffensis*, the early twelfth-century cartulary of the cathedral priory of Rochester; it is copied first in a Latin version and then in Old English.[28] Later copies of the Latin text are found in thirteenth- and fourteenth-century manuscripts from Rochester and in a somewhat different form from Canterbury cathedral. The Canterbury version makes it possible to restore some of the names that were subsequently erased from the *Textus Roffensis*.[29] It has been established, however, that the Latin text is secondary, being simply a translation of the Old English and having consistently later forms in its spelling of place-names; very probably the Latin version was the work of the compiler of the *Textus Roffensis*, who was working in c.1120.[30] In view of the fundamental importance of this document for the subsequent history of the bridge, a translation of the Old English text is included here, and an edition of both the Old English and the Latin texts is provided in Appendix C:

[28] Maidstone, Centre for Kentish Studies, DCR/R1, fos 164–7. There is a full facsimile: *Textus Roffensis*, 2 parts, ed. P.H. Sawyer, Early English Manuscripts in Facsimile, vii, xi, Copenhagen 1957, 1962. The Old English text was edited in BCS 1321 and in A.J. Robertson, *Anglo-Saxon Charters*, Cambridge 1939, no. 52; the Latin by W. Lambarde, *Perambulation of Kent*, London 1576, 419–24 and T. Hearne, *Textus Roffensis*, Rochester 1720, 379–82 and in BCS 1322.

[29] See below, Appendix C, 362–9.

[30] N.P. Brooks, 'Church, crown and community: public work and seigneurial responsibilities at Rochester bridge', in *Warriors and Churchmen in the High Middle Ages: Essays presented to*

This is the labour-service (*geweorc*) for the bridge at Rochester.

Here are named the estates (*þa land*) from which the labour is due.

First the bishop undertakes to construct (*to wercene*) the land pier on the [eastern] arm,[31] and to plank (*to þilliannæ*) three rods (*gyrda*), and to set in place (*to lycanne*) 3 beams (*sylla*): that is from Borstal, Cuxton, Frindsbury and Stoke.

Then the next pier pertains to Gillingham and Chatham: and one rod to plank and 3 beams to set.

Then the third pier pertains to the bishop once more; and two and a half rods to plank and 3 beams to set: from Halling, and from Trottiscliffe, and from Malling, and from [South]fleet, and from Stone, and from Pinden, and from Fawkham.

Then the fourth pier is the king's; and three and a half rods to plank and 3 beams to set: from Aylesford and all the lathe that lies thereto, and from Overhill, and from Oakleigh, and from the narrow estate (*þam smalanlande*), and from Cossington, and from Dowdes (*Dudesland*),[32] and from *Gisl[h]eardesland*, and from Wouldham, and from Burham, and from Eccles, [and from Stokenbury, and from Loose, and from Linton, and from *Lichebundesland*,][33] and from Horsted, and from Farleigh, and from Teston, and from Chalk, and from Henhurst, and from Haven [Street].

The fifth pier is the archbishop's; [and pertains] to Wrotham,[34] and to Maidstone, and to Wateringbury, and to Nettlestead, and to the two Peckhams, and to Hadlow, and to Mereworth, and to Leybourne, and to Swanton, and to Offham, and to Ditton, and to Westerham: and 4 rods to plank and 3 beams to set.

Then the sixth pier [pertains to] Hollingbourne and to all that lathe: and 4 rods to plank, and 3 beams to set.

Then the seventh and eighth piers are for the estate of the Hoo people (*to Howaran lande*) to construct; and four and a half rods to plank and 6 beams to set.

Then the ninth pier is the archbishop's, that is the land-pier at the west end; to [North]fleet, and to his Cliffe, and to Higham, and to Denton, and to Milton, and to Luddesdown, and to Meopham, and to Snodland, and to Birling, and to

---

K.J. Leyser, Oxford, ed. T. Reuter, London 1992, 1–20; for dating the compilation of the *Textus* to the episcopate of Ernulf (1115–1124), see *Textus Roffensis*, ed. Sawyer, ii, 18.

31 The Latin version has *in orientali brachio* where the Old English only has *on þone earm*, so it is possible that a word (*east, easterne*) has been omitted by the scribe of this leaf. The identification of the ninth pier as 'at the west end' leaves no doubt that the bridge is being described from east to west.

32 For the identification of *Dudesland*, see G. Ward, 'The lathe of Aylesford in 975', *Archaeologia Cantiana*, xlvi (1934), 7–26 (at 20) and J.K. Wallenberg, *Kentish Place-Names*, Uppsala 1931, 303. In the Latin text *Dudesland* comes at the end of the replacement leaf (f. 164); thereafter the hand of c.1120 takes over.

33 There is an erasure in the Latin and a gap in the Old English texts at this point, but the missing names are supplied (between square brackets) from the Latin version in London, British Library, Cotton Galba E.iv, f. 20. See below, Appendix C, 367–8.

34 *Wroteham* in the Old English text is the first word on f. 167, i.e. written by the scribe of the *Textus Roffensis* in c.1120.

Paddlesworth and all the valley-people (*dænewaru*):[35] and 4 rods to plank, and three beams to set.

The document was written on four consecutive folios of the *Textus Roffensis*: the Latin on ff. 164–5, the Old English on ff. 166–7. Unfortunately, however, the text has been tampered with. In both versions the first half of the document has been removed and the text has been rewritten on a replacement leaf in a later hand, probably of the very end of the twelfth century.[36] This means that the Old English text as far as the beginning of the fifth pier and the Latin text as far as the middle of the fourth pier are preserved in a manuscript of c.1200; but the second half of both versions is extant in a text of c.1120.

The reason for this rewriting is not hard to seek. The cartulary was regarded as a *textus*, a holy book, the honoured repository of the essential privileges and title deeds of the church of Rochester, which was probably kept close to or on the high altar.[37] The bridgework list, however, was an important prescriptive text whose regulations for the maintenance of the bridge had to be consulted whenever repairs were necessary. As estate organisation changed over the centuries, it was sensible to bring the estates assigned to particular piers up to date. The changes are unlikely to have been substantial. Both the format of the document and the language are broadly consistent in the two halves. There is no trace of spellings that would be natural for a scribe writing at the turn of the twelfth and thirteenth centuries.[38] The principal changes were probably made to the estates assigned to the bishop of Rochester's piers, that is the first and the third. By c.1200 the number of erasures or alterations to this early part of the document may have been so evident that an embarrassed Rochester scribe preferred to rewrite and replace the affected leaves.

Like most Old English administrative documents, the Rochester bridgework list is undated. Indeed, it bears no indication of the circumstances in which it was produced at all. It does not even make clear whether the document is a building contract for the construction of a new bridge (or a new wooden superstructure) or simply a regulation to govern repairs to an existing bridge.[39] Scholars have assumed that it was intended to fulfil the second role, which might explain its timeless quality. Moreover, since the work of the great eighteenth-century Rochester antiquary and bridge assistant, Dr J. Thorpe, they have dated the composition of the document to the reign of King Edgar (958–75), to c.975 or to 973x988.[40] Unfortunately this dating cannot be sustained. Noticing that certain piers are said

---

[35] The natural interpretation of *ealla þa dænewaru* as from *denu-ware* ('valley-people'), however, makes little topographical or historical sense. A possibility must be that the text should have read *dænware* and have referred to the inhabitants of the pig-pastures in the Weald ('denns') which were dependent upon distant Kentish manors.

[36] The dating ('s.xii/xiii') is that of N.R. Ker, *Catalogue of Manuscripts Containing Anglo-Saxon*, Oxford 1957, 447.

[37] *Textus Roffensis*, ed. Sawyer, i, 18–19.

[38] See the comments of P.R. Kitson cited in Appendix C, below, 363–4.

[39] I owe this point to the kindness of Mr C.R. Flight.

[40] J. Thorpe, *Antiquities of the Diocese of Rochester*, London 1782, 148; Ward, 'Lathe of Aylesford' (as in n. 32), 7–26; Robertson, *Anglo-Saxon Charters*, 351.

to belong to the bishop (nos. 1 and 3), to be the king's (no. 4) or the archbishop's (nos. 5 and 9), earlier scholars supposed that all the estates assigned to these piers would have belonged to those lords at the time of the document's composition. Since all the estates assigned to pier 1 and all except Pinden of those assigned to pier 3 were in the bishop of Rochester's hands in 1066 according to Domesday Book, it seemed reasonable to seek a time when all the estates allotted to the piers of the bishop, the archbishop and the king could have been within their lordship. But the attempt fails at the first hurdle, namely the estates of the church of Rochester, for there is no time, either in the later tenth century or later, when Malling and Fawkham were in the bishop's hands,[41] while Wouldham (pier 4) still remained with the king,[42] and Snodland and Denton (pier 9) belonged to the archbishop.[43]

Such a procedure would only be acceptable if we could be sure both that the text of the document represented accurately its content at the time of its composition and that the estates assigned to the lords' piers were indeed intended to be lists of their estates. Neither assumption can stand scrutiny. We cannot, of course, tell whether the text copied by the scribe of the *Textus Roffensis* in c.1120 had been emended before that time, but we do know that the opening section of the document (including both of the bishop's piers and most of the king's fourth pier) was subsequently so altered as to necessitate its rewriting on a new leaf by c.1200. In a book belonging to the cathedral community at Rochester, these changes are most likely to have affected the bishop's piers.

It is more sensible therefore to consider the archbishop's piers (5 and 9), since the early medieval history of the estates of the archbishops and the cathedral community at Canterbury are as well documented as those of Rochester;[44] while for these piers we do at least have the text as it was written by the scribe of the *Textus Roffensis* about the year 1120. We find that the first two estates listed under pier 5 (Wrotham and Maidstone) and the first under pier 9 (Northfleet) were indeed major archiepiscopal manors before the Norman conquest and are likely to have been very early possessions of the see;[45] but of the remaining eleven estates

---

[41] Campbell, *Charters of Rochester* (as in n. 22), no. 28 (S 514) is a purported royal grant of Malling to the see in c.942. Fawkham ought to have passed to Rochester by c.975 on the death of Brihtwaru, the widow of Ælfric, according to Robertson, *Anglo-Saxon Charters*, no. 59 (S 1457, perhaps of the early 980s) and D. Whitelock, *Anglo-Saxon Wills*, no. 11 (S 1511, probably of 973x5).

[42] According to Robertson, *Anglo-Saxon Charters*, no. 41 (S 1458), a statement of Rochester's claim to Wouldham, perhaps dating from 995, Wouldham had been granted by King Eadmund to Ælfstan (939x46) who eventually bequeathed it to Archbishop Dunstan seemingly on behalf of Rochester between 964 and 988. Thus it should not have been in royal hands after 946.

[43] The bishop of Rochester recovered his title deeds to Snodland, which had been stolen on behalf of Ælfric, as a result of litigation at London between 964 and 975, but seems not to have secured the estate until the death of Ælfric's widow, Brihtwaru (probably before 975). See Robertson, *A-S Charters*, no. 59 and Whitelock, *Wills*, no. 11 (as in n. 41). There is no evidence that Snodland or Denton (bequeathed directly to Rochester in Whitelock, *Wills*, no. 11) were ever in the hands of the archbishop.

[44] Brooks, *Church of Canterbury*, passim.

[45] Ibid., 106, 131.

assigned to the fifth pier only East Peckham, and of the nine assigned to pier 9 only Cliffe and Meopham were Canterbury estates in that they belonged either to the archbishops or to the cathedral community.[46] It seems clear that there had never been any intention that piers 5 and 9 should be repaired only by archiepiscopal or Christ Church estates; the archbishop's responsibility for these piers was rather a matter of coordinating a workforce drawn from estates of different lords. Doubtless he would have delegated the task to a reeve or to a tenant from the estates at the head of the lists, that is from Wrotham and from Northfleet. The fourth pier, which is said to be 'the king's', tells the same story. The first estate listed, Aylesford, was the principal royal manor in West Kent in the Middle Ages. But none of the other nineteen estates were in the king's hands in 1066; most are likely to have long been in lay hands, but Wouldham seems to have belonged to Rochester from 988,[47] and Farleigh may have belonged to Christ Church, Canterbury from 961 or thereabouts.[48]

If the estates assigned to piers did not in origin belong to the lords responsible for those piers, then we must abandon the attempt to date the document in terms of estate history. We are left only with linguistic means of establishing when the document was composed. Fortunately the scribe of the *Textus Roffensis*, though he made occasional slips, was normally accurate in reproducing the wording and to a considerable extent the spelling of his exemplars.[49] Moreover with at most two minor exceptions, the language of the first half of the text, which is written on the replacement leaf, is consistent with that of the second half. The document is written in good Old English with some traces of Kentish dialect, but with a number of features that place its composition in the eleventh century rather than in the 'classical' period of the late tenth.[50] It is therefore likely that the scribe of the *Textus Roffensis* was copying a document that had been composed in the first half of the eleventh century. Linguistic dating cannot, of course, be precise. An elderly English monk of Rochester could have composed it in the years immediately following the Norman conquest, but the later after 1066 the less likely it is that an administrative document of this type affecting the major landowners of a substantial part of Kent would have been composed in Old English rather than in Latin.[51]

[46] DB i, f. 3, 4b. Cliffe was said to have been given by the priest-abbot Werhard in the early ninth century (BCS 402; S 1414); Meopham was bequeathed to Christ Church by Brihtric and Ælfswith in ?973x5 (Whitelock, *Wills*, no. 11; S 1511).

[47] For the recovery of Wouldham by Archbishop Dunstan (d.988) for Rochester, see Robertson, *A-S Charters*, no. 41 (S 1458).

[48] For Eadgifu's supposed grant of Farleigh to Christ Church in 961, see BCS 1065 (S 1212).

[49] *Textus Roffensis*, ed. Sawyer, ii, 13–14; *Charters of Rochester*, ed. Campbell, xiii–xiv.

[50] See below, Appendix C, 363–4 for the detailed linguistic analysis of Mr P.R. Kitson, to whom I am much indebted.

[51] The Old English aristocracy of Kent was replaced by Normans very soon after 1066. See J. Le Patourel, *The Norman Empire*, Oxford 1976, 34, 40–8. For post-conquest OE texts see D.A.E. Pelteret, *Catalogue of English Post-Conquest Vernacular Documents*, Woodbridge 1990, passim.

The Reconstruction of the late Anglo-Saxon Bridge

The bridgework list assigns specific numbers of beams and exact quantities of planking, measured in terms of *gyrda*, to groups of estates. Each group is responsible for one of the nine piers of the bridge, except that the men of Hoo had to repair both the seventh and the eighth pier. These were practical arrangements for the repair of an actual bridge, so it is not surprising that it is possible to reconstruct the basic form of the bridge at Rochester from the details in the document (Fig. 4). We are told of nine piers, two of which were 'land-piers' or abutments. Each group of estates had to provide three beams or 'sills' (*sylla*), apart from the men of Hoo who had to provide six beams for their two piers. It therefore seems clear that the gaps between the piers were each spanned by three beams, and that these supported the timber roadway of planks laid across them.[52]

A bridge with seven piers in the river and with abutments on each bank should have had eight spans, but the document specifies nine sets of beams and planking, so either the first (the bishop's) or the last (the archbishop's) set of three beams must have been carrying the roadway from the river-bank further onto the land (Figs 4a, 4b). The timber specified in the list refers only to the beams and planking of the superstructure or carriageway. Nothing is said of any timber piles in the river-bed, nor of other wooden members belonging to the structure of the piers themselves, nor of any bracing struts supporting the beams. Thirteenth- and fourteenth-century records, moreover, make clear that the piers were of stone at that time and that the same arrangements for repair were then still in force.[53] It is reasonable to conclude that the piers of the late Anglo-Saxon bridge were already of stone (and were basically of Roman origin) and that they were not expected to need much maintenance, so that the particular obligations of the groups of estates did not need to be specified further.

It may be presumed that the timber carriageway was continuous, as is normal for the wooden superstructures of stone-piered bridges. In that case the measurements of the planking, which total 26½ *gyrda*, ought to give us the total length of the timber roadway. The Old English *gyrd* was the rod, pole or perch of 5½ yards or 16½ feet.[54] The bridge roadway would therefore have been 437⅓ feet long, but the

---

[52] The Latin version in *Textus Roffensis* has an additional sentence specifying that the beams had to be of sufficient size that they could well carry both the weight of the planks lying upon them and of all the traffic crossing the bridge. See Appendix C, 366–7.

[53] Below, 38–9 and n. 94.

[54] P. Grierson, *English Linear Measurements*, Stenton Lecture, Reading 1971; for the Roman origin of this perch, see P. Kidson, 'A metrological investigation', *Journal of the Warburg and*

actual length between the bridge abutments would be 415¼ or 420¼ feet, depending on whether the overland extension of the carriageway was at the east or west end. These are certainly figures of the right order of magnitude. The modern bridge built on the same site between 1851 and 1856 is 485 feet in length, but we would expect the fast-flowing Medway to have carved a wider stream during the intervening years at this narrow point immediately upstream from the acute angle in its course (Fig. 1).

Reconstruction in this simple form as a bridge with stone piers and a timber roadway of planks resting on three beams means that the bridgework list is complete in itself. It is not necessary to suppose that there were once missing texts that had specified obligations to produce other timber and supplies for the bridge. It also makes clear that the late Anglo-Saxon bridge at Rochester was a typical Roman bridge with stone piers and timber superstructure as found throughout Europe north of the Alps. The remains of the massive Roman pier-foundation discovered in 1851 encourages the belief that the late Anglo-Saxon bridge was indeed still using the Roman stone piers. What cannot be determined is whether the timber roadway had had a continuous history of use and piecemeal repair since Roman times or whether the bridgework list is documenting an Anglo-Saxon replacement of a more elaborate (conceivably stone-arched) but ruined Roman superstructure. To judge from the evidence of bridgework in Anglo-Saxon charters, however, we should certainly expect that the bridge at Rochester had had a continous history of use and repair at least from the early eighth century.

Early attempts to reconstruct the late Anglo-Saxon bridge assumed that the piers had been equally spaced across the river.[55] But it is difficult to understand, in that event, why the groups of estates assigned to each pier should not have been of equivalent extent and have had to provide identical amounts of planking. It is much more likely that the diverse measurements of planking tell us the length of the roadway to be covered and therefore the distance between the centres of the bridge-piers. Reconstructed in this form (Fig. 4), either as 4a or 4b, it may be noted that there is a tendency for the spacing between the piers to be longer at the western end, that is on the outside of the bend where the stream and tide would be faster

Courtauld Institutes, 53 (1990), 71–97; for a recent demonstration that a shorter Germanic perch of 4.65 metres was also in use in Anglo-Saxon England, see E.C. Fernie, 'Anglo-Saxon lengths and the evidence of buildings' and P.J. Huggins, 'Anglo-Saxon timber-building measurements: recent results', *Medieval Archaeology*, 35 (1991), 1–5, 6–28.

[55] S. Denne (?), *History and Antiquities of Rochester and its Environs*, London 1772, 44–5 erroneously allocated 4 beams to the sixth pier and supposed that the bridge had nine piers but ten equal spans of 43 feet! Denne was copied by E. Hasted, *History and topographical Survey of the County of Kent*, ii, Canterbury 1782, 15–16. The only attempt at a scaled drawing of the reconstructed Anglo-Saxon bridge was by J. Essex, 'A description and plan of the ancient bridge at Rochester, collected from two MSS published in Lambarde's "Perambulation of Kent"', *Archaeologia*, vii (1785), 395–401. He corrected some of Denne's errors, but believing the piers to have been of wood produced a plan which required 97 or 98 beams, the additional 70 being provided 'by different persons or places in the county', not to mention an uncertain number of 'joists', 'braces' and 'scantling'. Despite such imaginative departures from the texts, Essex's plan has *faute de mieux* been the one reproduced subsequently.

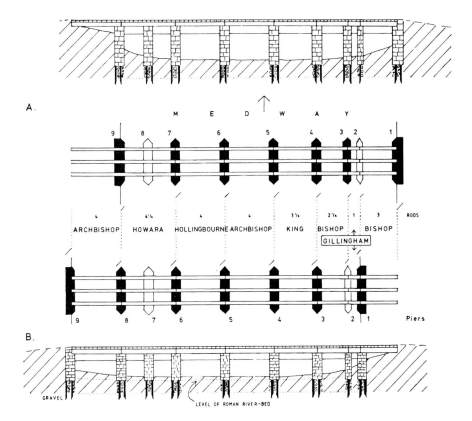

Figure 4. Alternative reconstructions (A and B) of the Anglo-Saxon bridge at Rochester, showing the nine piers and the beams of the timber superstructure, their allocation to lords and estates, and the measurements in rods and perches.

and the water deeper. Indeed this pattern of increasing spans towards the outside of the river's bend may have originally been even more regular. One possible explanation why the men of Hoo should uniquely have been responsible for two piers is that they originally had had to plank their four and a half rods of the carriageway and to provide beams for a single span, the largest in the bridge; when that task had proved too great for the available timber, they had had to provide an additional supporting pier to make their section of the bridge secure. The very short length of planking and beams (just one rod) for which the men of Gillingham and Chatham were responsible from the second pier might have had a similar origin (Fig. 4a). If, however, their responsibility was to span the gap between their second pier and the bishop's abutment (Fig. 4b), then it would fit a pattern common among medieval bridges of having a short first span; it may be that this section of the roadway was intended to be removable for defensive purposes.[56]

The wooden superstructure implied by the Rochester bridgework list raises questions both about the forestry practice and about the engineering and carpentry skills of early medieval England. It is likely that the principal timbers were of oak, either from the Weald or from the London clay of North Kent. If the beams provided by each group of estates had stretched from pier-centre to pier centre, the longest beams would have been of four rods, that is 66 feet long; if the men of Hoo had originally had to provide beams of 4¼ rods, these would have been of 72 feet 4 inches. That is improbably (but not impossibly) long. When grown closely together in competitive 'high forest' conditions, oaks will attain 30–40 metres (c.100–130 feet) which would produce some timbers of the length required. In the thirteenth and fourteenth centuries, however, when the rooves and spires of cathedrals were being built, about 50 feet seems to have been the limit of straight oak timbers then available in England.[57] Whilst it may be that difficulties of transport were then in reality the controlling factor, it seems unlikely that timbers at least 15–16 feet longer than the thirteenth-century maximum were available in late Anglo-Saxon Kent. An altogether more plausible interpretation is that the stone piers of Rochester bridge were of sufficient width to reduce the length of timber required to manageable proportions.

It has also to be asked whether a bridge of this form could indeed have stood for several centuries. The crucial question here is not so much the availability of timber of the required length, but rather the unsupported length that the timber girders would be required to span, that is the distance between the piers. Engineering

[56] When Simon de Montfort sought to capture the town and castle in 1264, he found that the burgesses had removed one section of the roadway and fortified their end of the bridge. See below, 37. Reconstruction 4b might be preferred to 4a, if the bridgework list's distinction between the eastern *arm* and the west *end* is significant.

[57] O. Rackham, *Trees and Woodland in the British Landscape*, London 1976, 75; id., *Ancient Woodland: history, vegetation and uses*, London 1980, 147, 152–3, 303. Rackham's figures derive from forests and churches in the Midlands and East Anglia, but he does cite the forest of Fontainebleau where oaks of over 100 feet in height are common. For evidence on the size of oaks when grown closely spaced, I am indebted to Dr P.S. Savill of the Department of Plant Sciences, University of Oxford. See also P.S. Savill and M.J. Spilsbury, 'Growing oaks at closer spacing', *Forestry*, lxiv (1991), 373–84.

principles suggest that seasoned oak beams of 1½ foot square section would bear the likely weight of planking and of carts crossing it, so long as the gaps to be spanned were less than 50 feet.[58] Unfortunately we do not know the width of the piers. The Roman pier-foundation removed in 1850 was at least as wide as the Strood pier of the new bridge (17 foot 8 inches). Had the Roman piers each been 23 feet (7 metres) wide, like those of the second-century bridge at Trier, then the longest beams would have had an unsupported span of 43 feet. An oak trunk 50 feet long and adzed or sawn to a square section of 1½ feet would weigh about 4 tons. Transport to Rochester could doubtless have been facilitated by floating the trunks down the Medway, but the task or raising such timbers onto the piers would itself have been a considerable engineering feat. Once again everything that one can learn or deduce about Rochester Bridge increases ones admiration both for its original Roman builders and for the generations of Anglo-Saxons who laboured to keep it in repair.

[58] I am grateful to Dr G.W.E. Milligan, Fellow in Civil Engineering of Magdalen College, Oxford, for guidance on the principles involved. The main problem is less the ability of the beams to support the weight than the dangerous flexibility of the timber roadway. The rigidity of the bridge would of course have been improved the more firmly the beams were secured into the structure of the piers or if there had been some diagonal bracing of the beams from a lower point on the piers, despite the silence of the document. His calculations were based on a carriageway 6 metres (approx. 19½ feet) wide, with planking 5 centimetres (approx. 2 inches) thick; they suggest approximate absolute limits of 30 foot spans for 12-inch square beams, 40 foot for 15-inch square beams and 50 foot for 18-inch square beams.

The Territory of the
late Anglo-Saxon Bridge

The identification of the estates assigned to the repair of the nine piers in the Rochester bridgework list is not a difficult task. The fact that after the completion of the new stone bridge in 1392 the Anglo-Saxon contributory estates were still ultimately liable for the repair of the bridge meant that they elected bridge wardens every year until 1908. Thus there was a continuing tradition of the bridgework territory and it was possible for Dr J. Thorpe, the Rochester antiquary and bridge assistant, to publish in 1731 a list identifying all except three (*Dudesland, Gisleardesland,* and *Þam smalanlande*) of the fifty-four names in the *Textus Roffensis* version of the document in terms of contemporary manors and parishes.[59] In the seventeenth and eighteenth centuries the bridge clerks were still using the parish system to notify the contributory estates of the need to send householders to participate in the elections, and were still distraining them when they failed to do so.[60] This continuity makes it possible to map the bridgework territory with some confidence. Forty-two of the bridgework estates have names which are also those of ancient ecclesiastical parishes whose boundaries were mapped in the Tithe Awards of the mid-nineteenth century. Parish boundaries commonly coincide with those of estates of the late Anglo-Saxon and Anglo-Norman periods, since it was at those times that the parishes were being defined. No less than ten of the estates in the bridgework list have extant pre-conquest charters with detailed boundary clauses. In every case the bounds agree in whole or in part with those of the nineteenth-century parishes.[61] It therefore makes sense to use parish boundaries as a guide to the extent of the territory that had to contribute to the repair of Rochester Bridge.

When the bridgework estates are mapped using parish boundaries (Fig. 5), it becomes clear that the bridgework territory very largely coincided with one of the Kentish 'lathes' (the name used for the six or seven medieval sub-divisions of Kent), namely with the region known in Domesday Book as the lathe of Aylesford. At first sight it appears that only about half of the territory of the lathe was

---

[59] J. Thorpe, *A List of the Lands Contributory to Rochester Bridge,* 1731. Throughout this section my understanding of parochial and estate histories has benefitted from the generous advice of Mr C.R. Flight, in particular for the information on parishes and chapels incorporated into nn. 63, 66 and 67.

[60] See Gibson, below, 130–4.

[61] The charters are as follows: *Charters of Rochester,* ed. Campbell, nos. 12 (Trottiscliffe), 14 (Broomy/Bromhey), 15 (Halling), 17 (Borstal), 27 (West Malling), 28 (Cuxton) and 31 (Wouldham) [S 129, 130, 37, 165, 321, 514 and 885]; BCS 562 (Haydon/Haven Street), 576 (Farleigh) and 741 (Meopham) [S 1276, 350 and 447].

assigned to bridgework; but most of the apparent omissions can be explained so that it becomes clear that virtually the whole lathe was intended to be liable to bridgework at Rochester. Thus the largest group of parishes that are not listed are those surrounding Hollingbourne. They comprised the hundred of Eyhorne in the thirteenth century and later. But the bridgework list assigns the sixth pier not just to Hollingbourne, but also to 'all that lathe', though it does not explain the extent of the territory or 'lathe' dependent upon Hollingbourne. That it was indeed the later hundred of Eyhorne was made clear both in the *Quo Warranto* inquests of 1279 and in the thirteenth-century version of the bridgework list from Canterbury which allocate the sixth pier to the hundred of Eyhorne and then apportion responsibility to estates in every parish in the hundred.[62]

Several other estates, seemingly omitted from the bridgework list, prove upon investigation to have been included under other names. Thus Strood, the parish at the western bridgehead, is not included; nor, however, is it found in Domesday Book. The estate and the parish of Strood were in fact twelfth-century creations, carved out of the episcopal manors of Cuxton and Frindsbury, for the bounds of Cuxton in a late ninth-century charter include the southern half of Strood parish, placing the northern boundary of Cuxton along 'the old street', that is along Watling Street itself.[63] Similarly the parishes of Ryarsh and Addington seem not to have become separate estates until after the bridgework list had been composed; Domesday Book shows them to have been in lay hands in both 1066 and 1086, but an eighth-century charter establishes that Birling (which is a bridgework estate) adjoined Trottiscliffe on both the east and the south in 788 and therefore must have included at that time the later parishes of Ryarsh and Addington (Fig. 5).[64] In comparable fashion Hunton, which is not recorded as a bridgework estate, was at the time of the Domesday survey a part of East Farleigh (a manor of the monks of Christ Church, Canterbury) and was held by their steward, Godfrey.[65] Other parishes omitted both from the bridgework list and from Domesday Book may likewise have only become jurisdictionally separate estates after the composition of the list, whatever the antiquity of the settlements within them. Stanstead, Ightham and Shipbourne therefore seem likely to have been considered parts of Wrotham;[66] Ifield, Cobham and Shorne parts of Chalk; Gravesend part of Milton; the Isle of

[62] See Appendix C, 367–9.

[63] *Charters of Rochester*, ed. Campbell, no. 27 (S 321). Ecclesiastically Strood was a chapel of Frindsbury (*Textus Roffensis*, ed. Sawyer, f. 221 margin) until the 1190s when the church was given to Strood hospital by Bishop Gilbert of Rochester.

[64] Ibid., no. 12 (S 129).

[65] The Domesday record of East Farleigh (DB, i, f. 4v; *DB Kent*, 3/5) records that Godfrey holds ½ sulung of the 6 sulungs of the manor; *Domesday Monachorum* identifies this as Hunton (ed. D.C. Douglas, London 1944, 95).

[66] See A. Everitt, *Continuity and Colonization: the evolution of Kentish Society*, Leicester 1986, 207, Map 13, 271–2. That Stanstead was part of Wrotham is shown by the fact that the whole western boundary of Trottiscliffe was formed by Wrotham in a charter of 788 [see *Charters of Rochester*, ed. Campbell, no. 12 (S 129)] and by its listing as a chapel of Wrotham in *Textus Roffensis*, f. 221 margin. Shipbourne's ecclesiastical links, however, were with Tonbridge and it may be that it should be excluded from the lathe.

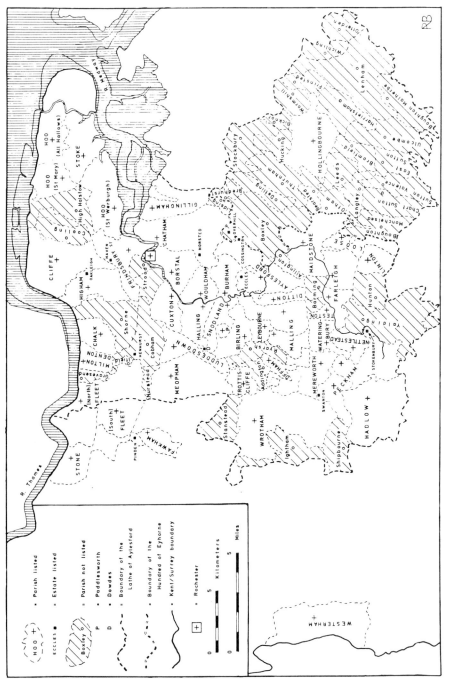

Figure 5. Map of the estates owing bridgework at Rochester, showing their relationship to the lathe of Aylesford.

Grain and Lidsing parts of Gillingham;[67] and High Halstow part of the territory of the Hoo people (*Howare*).

We are left with just five parishes in the lathe of Aylesford which existed as separate manors at the time of Domesday Book, but are not listed in the bridge-work list: Allington, Barming (East and West),[68] Cooling, Nurstead and Yalding. There is no evident reason why they should have escaped bridgework. In 1086 all were held by laymen, either by Richard fitzGilbert, lord of Tonbridge (East Barming and Yalding), or by Norman tenants of Bishop Odo of Bayeux; in 1066 all had been held by Anglo-Saxons, either directly from King Edward or from powerful magnates, Earl Leofwine (Cooling) and Æthelnoth Cild (Allington).[68] One of these estates, Cooling, had already been in lay hands in the early ninth century and had been disputed in the early tenth between Eadgifu, wife and widow of King Edward the Elder, on one hand and Goda and his descendants on the other. Eventually Eadgifu proved her title in Edgar's reign and gave Cooling to Christ Church, but it may be doubted whether the grant endured long beyond Edgar's reign since Cooling was in lay hands once more in 1066.[70] It seems unlikely that Cooling had received a unique exemption from bridgework, conceivably as a favour to the widow-queen Eadgifu; more probably the estate, being situated in the Hoo peninsula, was considered to be part of the territory of the *Howare* and therefore had to contribute to piers 7 and 8.

A similar explanation can be offered for three of the four remaining omissions: Allington, Barming and Yalding. They may have been considered part of the 'lathe that lies to' Aylesford, to which the fourth pier was assigned. Certainly Allington and Barming adjoin Aylesford, while Yalding had medieval tenurial links with Aylesford in the form of a shared 'denn' in the Weald.[71] The final omission, Nurstead, seems more likely to have been carved from a parent manor at North-fleet, perhaps at some time between the composition of the bridgework list and the Domesday survey.[72] What seems clear is that the obligation of repairing Rochester Bridge was in origin a territorial one, falling upon the whole lathe of Aylesford. Given the inadequacy of our knowledge of Anglo-Saxon estate history and the fact that the text of the document has been subject to alterations and erasures, it should not suprise us that we cannot provide certain explanations for every omission from the list.

---

[67] Grain was a separate parish by the twelfth century (*Textus Roffensis*, f. 221v) but was part of the archiepiscopal manor of Gillingham; Lidsing was a chapel of Gillingham (Ibid., f. 221v margin).

[68] Domesday Book records no pre-Conquest tenant of West Barming, which may have only been separated from East Barming after 1066.

[69] DB, i, ff. 7r, 7v, 8v, 9r, 14r (*DB Kent*, 5/41, 5/55, 5/101, 5/106, 5/113, 11/1, 11/2).

[70] BCS 326 (S 163); for Eadgifu's recovery of Cooling and grant to Christ Church, see F.E. Harmer, *Select English Historical Documents of the 9th and 10th Centuries*, Cambridge 1914, no. 23 (S 1211). Christ Church still claimed Cooling in spurious *pancartae* of the eleventh century: J.M. Kemble, *Codex Diplomaticus Ævi Saxonici*, 6 vols, London 1838–48 [hereafter cited as KCD], no. 715 (S 914) and Robertson, *A-S Charters*, no. 95 (S 1047).

[71] Everitt, *Continuity and Colonization*, 149.

[72] It is not clear whether the northern boundary of Meopham in BCS 741 (S 447) includes or excludes Nurstead.

Five estates which lie outside the lathe of Aylesford are nonetheless included in the bridgework list (Fig. 5). Four – Southfleet, Stone, Pinden and Fawkham, the last properties assigned to the bishop of Rochester's pier (no. 3) – are adjacent estates on, or close to, the north-eastern boundary of the lathe. But Westerham, the last estate assigned to the archbishop's pier (no. 5), lies a good five miles to the west of the nearest part of the lathe and is actually on the county boundary with Surrey. All five may represent alterations to an original territorial scheme for the bridge's repair. The four assigned to pier 3 come from that part of the *Textus Roffensis* that was rewritten at the end of the twelfth century and presumably represent an attempt by the bishop to adjust the burden of bridgework more evenly over his estates, whether they were in the lathe or not. Here as elsewhere in the document we see the seigneurial interest beginning to override the original territorial principle; for it was doubtless very much easier for the bishop's reeve to coerce men from Rochester estates to provide the necessary labour than to use the court of the lathe to secure labour from the men of different communities and other lords.

It is less easy to explain how Westerham came to be added at the end of the estates liable for the fifth (the archbishop's) pier, since it was neither an archiepi-scopal nor a Christ Church estate. It is therefore instructive that the men of Westerham are the only community who are known to have objected to being required to contribute to the bridge. In 1310–11 after the timber roadway of the fifth pier had collapsed, the tenants of Westerham refused to contribute; William Mot, the king's bailiff, therefore distrained a horse and five cows from them; whereupon he was attacked, beaten and forced to release the animals by Richard Trewe and Hamon le Brun of Westerham. In 1340 when the fifth pier again needed repair an inquisition held before Roger of Southwick and John Frere of Strood on 1 March identified what vills were liable; when the men of Westerham objected once more, the jurors reassembled on 26 June and swore that the men of that vill were bound to the repair of the pier 'by reason of the lands and tenements which they hold in that vill like the other vills assigned to the repair and support of the aforesaid pier'.[73] There was, it would seem, no appeal against the evidence of the bridgework list, however unreasonable it might be. Tenants in the listed vills were liable for bridgework. By that time the connection between the listed estates and the lathe of Aylesford was perhaps no longer evident, and the lathe itself had long since ceased to function as an effective territory or court. We cannot guess whether Westerham had been added to the fifth pier for some temporary tenurial reason or whether it was perhaps just a scribal error at some stage in the document's trans-mission.[74]

The impression that in the Rochester bridgework list we are looking at a terri-toral system in a state of partial disintegration is confirmed if we look at the

---

[73] C.T. Flower, *Public Works in Medieval Law*, Selden Soc., xxxii, London 1915, 203–9 but with 'sulungs' misunderstood as 'shillings'. Cf. Brooks, 'Church, crown and community' (as in n. 30), 15 where the men of Westerham's tenements *in eadem villa* are wrongly interpreted as lying in the town of Rochester, although the reference can only be to the 'vill' of Westerham.

[74] Conceivably a mistake for a vill within the lathe of Aylesford, such as Ightham (*Ehteham*), or Wester in Linton (*Westerey*) or West Malling.

territories that seem to have been assigned to the individual piers (Fig. 6). The estates assigned to the second and sixth piers both form coherent territories, the medieval hundreds of Chatham and Eyhorne respectively, but no such geographical and administrative sense characterizes the other pier-territories. Piers 1 and 5 each have a core territory but with a number of outliers; piers 4 and 9 each have improbably distended territories with one major outlier, whilst pier 3 has a territory formed of detached fragments without any core at all. It seems likely that many, perhaps all, of these irregularities are consequences of the bishop of Rochester's desire to have his piers repaired by men from Rochester estates and of the archbishop's comparable wish that his great manor of Maidstone should be assigned to his pier (no. 5); the removal of Canterbury and Rochester estates from other pier-territories will have had knock-on effects, necessitating further adjustments. It may be that Westerham came to be assigned to Rochester Bridge in some such process of compensation. The king's pier (no. 4) may also have achieved its astonishingly elongated territory as a result of this process. Other communities, such as the Hoo people, may have been less well placed to secure assistance with their burden of two piers when the episcopal estates at Stoke and Broomy (part of Frindsbury) were transferred to the first pier; the island of Grain, part of the archbishop's manor of Gillingham, may also have originally been in the territory of the adjacent Howare.

While such alterations to the pier-territories may have started from a wish to suit seigneurial needs, there may also have been some continuing need to ensure that the work was distributed reasonably. We have evidence that the late Anglo-Saxon burden of bridgework (like the related obligation of boroughwork) was levied on the traditional assessments, that is on the basis that one man served from every hide (or, in Kent, from every sulung).[75] Certainly the sulung assessments of Kentish estates, as recorded in the Domesday survey, were still determining obligations to repair particular piers in the fourteenth century.[76] If, therefore, we compare the length of planked roadway that each pier-territory had to provide with the assessment of the estates in *Domesday Book*, we find that the disparities are not great:

> Pier 1 (3½ rods of planked roadway) 19½ sulungs; pier 2 (1 rod) 12 sulungs; pier 3 (2½ rods) 26½ sulungs; pier 4 (3½ rods) 27 sulungs 3 yokes; pier 5 (4 rods) 49 sulungs; pier 6 (4 rods) 55 sulungs; pier 7 & 8 (4½ rods) 55½ sulungs; pier 9 (4 rods) 43 sulungs, 3 yokes.[77]

On average we find 11 sulungs responsible for each rod of planked roadway. Somewhat surprisingly the bishop's first pier and the king's fourth pier are the ones that appear overburdened. Even there the disparity may have been more apparent than real: the territory of the first pier surrounded the episcopal city of Rochester itself, which had no assessment and is not listed; the figure for the fourth pier is

---

[75] Brooks, 'Church, crown and community' (as in n. 30), 2–3, 11–12.

[76] See below, 38–9.

[77] For the Domesday assessment of the estates assigned to each pier, see Brooks, 'Church, crown and community', 18–20.

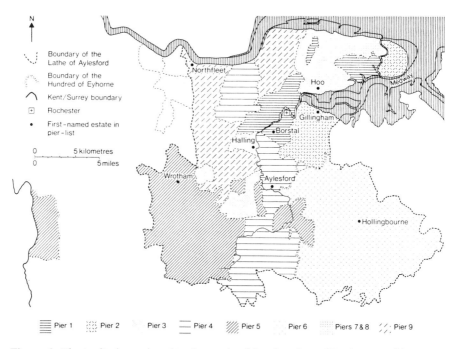

Figure 6. The territories assigned to the repair of the nine piers of Rochester Bridge.

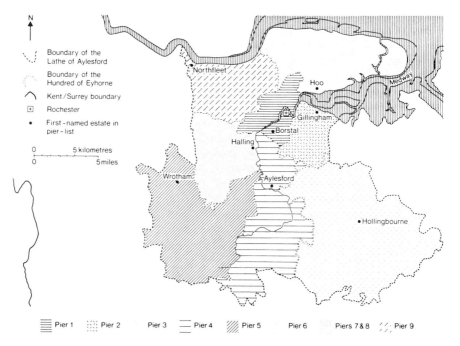

Figure 7. Conjectural reconstruction of the original pier-territories of Rochester Bridge as they may have existed in the seventh or eighth century.

also falsely low, since not only were many small estates listed under this pier whose assessment is unrecorded, but also a territory, or 'lathe', dependent upon Aylesford, which is also of unknown extent and assessment.[78]

Another indication that the pier-territories were not entirely arbitrary may be found in their relation to the structures of lordship in early medieval Kent. Professor Everitt identified almost fifty early estate-centres in Kent primarily on the basis of the survival of traces of their superior status in later manorial arrangements.[79] Of the nine situated in the lathe of Aylesford, all except Rochester itself were included in the bridgework list either as the first- or the second-named estate assigned to the piers:

> Pier 1 [Rochester]; pier 2 – ; pier 3 Trottiscliffe (2); pier 4 Aylesford (1); pier 5 Wrotham (1), Maidstone (2); pier 6 Hollingbourne (1); pier 7 & 8 Hoo (1); pier 9 Northfleet (1) and Cliffe (2).

Everitt also identified all these nine centres as early 'minsters' or mother-churches and recent work on the territorial organisation of the early Anglo-Saxon church in other parts of England has emphasized how closely it mirrored the structure of lordship in 'Middle Saxon' England.[80] It is therefore unlikely that the distribution of the most important estate-centres so evenly among the piers of the bridge is accidental. Only pier 2 lacks such a centre and that was the pier which had the shortest length of roadway to provide.

We may suspect that behind the complexities of the bridgework document as we have it in the *Textus Roffensis* and behind the text as it had been composed in the early eleventh century lay a system in which every pier of Rochester Bridge was supported by a territory forming a coherent geographical unit and normally dependent upon a major estate-centre. Figure 7 represents a highly conjectural attempt to reconstruct the form of the pier-territories as they may have existed in the seventh, eighth or ninth centuries. The exact distribution of parishes between piers 3, 4, 5 and 9 is inevitably somewhat arbitrary and is intended only to indicate the sort of original pattern from which the arrangements of the extant document could have derived. In its original form the arrangements for Rochester Bridge may simply have allocated particular peoples (such as the *Howare*) or particular estate-centres and their territories ('Hollingbourne and all that lathe') to the piers.

The precise lists of estates and the involvement of the greatest lords in the document as we now have it would reflect the growth and fragmentation of lordship in the middle and late Anglo-Saxon periods, the development of a manorial economy and of village nucleation. In this context it is well to remember that the

---

[78] The estates listed under the fourth pier but not named in Domesday Book are Overhill, *þam smalanlande*, Cozenton, Dowdes, *Gisleardesland*, Loose, Linton and *Lichebundesland*. It is also possible that the Domesday assessment of the manor of Aylesford at one sulung is the product of a reduction by the king in favour of his own estate.

[79] Everitt, *Continuity and Colonization*, 69–92.

[80] Ibid., 187–96; *Minsters and Parish Churches: the local church in transition 950–1200*, ed. J. Blair, Oxford Committee for Archaeology, 1988.

lathe of Aylesford appears to have been known in the eighth and ninth centuries as the territory of the *Cæsterware* or *Cæstersæte*, that is the people dependent upon the 'chester' (Rochester).[81] It seems entirely appropriate that bridgework at Rochester should have originally been performed by all the *Cæsterware* and natural to wonder what relation (if any) this early Anglo-Saxon territory may have had to the territory that had had to support the Roman bridge in late-Roman times. It is conceivable that the city-territory of *Durobrivae* was essentially the same as the lathe of Aylesford and that some sense of territorial responsibility had been maintained across the divide of the Dark Ages. It must be allowed, however, that the names of the individual estates, and of those that head each pier's list in particular, show little or no sign of Roman origin. Names in *-ham* (Wrotham), in *-ingaham* (Gillingham), in *-ingas* or *-ing-* (Halling, Hollingbourne) are English names that are likely to have been formed in the sixth, seventh or eighth centuries.[82] They would allow an origin for the bridgework scheme in the seventh or eighth century, but not earlier unless there had been a wholesale renaming of Celtic and Roman estates.

[81] BCS 199 (S 31) of c.747; Campbell, *Charters of Rochester*, nos. 4, 16 (S 30, 157) of 762 and 801. All these charters concern estates within the later lathe of Aylesford.

[82] M. Gelling, *Signposts to the Past*, London 1978, 105–112; J.M. Dodgson, 'The significance of the distribution of the English place-names in *-ingas*, *-inga-* in South-East England', *Medieval Archaeology*, x (1966), 1–29; id., 'Place-names from *-ham* distiguished from *-hamm* in relation to the settlement of Kent, Surrey and Sussex', *Anglo-Saxon England*, ii (1973), 1–50.

The Bridge from 1066 to the 1380s

After the Norman conquest, and more especially in the twelfth, thirteenth and fourteenth centuries, Rochester Bridge enters recorded history with increasing frequency. The testimony of chronicles and increasingly of records (first those of the cathedral priory of Rochester and then, from the thirteenth century, the chancery enrolments of the various offices of royal government) enable us to fill out the story of the bridge and of the constant struggle to maintain it in usable condition. The entry of the bridgework list into the great cartulary of the cathedral priory, the *Textus Roffensis*, in the time of Bishop Ernulf (1115–1125) is itself a reflection of the growing importance of the written word in Anglo-Norman England. We cannot tell whether it had also been occasioned by a recent collapse and repair of some section of the bridge. Only a few years later a general writ-charter of King Henry I in favour of the monks of Rochester confirmed them in possession of all the lands and rights that they had had in the reigns of William the Conqueror and of William Rufus: among these rights was specified the fourth penny of tolls by land and water at Rochester and also of ferry dues when the bridge was broken.[83] The community's right to a quarter of the ferry payments may roughly reflect the fact that two of the nine piers of the bridge were the responsibility of the bishop, a burden which was met from the priory's estates. In later centuries when any section of the bridge was down, we hear of ferry payments being devoted to the repair of the bridge.[84]

Among the principal benefactors of Rochester cathedral in the early twelfth century was Ansfrid, lord of Allington and sheriff of Kent in the early 1130s, and his wife, Mabel, who had two sons, both named William. The younger William, when newly made an esquire (*tyro*), rode through Rochester and coming to the bridge rashly neglected to dismount and to lead his horse across, as was customary. The terrified horse leapt off the bridge into the stream, drowning the unfortunate rider. The event was remembered in the cathedral because the dead William's tunic was made into a dalmatic for use on 'white feasts', whilst the sale of the horse paid for the pyx (*eucharistia*) which hung above the high altar.[85]

---

[83] *Regesta Regum Anglo-Normannorum 1066–1154*, ii (*1100–1135*), ed. C. Johnson and H.A. Cronne, Oxford 1956, no. 1867, where it is dated 1130x3. The charter is written in both a Latin and an Old English version. For the OE version, see Pelteret, *English Post-Conquest Vernacular Documents*, no. 49. The same rights were confirmed by Henry II in 1176–7 (London, British Library, Cotton Ch. VII.7).

[84] Below, 39.

[85] *Registrum Roffense*, ed. J. Thorpe, London 1769, 119. For the dates of Ansfrid's shrievalty, see J.A. Green, *English Sheriffs to 1154*, Public Record Office Handbooks, xxiv, London 1990, 17, 50.

The fact that it was unsafe to cross the bridge on horseback or in high winds is confirmed in later episodes. Thus a member of Edward I's household hired a horse from Richard Lamberd, a citizen of Rochester, on 18–19 February 1300, which was blown off the bridge and drowned; the king's wardrobe made a payment of 12 shillings to Lamberd for his loss.[86] A number of further individuals who drowned in the Medway after falling from the bridge can be gleaned from deaths recorded as being accidental rather than criminal in the thirteenth-century eyre rolls: Christiana, wife of Eymer of Gillingham, in the roll of 1261–3 and John le Fevere, who lost his footing when standing on one of the beams of the bridge, in that of 1292–4. Regrettably the brief entries in the eyre rolls include no details about the condition of the bridge. Thus when Ralf Lomb of Strood met Wulstan Edwyne of Worcester when crossing the bridge at night, 'each killed the other', but the roll of 1313–14 does not specify whether they slew each other on the bridge or whether they fell and drowned because part of the roadway was then so narrow that passing was perilous.[87]

A story with a happier ending is that of 'The harper at Rochester', in which a minstrel recounts in ninety-nine lines of French (or rather Anglo-Norman) verse how a gust of wind blew him off the bridge as he was crossing at Rochester. As he was borne down the Medway, he played lustily on his harp, appealing all the while to the Virgin Mary. In consequence he was not drowned, but gained the bank a league downstream and to the applause of a gathering crowd gave thanks to 'Our Lady' in a church there. His song is written in a hand of c.1300 in a loose quire now bound up with a late thirteenth-century manuscript from St Mary's, Dover.[88] That may be the provenance of the song, hence its emphasis on the Virgin. Whether this *fabliau* is history or simply fiction intended to amuse a Dover audience does not matter. The story depended upon the notorious dangers of crossing Rochester bridge (. . . *un punt mu perilye, dunt maint home fu deschus*) and could not have seemed too far-fetched to contemporaries. None of these episodes refers to any balustrade or handrail on the bridge, not even to its inadequacy or poor repair. The absence from the Rochester bridgework list of any reference to the provision of a timber fence of posts and rails on either side of the roadway therefore suggests that there was indeed no such protection for those using the bridge. Apparently the carriageway was a wooden platform without fences or guiderails on either side.[89] It

---

86 *Wardrobe Account, 28 Edward I*, Society of Antiquaries, London, 1787, 28, 30. A convenient summary is in W.B. Rye, 'Visits to Rochester and Chatham 1300–1783', *Archaeologia Cantiana*, vi (1864–5), 43–82 (at 44–5).

87 London, P[ublic] R[ecord] O[ffice], JUST 1/369, m. 38 and JUST 1/371, m. 46 for Christiana; JUST 1/374, m. 68 and JUST 1/376, m. 66 for John Le Fevere; JUST 1/383, m. 74 for Ralf Lomb and Wulstan Edwyne. The Eyre rolls, which also record numerous persons who fell from boats into the Medway and drowned, particularly when the bridge was under repair, are conveniently listed by D. Crook, *Records of the General Eyre*, PRO Handbooks, xx, London 1982.

88 London, British Library, Cotton Cleopatra A xii, ff. 68r–69v (old foliation 64r–65v). The song 'Del harpur a Roucestre' follows an Anglo-Norman poem on William the Conqueror and his three sons, written in the same hand and was printed by F. Michel, *Roman d'Eustache le moine*, Paris 1834, 108–111.

89 For a representation of exactly such a bridge see the thirteenth-century seal of Innsbruck

seems surprising that the citizens of Rochester should have failed to provide them, apparently being content to leave the contributory estates to maintain the bridge in this simple but dangerous form.

In the thirteenth century Rochester Bridge had figured prominently in the warfare between English kings and their baronial opponents, in particular because Rochester castle was of key strategic importance for the control of routes between London and the Channel. In 1215 when the settlement of *Magna Carta* rapidly degenerated into civil war, the barons secured the castle with a garrison under William de Albini with the intention that it could be relieved, when necessary, from their stronghold of London. On 12 October, however, John's forces entered the town from the east and found the bridge defended by Robert fitzWalter and 60 knights. Although baronialist writers claim that the king's attack on the bridge was beaten off, by the following day John had succeeded in seizing and breaking the bridge (*confractis pontibus*). Since the castle could no longer be relieved from the west, its siege and ultimate fall (28 October) were assured.[90] Unfortunately we know nothing of the extent of the damage that John's troops inflicted upon the bridge, nor of how long it took for repairs to be effected – presumably during the minority of Henry III.

The bridge and the castle were once more the focus of military activities in the spring of 1264, when the castle was held for Henry III by John, earl of Warenne, and Roger Leyburn. Simon de Montfort organised a joint attack by his own forces from London and Gilbert de Clare's from Tonbridge. The burgesses of Rochester had broken the bridge and had fortified their end. But on the second day of the assault (18 April) Earl Simon succeeded in firing the elaborate fortifications that had been built on the bridge – the use of Greek fire is mentioned in one account – and then entered the city. The siege of the castle was, however, soon abandoned (26 April), when the king's army threatened London.[91]

Much has been made by Kentish antiquarians of the brief chronicle accounts of these events in 1215 and 1264: in particular they suggested that John had attempted to burn the bridge but that Fitzwalter had put out the fire, and that Simon de Montfort's fireships had started a blaze which had consumed the whole bridge, as well as the timber tower upon it.[92] Unfortunately we have no firm evidence of the extent of the damage on either occasion or of the nature of the repairs that were necessary. What is clear, however, is that by the mid-thirteenth century the strategic role of the bridge in the defence of the town in the first instance, but thence of the whole kingdom, was coming to be recognized. Nothing is known of the form of the timber tower and fortifications that the citizens had erected in 1264. Two

---

reproduced by S. Rigold, 'Structural aspects of medieval bridges', *Medieval Archaeology*, xix (1975), 15, fig. 14.

[90] Ralf of Coggeshall, *Chronicon Anglicanum*, ed. J. Stevenson, Rolls Series 66, London 1875, 175; Barnwell Annals, preserved in Walter of Coventry, *Memoriale*, ed. W. Stubbs, Rolls Series 58, London 1873, ii. 226–7.

[91] Matthew Paris, *Flores Historiarum*, ed. H.R. Luard, Rolls Series 95b, London 1890, ii. 489–90; Annals of Dunstable in *Annales Monastici*, ed. H.R. Luard, Rolls Series 36c, iii. 230–1.

[92] Denne, *History of Rochester*, 45–6; Hasted, *History of Kent*, ii, 17–18.

generations later an inquisition of the year 1343 reveals that by that time (perhaps in consequence of the war with France) the king had extended the bridge at its western end by providing a barbican or double tower with a drawbridge (*pons tractivus*), while the master of the hospital of St Mary at Strood was responsible for the wharf and its buildings on the western bank.[93]

From the reign of Edward I the quality of our information about repairs to the bridge improves, so that we can compile a reasonably complete account of the last century of the first bridge's history. The picture that the sources provide is of a bridge that was becoming increasingly difficult to keep in use. On no fewer than nineteen occasions between 1277 and 1381 the bridge was broken and substantial repairs were necessary. Serious collapses of the timber roadway or of the piers that supported it were still occasional events until the 1340s; thereafter they became frequent until the final collapse of 1381. Despite developments in royal administration and the unevenness of the surviving records, the procedure adopted on each occasion seems to have been much the same. When the bridge became unusuable, the king appointed two or three leading officials or Kentish notables to hold an inquisition or commission to enquire from a jury of 'worthy and lawful men' of the county in order to determine who was responsible for the upkeep of every pier of the bridge and section of the carriageway. On each occasion the jurors swore to the arrangements as they are essentially found in the Rochester bridgework list. Records of such inquisitions or commissions survive from 1277, 1280, 1310, 1332, 1339, 1343, 1344, 1350, 1354, 1355, 1359, 1360, 1361, 1363, 1364, 1369, 1375, 1377, and 1381/2.[94]

Often the jurors went on to specify exactly how the burden of the repairs of the particular damaged pier or roadway was to be divided amongst the listed estates in terms of their assessment in sulungs, yokes and acres. The record of one such inquisition, perhaps either that of 1277 or of 1280, has been preserved in the registers of Canterbury cathedral priory and is printed here in Appendix C, no. III.[95] On this occasion the fourth and sixth piers had been damaged and the jurors provided details of the assessments of the estates assigned to their repair; indeed they went further and gave information about every tenement, even down to the

---

[93] Inquisition of 23 June 1343 held before J. de Vyelestone, *Calendar of Inquisitions Miscellaneous*, ii, *1307–49*, 459–60 (no. 1846); the king's drawbridge had to be repaired in 1375 (see below, n. 94).

[94] 1277 (*Calendar of Inquisitions Miscellaneous, 1219–1307*, London, 1916, no. 1061); 1280 (*Cal. Pat. Rolls, 1272–81*, 414; 1310 (*Cal. Pat. Rolls, 1307–13*, 331; 1332 (*Cal. Pat. Rolls, 1330–4*, 284; 1339/40 (C.T. Flower, *Public Works in Medieval Law*, i, Selden Society, xxxii (1915), 203–9; 1343 (*Cal. Inq. Misc., 1307–1349*, 459–60); 1344 (*Cal. Pat. Rolls, 1343–5*, 425); 1350 (*Cal. Pat. Rolls, 1348–50*, 526); 1354 (*Cal. Pat. Rolls, 1354–8*, 67); 1355 (Ibid., 230); 1359 (*Cal. Pat. Rolls, 1358–61*, 280); 1360 (Ibid., 485); 1361 (PRO, E101/509/2); 1363 (*Cal. Pat. Rolls, 1361–4*, 444); 1364 (Ibid., 543); 1369 (*Cal. Pat. Rolls, 1367–70*, 343); 1375 (PRO, E/101/480/4); 1377 (*Cal. Pat. Rolls, 1377–81*, 53); 1381/2 (*Cal. Pat. Rolls, 1381–5*, 136.

[95] Below, 367–9. A similar list specifying the sulungs assigned to the estates assigned to the fifth pier is found in the record of the inquisition of 8 April 1340 recorded on the Coram rege Roll, Easter, 14 Edward III, m. 45 and printed by C.T. Flower, *Public Works in Mediaeval Law*, i, Selden Society, xxxii, London 1916, 204–8 (at 206).

level of 'the heirs of Thomas de la Dane's five acres' in Hollingbourne and of many other tiny holdings. It is evident from these lists that the actual work was to be done by the peasant tenants of the estates, and it is instructive that for the fourth pier the jurors omitted to declare (or the scribes to record) that this pier was 'the king's'. They also made no mention of the fact that the first named estate should have been the royal manor of Aylesford.[96] It is difficult not to suspect that Edward I's government was more willing to see that the work was allocated than it was to enforce the obligations from the king's own manors.

After this repair to the fourth and sixth piers, it was the fifth pier that had to be restored in 1310–11, the wharf at the west end in 1332, the fifth again in 1339–40, the first and third in 1343, the king's drawbridge in 1375, whilst in 1354–5 the astonishing sum of £534 6s. 8d. had been spent on repairs to the whole structure and the expense shared among the contributory estates.[97] Even this incomplete listing makes clear that in the late thirteenth and fourteenth centuries almost all parts of the bridge were causing concern. An increasingly strident tone is detectable in the writs setting up the inquisitions and authorizing the repairs, protesting at the bridge's neglected and perilous state, at the failure of the estates and persons responsible to keep it in a state of good repair, and at the inconvenience, delays and dangers to travellers of the ferry that was used when the bridge was broken. Here the public records confirm the evidence of the song of 'The harper at Rochester' and of those who drowned after falling from the bridge that at times when it was in use, the bridge had become notoriously dangerous. When the bridge was broken, however, the ferries seem to have been even more hazardous. The Kentish eyre rolls record several named individuals, as well as groups of unknown *extranei* and pilgrims, who drowned when they fell from boats when crossing the river in stormy weather at times when the bridge was down.[98]

At one level the evidence of the last century of the first bridge's history is a splendid witness to the practicality of the traditional arrangements for its repair and to the efficiency of English medieval government. Time and time again, as repairs became necessary the burden was indeed allocated to the communities that had borne the responsibility for centuries in accord with the sworn testimony of lawworthy jurors of the county. When a section of the bridge had collapsed, the king granted to named individuals the right to operate a ferry, requiring them to present a full account of the income so that the proceeds could be put to the needs of the bridge and the fourth penny could indeed be paid to the cathedral priory, as had been customary at least since Henry I's charter of 1130x3.[99] In the mid-fourteenth century when the bridge was broken almost annually, the repairs were sometimes

---

96 A more charitable interpretation would suggest that the king's construction of the barbican and drawbridge at the west end (above n. 93) had necessitated some redistribution of the crown's responsibilities.

97 See the references in n. 92, above.

98 Eyre of 1292–4: PRO, JUST 1/374, m. 67d and JUST 1/376, m. 65d (*quidam peregrini ignoti* and John Edward of Strood). Eyre of 1313–14: PRO, JUST 1/384, m. 74d (*quidam extranei*).

99 Above, 35.

effected very speedily: one pier collapsed on 28 September 1361; but by 18 October the ferry could be discontinued since the repairs had been completed.[100]

But at another level it must have been increasingly evident that this marvellous relic of the Roman past, this triumph of Roman engineering skills, had become a liability. Its days were numbered and the effort of keeping the ruinous structure in any state of repair was less and less profitable. The sources do not make clear to what extent it was the timber superstructure with its huge oak beams that was proving difficult to renew effectively (perhaps because of a lack of adequate timber), or whether it was rather the masonry structure of the Roman stone piers themselves which was finally giving way to the centuries of tidal pressure and the inexorable rise in the mesne water level. In the end it was the severe winter of 1380–1, when (despite the tidal flow) the Medway froze above Rochester, that was the occasion of its final fall. A sudden thaw about the time of Candlemas, the feast of the Purification of the Virgin Mary (2 February), brought a huge head of water and vast ice floes onto the bridge, so that their combined weight carried away 'the great part of the bridge'.[101] It was not immediately apparent that this was indeed to be the end of the old bridge. It was several years before a practical design could be agreed, or the necessary political will and financial resources found, to build a new stone bridge at Rochester. It was therefore some time before the possibility of restoring the old bridge was finally abandoned. But Candlemas 1381 does indeed mark the natural termination of the history of the first bridge. Its sad final decade as a broken ruin before the completion of the new bridge in 1392 is better considered as the preamble to the story of the new bridge.

[100] PRO, E101/509/2.
[101] *The Westminster Chronicle, 1381–1394*, ed. L.C. Hector and B.F. Harvey, Oxford 1982, 2–3.

Rochester Bridge

1381–1530

The New Bridge

1381 – 1530

'About the feast of the Purification of the Blessed Virgin this year a great part of Rochester Bridge was destroyed. Ice had formed in vast quantities, and when it broke up, with the onset of milder weather, the massive pressure of the floes which had composed it wrecked the bridge.'[1] So the author of the *Westminster Chronicle* opens his work. He informs us, with greater precision than that of any other authority, how the old bridge had met its last calamity about the beginning of February 1381. A reliable source from three months after the accident adds the further detail that the bridge had fallen at a time of storms and floods.[2] The bridge had been known to be in need of repair for some years, but in spite of the king's having appointed commissioners to organise the necessary building operations, not enough had been done.[3] The chronicler implies that the fall of the bridge was an event of national importance. Perhaps he saw it as a portent of the collapse of traditional authority in Kent only a few months later, since he rapidly takes his reader on to the dramatic events of the Peasants' Revolt. But for its strategic importance alone the loss of the bridge was a matter for concern, since it impeded communications from London to Canterbury and the Kent channel ports.

The restoration of the bridge was the responsibility of the 'persons, towns, places and districts' committed by long-established custom to its maintenance. The need to provide an alternative means of crossing the Medway supplied an additional local source of funds for repairs; a ferry was quickly established, and in May the king entrusted its revenues to two local appointees who were to spend any proceeds on the bridge. The need to get the repairs in hand was pressing because having to cross the river in small boats was both inordinately inconvenient and potentially dangerous.[4] But the size of the task in hand soon revealed the incompatibility between available local resources and the national interests at stake. The problem of cash was acute. The burden of supporting the bridge was so heavy, it was later observed, that those unfortunate enough to be subject to it were almost destroyed and brought to nothing.[5] In addition, the administrative weaknesses of traditional arrangements were thoroughly exposed. There were ambiguities about just who was responsible and there were problems in compelling contributors to

---

1 *The Westminster Chronicle, 1381–1394*, ed. L.C. Hector and B.F. Harvey, Oxford Medieval Texts, Oxford 1982, 2–3.
2 PRO, C.66/310, m. 17.
3 PRO, C.66/297, m. 1d.
4 PRO, C.66/310, m. 17. The word 'feria' here means ferry, not fair; cf. 'totum proficuum ferie siue passagii', in PRO, C.66/314, m. 20. The danger of the river crossing is stated here, and even more emphatically in PRO, C.66/316, m. 29.
5 PRO, C.62/52, m. 5, edited in *Rot. Parl.*, iii, 289b–290b. The original petition is PRO, S.C.8/85.

pay their share. Some men were inclined to collect money and materials for the bridge and then hang on to them, so that it was unclear what was available and who had what. Two royal commissions were appointed to sort out these disorders in the following years.[6] The problems were perhaps insurmountable. Certainly whatever was done to mend the bridge during the two years after its destruction was not enough. In March 1383 travellers were still dependent upon a ferry crossing.[7]

In that month a new initiative redefined both the problems to be solved and the resources to be devoted to solving them. A new bridge would be built at a new crossing point considered better and safer, a hundred yards upstream from the old bridge between the northern bastion of Rochester castle on the eastern bank and Strood Hospital on the opposite side of the river. William Lambarde later commented that the new site was preferable to the old 'both for the fastnes of the soile and for the breaking of the swiftnes of the streame'.[8] The new bridge was planned to be bigger than the old one, presumably because in practice the amount of traffic was thought to warrant it. Because of its new position it was also longer.[9] The structure was to be wholly of stone, unlike the old bridge with its wooden beams and planks.[10] It was decided to complete limited repairs on the old bridge so that it could be used by pedestrians and riders until the new one was ready. Thomas Dodmere and Richard Purveyour were appointed to impress stonemasons, carpenters and labourers and to commandeer building materials and transport for both bridges.[11] The planning of these operations must have involved Henry Yevele from its earliest stages. He was the best English architect of his day, and knew all about big bridges from many years of service as a warden of London Bridge.[12] In February 1383 the king had appointed him one of four supervisors of expenditure on the old Rochester Bridge,[13] but his interest in the work is likely to have gone back earlier; he was the most obvious consultant with whom to discuss the technical difficulties of the case. It is unlikely that any one else involved with the bridge would have had the knowledge and confidence to propose moving and enlarging it.

One of the local figures most involved from the beginning of the new bridge was Sir John de Cobham. His family seat at Cobham was only 3½ miles from the bridge and he was one of the customary contributors to the maintenance of the old structure. Sir John was a leading figure in Kent county society. He had been one of

[6] PRO, C.66/312, m. 25d, C.66/314, m. 2d.

[7] *Cal. Pat. R., 1381–5*, 241.

[8] *Rot. Parl.*, iii, 354b; W. Lambarde, *A Perambulation of Kent*, 1st edn, London 1576, 303; RBT, The Bridge Mapps (1663–1717), map 9. Hasted estimated the distance at forty yards, but this is too short (E. Hasted, *The History of Kent*, 2nd edn, 12 vols, Canterbury 1797–1801, iv, 78). The two bridges were not parallel; my measurement, from the centre of the Roman bridge to the centre of the new bridge in mid stream, corresponds to that of A.A. Arnold, 'Rochester Bridge in 1561', *Archaeologia Cantiana*, xvii (1887), 213.

[9] PRO, S.C.8/119; *Cal. Pat. R., 1381–5*, 239, 243.

[10] *Rot. Parl.*, iii, 354b.

[11] PRO, C.66/314, m. 2d.

[12] J.H. Harvey, *Henry Yevele, c.1320 to 1400: The Life of an English Architect*, London 1944, 28–9, 40.

[13] PRO, C.66/314, m. 20.

the commissioners appointed to look to the safety of the bridge in October 1377. A
year after the fall of the bridge he had been one of the commissioners appointed in
February 1382 to find out who was responsible for repairs, and in March 1383 he
was appointed with Henry Yevele to supervise the spending of money from the
ferry on the repair of the old bridge.[14] Sir John participated in the project for a new
bridge from the outset. He was involved in the new arrangements authorised in
royal documents issued on 18 and 20 March 1383. The profits of the Medway ferry
were devoted to repairing the old bridge, at least in the first instance, but the king
granted for seven years a special bridge toll on the old bridge to help pay for the
new one. Sir John was appointed with Henry Yevele and others to supervise the
spending of these various sums. On 7 March Sir John was also appointed to a
commission to establish who in Kent had money and materials belonging to the
bridge.[15] He had known Henry Yevele for a number of years, and Yevele had
designed buildings for him at Cobham and Cooling and in London, so the two men
knew how to co-operate.[16] But none of the evidence from the early 1380s suggests
that Sir John was making any outstanding personal contribution to the finances of
the project.

Sir John's deeper involvement with the new bridge came only some years after
the new bridge was begun, and it hinged upon an alliance with the Cheshire knight,
Sir Robert Knolles.[17] The two men were associated in local defence in July 1385
when they were both principal captains to guard southern England while Richard II
was engaged on his Scottish expedition.[18] They co-operated as the feoffees of some
lands in Norfolk in the summer of 1387.[19] But the two men no doubt knew each
other, despite their very different origins, through service of the crown over many
years. Both were national figures with long and distinguished careers. Sir John had
served in the French wars in his younger days, but during the last ten years had
been employed more as a diplomat. He was a member of the king's council.[20] Sir
Robert's war record had been exceptionally long, adventurous and profitable, and
had come to an end about the time the old bridge collapsed. He was in London at
the time of the Peasants' Revolt, and distinguished himself in organising the
citizens of London to resist the rebels. He had an interest in Kent as the trustee for
the heirs of John, Earl of Pembroke, in respect of an estate of 1,000 acres at Elmley
in the Isle of Sheppey.[21]

In the summer of 1387 Sir John and Sir Robert joined forces to carry through
the works at Rochester Bridge. For Sir John this was an intensification of his

[14] PRO, C.66/297, m. 1d, C.66/314, m. 20; *Cal. Pat. R., 1381–5*, 235.

[15] *Cal. Pat. R., 1381–5*, 239–40, 243, 262.

[16] Harvey, *Henry Yevele*, 30, 37–9.

[17] For a discussion of the significance of Sir Robert's Cheshire background for his career, see M.J.
Bennett, *Community, Class and Careerism*, Cambridge 1983, 162–91, 205–7.

[18] *Cal. Pat. R., 1385–9*, 80.

[19] *Cal. Pat. R., 1385–9*, 327–8.

[20] *Dictionary of National Biography*, 22 vols, Oxford 1921–2, iv, 611–12.

[21] J.C. Bridge, 'Two Cheshire Soldiers of Fortune of the XIV Century: Sir Hugh Calveley and Sir
Robert Knolles', *Journal of the Chester Archaeological Society*, xiv (1908), 201–5, 220.

Knolles

earlier involvement; for Sir Robert it was something new. Sir Robert's Kentish connections were tenuous, and he seems to have been drawn to the bridge as a worthy cause. The bridge was on the route both to the battlefields of France and to the shrine of St Thomas, so the nationalism of his active years and the piety of his old age may equally well have been his motives for action. Lambarde surmised that Knolles was aiming 'some way to make himselfe as well beloued of his countrie men at home as he had been euery way dread and feared of straungers abroad'.[22] It was probably as a result of a recent agreement between Sir John and Sir Robert, and between them and the king, that on 8 July 1387 Richard II revoked his earlier grants of revenue from the ferry and from pontage. We are told simply that this action was taken 'for certain reasons propounded before us and our council', but such a step suggests that alternative finances for the bridge works had become available.[23] The following month Sir John and Sir Robert were associated with Henry Yevele, John Clifford, the chief mason of London Bridge, and Sir William Rickhill in obtaining a recognisance in £360 from masons and quarrymen of the Maidstone area, probably to secure the performance of a contract for materials for the bridge.[24] The first unambiguous evidence of a new deal is in a royal grant of 18 March 1388 that describes the bridge wardens as deputies of Sir John and Sir Robert. At this time the wardens were dependent upon Sir John and Sir Robert for money. A similar grant of 22 October 1390 shows the same structure of responsibility.[25]

From 1388, then, Sir John de Cobham and Sir Robert Knolles were recognised as the principal donors to the bridge. Sir Robert's purse seems to have been the longer. An account of Robert Rowe as bridge warden for the twelvemonth ending 26 June 1392, the earliest wardens' account to have survived, is described as recording 'all receipts and expenses on Rochester Bridge in the name of Sir Robert Knolles, knight'. The main receipts recorded in the account are £250 all received at various times in the year from Sir John Drewe.[26] Drewe was parson of Harpley in Norfolk. He was also Sir Robert's private clerk, was associated with his business affairs over many years, and was eventually to be one of his executors.[27] The evidence here is consistent with Sir Robert's being the sole source of funds. Rowe may have kept a separate account for Sir John's money, though that would surely have required some complex accounting fictions. In later days there were some who associated the bridge more with Sir Robert than with Sir John, like Thomas of

---

22 W. Lambarde, *A Perambulation of Kent*, 1576 edn, 314.

23 PRO, C.66/324, m. 36.

24 Harvey, *Henry Yevele*, 41–2.

25 *Cal. Pat. R., 1385–69*, p. 416; *Cal. Pat. R., 1388–92*, 316, 329. In March 1388 the purveyors of materials for the bridge were instructed to act 'per auisamentum et assignacionem Roberti Rowe et sociorum suorum deputatorum dilectorum et fidelium nostrorum Johannis de Cobeham et Roberti de Knolles chiualer', PRO, C.66/325, m. 28.

26 RBT, account 1391–2.

27 *Cal. Pat. R., 1385–9*, 327–8, *Cal. Pat. R., 1391–6*, 660, *Cal. Pat. R., 1405–6*, 182, 319; RBT, account 1424–5; Bridge, 'Two Cheshire Soldiers of Fortune', 219–23.

Plate 1. Brass in Cobham church of Sir John de Cobham who died in 1407.

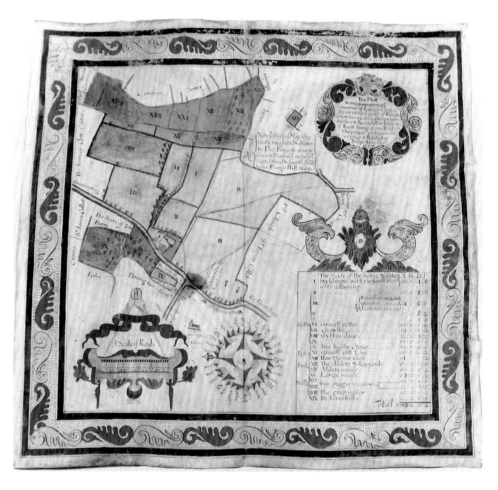

Plate 2. Estate Map drawn in 1659 of the Manor of Langdon given to the Bridge Wardens in 1399.

Plate 3. Royal Grant from Henry VI to the Bridge Wardens for support of the Bridge Chapel in 1442.

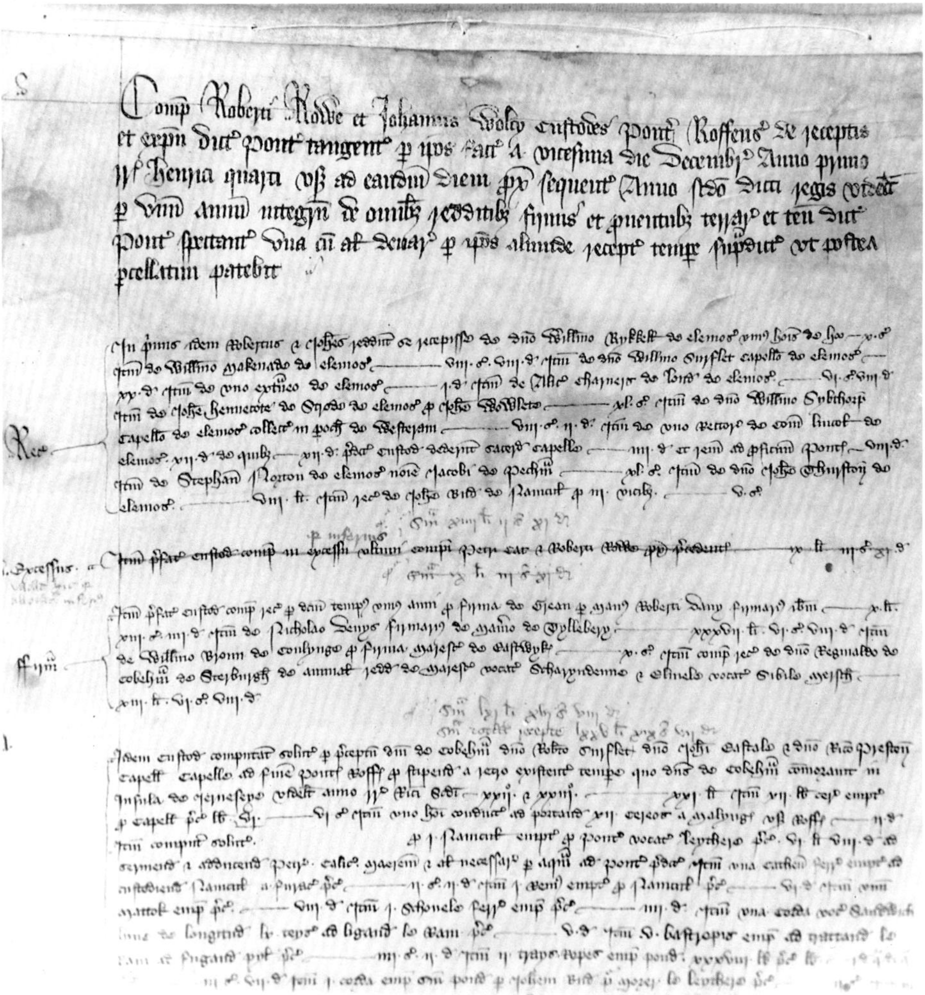

Plate 4. Account roll of Bridge Wardens Robert Rowe and John Wolcy, 1399–1400.

Walsingham, whose chronicles make much of the former's enormous wealth and charitable giving.[28]

The bridge was nearing completion in the autumn of 1391. The construction of two large piers of the bridge was begun only in Richard II's fourteenth year, ending 22 June 1391.[29] But that was perhaps the last major operation on the main structure. In a petition presented to the November parliament of 1391 the new bridge is spoken of as an accomplished fact.[30] The unusual sales of surplus materials recorded in the account of 1391–2 has been explained as evidence that the work was nearing completion.[31] It may also be relevant that of the £250 received from John Drewe that year, £170 had been received by the end of November 1391. One last part remaining to be completed in 1391 was outside the control of Sir John and Sir Robert. This was the drawbridge between two of the piers with the winding chamber above it, which was the responsibility of the king. He assigned responsibility for it to successive controllers and clerks of his works and it was not finally completed until 1397 or 1398.[32] We do not know what was done to celebrate the completion of the bridge as a whole, or at what point the first pedestrians, riders and carts were able to trundle over it.

Thomas of Walsingham described the new bridge as 'sumptuosissimus', which can be translated as 'magnificent'.[33] It is hard to know how close the surviving pictures of the eighteenth century can take us to what was there in 1391. Medieval bridges were vulnerable structures, especially when they were large and built over a tidal river, and Rochester Bridge must have been one of the most difficult in England to maintain. By the time the bridge was eventually demolished in 1857 it had been patched and rebuilt over and over again. But until the engineering wonders of the industrial revolution drew men's fancies in other directions, the bridge retained the fascination it had exercised on its first admirers. In 1561 it was described as 'so notable a monument . . . that besydes the bryge of London and Brystow none in the realm (is) to be compared to yt'.[34] As late as 1782 it could be said that 'the bridge, for height and strength, is allowed to be superior to any in England, excepting those at London and Westminster'.[35] These comments should not be accepted too literally; their authors are likely not to have known some of the biggest bridges of England away from the London area, like those of Newcastle upon Tyne in the North-East, or Bideford and Barnstaple in the South-West (Table 1).

---

28 *The St. Alban's Chronicle, 1406–1420*, ed. V.H. Galbraith, Oxford 1937, 22; Thomas Walsingham, *Historia Anglicana*, ed. H.T. Riley, Rolls ser., London 1863–4, ii, 277.

29 RBT, undated account c.1392.

30 PRO, C.62/52, m. 5.

31 J. Becker, *Rochester Bridge, 1387–1856: A History of its Early Years*, London 1930, 9.

32 PRO, C.66/341, m. 17, C.66/345, m. 10, C.66/347, m. 7, C.66/349, mm. 16, 17; H.M. Colvin, ed., *The History of the King's Works*, 6 vols, London 1963–73, ii, 814–15.

33 *The St. Alban's Chronicle*, ed. Galbraith, 22. The relevant passage is translated in Bennett, Community, Class and Careerism, 183.

34 Arnold, 'Rochester Bridge in 1561', 225.

35 Hasted, *History of Kent*, iv, 77.

Table 1

The dimensions of some large medieval English bridges

Bridge	First built in stone	Length feet	Number of openings	Width feet
London	1176–1209	906	20[a]	20
Newcastle	from 1248	711	12	?
Bristol	mid 13th c.	216	4	15
Barnstaple	late 13th c.	700	16	?
Bideford	late 13th c.	677[b]	24	?
Rochester	1383–91	560	11[a]	14

[a]   including one drawbridge opening
[b]   existing structure

Sources: J.C. Bruce, 'The Three Bridges over the Tyne at Newcastle', *Archaeologia Aeliana*, new ser., x, pp. 2–11; J. Dalloway, *Antiquities of Bristow in the Middle Centuries*, Bristol 1834, 27; G. Home, *Old London Bridge*, London 1931, 24–5; W.G. Hoskins, *Devon*, London 1954, 330 (Barnstaple), 335–6 (Bideford).

The total length of the new Rochester Bridge was 560 feet and it was 14 feet wide. Where the old bridge had had nine piers, including those on either bank of the Medway, the new one probably had twelve. It is likely that the foundations of the bridge, at least, remained fixed in the course of successive rebuilding between 1391 and the eighteenth century. If so, then, there were eleven openings between the piers, all arched except for the seventh opening from the Rochester bank, which was crossed by the royal drawbridge and surmounted by the winding-house.[36] These dimensions were smaller than those of the similarly constructed London Bridge which was 906 feet long, 20 feet wide and had twenty openings including a drawbridge.[37] Bristol bridge was impressive in a different way. It was 216 feet long with only four arches, but it was high and broad – more than 15 feet wide if the houses are included – and the houses on it were particularly fine.[38]

The opposite banks of the Medway where the bridge abutted were built up with stone walling, called the east breast and the west breast.[39] The stone piers across the river were of differing dimensions, and the width of the arches varied too because of irregularities in the riverbed. The same was true of other long medieval arched bridges.[40] As in the case of London Bridge, and many other bridges built since the eleventh century, the piers were built upon structures called staddles. A member of

[36] Becker, *Rochester Bridge*, 9–10. The location of the drawbridge is known only from much later pictures.
[37] G. Home, *Old London Bridge*, London 1931, 24–5.
[38] J. Dallaway, *Antiquities of Bristow in the Middle Centuries*, Bristol 1834, 27; J. Millerd, *Plan of Bristol*, 1673. I owe these references to Dr Simon Penn.
[39] RBT, account 1398–9, 1400–1, 1424–5.
[40] Home, *Old London Bridge*, 26–7.

the firm of contractors who removed these foundations of the bridge after its demolition described them as having been constructed by driving iron-tipped piles, mostly of elm, close together into the riverbed to establish a base about 45 feet long by 20 feet wide. Around each platform a protective barrier was made with further piles tied together, and the cavity so formed was packed with chalk, thereby creating a platform of about 95 feet by 40 feet. Both upstream and downstream these platforms were pointed to allow tides to run in and out with minimal resistance. The top and sides of each platform were boarded over with elm planks. Modern writers call such platforms starlings (a word deriving perhaps from 'staddling') and reserve the word staddles for the bases upon which the piers of a bridge rested. The functional difference is indeed an important one; starlings were constructed to resist the force of the river while staddles had to bear the weight of the bridge. In the early Rochester Bridge accounts, however, the whole structure at the foot of each pier was called a staddle, and this usage will be followed here. The demolition of these structures in the nineteenth century involved the removal from the riverbed of over 10,000 piles.[41]

The roadway across the bridge was paved with ragstone, and was kept clear of accumulated rubbish by being cleaned from time to time each year.[42] There were gutters to allow rain to run off the surface.[43] Unlike the bridges at London and Bristol there were never any houses on Rochester Bridge in the later Middle Ages, partly perhaps because the city of Rochester was less in need of building, but chiefly because of the vulnerability of the bridge to being undermined by the waters beneath it. By the east breast, at the Rochester end of the bridge, was a counting house, which occurs in the records from 1398–9 onwards. It was thatched with rushes and had a chimney. There was also a storehouse for bridge equipment which is first recorded in 1399.[44] Since there were no regular tolls to be collected this building presumably functioned as the bridge office, where financial records were compiled and stored.

A further addition to the bridge complex was the bridge chapel, which was described as 'newly erected' in mid January 1393.[45] Large medieval bridges always had chapels associated with them, and often built on them, as at London and Bristol.[46] The chapel belonging with Rochester Bridge stood opposite the head of the bridge on the Rochester bank. It was built by Sir John de Cobham, and was

---

[41] A.A. Arnold, 'The Earliest Rochester Bridge; Was It Built by the Romans?', *Archaeologia Cantiana*, xxxv (1921), 134; Becker, *Rochester Bridge*, 7–8; M.N. Boyer, *Medieval French Bridges*, Cambridge, Mass., 1976, 84–5. The earliest use of the word starling noted in OED (under starling[2]) is from c.1684.

[42] RBT, accounts 1398–9, 1400–1, 1402–3, 1403–4. The use of rag for paving the bridge is attested in 1426–7: 'In cariagio de rag per aquam ad dictum pontem pro paviamento eiusdem, ijs viijd' (RBT, account 1426–7).

[43] RBT, account 1414–15.

[44] RBT, accounts 1398–9, 1400–1, 1410–11.

[45] Becker, *Rochester Bridge*, 13.

[46] R. Hall Warren, 'The Medieval Chapels of Bristol', *Transactions of the Bristol and Gloucestershire Archaeological Society*, xxx (1907), 182–3; Home, *Old London Bridge*, 47. For a broader discussion, see Boyer, *Medieval French Bridges*, 53–5.

particularly associated with him. In January 1395 he obtained royal licence to found a chantry there whose three chaplains were eventually to be supported out of the bridge endowment.[47] In the short term, however, he was obliged to support them from his own income. The unique responsibility of Sir John for the chaplains in the early years is established by the misfortunes that afflicted them in 1397. In that year Sir John's past caught up with him when he was impeached by the commons for his association with Richard II's opponents eleven years earlier. He was lucky to escape with his life, but was spared on account of his age, and was banished to Jersey instead. He returned to England only after Henry Bolingbroke's triumph over Richard II in 1399.[48] All this time the three chaplains had received no stipends. It was only on Sir John's return from exile that the wardens were authorised to spend £21 to make up the arrears.[49]

The future maintenance of the bridge was a question which already exercised the minds of its two principal benefactors at the time when its construction was nearing completion. It was too vulnerable to be left to take its chance; like the old one it needed some institutional structure to take care of it, and the burden of financial responsibility had to be defined for future years. There was no question of the bridge being a private possession of Sir John, Sir Robert and their heirs. Nor was it intended that the upkeep of the bridge should be financed by tolls on those who used it. Conservatism supplied one of the answers to the problem. People in Kent who had been responsible for the old bridge could be made responsible for the new one. In the parliament of November 1391 Sir John and Sir Robert petitioned that the responsibility for maintaining the new bridge should be reapportioned between the old contributors, and to this end they supplied a schedule of responsibilities for the old bridge copied from records in the royal exchequer – a transcript, in fact, of the Latin version of the text relating to bridgework from the *Textus Roffensis*.[50] As in the past the contributors should choose annually two of their number to be wardens with responsibility for keeping the bridge and accounting for the sums of money received for its maintenance. This was granted by the king; hundreds of years of tradition were not to be sacrificed in a moment of need. The responsibility of the contributors was the subject of another petition in Parliament in 1397, and it was confirmed by royal letters patent in January 1399.[51]

Some petitions of Sir John and Sir Robert to the crown from this period show that they were attempting to allocate responsibilities precisely.[52] Calculating the length of the bridge at 566 feet 1⅛ inches they divided it up between the contributing parishes so that the groups responsible for each pier of the old bridge should be

---

[47] PRO, C.66/341, m. 30. The original petition which these letters patent answer is PRO, S.C.8/147.

[48] *Dictionary of National Biography*, iv, 612; A. Tuck, *Richard II and the English Nobility*, London 1973, 219.

[49] RBT, account 1399–1400.

[50] PRO, S.C.8/85 ('Domesday pour le pount de Roucestr' selonc leschequer'): cf. Textus Roffensis, ff. 164v–165v. Two petitions in which the burdens of maintaining the new bridge are allocated seem to date from this same occasion: PRO, S.C.8/86, 119.

[51] *Rot. Parl.*, iii, 289b–290b, 354b; *Cal. Pat. R., 1396–9*, 454.

[52] PRO, S.C.8/86, 119.

responsible for a given length of the new one. Table 2 records the results of their planning. It shows that the villages responsible for the first pier of the old bridge – Borstal, Cuxton, Frindsbury, Stoke, Gillingham and Chatham – were supposed to be responsible for 64 feet 0¾ inches of the new bridge, and so on. The scheme can never have been of any practical significance, and indicates the difficulties implicit in transferring the traditional obligations to the new bridge.

Table 2

The plan of Sir John de Cobham and Sir Robert Knolles for allocating responsibility for the new bridge, 1391

Old responsibility (pier of old bridge)	New responsibility (length of new bridge)	
	feet	inches
1	64	0¾
2	21	4¼
3	53	4⅝
4	74	8⅞
5	85	6
6	85	6
7 and 8	96	0⅝
9	85	6

Source: PRO, S.C.8/119.

But in other respects the building of the new bridge encouraged new thinking about the apparatus of management. The sums of money which the support of the bridge would require were greater than what could be imposed upon the local communities of Kent without risking a repetition of the disaster of 1381. And so in 1391, alongside their appeal for the maintenance of old responsibilities, Sir John and Sir Robert petitioned for the wardens to be authorised to hold property up to the annual value of 500 marks (£333 6s. 8d.). The king's permission was necessary because the bridge establishment was permanent, like a monastic house; its lands would not pass from one individual to another, like those in the hands of landowning families, and some of the rights exercised by feudal superiors would consequently become impossible to exercise. After the Statute of Mortmain of 1279 perpetual institutions of this sort were allowed to acquire property only if they were given special licence to do so by the crown. In 1391 the king agreed to the principle behind the request of Sir John and Sir Robert but responded by limiting acquisitions for the bridge to an annual value of 300 marks (£200). However, no formal authorisation was granted for the bridge to acquire even this amount of land, and for some reason the sum required was soon assessed at an even lower figure. A petition from the wardens dating from the early 1390s asked for licence to acquire properties to the value of 200 marks (£133 6s. 8d.). This was the sum eventually authorised in January 1395. In fact the 200 marks had to maintain Sir John's chaplains as well as the bridge itself, so it was a severe reduction from the original request.[53] The ability to acquire property was nevertheless to be of considerable importance in the future finances of the bridge. From this period until the 1440s the multiplication of rent-yielding endowments gave the wardens a rising annual income that soon superseded any regular financial responsibilities on the part of the former contributors. The wardens' accounts show that in 1398–9 and 1399–1400 receipts of alms included contributions from local parishes and property owners which, because of the repetitive structure of many of the sums concerned, probably represent traditional obligations, though some may have been voluntary donations (Table 3). This was the last occasion on which the former contributors to the bridge were asked to contribute. After 1400 such receipts disappear from the wardens' accounts.

Table 3

Alms received from parishes and landowners in 1398–9

Parishes	£	s	d	Landlords	£	s	d
Higham	1	10	0	James Pekham	3	6	8
St Werburgh, Hoo	1	10	0	Prior of Rochester	2	0	0
Chatham	1	10	0	John Frennyngham	2	0	0
Rochester	1	5	0	Abbot of Boxley	2	0	0
Cobham	1	0	0	Reginald Pympe		13	4
Shorne	1	0	0	Master of Cobham College		13	4
Whetestede		17	5	John de Cosyngton		6	8
Halstow, Hoo		10	0	Stephen Norton		6	8
St Mary, Hoo		10	0	John Topcleve		6	8
St Margaret by Rochester		10	0	Isabelle Wareys		6	8
All Saints, Hoo		8	10	William Champeneys		6	8
Strood		6	8	William Chesyldenne		6	8
Gravesend		6	8	Peter Culpeper		6	8
Cliffe		5	1	Master John Hoke		3	4
				Nicholas Hobbe of Strood		3	4
				John Totesham		3	4
				John Barbour of Wrotham		3	4
				The parson of Bromleigh		3	4
				John Underwode		1	8
				William Clerc of Trottiscliffe		1	8
				William Godyng of Hadlow		1	8
				William Gode of Trottiscliffe		1	8
				John Eldeham of Strood		1	0

Source: RBM/1B.

[53] PRO, C.62/52, m. 5, C.66/341, m. 30, S.C.8/86.

The acquisition of property meant that the bridge establishment had to develop in other ways as well. The legal status of the bridge wardens as the temporary appointees of an amorphous group of Kent parishes and landowners was impossible to define in law, and yet properties to be acquired for the bridge would have to be vested in some definite owner or owners. A trust might have been a solution, but this would have created a complex tripartite distinction between wardens, trustees and the wider group of interests responsible for the bridge, and a trust would have required frequent renewal. A simpler solution to the problem was proposed by Sir John and Sir Robert in 1391. They petitioned the crown that the wardens could sue or be sued as such rather than as individuals, which would mean that any lawsuit concerning the bridge could continue uninterrupted by the replacement or death of particular wardens.[54] But a yet more satisfactory resolution of the legal problem was found in 1399 by extending concepts more commonly associated with town government. Richard II now granted that those who were liable to contribute to the bridge, and who were already responsible for appointing the wardens, should be regarded as a 'commonalty of themselves' for the purpose of maintaining the bridge. From this time forward the property of the bridge was to be legally vested in the Wardens and Commonalty. The commonalty should be responsible not only for choosing wardens but also for appointing auditors to scrutinise their accounts. This formula immediately placed the bridge establishment in a recognised legal framework of rights and responsibilities. Its continuous existence was identified with the commonalty rather than the wardens who happened temporarily to be in charge.[55] When this constitution was confirmed by the king in parliament in 1421 the commonalty established its right to have a common seal for all the business of the bridge.[56] The surviving bronze seal in the British Museum duly carries the inscription SIGILLUM GARDIANORUM COMMUNITATIS PONTIS ROFFENSIS – 'the seal of the Wardens of the Commonalty of Rochester Bridge.[57]

Having received authorisation from the crown to endow the bridge with land, Sir John de Cobham and his circle took the lead in doing something about it. Sir Robert Knolles did not participate in this aspect of the new foundation. Properties were acquired for the purpose by a consortium of feoffees comprising Sir John himself, Reginald de Cobham and Ralph de Cobham, together with William Rickhill and William Makenade, both of whom were justices of the peace in Kent.[58]

Two of the earliest acquisitions were donated by Sir John de Cobham himself, according to the Chaplains' Memorandum Book.[59] One of these was a collection of properties on the Isle of Grain containing 80 acres of land and 900 acres of marshland and with rents totalling 30s.[60] Part of this was known in the eighteenth

54 PRO, C.62/52, m. 5.
55 PRO, C.66/351, m. 31.
56 *Rot. Parl.*, iv, 148b–9b.
57 Becker, *Rochester Bridge*, 100.
58 *Cal. Pat. R., 1396–9*, pp. 237, 488.
59 RBT, Chaplains' Memorandum Book, f. 3v.
60 PRO, C.66/351, m. 11.

century as the manor of Rose Court, comprising the blocks of marshland to the east of Yantlet Creek marked on modern Ordnance Survey maps as North Level and Grain Marsh. There were also several parcels of marshland lying south of this, to the east of Colemouth Creek by its junction with the Medway. The eighty acres of arable were in dispersed parcels, one next to Grain church and the others scattered up to three-quarters of a mile away.[61] Sir John also gave the reversion of the small manor of East Tilbury in Essex, whose most valuable asset was the profits of the ferry from East Tilbury to Higham. Grain and Tilbury were between them supposed to be worth a clear forty marks (£26 13s. 4d.).[62] To these gifts another member of the family, Reginald de Cobham, contributed an annual rent of 40 marks from the manor of Sharnden and from a marsh in Elmley Marshes.[63]

The acquisitions through the Cobham family also included the reversion of some property in Cornhill which was currently held by the London draper William Wangford. The Chaplains' Memorandum Book speaks of this as a gift from Wangford himself, but the reality may have been more complicated. We know that in October 1391 Sir John was paying off a debt to William Wangford of £200.[64] The site was a block of tenements with a frontage of 130 feet along Leadenhall Street and frontages of 100 feet along either side of Shaft Alley in the parish of St Andrew Undershaft. The shaft in question was a maypole that lay along over the doors and under the eaves of the houses on one side of the Alley, till one Sunday in 1549 the bridge tenants chopped it up as a papist idol.[65]

Sir John's impeachment in 1397 put a temporary halt to his plans because all his properties, including these, were forfeited to the crown. But Richard II was willing to allow the endowment of the bridge to go forward. In February 1399, only a few weeks after having authorised the contributors to the bridge to be considered a commonalty at law, he gave effect to the fulfilment of Sir John's wishes. A few months later, having been recalled from exile by Henry Bolingbroke, Sir John confirmed these endowments to the bridge four days before Richard II's 'abdication'. The gifts were ratified by the new king within a month of his coronation.[66]

In February 1399 Richard II had also authorised William Makenade and Stephen Bettenham to make over to the Wardens and Commonalty of the bridge the reversion of Langdon manor on the death of the widowed Alice Potyn. The reversion of the manor had presumably been bequeathed by the late Nicholas Potyn, whom the

---

[61] RBT, The Bridge Mapps (1663–1717), maps 4a, 4b, 5; Hasted, *The History of Kent*, iv, 253. See too J.H. Evans, 'The Rochester Bridge Lands in Grain', *Archaeologia Cantiana*, lxviii (1954), 184–96.

[62] PRO, C.66/351, m. 11.

[63] PRO, C.66/351, m. 11; RBT, accounts from 1399–1400 to 1402–3. This rent had previously been granted to Cobham College as an interim endowment: RBT, E56.

[64] RBT, Chaplains' Memorandum Book, f. 3v; Kent RO, U601/E22. See, too, Becker, *Rochester Bridge*, 41.

[65] RBT, The Bridge Mapps (1663–1717), maps 7, 8; J. Stowe, *A Survey of London*, ed. C.L. Kingsford, 2 vols, Oxford 1908, i, 143–4; Becker, *Rochester Bridge*, 41–2.

[66] *Cal. Close R., 1399–1401*, 114–15; *Cal. Pat. R., 1399–1401*, 127; Hasted, *The History of Kent*, vi, 336–7. Stephen de Bettenham and William Makenade granted the reversion of Langdon to the wardens on 17 July 1402: RBT, E64.

Chaplains' Memorandum Book remembered as its donor.[67] The Langdon property was a compact block of land of 168 acres lying to the east of the manor house, which stood just north of Goodnestone in the parish of Faversham.[68] In spite of having been acquired in reversion, Langdon was in the wardens' hands long before the death of Alice Potyn. She received in exchange an annuity of £13 6s. 8d. for eleven consecutive years from 1400–1, presumably until she died.[69]

In April 1400 Robert Rowe was authorised to give the bridge some properties in Rochester, the neighbouring parish of St Margaret, and in Frindsbury on the opposite bank of the Medway. These were properties which had been specially acquired for the bridge by its friends and patrons; the tenement in Rochester later known as the Star had been acquired in 1395 by Rowe together with Sir John de Cobham, William Makenade and John Flemyng.[70] Robert Rowe was also licensed to give Eastwick marsh, which lay on the southern shore of the Thames between Egypt Bay and St Mary's Bay.[71] In November 1401 a similar licence authorised John de Frenyngham and William Makenade to convey to the Wardens and Commonalty of the bridge the manor of Nashenden, in the parish of St Margaret's. Frenyngham and Makenade had received the manor on behalf of the bridge from James de Peckham, who according to the Chaplains' Memorandum Book was the real donor. The manor was a long thin block of land lying mostly south of the road from Rochester to Maidstone and stretching from the manor house, now Nashenden Farm, southwards and eastwards, past the eastern edge of Monk Woods.[72] The bridge was also promised the reversion of a small and scattered property in Dartford, given by John de Frenyngham; it would come into their hands following the deaths of John de Frenyngham and his wife. The property as described in 1411 comprised a messuage, a wharf, three virgates of land, 35 acres of meadow, 6 acres of pasture and rents amounting to 4s. The main block of property here was on either side of the River Darent; the wharf was in the angle between Hythe Street and the river, and there were meadows belonging to the bridge on the opposite bank.[73] John de Frenyngham and William Makenade were also authorised to give the bridge 200 acres of pasture in Aylesford.[74]

In practice some of these gifts to the bridge took time to be effective, particularly when the bridge acquired only a reversionary interest. And some of the gifts never took effect because of some defect in title or for some other reason. Forty marks from Sharnden and Elmley were paid in the four years up to 1402–3, but then

[67] PRO, C.66/351, m. 11; RBT, Chaplains' Memorandum Book, f. 3v.
[68] RBT, The Bridge Mapps (1663–1717), map 3.
[69] RBT, accounts from 1400–1 to 1410–11.
[70] Cal. Pat. R., 1399–1401, 277–8; RBT, E7.
[71] Cal. Pat. R., 1399–1401, 277–8; RBT, The Bridge Mapps (1663–1717), map 6.
[72] RBT, Chaplains' Memorandum Book, f. 3r; RBT, The Bridge Mapps (1663–1717), map 11; Cal. Pat. R., 1401–5, 22; Hasted, The History of Kent, iv, 166–8.
[73] RBT, E42; RBT, Chaplains' Memorandum Book, f. 3r; RBT, The Bridge Mapps (1663–1717), map 1; Cal. Pat. R., 1401–5, 22; Cal. Pat. R., 1408–13, 293.
[74] Cal. Pat. R., 1401–5, 22.

disappeared from the accounts.[75] The bridge never received any income from pasture in Aylesford. The establishment of a regular annual income was nevertheless rapid. Though several new properties were acquired from time to time over many years, the foundations of the late medieval endowment of the bridge were laid very quickly between 1399 and 1405. Of the properties that became a permanent part of the endowment, the manor of Grain was the first to yield any revenue (1398–9), followed by the manor of East Tilbury and the marsh at Eastwick (1399–1400), the manors of Langdon and Nashendon (1400–1) and some minor Rochester properties (1404–5).[76] By the time Sir John de Cobham died in 1408 the wardens were accounting for a gross annual income from rents of over £60. The details of the rent income of the bridge in 1407–8 are shown in Table 4.

Table 4

Rents paid to Rochester Bridge in 1407–8

	£	s	d
Grain manor	10	0	0
East Tilbury manor	33	6	8
marsh at Eastwick		13	4
Langdon manor	10	13	4
Nashenden manor	8	0	0
marsh by Boley in Rochester		4	0
a house in Rochester		7	0
TOTAL	63	4	4

Source: RBT, account 1407–8.

The endowment and maintenance of the rebuilt and re-established Rochester Bridge depended heavily upon leading figures in Kent society. The commonalty of the bridge illustrates, however dimly, the necessity and capacity for county families to co-operate for practical purposes.[77] Of the donors and feoffees we have mentioned, Sir John de Cobham, Sir Reginald de Cobham, Stephen Bettenham, William Rickhill, William Makenade and John de Frenyngham were all pillars of local society as justices of the peace and royal commissioners. So was Nicholas Potyn whose manor of Langdon was promised to the bridge. The ordinary management of the bridge also occupied these same leaders of the local community from time to time. References to the commonalty of the bridge at work are few and do not offer any clear perception how its affairs were organised, how responsibilities were allocated or how new wardens were elected. But the accounts show many details

---

[75] RBT, accounts from 1399–1400 to 1402–3.

[76] RBT, accounts from 1398–9 to 1404–5.

[77] For a more general survey of the leaders of Kent county society in this period with some details of individual biographies, see B. Webster, 'The Community of Kent in the Reign of Richard II', *Archaeologia Cantiana*, c (1984), 217–29.

from these early days of how the bridge depended upon members of the commonalty pulling their weight.

William Makenade of Preston, near Faversham, for example, acted in various capacities on behalf of the Wardens and Commonalty.[78] In 1398–9, together with William Rickhill and the Archbishop of Canterbury, he authorised the wardens to spend 15s. 3d. on the 'east lok' of the bridge, perhaps meaning the channel through the easternmost arch, beside the east breast.[79] In 1400–1 he was a co-feoffee with a number of other local landlords (Richard Charles senior, Richard Charles junior, James Pekham and John Frenyngham) who alienated 120 acres of land in Buckmore and Sylewode which were added to the Nashenden estate.[80] In 1403–4 he conveyed 100s. to an agent undertaking to obtain a royal licence for the Wardens and Commonalty to buy Nashenden manor.[81] He and John Beaufitz authorised the wardens to pay 73s. 4d. on unspecified administrative expenses in 1405–6, and in the same year he was made responsible for taking 3s. 3d. from bridge funds to pay a court fine at Faversham Abbey.[82] His death interrupted an attempt to take out letters patent for acquiring John Frenyngham's property in Dartford, so that the wardens had to pay all over again for a new one in 1410–11.[83]

Sir William Rickhill, justice of common pleas from 1389, and lord of the manor of Ridley between Rochester and Sevenoaks,[84] was another member of the commonalty who was on occasions useful during the early years of the new bridge. In 1398–9 he was active as an intermediary for collecting the contributions to the bridge recorded in Table 3. A shilling was recorded as received from Sir William 'for John Eldeham of Strood', 6s. 8d. 'for John Topcleve', 6s. 8d. 'for Isabelle Wareys', 20s. 'for Shorne', 6s. 8d. 'for William Champeneys' and 8s. 10d. 'for the parish of All Saints in Hoo', and there are numerous other examples.[85] Again in 1399–1400 Sir William conveyed to the wardens 10s. given in alms by a man of Hoo.[86] The account of 1398–9 records his having paid three instalments of the rent due from the manor of Grain, apparently again as an intermediary agent rather than as tenant; on another occasion the rent was delivered by Sir John de Cobham.[87] These last arrangements represent an early stage in the commonalty's acquisition of property before any regular procedures for rent collecting were established.

The wardens themselves were inevitably responsible for most of the day-to-day business, though they were dependent upon leading representatives of the

78 Makenade was described as of Preston in 1395: Kent RO, DRc/T583. Macknade is a placename in Preston: J.K. Wallenberg, *The Place-Names of Kent*, Uppsala 1934, 292.
79 RBT, account 1398–9.
80 RBT, account 1400–1.
81 RBT, account 1403–4.
82 RBT, account 1405–6.
83 RBT, account 1410–11.
84 *Dictionary of National Biography*, xvi, 1149.
85 RBT, account 1398–9.
86 RBT, account 1399–1400.
87 RBT, account 1398–9.

commonalty to authorise many of their actions and to audit their accounts. Throughout the period of the construction of the new bridge, and during the three decades thereafter, attention must focus on Robert Rowe, who was one of the key figures in the management of bridge affairs throughout the period. His first recorded connection with the bridge was in February 1383, when he replaced Nicholas Heryng as a royal appointee charged with spending the profits of the Medway ferry for repairing the old bridge. Although not described as such, this means that he was one of the bridge wardens. His colleague in office at this time was the master of Strood Hospital.[88] Rowe was confirmed in this position when the new bridge was projected in March. In November 1384 and in June 1385 the king acted on his request to appoint auditors for the wardens' accounts of pontage, and on the grounds that he was responsible for collecting pontage by royal appointment he was replaced in 1385 as a collector of taxes in Kent.[89] He is named as a bridge warden in 1387, 1388 and 1390, and was responsible for all the earliest surviving accounts from 1391–2 to 1415–16. In 1398–9 he was paid a stipend of £6 13s. 8d. for his work as warden, and it is likely that he received the same sum every subsequent year in office. In 1399–1400 the same sum was said to have been allowed him by Sir John de Cobham on account of his great labour.[90] He continued in office until at least 1415–16.[91] Robert Rowe's fellow warden for the whole period from 1398–9 to at least 1415–16 was John Wolcy. He was paid less than Robert Rowe – only £2 in 1399–1400 and 1400–1 and £4 in 1411–12,[92] and in some years nothing at all[93] – because he was less constantly at work on bridge business.

As Rowe's explicit subordination to Sir John implies, the wardens were not drawn from a social rank as distinguished as the leaders of the commonalty of the bridge. Robert Rowe came from near Aylesford; his family gave its name to the estate called Rowe Place.[94] He also held land in Strood from Sir John de Cobham and from Rochester Priory, some of which at least he gave to Strood Hospital.[95] But neither Rowe nor Wolcy was ever included in commissions of the peace, commissions of array or commissions of sewers for Kent, and their social status was not comparable to that of the knights of the shire on whose behalf they served. The very long period the two men were in office suggests that even in the early years of the new bridge establishment the constitutional apparatus of the bridge did not need to be very active. It seems unlikely that there were annual elections of

---

[88] For the masters of Strood Hospital in this period, see A.C. Harrison, 'Excavations on the Site of St Mary's Hospital, Strood', *Archaeologia Cantiana*, lxxxiv (1969), 156–8.

[89] PRO, C.66/318, m. 11d, C.66/320, m. 14; *Cal. Fine R., 1383–91*, 79.

[90] RBT, accounts 1398–9, 1399–1400.

[91] RBT, accounts from 1398–9 to 1415–16.

[92] RBT, accounts 1399–1400, 1400–1, 1411–12.

[93] RBT, accounts 1406–7, 1407–8.

[94] Kent RO, DRc/T583; *Cal. Fine R., 1383–91*, 79; Hasted, *The History of Kent*, iv, 435; Wallenberg, *Place-Names of Kent*, 146.

[95] Kent RO, DRc/602, 603.

bridge wardens between 1398 and 1415, and there is nothing in the accounts to suggest that they were audited annually. From the beginning of the new arrangements it was apparently understood that it was up to the wardens to organise election meetings and auditing procedures, and that in the absence of such initiative the operation of keeping the bridge would roll on with little formality from year to year.

Maintenance and Rebuilding

As Sir John de Cobham and Sir Robert Knolles had recognised in 1391, the upkeep of the new bridge required continuous expenditure and constant vigilance. Tides in the Medway pulled hard on the bridge, making the river foam noisily as it passed between the platforms supporting the masonry piers. The chalk bed of the river and the packing of the staddles were continuously eroded by the force of the waters. The wardens had to maintain a check on the depth of water passing under the bridge to alert them to possible danger. They had to be continuously strengthening weakened foundations. So the completion of the bridge in about 1391 did not mean the cessation of bridgework. Every year the timber piles that were the chief strength of the staddles were reinforced by dozens of new ones, the outer wooden framing was repaired or renewed, and hundreds of tons of chalk and stone were dug and packed into them. From time to time materials were tipped into the river under the bridge to raise the level of the riverbed and protect the foundations, as in 1398–9 when 64 'tontights' of chalk were used for this purpose or in 1400–1 when 197 tons of chalk were dug to be thrown on the staddles and into the water.[1] The bridge was also weakened, year after year, by the hammering of the traffic passing over it. A fifteenth-century petition on behalf of the bridge speaks distinctly of 'the shakyng of cartes that heuy laden continually passen ouer it'.[2] Over the ten years from December 1398 to November 1408 the wardens spent on average about £25 a year on maintenance work. In later years the sums were higher still (Appendix B). The wardens employed a workforce of carpenters, masons, boatmen and labourers whose livelihood depended chiefly upon the ongoing work of keeping the bridge in good order.

Expenditure on the bridge went partly on materials themselves and partly on their carriage by land or water as far as the bridge. The wardens needed to lay their hands on large quantities of elm trees for making piles, which could be tipped with iron and beaten into the riverbed with the help of two pieces of apparatus called the gin and the ram. The gin, which was moved from staddle to staddle according to where work was taking place, was lifting gear employing a rope coiled round a central spindle. It was essential for getting piles up and set into position before they could be driven into the riverbed. The ram was the essential pile-driving equipment, whose main feature was a heavy weight to be raised and lowered on to the head of each pile in turn. Work on the staddles of this sort was restricted to certain states of the tide, so that the workers engaged in it were paid by the tide rather than by the day and were often called tidemen.

---

[1] RBT, accounts 1398–9, 1400–1; Hasted, *The History of Kent*, i, 278.
[2] PRO, S.C.8/137.

The bridge crossed the Medway just to the north of the point where the river breaks through the North Downs. On the eastward bank the line of the hills approaches from the southeast, the end of the low ridge coming down into the valley by the bridge estate at Nashendon manor, two miles south of the bridge itself. On the westward bank of the river the main downland ridge advances from the southwest to the north of Snodland and Halling, and abuts against the Medway at Cuxton. The steeper slopes of the downs, in the fifteenth century as in the twentieth, were covered with a ribbon of woodland, sometimes broader, sometimes narrower, that could serve the Wardens and Commonalty as a valuable resource. Beyond Cuxton on the northern side of the river another low and broken ridge of land stretches from Cobham and Strood northeastward into the centre of the Hoo peninsula, and this too was wooded at its higher altitudes. At the time when the new bridge was under construction, its projectors had had carte blanche, on the authority of Richard II, to take any timber they required for the work, except on the land of the church, and they had duly caused the felling of thousands of trees from the downlands in the immediate vicinity of the bridge.

Their requirements then had exhausted local reserves until the woods had time to grow again. In the decades that followed the completion of the bridge the main sources of timber were higher up the Medway between Aylesford and Maidstone. In several years the wardens sought their supplies at Aylesford itself[3] or at 'Gervayssisforstall' (unidentified), where there was apparently a timber yard by the river.[4] The woodland on and below the scarp of the North Downs around Boxley was another regular source of supply in the early decades of the fifteenth century.[5] Other recorded sources up to 1420 were Allington,[6] Birling,[7] 'Bottylle' (unidentified),[8] Ditton,[9] East Malling,[10] Maidstone,[11] Millhall,[12] New Hythe,[13] Preston in Aylesford,[14] Romacres in Oare,[15] Tottington in Aylesford[16] and Weavering in Boxley.[17] Timber from this part of the region was most conveniently brought to the bridge by being dragged down to the river at one of the numerous wharves along

---

3 RBT, accounts 1400–1, 1409–10, 1414–15, 1415–16.
4 RBT, accounts 1406–7, 1407–8, 1413–14, 1415–16. 'Fore-stall' signifies the place in front of a farm house: A.H. Smith, *English Place-Name Elements*, 2 vols, Cambridge 1956, i, 184. There are several examples of it in place-names near Rochester – such as Hanslett's Forstall and Painter's Forstall in Ospringe, Bell's Forstall in Throwley – but I have not been able to identify 'Gervayssisforstall'.
5 RBT, accounts 1400–1, 1414–15, 1415–16.
6 RBT, accounts 1398–9, 1402–3.
7 RBT, account 1400–1.
8 RBT, accounts 1402–3, 1412–13, 1413–14, 1415–16.
9 RBT, account 1402–3.
10 RBT, account 1400–1.
11 RBT, account 1412–13.
12 RBT, account 1415–16.
13 RBT, account 1412–13.
14 RBT, account 1415–16.
15 RBT, account 1400–1; Wallenberg, *Place-Names of Kent*, 289.
16 RBT, account 1414–15; Wallenberg, *Place-Names of Kent*, 146.
17 RBT, account 1400–1; Wallenberg, *Place-Names of Kent*, 135–6.

its banks and shipped along the Medway in one of the lighters belonging to the bridge. The movement of heavy timber required the assistance of equipment called the tug, or the trug, which was drawn by four or five horses.[18] The sources of timber during the 1420s and 1430s were much the same as those already listed. From this period we can add 'Cotoron' (unidentified),[19] Islingham in Frindsbury,[20] 'Fyssheresford' (unidentified),[21] Strood,[22] and, towards the end of the thirties, Chatham,[23] Higham,[24] Cobham[25] and Frindsbury.[26]

Aylesford and Boxley remained important sources of supply during the 1440s and 1450s; in 1445–6 the wardens had a sawpit made at Monkdown Wood so that timbers could be cut into planks there.[27] The wharves at 'Lowyneshole' and New Hythe were amongst those most frequently visited by the bridge boats for carrying timber downstream. But from the late 1430s woods nearer to Rochester and Strood were becoming sufficiently renewed for the wardens to be able to buy elms from them in large numbers. Snodland became a regular source from 1447–8 onwards.[28] Other more local supplies in these decades came from Burham,[29] Delce,[30] Frindsbury,[31] Gillingham,[32] Halling,[33] Higham,[34] Holwood,[35] Hoo,[36] Hoo Street,[37] Horsted in Chatham,[38] Nashenden,[39] and Strood.[40] Because of the closer proximity of supplies in this period, it became more common for timber to be brought to the bridge by land transport.

By the 1460s and 1470s the effects of late fourteenth-century felling were finally overcome. No longer did the wardens buy timber from Aylesford or Boxley, or even from Snodland and Burham. The recorded sources from this period were

---

[18] RBT, accounts 1414–15, 1444–5.
[19] RBT, account 1428–9.
[20] RBT, accounts 1425–6, 1426–7, 1428–9; Wallenberg, *Place-Names of Kent*, 115.
[21] RBT, account 1425–6.
[22] RBT, account 1428–9.
[23] RBT, account 1438–9.
[24] RBT, account 1438–9.
[25] RBT, account 1439–40.
[26] RBT, account 1439–40.
[27] RBT, account 1445–6.
[28] RBT, accounts 1447–8, 1449–50, 1450–1, 1451–2, 1452–3, 1456–7, 1457–8.
[29] RBT, accounts 1443–4, 1456–7.
[30] RBT, account 1445–6.
[31] RBT, accounts 1447–8, 1451–2, 1452–3.
[32] RBT, account 1445–6.
[33] RBT, account 1452–3.
[34] RBT, accounts 1438–9, 1447–8, 1449–50, 1450–1.
[35] RBT, account 1444–5.
[36] RBT, accounts 1444–5, 1449–50.
[37] RBT, accounts 1444–5, 1450–1, 1456–7, 1458–9.
[38] RBT, accounts 1443–4, 1444–5, 1451–2, 1452–3, 1456–7, 1457–8; Wallenberg, *Place-Names of Kent*, 128.
[39] RBT, account 1444–5.
[40] RBT, accounts 1447–8, 1451–2.

all quite close to the bridge: Birling,[41] Borstal,[42] Chatham,[43] Cuxton,[44] Islingham,[45] Frindsbury,[46] Gillingham,[47] Holwood,[48] Hoo Street,[49] Horsted,[50] Little Delce,[51] Nashenden,[52] Rochester[53] and Wouldham.[54] The main exceptions to the local nature of supplies concerned timber needed for special purposes. Timber bought at Millhall in 1476–7 was required for the gin; this must have been a timber of exceptional hardness, probably oak.[55] And the wardens often sent as far as Maidstone for special sorts of laths they required and for 'asseres' of oak. The attraction there was the fairs of the Translation of St Edmund, St Faith and SS Philip and James, which must have had a distinctive line in these sorts of timber.[56]

Table 5

Elms bought and used for piles, 1436–1446

Year	Bought	Used
1435–6	237	190
1438–9	89	132
1439–40	86	34
1443–4	88	160
1444–5	200	200
1445–6	183	180

Source: RBT, accounts, 1435–6 to 1445–6.

The amount of timber required by the bridge varied from year to year depending on the amount of work in hand. Table 5 shows the number of elms used for making piles during some years for which there is exact information between 1436 and 1446. The figures give some impression of the range of variation between some more normal years, like the first four in the table (with an average consumption of 129 elms a year) and years of heavier reconstruction like 1444–5 and 1445–6

---

41 RBT, account 1464–5.
42 RBT, account 1478–9.
43 RBT, accounts Feb.–Sept. 1467, 1467–8, 1471–2, April–Sept. 1476.
44 RBT, account June–Sept. 1466.
45 RBT, accounts 1461–2, 1476–7.
46 RBT, accounts 1467–8, April–Sept. 1476, 1476–7, 1478–9, 1478–9.
47 RBT, accounts 1460–1, 1461–2, June–Sept. 1466, Feb.–Sept. 1467.
48 RBT, accounts 1463–4, June–Sept. 1466, Feb.–Sept. 1467, 1467–8, Feb.–Sept. 1469, 1469–70, 1471–2, 1478–9.
49 RBT, account 1464–5.
50 RBT, account 1461–2.
51 RBT, accounts 1461–2, 1473–4.
52 RBT, account 1473–4.
53 RBT, account Feb.–Sept. 1467.
54 RBT, account 1460–1.
55 RBT, account 1476–7.
56 RBT, accounts 1451–2, 1452–3, 1456–7, 1457–8, 1458–9, 1460–1, 1463–4, Feb.–Sept. 1469, 1469–70, 1471–2.

(averaging 190 a year). These requirements alone were a major source of demand for the local timber economy, and they do not represent the total impact of the bridge upon the local market since timber was required in other forms as well. The accounts used for Table 5 also record the acquisition of 54 'porterpeces' or 'porteres' in 1439–40, 1443–4, 1444–5 and 1445–6 for use on the staddles of the bridge,[57] 53 pieces of timber in 1438–9 for repairs at Grain and Tilbury,[58] 1000 'daubynglaths', for buildings at East Tilbury, in 1435–6,[59] and 1850 'teilelathes', many of which were used to repair buildings at Rochester, in 1443–4.[60]

The configuration of the North Downs, besides its influence upon the distribution of woodlands around Rochester, affected the location of accessible chalk deposits. Chalk was even more difficult than timber to transport over long distances, so in effect the wardens had to secure their supplies at those points where there were chalk quarries beside the river. One source they used regularly up until 1414 or shortly afterwards, was Cuxton. They engaged in no quarrying on their own account there. All the chalk they bought at Cuxton between 1399 and 1414, amounting to over 1200 tons, was paid for by the ton, usually at a price of 3d. a ton, though the wardens were often able to negotiate a discount. The other major source of chalk was at a property called Walshes in Frindsbury, less than a mile downstream of the bridge on the opposite bank from Rochester.[61] The arrangements they made at Walshes were more variable. In 1400–1 and 1401–2 the wardens employed a team to mine there and paid nothing for the chalk beyond their labour costs. In 1402–3, 1403–4 and 1404–5 they obtained chalk there without paying even the mining costs, perhaps because it was left over from earlier quarrying. Between 1405–6 and 1407–8 they bought chalk ready mined at prices between 2d. and 3d. a ton. In 1409–10 and 1410–11 they paid 1d. a ton for chalk and then themselves paid the mining costs. Then in the years 1411–12, 1412–13 and 1413–14 all the chalk acquired by the wardens was bought at 3d. a ton; this chalk may not have come from Walshes in the first two of these years, but several hundred tons were purchased there in the third.[62] These different arrangements at Walshes appear to represent jockeying for an acceptable agreement on the part of the landlord at Walshes. Up to 1404 he was prepared to let the wardens take chalk from his land for nothing, but he changed his mind about 1405 and converted his relationship with the wardens to a commercial one.

---

[57] RBT, accounts 1439–40, 1443–4, 1444–5, 1445–6.
[58] RBT, account 1438–9.
[59] RBT, account 1435–6.
[60] RBT, account 1443–4.
[61] John Walshe occurs as the owner of property in Frindsbury between 1355 and 1398: RBT, E50, E51, E53.
[62] RBT, accounts from 1400–1 to 1413–14.

Table 6

Chalk acquired for Rochester Bridge

	Total tons	Bought tons	Dug tons
1398–9	166	166	0[1]
1399–1400	?	?	?
1400–1	197	0	197
1401–2	765	243	522[2]
1402–3	?	?	?
1403–4	443	84	359[3]
1404–5	162	162	0
1405–6	659	339	300
1406–7	557	257	300
1407–8	750	350	400
1409–10	1117	797	370
1410–11	295	95	200
1411–12	209	209	0
1412–13	82	82	0
1413–14	515	515	0
1414–15	522	0	522
1415–16	396	0	396[4]
1423–4	650	0	650
1424–5	900+	0	900+
1425–6	900	0	900
1426–7	900	0	900
1428–9	1600	0	1600
1429–30	1000	0	1000
1430–1	1200	0	1200
1435–6	1800	0	1800
1438–9	2234	0	2234
1439–40	1217	0	1217[5]
1443–4	1367	0	1367
1444–5	2417	0	2417
1445–6	2542	0	2542
1447–8	824	0	824
1449–50	983	0	983
1450–1	767	0	767
1451–2	1567	0	1567
1452–3	733	0	733

	Total tons	Bought tons	Dug tons
1456–7	1383	0	1383
1457–8	967	0	967
1458–9	1600	0	1600
1460–1	767	0	767
1461–2	1417	0	1417
1463–4	983	0	983
1466–7	1117	0	1117
1467–8	1067	0	1067
1469–70	1033	0	1033
1471–2	817	0	817
1472–3	817	0	817
1473–4	633	0	633
1475–6	1567	0	1567
1476–7	2500	0	2500
1478–9	1667	0	1667

1 The account records the purchase of 166 t. 'dez quel cij tonnetith sount prestes a Burgham melle desur lewe et lxiiij tonnetyth sount getes en lewe al pount de Rouchestre pur ffounder del ewe'.

2 A labourer was paid 'pur fower myner ccxv tonntight de croye a Walsshes', but other labourers were employed in the same task under Budd's supervision and 522 t. were carried from Walshes to the bridge.

3 In the purchases 84 t. are recorded as bought at Cuxton. The transport accounts include 84 t. 'de croye de William de Chetham' (presumably the 84 t. bought at Cuxton) and 359 t. 'de croye de Walsschis et de Cokkelstane', all carried to the bridge.

4 22 lighter loads, each containing 18 t. (cf. R.B.T., account 1414–15)

5 73 boatloads 'et singule navicule continent c tontigh[t]'. From this account onwards the chalk is measured by boatload.

Source: RBT, accounts, 1398–9 to 1478–9.

From 1414, however, there was a permanent change in the bridge's acquisition of chalk. Up till then, as we have seen, the bridge authorities had been obliged to buy a large proportion of the chalk they required. From that date they never bought chalk, but mined everything they required without any payment of royalties. And from that date their activities were confined to the quarry at Walshes. Table 6 shows the amounts of chalk used in bridge maintenance from year to year. The columns distinguish between quantities which were bought ready-mined and those whose mining the wardens paid for, and the figures show clearly the change in circumstances from 1414–15 onwards. The change at this point occurred because, as we shall see, the quarry had been given to the commonalty of the bridge. Shortly afterwards the wardens also began to receive an annual rent for lands and a marsh at Walshes though there is no record of the formal acquisition of any title to these properties until 1438.[63] The gift had obvious implications for the normal range of operations funded and directed by the wardens, since these now included quarrying operations through most of the year. The cost of quarrying chalk was reduced to a formula: 5s. for each 100 tons between 1428–9 and 1430–1, 4s. for each 100 tons between 1435–6 and 1449–50.[64] All told maintenance of the bridge consumed around 100,000 tons of chalk during its first hundred years, to judge from the 49 years between 1398–9 and 1478–9 for which we have figures, and most of this came from Walshes. On top of these various charges the wardens had to meet the costs of transporting any chalk they acquired to the bridge. The combined cost of carrying chalk from the quarry to the river and then shipping it up river to the bridge was fixed at 14s. for each 100 tons between 1428–9 and 1449–50.[65]

The wardens were long able to use the foundations of the old bridge as a source of ragstone. In September 1393, not long after the completion of the bridge, Richard II had appointed a commission of friends of the bridge, including Sir William Rickhill, William Makenade, John Frenyngham, James Pekham and Nicholas Potyn, to examine the old bridge and remove whatever was likely to be detrimental to the new one. This was in response to the discovery that the remains of the old bridge were impeding the rise and fall of the Medway to such an extent that the riverbed was being swept away and the foundations of the new bridge were weakened. The same commissioners were given powers to raise funds from the regular contributors to finance this operation.[66] In practice the clearing away of the old bridge took place over many years, and soon became a normal part of bridge maintenance rather than a special operation. Materials from the old bridge were systematically absorbed into the new one, mostly into packing the staddles. Stone and timber were removed in 1398–9 in unspecified quantities. In 1400–1, more precisely, 55 tons of ragstone were taken from the old bridge and in 1401–2 boatmen were paid to get together 342 tons of ragstone from the staddles of the old bridge and carry them to the new one for filling up the staddles.[67] A further 216 tons of ragstone was taken in 1403–4.[68] Later details do not give such quantitative precision, but such operations continued as late as 1415–16.[69] Some cut stone from the old bridge was also available, and could be used in maintenance work.[70]

Other sources of stone became more important in the course of time as the wardens had to purchase supplies. In 1409–10 the extensive repairs to the bridge required the purchase of about 400 tons of ragstone and 22 tons of 'bordor' stone,

[63] A.A. Arnold, 'Quarry House, on Frindsbury Hill', *Archaeologia Cantiana*, xvii (1887), 170.
[64] RBT, accounts from 1423–4 to 1449–50; the breakdown of costs is taken from RBT, accounts 1428–9, 1444–5.
[65] RBT, accounts from 1423–4 to 1449–50.
[66] PRO, C.66/338, m. 20d.
[67] RBT, accounts 1400–1, 1401–2.
[68] RBT, account 1403–4.
[69] RBT, accounts 1405–6, 1406–7, 1412–13, 1413–14, 1415–16.
[70] RBT, account 1400–1.

though the source of this material is not stated.[71] In the 1420s the principal source of stone was John Cartere, who sold the wardens 54 tons of ragstone and 4 carts of 'bordour' in 1423–4, 6 tons in 1424–5 and 90 tons in 1425–6; this stone probably came from Faversham.[72] The work under way in 1425–6 required altogether the purchase of 130 tons of ragstone at 5d. a ton, 6 tons of large ragstone at 10d. a ton, 163 feet of ashlar at nearly 4d. a foot and 92 long stones called 'endestones' at 8d. each, and most of this came from inland in Kent; some at least of the rag, the ashlar and the endstones were carried by water from 'Lowynyshole' and other places on the Medway.[73] Ragstone was again shipped from 'Lowynshole' in 1429–30 and 1430–1.[74] Maidstone was also a source of ragstone in the middle decades of the fifteenth century.[75] The stone needed for the bridge was evidently not quarried very locally, but it must have been chiefly Kentish, which is not surprising since ragstone from the Medway area was one of the main materials used for building London Bridge.[76]

Some other materials needed for the bridge could be obtained within the local economy of the Medway estuary. Sand was used chiefly for mixing cement, but it was sometimes spread on the surface of the bridge, as for a visit of Henry VI in 1435–6.[77] It was brought by the boatload either from Sheerness or from Halling.[78] Clay, which was also used for the bridge surface, was brought from Sheerness.[79]

Operations at the bridge required a great deal of ironwork each year. Levers and crowbars were wanted for manoeuvering stone. The ram, the gin and the tug all had iron parts that needed periodic renewal. Picks and shovels were used in quarrying operations. And the maintenance of the bridge boats required nails, anchors and hinges for the rudders. The wardens bought other iron spikes, clasps, plates, staples, bolts and hooks whose purposes are uncertain. But the heaviest consumption of iron was for 'pile shoes' – the iron tips fitted to elm piles in preparation for their being beaten into the riverbed. These were unstandardised, but always weighed several pounds each, and in a busy year the riverbed consumed hundreds of pounds of iron. In the two years 1444–6 the wardens bought 227 pile shoes weighing 1059 lb in all.[80] Most of the iron work was obtained very locally. All the accounts from the second quarter of the fifteenth century, and a few years either

---

[71] RBT, account 1409–10.

[72] RBT, accounts 1423–4, 1424–5, 1425–6. The account of 1423–4 says this stone was paid for 'cum cariagio usque ffeversham', but this would make more sense if it meant that the carrier had gone to Faversham to fetch it back to the bridge.

[73] RBT, account 1425–6. In the following year rag was carried by river from 'le ffyshous' and elsewhere, RBT, account 1426–7.

[74] RBT, accounts 1429–30, 1430–1.

[75] RBT, accounts 1430–1, 1443–4.

[76] Home, *Old London Bridge*, 38.

[77] RBT, account 1435–6.

[78] RBT, accounts 1428–9, 1429–30, 1430–1, 1438–9, 1439–40, 1445–6, 1450–1, 1451–2, 1452–3 (Sheerness); RBT, accounts 1449–50, 1457–8, 1460–1, 1476–7 (Halling).

[79] RBT, accounts 1444–5, 1457–8.

[80] RBT, accounts 1444–5, 1445–6.

side, show that the main supplier to the bridge was John Smith of Chatham, who repaired iron equipment and manufactured any iron tools or parts that the bridge-work required, often supplying the iron for the job.[81] From the middle of the 1450s Thomas Smith took his place, and though we do not know where he worked he was evidently local because of the number of minor contracts he received and the absence of associated carriage costs.[82] Another item for which the wardens depended on local industry was ropery. The towlines, hawsers, cables and traces bought each year were needed for the ram, the gin and the tug as well as for the bridge boats. We do not usually know exactly where the bridge's suppliers were operating, but in the later 1440s the chief one was Roger Roper of Chatham.[83]

London was so close to the Medway estuary by boat that it can be included in the wardens' local sources of supply. The wardens' visits there were sometimes accompanied by the purchase of necessary materials, but they also made use of friends of the bridge living there to negotiate on their behalf.[84] London's import-ance was secondary to Kentish sources for the major material requirements of the bridge, but it was nevertheless important in several respects. The city supplied imported products which could not be obtained locally, such as the 250 lb of resin bought in 1439–40 and the 562 lb of resin bought from John Bolle of London a few years later.[85] Coal was also bought there sometimes.[86] Other occasional pur-chases recorded are grease for the engine, pitch and lime.[87] London was sometimes a better source for bulk purchases than local dealers. Though most ironwork was obtained from near Rochester it was not unusual for large consignments of iron to be shipped from London to be supplied to local smiths.[88] The wardens also depended from time to time on the products of London manufacturing industry. Nails were quite often bought in London ready made. A particularly large consign-ment was that of 4000 'prig' nails bought from John Irenmonger of London in 1447–8. The wardens again bought exceptionally large quantities of prigs and other nails from John Portlowe of London twenty years later.[89] In the mid 1440s the wardens bought large quantities of London bricks. In 1443–4, for example, they bought 3500 bricks from John Bolle and another 2000 at Baynard Castle, and had them all transported by boat from the Tower of London.[90] Other miscellaneous purchases recorded from time to time are ropes, tiles, oars for the large bridge boat, shovels and baskets.[91] When the wardens were reconstructing the Crown Inn in

---

[81] RBT, accounts from 1423–4 to 1452–3.
[82] RBT, accounts from 1456–7 to 1478–9.
[83] RBT, accounts from 1444–5 to 1450–1.
[84] This was particularly the case when William Sevenoke was active in bridge affairs: RBT, accounts 1414–15, 1415–16.
[85] RBT, accounts 1439–40, 1445–6.
[86] RBT, account 1439–40.
[87] RBT, accounts 1398 (grease), 1414–15 (pitch), 1415–16 (lime).
[88] RBT, accounts 1414–15, 1415–16, 1423–4, 1444–5, 1445–6, 1451–2, 1469–70.
[89] RBT, accounts 1423–4, 1447–8, Feb.–Sept. 1467, 1467–8.
[90] RBT, accounts 1443–4, 1445–6.
[91] RBT, accounts 1414–15 (ropes), 1415–16 (ropes), 1423–4 (cable), 1445–6 (tiles), 1456–7 (oars), 1467–8 (shovels and baskets).

1424–5, they sent the inn signs to London to be painted; the signs travelled by water and were unloaded at Billingsgate.[92]

When the bridge was first set up, there was some uncertainty about how much its upkeep would require over the years. As we have seen, Sir John de Cobham and Sir Robert Knolles had wanted to play safe by securing an annual income of £333 6s. 6d., and the king eventually agreed to allow the Wardens and Commonalty to acquire property to the value of £133 6s. 8d. Appendix B shows the annual expenditure of the wardens in those years for which the accounts are extant. From this it can be deduced that Sir John and Sir Robert had been excessively apprehensive and that the sum finally authorised by the king was not unduly mean. This may be, of course, because the king's figure was determined after the wardens had had several years of experience in managing the bridge. The amount spent on maintaining the bridge fluctuated sharply from year to year but averaged only £65 between 1398–9 and 1478–9. The cost of maintaining the chapel, another charge on the establishment, averaged £16 a year. On the basis of these figures an annual income of £133 6s. 8d. should have been enough for the purpose. There is no reason to suppose that the Wardens and Commonalty ever felt that their work was jeopardised by the king's decision, or that they would have wanted to spend more on the bridge had their income been higher.

In spite of the endeavours of those responsible for its upkeep, there were numerous periods of anxiety, and some real disasters in the course of history of the bridge between 1391 and 1532. The major structural problem came only about twenty years after the new bridge had been completed, and within a year or two of the deaths of Sir Robert Knolles (in 1407) and Sir John de Cobham (in 1408). The bridge was evidently in jeopardy in 1409–10 when large cracks appeared in the stonework. Advice was sought from competent masons. Stephen Lote came to see the problem; he and his clerk were paid their expenses for two days, and in the presence of the Prior of Rochester, representing the commonalty of the bridge, he gave his advice about what to do. The advice of John Kotys was also sought, and he was paid expenses for two days. A third opinion was sought from another mason; Robert Rowe and William Chaumpenays had to ride over to Rainham to consult him because he was ill. The treatment of the problem included closing cracks in the stonework with a cement made from crushed Flemish tiles and pitch. But most of the expense was incurred by an intensified restoration of the staddles. The wardens bought 382 pieces of timber for piles and other necessities, 405 tons of ragstone for the bridge foundations and 1,167 tons of chalk. Total expenditure on the bridge in 1409–10 shot up to about £156, about six times as much as in a normal year of the previous decade.[93]

After this scare, and another in 1412–13 when some of the bridge's workforce were paid extra 'on account of great fear that the bridge was in danger', the normal level of spending on maintenance went up. Between 1410–11 and 1415–16 the wardens spent on average about £75 a year on bridgework. But this did not prevent

[92] RBT, account 1424–5.
[93] RBT, account 1409–10.

a major disaster in the 1420s when two arches broke and had to be taken down and rebuilt in new stone. The account for 1423–4 details these operations as the 'new work'.[94] Appendix B shows a peak of expenditure on bridge maintenance in 1425–6 as a result of these activities. The necessary reconstruction was completed only in 1426–7, when a paver was employed to pave the new work and a labourer was employed to clean the bridge after it had been finished.[95]

Within ten years another structural difficulty had arisen as a result of problems with the abutments of the bridge on to the banks at either end. It was no doubt to meet the costs of the necessary structural work that in 1431 the king granted the wardens the right to collect tolls on the bridge for seven years.[96] In 1430–1 the wardens were shoring up the east breast of the bridge with new stonework, and constructed there what the accounts describe as a 'new pier'.[97] But the west breast of the bridgework was also needing repairs, and the wardens alleged that the problem arose from neglect of the river banks by the abbess of Denney, the master of Strood Hospital and others who had lands beside the bridge. Erosion on either side of the west breast was exposing the stonework of the bridge to increased water and threatening to undermine the bridge abutment on the Strood bank. In 1431 the wardens petitioned in Parliament for the abbess and the master of Strood Hospital to be called into Chancery for their responsibilities in this matter to be examined.[98] There are no accounts for the four years from Michaelmas 1431, and it was presumably in these years that the bulk of the work on the west breast was carried out. But it was still in progress in 1435–6, when the operation required 52 small elms, 11 cartloads of thorns, 6 wooden boards, 52 hurdles, 500 nails and 505 tons of chalk from Walshes. In 1438–9 the work was continuing only in a desultory way, but there was another spurt of activity on the 'new work called west breast' in 1439–40, involving amongst other things the building of 3½ perches of new walling in ashlar. The west breast had been the major maintenance work for the 1430s.[99]

The next peak of expenditure was in 1445, when the bridge broke so severely as to be unusable for over seven months. There was serious trouble at the end of March. An advisory team of John Gonell, master carpenter, some other carpenters and six stonemasons was invited to Rochester to view the bridge and give their opinions about what was to be done; they were there on Maundy Thursday and Holy Saturday (25 and 27 March). They recommended urgent attention to the staddles. This meant speeding up the work of getting chalk from Walshes up to the

[94] RBT, account 1425–6.

[95] RBT, account 1426–7.

[96] PRO, C.66/429, m. 17. The account of 1430–1 includes a receipt of 7s. 3d. from tolls 'pro passagio diuersarum rerum venalium cariatarum per et subtus pontem licencia regis inde acquesita'. No receipts of this kind were recorded in 1435–6.

[97] The wardens paid £8 16s. 8d. to John Cartere 'pro M^l assheler emptis pro le eastbrest ad finem pontis'. There are other references to work on the east breast. Sand was carried in March 1431 'pro novo pere' a couple of months later sand and other things were again carted 'ad murum novi pere': RBT, account 1430–1.

[98] PRO, S.C.8/26.

[99] RBT, accounts 1435–6, 1438–9, 1439–40.

bridge. A call was made for assistance from owners of wheeled vehicles, and several men responded by lending carts of the characteristic Kentish type known as a *curtena*.[100] Robert Soutere was paid to use his *curtena* with four horses for carrying chalk at Walshes by day and night to accelerate the process of getting chalk down to the boats. Two other *curtene* were simultaneously employed for two days, and two for a day and a half. Seven labourers were deployed during the daytime for digging chalk, and filling up the carts. But after only two and a half days and two nights of this work an arch of the bridge collapsed, sometime in Easter Week. A ferry was instituted for travellers on Low Sunday (4 April),[101] and a boat was purchased for the ferry from John Coste of Hoo shortly afterwards. The king subsequently granted this ferry to the citizens of Rochester in 1446.[102]

Immediately after the disaster Richard Smith, one of the wardens, went to Maidstone to obtain the appointment of a commission to commandeer workers and timber on behalf of the bridge. He then went to London for three months to collect alms on behalf of the bridge. The size of the operation needed is apparent from the figures in Tables 5 and 6, which record the acquisition of 383 piles and 4,959 tons of chalk for rebuilding defective staddles in the two years 1444–6. Special searches for timber were conducted by John Gonell and John Hassok, and later in the year by Gonell and Thomas Broke. In May 1445 a new tug with two oxen was bought from Thomas Coppyng, who spent four days at Boxley showing the bridge employees how to use it, but who was later paid for operating it himself. Teams of carpenters were employed not only on the staddles and at 'le framingplace' by the bridge but at Boxley, Loose, Wateringbury and elsewhere where there was timber to be cut. Gonell and Hassok – later on Gonnel and Broke – had the task of going out to check on what was done. John Gonell was the principal adviser of the wardens at this time. This was because the decision had been taken not to replace the fallen arch as it had been but to replace it with a wooden structure which could be manoeuvred into position.[103]

After three or four months of intensive work on the staddles Richard Beke the stonemason came from Canterbury for three days and nights to look over the bridge with John Gonell. Although the former arch was not to be replaced, some weaknesses needed making good and a certain amount of patching up was necessary. In September the wardens bought 20 tons of hassock stone and 222 tons of ragstone, some of which was probably wanted for the staddles. But little stonework was done on the bridge until October and November when John Stile and Roger Rowe worked for a number of weeks inspecting and repairing several arches of the bridge, helped by John Hopper who mixed the cement. However, the amount of stonework, the total cost of which was £3, was remarkably small in comparison with the amount of timber work. And the final phase of the work did not involve

[100] For this vehicle, see J. Langdon, *Horses, Oxen and Technological Innovation: the Use of Draught Animals in English Farming from 1066–1500*, Cambridge 1986, 153.
[101] RBT, account 1444–5.
[102] Hasted, *The History of Kent*, iv, 79.
[103] RBT, account 1444–5.

masons at all. In November nine labourers were employed to help the carpenters put up 'posts, braces and other parts of the bridge'. Four labourers helped the carpenters 'to erect the bridge' for one day and a team of sixteen labourers was employed for four days to assist the carpenters 'to erect the bridge'. On 22 November the ferry was discontinued, and the bridge was open to traffic once more. As a finishing touch John Hoppere was employed to coat the main beams and posts of the bridge with resin.[104]

Part of the bridge broke again in the spring of 1465. The accounts for the year 1463–4, instead of being closed at Michaelmas 1464, were allowed to run on. Whether this was because of some problem in the management of the bridge or because of the difficulty of getting the accounts audited is not clear, but it meant that details of income and expenditure after that Michaelmas were added at the end of the account. These receipts include a sum for tolls levied on carts crossing the bridge between Michaelmas 1464 and the day the bridge was ruined, together with another sum received from the Tilbury ferry for the same period. There is no unambiguous evidence when this accident happened, but the most likely date is sometime early in March 1465. The 1463–4 account was allowed to run on until 9 March, but the expenditure up to that date includes nothing that can be interpreted as urgent repair work nor any receipts from a ferry across the Medway. The wardens accounted for Tilbury ferry only up to the ruin of the bridge perhaps because that was when the account was finally closed. The following wardens' account has not survived, so the extent of the damage at this time, and the problems incurred in putting it right, are not recorded.

We now enter a period when the bridge muniments are less perfectly preserved, and when references to accidents to the bridge are inevitably more scanty. But there is abundant evidence to show that the bridge faced a major crisis in the early Tudor period. Major works were under way in 1489, when the king appointed three commissioners to provide boats, wagons and carts to carry construction materials for the bridge and authorised them to impress stonecutters and other workmen for work at Rochester Bridge and elsewhere.[105] In this year Cardinal Morton encouraged donations to the bridge by granting donors forty days remission from purgatory. The bridge, according to his letter of indulgence, was so broken and weakened that various parts of it threatened to fall down; it would collapse unless repairs were undertaken quickly.[106] In 1491–2 the wardens acquired a new charter, probably relating to the special problems of reconstruction though its terms are unknown.[107] Morton took personal responsibility for the work, gave large sums of money, and was subsequently enrolled on the list of benefactors of the bridge.[108] It seems likely that the bridge did fall. Certainly what ensued was more than a

---

[104] RBT, accounts 1444–5, 1445–6.

[105] PRO, C.66/569.

[106] Lambeth Palace Library, Archbishop Morton's Register, vol. 1, f. 25r.

[107] The charter is mentioned in a letter written in 1561: PRO, S.P.12/19, item 27. I owe this reference to Dr Gibson.

[108] RBT, account 1500; *The Itinerary of John Leland in or about the Years 1535–1543*, ed. L.T. Smith, 5 vols, London 1907–10, iv, 44.

patching-up operation. The work dragged on for years. The account of 1500 records an expenditure of £394 0s. 6½d. on bridgework, a sum over a third greater than that of any recorded year in the fifteenth century, and this was before the sixteenth-century inflation had started.[109] Expenditure on the bridge during the twelve months following Michaelmas 1507 was £159 11s. 2d., which was high by normal standards even if it represents some decline in activity since 1500.[110]

The bridge was unserviceable for many years while this rebuilding was under way. In 1492 and 1494 Henry VII's privy purse expenditure included gifts to the ferry boat at Rochester, implying that the bridge was closed even to the king.[111] Traffic through Rochester was seriously disrupted. When in October 1495 the wardens granted the Crown Inn in Rochester on a five-year lease, the rent was only £4, though it had been £12 in 1478–9. The lease provided for the terms of the lease to be renegotiated 'if it happyn the seid brigge for to be made within the seid terme of v yeres so that horsse and manne may conveniently passe ouer hit'.[112] The clause was not invoked. The bridge was not passable in 1500, the year of Morton's death, nor for a long time afterwards. The accounts from June 1507 to Christmas 1508 show that a ferry was operating throughout the period.[113] In 1514 petitioners of the crown from Rochester commented that the crossing from Rochester to Strood 'by long season hathe been and yet is only by bootes to be feryed ouer the swyft water of Medway ronnyng vnder the same our citie of Rouchester, whiche passage is not only right jeopardous, tedeous and grett lett to all suche as shall passe by the sam but also many persons haue been therby putt in grett fere of theyr lyves and dyuers of them drownyd and so perished, and that the same contynuance of that passage by bootes of necessite must be vsid and had vnto suche tyme as the said new brydge, whiche of stonewerke is ther substauncially begoun and well toward the perfite perfourmance of the same, be hooly endyd, onles sum other spedy and light work for the tyme ther for the said passage may be provided'.[114]

The object of this petition was for permission to build a temporary wooden crossing which would be a convenience for travellers and a source of bridge tolls until the new bridge was complete. In the Rochester petition the proposed construction is described as 'a brydge of tymbre to be wrought, sett and adioyned betwene and to the said stonewerk of the said bridge and the rype or banke of the sayd water toward our said citie of Rouchester'.[115] In May 1514 the wardens were duly licensed by Henry VIII to proceed with this plan. This grant was confirmed in October 1517, implying that the stone bridge was still incomplete.[116] The new

[109] RBT, account 1500.

[110] RBT, account 1507–8.

[111] Rye, 'Visits to Rochester and Chatham', 48.

[112] RBT, lease of the Crown Inn, 12 October 1495, and account 1478–9.

[113] RBT, accounts 1500, 1507–8.

[114] PRO, C.86/406. There is a draft of this petition in the RBT muniments. It requests specific tolls which were not included in the petition eventually submitted.

[115] Ibid.

[116] L.P., i(2), no. 2964(10), p. 1279; L.P., ii(2), no. 3734, p. 1176.

stonework was substantially completed by 1522; the accounts of 1522–4 record no income from a ferry or footbridge tolls. Even then some of the finishing off remained to be done. Lambarde noted that 'Archbishop Warham added to the coping of the bridgwoorke those iron barres which do much beautifie the same, entending to have performed it thorowe out: but either wanting money by the losse of his prerogatives, or time by prevention of death, he left it in the halfe, as you may yet see it'.[117] It was perhaps for these finishing stages on the coping of the bridge that John Warner and John Otterbury were authorised to take timber and other materials for the bridge, as well as craftsmen, workmen and labourers, in 1532–3.[118] Archbishop Warham died on 22 August 1532.[119]

It is difficult to know how to assess the work of 1489–c.1532 in the history of the bridge. It was a much longer project than the building of the first stone bridge between 1383 and 1391–2. The petition of 1514, with its description of the 'new brydge' as 'substauncially begoun', and its request for tolls 'to be imployed to the bylding and fyneshing of the said new stonebrydge', implies that Henry of Yevele's bridge was in effect rebuilt. This must be the origin of the myth retailed by the Marquis of Winchester in 1561 that Rochester Bridge was 'removed and converted to stone at the charge of the Cardinall and of the cuntry'; he had confused Morton's role in the history of the bridge with that of Sir John de Cobham and Sir Robert Knolles a hundred years earlier.[120] Perhaps the bridge was rebuilt on the same foundations as the earlier one and to the same dimensions. But it was newly constructed, and we must suppose that it was altered in detail.

Considering the amount of replacement of materials that took place even in normal years, and then the crises which required much more extensive reconstruction in 1409–10, 1423–7, 1445–6, 1465, 1489–1517 and 1532–3, it is difficult to think of the Rochester Bridge of Elizabeth's reign as an ancient monument. It was a structure subject to constant partial replacement and had been rebuilt once. Shortage of funds does not seem to have been the main problem; had it been so a solution could have been found within decades of the new bridge's completion in 1391. The need for constant replacement and alteration was, rather, implicit in the problem to be solved at Rochester and the inadequacy of the technology available for solving it. The history of the bridge between 1391 and 1532 implies that in this period it was impossible, given the violence of the tides in the Medway, to build a bridge which would not fail every twenty years or so.

[117] W. Lambarde, *A Perambulation of Kent*, reprinted Chatham, 1826, 354. This passage was not in the 1576 edition.

[118] *L.P.*, vi, no. 418(17), p. 30.

[119] E.B. Fryde, D.E. Greenway, S. Porter and I. Roy, *Handbook of British Chronology*, Royal Historical Society, London 1986, 234.

[120] Arnold, 'Rochester Bridge in A.D. 1561', 222.

Income

The sums received each year from the 1390s by the wardens of Rochester Bridge are shown in Appendix B. They can be divided, without great problems of ambiguity, between two main categories: regular income (most of which derived from property) and irregular income (most of which derived from gifts). The importance of this distinction can be seen in Table 7. The normal income of the bridge changed greatly in the course of the period, but it did so in a manner that has a readily apparent shape to it – rapid growth up to and including the first decade of the fifteenth century, slower growth up to and including the forties, then contraction to a lower level in the 1460s and 1470s and only mild recovery thereafter. This pattern, we might guess, was shaped by long-term changes affecting the number of assets owned by the bridge and by variations in the level of rents they could demand.

Table 7

Average annual receipts of the Wardens of Rochester Bridge
for each decade, 1390–1529

(number of years averaged in brackets)

	Regular			Irregular			TOTAL		
	£	s	d	£	s	d	£	s	d
1389/90–1398/9 (1)	19	9	0	25	11	4½	45	0	4½
1399/1400–1408/9 (9)	80	12	4¼	1	11	5	82	3	9¼
1409/10–1418/19 (7)	82	13	0½	44	15	1¾	127	8	2¼
1419/20–1428/9 (4)	96	12	4	83	0	6	179	12	10
1429/30–1438/9 (4)	110	13	3¾	19	10	3	130	3	6¾
1439/40–1448/9 (5)	130	6	7	76	9	6½	206	16	1½
1449/50–1458/9 (6)	111	14	0½	12	5	2	123	19	2½
1459/60–1468/9 (4)	101	6	5¾	1	4	7	102	11	1¾
1469/70–1478/9 (7)	103	18	6	2	1	0	105	19	6
1499/1500–1508/9 (2)	108	1	0	56	7	8	164	8	8
1519/20–1528/9 (2)	96	19	1		5	4¼	96	19	1¼

Source: RBT, accounts, 1398–9 to 1522–4.

By contrast, the irregular income of the bridge was highly volatile from decade to decade and had a less coherent pattern of growth and decline. These averages are sensitive to exceptional figures for particular years. The high figure for the 1420s, for example, is owing to high receipts from alms between 1423–4 and 1425–6 when the bridge was being repaired. The high figure for the forties is similarly the consequence of exceptional receipts in 1445 after the collapse of the bridge. The early sixteenth-century figures show the effects of income from the ferry while the bridge was being rebuilt. Changes in irregular income, as these examples imply, were the result of sudden variations in the fortunes of the bridge rather than any longer patterns of historical change. This means that these averages, being based on less than complete evidence, are less reliable than those for normal income.

The growth of regular income in the early decades of the fifteenth century can be easily explained as a direct result of the acquisition of property, the beginnings of which we have already observed. If we take the receipts for 1443–4, when income from property was at its peak, and list the properties in the sequence in which they first yielded rent to the bridge foundation (Table 8), the force of this explanation can be appreciated. The figures here account for the build up of rent income only approximately, since some rents had changed from earlier levels, but comparison with Table 4 will put this complication into perspective. The rents collected from Grain manor and Langdon manor were together £5 17s. 1d. higher in 1443–4 than they had been in 1407–8, but the other rents remained unchanged. This implies that only 7 per cent of the increase in rent income between 1408–9 and 1443–4 was the result of rent increases.

The total receipt from property in 1443–4 corresponds very closely to the 200 marks which Richard II had authorised the Wardens and Commonalty of the bridge to acquire, and it had taken almost fifty years to get there. The new rents of the second decade of the fifteenth century were the consequence of earlier provision. As we have seen, the reversion of John de Frenyngham's property in Dartford had been granted in 1401 and that of Wangford's rents in Cornhill, London, as far back as 1399. These two properties first contributed to the income of the bridge in 1411, and in that year the wardens took out a new license to acquire Dartford property in mortmain.[1] Later additions to the bridge rent income were all the result of gifts made after the founders of the new bridge were dead.

The most important of these later acquisitions were various properties in Rochester which came into the hands of the wardens during the 1420s. Sometime between 1416 and 1423 the list of rents in the city was lengthened by the acquisition of some properties which had been owned by William Mymmes, including a corner tavern and cellar with some cottages and other buildings. These included a tenement called the Pewterpot with a stable next to it.[2] A yet more important acquisition in Rochester was the Crown Inn, which first paid a rent to the bridge in

---

[1] RBT, E42; *Cal. Pat. R., 1408–13*, 293. A schedule of the costs of acquiring new letters patent for the Dartford property is affixed to the back of RBT, account 1410–11.
[2] RBT, accounts 1415–16, 1423–4.

Table 8

Properties belonging to Rochester Bridge in 1443–4,
listed in order of the date when they first yielded rent

	Rent in 1443–4			Running total		
	£	s	d	£	s	d
first payment by 1398–9						
Grain manor	14	9	1	14	9	1
first payment by 1408–9						
East Tilbury manor	33	6	8			
marsh at Eastwick		13	4			
Langdon manor	12	1	4			
Nashenden manor	8	0	0			
Rochester rents (1)		11	0	69	1	5
first payment by 1418–19						
land at Dartford	6	0	0			
London rents	17	7	0	92	8	5
first payment by 1428–9						
land at Walshes	1	0	0			
Little Delce manor	6	0	0			
Rochester rents (2)	6	11	4			
The Crown, Rochester	14	13	4	120	13	1
first payment by 1438–9						
rent from Lidlez in Sheppey	2	0	0	122	13	1
first payment by 1443–4						
Northfleet mill	10	13	4			
limekiln	1	0	0	134	6	5

Source: RBT, account 1443–4.

1426–7.[3] It stood in a prime site on the corner where the approach road to the bridge joined Rochester High Street, only a hundred yards or so from the bridge chapel.[4] In the wardens' account of 1450–1 it was called the King's Inn, and this alternative name often occurs in later accounts.[5] The wardens' interest in this property went back to 1415–16, if not earlier. In that year Sir William Neubold spoke several times to Thomas Langley, Bishop of Durham and a prominent

---

3 RBT, account 1426–7.
4 The public house now called The Norman Conquest stands on part of the site.
5 The inn is called the King's Inn in the Rochester rents of 1450–1, in every documented year between 1452–3 and 1463–4, and again in 1466–7 and 1472–3. It was called the Crown, however, in the rent accounts of 1451–2, 1466–7 and 1469–70. In some accounts it is called the Crown in the repairs account even though it is called the King's Inn in the rent account, as in 1458–9, 1460–1 and 1461–2.

member of Henry V's council, in the expectation that he would buy the inn on behalf of the bridge. Roger Ferour was consulted in London about the legal side of the acquisition.[6] The bishop's interest no doubt stemmed from the strategic importance of the bridge in the war effort. The course of the later negotiations between the wardens and the bishop is unknown because of the loss of the accounts for the seven following years, which include most of the seven-year period when Langley was Chancellor of England. But the bishop was certainly as good as his word, and was long remembered as one of the benefactors of the bridge.[7] The Crown Inn was in the hands of the wardens by the summer of 1424, when one of the wardens and others representing the bridge spent nine days in London trying to lease it.[8] In the event another strategy was pursued, perhaps because the wardens were unable to obtain a tenant on satisfactory terms. During the course of the following two years they spent £78 10s. 9d. in restoring the inn and its outbuildings and supplying new inn signs. They allowed a further £20 to a new lessee for stocking it up. Then they leased it for nine years from Christmas 1426 at an annual rent of £13 6s. 8d. The continuing interest of the Bishop of Durham during these expensive operations is evident from the fact that John Tannere, his carpenter, went to view the repairs in the course of 1424–5. It was probably on business connected with the inn that John Depyng and John Clyfton spent four days in London to get an audience with the bishop in the same year.[9] And again in 1428–9 the same John Tannere came to Rochester 'to inspect the new inn belonging to the bridge'.[10]

Of the other properties acquired by the bridge in the earlier fifteenth century, the land at Walshes in Frindsbury first occurs in the list of rent receipts in 1423–4, though it may already have been contributing to the income of the bridge a few years before this since there is a gap in the series of wardens' accounts between Michaelmas 1416 and Michaelmas 1423. The property lay in a number of adjacent blocks of which the largest ran along the northern shore of Limehouse Reach. Its acquisition was linked with the rights of the bridge in the chalk quarry and the wharf, near which the wardens had a limehouse in the fifteenth century. It was described in 1663 as belonging to the manor of Islingham.[11] The Chaplains' Memorandum Book links the acquisition of this property to that of the Crown Inn: 'Syr Thomas Langley bysschop of Dyrham yaff and mortaysed the Crowne wyth iij other rentes wyth a grownde called Walsches ierly wurth xxj marke vj s. viij d.' Langley would have bought the property on behalf of the bridge because of its importance as a source of chalk.[12]

Little Delce was added to the rent-paying properties in 1428–9. The manor

---

6 RBT, account 1415–16. For Thomas Langley's public career in the early years of the war, see R.L. Storey, *Thomas Langley and the Bishopric of Durham, 1406–1437*, London 1961, 31–6.

7 *The Itinerary of John Leland*, iv, p. 44.

8 RBT, account 1423–4.

9 RBT, accounts 1424–5, 1425–6.

10 RBT, account 1428–9.

11 RBT, The Bridge Mapps (1663–1717), map 2; RBT, account 1423–4; A.A. Arnold, 'Quarry House, on Frindsbury Hill', *Archaeologia Cantiana*, xvii (1887), 169–80.

12 RBT, Chaplains' Memorandum Book, f. 3v.

house stood just over a quarter of a mile south of Rochester on the road to Maidstone. Like Nashenden it was a long, thin manor; it stretched southwards to abut upon the middle of Nashenden manor. Today the northern part of Little Delce manor is a suburb of Rochester. The middle part is occupied by Borstal School and the Youth Custody Centre, and the southern part by Rochester Airport.[13] The property was given to the bridge by William and Charles Snayth, the former having acquired it by right of his wife.[14] But there was some complication in the transfer of the property, since the wardens' accounts record that John Skynnere had been paid 40 marks for the manor by annual instalments between 1427 and 1430, and there was litigation with Skynnere in the king's courts to confirm the title. The formalities of seeking royal consent for this acquisition and formally conveying the property to the wardens were completed only in 1439, and the king's licence was not in fact issued until 1440.[15]

The new income from Sheppey recorded in Table 8 was described as an annual rent of £2 from lands and tenements called Lyles or Lydles in Leysdown which were part of the manor of Tunstall. The rent was given to the bridge in 1407 by William Cheyne of Sheppey, a man sufficiently wealthy to be appointed to commissions of the peace in Kent in 1416, 1418 and 1422. But the wardens had to wait until his death for the gift to become effective; the first instalment is recorded in 1429–30.[16] In later accounts this income is described as 'Paytevynesrent' after the name of a former tenant of the property.[17]

Northfleet Mill, the last main acquisition to be considered here, does not appear on any account before the early forties. It came from the estate of John Darell, who had died a few years earlier. In his lifetime Darell had been an important friend of the bridge. The Chaplains' Memorandum Book notes that he 'yaff to the reparacion of the sayed brygg xl mark'; that was probably in the early 1420s. He had also given the wardens his advice from time to time. The account of 1438–9 records the relevant discussions with Darell's widow and executors for the acquisition of Northfleet Mill.[18]

In 1442 the wardens were complaining that the profits of the bridge were so diminished that they were having difficulty in funding the costs of divine service in the bridge chapel. It is difficult to see what they meant, unless the loss of accounts from the years from Michaelmas 1440 to Michaelmas 1443 conceals some short-term crisis. It may be that the wardens were already exceptionally concerned about the state of the bridge and could foresee that heavy expenditure would be needed. Or alternatively they were playing on Henry VI's weakness for pious causes. Their request was successful to the extent of a royal grant of £5 a year which had previously been paid into the exchequer by St Augustine's Abbey in Canterbury,

---

[13] RBT, account 1428–9; RBT, The Bridge Mapps (1663–1717), map 10.

[14] RBT, Chaplains' Memorandum Book, f. 3v; Hasted, The History of Kent, iv, 171–3.

[15] RBT, accounts 1428–9, 1429–30, 1439–40; RBT, E44; PRO, C.143/448/19, C.66/450, m. 2.

[16] RBT, E68; RBT, accounts 1429–30, 1430–1, 1435–6; Hasted, The History of Kent, vi, 269. This rent had once belonged to Sir Robert Knolles: RBT, E66.

[17] RBT, accounts 1430–1, 1435–6.

[18] RBT, accounts 1438–9, 1443–4.

though the wardens' accounts show that the grant was never put into effect.[19] On this occasion the plea of poverty was not one that a dispassionate observer could have taken seriously. But within a short while the wardens had more cause for concern. By contrast with the period when the property of the bridge was being built up, the decades after 1443 were a period of financial gloom as their regular income began to decline. Table 7 suggests the dimensions of this decline – a fall of 22 per cent in regular income between the 1440s and the 1460s.

Table 9

Properties rented by Rochester Bridge in 1478–9 and 1556–7

	1478–9			1556–7		
	£	s	d	£	s	d
Grain manor	6	13	4	7	0	0
East Tilbury manor	26	5	0	13	15	4
marsh at Eastwick	–	–	–		10	0
Langdon manor	8	0	0	9	0	0
Nashenden manor	8	0	0	10	2	9
Rochester rents	25	1	7	14	6	4
land at Dartford	6	6	8	4	13	4
London rents	15	10	11	19	15	4
land at Walshes	1	0	0	2	6	8
Little Delce manor	5	15	1	6	13	4
rent from Lidlez in Sheppey	–	–	–	2	0	0
Northfleet mill	–	–	–	–	–	–
a lime-kiln	–	–	–	–	–	–
rent from Great Delce	–	–	–	1	6	8
Cockamhill	–	–	–		2	10
TOTAL	102	12	7	92	12	7

Source: RBT, accounts 1478–9 and 1556–7.

Table 9 shows the last figures available from the fifteenth century. Despite some recovery since the trough of the depression in the 1460s, income from rents remained below its former level. This was in spite of the fact that the Wardens and Commonalty had further increased the number of properties they owned in Rochester. They had acquired properties called the Fleur-de-lis, the Horseshoe and the Copped Hall which together should have raised their total annual income by some 7 per cent above the level of 1443. Indeed, the total rent income from Rochester was higher than it had been in the past. But this increase was more than offset by the fact that some rents had been temporarily or permanently lost, some properties were no longer tenanted, and some tenants had had reductions in their

19 *Cal. Pat. R., 1441–6,* 70; *Cal. Close R., 1435–41,* 24.

rent. In the first category comes Northfleet mill. Its rent had been reduced from
£10 13s. 4d. a year between Michaelmas 1443 and Michaelmas 1446 to £7 6s. 8d.
a year between Michaelmas 1449 and Michaelmas 1453, after which the mill
disappeared permanently from the wardens' accounts. Sheppey was a casualty of
the mid-sixties depression. It paid in 1463–4, but not subsequently, though the
wardens eventually recovered this rent, as can be seen from the evidence of
1556–7.[20] In the second category, of properties that paid no rent in 1478–9 because
they were simply untenanted, was the lime-kiln (always described in the accounts
as the lime-oast).[21] This had last been leased in 1450–1; in the following year it was
described as ruined and unleased.[22] The marsh at Eastwick, too, had been untenanted for four or five years for want of a lessee. Many of the urban properties of
the bridge were similarly untenanted; the wardens accounted for lost income of £1
6s. 9d. in London and £3 0s. 5d. in Rochester from this cause. And finally, in the
third category, there had been rent reductions on a number of the bridge estates.
Comparison between Tables 8 and 9 shows the extent of the losses of income from
this cause at the manors of Grain, East Tilbury, Langdon and Little Delce. The rent
of the Crown Inn in Rochester had also fallen from £14 13s. 4d. to £12. The few
increases in rent, at Dartford and on some Rochester properties, were barely
significant by comparison. The 7 per cent increase in income which would otherwise have resulted from the acquisition of new tenements in Rochester was
swamped by a general loss and reduction of rent by 28 per cent, so that in the event
total rent income was down by about 24 per cent.

The rent income of the bridge cannot be described in detail after 1479 because
accounts are fewer, less consistent with each other and less informative. None of
them gives details of the separate rents from different properties, so that it is
impossible to analyse the extent to which changes in the wardens' income resulted
from movements of rent or from acquisitions and losses of property. The first
column of Table 11 summarises what is known. The implication of these figures is
that there was no clear recovery in the normal rent income of the bridge during the
first half of the sixteenth century. Indeed the gross receipts from rent in the two
years from Michaelmas 1522 to Michaelmas 1524 were no better than those of the
depressed years of the 1460s and 1470s, and those of 1507–8 were even worse.

The receiver's account for 1556–7 enables us to see for the first time since
1478–9 what properties the bridge could lease; the information is included in Table
9. Very little rentable property had been gained or lost since the 1470s, and the
overall picture is one of surprising stability. There is little pattern to the movement
of rents relative to each other. The London rents were slightly up, the Rochester
ones quite a lot down. The manors of Grain, Langdon, Nashendon and Little Delce
were all worth more than they had been, and rents had been re-established from
Eastwick (described in 1557 as 'the landes in Halstowe') and from Sheppey. But

---

[20] RBT, accounts 1463–4, June–Sept. 1466, Feb.–Sept. 1467, 1467–8.
[21] 'le lymhost', RBT, accounts 1443–4, 1444–5, 1445–6; 'le lymoste', RBT, account 1447–8; 'le
      lymeoste', RBT, accounts 1449–50, 1450–1.
[22] RBT, accounts 1450–1, 1451–2.

Table 10

Average annual net income from the property of Rochester Bridge
for each decade, 1390–1479

(number of years averaged in brackets)

	Total rents			Rents and taxes paid			Maintenance of property			Net income from rent			Net income as a percentage of total rents
	£	s	d	£	s	d	£	s	d	£	s	d	%
1389/90–1398/9 (1)	18	13	4	–	–	–	–	–	–	18	13	4	100
1399/1400–1408/9 (9)	80	12	4¼	16	17	6¼	5	10	6½	58	4	3½	72
1409/10–1418/19 (7)	81	12	1	8	2	11	5	19	3½	67	9	10½	83
1419/20–1428/9 (4)	95	5	7	1	7	3¾	19	0	6¾	74	17	8½	79
1429/30–1438/9 (4)	109	16	0	3	12	8	14	18	8½	91	4	7½	83
1439/40–1448/9 (5)	127	7	1½	11	15	2¼	17	2	11¼	98	9	0	77
1449/50–1458/9 (6)	110	2	8¼	2	3	1¾	24	11	8	83	7	10½	76
1459/60–1468/9 (4)	98	5	11¼	5	10	6¾	28	7	2½	64	8	2	66
1469/70–1478/9 (7)	103	3	7½	2	13	2½	19	16	9¼	80	13	7¾	78

Source: RBT, accounts 1398–90 to 1478–9.

Table 11

Annual rents from land in documented periods, 1500–1528

Year	Total rents			Rents and taxes paid			Maintenance of property			Net income from property			Net income as a percentage of total rents
	£	s	d	£	s	d	£	s	d	£	s	d	%
1.i.1500–31.xii.1500	95	19	0¾	3	2	4	7	11	10	85	5	8	89
29.ix.1507–29.ix.1508	71	11	3		10	1	11	3	8	59	17	6	84
29.ix.1522–29.ix.1524	192	0	10	3	18	6½	24	5	4	163	16	11½	85
29.ix.1527–29.ix.1528	108	2	8	–	–	–	16	5	4	91	17	4	85
29.ix.1556–29.ix.1557	92	12	7	1	9	5½	–	–	–	91	3	1½	98

Source: RBT, accounts 1500, 1507–8, 1522–4, 1527–8, 1556–7.

the Thamesside properties of Dartford and East Tilbury were worth less. All told the bridge rents were less valuable than they had been, despite the addition of a few new ones. The chief loss of income had been in Rochester itself. But the documentation is not rich enough to say whether 1556–7 was a representative year for the mid sixteenth century or to explain why the rents in that year were no higher.

Tables 8 and 9 contain only income from rents that was actually collected, so in that sense they represent the real value of the bridge properties over the years. Nevertheless there were costs to offset against income which reduced the amount available for spending on the bridge and chapel. The costs of rent-collecting are difficult to separate systematically from other administrative costs, though they probably did not change very much from year to year. The wardens also had to pay some rents for properties which they held from other lords. In addition the wardens were obliged to spend money to maintain their estate, and this could dramatically reduce the net value of particular properties in certain years. Tables 10 and 11 make some allowance for these expenses on the strength of the information in the account rolls. The balance between gross and net income was evidently variable. In the years from 1400 to 1411 net receipts were depressed by the annuity of £13 6s. 8d. payable to Alice Potyn.[23] The tendency for landlords' maintenance costs to rise in periods of depressed property values accounts for the exceptionally low net income of the 1460s. By contrast in the early sixteenth century a higher proportion of the income from rents was available for expenditure on the bridge, which perhaps signifies that the wardens were able to pass on more of the costs of maintaining property to tenants. In spite of such variations, the figures suggest the extent to which available income normally fell short of gross income from rents. And these must be minimum figures, since the charges shown against rent income in Tables 10 and 11 omit all administrative costs.

Regular sources of income were dominated by income from rents; nothing else made much difference to the movement of the figures in Table 7. Nevertheless, before leaving this aspect of the finances of the bridge, some notice should be given to the minor recurrent sums. The bridge wardens made a small amount in some years by hiring out the boats belonging to the bridge. The highest annual income recorded from this source was £1 11s. 0d. in 1414–15, when they received 21s. from 'batylage' from the Bishop of Durham and 10s. from other people on various occasions.[24] Another recurrent source of small sums from 1412 onwards was the lease of fishing from the staddles. But the largest sum recorded from this source was £1 3s. 4d. in 1415–16.[25] Of slightly more weight were the receipts from the custom paid by carts crossing the bridge between 1445 and 1479, though the sums involved are surprisingly small; the largest recorded figure was £6 in the depression year 1463–4.[26] The costs of collecting this particular income seem to have prevented its being systematically exploited. Finally, the wardens derived small sums from sales of surplus material from time to time. The most remarkable

[23] RBT, accounts from 1399–1400 to 1410–11.
[24] RBT, account 1414–15.
[25] RBT, account 1415–16.

[26] RBT, account 1463–4. The figures are recorded in Becker, *Rochester Bridge*, 60–1.

instance of this was in 1457–8 when the wardens organized the manufacture of 76 quarters of lime, all of which they sold to various local buyers.[27] The £5 1s. 4d. they earned from this enterprise was higher than their income from sales in any other recorded year.

The irregular income of the bridge must include some sources of income which were only available in periods of acute difficulty. Income from ferry boats, for example, was available only when the bridge was impassable. There is no record of the doubtless considerable sums derived from this source between 1381 and 1387, but they are likely to have been around £100 a year. The wardens received £62 19s. 1d. from the ferry between 4 April and 21 November 1445. Later figures are rather lower – £67 17s. 4d. for a full twelve months in 1500 and £86 12s. 8d. during an eighteen-month period from Midsummers Day 1507 to Christmas 1508.[28] The bridge was also more likely to be given privileged rights to collect money in periods of special need. In 1383, when the bridge was down, Richard II authorised John Shropshire and John Bregge, junior, to collect donations for the repair of the bridge, with the right to arrest unauthorised collectors, though they had stopped collecting by the time of the first surviving account in 1391–2.[29] And in some moments of need ecclesiastical dispensation was granted for spiritual privileges to accompany donations to the bridge. Archbishop Courtenay granted indulgences for gifts to the bridge during the course of its construction.[30] Collections of this sort could draw numerous small gifts from passing travellers and others. Such a scheme operated for some years from the time of the crisis of 1409–10. In that year £6 12s. 11¾d. was collected by various people around Rochester as 'pardoun' money, and similar, though smaller receipts were recorded in most years up to 1415–16. In 1412–13 the pardon money is described as having been 'received in the box and collected in the country', implying that there was some collecting box in the bridge chapel or in some other suitable position near the bridge. In following years the dwindling and barely significant receipts from pardon money were entirely from this box.[31] Similar policies were pursued later in the history of the bridge. In 1428–9 John Man the hermit was appointed procurator of the bridge, with a royal licence to collect alms anywhere in England.[32] And in 1472–3 the wardens obtained letters patent to collect alms for bridge work for three years, as well as letters of indulgence to alms-givers from various bishops. That year they gave 4d. to a preacher who appealed on their behalf to the faithful at St Paul's Cross in London. The sums from this source remained small – only £1 16s. 5d. in 1473–4.[33]

The endeavours of the wardens and other members of the commonalty of the bridge to attract larger donations from wealthier individuals were more sustained in

---

[27] RBT, account 1457–8.
[28] RBT, accounts 1444–5, 1500, 1507–8.
[29] *Cal. Pat. R., 1381–5*, 273, 275; RBT, account 1391–2.
[30] F.R.H. DuBoulay, *The Lordship of Canterbury: An Essay on Medieval Society*, London 1966, 169.
[31] RBT, accounts from 1409–10 to 1415–16.
[32] RBT, account 1428–9.
[33] RBT, accounts 1472–3, 1473–4.

years of difficulty than at other times, which is why receipts from this source were at their highest in 1409–10 (£103 5s. 8d.), 1423–4 (£111 12s. 0d.), 1425–6 (£200 9s. 6d.) and 1444–5 (£171 19s. 4d.). In such moments the wardens endeavoured to tap the wealth of Londoners in particular. In 1409–10 the principal agent in collecting donations was 'Sir Harry' (perhaps Henry Bourne, clerk), one of the chaplains employed to officiate in the bridge chapel. He was paid £13 8s. 2d. for his expenses in going to London and elsewhere on bridge business, and during the course of the year submitted to the wardens an account of gifts and donations to the bridge from London and elsewhere. The list of twenty names contained eleven from London and three from Southwark and included the comment that 6s. 8d. remained uncollected in the hands of a London man.[34] In 1424 the chief fund-raiser in London was William Sevenoke, a notable citizen of London, who drew up an indenture with the wardens for his successes between 24 June and 29 September. They included £40 from the executors of Richard Whittington, the rich and worthy citizen who was thrice lord mayor of London, though 7s. 8d. had to be deducted from this sum because the coin in which it was paid, like other coin received in this period, was of deficient weight.[35] By 1425–6 though William Sevenoke still helped the bridge in this capacity the main intermediary between London and the wardens was the king's justice, John Martyn, who was also the wardens' tenant for the manor of Langdon. Amongst other receipts he was able to raise £26 13s. 4d. for the souls of Thomas Arundel, Archbishop of Canterbury, Guy Mone, Bishop of St David's and William Maydeston.[36] In 1444–5 most of this work was apparently done by the wardens, and particularly Richard Smith, who made some prolonged stays in London asking and negotiating for funds for the bridge. He was responsible for netting a very large donation from the executors of Lord Fanhope. John Wigmore, one of the bridge chaplains, was also in London for part of the year on the same mission.[37]

Table 12, which records only the largest known donations to the bridge, shows that though these were bunched in the years of greatest need there was also a pattern of donations to the bridge in the ordinary course of events. And there can be no doubt that the gentle flow of gifts and legacies owed a great deal to deliberate public relations activities on the part of the bridge authorities even in years when there was no imminent crisis. A case in point is the pursuit of a donation from the executors of Cardinal Beaufort, Bishop of Winchester, who died on 11th April 1447 leaving a great fortune for dispersal by his executors. The residue of the estate was to be spent in pious and charitable uses. Not surprisingly there were many applicants. A begging letter from Oxford university was rewarded to the tune of 500 marks (£333 6s. 8d.) and Exeter College, Oxford, was given a tenth of this

[34] RBT, account 1409–10. 'Sieur Henry, chapellayn de la chapelle al dit pount' (RBT, account 1410–11) is probably to be identified with Henry Bourne, clerk (*Cal. Pat. R., 1408–13*, 293).
[35] RBT, account 1423–4.
[36] RBT, account 1425–6.
[37] RBT, account 1444–5.

sum. The city of Exeter asked for money to rebuild its bridge.[38] But from the accounts of the wardens of Rochester Bridge we can see some of the effort that had to go into such petitioning for funds. Three representatives of the bridge rode on horseback to London on February 8th to speak with the late bishop's executors and to ask for alms for the bridge, and they were there for four days. Later the same month William Saunder, clerk, and his servant made the same trip for the same purpose and were paid their expenses for three days. This is the background to the gift of £30 in 1447–8 recorded in Table 12. In later years the wardens made additional attempts to attract the favour of the cardinal's executors. In November 1449 Henry Baker, one of the wardens, was again in London for four days to communicate with them, and it may have been on this occasion that the cardinal's treasurer was given a small gift of wine to earn his goodwill. Negotiations continued into the following year; William Porte, one of the executors, was made a present of some wine sometime around Easter, and another present of wine to the executors was given in the late summer. But there is no indication in the rolls of 1449–50 or 1450–1 that this second initiative was rewarded.[39]

The circumstances of this appeal were not exceptional, as far as the Wardens and Commonalty were concerned. The only unusual feature in the case was the size of Cardinal Beaufort's estate. In other respects – the need to sue for consideration, to travel, to wait, and to offer presents – the pattern repeated itself many times, and each success was the outcome of an assiduous campaign. In 1447–8, besides their approaches to the cardinal's executors, the wardens gave presents of wine to the chancellor, to Richard Bain, to John Throgmerton's wife, to the executors of John Gillyngton of 'Wantnare', to the Archdeacon of Richmond, to a kinsman of the Archbishop of York, to the Archbishop of York's treasurer, to a chamberlain of the Archbishop of Canterbury, and to an executor of Lord Fanhope. Some of these are said to be for goodwill, but some were clearly associated with petitions for alms. Other recorded approaches for alms were made to the Archbishop of Canterbury, to an executor of William Estfeld, knight, to the executors and feoffees of William Seprawns, knight, and to the cardinal of York. Such work involved a lot of travelling about. To see the Archbishop of Canterbury both wardens went to Maidstone. One of the wardens went to Maidstone to see Sir William Seprawns's executors, and two clerics were sent to Wye to approach the cardinal of York.[40]

Even when a promise of money was more easily gained it was often a different matter to collect it. In the year 1414–15 Henry V made two separate donations to the bridge, one of £13 6s. 8d. and the other of £20. The first was promised, perhaps, when the king passed over the bridge on his way to France, the second when he recrossed it on his triumphant journey home. But the matter was not as simple as the receipt side of the account would imply. That year's expenses contained a separate section to detail costs incurred 'for the alms given by our lord the

[38] G.L. Harriss, *Cardinal Beaufort: A Study of Lancastrian Ascendancy and Decline*, Oxford 1988, 379–82.
[39] RBT, accounts 1447–8, 1449–50, 1450–1.
[40] RBT, account 1447–8.

Table 12

Recorded donations to Rochester Bridge of £10 and more, 1398–1479

Year	Donor	£	s	d
1409–10	John Mokkyng of Notstede	33	6	8
1409–10	Robert Legh of Southwark	11	6	8
1409–10	William Walderne of London	14	0	0
1409–10	John Geboun of Sandwich	20	0	0
1414–15	King Henry V	33	6	8
1414–15	Robert Chechele of London	25	0	0
1415–16	—— Chechele of London and William Croumer of London	62	13	4
1423–4	legacy of William Lenne, citizen of London	20	0	0
1423–4	executors of Richard Whittington	40	0	0
1423–4	William Cambregg	20	0	0
1423–4	William Symmes	10	0	0
1423–4	William Olyver	10	0	0
1423–4	executors of Geoffrey Wymond	10	0	0
1425–6	Thomas Knolles, citizen of London	13	6	8
1425–6	Thomas Arundel, bishop, and William Mayston	20	13	0*
1425–6	executors of John Hadersham	10	0	0
1425–6	John Lane of London	13	6	8[1]
1425–6	John Darell	20	0	0
1425–6	executors of John Drewe	20	0	0
1425–6	John Martyn	26	13	4
1429–30	legacy of John Shadworthe, citizen of London	10	0	0
1430–1	legacy of John Sergant, citizen and armourer of London	10	0	0
1438–9	legacy of Robert Chichele	20	0	0
1438–9	Richard Cleterowe	40	0	0[2]
1438–9	executors of John Langdon, bishop of Rochester	20	0	0[3]
by c.1440	Thomas and Bartholomew Wode	20	0	0*
by c.1440	Isabel Russe	10	0	0*
by c.1440	John Penne	10	0	0*
1443–4	Thomas Glovere	10	0	0
1444–5	executors of Thomas Glover, late warden of the bridge	10	0	0
1444–5	wife of John Throgmerton, esq.	13	6	8
1444–5	Master John Stopyndon, clerk of the rolls	10	0	0
1444–5	executors of John Langdon, late bishop of Rochester	10	0	0
1444–5	John Michell, late of London	10	0	0
1444–5	executors of John Cornwaill, knt., Lord Fanhope	100	0	0
1447–8	executors of the bishop of Winchester	30	0	0
1450–1	executors of Gilbert Cooke of London	13	6	8
1451–2	executors of Ralph Holand, citizen and draper of London	10	0	0
1465–6	executrix of William Holt, citizen and fellmonger of London	40	0	0*

Year	Donor	£	s	d
1465–6	executors of Geoffrey Boleyn	100	0	0*
1465–6	executors of William Middilton, citizen and grocer of London	100	0	0*
1472–3	legacy of Richard Lee, knt.	10	0	0

1 to be paid over two years (Chaplains' Memorandum Book, f. 4r)
2 to be paid over six years
3 to be paid over two or three years (Chaplains' Memorandum Book, f. 3v)

Source: RBT accounts 1409–10, 1423–4, 1425–6, 1429–30, 1430–1, 1438–9, 1439–40, 1444–5, 1447–8, 1450–1, 1472–3. Gifts marked with an asterisk are recorded only in the Chaplains' Memorandum Book, ff. 3v–5r.

king'. We learn there that in winning the first donation Sir William Neubold, probably the senior chaplain in the bridge chapel, had spent 14s. 3d. at Rochester in gaining goodwill amongst the king's entourage. His success there entailed spending a further £1 2s. 4½d. in the course of ten days away from Rochester, first in Canterbury and then in London, in the course of which he had to meet both his own expenses and those incurred 'around the officers of our lord the king'. A petition to the king had cost 1s. 6d. to be drawn up. The second gift implied further expenditure, though it was apparently a more spontaneous gesture than the first on the part of the king or his almoner. On this occasion the wardens made no payments to earn the goodwill of the king's officers, but they had to pay to get the money after the gift had been promised. Sir William again left home for ten days on a tour that took him to London, Kennington and Mortlake. He then had to go to Canterbury for six days. To get a warrant to receive the king's £20 he had to go to Mortlake, and from there to Aylesford. Then he had to go again to Mortlake and Kennington to receive the money, apparently to no avail. Then later in the year, or even perhaps early in 1416, a further expenditure was ascribed to a six-day visit to Dartford and London to receive the king's £20 from the hands of Lord Fitzhugh, the king's chamberlain. The combined cost of all this travelling was £2 2s. 9½d. These allowed expenses, which make no allowance for at least a month of Sir William's time, add up to over ten per cent of the total amount of the king's gifts.[41]

The irregular income of the bridge, then, was not made up chiefly of windfalls. It was earned by a time-consuming and sometimes frustrating process of waiting upon other people. In the middle decades of the fifteenth century this business was taken very seriously even in years of ordinary expenditure. The petition to Henry VI in 1442 was in this respect part of the annual routine, and probably represented an automatic response to the king's visit to Rochester in the first week of the year,[42] even if the wording of the petition had to be devised to suit the king's proclivities. Between 1409–10 and 1451–2 there were donations in most recorded years and a

41 RBT, accounts 1414–15, 1415–16. For Henry, Lord Fitzhugh, see J. Catto in G.L. Harriss, ed., *Henry V: The Practice of Kingship*, Oxford 1985, 86, 93.
42 B. Wolffe, *Henry VI*, London 1981, 363.

number of large ones, as recorded in Table 12. In the third quarter of the fifteenth century this fund-raising activity was less assiduously performed, with predictable implications for the sums of money that were donated to the bridge. It is interesting that the income from donations, as suggested in Appendix B, and the number of large donations recorded in Table 12, fell off in the third quarter of the fifteenth century, just at the same time that the rent income of the bridge was also declining. In the fourteen years for which there are accounts from 1456–7 to 1478–9 there was one donation of more than £10, and the Chaplains' Memorandum Book records only three others.[43] One of the reasons for this may have been simply declining effort on the part of the Wardens and Commonalty. There is something of a parallel in the years from 1400–1 and 1407–8 when there were no donations to the bridge at all, presumably because no one asked for any. But it would be unjust to attribute the decline in donations from the 1450s wholly to the lethargy of the men responsible for the bridge. The economic environment was generally less favourable for the Wardens and Commonalty at this time than in earlier decades because landlords other than the wardens were suffering from reduced incomes from rents. In a period when money was short, it was bound to be even harder to raise donations than it had been in the decades before 1450, so that the expenditure of time and trouble in this direction was less easily justifiable than it had been in the past.

The early Tudor period saw a resurgence of donations to the bridge made necessary by its weakened state. The rebuilding of the bridge after 1489 was not, on past experience, something which could have been contemplated from the ordinary income of the bridge and it necessarily depended upon a renewed flood of gifts to the fabric. The largest single item in the receipts of Richard Symondes, the surveyor and sole warden for 1500, was £307 0s. 6d. received by mandate from Cardinal Morton at various times and from other people whose names were not recorded in the account.[44] The archbishops of Canterbury were the major donors in this period, performing both the financial and the supervisory role which Sir John de Cobham and Sir Robert Knolles had done in the later 1380s. There were smaller donations and bequests of which we know little. John Crouch, for example, bequeathed £3 6s. 8d. 'to the reparacion of the grete brigge at Rowchestre' in 1492.[45] A Rochester merchant, John Warner, was long remembered for having contributed to the final coping of the bridge.[46] The bridge continued to be regarded as a fit object for charitable giving. Richard Chetham, the prior of Leeds was criticised by one of the canons there in 1511 for committing the priory to supporting the repair of Rochester Bridge.[47] As John Weever wrote in his poem 'The Mirror of Martyrs', published in 1601:

[43] RBT, accounts from 1456–7 to 1478–9; RBT, Chaplains' Memorandum Book, f. 4v.
[44] RBT, account 1500.
[45] Testamenta Cantiana: A Series of Extracts from Fifteenth and Sixteenth Century Wills relating to Church Building and Topography, West Kent, ed. L.L. Duncan, London 1906, 64.
[46] The Itinerary of John Leland, iv, 52.
[47] Kentish Visitations of Archbishop Warham and his Deputies, 1511–12, ed. K.L. Wood-Leigh, Kent Records, xxiv, Maidstone 1984, 40. I owe this reference to Dr Gibson.

Warham, th'archbishop once of Canterbery,
The iron barres upon the bridge bestow'd:
Warner the copings did reedifie
And many since their liberall minds have show'd,
Whose deedes in life (if deedes can Heaven merit)
Made them in death all heavenly joyes inherit.[48]

Perhaps not all money given to the bridge was given so liberally. In their Kentish visitations in 1511 Archbishop Warham and his deputies were mindful of the bridge as a potential beneficiary of the penalties they imposed. At Hoath chapel in Reculver the churchwardens and parishioners were required to provide a pix and chrismatory, and to undertake certain repairs, on pain of 40s. to the repair of Rochester Bridge. And at Chartham the executor of Robert Shefeld was ordered to pay 18s. belonging to the church there on pain of 20s. to the bridge.[49]

[48] 'Rochester Bridge: A Poem Written in A.D. 1601', ed. W.B. Rye, *Archaeologia Cantiana*, xvii (1887), 162.
[49] *Kentish Visitations*, ed. Wood-Leigh, 78, 171. I owe these references to Dr Gibson.

Administration

The principal surviving records of the bridge from the fifteenth century are the annual accounts of the wardens, who as individuals had continuous responsibility during their terms of office. We accordingly know more in detail about them than about the commonalty of the bridge which they represented. The wardens' duties, for most of the fifteenth century, had varied very considerably from person to person and from year to year, depending on how much help they received from other members of the bridge establishment and from members of the commonalty. Though it was normal to appoint two, their duties and status were not equal. Robert Rowe and John Wolcy, as we have seen, were paid different sums for different levels of responsibility in the early fifteenth century, and this custom persisted. The wardens took £10 between them every year, but it was divided unequally. In 1443–4, for example, Richard Smith was expecting to get £6 13s. 4d. and John Cust only £3 6s. 8d.[1] In the sixteenth century accounting for receipts and accounting for expenditure came to be two different tasks, but differences between the two wardens in the fifteenth century are not explicable along these lines since both wardens are often said to be responsible in accounting for particular receipts and expenses. In the account for 1415–16, for example, Robert Rowe and John Wolcy jointly accounted for the fact that there was no rent from the marsh adjoining the Boley, one of the bridge properties in Rochester, and they both accounted for paying the expenses of the chapel.[2]

If we take the account of the year 1449–50, we can see something of the work entailed when there was relatively little support from the commonalty or the bridge chaplains. It was a year when total administrative costs were modest, so not a year of exceptional stress. As usual, one of the wardens took a stipend of £6 13s. 4d. and the other of £3 6s. 8d. The account does not say which was which, but the busier warden was demonstrably Henry Hunte, and it was no doubt he who took the larger salary. When his colleague, the clerk William Saunder, died in 1452, Hunte continued in office alone for a year at a salary of £6 13s. 4d., which would imply that he was carrying on work he had done before. The year 1449–50 was one of relatively light maintenance work on the bridge (to a total expenditure of £35 19s. 4½d.) and relatively heavy expenditure on repairs to property (to a total of £32 7s. 5d.), all of which had to be accounted for. Table 13 gives details of Hunte's travels on bridge business in this year as they are recorded in the wardens' expenses. Much of this travelling was the direct consequence of the repair of bridge properties. The frequent visits to East Tilbury, for example, are to be explained by the expensive repairs to the manor buildings and the bridge there, though on one occasion Hunte

[1] RBT, account 1443–4. [2] RBT, account 1415–16.

went there to hold the Easter term leet court. Northfleet mill was being repaired, and Hunte's three visits to Northfleet were to supervise that. There were also improvements under way at Langdon manor, especially to the gatehouse. But the normal course of bridge maintenance also involved travel, in search of materials. The first visit to Snodland was to buy elms from William Combes, and the second visit was to choose more elms there. The first visit to Maidstone, to coincide with the St Faith's fair there, was to purchase laths. And then there were journeys to discuss bridge affairs with other people, such as the trips to London; there were only two this year, the first being to ask for alms from Cardinal Beaufort's executors. Since Hunte was not in Rochester for much of the time, he cannot have been responsible for the supervision of daily routine. His colleague did little travelling on bridge business. He accompanied Hunte to East Tilbury to hold the Easter court there, and again accompanied him to Dartford in May, but he is not recorded to have made other trips.

From innumerable details in the accounts it is plain to see that the commonalty of the bridge, the body of people bound by tradition to contribute to the upkeep of the bridge, continued for some time after the 1390s as the main authority for the maintenance of the bridge structure. A detail from the 1420s indicates well a chain of responsibility. The wardens of 1424–5, Henry Rowe and John Marchaunt, included amongst their expenses the sum of £2 3s. 4d. for wine given to the General Chapter of the Carmelite Friars by William Sevenoke, presumably as an expensive exercise in public relations. This was at a time when William Sevenoke was the leading agent for bridge affairs in London. When the accounts came to be audited, some time in 1426–7, this expenditure was queried and referred to the commonalty of the bridge for approval. No opportunity to discuss the question arose until June 1427, but at that point the wardens petitioned to be allowed the sum in question and were apparently successful in making their case. The accounts for 1426–7 record that John Darell, John Beaufitz and other members of the commonalty were in Rochester on two occasions during the year 'to oversee the state of the bridge and to audit the wardens' accounts'. Perhaps the first of these meetings was the preliminary audit at which the wardens' expenditure from two years previously was queried. The second must have been a plenary meeting of the commonalty empowered to give the wardens a final decision.[3]

This episode illustrates most of the features which we know about the operations of the commonalty. In the person of William Sevenoke we can observe an individual member of the commonalty with an exceptionally high profile in bridge affairs who was inclined to take decisions on his own initiative. Sevenoke was a man with an extraordinary career. He had been raised as a foundling in Sevenoaks, and named after the village. His benefactor had sent him in due course to be apprenticed in London, and here he rose to be a major figure in the Drapers' Company. He retained an interest in Kentish affairs, however, and by his will founded the first

---

[3] RBT, accounts 1424–5, 1426–7.

Table 13

Henry Hunte's travels on bridge business in 1449–50

1449

Maidstone	6 October
East Tilbury	17 October
London	in week beginning 10 November (4 days)
Northfleet	in week beginning 17 November

1450

Dartford	in week beginning 5 January
Birling	21 February
Maidstone	in week beginning 23 February
London	in week beginning 23 February (3 days)
East Tilbury	in week beginning 30 March
Northfleet	12 April
Maidstone	17 April
Snodland	21 April
East Tilbury	2 May
East Tilbury	12 May
Snodland	18 May
East Tilbury	20 May
Dartford	in week beginning 25 May
Snodland	21 July
Langdon manor	in week beginning 7 September
Dartford	in week beginning 7 September
East Tilbury	in week beginning 7 September
? East Tilbury	in week beginning 14 September
Langdon manor	in week beginning 14 September
Northfleet	28 September

Source: RBT, account 1449–50.

endowed school in Kent at Sevenoaks.[4] Rochester Bridge was another of his interests. From various episodes we know that he was able to summon the wardens to London. In November 1423, for example, Henry Rowe was in London on bridge business for four days 'at the command of William Sevenoke', and both wardens were together in London for three days at some stage in 1423–4 'because William Sevenoke sent for them'. The bridge stonecutter, William Champenays, rode to London that year for discussions with William Sevenoke and Robert Chechele. Sevenoke also authorised the expenditure of 6s. 8d. as a fee for Richard Ryxton to

4 *Dictionary of National Biography*, xvii, 1214; W.K. Jordan, 'Social Institutions in Kent, 1480–1660', *Archaeologia Cantiana*, lxxv (1961), 68–9.

sue for a royal patent on behalf of the bridge.[5] The case of the Carmelites' wine also illustrates how the wardens' expenditure, even when it was expenditure by Sevenoke, was subject to an audit on behalf of the commonalty of the bridge. It shows too how the auditors might feel obliged to refer particular matters back to a meeting of the commonalty. But a further implication of this episode, and a matter of some importance for evaluating the commonalty in action, is that it had taken so long for the account of 1424–5 to be audited. It was evidently not the practice, even in the 1420s, for members of the commonalty to be called together every year either to audit the accounts or to discuss business. There is plenty to suggest, in fact, that gearing the commonalty into prompt action as a body created difficulties that were never satisfactorily resolved, and which became more intractable from the 1430s.

Unlike a borough, which by this time would have had a council regularly interposing its authority between the burgesses and the individual officers at their head, the contributors of Rochester Bridge had no formally elected intermediate body. References to the activities of the commonalty in the wardens' accounts concern either the acts of individuals like William Sevenoke, whose authority was not explicitly grounded in any particular office, or those of such individuals 'and others'. On 25 February 1446, for example, a party comprising John Bamburgh 'and other gentlemen of the country' assembled at Rochester to inspect the recent bridgework.[6] John Bamburgh was an active and senior member of county society in Kent at the time, a frequent commissioner of the peace between 1428 and 1447, so it is not surprising that he should be picked out by name.[7] But statements of this sort pinpoint the recurrent problem of leadership in the commonalty of the bridge. The wardens themselves were answerable to the contributors, and the contributors were answerable to the crown, but there was (so it seems) no one except the crown from above or the wardens from below who had any permanent interest in ensuring that the commonalty was in working order. In the absence of appointed leaders the functioning of the commonalty depended upon the energy of individuals in Kent society who were prepared to act, usually at the prompting of the wardens. It was symptomatic of the weakness of the commonalty as an organising body that the carefully devised legal structure devised for the bridge in 1399 was negligently observed from the 1430s. The king's grant of pontage in 1431 was issued not to the Wardens and Commonalty but to the 'wardens of the fabric of the bridge of the town of Rochester', almost implying that the wardens were responsible to the borough community.[8] And in 1440 a licence to acquire land in mortmain was granted to the wardens, with no reference to the commonalty.[9]

It was in this context that the role of the archbishops of Canterbury became increasingly important for the management of bridge affairs. Even in the early

5 RBT, account 1423–4.
6 RBT, account 1445–6.
7 *Cal. Pat. R., 1429–36*, 618–19; *Cal. Pat. R, 1436–41*, 584; *Cal. Pat. R., 1441–6*, 472.
8 The grant was made 'custodibus fabrice pontis ville de Rouchestre . . . in auxilium reparacionis et emendacionis pontis ville predicte': PRO, C.66/429, m. 17.
9 PRO, C.66/450, m. 2.

decades of the fifteenth century archbishops sometimes took a leading role in bridge affairs, as in January 1416 when several men were summoned to go and see Henry Chichele on bridge business and the wardens had to pay their expenses.[10] Within a few decades such episodes became more numerous, and more a matter of course. In Easter week 1445 Richard Smyth, one of the wardens, went to Archbishop John Stafford at Maidstone to ask for a commission for the bridge to be allowed to commandeer workers and timber. From the 1440s the archbishop was taking a prominent role in the calling of election meetings. In August 1446 Smyth was back in Maidstone asking the archbishop 'for a writ for putting other wardens in office'.[11] An extraordinary item in the wardens' account of 1449–50 was the £2 stipend paid to William Godfrey for his service as archbishop's beadle and reeve in Grain and Gillingham; this was because the bridge wardens had been elected in the archbishop's court.[12] The nuances of this bargain are obscure, but it implies that the archbishop had undertaken responsibility for co-ordinating a meeting of the commonalty under the auspices of his regular jurisdiction.

The archbishops also acquired a leading role in controlling bridge finances. A petition in parliament in 1437 requesting a thirty-year toll on carts on behalf of the bridge proposed that the wardens should account for the money before the Archbishop of Canterbury and the Bishop of Rochester.[13] But the scope of the archbishop's supervision was to become wider than that. In 1457 the pre-eminence of Thomas Bourgchier within the commonalty is explicit in the auditors' decision to seek his approval, with that of 'others' in laying on the wardens a payment of £10 for which their accounts were in deficit. After due consultation the wardens were freed from this obligation 'by the mandate of the venerable father in Christ Thomas Archbishop of Canterbury and the advice and consent of other gentlemen of the county'. This formula, perhaps a careless one, raises the archbishop to a uniquely authoritative position in the affairs of the commonalty.

In November 1466 a meeting was held in London between the warden, the clerk of works, their servants, the Archbishop of Canterbury, Sir John Fogge 'and other friends of the bridge' to renew the bridge corporation, to examine the current state of affairs and to make some provisions for the future. The very fact that William Testwode was warden on his own from June 1466 to February 1467 implies some breakdown in the management of the bridge.[14] The upshot of this meeting is not recorded, but it probably confirmed or reinforced the dominant role of the archbishop in the commonalty which had already become apparent in earlier decades. From this time on the wardens were answerable to the archbishop before all other members of the commonalty. In 1471–2 William Testwode, one of the wardens, went to Mortlake 'to talk to the archbishop of Canterbury about appointing auditors to deal with the wardens' account',[15] which clearly implies that the archbishop was acting on behalf of the commonalty in the performance of one of its principal duties. A similar responsibility is implied in the handling of William Testwode's

[10] RBT, account 1415–16.
[11] RBT, account 1445–6.
[12] RBT, account 1449–50.

[13] PRO, S.C.8/137.
[14] RBT, account 1466–7.
[15] RBT, account 1471–2.

account of the seven months from Michaelmas 1475 to 24 March 1476, which was audited by John Bam and John Beweley. After the audit Testwode went to Knole with the auditors, 'to show the lord archbishop of Canterbury the foot of the last account and to sue to him for a letter of proclamation for electing bridge wardens'.[16] This implies that the archbishop was responsible not only for accepting the accounts on behalf of the commonalty but also for initiating election procedures. The point is confirmed by the account for 1476–7, which records that William Testwode had to go to London 'to talk and sue to the lord archbishop of Canterbury for providing a bridge warden', and in the autumn of 1478 he was again in London for five days to communicate with the archbishop 'about holding an election of wardens'.[17]

But the new constitution of 1466, if such it was, had failed to solve the problem of weak organisation in the commonalty of the bridge. The archbishop's authority in Kent was not sufficiently great to overcome the apathy of Kentish society towards bridge affairs in this period. William Testwode was unsuccessful in all his attempts to get his accounts audited and to have an election held so that he could stand down from office. Shortly before his death he had even tried to persuade Sir John Fogg to intercede with the king on his behalf.[18] From March 1476 he was warden on his own, and he died in office late in 1478. His widow Joan submitted his account on Christmas Eve, 1478. Even then no election could be held. John Soneman, a former clerk of works at the bridge[19] stood in as sole warden for the year 1478–9, and experienced all the troubles that Testwode had had before him. His expenses included the costs of three attempts in August 1479 to sue to the archbishop for a letter directed to the contributors of the bridge to persuade them to attend an election. A letter was eventually obtained, at an additional cost of 5s. to the secretary who wrote it. But the contributors failed to turn up on the appointed day, and Soneman had to go to Trottiscliffe and back to Knole for further authority to proceed. Another election day was proclaimed by John Soneman himself one market day at Maidstone and again at Malling. Three men were each paid 1d. to advertise the elections in Maidstone, Malling and Rochester. An *ad hominem* approach to Lord Cobham, involving four trips to Cooling, was aimed at persuading him to attend the election. What happened next we do not know. Soneman was at least successful in getting auditors appointed, at the cost of another trip to Knole and another 5s. to the archbishop's secretary, and an audit was duly held at the end of his year in office.

Whether the problems of the 1470s have any long-term significance for the place of the bridge in Kentish society it is impossible to be sure in the absence of further accounts from the later fifteenth century. Arguably the vigour of the commonalty always depended on a handful of people, and periodic weaknesses were only to be expected, as in most amateur organisations. In the 1380s there had been problems in getting the proper audits even when the king himself was

16 RBT, accounts 1475–6, April–Sept. 1476.
17 RBT, accounts 1476–7, Sept.–Dec. 1478.
18 RBT, account 1478–9.

19 RBT, accounts 1458–9, 1463–4, Feb.–Sept. 1467, 1467–8, 1469–70.

appointing auditors for the accounts of pontage and the ferry profits.[20] On the other hand, the reluctance of men to attend bridge meetings or to serve as wardens appears to be something new from the 1460s, and it has similarities to the difficulties some urban communities found in appointing financial officers during the same period and later. The way initiative was allowed to pass to the archbishop also suggests more than a passing phase. In the account from 1500 the sole warden, Richard Symondes, is described as 'supervisor or warden of all repair works and rebuilding and money receipts of the bridge of the town of Rochester, whom the very reverend father in Christ, lord John Morton, late cardinal, by divine allowance archbishop of Canterbury, now deceased, by his mandate caused, ordained and established to occupy and exercise the said office'. Symondes was one of the chaplains employed to celebrate in the bridge chapel, so his appointment marked a considerable breach with earlier convention. He took a salary of £3 6s. 8d., that of the junior warden, on top of the £6 he received as a chaplain.[21] Archiepiscopal responsibility for the bridge in the years of its rebuilding is seen in its extreme form in 1502. In June that year the archbishop of Canterbury, Henry Dene, was himself a bridge warden together with Richard Symondes.[22]

The archbishop's assumption of responsibility for the bridge implies unambiguously that the existing establishment was inadequate. The reason is plain. The sort of men who had been appointed wardens in the fifteenth century, at least up to 1479, were of insufficient social standing to be able to mobilise effectively the energy and resources of the commonalty in a time of crisis. Like Robert Rowe in the early years of the century, they were from families below the ranks of the county gentry. Not one of the wardens known from the fifteenth century was ever appointed a commissioner of the peace at any time in his life. Henry Hunte, alias Henry Baker, who was a warden from Michaelmas 1438 for two years, and then again for at least seven years from Michaelmas 1446, was described as a yeoman in 1454.[23] William Testwode was described as a 'barbour' in 1444.[24] The wardens were invariably of a lower status than the men who audited their accounts on behalf of the commonalty, many of whom were stalwarts of county society – men like John Darell who was an auditor in 1427 and 1431, John Bamburgh in 1440, Richard Bam in 1440 and 1444, Richard Bruyn in 1444 and 1457, Edmund Chertsey in 1440, 1457 and 1464, John Rowe in 1457, 1464, 1467, 1468, 1469 and 1472, John Bam in 1464, 1467, 1468, 1469, 1470, 1472, 1473, 1474, 1476, 1477, 1478 and 1479, all of whom were justices of the peace at various times.[25] The

---

[20] PRO, C.66/318, m. 11d, C.66/320, m. 14.

[21] RBT, account 1500.

[22] Essex RO, D/Q/18/24. I owe this reference to Dr Gibson.

[23] *Cal. Fine R., 1452–61*, 85.

[24] RBT, account 1443–4.

[25] RBT, accounts 1426–7, 1430–1, 1439–40, 1443–4, 1456–7, 1463–4, 1466–7. Feb.–Sept. 1467, 1467–8, Feb.–Sept. 1469, 1469–70, 1471–2, 1472–3, 1473–4, 1475–6, April–Sept. 1476, 1476–7, 1477–8, 1478–9; *Cal. Pat. R., 1422–9*, 564–5; *Cal. Pat. R., 1429–36*, 618–19; *Cal. Pat. R., 1436–41*, 584; *Cal. Pat. R., 1441–6*, 472; *Cal. Pat. R., 1446–52*, 590; *Cal.Pat. R., 1452–61*, 668; *Cal. Pat. R., 1461–7*, 565–6; *Cal. Pat. R., 1467–77*, 617–18.

office of warden had been conceived as a routine administrative appointment, comparable to that of an estate steward. But experience had shown time and again that adequate management of the bridge called for considerable powers of leadership. Such a demand was incompatible with the low social standing of fifteenth-century wardens.

In the early sixteenth century there was some decisive rethinking. The wardenship of the bridge now passed back to the laity, but from this time it was associated with men of an appreciably higher status than ever before. In September 1506 one of the wardens was George Neville, Lord Bergavenny, and he was in this office for at least sixteen years, with the prior of Leeds as his fellow warden.[26] Sir George Brooke, Lord Cobham and Sir Christopher Hales, who were said to be in Rochester on bridge business in 1537 were probably the wardens at the time; certainly Lord Cobham was one of the wardens from at least 1545 until his death at Cooling Castle in 1559, and for most of this period his fellow warden was Sir Thomas Moyle.[27] Responsibility for taking an initiative in bridge affairs had been decisively assumed by leading landlords of Kent and had finished up in the hands of the nobility. None of the early sixteenth-century accounts record any payment to the wardens for the performance of their duties, which implies that the office had become an honorary one.

This change in the social status of the bridge wardens soon had implications for the normal structure of bridge management. In the years 1507–8 accounts were still drawn up in the name of the wardens, Lord Bergavenny and the prior of Leeds.[28] But the next formal account to survive – that for two years from Michaelmas 1522 to Michaelmas 1524 – describes itself as 'thaccomptes of John James master of the workis of theseide brydge aswell for all and singuler somes of money by hime and by euery other person and persons by his commaundemente knowlege and assignmente appointed to thuse and behof of theseide brige receyvid and hadd as of and for all maner of paymentes of money for provicons of stuffes, wages of workemens and laborours and other necc(ess)arye expensis hadd and made by hyme or by his commaund'. In other words, receipts and expenses were in the same account, but it was being rendered by a new officer called the master of the works, and no longer by the wardens. James had had a predecessor in the same position, since he recorded a sum of 'money received of Mr John Wright, clerke, late master of theseide workis'.[29] A fragmentary and less formal record from 1527–8 shows the same administrative structure; it is part of an annual account of receipts and expenses drawn up for Richard Short, 'surveyor and paymaster (*dispensator*) for the works and repairs of the bridge', and is the same office as that of John James under a different title. And there is another account which shows that

---

26 RBT, E11, E46, E47, E689, E1144. The accounts of these two wardens are extant for the period from 24 June 1507 to 29 September 1508: RBT, account 1507–8.

27 RBT, E723, E743; *L.P.*, xii(1), no. 63, p. 30; Arnold, 'Rochester Bridge in A.D. 1561', 215.

28 RBT, account 1507–8. An account for the period of three months from Christmas 1508 is compiled in the name of the bridge clerk, but this is an interim account of the sort bridge clerks had been compiling for some time: RBT, account 1508–9.

29 RBT, account 1522–4.

John Turke, 'in thoffyce of surveying and kepyng of the sayd bredge', was accounting for both the income and expenditure of the bridge from Michaelmas 1542 to 25 March 1544.[30] This suggests that the office of master of the works, or surveyor and paymaster, was created as a post of lieutenant for the wardens sometime between 1508 and 1522, soon after the status of the wardens themselves had risen so high that it was no longer appropriate for them to be directly responsible for routine operations. This officer, as his title suggests, had immediate responsibility for employing men to work on the bridge.

Less evident in the records of this period, but nevertheless capable of being traced, was the office of receiver. This officer was responsible simply for collecting rents, accounting for them, and making the money available to the master of the works. John James's account of 1522–4 does not name this officer, or record any stipend having been paid to him. But he accounts for 10s. received from Robert Canon 'late collector of the seid rentes and ffermes', as well as arrears from William Neve the rent collector in London. He also records 20s. spent 'for the costes of the auditour and receivour comynge ffrome London to Rochester to thaudite there'. The auditor got 13s. 4d. and the receiver 6s. 8d. on this occasion.[31] Richard Short's account of 1527–8 includes the sum of £6 1s. 8d. paid to Thomas Roydon, esq., at the rate of 4d. a day as 'receiver and surveyor of the bridge'.[32] None of the early sixteenth-century accounts contain any details of rents from particular properties, and this can now be explained as a result of the fact that the master of the works was not responsible for their collection.

Looked at in retrospect, then, the development of the government of Rochester Bridge can be said to have gone through two principal stages since the mid-fifteenth century, against a background of stagnant, and occasionally declining, income from rents. First of all, the commonalty of the bridge became lethargic in its sense of responsibility and depended upon the archbishop of Canterbury for any sense of initiative. Secondly, during a major reconstruction of the bridge the status of the two wardens was raised, and the office came to be normally occupied by at least one member of the county nobility. As a result, local responsibility for the accounts passed to subordinate officers by the 1520s, one essentially responsible for collecting money and the other for spending it. They were men of much the same social background as the former wardens. In effect a new aristocratic stratum had been grafted onto the bridge establishment at a time of exceptionally heavy expenditure.

The bridge wardens, and later the paymaster and receiver, headed a staff of subordinates whose work was essential for the smooth running of bridge affairs. On the clerical side of their duties the wardens acquired full-time assistance, though there was no formal arrangement until the second quarter of the fifteenth century, and for many years the wardens depended upon employing clerks at piece rates. But the bridge chapel with its three chaplains was part of the bridge establishment from the early days of the new bridge, and there was a period of about ten years from Michaelmas 1409 when first 'Sir Harry' and then Sir William Neubold were prominent in handling bridge affairs.[33] To take an extreme case, in 1415–16 William Neubold was much more active in the day-to-day management of the bridge than either of the wardens. It was he who normally made payments for construction materials and labour. He also travelled on bridge business in the course of the year – to London, Dartford, Maidstone and elsewhere – in order to make purchases, collect rents, inspect property and discuss the legal affairs of the bridge.[34] These were all things that in other years were the work of the wardens themselves. The assumption of responsibility by the chapel clerks was particularly advantageous to the bridge at this period because both the wardens were elderly; Robert Rowe, the senior warden, had been in office for twenty-six years by 1409 and was as much a part of the bridge as the stonework. After the retirement of Rowe and Wolcy, subsequent wardens had shorter periods in office and were usually quite active. But even active wardens welcomed assistance, and the distinctive features of the years 1409–c.1416 cannot be wholly explained by the age or infirmity of Rowe. Perhaps the employment of chaplains as administrators was queried by one of the several higher clergy who knew about bridge affairs. Certainly the bridge chapel was no longer a part of the administrative resources of the bridge in the 1420s and after as it had been earlier. Richard Symondes' appointment as sole warden in 1500 was a temporary aberration.[35]

The office of bridge clerk is first definitely attested in 1438–9, though it had been anticipated in some respects for a number of years. John Depyng was paid for holding manor courts at Grain in 1423–4, and later received an annual fee for holding courts on behalf of the bridge between 1424–5 and at least 1435–6.[36] In 1438–9, after two years whose accounts are missing, Robert Reynold was paid a stipend of 40s. as bridge clerk for the year; his duties were to itemise receipts and expenses month by month, hold courts and draw up the final wardens' account.[37] This office was one that was maintained at the same salary for the following hundred years. Reynold was succeeded by John Soneman at Michaelmas 1444; his duties are described as compiling and copying the wardens' annual account, entering items weekly and monthly, putting together the bridge muniments and holding courts.[38] One of his paper account books survives from 1466–7. It shows how expenses were noted week by week through a period of over a year. This record was the basis for the more structured annual account; a small cross was put in the margin by each entry as it was incorporated into the yearly figures.[39] The bridge clerk was also employed as an assistant to the wardens on some occasions when they needed to travel. In 1450, for example, Soneman accompanied Henry Baker to Dartford in January, both wardens to East Tilbury at Easter, and Henry Baker

---

[33] RBT, accounts from 1409–10 to 1415–16.
[34] RBT, account 1415–16.
[35] Symondes is described as 'sole wardeyn' in RBT, E1087.
[36] RBT, accounts 1425–6, 1426–7, 1428–9, 1429–30, 1430–1, 1435–6.
[37] RBT, account 1438–9.
[38] RBT, account 1444–5.
[39] RBT, account book 1466–7.

again to Langdon and Dartford in September. On 5 May he went to Grain, and was paid his expenses, as was the vicar.[40]

Soneman was in office until at least Michaelmas 1470; in his later years he is described as 'clerk of works'.[41] By Michaelmas 1471 William Bruyn had taken his place, and he remained in office until at least 1479.[42] After that it becomes impossible to discuss the bridge clerk's office in any very constructive way. Edward Mongeham, the bridge clerk in 1508–9, was one of the chaplains in the bridge chapel. He kept quarterly accounts on behalf of the wardens, and one of these has survived. It records payments to him of £1 10s. 'for his quarter wages for syngyng in the chappell' and £1 'for his quarter fee'.[43] The office is undocumented in the following two decades, but it is perhaps the same as that of the 'clerk of the courtes and attorney in the lawe' who received a fee in the years 1522–4.[44]

Besides their staff in Rochester, there was also the skeleton of a bridge administration in London, comprising two very dissimilar positions. One was the office of rent collector there, which first appears in 1423–4, though the office may have been instituted earlier since this account follows a gap of seven years in the series. Earlier on, someone had gone out from Rochester to supervise the Cornhill properties and collect the rents there. In 1412–13, for example, Sir William Neubold had been paid his expenses for collecting rents in London, which included 2s. paid for drink for the tenants when they paid their rents, as had been the custom in Wangford's time.[45] In 1423–4, however, Hugh Sharp was paid 18s. for collecting the rents, organising repairs and submitting an account.[46] This remained the core of the office in later years, though the collector was probably also responsible for finding tenants. The office was temporarily discontinued in the later 1470s when the wardens were receiving rents directly from the tenants.[47] But an account for 1522–4 shows that a London rent gatherer was still part of the bridge establishment at an annual fee of £1.[48]

The other London position was that of the retained attorney who would act on behalf of the bridge in legal matters. This idea went back to the late 1430s. The first bridge attorney, Henry Hykkes, received 6s. 8d. as an annual retainer for ten years from 1438–9.[49] The wardens had employed him before; in an action to secure Little Delce in 1428–9 they paid Hykkes two separate sums of 5d. and 3s. 4d. for his work as 'bridge attorney'. But they had not then retained him, and they had employed other attorneys on other occasions.[50] Hykkes was a local man, described

---

[40] RBT, account 1449–50.
[41] RBT, accounts 1463–4, Feb.–Sept. 1467, 1467–8, 1469–70.
[42] RBT, accounts 1471–2, 1478–9.
[43] RBT, account 1508–9.
[44] RBT, account 1522–4.
[45] RBT, account 1412–13.
[46] RBT, account 1423–4.
[47] RBT, accounts 1475–6, April–Sept. 1476, Sept.–Dec. 1478, 1478–9.
[48] RBT, account 1533–4.
[49] RBT, account 1438–9.
[50] RBT, account 1428–9. The wardens employed William Bery in another matter in 1428–9 and they employed John May to prosecute two tenants in Grain in 1435–6 (RBT, accounts 1428–9, 1435–6).

as of Rochester, and he was appointed several times as an assessor of taxes in Kent.[51] But his practice was evidently wider than local courts, since in 1444–5 he was described as 'bridge attorney at Westminster for prosecuting the suits of the bridge'.[52] By Michaelmas 1450 he had been succeeded by Thomas Heth, later described as 'attorney for the bridge at Westminster in all matters concerning the bridge'. He was retained till at least 1457.[53] For a number of years after that the wardens did not consider it worthwhile naming the bridge attorney in the accounts, but the practice was always maintained. From 1466 to 1479 the bridge attorney was John Nethersole.[54] The annual fee was always 6s. 8d. In the event of litigation the bridge attorney might be paid some categories of expenses, but he was not paid any additional fee.[55] This appointment has no direct analogy in the accounts of the early sixteenth century. In 1522–4, as we have seen the post of 'attorney in the lawe' had been amalgamated with that of 'clerk of the courtes'.[56] But again in 1544 the sum of £1 10s. was paid 'to Hampsthed attorney of thexcheker for hys dim' yer ffe to answer ther for the lordschypps that longeth to the bredge'.[57]

Other men who might be regarded as counsellors of the bridge were paid no regular fee. In 1473 Humphrey Starkey, 'counsellor of the bridge' gave his advice about how to recover £2 of rent from Leysdown that the tenant there had failed to pay, and for this the wardens gave him 6s. 8d., but this was described as a 'reward', implying a gift, not as a fee.[58] It was an unusual transaction, and implies that Starkey was not a member of the commonalty of the bridge. In fact a great part of the advice given to the wardens came, as in the past, from individual Kentish gentlemen who took an interest in bridge affairs and who could expect nothing but their expenses. In June 1436, for example, the wardens went from Langdon to Calehill for a discussion with John Darell, and later in the summer they had a discussion with John Darell and Geoffrey Landour in London 'about raising money assigned to the use of the bridge', but on both these occasions the only charge against the accounts was the wardens' travel expenses.[59]

Up until the end of the 1470s, as several examples have already shown, the auditors of the wardens' accounts were appointed *ad hoc* and paid expenses for their labours in coming to Rochester. There were invariably several men appointed for any one audit. In the following fifty years this procedure was altered in favour of a single stipendiary auditor who may be regarded as part of the bridge establishment. The account of 1500 does not include an auditor amongst the recipients of fees, but John Sedley was acting alone as auditor, with responsibility for inspecting the books and drawing up final annual account, and for this he was paid 15s. and his expenses. The auditors of the 1520s had similar obligations, and were

51 RBT, account 1438–9; *Cal. Fine R., 1422–30*, 294, 330; *Cal. Fine R., 1430–7*, 190.
52 RBT, account 1444–5.
53 RBT, accounts 1450–1, 1452–3.
54 RBT, accounts from June–Sept. 1466 to 1478–9.

55 RBT, accounts 1438–9, 1439–40.
56 RBT, account 1522–4.
57 RBT, account 1542–4.
58 RBT, account 1473–4.
59 RBT, account 1435–6.

included amongst those receiving an annual fee for their services. The auditor in 1522–4 received £2 for the two years. Hugh Fuller, the auditor in 1527–8 was paid £1 6s. 8d. for his fee, and for writing the accounts using his own paper and parchment.[60]

The wardens' presence at the bridge was frequently necessary. But they were not expected to be technical experts, and they had to employ men of sufficient quality to guarantee that maintenance and rebuilding would be carried out properly. A good deal of work on the bridge could be supervised from day to day by the master craftsmen to whom it was committed, and who no doubt understood the business better than the wardens. Already in the 1390s there was a core of staff there who could take responsibility for the regular operations. John Budde was employed in 1398–9 as surveyor of bridgework and guardian of the store of building materials, equipment and other movable assets belonging to the bridge, and then in 1399–1400 he was paid a yet larger stipend to guard the bridge and its store by day and night. One of his chief responsibilities was maintaining the boats belonging to the bridge and supervising the work of the tidemen. At first he did not work the whole year, but throughout the period from Michaelmas 1405 to Michaelmas 1408 he earned 1s. a week. He occupied a house belonging to the bridge in Horselane.[61] A similar position was later described more particularly in terms of responsibility for the boats, but the work included supervising the carriage of chalk and other materials by water. John Hendeman, the 'bargeman' in 1423–4, was paid 10d. a week through the year 'to guard the bridge boats'.[62] The office became known as that of 'the master of boats' when Simon Hert took it in the early 1440s, but the salary was simultaneously reduced to 8d. a week.[63] In 1522–4 the equivalent officer was described as 'the keper of the store house' at an average salary of £2.[64]

The team of tidemen who handled the boats was the nearest the bridge came to having a necessary complement of wage-earners, though the men were always paid by the tide – in effect, according to the number of times they were on the river – and their number varied considerably according to the amount of material to be shifted in the course of a year. In 1423–4, a year of heavy expenditure on the bridge, there were sometimes eighteen tidemen simultaneously in employment as well as the master of boats. In 1449–50, a year of low expenditure, there were never more than three.[65]

The more skilled work with timber and stone construction depended upon the direction of responsible individuals, but there were no established salaried positions. Specialists were hired according to the work in hand. In 1423–4 the number of carpenters at work on the bridge varied from three to six at different times of the year. One of these, William att Weye, was in a position of some authority. He was employed through much of the year, and was paid on one occasion for riding out into the countryside to look for timber. He was paid at the

---

[60] RBT, accounts 1500, 1522–4, 1527–8.

[61] RBT, accounts 1398–9, 1399–1400, 1400–1, 1402–3, 1403–4, 1404–5, 1405–6, 1406–7, 1407–8.

[62] RBT, account 1423–4.

[63] RBT, account 1443–4.

[64] RBT, account 1522–4.

[65] RBT, account 1449–50.

rate of 6d. a day, like other carpenters, but as a mark of distinction he was paid a bonus of 15s. as 'master carpenter' at the end of the financial year. William and John Champeneys were the only masons employed during the year, and only for a few weeks. William was allowed some responsibility; on one occasion he rode up to London for consultation with William Sevenoke and Robert Chichele, for which he received a bonus of 1s. 4d.[66] In ordinary years the bridge employed even fewer craftsmen and there is less indication of any rank amongst them. In 1449–50, for example, the account records only four carpenters working on the bridge during the year, all at 6d. a day: John Marchall for 168 days, Thomas Broke for 147 days, Simon Marchall for 97 days and William Johnson of Strood for 13 days. John Marchall and Thomas Broke each got a shilling as a Christmas present. No stone-work was necessary on the bridge that year, and no stonecutters were employed.[67]

Table 14

The bridge establishment, 1449–50 and 1522–4

	1449–50	Stipend		
Wardens (2):	Henry Hunte	£6	13s	4d
	William Saundre, clerk	£3	6s	8d
Bridge clerk	John Soneman	£2		
Attorney at Westminster	?		6s	8d
Chaplains (3):	John Coton	£6		
	Henry	£6		
	Roger Chaplain (½ year)	£3		
	John Bikerton (½ year)	£3		
Master of boats	John Toppe	£1	14s	8d
Rent collector in London	Nicholas Stone	£1	6s	8d
	1522–4	**Stipend**		
Wardens (2):[1]	George Neville, Lord Bergavenny	–		
	Richard Chetham, Prior of Leeds	–		
Master of the works	John James	£4		
Receiver	?	£6	1s	8d.[2]
Clerk of the courts and attorney in the law	?	£1	6s	8d
Auditor	?	£1		
Chaplains (3)	?	£18[2]		
Master of the store house	?	£2		
Rent collector in London	William Neve	£1		

[1] from RBT, E1144 (1522)
[2] from RBT, account 1527–8

Source: RBT, accounts 1449–50, 1522–4, 1527–8.

[66] RBT, account 1423–4.   [67] RBT, account 1449–50.

Table 14 summarises the state of the bridge establishment as it was in the middle of the fifteenth century and again, less satisfactorily, in the 1520s. It includes everybody who received a fixed stipend, but excludes the much larger number of people who were employed for shorter or longer periods by the day or by the job. The names of the wardens are supplied from a deed of 1522, and they served throughout the period to Michaelmas 1524.[68] By the 1520s the bridge establishment was a microcosm of Kent society. It was headed by a nobleman and a churchman, as representatives of the commonalty of the bridge. It was administered by a small group of educated professionals. And it offered employment to a varying number of specialised craftmen as well as to less well paid labourers.

---

[68] Richard Chetham had resigned as prior of Leeds by 4 March 1524: *L.P.*, iv (1), no. 147, p. 61.

Rochester Bridge

1530–1660

Decline of the Medieval System

At the beginning of the sixteenth century, following the trend established in the second half of the fifteenth century, the Archbishop of Canterbury and the ecclesiastical establishment exercised ultimate authority over Rochester Bridge affairs. Richard Symondes, a clerk serving in the Bridge Chapel, had been appointed sole bridge warden by Cardinal Morton in the closing years of the fifteenth century and served at least until 1502, when Archbishop Henry Dene himself joined Symondes as Senior Warden. Sometime after Dene's death in January 1503, they were succeeded by Richard Chetham (alias Richard Reynham), Prior of Our Lady and St Nicholas of Leeds.[1] Archbishop William Warham, Dene's successor, while not serving directly as a bridge warden, maintained a close interest in the bridge and contributed personally to the rebuilding of the bridge by donating the iron railings.[2]

As the sixteenth century progressed, however, the balance of power controlling Rochester Bridge shifted from the sacred to the secular, following the shift in national power from prelate to parliament. Between 1506 and 1530, and probably until his death in June 1535, George Neville, fifth Lord Bergavenny, served as Senior Warden along with prior Richard Chetham.[3] Resident at Birling in Kent and prominent in both county and national affairs, Neville was created Knight of the Order of Bath at the coronation of Richard III in 1483; he held the hereditary office of chief larderer, which he exercised at the coronation of Henry VIII in 1509 and again at the coronation of Anne Boleyn in 1532. He was appointed Lord Warden of the Cinque Ports in 1513, became a privy councillor in 1515, and served as captain of the army in France in 1514 and again in 1523. Not since the days of Sir Richard Knolles and Sir John de Cobham had such an important Kentish landowner taken charge of Rochester Bridge.

How long Sir George Neville and the prior of Leeds continued as bridge wardens remains unknown due to a gap in the records between 1530 and 1535. Neville, however, died in June 1535; and in 1524 Arthur Sentleger had replaced Richard Chetham as prior of Leeds, an office he held until the dissolution of the priory in 1536.[4] Sentleger may have briefly succeeded Richard Chetham as bridge

---

[1] Missing leases and accounts prevent precise dating of the early sixteenth-century bridge wardens. Richard Symonds returned an account for 1500 (RBT wardens account 1500), and his name appears with Henry Dene's on a lease dated 7 June 1502 (Essex Record Office, D/Q 18/24).

[2] Edward Hasted, *The History and Topographical Survey of the County of Kent*, iv (1798), 79.

[3] The names of George Neville and Richard Chetham appear together on leases between 1506 and 1530 (RBT E11, E46, E47, E689, E1144; and The booke of the Survey of the Bridge landes 1575–1577, f. 12r).

[4] *The Victoria History of the Counties of England: Kent*, ed. William Page, ii, St Catherine Press, 1926, 164.

warden; however, by 3 July 1535, when the names of wardens Sir George Brooke, Lord Cobham and Sir Christopher Hales appear on a Dartford lease, the shift from sacred to secular was complete.[5]

Like Neville, prominent both in county and national affairs, Hales served as counsel for the Corporation of Canterbury and was returned to Parliament for that city in 1523. In the county he served as a commissioner of the sewers for the Thames between Greenwich and Gravesend in 1525, as a commisioner to inquire into the estates held by Cardinal Wolsey in Kent in 1530, and as a commissioner of the sewers for Kent in 1536. On 29 December 1539 he joined other Kentish gentry and nobility to receive the Lady Anne of Cleves on her arrival at Dover, and in 1540 with Cranmer and Lord Rich he helped to establish the new foundation of Canterbury Cathedral that replaced the monks with secular clergy. On the national scene, appointed Solicitor-General in 1525, Hales rose to Attorney-General in 1529, in which office he conducted the proceedings against Sir Thomas More, Bishop Fisher, and Anne Boleyn, and succeeded Cromwell as Master of the Rolls in 1536.[6]

Like Hales, his fellow bridge warden Sir George Brooke, ninth Baron Cobham, also rose to national prominence under Henry VIII, having been summoned to Parliament in 1529. Appointed Lord Deputy of Calais by Henry, he continued in that office under Edward VI and Queen Mary until his death in September 1558. With dexterity he steered a steady course through successive changes of government. In the reign of Edward VI he sat on the Privy Council, was made a Knight of the Garter, and substantially enriched his estate with monastic property. After initially supporting Jane Grey, he quickly changed his allegiance to Mary; and although implicated in the revolt of his nephew Sir Thomas Wyatt and briefly imprisoned in the Tower, he so thoroughly assured Mary of his loyalty that he was later appointed to a commission to enquire about heretics.[7]

The final prominent player in Rochester Bridge politics during the first half of the sixteenth century was Sir Thomas Moyle, Speaker of the House of Commons under Henry VIII. Bridge records show him acting with Lord Cobham by 1542,[8] although he probably became a bridge warden after the death of Sir Christopher Hales in June 1541. Along with Hales he had received Anne of Cleves on her arrival at Dover, and like Lord Cobham he survived the political turmoil of the time, having been returned Member of Parliament under Henry VIII to represent the county of Kent in 1542 and Rochester in 1544, and again under Mary to represent Rochester in 1553 and 1554.[9]

From Archbishops Dene and Warham to Lords Bergavenny and Cobham, from Richard Chetham, Prior of Leeds, to Sir Christopher Hales and Sir Thomas Moyle, the authority for Rochester Bridge affairs passed during the first half of the sixteenth century from the Church to the nobility and landed gentry, keeping pace

5   RBT, The booke of the Survey of the Bridge landes 1575–1577, f. 9v.
6   *Dictionary of National Biography*, s.v. 'Hales, Sir Christopher.'
7   Esme Wingfield-Stratford, *The Lords of Cobham Hall*, London 1959, 58–63.
8   RBT, Account of John Turke, surveyor, 1542–1554.
9   *Dictionary of National Biography*, s.v. 'Moyle, Sir Thomas.'

Plate 5(a). Monument in Cobham church to Sir George Brooke, Lord Cobham (1497–1558), his wife Anne, and their ten sons and four daughters, including Sir William Brooke, Lord Cobham (1527–1597).

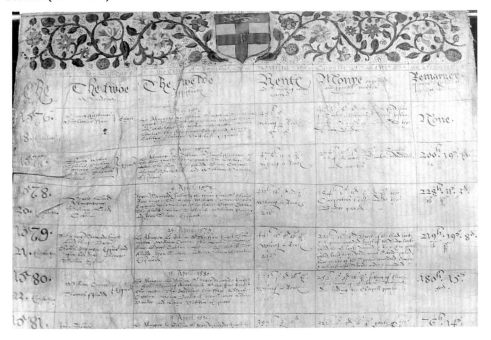

Plate 5(b). The Wardens Roll begun in 1585 by William Lambarde and Sir Roger Manwood.

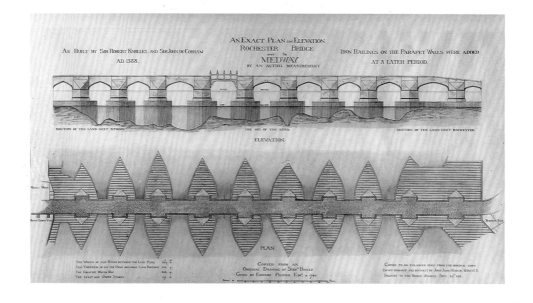

Plate 6(a). Plan and elevation of the medieval bridge showing the staddles and the riverbed.

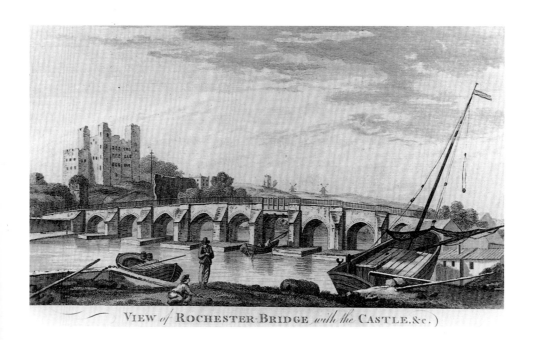

Plate 6(b). Print of Rochester Bridge showing boat with lowered mast passing under the drawbridge (from an original in the private collection of Michael Lewis).

VIEW of ROCHESTER-BRIDGE *with the* CASTLE.&c.)

Plate 6(b). Print of Rochester Bridge showing boat with lowered mast passing under the drawbridge (from an original in the private collection of Michael Lewis).

From 'Traffic & Potulies
Ed. Yates & Gibson 1994
pl 6b

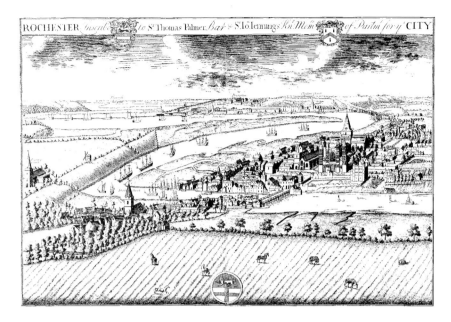

Plate 7(a). View of the Medway Towns inscribed to Bridge Warden Sir Thomas Palmer, Bart, published in John Harris, *History of Kent*, 1719.

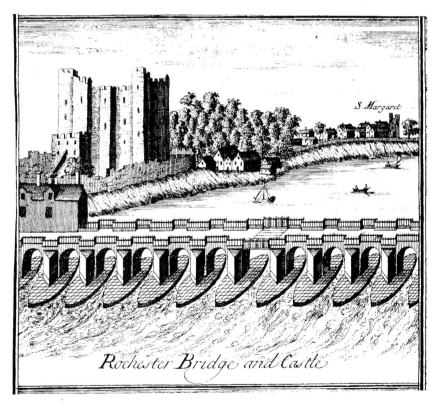

Plate 7(b). View of Rochester Bridge showing the 'great rush of water' at the arches, published in John Harris, *History of Kent*, 1719.

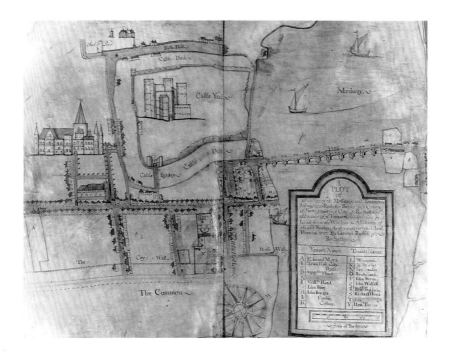

Plate 8(a). Plan of Rochester showing the bridge properties in 1717.

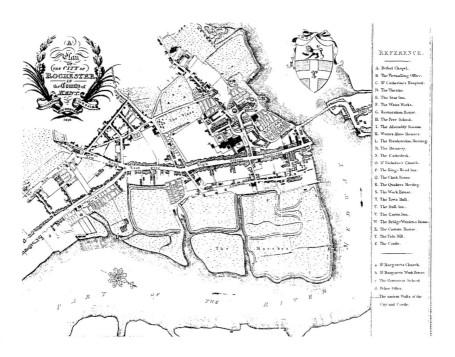

Plate 8(b). Plan of Rochester by R. Sale, published in *The History and Antiquities of Rochester and its Environs*, 1817.

with the progress of the Reformation. With it also passed the Bridge Chapel. Founded by Sir John de Cobham in January 1393 in honour of the Trinity, the Blessed Virgin Mary, and All Saints and named 'Allesoulen chapel', the Bridge Chapel had ministered for one hundred and fifty years to medieval pilgrims and travellers.[10] Three priests, each receiving an annual stipend of £6, had performed the office and celebrated mass daily and prayed for the souls of the founders and benefactors of the bridge.

In the sixteenth century the Bridge Chapel was still performing the wishes of its patron. The survey of monastic property undertaken by Henry VIII in 1534 reveals the names of the three priests – George Tilletson, Thomas Peron, and John Cokerell – and records that each received £6 for their singing according to the foundation of John Cobham and Robert Knolles.[11] Following the Chantries Act 1545, a second commission, issued on 14 February 1546 to Archbishop Thomas Cranmer and Bishop of Rochester Henry Holbeche, surveyed all chantries, chapels, hospitals, and colleges in Kent. Again the record shows three stipendary priests – George Richardson, Richard Albertson, and John Stacye.[12]

The end came swiftly for the Bridge Chapel early in the reign of Edward VI. On 4 November 1547 Parliament passed the second Chantries Act taking for the Crown all colleges, free chapels, and chantries in which a priest had been maintained during the five years prior to the passage of the statute. If the stipend of such priests formed part of a larger endowment, as in the case of Rochester Bridge, the amount of the stipend was converted to an annual rent-charge to be paid to the Court of Augmentations, the court established by Henry VIII to settle all claims arising from the suppression and sale of monastic and chantry property. In addition the statute specified that all movable goods, jewels, plate, and ornaments belonging to the chantries had become the property of the king.

The commission for the sale of chantry lands in Kent was issued in April 1548, and the return shows only one priest still resident in the Bridge Chapel, goods and ornaments valued at 14s. 6d. ob., and plate weighing forty-one ounces.[13] The vestments, candlesticks, mass books, and other goods – including a bell valued at 30s. – were surrendered to the commission on 31 May 1548 and sold back to John Burwell, paymaster and receiver of the bridge, for 50s.,[14] and the chapel itself was converted to a storeroom for the master carpenter of the bridge.[15] However, the

---

[10] Centre for Kentish Studies, Register of William Botlesham, DRb Ar1, ff. 145v–146v; *Kent Chantries*, ed. Arthur Hussey, Kent Records xii (1936), 234–35.

[11] *Valor Ecclesiasticus*. Printed by Command of His Majesty King George III. 1810, vol i, 110; Arthur Hussey, 'Chapels in Kent', *Archaeologia Cantiana*, xxix (1911), 251.

[12] 37 Henry VIII cap. 4, printed in *Statutes of the Realm*, iii, p. 988; PRO, E.301.29, mb 44d; Hussey, *Kent Chantries*, 238.

[13] PRO, E.301.28, item 210; Hussey, *Kent Chantries*, p. 239. The one remaining priest died in 1549, for the receiver's accounts for 25 February 1548–4 March 1550 include the following item: 'Item payd to alberson pryst of the Bryge now decessid for one hole yere vj^{li}' (RBT receiver's account 1548–1550, f. 14r.).

[14] Scott Robertson, 'Inventories of Parish Church Goods in Kent, AD 1552,' *Archaeologia Cantiana*, x (1876), 291.

[15] RBT, The booke of the Survey of Bridge landes 1575–1577, f. 4.

bridge wardens used both political influence and legal action to prevent the £18 annual stipend for the priests from falling into the hands of the Crown.

Junior Warden Sir Thomas Moyle had been appointed receiver for the Court of Augmentations in 1537 and had later been promoted to the chancellorship of that court.[16] Senior Warden George Brooke, Lord Cobham had used his influence as privy councillor to Edward VI to exempt Cobham College from the Chantries Act and had arranged for its private surrender to himself.[17] Both men knew how the system worked and how to work the system. Both men had personally profited from the national land grab. The Crown's chances of converting the annual priests' stipend into an annual rent-charge were remote. Bridge accounts show payments to bridge attorney Remsey for a supplication in the augmentations court disputing the claimed rent-charge, and a further payment 'for sir Thomas moyle chargis at Rochester one day & nyght and lokyng vppon the Evidences in the Chapell with dyuers other accompanyng hym xiiij^s viij^d.'[18] No record of the supplication survives among the proceedings of the augmentations court, nor were further claims forthcoming from the Crown. Not, that is, until 1577.

On 6 May 1577 Sir John Abington, Receiver General for Kent, sued the bridge wardens in the Court of Exchequer for twenty-eight and one-half years of arrears, totalling £513, due to the Crown under the Chantries Act of 1547 for the £18 annual stipend of the three priests.[19] Again the bridge wardens turned to friends in high places. With the help of assistant warden Sir Roger Manwood, Justice of the Common Pleas, bridge wardens Sir Thomas Wotton and Nicholas Barham, Serjeant-at-law, successfully argued that the Chantries Act, which had suppressed only chantries that had been supporting a priest in the five years preceding the passage of the statute on 5 November 1547, did not in fact apply to the Bridge Chapel. They maintained that since 1539 the annual stipend for priests had been diverted to the repair and maintenance of the bridge and that no money had been paid for worship in the chapel. They also argued successfully for a change of venue from the Court of Exchequer to the more friendly ground of the court of assizes in Kent, presided over by Sir Thomas Gawdye and Sir John Southcote, both members of the 1571 and 1574 commissions to investigate Rochester Bridge. Surviving accounts of John Turke, surveyor, and John Burwell, paymaster, do show regular payments for the priests' wages and numerous expenses for wine, wax, and washing of the chapel gear during the five years between November 1542 and November 1547;[20] nevertheless, when the case came before Southcote and Gawdye at Canterbury Castle on 3 July 1577, the bridge wardens were exonerated. For his work Roger Manwood received £30 9s. 10d.,[21] and an Inspeximus of exoneration under

---

[16] *Dictionary of National Biography*, s.v. 'Moyle, Sir Thomas.'

[17] 1 Edward VI cap. 14, clause xxxiii, printed in *Statutes of the Realm*, vol. iv, pt. 1.

[18] RBT, receiver's accounts 1548–1550, ff. 12r, 15r.

[19] PRO, E.363/408, rot. 64.

[20] RBT surveyor's account 1544, mb 3–4; paymaster's account 1544–1545, ff. 2v, 3v, 5r, 7v, 8r, 10v, 13r; paymaster's account 1545–1546, ff. 2v, 5v, 6v, 8r, 9v; paymaster's account 1547–1548, ff. 3v, 4v, and 14r.

[21] RBT, Wardens Accounts, vol. i, f. 27v.

the great seal, dated 7 February 1578, in the archives of Rochester Bridge still attests to the alleged innocence of the bridge wardens.[22]

If Sir Thomas Moyle had paid as much attention to the estates of Rochester Bridge as he did to the estates of suppressed monasteries, and if Lord Cobham had paid as much attention to the fabric of Rochester Bridge as he did to the fabric of Cooling Castle and Cobham Hall, Rochester Bridge might have been spared the misfortunes of the 1550s and 1560s. Neither did, however, and the bridge suffered. Aside from signing leases and making occasional inspections of the bridge, the wardens left the day-to-day running of the bridge primarily to subordinate officers. In 1546, when John Burwell served as paymaster, William Cobham as receiver of revenues, and John Gryffyn as master carpenter, other officers included an auditor, an accountant, a rent collector for the London rents, and an attorney on retainer in the Court of Exchequer.[23] During the next decade personnel changed frequently. John Foule became receiver in 1548, followed by Alan Wodd in 1553; and Richard Skelton became paymaster in 1549, followed by Nicholas Brydges in 1555. In the late 1550s, when matters came to a head, John Wilkins, servant of Lord Cobham, was serving as receiver; Edmund Tynte, servant of Sir Thomas Moyle, as auditor; Richard Watts, master surveyor and clerk of the works at Upnor Castle, as paymaster; and Richard Cowdale as the master carpenter.

The main problem was money. The surviving accounts rendered by the receiver and paymaster during the 1540s and 1550s show that rent revenue never recovered the high level of the mid fifteenth century. Between Michaelmas 1546 and Michaelmas 1548 annual rental income was £96 8s. 8d; between Michaelmas 1555 and Michaelmas 1556 rental income had dropped to £92 12s. 7d.[24] An undated 'Rentall of the lands and tenementes apperteynynge to the bridge of Rochester as ye profytts are now,' probably drawn up around 1550, puts the total revenues at £92 3s. 1d.[25] Rental income continued its slow decline during the 1560s and 1570s; the rental commissioned by Sir Roger Manwood in 1575 showed gross rents of only £90 7s. 6d.[26]

The reason, according to Manwood, was mismanagement. In 'A true discourse of the auncyent wodden and present stoned bridge at Rochester' Manwood points to the problem:

> it followed in continewance of tyme; and by abvse; that the landes proper of the said bridge were from tyme to tyme demised & letten by the two wardens of the said bridge alone without thassent of the commonaltie, making leases of the same landes vnto theire frendes and Servantes for greate termes of yeares, and at tholde Rents, not respecting that because the charges of Stone and Timber and other provision and caryages, and the Wages of Masons, Carpenters, Laborers, and other like were not had for tholde Rates or prices but

[22] RBT, MS 1178.
[23] RBT, Paymaster's accounts 1545–1547, f. 9v.
[24] Ibid., f. 7r; Paymaster's accounts 1547–1551, f. 1v.
[25] RBT, rental c.1550, mb. 3.
[26] RBT, The booke of the Survey of the Bridge landes 1575–1577.

treble, or Quadruple in price, Soe ought the Landes to have ben ymproved and letten for treble or Quadruple. By reason of which negligence the yerelie charge of reparacions did soe farre surmownte the yerelie Revenewes, as in processe of tyme the Bridge grewe into greate Ruyne and decaye.[27]

Table 15 reveals the truth of Sir Roger Manwood's charges. Compared with mid fifteenth-century income, annual rents in the sixteenth century remained largely unchanged or lower. In 1450 The Crown Inn rented for £14 13s. 4d.; in 1575 the rent had dropped to £4. In 1450 the manor of South Hall in East Tilbury with its lucrative ferry across the Thames rented for £33 6s. 8d.; in 1575 the rent had dropped to £13 13s. 4d., the ferry having fallen into disrepair described as 'being indeed of very smale valewe.'[28] The manors of Langdon, Little Delce, Rose Court, and Nashenden showed marginal increases, but the total London rents remained the same at £18 19s. 8d.

Table 15

Mid sixteenth-century leases

Property	Annual rent						Term	Date
	1450			1575				
	£	s	d	£	s	d	years	
London tenement					26	8	72	1530
Dartford	6			4	13	4	60	1535
Nashenden Manor	8			10			40	1544
London tenement					10		61	1544
Rose Court Manor	6	13	4	7			40	1545
Southhall Manor	33	6	8	13	15	4	30	1552
London tenement				3	13	4	40	1552
The Crown	14	13	4	4			50	1553
London tenement				1	4		31	1554
London tenement					14		31	1554
London tenement					13	4	31	1554
London tenement					8		30	1554
Little Delce Manor	6			6	13	4	50	1559
Langdon Manor	8			10			40	1559

Source: RBT Wardens' Accounts 1450–1, Survey 1575–1577.

---

[27] RBT, A true discourse of the Auncyent wodden and present stoned bridge at Rochester, and of the landes proper & contributorie therto, and of the verie causes of the decay of the said stone Bridge; & for the course taken for reformacion therin: collected & written by Sir Roger Manwode knighte Lord chiefe Baron of her Majesties Exchequer in the yere of our Lord Christe 1586 and of the Raigne of Quene Elizabeth the xxviij[th] at which tyme he was secondlie one of the wardens of the sayde Bridge., ff. 15v–16r. Hereafter referred to as 'A True Discourse.'

[28] The booke of the Survey of Bridge landes 1575–1577, f. 10r.

The average length of lease granted between 1530 and 1560 was 43 years, thus preventing the low rents from keeping pace with the rising prices of stone and timber and the rising cost of workmen's wages. Nor were the rents always collected. In 1544, when rental income should have been £96 8s. 8d., the paymaster John Burwell received only £54 6s. 4d. from the receiver of revenue William Cobham. In 1545 he received only £79 2s. 2d. When William Cobham died in 1547, he left a debt owed to the bridge of £38 either uncollected or not handed over.[29] Burwell's successor as paymaster, Richard Skelton, fared little better, receiving only £78 16s. in 1549 and £38 13s. 4d. in 1550 from the receiver of revenue John Foule.[30] Part of the problem may have been the favouritism alluded to by Manwood. At least one of the long leases at low rents, that for Rose Court manor in the Isle of Grain, was granted by Lord Cobham to his servant John Wilkins, who himself later served for almost twenty years as receiver of revenue.[31]

Problems with revenue from the estate inevitably produced problems with repair of the fabric. In 1557 a royal commission described the bridge as 'fallen into suche greate ruyne and decaye that the comon passage over the same is like vtterlie to faile in shorte tyme to come (if spedy remedie be not the soner had and provided for the same) which wolde not only be to the grete perill lett and hinderaunce of all manner of persones having occasion to passe over the same but also to the vtter decay of oure Citie of Rochester and annoyaunce of diuers other Cities townes and the parties therunto adioynyng.'[32] On 21 May 1557, therefore, Queen Mary authorised George Brooke, Lord Cobham and Sir Thomas Moyle to charge a toll for passage over and under the bridge for the next four years. In addition, the bridge wardens were granted a charitable brief, that is, permission to ask and receive charitable alms once a year for the following four years in every parish in the county. No evidence survives that the bridge wardens pursued the second remedy,[33] but they wasted little time in following the first.

Bridge workmen, supervised by master carpenter Richard Cowdale, immediately set about building a gate at the Rochester end of the bridge, and by 2 June the gathering of the toll began. Additional payments appear for 'an Iron boxe to putt the Toll money in the iiij[th] daye of Julye – x s.,' for a 'chayne & lock for to fasten the boxe at the gate – xij d.,' for 'a hangyng hammer to knock at the seid gate – xvj d.,' and for 'writtyng in parchement the Rates of the toll of the bridge accordyng to the Comyssion – vj d.'[34]

---

[29] RBT, paymaster's accounts 1544–1545, f. 4v; ibid. 1545–1547, f. 1v; ibid. 1545–1551, f. 1v.

[30] RBT, paymaster's accounts 1545–1551, ff. 18v, 32r.

[31] RBT, MS 3007.

[32] PRO, C66.910, mb. 19d.

[33] No receipts from this brief appear in the receiver's accounts for these years. In the neighbouring parish of St Nicholas, Strood, furthermore, no payment to Rochester Bridge is recorded in the churchwardens' accounts between 1557 and 1561. (See Henry R. Plomer, trans. *The Churchwardens' Accounts of St Nicholas, Strood.* Kent Records, v (1927).) Few churchwardens' accounts survive in Kent for that period, but if no payment occurred where it is most likely in a parish bordering on the bridge, it probably did not occur elsewhere in Kent.

[34] RBT, paymaster's accounts 1557–1558, ff. 6v–7r.

Table 16

Rochester Bridge toll charges, 1557–1561

Cart	4d.
Horse and rider	1d.
Horse with pack or burden	2d.
Horse led or driven	1d.
Bulls, oxen, cows, steers, bullocks or heifers	1d. each
Calves led or driven	ob. each
Sheep	1d. every four
Sows, hogs, boars or gilts	ob. each
Boats (1–6 tonnes load)	2d.
Boats (7–12 tonnes load)	4d.
Boats (over 12 tonnes load)	ob. per tonne

Source: PRO, C66.910, mb. 19d.

In August a penthouse was built at the gate for the toll collectors, and later that month a payment occurs for 'ij greate lanthorns for the portare*s* of the gate – ij s. vj d.'[35] The latter appear to have been safety precautions to protect the toll collectors in gathering what must have been an unpopular charge, for on 16 August paymaster Nicholas Bridges submitted an indictement at the quarter sessions court at Sittingbourne against John Bocher of Sittingbourne 'for drawyng his sworde ageynst them that receved the Toll of the bredge.'[36] Even in better times the east end of the bridge below the castle wall was a lonely place on a dark night. 'The booke of the Survey of the bridge landes' records in 1577 that the toll collector's house at the bridge entrance remained unoccupied because 'it is not thought meete by thinhabitants that eny shuld dwell therin least the aptnes of the place shuld be thoccasion of Robberyes and other mischeifes.'[37]

Collection of the toll was not only dangerous, but also inefficient and costly. Indentures showing toll money received by John Wilkins from the porters of the bridge reveal a steady decline in monthly toll revenue during the four-year period from almost £11 per month during the first year to less than £4 per month during the last year. Over all the average monthly toll collected amounted to only £6 5s. 8d.

While income from toll collection declined, the cost of collecting the toll remained high. In addition to the initial capital cost of constructing the gate and building the toll keeper's cottage, the bridge wardens employed two porters at 8d. per day to gather the toll. A summary account returned on 21 May 1561, when the

---

[35] Ibid., f. 7r.
[36] Ibid.
[37] The book of the Survey of bridge landes 1575–1577, f. 4r.

commission for the toll expired, shows that out of the £301 11s. 10d. total receipts from the toll, £103 4s. was paid out for the wages of the porters, or an average monthly wage of £2 3s. to collect an average monthly toll of £6 5s. 8d.[38]

Table 17

Toll proceeds, 1557–1561

Time	Amount collected			Average monthly toll		
	£	s	d	£	s	d
20 June 1557–19 June 1558	129	10		10	15	10
20 June 1558–19 June 1559	85	4		7	2	
20 June 1559–29 September 1559	15			5		
29 September 1559–21 May 1561	71	17	10	3	11	10
Four-year totals:	301	11	10	6	5	8

Source: RBT, Toll indentures, 1557–1561.

Repair of the bridge did begin during the summer of 1557. On 6 August Lord Cobham met with the surveyor, master mason, and master carpenter of London Bridge 'to vewe the feul*tes* & decayes of the bredge.'[39] Little progress, however, was made, due both to inefficient administration and insufficient money. To make matters worse, both bridge wardens died – Lord Cobham on 29 September 1558 and Sir Thomas Moyle at his manor in Eastwell in 1560. When Edmund Tynte, Moyle's servant and auditor of the bridge, came to Rochester to audit the accounts in November 1560, the receiver of revenue John Wilkins refused to render his account claiming that he had not collected many of the rents and that 'he had suche busynes of my lord Cobham his master that he could not then attend the same.'[40] When Tynte pressed the matter with William Brooke, the new Lord Cobham, he received the same answer. Moyle promised to intervene, but died before the meeting could take place. The informal system of checks and balances, whereby Lord Cobham's servant received the money and Sir Thomas Moyle's servant audited the books, had broken down irrevocably. When Wilkins finally submitted his accounts on 21 May 1561, rent arrears had mounted to £100 18s. ob., an amount higher than the entire annual rental income of £92 3s. 1d. Revenue from the toll had slowed to a trickle – only £31 11s. 2d. since Michaelmas 1559 after the toll keepers' wages had been subtracted. Bridge affairs had sunk to such a low ebb that on 12 July 1561 Queen Elizabeth herself intervened.

[38] RBT, The State of the Revenewes and Collection of Tolle belonging to the Bridge of Rochester, 20 June 1557–21 May 1561.
[39] RBT, paymaster's account 1557–1558, f. 7r.
[40] RBT, letter, Edmund Tynte to Sir Richard Sackeville, 25 August 1561.

The Elizabethan Commissions

Queen Elizabeth was no stranger to Rochester Bridge nor to Cobham Hall, residence of William Brooke, tenth Baron Cobham, who had succeeded to his father's title and to his father's position of bridge warden in September 1558. On three progresses through Kent during her reign, Elizabeth visited Rochester, where she viewed first-hand both the decay and the repair of Rochester Bridge. On her first progress Lord Cobham entertained her at Cobham Hall on 17 July 1559 in 'a banqueting house made for her Majesty in Cobham Park, with a goodly gallery thereto composed all of green with several devices of knotted flowers, supported on each side with a fair row of hawthorn trees, which nature seemed to have planted of purpose in summer to welcome her Majesty and to know her lord and master.'[1] In 1573, Queen Elizabeth stayed at the Crown Inn, 19–23 September; was entertained by former bridge paymaster and MP for Rochester Richard Watts at Satis House on Boley Hill, 23–24 September;[2] and again visited William, Lord Cobham at Cobham Hall on 24 September. In 1582, during her last progress into Kent at the departure of the Duke of Alençon, the queen stayed at the Crown Inn, 1–3 February, and with bridge warden Sir Roger Manwood at Canterbury, 5–6 February, and on her return journey visited the widow of Richard Watts at Satis House, 14–16 February. When the bridge wardens built their audit chamber in 1586, a stained glass window displaying the arms of the queen commemorated the royal connection with the bridge and bridge wardens.[3]

The relationship between Queen Elizabeth and her favourite William, Lord Cobham, moreover, extended far beyond that of royal guest and host. Summoned to Parliament on 5 November 1558, Lord Cobham was well acquainted with politics and power. Having represented Hythe in Parliament from 1547 to 1552 and Rochester in 1555, William Brooke had been appointed Lord Warden of the Cinque Ports and Constable of Dover Castle in the final days of Queen Mary's reign. Queen Elizabeth confirmed these appointments on 28 April 1559 and a month later added the post of Lord Lieutenant of Kent, all positions which he held until his death in 1597. Having undertaken several diplomatic missions for the queen, including breaking the news of Queen Mary's death to Philip in 1559, Lord Cobham was nominated Knight of the Garter in 1578, appointed to the Privy

---

[1] Raphael Holinshed, *Chronicle of England, Ireland, and Scotland*, as quoted by Esme Wingfield-Stratford, *The Lords of Cobham Hall*, London 1959, 64.

[2] Local legend attributes the name Satis House to this occasion. When Richard Watts apologised for the smallness and inconvenience of his house, the queen is said to have replied, 'satis'. (See Edward Hasted, *The History and Topographical Survey of the County of Kent*, 2nd edn (1798), vol. iv, 162.)

[3] RBT, Wardens Accounts, 1586–1687, vol. ii, f. 149v.

Council on 19 February 1586, and made Lord Chamberlain of the Royal House-hold on 8 August 1596.[4]

The relationship with Elizabeth was personal as well as political. His first wife Dorothy Neville, daughter of George Lord Abergavenny, having died on 22 September 1559, Lord Cobham chose as his second wife Frances Newton, one of the queen's ladies of the bedchamber. Their wedding was celebrated on 25 February 1560 at Westminster Palace in the presence of Queen Elizabeth, who became godmother for their eldest son. A daughter, Elizabeth, later married Robert Cecil who succeeded his father William Cecil, Lord Burghley as Queen Elizabeth's Secretary of State.[5]

If position and political influence could have saved Rochester Bridge from impending disaster, William Brooke, Lord Cobham was the man. However, surviving evidence suggests that he did little to avert the crisis. The two leases that bear his name show him acting with Sir Thomas Moyle in 1559 to lease Little Delce manor for 50 years at the peppercorn rent of £6 13s. 4d. and Langdon manor for 40 years at £8. Collection of rents was left to his servant John Wilkins, and when Sir Thomas Moyle died in 1560, William Brooke privately persuaded his brother-in-law by his first marriage, Henry Neville, Lord Abergavenny to act as fellow bridge warden. Neither Neville nor Brooke was elected by the commonalty, nor did either peer take an active interest in bridge affairs; indeed, when Queen Elizabeth created a commission to investigate the decay of Rochester Bridge on 12 July 1561, neither Lord Cobham nor Lord Abergavenny appears in the list of commissioners.

The commission was addressed to Sir Richard Sackville, Nicholas Wotton, Thomas Wotton, Warham Seintleger, Benjamin Gunstone, William Winter, Robert Rudstone, Roger Manwood, William Lovelace, and Thomas Henley.[6] The main business of the commission, however, was carried out by three commissioners: Sir Richard Sackville of Knowle, knight of the shire, privy councillor, and undertreasurer of the exchequer; Nicholas Wotton, privy councillor and dean of Canterbury Cathedral; and William Lovelace, barrister and MP for Canterbury.

The commissioners were charged to examine all written evidence of the bridge foundation and estate, to review all accounts of rents and tolls for the past seven years, to survey the 'ruyne and decaye' of the bridge, and to take immediate steps for its repair including hiring of surveyors, collectors, workmen, and other officers. The commission was to remain in force until 24 June 1562, with a preliminary report being returned by the feast of All Saints 1561 certifying what steps would be taken.[7] The first meeting of the commissioners was set for 18 August.

---

[4] *Burke's Peerage and Baronetage*, s.v. 'Cobham'; and *Dictionary of National Biography*, s.v. 'Brooke, Henry.'

[5] Smith, *Rochester in Parliament*, 96; and Esme Wingfield-Stratford, *The Lords of Cobham Hall*, London 1959, 66–67.

[6] PRO, C.66.964, mb. 8. A contemporary copy of the commission also survives in the Rochester Bridge Trust archives.

[7] A summary of the early proceedings of the commission is found in a draft report in the Rochester Bridge Trust archives entitled, 'The Certificate made y[e] x[th] day of november in the iij[de] yere off y[e] reigne off our sove*r*aigne lady Elyzabeth by the grace off god Queen off Irelond

Meanwhile, having interviewed the receiver of revenue John Wilkins, Nicholas Wotton discovered that 'Wilkins hath no kynde of wrytinges to shewe me, nor knoweth not wher eny ar,' that the paymaster Richard Watts retained in his house the only coffer '& keepeth it withowte locke & keye,' and that the auditor Edmund Tynte was in Devonshire. He suggested to Sackville that an approach be made to Lord Cobham: 'Yf we haue authorite sufficyent to calle the wardens of the bridge it wer meete they wer callidde for of theym we oughte to be fullye instructidde of all thinges aperteyning to this mater.'[8] Three days later, having taken legal advice from Lovelace, Wotton wrote again to Sackville, urging that the bridge wardens be required to cooperate with the commissioners and that William Brooke, as executor for his father, and Sir Thomas Kempe and Sir Thomas Fynche, executors for Sir Thomas Moyle, 'enforme vs by them selfes or other sufficiently authorysidd by theym, of all thynges don by the sayd late Lord Cobham, or Sir Thomas Moyle, or yn the tyme whyle they were wardens, concerninge the sayd bridge.'[9] On the advice of Lovelace, Wotton also urged that the commissioners summon the mayor and aldermen of Rochester and 'reqwyre theym to be assistent vnto vs for the better enformacion of vs how to come to the perfite knowledge of the state of the bridge.'

At their first meeting on 18 September the commissioners assembled at Rochester, read the commission, and then adjourned to inspect the bridge. Many of the protective piles around the perimeter of the staddles had decayed, exposing the staddles to the force of the current. The greatest danger centered on the second pier from the Rochester side, where the tide had scoured a deep gully under the second arch and threatened to destroy the very foundation of the pier. Indeed, two weeks later on 2 September John Wilkins reported to Sir Richard Sackville, 'There brake owte of the seconde Locke next the Towne synce your honors being here xl peces of Tymbre, none lefte in the space of fyftie foote but only the piller.'[10] Having consulted with John Nycolls, comptroller, and Thomas Harper, master carpenter of London Bridge, and having discovered that repairs could cost as much as £2,000, the commissioners then reconvened to decide how that sum could be raised.

The commissioners faced two problems: in the long term how to raise the formidable sum of £2,000 to renew the foundations of the bridge and in the short term how to raise immediately a sum sufficient to prevent the imminent collapse of the bridge before winter. Sir Richard Sackville had learned from Edmund Geste, Bishop of Rochester, about the ancient system of taxing the contributory parishes

France & Ingelond defendor off ye fayth &c by the Comyssyoneres appoynted by herr hyghnes for the reparacion off rochester brydge vnto hyr maiesties pryvye counsell.' Hereafter referred to as 'Certificate.'

[8] RBT, letter, Nicholas Wotton to Sir Richard Sackville, 28 July 1561. This letter and other correspondence pertaining to the work of the commissioners have been published by A.A. Arnold in 'Rochester Bridge in AD 1561,' *Archaeologia Cantiana*, xvii (1887), 212–40.

[9] RBT, letter, Nicholas Wotton to Sir Richard Sackville, 31 July 1561.

[10] RBT, letter, John Wilkins to Sir Richard Sackville, 2 September [1561].

for the repair of the early medieval wooden bridge,[11] but he did not know that statutes of 21 Richard II and 9 Henry V had transferred that obligation to repair from the old wooden bridge to the stone bridge of Sir Robert Knolles. Indeed, drawing on the distinction between the two bridges in the 1492 charter, he determined that 'those which of auncyent tyme ware bownden dystinctlie to the reparacons and mayntenance of the partes of tholde Rochestre bridge arre not by lawe chargeable to the mayntenance of this bridge.'[12] Therefore, the commissioners, on the advice of the Lord Treasurer, William Pawlett, Marquis of Winchester, resolved to tax the entire county.[13] A statute of 32 Henry VIII for repairing bridges authorised the justices of the peace to levy a tax throughout the shire for the repair of bridges, if the bridge were situated outside of a city or incorporated town and if it could not be discovered who was responsible for its repair.[14] The Lord Treasurer had calculated that after collection charges and rebates to the Cinque Ports the tax, or fifteenth, would yield £1200, 'which money take and gyue thanks and you may haue yt, for yt ys a good begynnynge & if that be well spent yt shalbe a good occasion to moue the cuntrey to gyue you more.'[15] Thus the commissioners decided to present the bridge at the next quarter sessions at Canterbury on 23 September and, meanwhile, to summon the magistrates to Maidstone on 25 August to acquaint them with the plan.

To meet the immediate need for money, the commissioners resolved to appeal to the queen herself for a loan of £300 to be repaid from the proceeds of the tax. A letter, signed by all ten commissioners and dated 18 August 1561, was accordingly dispatched to Sir William Cecil, Lord Burghley seeking his assistance to obtain the loan and soliciting the Privy Council to send letters to all justices of the peace in Kent to ensure their cooperation in levying the tax.[16] Cecil's reply was not encouraging. 'When I cam to require onely a prest of iij^c ^{li} I saw hir Maiesty as you ar wont to see draw backward and devise argument ageynst it, alledgyng that it was a symple contrey that wold not strayne themselves so farr as to procure iij^c ^{li}, to the help of so necessary and public a work.'[17] The commissioners had to look elsewhere for their loan.

On 25 August Sir Richard Sackville delivered a vigorous speech to the justices of the peace assembled at Maidstone, appealing both to their self interest and their public spirit. 'One of the cheif ornaments and garnyshyngs of the Shire,' Rochester Bridge provided for the passage and repassage not only for Her Majesty's subjects and foreign ambassadors but also for 'the besyness of spedy transportyng of ordenaunce shot artyllyry and men for the defence of thosse in thys shere.' Repairs

---

[11] RBT, letter, Edmund Geste to Sir Richard Sackville, 17 August; the obligation of the contributory parishes is recorded in the earliest surviving register in the Diocese of Rochester, known as the Textus Roffensis, see above pp. 16–20.

[12] PRO, SP12/19, item 27, letter to William Cecil, Lord Burghley.

[13] RBT, letter, William Pawlett to Sir Richard Sackville, 20 August 1561.

[14] 32 Henry VIII cap. 5, printed in *The Statutes at Large*, ii, pp. 153–55.

[15] RBT, letter, William Pawlett to Sir Richard Sackville, 21 August 1561.

[16] PRO, SP 12/19, item 27.

[17] RBT, letter, William Cecil, Lord Burghley to Sir Richard Sackville, 21 August 1561.

begun before winter would cost £2,000; repairs delayed would cost more than 20,000 marks. Less than £20 remained in the bridge coffers. Then turning to the letters from the Privy Council addressed to each magistrate, Sackville concluded, 'And before the openyng of them, I can no les then say thys much vnto you, wyche ys that as the kepyng of yt standyng & in good repayer shal be most and chefflyest to the benefyt of the Inhabitantes of thys shere, & so the deyty of ye same shalbe the cheff charge & detryment to them, so resson ys, that whoso consyder the same, that yf no lawe tyede & bownde us to the repayryng of yt that for that respecte whe wold offer the same to be done by us for owre owne benefyts and every man indeavour hymself to arme hymself with good perseveringe for to amerse suche as shall seme to be ignorant & forgetfull how to do good to them selfes and chefly to take from thys Contrey that blot that ther neglygence hauth robbed ther awncesters & predecessers of that gret honour that this Shere reseved by the gret charge and dylygence of so goodly an ornament as that bryge was & yet ys vnless they wyllfully dystroye the same in the denyyng of ther small helpe.'[18]

When Sackville had finished speaking and the magistrates had read their letters from the queen, notes the preliminary report, 'The Justices shewed theym selves verye well contentyd therwith and graunted their ayde therin.'[19] The fifteenth was ordered to be levied, and collectors of the tax were appointed. Nicholas Wotton and Sir Richard Sackville each having offered to contribute £50, the remaining commissioners and magistrates also voted to make their own contributions, everyone according to his means, toward the £300 loan so that the repairs could begin before the winter.

To satisfy completely the provisions of the statute of 32 Henry VIII under which they were proceeding, however, Lovelace had advised the commissioners to present the bridge at the September quarter sessions before beginning to collect the tax. Meanwhile, they proceeded to collect the loan and to reorganise the administration of the bridge. Lovelace and Wotton gathered the counterpart leases and accounts from former auditor Edmund Tynte and gave instructions for a survey of the bridge lands. At their first meeting on 18 August the commissioners had also appointed officers: Robert Dean, later replaced by Thomas Culpepper in March 1562, to be general purveyor of timber and stone; John Watts, alderman of Rochester, to be clerk of the works; the Revd. Martin Collins and John Symkyns, prebendaries of Rochester Cathedral, to be surveyors and auditors of the works; and John Wilkins to be general receiver of the tax.[20] Although the latter appointment was no doubt made out of deference to William Brooke, Lord Cobham, Lovelace and Wotton insisted – with good reason – that Wilkins give his bond

---

[18] RBT, speech, Sir Richard Sackville, Maidstone, [25 August 1561].

[19] RBT, Certificate, 6.

[20] Ibid., 4. Although Richard Watts was not reappointed paymaster of the bridge, he evidently continued to hold the bridge wardens in high regard. After his death the Wardens and Commonalty of Rochester Bridge were party to the indenture quadripartite, along with Thomas and Marian Pagitt, the mayor and citizens of Rochester, and the Dean and Chapter of Rochester Cathedral, that established the administration of Watts Charity. See E.J.F. Hinkley, *A History of the Richard Watts Charity*, Rochester 1979, 121–35.

before receiving the tax.[21] Fifteen years later, when Wilkins died, the bridge wardens recovered from his widow arrears remaining in his possession for the 'Toll and fyfteene towarde the reparations of the same Bridge levied within the Countie of Kent' amounting to £518.[22]

Collection of the loan advanced slowly. On 2 September Wilkins had received only £130; ten days later, having still received less than half of the promised loan, he wrote to Sir Richard Sackville complaining that money 'commethe yn verye slowlye' and listing the names and outstanding amounts.[23] As they waited for the quarter sessions day, Nicholas Wotton and William Lovelace sought a contribution from the mayor and aldermen of Canterbury, which along with the Cinque Ports was exempt from the fifteenth, and on 8 September received a gift of 40 marks.[24] The following week commissioners Nicholas Wotton, Robert Rudstone, Thomas Wotton of Boughton Malherbe, and William Lovelace solicited a similar voluntary assessment from the citizens of Romney Marsh, from whom they received £4 2s. ob.[25]

On 23 September Lovelace and Wotton had arranged for the presentment of the bridge by the quarter sessions jury at Canterbury Castle. The jury readily recognised the problem – 'That same bridge is so far broken, ruptured, and ruinous, and in such decay that by reason of the aforesaid breaking down, ruin, breach, and decay of this same bridge within a short time this same bridge will collapse'[26] – but they did not so easily grant the solution. The statute of 32 Henry VIII required the justices of the peace to tax the shire only if the ruined bridge stood 'without City or Town Corporate.' The City of Rochester had always claimed ownership of the shore, river, and riverbed, and as Lovelace later wrote to Sackville, the presentment was obtained only 'with some difficultie for that it was mytche dowted to them whether it were within the Citie of Rochester or no.'[27] The jury, however, eventually declared that they did not know who was responsible for repairing the bridge, and accordingly the tax was ordered to be levied throughout the whole county.

John Wilkins began receiving money from the collectors on 5 October, but difficulty and delay plagued the collection. Queen Elizabeth had issued a proclamation on 15 November prohibiting the use of Spanish money; and at least one collector, Thomas Hamon, from the lathe of St Augustine, had accepted payment in foreign coins that ceased to be legal tender before he rendered his account to John

---

21 RBT, letter, William Lovelace to Sir Richard Sackville, 17 September 1561; letter, William Lovelace and Nicholas Wotton to Sir Richard Sackville, 30 September 1561.
22 RBT, wardens accounts 1576–1577, vol. i, ff. 4r, 17v.
23 RBT, letters, John Wilkins to Sir Richard Sackville, 2 September 1561 and 12 September 1561.
24 RBT letters, William Lovelace to Sir Richard Sackville, 4 September 1561 and 8 September 1561.
25 RBT, letter, Nicholas Wotton to Sir Richard Sackville, 12 September 1561.
26 RBT, presentment, County of Kent, Quarter Sessions, 23 September 1561.
27 RBT, letter, D.B. Lewis, Rochester Town Clerk to Rochester Bridge Clerk, 27 December 1845; letter, Nicholas Wotton and William Lovelace to Sir Richard Sackville, 30 September [1561].

Wilkins on 18 November.[28] Other collectors had difficulty persuading people to pay. On 22 November, therefore, the Privy Council sent a second letter to the justices of the peace requiring the magistrates to warn the constables and collectors to complete their collection by 1 January. Anyone refusing to pay the tax would then be summoned to appear before the Privy Council.[29] Eventually the tax was collected, and accounts of the general receiver John Wilkins, covering 1 October 1561 to 16 February 1564 show the following receipts after allowances for the collectors and rebates to the Cinque Ports:

Table 18

Revenue from the Fifteenth levied August 1561

	£	s	d
Lathe of Shepewaye	117	12	2 ob.
Lathe of Saynt Augustyens	205	6	11 ob.
Lathe of Scraye	377	19	1
Lathe of Aylesford	297	16	3 qu.
Lathe of Sutton at Hone	176	8	10 ob.
Mayor and Commonaltie of Rochester	13	13	1 ob.
Mayor and Commonaltie of the Citie of Canterburye	23	6	8
Total receipts:	1212	3	2 qu.

Source: RBT, account of John Wilkins, receiver.

Of this amount £316 11s. 4d. was handed over to purveyours Robert Dean and Thomas Culpeper, and £835 18s. 3d. was distributed to the workmen for wages and tools. A further account rendered on 31 May 1564 by Thomas Culpeper, purveyour of 'Tymber, Stone, Bricke, Lyme, Iron, leade, Artificers, Workemen and of all other thinges whatever neadefull for the Repaire and Amendemant of the saide Bridge' shows payments of £142 18s. 2d. ob. for timber, £39 9s. 8d. for stone, £56 7s. for iron fittings and tools, £11 2s. 2d. for lead, 21s. 4d. for bricks, £14 2s. 10d. ob. for rosin, pitch and tar, £27 15d. for ropes, 40s. 6d. for broom faggots, £10 11s. ob. for cartwheels, shovels, and tools, £7 13s. 10d. for the bridge boat, £20 3s. 2d. for carriage of materials, £35 19s. 11d. for wages of workmen and labourers felling trees and sawing timber, and 68s. 8d. for officers of London Bridge who came to Rochester to advise on repairs in May 1562.[30]

The major repair work started during the spring of 1562 and continued until the

---

[28] RBT, letter, Thomas Hamon to Nicholas Wotton, 25 November [1561]; letter, Nicholas Wotton to Sir Richard Sackville, 25 November 1561; Arnold, 234.

[29] RBT, 'A letter ffor ye Counsell to wryte to ye sheryff of Kent & ye Justices there for Rochester brydge ... from the Court at Sainte James the xxij[th] of November.'

[30] RBT, account of Thomas Culpeper, purveyour, 22 March 1562–31, May 1564.

spring of 1564. To prevent further deterioration during the winter months, a coffer dam had been constructed around the second pier, protecting the undermined foundations of the pier from the swift river current. Timber for renewing defective piles and stone for repairing the pier were stockpiled in readiness at the Rochester quay. In March 1562 a rammer for a 'run*n*yng gynne' was borrowed from London Bridge in order to drive the piles; and as soon as danger from winter storms had passed, the repair of the staddles began.[31]

While repair of the bridge foundations continued, the commissioners deliberated and devised a final report to the Privy Council which was drafted in December 1564.[32] Between the original decisions of the commission in August 1561 and the writing of their final report, the commissioners had discovered the statutes of 21 Richard II and 9 Henry V regarding the liability of the contributory parishes for the repair of the stone bridge. This discovery placed them in a doubly awkward position. Not only was the commission bound to reinstate a long forgotten obligation on the landowners of the contributory parishes, but they no longer had a legal basis for the tax they had levied on the entire county. William Lovelace, writing to Nicholas Wotton, confessed himself 'per*p*lexed what were best to do lykely to take a good successe & to coverre ye better our fformer doyng*es* off ignorans not knowyng th*at* now we know.'[33]

In the end the commissioners certified that £1,200 had been spent on repairs and that a further £200 should be spent to repair the wooden wharf at the Strood end of the bridge and the stone wharf at the Rochester end 'w*h*ich by means of the gullinge of the water vnder the fundacyon of it must be taken downe and newlye made.'[34] The commissioners went on to recommend that not less than £200 annually would be needed to maintain the bridge and noted that the annual revenue from the estate ammounted to only £98 12s. 10d. ob. They reported that the wardens had not been elected annually, as required by the letters patent of Richard II, and that the electors of the wardens were no longer known. To cover their mistake in charging the entire county, they blamed the commonalty for not cooperating. 'For that sitche of the Countrye as were Contrybutoryes to the woodden brydge before the newe Stone brydge was buylded, clayme not to be chargeable to the rep*ar*acions of the same Stone brydge. And the tyme is so farre past syns any sytche chardge was putt in vse that the Townes Landes or p*er*sons are not knowen.'[35] Finally, they left the reformation of the commonalty in the hands of the Privy Council, recommending the appointment of another commission composed

---

[31] RBT, letters from Martin Colyn and John Symkins to Sir Richard Sackville, 26 September 1561, 13 October 1561, 18 October 1561, and 20 March [1562].

[32] RBT, 'The Certyfycat made the   daye of   In the vj^th yere of the Reigne of our most dred Soveraigne ladye Queene Elizabethe: By the Commyssion*er*s appoynted by hyr highnes for the Survey of the estate of Rochester Brydge and the Reparacons of the same, touchinge their doyng*es* therin By certene of the sayd Comyssyon.' Although this draft report is dated only by regnal year, a letter from Lovelace to Nicholas Wotton, dated 23 December [1564] fixes the drafting of this report in late 1564 or early 1565.

[33] RBT, letter, William Lovelace to Nicholas Wotton, 23 December [1564].

[34] RBT, draft report of William Lovelace, 3.

[35] Ibid., 4–5.

of 'the gretter numbre off ye wyse heddes of the shyre' and the creation of a new corporacion 'for the government & perpetual mayntenance of the brydge & for the good ordering of the landes & revenues belongyng to Rochester brydge.'[36]

This second Elizabethan commission was appointed on 1 August 1571 and ordered to report to the Privy Council before 25 December 1572. Headed by Sir Edward Fynes, Lord Admiral and member of the Privy Council; bridge wardens Henry Neville, Lord Abergavenny and William Brooke, Lord Cobham; and Sir William Cecil, Privy Councillor and Lord Treasurer; the commission did indeed assemble – to use Lovelace's phrase – 'the gretter numbre of ye wyse heddes of the shyre.' Sir Richard Sackville had died in 1566 and Nicholas Wotton in 1567, but five other members of the first commission – Sir William Lovelace, serjeant-at-law and MP for Canterbury; Sir Roger Manwood, serjeant-at-law and MP for Sandwich; and landowners Thomas Wotton, Robert Rudstone, and Thomas Hendley – also served on the second. Other commissioners included John Southcote, justice of the queen's bench, and Thomas Gawdy, serjeant-at-law, both justices of the assizes in Kent; Nicholas Barham, serjeant-at-law and MP for Maidstone; Hugh Cartwright of East Malling, surveyor and under-sheriff of Kent and MP for Rochester in 1558; Sir Thomas Kempe of Wye, former sheriff in 1564 and knight of the shire in 1559; landowners John Cobham, Sir William Damsyll, William Cromer, and Robert Alcock; the mayor of Rochester and the dean of Rochester Cathedral; and the mayor of Canterbury and the dean of Canterbury Cathedral.

Once again the bridge had fallen into wrack and ruin. 'By reason of the greate rageynge and frettinge of the salte water and of the fearcenes of the swyfte water course and passage vnder the same the Bridge ys growen to greate decaye and so Without spedye prouysion and good foresight is lyke in shorte tyme to be in perell of vtter ruyne to the greate dishonor of our Realme and to the greate anoyaunce of our comonwealthe.'[37] The commissioners were charged to use their wisdom and discretion to make necessary repairs, but the main thrust of the commission propelled the commissioners toward reformation of the commonalty. Citing the statute of 21 Richard II and the neglect of its provisions for the contributory parishes to repair the bridge, to elect wardens, and to audit the accounts, the commission charged the commissioners by inquisition of jury and examination of all evidence and writings to determine which parishes and persons ought to be contributory to the maintenance of the bridge and to devise a scheme of ratable contributions. The commissioners were further charged to survey the lands belonging to the bridge, to recall leases granted by the wardens without the consent of the commonalty, and to make new leases. Finally, the commissioners were authorised to review the rules, ordinances, customs and orders governing the bridge and to make such changes as they thought fit.

No evidence survives of the work of these commissioners, although an undated report, entitled 'Devyses orders and rules for a newe corporacon for the mayntenance

[36] RBT, letter, William Lovelace to Nicholas Wotton, 23 December [1564]; draft report, 5.
[37] PRO, C.66.1077, mb. 26d–27.

of Rochester brydge' and bearing the annotations of Lovelace, may originate from this time. This report called for a new corporation consisting of the mayor and aldermen of the City of Rochester and the Dean and Chapter of Rochester Cathedral. Each group would elect one warden annually, the wardens would submit annual accounts, and the corporation would make an annual inspection of the bridge. Terms of leases would not exceed ten years, and new letters patent would provide for an annual income of £200. Furthermore, the letters patent would be copied into the minutes of the Dean and Chapter of Rochester Cathedral, the mayor and aldermen of the City of Rochester, the Dean and Chapter of Canterbury Cathedral, the mayor and aldermen of Canterbury, and the mayor and aldermen of Maidstone so 'that the right vse and order of the same maye not be secrette and misvsed, But be openlie vnderstoode to the worlde.'[38] Whether this proposal dates from the first commission of 1561 or the second commission of 1571 remains uncertain, for the Privy Council apparently took no action on the recommendations except to establish yet another commission.

The third Elizabethan commission resulted in part from the personal inspection of the bridge by Queen Elizabeth during her progress through Kent in September 1573, when William Cecil, Lord Burghley took the opportunity to acquaint her with the necessity of reforming the commonalty and increasing the revenue of the bridge.[39] Created on 8 November 1574, the third commission retained most of the members of the second, adding Edmund Geste, Bishop of Rochester; Sir Richard Baker of Sissinghurst, former MP for Romney and high sheriff of Kent; Henry Cobham, diplomat and brother of William, Lord Cobham; Thomas Fane, surveyor of Kent; landowners Robert Binge and Thomas Coppinger; and Sir Walter Mildmay, who had replaced Richard Sackville as chancellor and under-treasurer of the exchequer.[40]

The commission assembled on 8 February 1575, started their investigation by appointing committees, and ordered initial reports to be made before Easter. Roger Manwood, Nicholas Barham, William Lovelace, Richard Baker, and Thomas Wotton were directed to examine all statutes, writings, and evidence concerning the bridge and the estate. Gilbert Hide, the bridge auditor, was ordered to search the records of the exchequer, and the deans of Canterbury and Rochester were ordered to search through the registers and records of their cathedrals. William Cromer, Robert Binge, and Thomas Fludde were assigned to survey the estate; and Henry, Lord Abergavenny, William, Lord Cobham, Thomas Willoughby, John Cobham, and Thomas Coppinger were assigned to survey the bridge and draw up plans for its repair. Finally, Lord Abergavenny, Lord Cobham, the deans of Canterbury and Rochester, Thomas Kempe, Richard Baker, Thomas Wotton, John Cobham, and Thomas Coppinger were ordered to audit all accounts of the toll and tax and all

[38] RBT, 'Considerations for the repaire of Rochester Bridge, and safetie of the Revennewes thereof,' 3.
[39] William Lambarde, *A Perambulation of Kent: conteining the Description, Hystorie, and Customes of That Shire*, London 1576; reprinted Chatham 1826, 355.
[40] PRO, C.66.1108, mb 32d.

other rents and revenues. On 13 April the commission empanelled two juries, charging them to discover and record the owners, lessees, and value of all lands in the contributory parishes, to determine the value and present rents of the estate proper, and to survey the bridge itself, estimating the cost of repairs and establishing the extent of embezzlement of tools and supplies. The committees and juries continued to meet throughout the spring, summer, and autumn of 1575. The juries were further instructed to investigate the concealment of quitrents; and John Wilkins and Thomas Culpeper were pressed to render fuller accounts, the latter finally being bound upon his recognizance to appear before the Lord Treasurer William Cecil to account for money received from Wilkins during his tenure as purveyour for the bridge.

The real work of this commission, however, was carried on by Lord Burghley and Sir Roger Manwood in the court of Star-chamber on 25 November 1575. As Manwood rightly judged, the crux of the bridge problem was mismanagement of the estate, the 'leases made of the Bridge landes at an vnder valewe by Wardens of honor and of worship for preferrement of theire frendes and servantes and to the preiudice and great decaye of the Bridge.'[41] Cecil and Manwood had privately agreed that if Manwood could devise a plan to frustrate the existing leases of the bridge estate, Cecil would guarantee the approval of Queen Elizabeth. The estate could then be relet at trebled values, sufficient revenue to maintain the bridge would be provided, and 'justice might be done.' To cover themselves, however, Cecil and Manwood had first arranged for the commission under the great seal authorising them 'to heare and determyne aswell all matters & thinges whatsoeuer touching or concerning the said bridge, or the Revenewes, accomptes, decayes or reparacons of the same, as also the landes contributary to the maintenaunce of the said bridge & all circumstances touching the premisses, as well by taking Inquyeries, as by such other waies & meanes as to the commissioners aforesaid should be thought mete and convenyent.'[42] Having received carte blanche from the queen, they then proceeded to execute their plan.

The statute of 22 Richard II, contended Manwood, had granted the bridge estates to both the wardens and the commonalty. The statute permitted the wardens to 'keep, oversee, support, and maintain the same Bridge from time to time, in the name of the whole Community aforesaid,' it allowed the wardens 'to implead others, or be impleaded by others, concerning Lands, Tenements, Rents or Services;' and it held the wardens responsible 'for all manner of Issues, Rents, and Revenues, arising and proceeding from such Lands and Tenements;'[43] but it did not specifically state that the wardens could grant leases in the name of the commonalty. Manwood argued, therefore, that since the leases had been signed by the wardens without the consent of the commonalty, the leases were invalid and could be lawfully frustrated.

[41] Sir Roger Manwood's account of the proceedings of the commission is found in 'A true discourse of the auncyent wodden and present stoned bridge at Rochester,' op. cit., ff. 16r–20v.
[42] Ibid., f. 16r.
[43] A Collection of Statutes concerning Rochester Bridge, London 1733, 8.

The lessees of the bridge estates, therefore, were summoned to appear in London with their legal counsel on 14 November 1575 to give answer whether they would surrender their leases or defend them in law. Having requested time to inspect the leases at the chambers of Justice Manwood on 21 November and still finding themselves unable to give answer, the lessees were ordered to appear with their counsel before the court of Star-chamber on 25 November. There before the Lord Chief Justice, Lord Burghley, Lord Abergavenny, Lord Cobham, serjeant-at-law Barham, serjeant-at-law Lovelace, and other bridge commissioners, Justice of the Common Pleas Roger Manwood presented his case of impeachment against the leases: the former bridge wardens had not been elected by the commonalty, their accounts had not been audited by the commonalty, and the leases at low rents signed by wardens having no legal standing had not been granted with the consent of the commonalty. Furthermore, the low rents, which no longer supported the maintenance of the bridge, placed an unjust tax burden upon the commonalty. After reply from counsel for the defendants, the matter was referred to the Lord Chief Justice and further debated in his chambers on 27 November. The Lord Chief Justice having delivered his opinion in favour of the bridge commissioners, the defendants, rather than contest their case in the courts, surrendered their leases. At the next meeting of the Star-chamber on 29 November Lord Burghley declared that the lessees should compound for new leases at higher rents.

That justice was done – to use Judge Manwood's phrase – remains open to debate just as in the debatable quashing of the case against the bridge wardens for recovery of the chapel rent-charge in 1577 when Manwood received £30 9s. 10d. for his services. In the course of his rise from Serjeant-at-Law to Judge of the Common Pleas to Lord Chief Baron of the Exchequer and member of the court of Star-chamber, Judge Manwood rarely scrupled at injustice to see that justice was done, including selling one of the offices in his gift, which earned him the censure of the queen, and offering Lord Burghley five hundred marks for the vacant chief justiceship of the queen's bench, which earned him the censure of the Privy Council.[44] Nevertheless, even an unscrupulous judge can interpret the law justly, and Manwood's successful impeachment of the bridge leases, supported by the Lord Chief Justice himself, released the bridge wardens from their self-imposed penury and formed the foundation for the reformation of the commonalty. After the Star-chamber proceedings little else remained for the bridge commissioners to do except to draft the legislation that became the Rochester Bridge Act 1576.

---

[44] *Dictionary of National Biography*, s.v. 'Manwood, Sir Roger.'

The Elizabethan Statutes

The passage of the Rochester Bridge Act 1576 marked the start of a new administrative system for the bridge that lasted until the twentieth century. Entitled 'An Acte for the perpetuall mayntenaunce of Rochestre Bridge,' the statute established the annual election at Rochester Castle of two wardens and twelve assistant wardens on the day after the general quarter sessions of the peace following Easter.[1] The outgoing wardens were bound upon forfeit of £10 to account to the incoming wardens for all rents and revenues received, and accounts were to be rendered at the Crown Inn by Thursday of Whitsun week. No leases were to be made without the consent of both wardens and the majority of assistant wardens, and all leases were to be entered in a register kept in a chest with the common seal and evidences of the estate. A terrier of lands and rents was required every seven years. Should the revenue from the estate prove insufficient to maintain the bridge, the Wardens and Assistants were authorised to tax the contributory parishes or assess contribution money based on the land values recently established by the juries and bridge commissioners.

This reconstitution of the commonalty after almost a century in abeyance met with inertia on the part of the landowners and diffidence on the part of the newly elected Wardens and Assistants. After an initial burst of support, the amorphous group of landowners in the contributory parishes lost their enthusiasm for assembling at Rochester Castle on election day, and the annual elections were carried out with great difficulty. For their part the Wardens and Assistants expressed uncertainty about their power to tax the commonalty and doubt about their power to enforce a tax if it were levied. As a result, in 1585 Parliament passed a second statute, entitled 'An Acte of Explanacion and Addicion unto the late Statute for the mayntenance of Rochester Bridge,' clarifying the tax clause of the 1576 statute, further defining the electors of the wardens, and adding enforcement powers.[2] Both statutes, incidentally, Sir Roger Manwood notes were 'obteyned by the travayle of the saide Sir Roger Manwood withowte anye fees in the higher howse or lower howse of parlyament to Lo: Chauncelor or Speaker, or other Mynisteres or Clerkes and soe not one peny charge to the Brydge thowghe dyverse other lyke parlyament Bylles haue paide and borne the same Chardges.'[3] As the Wardens and Commonalty eventually accustomed themselves to the new responsibilities established by

---

[1] 'An Acte for the perpetuall mayntenaune Rochestre Bridge,' 18 Elizabeth I, *A Collection of Statutes concerning Rochester Bridge*, London 1733, 10–11.

[2] 'An Acte of Explanacion and Addicion unto the Statute for the mayntenance of Rochester Bridge,' 27 Elizabeth I, *A Collection of Statutes concerning Rochester Bridge*, London 1733, 12.

[3] RBT, 'A true discourse of the Auncyent wodden and present stoned bridge at Rochester,' f. 20v.

these two Elizabethan statutes, the problems that had plagued Rochester Bridge for centuries gradually faded into the past.

The first and fundamental problem was power. The 1576 statute decreed the annual election of two wardens and twelve assistant wardens, but it did not address the problem of ultimate authority. 'Be it ordeyned and enacted by thauthority of this present Parliament, that on the morrowe after the generall Quarter Sessions of the peace, holden in the said Countie of Kent, next after the feast of Easter next coming, the Wardens and Commonalty of the Landes contributory to the said Rochester Bridge, *or as many of them as conveniently may*, shall assemble themselves at the Castell of Rochester, nere to the said Rochester Bridge, and there, by the moste number of their voyces then present, to make an Electyon of twoo Persons of the same Commonaltie to be the Wardens . . . and of twelve Parsons of the said Commonaltie to be Assistants to the said two Wardens, for one hoole yere after the next day of Pentecost then next ensuinge: And so from thenceforth for ever, at the said daye and place, a yerely Election to be made of twoo Wardens for the said Bridge, and of twelve Assistaunts.'[4] Once again the fate of the bridge depended upon that nebulous federation of parishes, the commonalty of lands contributory to Rochester Bridge.

Just where the foundation should have been strongest, it was weakest. For three hundred years since the first recorded writ of inquisition to determine responsibility for repairing the bridge in 1277, royal commissions had tried to force the commonalty to act, and they had failed. Successful operation of the commonalty depended on good will and cooperation for the common good, but no one, neither archbishop nor king's council, could compel it to cooperate. The 1576 statute, optimistically entitled 'An Acte for the perpetuall mayntenaunce of Rochestre Bridge,' established the mechanism for electing bridge wardens and assistant wardens 'thenceforth for ever,' but failed to ensure that the perpetual motion machine would start. For the next three hundred years the bridge wardens tinkered with the election mechanism, fine tuning it with further statutes in 1585, 1702, and 1876, before trading it in for an entirely new administrative model designed by The Rochester Bridge Act 1908.

At the first election on 2 May 1576, over one hundred persons from the commonalty assembled at Rochester Castle. In 1577 attendance dropped below one hundred and continued to decline over the next decade. By the time the bridge wardens reformed the election procedure in 1585 to require the presence of the electors, only a handful of parishes in the commonalty were represented at the annual election.[5]

The 1585 statute further defined the electorate as at least two householders from every parish having at least four householders and situated within seven miles of the bridge. It also prescribed penalties for absence from the election. In part the

---

4 *Collection of Statutes*, 10 (italics mine).
5 RBT, The yearelie Elections of the twoe wardeins and twelve Assistant*es* of Rochester Bridge, and of other officers there, from the tyme of the Statute made in the eighteenth yere of the Raigne of Quene Elizabeth, ff. 42, 42v, 46v. Hereafter referred to as 'The Yearelie Elections.'

statute reads, 'yt is further ordeyned and inacted by authoritie aforesaide, that everie yere at the Election of the saide twoe Wardens and xii Assistaunts (by the said former Statute lymyted) Twoe at the leaste of howseholders, Inhabitaunts of everie parrishe, in whiche there are fowre howseholders at the leaste, within vii myles of the saide Bridge, and wherein anye of the saide contributorie lands doe lye, shalbe present to gyve theire voyces at the same Election, upon payne of Tenne Shillings, to be forfeited by the Inhabitaunts of everie suche parishe making defaulte of suche apparaunce.'[6] At last the bridge wardens had the means to start their perpetual motion machine.

On 21 April 1585 at the first election following the passage of this statute, twenty-three parishes failed to appear, and £11 10s. in fines was levied, 'all which was discharged by assent for that they of the sayde parishes could not have reasonable forewarning of this theire duetie of appearaunce, which happened within xxij dayes after thend of that Session of Parliament 27 Elizabeth.'[7] After 1585 attendance at elections improved. The number of defaulting parishes dropped to fourteen in 1586, dwindled to four in 1590, and then continued at an average forfeit rate of four parishes each year for the next seventy years.

Administration of the forfeit system, however, proved difficult and the collection cumbersome. Unlevied and uncollected fines passed from one year's accounts to the next during the 1590s. Some parishes paid, and others defaulted. Arrears had amounted to £38 in 1603, when the following note appeared in the account book: 'This some of xxxviij[li] is omitted out of this accompt and to be left out of any future Accompt bycause by the negligence of the Collectors it doth not appear who hath paid and who not.'[8] Beginning in 1602, the bridge wardens hired a messenger to remind parishes of their obligation before each election, yet neither attendance nor collection of fines improved dramatically. Over the next decade arrears again climbed to £14 10s. in 1613.[9]

Even when the fines were levied, the effort and expense of enforcement threatened to outweigh the value of the fine collected. Warrants, signed and sealed by the bridge wardens, authorised the Bridge Clerk and other collectors 'to take distresse either of Cattle or other goodes of any the Inhabitantes of the severall parishes . . . to make sale thereof, and to detaine for the vse of the said Bridge the several somes by them severally forfeited.'[10] In 1586 the bridge wardens paid twenty shillings 'To Mr Bettes for gathering the forfeytures of the parishes aforesaid for this first difficulte tyme,'[11] and similar payments in succeeding years often amounted to a significant percentage of the total collected. When Bridge Clerk William Somer served a warrant on the parishes of Aylesford, Northfleet, Milton, Chalk, Higham, and Strood in 1638, for example, it cost 17s. 10d. for his horse hire and travelling expenses, or just over twenty-five per cent of the £3 10s. collected. The time lapse

[6] *Collection of Statutes*, 12.
[7] RBT, The Yearlie Elections, f. 47.
[8] RBT, Wardens Accounts, IV, f. 3.
[9] Ibid., III, f. 368; IV, ff. 14, 61, 103; V, f. 107v.

[10] RBT, MS 1142.
[11] RBT, Wardens Accounts, II, ff. 107, 197v, 242, 288.

between the missed election and attempted collection often compounded the difficulties of administration. The warrant to Bridge Clerk John Atkins in May 1657 cites nineteen parishes for twenty-seven absences over a period of seven years from 1651 to 1657.[12]

Other parishes claimed exemption under the seven-mile rule. Faversham was declared outside the seven-mile radius in 1588, followed by Thurnham, Offham, Wrotham, Southfleet, and Allhallows, Hoo in 1599. Ditton, East Malling, West Malling, Trottiscliffe, Leybourne, and Maidstone were measured in 1621 after five years of agitation, but all were judged to lie within seven miles of the bridge. The most persistent offenders – East Malling, Trottiscliffe, Leybourne, and Stoke – again petitioned the bridge wardens to measure the distance to their parishes on 25 April 1639 and agreed to pay the Bridge Clerk William Somer five shillings per day for his pains and one shilling to his labourer.[13] No record survives of the outcome, except for a payment of three shillings 'for charges of expence at the measuring of the distance betweene the Parrishe of East Malling and Rochester Bridge in the year 1639,'[14] and no satisfactory resolution was reached. All four parishes continued to default on election day, and the bridge wardens continued to levy fines. Although the thirty-five parishes obligated to send electors each missed an average of eight times between 1585 and 1660, East Malling defaulted 30 times, Trottiscliffe 32 times, and Leybourne and Stoke each 18 times.

In 1621 the bridge wardens added positive reinforcement to negative punishment in order to ensure attendance on election day. In addition to the system of levying ten-shilling fines against defaulting parishes, the bridge wardens George Bing and Sir George Fane decided to pay one-shilling rewards to those attending. Among the expenses for the 1621 election appears the following item: 'Geven to the Comynaltie at the Election daye by the gentlemen's Comandment – xxˢ.'[15] Attendance increased in 1622 to thirty parishes and continued at an average of twenty-eight for the next forty years. The 1585 statute explicitly stated, 'the Expenses of the saide Wardens, Assistaunts, or Inhabitants, at the saide Election daye, to be paied or borne at theire owne chardges, everie man to beare his owne chardge.'[16] Nevertheless, the reward system continued, increasing to eighteen pence per parish in 1638 and gathering authority with age. By 1648 the reward had become a time-honoured custom, witness the payment that year 'to xxviijᵗⁱᵉ parishes that came to give their voyces at the Ellecion of the wardens and assistantes according to the Custom at xviijᵈ yᵉ parish.'[17] A year later in 1649 it was described as 'according to yᵉ auncient custome.'[18]

In reality the provision of the 1585 statute prohibiting the payment of election expenses had never been enforced. The now time-honoured custom of dinner after the meetings of the Wardens and Assistants goes back at least as far as 1577 when

[12] RBT, MS 1175.
[13] RBT, The Yearlie Elections, f. 98v.
[14] RBT, Wardens Accounts, VIII, f. 316v.
[15] Ibid., VI, f. 92v.

[16] Collection of Statutes, 12.
[17] RBT, Wardens Accounts, IX, f. 275.
[18] Ibid., f. 318v.

the following item appears in the accounts: 'Paid the xvij[th] of Aprill 1577 for a dynner for the Wardens and assistauntes of the said Brydge assembled at Rochester aforesaid for the election of newe wardennes of the same Brydge and for their horse meate – ljs vd.'[19] Unabated by the passage of the 1585 statute, the custom of providing dinner and expenses on election day eventually came to include not only the bridge wardens and assistant wardens, but also their servants, the bridge workmen, and the householders attending the election. In 1640, for example, the following list of election expenses appears in the wardens' accounts:[20]

In primis paied to Mr Philpott for 13 ordinaries for the gentlemen at 5s a peece	iij[li]	v[s]	oo
Item paied for 23 ordinaries for the Servantes at xviij[d] a peece	j[li]	xiiij[s]	vj[d]
Item paied for Wyne	j[li]	iij[s]	vj[d]
Item paied for fyer	oo	j[s]	viij[d]
Item paied for Tobaco	oo	j[s]	vj[d]
Item paied for paper	oo	oo	iiij[d]
Item paied for bread and beere before dynner and after	oo	iij[s]	viij[d]
Item paied for horsemeate	oo	xvij[s]	x[d]
Item paied for Mr Marsham Mr Barnham and Mr Duke for their supper over night	j[li]	xvj[s]	xj[d]
Item given to the Oastler	oo	j[s]	oo
Item paied to the Carpenters and Lightermen for their dynners at xij[d] a peece being of them 8	oo	viij[s]	oo
Item given at the Election for the Apparance of 25 Parrishes that cam to giue their voyces at xviij[d] the parishe	j[li]	xvij[s]	vj[d]

In all the bridge wardens spent £11 11s. 5d. on election expenses that year. Whether through incentives like these or through the threat of distress and sale of property, however, the Wardens and Commonalty did in the end manage to assemble sufficient representation to conduct with reasonable success the annual election of two wardens and twelve assistant wardens until the reform of the election procedure in 1908.

Having established a firm power base, the bridge wardens then tackled the problem of administrative disarray. While the three Elizabethan commissions had investigated, deliberated, and legislated, the day-to-day supervision of the bridge had been left to the subordinate officers elected by the 1561 commission: John Watts, paymaster; John Wilkins, receiver; Thomas Culpeper, purveyor; and Gilbert Hyde, auditor, whose last assignment before being replaced in 1577 by the four auditors elected annually by the commonalty was to sort out the tangled accounts

[19] Ibid., I, f. 16.   [20] Ibid., VIII, f. 314v.

of John Wilkins, who had died in 1575 still owing the bridge wardens £518. In 1576 Richard Harlowe, jurat and mayor of Rochester, was appointed receiver and paymaster at a salary of £8, followed by Philip Symonson in 1593, Hugh Southerne in 1599, James Catlett in 1620, William Somer in 1632, John Atkins in 1645, and Matthew Inwood in 1657. Initially the bridge wardens also employed a clerk – Thomas Farall in 1575, John Springfeelde in 1580, and William Beane in 1584 – at an annual wage of forty shillings to write out the accounts. In 1603, however, the positions of paymaster and clerk were combined, and other duties were gradually added. In 1660, for example, Matthew Inwood received £10 for acting as Bridge Clerk, £4 as paymaster, £2 13s. 4d. as wood reeve of the bridge woods, and £4 as overseer of the carpenters, masons, and lightermen. The other chief officer was a master carpenter. At first the bridge wardens relied on the officers of London Bridge, paying Thomas Harper £20 annually for his advice. Beginning in 1584, however, the bridge wardens employed their own master carpenter William Haywoode, followed by William Sherland in 1589, Elias Blackett in 1600, Robert Cozens in 1620, and Nathaniel Franke in 1627.[21]

Unlike the absentee bridge wardens of the mid-sixteenth century, however, the newly elected Wardens and Assistants did not leave the administration of the bridge to the bridge officers. The 1576 statute provided for the election of two wardens, twelve assistant wardens, and four auditors, and at the first election on 2 May 1576 the new administrative system began to function. Seven members of the first court of Wardens and Assistants had previously served on the Elizabethan commissions: Thomas Wotton of Boughton Malherbe; Nicholas Barham, town recorder of Maidstone; Warham St Leger of Leeds Castle; Thomas Fane of Lynton; William Lovelace of Canterbury; and former bridge wardens William, Lord Cobham and Henry, Lord Abergavenny of Birling Manor. The remaining assistants included Thomas Lovelace, Thomas Watton, Sir Thomas Fludd of Milgate in Bearsted, George Catlyn of West Malling, and Henry Brokhull of Aldington beside Thurnham. Sir James Fitzjames of West Malling and Sir Thomas Fane of Baddeshill were elected wardens, and Lords Abergavenny and Cobham, Thomas Wotton, and Thomas Fludd were elected auditors.[22]

Beginning with this first election the Wardens and Assistants were drawn from a closely knit group of established county families. Of the 100 bridge wardens and assistant wardens elected between 1576 and 1660, one-half came from just twenty families including two Botelers, two Coppingers, two Fludds, two Hales, two Lennards, two Lovelaces, two Levesons, two Painters, three Barnhams, three Cobhams, four Culpepers, and four Sedleys. Often son followed father in an unbroken line of succession. Sir Thomas Walsingham (1615–1630) of Scadbury, for example, was succeeded by his son Sir Thomas Walsingham (1630–1658). Robert Bing (1594–1595) of Wrotham was followed by his son George Bing

---

21 Ibid., I, ff. 26v, 27v, 40v, 51r; ibid., X, f. 305v; The Yearelie Elections, ff. 50v, 54r, 60v, 61v, 79v, 87r.

22 RBT, The Yearelie Elections, f. 42r.

(1596–1616) and his grandson George Bing (1619–1624). Sir Peter Manwood (1598–1621) of Hackington-next-Canterbury followed his father Sir Roger Manwood (1578–92). Peter Bucke (1602–1627) of Eastgate House in Rochester was followed by his son Peter Bucke (1628–54) making an unbroken tenure of 53 years, and Thomas Duke (1587–1605) was followed by his son Edward Duke (1606–1637) and his grandson George Duke (1638–1660) for a combined tenure of 74 years. In other families, as in the Fanes of Tudeley and Mereworth, several members served simultaneously. Sir Thomas Fane (1576–1588) and his brother Thomas Fane MP (1576–1593) both sat on the original court of Wardens and Assistants, followed by the two sons of the former, Sir Francis Fane, 1st Earl of Westmorland (1601–1628) and Sir George Fane (1613–40), and his grandson Sir Mildmay Fane, 2nd Earl of Westmorland (1625–1649).[23]

Even more of the Wardens and Assistants were related by marriage. The Fanes, who contributed five court members over three generations, were related by marriage to the Botelers of Teston, to the Culpepers of Bedgebury, and more significantly to the Nevilles of Birling through the marriage of Sir Thomas Fane (1576–1588) and Mary, daughter of Henry Neville, Lord Abergavenny (1560–1586) through whom the titles of Lord Despencer and Baron Burghersh, as well as the castle and manor of Mereworth, passed to the Fane family. Henry, Lord Abergavenny (1560–1586), in turn, was son of George, Lord Abergavenny (1506–1535), brother-in-law of Sir Warham St Leger (1576), who married his sister Ursula Neville, and brother-in-law of William, Lord Cobham (1559–1597), who married his sister Dorothy Neville. The Lords Cobham had their own dynasty of bridge wardens descending through Sir George Brooke (1535–1559), Sir William Brooke (1559–1597), Sir Henry Brooke (1597–1603), his brother-in-law Thomas Coppinger (1577–1578), and Sir William Brooke (1625–1643). Altogether thirteen members of these three families served as bridge wardens and assistant wardens during the sixteenth and early seventeenth centuries.[24]

Similar marital ties connected other wardens and assistant wardens. The Levesons of Halling, the Harts of Lullingstone, and the Walsinghams of Scadbury were all related by marriage to the Manwoods of Hackington. Margaret, daughter of Sir Roger Manwood (1578–1592), married Sir John Leveson (1586–1614); Anne, a second daughter of Sir Roger Manwood, married Sir Percival Hart (1596–1598, 1617–1637); and Sir Roger's son Sir Peter Manwood (1598–1621) married Frances, sister of Sir Percival Hart to doubly unite the two families. Their daughter Elizabeth, in turn, married Sir Thomas Walsingham (1631–1658), son of Sir

---

23 Records of the tenure of the Wardens and Assistants have been compiled from 'The Yearlie Elections' and from the wardens roll begun by William Lambarde in 1585. See also *The House of Commons 1558–1603*, s.v. 'Byng, George'; ibid., s.v. 'Byng, Robert'; ibid., s.v. 'Manwood, Peter'; ibid., s.v. 'Manwood, Roger'; ibid., 'Fane, Francis'; ibid., s.v. 'Fane, George'; ibid., s.v. 'Fane, Thomas'.

24 *Burke's Peerage, Baronetage, and Knightage*, 105th edn (1970), s.v. 'Abergavenny'; ibid., s.v. 'Cobham'; ibid., s.v. 'Westmoreland'; *Dictionary of National Biography*, s.v. 'Fane, Sir Thomas'; ibid., s.v. 'St. Leger, Sir Warham'; ibid., s.v. 'Brooke, Henry'.

Figure 8

Family ties between the Fanes, Nevilles and Brookes

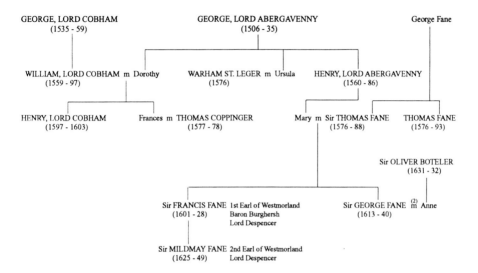

Thomas Walsingham (1615–1630). The Barnhams of Hollingbourne and Boughton Monchelsea – another family dynasty composed of Martin Barnham (1589–1595), his son Francis Barnham (1629–30) and his grandson Robert Barnham (1633–1644) – were related both to the Lennards of Chevening through the marriage of Francis Barnham to Elizabeth, daughter of Sampson Lennard (1602–1603), and to the Honywoods of Pett's Court in the parish of Charing through the marriage of Francis Barnham's sister Alice to Robert Honywood, parents of warden Sir Robert Honywood (1654–1660). Often a son-in-law of one of the wardens or assistants was appointed, such as George Bing (1596–1616), who married the daughter of William Cromer (1578–1598), or Sir Edward Hales, Bart. (1621–1643), who married the daughter of Thomas Wotton (1576–1586). Kentish historian William Lambarde (1581–1601) was both son-in-law of George Multon (1579) through his first marriage and stepfather of Sir Maximilian Dalyson (1604–1631) through his second marriage.[25]

This same closely knit group of county gentry and nobility filled numerous county and national offices during the late sixteenth and early seventeenth centuries. Many wardens and assistant wardens were active county officials. Nicholas

25 *The House of Commons 1558–1603*, s.v. 'Leveson, John'; ibid., s.v. 'Hart, Percival'; ibid., 'Byng, George'; ibid., 'Cromer, William'; *Dictionary of National Biography*, s.v. 'Walsingham, Sir Thomas'; ibid., 'Manwood, Sir Roger'; ibid., 'Manwood, Sir Peter'; ibid., 'Barnham, Sir Francis'; ibid., 'Honywood, Sir Robert'; ibid., s.v. 'Hales, Sir Edward'; ibid., 'Lambarde, William'; Frederick Francis Smith, comp. *Rochester in Parliament* (1933), 109.

Barham of Barham Court in Teston acted as town clerk and recorder of Maidstone, Roger Manwood as recorder of Sandwich; John Parker as recorder of Gravesend, and Henry Clerke as recorder of Rochester. Fourteen of the Elizabethan wardens and assistant wardens were appointed justices of the peace, and nine served as sheriff of the county. William Lovelace was a justice of assize for Kent, and ecclesiastical lawyer William Lewin, LLD, held the posts of judge of the prerogative court of Canterbury and chancellor of Rochester.

The high profile of the Wardens and Assistants in community and county affairs inevitably attracted new duties. In 1593, for example, the Wardens and Commonalty of Rochester Bridge were made party to the indenture quadripartite between Thomas Pagitt and Marian his wife, late widow of Richard Watts, the Dean and Chapter of Rochester Cathedral, the mayor and aldermen of Rochester, and the bridge wardens for the administration of the Richard Watts Charity in Rochester. By this agreement the city appointed an overseer of the poor to administer the almshouses and the House for Six Poor Travelers, and either the dean or the bridge wardens annually audited the accounts.[26] In 1597, when Sir William Brooke, Lord Cobham died, bridge wardens Sir John Leveson, Thomas Fane, and William Lambarde, his executors, were directed to establish the New College of Cobham to provide lodging and 6s. 8d. monthly for twenty poor people. The 1598 statute confirming Lord Cobham's will directed 'that the wardens for the time being of Rochester Bridge, which be continually chosen of such persons as be of great estimation and credit in the county, who noe doubt will be faithfull and carefull for the due performance of soe honourable and charitable a work, should be made a body corporate as the Presidents of the New College of Cobham, and have the government of the said College' – a duty which the twentieth-century bridge wardens still perform.[27]

Other wardens and assistant wardens of the period held national offices or positions at court. Thomas Fane served as Lieutenant of Dover Castle and Deputy Warden of the Cinque Ports under William, Lord Cobham; and in 1597 Henry, Lord Cobham succeeded to his father's posts of Lord Warden of the Cinque Ports, Constable of Dover Castle, and Lord Lieutenant of Kent, positions which he held until he was imprisoned and attainted for complicity in the Raleigh conspiracy in 1603. Sir Thomas Walsingham was appointed chief keeper of the queen's wardrobe, in which role he performed in many of the court masques and entertainments; and Sir John Leveson served as gentleman of the privy chamber and member of the royal household of James I. One in three bridge wardens held knighthoods, and six were baronets. It was in Parliament, however, where the Wardens and Assistants most distinguished themselves, for 37 of the 100 Rochester Bridge wardens elected between 1576 and 1660 also sat in Parliament.[28] During the thirty years between

[26] E.J.F. Hinkley, *A History of the Richard Watts Charity*, Rochester 1979, 121–35.

[27] An Act for the Establishment of the New Colledge of the poore at Cobham in the County of Kent, 39 Elizabeth, cap. 32; A.A. Arnold, 'Cobham College,' *Archaeologia Cantiana*, xxvii (1905), 64–109.

[28] P.W. Hasler, *The House of Commons 1558–1603*, London, 1981, i, 392, 495, 511, 524, 562–3, 578–9; ii, 102–4, 143–4, 265, 460–2, 464, 467–8, 491–3; iii, 14–17, 122; Frederick Francis Smith, *Rochester in Parliament 1295–1933*, London 1933, 96–118; J.M. Russell, *The History of*

1590 and 1620 seven or eight out of the two wardens and twelve assistants elected in any given year were either present or former members of Parliament.

Table 19

Rochester Bridge Wardens and Assistants in Parliament, 1555–1660

1555

Robert Bing	Steyning
William Brooke	Rochester
Roger Manwood	Hastings

1557–1558

Roger Manwood	Sandwich

1558–1559

Robert Bing	Abingdon
Roger Manwood	Sandwich

1562–1563

Nicholas Barham	Maidstone
William Lovelace	Canterbury
Roger Manwood	Sandwich

1571

George Catlyn	Rochester
William Cromer	Hythe
Sampson Lennard	Dunheved
William Lovelace	Canterbury
Roger Manwood	Sandwich

1572

George Catlyn	Rochester
William Lovelace	Canterbury
Roger Manwood	Sandwich

1584

George Bing	Rochester
Sampson Lennard	Bramber
John Leveson	Bossiney

1586

Sampson Lennard	St Mawes
William Lewin	Rochester

1588–1589

Henry Brooke	Kent
Thomas Fane	Dover
Sampson Lennard	Christchurch
William Lewin	Rochester
Peter Manwood	Sandwich
Edward Neville	New Windsor

Maidstone, 1881 rptd. 1978, 409; J. Cave-Browne, 'Knights of the Shire for Kent from AD 1275 to AD 1831,' *Archaeologia Cantiana*, xxi (1895), 198–243.

1592–1593

Henry Brooke	Hedon
Levin Buffkyn	Maidstone
Thomas Fane	Dover
Thomas Fludd	Maidstone
Sampson Lennard	St Germans
William Lewin	Rochester
Peter Manwood	Sandwich

1597

Thomas Fane	Dover
Thomas Fludd	Maidstone
Percival Hart	Kent
Sampson Lennard	Rye
John Leveson	Maidstone
Peter Manwood	Sandwich
Thomas Walsingham	Rochester

1601

Francis Fane	Kent
George Fane	Dover
Thomas Fludd	Maidstone
Percival Hart	Lewes
Sampson Lennard	Liskeard
John Leveson	Maidstone
Peter Manwood	Sandwich
Thomas Walsingham	Rochester

1603–1604

Francis Barnham	Grampound
George Bing	Dover
Francis Fane	Maidstone
George Fane	Sandwich
John Leveson	Kent
Peter Manwood	Saltash
John Scott	Kent
Thomas Walsingham	Rochester

1614

Francis Barnham	Grampound
Francis Fane	Maidstone
George Fane	Dover
Sampson Lennard	Sussex
Peter Manwood	Kent
Thomas Walsingham	Kent
Thomas Walsingham, Jr	Poole

1620–1621

Francis Barnham	Maidstone
Henry Clerke	Rochester
Francis Fane	Maidstone
George Fane	Kent
Peter Manwood	New Romney
Thomas Walsingham, Jr	Rochester

1623–1624

Francis Barnham	Maidstone
Maximiliam Dalyson	Rochester
Francis Fane	Peterborough
George Fane	Maidstone
Thomas Walsingham, Jr	Rochester

1625

Henry Clerke	Rochester
Mildmay Fane	Kent
Thomas Walsingham, Jr	Rochester

1625–1626

Francis Barnham	Maidstone
Henry Clerke	Rochester
George Fane	Maidstone
Edward Hales	Kent
Thomas Walsingham, Jr.	Rochester

1627–1628

Francis Barnham	Maidstone
William Brooke	Rochester
Thomas Culpeper	Tewkesbury
George Fane	Maidstone
Thomas Walsingham, Jr	Rochester

1640 (short)

Francis Barnham	Maidstone
George Fane	Maidstone
Thomas Walsingham, Jr	Rochester

1640 (long)

Francis Barnham	Maidstone
Edward Hales	Queenborough
Richard Lee	Rochester
Augustine Skinner	Kent
Thomas Walsingham, Jr	Rochester

1653

John Parker	Rochester

1654

Richard Beale	Kent
William James	Kent
John Parker	Rochester
Augustine Skinner	Kent
Ralph Weldon	Kent

1656

John Parker	Rochester

1658–1659

William James	Kent
Thomas Style	Kent

	1659	
William James		Kent
Thomas Style		Kent
	1660	
Robert Barnham		Maidstone
John Marsham		Rochester

The collective leadership of these bridge wardens, each serving for an average of twelve years, gradually transformed the administration of Rochester Bridge. Under the influence of William Lambarde, Kentish historian and keeper of records in the Tower, proper record keeping was organised. The unbroken series of wardens' accounts, the register of the yearly election of the officers ('the whyte lidgier booke'), and the register of leases ('the redd ligier booke') all began in 1576; and in the same year Henry, Lord Abergavenny presented to the bridge wardens a new common seal, made of silver, 'to be vsed about the affayres of the said Brydge.' The first annual inventory of timber, tools, and supplies, entitled 'A true note of all suche thinges as in the daye of exhibiting this Accompt doe apperteyne vnto the Bridge of Rochester' was presented to the Whitsun meeting on 22 May 1578.[29] In 1585 bridge wardens William Lambarde and Sir Roger Manwood began the wardens' roll, a series of parchment membranes stitched end to end and measuring some 32 feet in length, which lists the names of the Wardens and Assistants, receipts, expenses, and balance year by year from 1576 to 1908. In 1590 a new chest was purchased to keep the bridge records, replacing the old chest built in 1557;[30] and between July and September 1585 the first Bridge Chamber was constructed, comprising the upper storey of a newly built house adjoining the old chapel on the north.[31] This audit chamber, which featured a stained glass window of Normandy glass displaying the arms of Queen Elizabeth, was replaced in 1627 with a new audit chamber costing £101 4s. 5d. ob. and furnished with tables, two red leather chairs, and twelve stools for the meetings of the Wardens and Assistants.[32] On the walls of the audit chamber were hung three wooden boards or tables prominently displaying the 'Advertisements of good Orders' or rules for administering the bridge estate.

First devised in 1585 by Sir Roger Manwood and William Lambarde, these 'Advertisements of good Orders' were faithfully copied year by year into the annual account book, and additional orders were added from time to time. The first order required that all evidences of the bridge estate be copied verbatim 'to avoyd the often handeling of the Originals themselues, and the daunger of breakinge

[29] RBT, Wardens Accounts, i, ff. 16r, 28v.
[30] RBT, paymaster's accounts, 1557–1558, ff. 11v, 16r; ibid., Wardens Accounts, ii, f. 333r.
[31] RBT, Wardens Accounts, ii, ff. 68v–86v.
[32] RBT, Wardens Accounts, ii, f. 149r–v; vii, ff. 72r–73r.

Seales, and the losse, or defacement of them.'[33] Through the industry of William Lambarde over the next decade, these documents were gathered or exemplified from originals in the Tower and transcribed into 'the blacke lidgier booke' entitled 'A Kalendar of the Evidences of Rochester bridge hitherto discovered & copyed into the blacke lidgier booke of the said Bridge, remaynïng in the Closett of the Bridge Chamber 10 Iunii 1595 et 37 Elizabethe Regine, Sir Thomas Flud Knight and Wm Lambard Esquiour then being Bridge Wardens there.' The second order required that all leases not yet registered in 'the redd ligier booke' be called in and recorded. Other orders dealt with management of the estate, including the periodic survey of the bridge properties, particularly in London, 'that they runne not into decaye'; the keeping of the Court Baron of the bridge lands and manors at least once in every three or four years; the maintenance of the bridge woods; the recovery of any lands and rents overlooked in the 1575 survey; the recovery of rents for 'fishinges, battilage and customes vpon the water, that aunciently were payed to the bridge'; and the requirement of sureties for all new leases.

The wardens added three additional orders in 1588 and a fourth in 1589 concerning new leases. The 1576 statute had given the sitting tenants preference in the renewal of their leases, but as time went on, procedures had to be devised for the granting of leases to new tenants. Applications in writing, setting forth the arguments for the granting of a lease, were required from prospective tenants and considered on assembly days of the Wardens and Assistants. After debate on all applications, the decision would be deferred until the next assembly day when the majority vote of the Wardens and Assistants, as required by the 1576 statute, would decide the lease. Between the original application at the first assembly and the decision at the second, one of the assistants was required to survey the property for repairs.[34] Finally, no new lease could be sealed until the Bridge Clerk had first registered it in the 'redd lidgier booke.'[35] These twelve 'Advertisements of good Order', copied annually into the wardens' accounts and displayed prominently on the walls of the Bridge Chamber, served as a constant check against the mismanagement of the estate that had crippled the bridge finances in the early sixteenth century.

The sixth order – 'That some conference be had for discoverie of the right of the bridge in certaine Landes, and rentes, wherof there is no full declaration in the booke of Survey' – involved the Wardens and Assistants in considerable expense and litigation during the late sixteenth century. Where possible, the Wardens and Assistants solicited help from their tenants, even offering incentives for land recovered. The lease for Nashenden Manor in 1588, for example, required tenant William Betts to demande, levy, and account for 'sundrie Quitrents, customes, and Services due to the sayde demysed manor' which 'haue bin for the space of certaine yeares iniuriouslye witholden by suche persons as of righte and duetie ought to paie the same.'[36] The lease for the tenement, wharf, and meadows in

---

[33] Ibid., f. 112v.
[34] Ibid., f. 248v.

[35] Ibid., f. 294r.
[36] RBT, register of leases, i, f. 93v.

Dartford, granted to Giles, Lord Pawlett on 12 June 1577, contained a recovery clause allowing the tenant, if he could regain posssession, to lease for 3s. 4d. an acre any lands that 'of righte ought to belonge and apperteine to the said Bridge which at this time are withholden and deteined by other persons.'[37] The incentive worked, for an agreement signed on 23 February 1578 reveals that Lord Pawlett recovered from Nicholas Byer ten acres of fresh marsh that 'the same Nicholas Byer dothe agree he ought to holde as fermer to the Brydge of Rochester.'[38]

Other disputes were not so quickly solved. The 1575 survey of East Tilbury Manor alleged that one Richard Champion occupied a tenement and 25 acres of land thought to belong to the manor 'but he denyeth to pay eny rent for the same.' Legal proceedings began in 1597, when the bridge wardens paid £9 10s. to their tenant Isaac Gesling for 'costs and charges in Lawe in the Suite of a Comon claymed to be parcell of the manor of East Tilberie in Essex, but recovered by Richard Champion Esquior.' Over the next three years the wardens paid an additional sum of £20 before the case was concluded in April 1600.[39] Nor were all of the bridge wardens entirely cooperative. William Cromer, bridge warden from 1578 to 1598 and one of the original surveyors of the estate in 1575, involved his fellow wardens in a long-running dispute over an annual rent-charge arising from three hundred acres of marsh on the Isle of Sheppey. In October 1588 the wardens paid 6s. 8d. 'to a speciall messenger sent diuerse tymes to Tunstall to Mr Cromer, and into Shepey about the servinge of certaine writtes according to the appointement of my Lord chieffe baron concerning a certaine Rent charge due to Rochester bridge out of certaine landes in shepey aforesaid called Bartlemew, Nuttes & churchfield, & alsoe for certefieng the said Lord chefe baron of the serving of the said writtes at London.' Ultimately, surveyor William Cromer proved to be no match for Lord Chief Baron Sir Roger Manwood, however, for the 1592–1593 accounts record receipts from William Cromer of £12 for nine years of rent arrears and £26 13s. 4d. for 'expenses in lawe layde out in the behalfe of the said bridge concerning a certaine suite betweene him the said Wm Cromer esquior and the wardens of the sayde Bridge.'[40]

In 1589 the bridge wardens even solicited help from the Crown to regain control of disputed lands originally granted to the Wardens and Commonalty by John de Cobham in 1399. On 18 January 1589 Queen Elizabeth granted a commission to William Lewyn, LLD, Sir Thomas Sandys, Thomas Fane and Sir Henry Brooke to survey and enquire into certain marshland in the manor of Sherinden and the Isle of Elmeley. The outcome of this enquiry was apparently unsuccessful, but for many years the Wardens and Assistants continued to include 40 marks rent out of Sherinden and Elmeley on their annual list of 'Advertisements for certain rent concealments.'

---

[37] RBT, MS E1088.
[38] RBT, MS 3026.
[39] RBT, The book of the Survey of bridge landes 1575–1577, f. 10v; Wardens Accounts, iii, ff. 169v, 211v, 244r, 249r, 280v, 283v.
[40] RBT, Wardens Accounts, ii, ff. 228r, 411r, 411v.

To consolidate their gains in recovering the bridge estate, the Wardens and Assistants hired cartographer Philip Symonson to draw a series of estate maps. Symonson, who also served as bridge receiver and paymaster between 1593 and 1598, was paid £6 12s. 4d. in 1595 for 'plotting yᵉ manors' of Nashenden, Little Delce and East Tilbury and 20s. in 1596 for 'plotting the marshe called Eastweke marshe in the parishes of St. Maries and Halstowe.'[41] In addition to these maps the Rochester Bridge Trust archive holds maps of Langdon Manor and the Dartford estate also drawn at this time and attributed to Philip Symonson.

The careful attention to the establishing of title, granting of leases, and exercising of manorial rights long neglected steadily increased the value of the bridge estate. Surrender of the leases, following the Star-chamber ruling on 29 November 1575, and the subsequent re-letting of the property by the first elected court of Wardens and Assistants in 1576 produced a dramatic rise in revenue.

Table 20

Increase in selected rents

	1575 rent			1576 rent			% increase
	£	s	d	£	s	d	
The Crown Inn	4			8			100
Dartford	4	13	4	11	17	6	160
East Tilbury Manor	13	15	4	25			82
Langdon Manor	10			25			150
Little Delce Manor	6	13	4	16	5	8	144
Nashenden Manor	10			30			200
Rose Court Manor	7			24	11	4	250
Average increase:							155

Source: RBT, Register of Leases, vol. i.

Unfortunately, comparison of total rental income for these two years is not possible due to the accumulated amount of rent arrears and the large number of properties held without lease before the 1576 statute came into effect. The comparison of new leases on selected properties with the rental value established in the 1575 survey, however, indicates that most rent increases varied between 100 per cent and 200 per cent. One property, Rose Court Manor, formerly leased to the late receiver of revenue John Wilkins and in 1576 leased to Sir Roger Manwood who had married Wilkins' widow, increased 250 per cent. Overall, the rent increases averaged 155 per cent on the properties in Table 20.

[41] Ibid., iii, ff. 92r, 169v.

Over the next seventy-five years rental income continued to rise. Table 21 shows the rents on the same selected properties in Essex and Kent checked at twenty-five-year intervals in 1575, 1600, 1625, and 1650. Rent increases between 1575 and 1650 vary between 200 per cent on Little Delce Manor in the parish of St Margaret's, Rochester and 471 per cent on Rose Court Manor in the Isle of Grain. The average rent increase on these properties during the period amounted to 295 per cent.

Table 21
Rent increases on selected properties, 1575–1650

	1575			1600			1625			1650			% increase
	£	s	d	£	s	d	£	s	d	£	s	d	
Crown Inn	4			8			8	10		15	3	4	279
Dartford	4	13	4	15			15	10		17			272
East Tilbury	13	15	4	30			42			46			224
Langdon Manor	10			30			40			47			370
Little Delce	6	13	4	18	5	8	18	10		20			200
Nashenden	10			32			32			36			260
Rose Court	7			25			25	10		40			471
Average increase between 1575 and 1650:													295

Sources: RBT, 1575 Survey; Wardens' Accounts, iii, ff. 336r–338r; ibid., vi, ff. 309r–311r; ibid., x, ff. 25r–26v.

Total rental income for the seventy-five-year period, led by sharp increases in the London and Rochester rents, rose even more dramatically as shown in Fig. 9 below. Essex and Kent rents, excluding Rochester, yielded £56 13s. 8d. in the 1575 survey. This figure had climbed to £164 3s. 7d. ob. by 1600, £190 12s. 7d. by 1625, and £220 17s. 10d. by 1650, representing an increase of 288 per cent. Special attention to the London properties in the 'Advertisements of good Order' produced an even higher rate of increase in the London rents. Rental income from all London properties amounted to £22 8s. 8d. according to the 1575 survey. By 1600 the London rents had risen to £51 8d.; by 1625, to £66 6s. 8d.; and by 1650, to £108 6s. 8d., making a total increase of 383 per cent. Rochester rents rose highest of all. From £10 19s. 6d. in 1575, rental income in Rochester swelled to £34 1s. in 1600, to £44 10s. 4d. in 1625, and to £63 10s. in 1650, producing during the period an increase of 478 per cent. Proportionally, rents from the farms and manors in Kent and Essex represented 63 per cent of the total income in 1575, London rents 25 per cent, and Rochester rents 12 per cent. By 1650, farm income had dropped to 56 per cent of the total, while London rents climbed to 28 per cent and Rochester rents to 16 per cent.

Figure 9

Rental income on all properties, 1575–1650

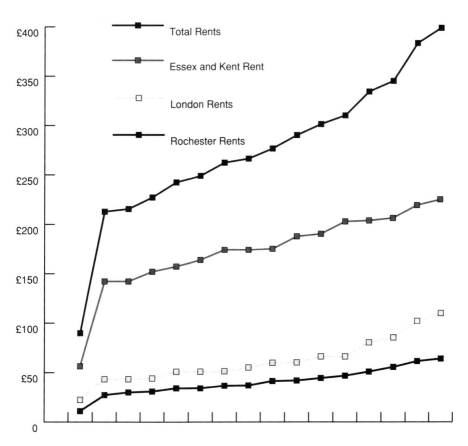

Source: RBT, 1575 Survey; Wardens Accounts, i, ff. 53v–56r; ii, ff. 107v–111v, 341–345r; iii, ff. 137–139v, 336r–338r; iv, ff. 156–158; v, ff. 21–23r, 249–251v; vi; ff.97–99r, 309–311r; vii, 231–233r, viii, ff. 130–132r, 373–375r; ix, ff. 190–193v; x, ff. 25r–26v.

Much of the growth in rental income resulted from the surrender of leases in 1575 and the re-letting of properties at realistic values. Between 1575 and 1580, for example, total rental income increased 135 per cent from £90 7s. 6d. to £212 11s. 6d. Nevertheless, during the next seventy years rental income continued to climb steadily to £249 5s. 3d. in 1600, £301 9s. 7d. in 1625, and £393 4s. 6d. in 1650, making an overall increase of 336 per cent.

Furthermore, this increase in rent revenue represented a significant increase in real income for the bridge wardens. During the same period, wages for the master carpenter rose 50 per cent from 16d. per day in 1575 to 24d. per day in 1650. Wages for

Figure 10

Percentage increase of rental income and costs, 1575–1650

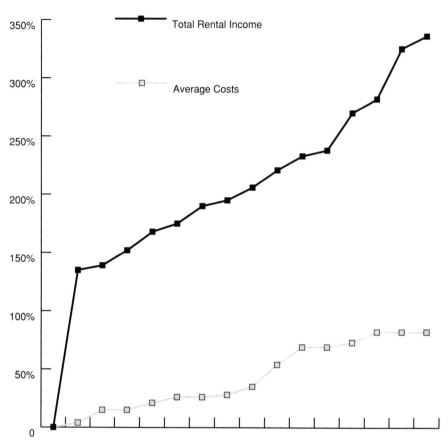

labourers rose 100 per cent from 8d. to 16d., for masons 83 per cent from 12d. to 22d., and for a sawyer and his mate 33 per cent from 24d. in 1575 to 32d. in 1650. For a team and driver to carry chalk from Frindsbury, the bridge wardens paid 3s. per load in 1580, compared with 5s. 4d. in 1650 – an increase of 77 per cent. Even provisions subject to high inflation, such as the frequent purchase of elm timber for piles, rose only 150 per cent from 8s. per tonne in 1575 to 20s. in 1650. Fig. 10 shows the average percentage increase at five-year intervals for the above wages and supplies compared with the percentage increase in total rental income. Between 1575 and 1580, when rental income increased 135 per cent, average costs increased only 4 per cent. By 1600, rental income had increased 175 per cent over 1575; average costs had increased only 26 per cent. By 1625, rental income had increased 233 per cent; average costs had increased only 69 per cent. Altogether during the seventy-five years from 1575 to 1650 rental income increased 336 per cent and average costs just 82 per cent.[42]

The steadily increasing revenue from the estate, coupled with the much lower inflation in wages and building costs, gradually placed the Wardens and Assistants in a secure financial position. Neither financial security nor even financial solvency came immediately, however, in spite of the best efforts of the Wardens and Assistants to improve the estate after the 1576 statute. Average annual expenses for repair and maintenance of the bridge between 1576 and 1650 equalled £294 4s. 8d. For the same period average revenue from rents equalled only £281 10s. 6d. This imbalance between revenue and expense repeatedly left the bridge wardens tottering on the brink of deficit spending. During one year in five between 1576 and 1650 the annual surplus fell below £50, and six times the bridge wardens' accounts carried a deficit into the next financial year.

At first the problem was masked by the bridge wardens' success in collecting arrears owed to the bridge by past bridge officers and tenants. When John Wilkins, receiver of revenue, died in 1575, he still owed the bridge wardens not only for the tax levied throughout the county in 1561, but also for the toll collected between 1557 and 1561. In 1576 the accounts include the receipt of £366 from the late John Wilkins and Elizabeth his widow, and a second instalment amounting to £151 19s. 2d. was forthcoming in 1577.[43] In the same year bridge wardens Thomas Wotton and Thomas Hendley collected £19 0s. 7d. ob. from Thomas Culpeper, former purveyor of materials during the 1561 commission, and £7 10s. from the widow of Robert Seathe 'in parte of payment of xv[li] x[s] iij[d] q. due vpon the foote of an accompte made by the said Robert Seathe one of the Collectoures of a ffyfteene (towarde the Reparations of the said Brydge) by hym levyed within the Lathe of saynte Augustines.'[44] These receipts, together with the successful collection of rent arrears in 1577, swelled the total receipts to £453 3s. in 1576 and £478 16s. 2d. in 1577 – sums not equalled for the next 25 years.

During the ten years following the 1576 statute, however, the cost of repairs remained high; and in spite of the initial dramatic rise in rents, revenue remained low. Average annual maintenance expenses between 1576 and 1585 totaled £288 2s. 2d., while average revenue from rents yielded only £209 0s. 3d., leaving an average annual shortfall of £79 1s. 11d. During 1576 alone extensive repairs amounted to £458 8s. 3d. As the expense of repairs steadily eroded the arrears collected from John Wilkins, the annual surplus dropped from £228 in 1578 to £219 in 1579, £180 in 1580, £76 in 1581, £28 in 1582, and £19 in 1583.[45]

To augment the shrinking surplus, the bridge wardens first resorted to policies practiced by their mediaeval predecessors: the solicitation of gifts and the

---

42 These statistics compare favourably with the research of E.H. Phelps Brown and Sheila V. Hopkins, 'Seven Centuries of Building Wages,' in *Essays in Economic History*, ed. E.M. Carus-Wilson, ii (1962), 172, who found that wages of building craftsmen and labourers in Southern England rose 70 per cent between 1575 and 1650.

43 RBT, Wardens Accounts, i, ff. 4r, 17v.

44 Ibid., f. 17v.

45 Ibid., ff. 40v, 51r, 64v, 76v, 88r, 98r.

collection of fines. Many of these gifts came through the efforts of Thomas Wotton, and others came directly from bridge wardens Thomas Hendley, Thomas Fludd, and William Lewyn.[46] In 1581, for example, the wardens received £4 'towarde the reparations of the said Brydge' from John Yong, Bishop of Rochester; and in 1582, when the surplus sank to £28, the wardens received a further gift of £4 from the dean and prebendaries of Rochester Cathedral and £20 from the dean and prebendaries of Canterbury Cathedral.[47] In 1583, when the surplus dropped to £19, only the receipt of gifts totaling £50 kept the accounts in the black. In 1584, additional gifts amounting to £45, combined with £49 2s. 8d. realised from the sale of the lead roof of the house dismantled to make way for the audit chamber, produced a short-lived surplus – the first increase in seven years.[48] With the extra expense of constructing and furnishing the Bridge Chamber, however, the temporary surplus plunged from £71 7s. 8d. in 1584 to a deficit of £58 15s. 6d. in 1585.[49] That year Junior Warden William Lambarde reached into his own pocket to lend the bridge £40 'to be imployed vpon necessarie causes of repayring the sayde bridge.'[50]

In addition to soliciting gifts, the bridge wardens also benefitted from fines levied by bridge warden Dr. William Lewyn, judge of the prerogative court of Canterbury and chancellor of Rochester, just as earlier in the century Archbishop Warham had made Rochester Bridge the beneficiary of fines levied during his visitation of the Diocese of Canterbury in 1511. In 1582 the wardens received 20s. from William Cole of the parish of St. Mary's, Hoo "in redemption and release of corporall punishement for a lewde offence likelye to be imposed vpon hym, towarde the reparations of the same Brydge," and in the following year £6 13s. 4d. in fines from similar offences was awarded to the bridge after the solicitation of Senior Warden Thomas Wotton, Junior Warden Henry Brockehill, and John Sommer.[51]

These methods of raising revenue, however, could not support the bridge indefinitely, and the bridge wardens looked toward a new source of income: taxation. The 1576 statute had permitted taxation of the commonalty, or contributory lands, 'at such tyme and tymes onely, as the Rents or other profytts of the Landes proper and belonginge to the sayde Brydge, from tyme to tyme dewe and payable to the wardens and Commonaltye of the sayde Brydge, shall not be suffycient to accomplyshe the repayer and mayntenans of the sayde Brydge.'[52] Although the 1576 statute allowed taxation of the commonalty to meet the annual deficits, it did not expressly state who should levy the tax or how the tax would be collected. Without clear authority the Wardens and Assistants hesitated to proceed. The preamble of the 1585 statute stated the problem precisely: 'Yet for want of (expresse) woords, lymyting, that the saide Wardens and Assistants shoulde taxe the saide contributorie Lands in suche case of wante, as aforesaide, the same Wardens and

[46] Ibid., i, ff. 67v, 79r, 91r; ii, f. 2v.
[47] Ibid., i, ff 67v, 79r.
[48] Ibid., i, ff. 90v–91r; ii, ff. 2v–3r.
[49] Ibid., ii, f. 62v.

[50] Ibid., ii, f. 35v.
[51] Ibid., i, ff. 79v, 91v.
[52] Collection of Statutes, 11.

Assistaunts hetherto have bene dowbtfull, and have forborne to make suche Taxe, and therebie have bene forced, upon theire owne credites and frendshipps, to procure the wante aforesaide to be supplied by some benevolent Loanes and Gifts of sondry Persons; a matter very difficulte, and not to be trusted upon for perpetuall mayntenance of the saide Bridge.'[53] To clarify the uncertainty, the 1585 statute authorised the Wardens and Assistants, assembled at the accustomed place of election, to levy a bridge rate on the parishes forming the commonalty. The statute also added enforcement powers. If a parish did not pay the rate, the bridge wardens were authorised to seize and sell the goods and chattels of any landowner in the parish.

To facilitate collection of the tax, the bridge wardens proceeded to reorganise the commonalty. From ancient times each parish or group of parishes in the commonalty had been responsible for a particular arch or pier of the bridge and had been taxed only if that pier needed repair. In 1585, however, the Wardens and Assistants voted to divide the commonalty into four, three, or two divisions to bear proportionally any surcharge levied on the commonalty. After extensive consultation throughout the following year, on 26 April 1587, when the surplus for the year had dropped to a dangerous low of £6 17s. 1d., the following three divisions were established:[54]

1. Borstall, Cuxton and the rest limited to the first arche
   Wrotham and the rest limited to the fyveth arche
   Gillingham & the rest limited to the second arche
   Northflete, Cliff, and the rest limited to the nyneth arche

2. Hooe and the rest limited to the Seventh & eight Arches
   Halling and the rest limited to the third arche
   Burham, Wouldham and the rest limited to the fourthe arche

3. Boxley, Eyhorne, Lenham and the rest limited to the sixth arche

Each group of parishes henceforth would bear responsibility for one-third of any surcharge required to balance the accounts and maintain the bridge.

In the event, however, no tax was ever levied. After the first difficult decade, rent revenue gradually began to keep pace with expenditure for bridge maintenance and repairs. Rent arrears did cause a deficit of £19 17s. 9d. in 1593, and major repairs amounting to £555 9s. 6d. caused a further deficit in 1619, forcing the bridge wardens to borrow £17 5s. 11d. from Cobham College. These deficits, however, were clearly anomalies rather than the norm in the years before the Civil War. The average annual surplus for the remainder of the sixteenth century was £49 2s. 6d., and during the first half of the seventeenth century the average surplus was well over £100.

---

[53] Ibid., 12.
[54] RBT, The Yearlie Elections, f. 20v.

Figure 11

Average annual surplus, 1585–1660

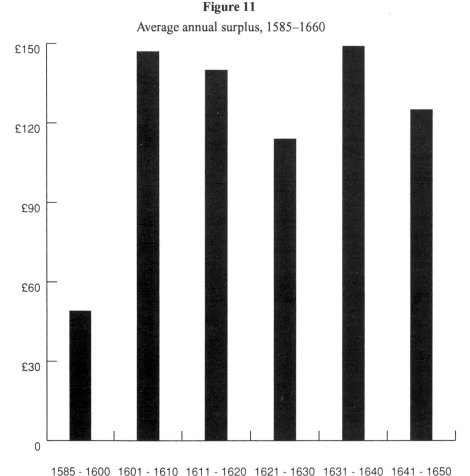

Source: RBT Wardens Accounts

Fig. 11, showing the average annual surplus decade by decade for the first half of the seventeenth century, illustrates the much improved financial position of the Wardens and Assistants. Just before the end of the Commonwealth period in 1659, furthermore, total receipts amounted to £712 14s. 6d., and total expenses equalled £338 6s. 11d., leaving after allowances for rent arrears a healthy surplus of £330 3s. 2d. – an amount almost four times higher than the entire income of the bridge before the 1576 statute. No longer did the bridge wardens need to raise revenue from charitable gifts, from taxes, or from tolls as they had done one hundred years before in order to repair and maintain the bridge.

Having solved the financial problem, the Wardens and Assistants could in turn attend to the timely repair of the bridge fabric. During the Elizabethan and

Jacobean years, as in preceding centuries, bridge maintenance demanded constant vigilance against the ravages of salt water and tide. The ten stone piers of the bridge rested on foundations called staddles, consisting of hundreds of elm piles driven into the riverbed to form platforms pointed at both ends and measuring 95 feet by 40 feet. To protect the piles from the salt water, chalk filled the spaces between the piles, and elm planks surrounded the perimeter and covered the top of each staddle. Nevertheless, between these wooden islands the swift current gouged deep gullies in the riverbed which repeatedly undermined the staddles and threatened to weaken the foundation of the stone piers and arches. To prevent potentially expensive repairs to the masonry, then, bridge workmen took annual soundings of the riverbed around and between the staddles (sounding charts survive from 1613 to the mid-nineteenth century), filled the deepest holes with chalk, and renewed defective or rotten piles and planking. Except for occasional repaving of the roadway or renewing of the drawbridge or repair of the wharves at either end of the bridge, this staddle work accounted for most of the £294 4s. 8d. expended each year on average for bridge repair and maintenance between 1576 and 1650.

The year from Pentecost 1622 to Pentecost 1623, during which the bridge wardens spent £298 18s. 5d. on maintenance and repair, most closely approximates the average expenditure and aptly illustrates the constant struggle of the bridge workmen against weather and water.[55] From 10 June to 29 November 1622 and from 3 March to 31 May 1623 the bridge wardens employed a full-time master carpenter and his mate, four lightermen to operate the bridge boat, and a general labourer named John Haggart. Each worked 210 days, no work traditionally being carried out during the inclement winter months. A sawyer and his mate and one additional carpenter were employed two-thirds time in the timberyard at the Strood end of the bridge, and one man with his team and driver were employed to dig and carry chalk at the Frindsbury quarry two or three days each month. In addition two masons were hired during September to make repairs to the land pier at Strood, and three bricklayers were hired in March to build a sundial at the Rochester end of the bridge. The master carpenter Robert Cozens earned an annual fee of £5 plus 2s. per day, his mate earned 16d. per day, the sawyer and his mate earned 2s. 8d., the lighter crew earned 14d. and the master 16d., and the chalk team earned 5s. 4d. Altogether the bridge wardens paid £138 0s. 10d. that year for labour.

On 12 June the lightermen took soundings around the point of each staddle and in the channel between each staddle. Depths ranged from 26 feet along the Strood wharf to 8 feet on the upper side of the second pier from Rochester; those registering 18 feet or more were scheduled for filling.[56] During the year the lightermen ferried 32 loads of great chalk from Frindsbury to dump in the riverbed and 13 loads of small chalk to pack in the staddles, one load of gravel for the Strood end of the highway, and ten loads of rubbish to fill holes in the timberyard and quay at Strood.

---

[55] RBT, Wardens Accounts, vi, ff. 157r–182v.
[56] RBT, Eng. C 5/8, 'The soundes of the Gullitts and points of the Stadles of Rochester Bridge taken the 12 die Iunij 1622.'

When not carrying chalk, the lightermen worked with the carpenters. From June through August they repaired the downstream side and breast of the third staddle from Strood, in September and October they moved to the upstream side and breast of the fifth staddle from Strood, in November they constructed an extension to the Strood quay, and during the spring they moved to the land staddle on the Rochester side. During high tides, when the staddles were covered with water, the carpenters occupied themselves in the timberyard making trunnels, or cylindrical oak pins, two feet in length used to fasten timbers together below the water line. During September the carpenters and lightermen used the time between the tides to remove the upper tier of planks from the drawbridge, renew the two thirty-foot bearers underneath, and replace the planks.

Staddle repair was slow work and labour intensive. On the third staddle, for example, defective piles were drawn, and 31 new piles, ranging from ten feet to eighteen feet in length and tipped with iron pile shoes, were driven into the riverbed. To drive the piles, bridge workmen used a six-man beetle, an implement that consisted of a heavy weight or head with six handles. Requiring six men to lift, the weight was then dropped onto the pile, ramming it into the riverbed. From side to side across the staddle heavy timbers called reasons were spiked on top of the piles in order to hold them vertical. Joists were then laid lengthwise on top of the reasons and fastened with stoppers driven into the piles and spiked to the joists. Around the outside of the third staddle 153 feet of new vertical binding planks were spiked to the piles, and 874 feet of binders were laid horizontally across the joists to cover the top of the staddle after spaces between the piles had been packed with two loads of small chalk. Similar repairs to the other two staddles accounted for 36 pile shoes, 314 pounds of spikes, 1585 6d. nails, 634 feet of oak timber, and almost 2000 feet of elm timber. Together with other provisions during the year – including tools and chalk baskets for the lightermen, rope, grease, tar, lime, and stone – these materials cost £154 15s. 7d.

Among the year's expenses also appear numerous repairs for the ten royal beasts mounted on the drawbridge. Four years before in July 1618, the bridge wardens had commissioned the carving of the royal beasts of James I to decorate the drawbridge: a lion, a unicorn, a buck, a greyhound, a bull, a boar, a dragon, a leopard, a talbot, and a panther.[57] During 1622, however, accidents and vandalism plagued the drawbridge, necessitating constant repairs to the heads. In June John Vidgeon was paid 4d. 'for settinge on the horns of the Booll', and John Childs received 12d. 'for makinge of a newe horne for the vnicorn & settinge yt on.'[58] In October the carver was paid 14s. 'for cutting of a newe Beast & mending of the other that was broken from the drawbridge by overthrowinge of John Clarkes

[57] RBT, Wardens Accounts, vi, ff. 5v, 7v, 12r, 14v, 15v, 44v, and 47v. S.W. Wheatley, 'Heraldic Decoration of the Drawbridge of the Medieval Bridge of Rochester,' *Archaeologia Cantiana*, lxiii (1951), 140–43, although admitting that the unicorn did not appear as a royal badge or supporter before the accession of James I, mistakenly identifies these royal beasts with Henry VIII and Jane Seymour and dates their construction between 1536 and 1537.
[58] Ibid., f. 158Av.

waggon with a load of strawe,'[59] and in November John Meller received 2d. 'for taking vpp of the beast when yt was strooke from y[e] drawbridge.'[60] In April the bridge wardens again paid 2d. 'to a pore man that brought the Buckes horn when yt was last broke of' and 4d. 'for a sockitt for the Buckes horn.'[61] Finally in May they bought two new heads, paying Philip Ward of Rochester 40s. 'for paintinge & gildinge of the two newe Beastes vppon the drawbridge.'[62]

Mending of the unicorn's horn and gilding of new beasts notwithstanding, from Pentecost 1622 to Pentecost 1623 the Wardens and Assistants did effectively administer the repair and maintenance of the bridge. Revenue that year from the bridge estate produced £294 17s. 3d., and repairs cost £298 4s. 8d., causing only a small claim of £4 14s. 9d. on the previous year's surplus of £36 7s. 4d. Two wardens and twelve assistants were elected by the commonalty gathered at Rochester Castle on 2 May 1622, and the accounts for the year were duly approved by the commonalty at the following audit assembly on 7 June 1623. One by one the problems of bridge maintenance, finances, estate management, administration, and authority – problems that had troubled Rochester Bridge for centuries – had faded into the past. The reformation of Rochester Bridge prompted by the Elizabethan statutes of 1576 and 1585 had finally established effective and efficient administration of the bridge in the years leading up to the Civil War and Commonwealth.

[59] Ibid., f. 166v.
[60] Ibid., f. 168v.

[61] Ibid., f. 173v.
[62] Ibid., f. 177v.

The Civil War and Commonwealth

The decorated drawbridge featured yet again in the history of Rochester Bridge during the royalist uprising in May 1648. Following the county assizes in early May, Kentish petitioners had solicited support for a peaceful assembly of the county at Blackheath and a march to Parliament to present their grievances. By 21 May, however, zealous Cavaliers had inflamed the royalists to revolt. Rebels seized the castles of Walmer, Deal, Sandgate, and Sandown and occupied the towns of Sandwich, Faversham, Sittingbourne, and Rochester with their ordnance and magazines. The gates at the east end of Rochester Bridge were shut, a guard was stationed, and two pieces of ordnance were mounted upon the bridge. On 30 May, the day appointed for the petitioners to assemble, the parliamentarian army comprised of four regiments of horse and three regiments of foot soldiers led by General Fairfax occupied Blackheath and on Wednesday, 31 May, began their march into Kent. One regiment under Major Gibbons headed south through the Weald to relieve the siege of Dover Castle; the main force under Fairfax crossed the Medway at East Farleigh and engaged the royalists in the battle of Maidstone on Thursday 1 June and Friday 2 June; the remaining regiment under Major Husbands marched toward Rochester to secure the bridge there.[1]

A letter from a parliamentarian eyewitness, dated 'Gravesend 2 June 1648' and published under the title 'Bloudy Newes from Kent Being a Relation of the great Fight at Rochester and Maidstone', gives the following account of the battle at Rochester Bridge on 1 June:

> Since my last, here hath hapned a great Engagement betwixt the two armies, the manner thus: The Lord Generall having entered Kent, and forced the Enemy to withdraw from Deptford, Greenwich, Blacke-Heath, and other places, they pursued them towards Rochester, where the Enemy with the greatest part of their Forces made a stand, and drew up into two distinct Bodies, and after some consultation, they resolved not to fight in the field, but to make good Rochester bridge, and the River and Foords at Maidstone, and Alsbury; this was unanimously assented to and the Kentish forces presently marched over Rochester bridg, and left as many horse and foot to defend the place, as the town could contain, and the rest of the forces marched to make good the passages at Maidstone, and other places; and in the Rivers where the horse might possibly get through, they fastned barrows, and many sharpstakes in the bottome. At Rochester they bestirred themselvs to the utmost, to make their Fortifications good; drawing up the bridge, and casting up workes where

1 See Henry Francis Abell, *Kent and the Great Civil War*, Ashford 1901, 178ff. and Alan Everitt, *The Community of Kent and the Great Rebellion 1640–60*, Leicester University Press 1973, 231–70.

need was, & planted 4 piece of Ordnance at the bridge foot: they also planted 40 of their greatest pieces upon the workes neer the River, and about the town for the defence of themselves against the army, whom they expected hourly; and upon Thursday night last, the Lord Generall with his forces drew neer the town, which gave a strong allarm to the Kentish men, but they resolved to stand to it: the army was divided into parties, some of them being designed to fall on at Maidstone, another party at Alesford, and the main body to fall on at Rochester, which they did, and fought gallantly against the Kentish-forces at Rochester bridge, the Kentishmen also stood it out stoutly, and often cryed out, hey for King Charles, this dispute lasted long, and many men were slain on both sides, it is said, about 500. some of them being persons of quality as a Colonell, a Captaine, and many others; likewise many are dangerously wounded, & it is feared, much bloud will be spilt before the bridge can be taken; this business by some is thought to be much greater then it is; for they give out, that when the Parliaments Forces were engaging at Rochester bridge that the ship called the Swallow lying above the bridg, and Rainbow lying below the bridge, charged with case-shot, discharged themselves upon the Parliaments Forces, and killed 500 of them, insomuch that the souldiery were forced to retreat; which the Kentish men perceiving, sallied out of Rochester with their whole body of horse, pursued them, took 12 piece of Ordnance, some arms, some prisoners, all their Carriages. Also they say, that Col. Burkestead, Col. Rich, and divers others are slain; but I give you this Relation not for any real truth I suppose to be in it, but that you may see the various rumours that are spread abroad, therefor you may take it rather for a report of those that would have it so, then for a certainty that it is so.[2]

Although the royalists had succesfully defended Rochester Bridge, defeat at the battle of Maidstone caused general alarm among the victorious troops at Rochester. When Fairfax marched up the east side of the River Medway and entered Rochester on Saturday, 3 June, the rebels under Lord Goring had already fled towards Gravesend where they crossed the Thames into Essex. Before leaving Rochester Bridge, however, the royalists threw the drawbridge into the river to prevent Fairfax from following them, as described in a further letter dated 'Rochester 3 June 1648.'

Yesterday we had intelligence that the Enemy went about three in the afternoon out of Rochester towards Gravesend, they broke up the bridge that no horse might passe: the Town were very glad they were gone Major *Brown* Governour of Upnor Cast. as they upon their going away overturned their carriages of their ordnance, and the women of the Town helpt to throw down the workes, they were not full 3000 that marched out of that Town.[3]

Bridge wardens' accounts for that year, verifying the military reports, include a

[2] British Library, Thomason Tracts E.445.36, Bloudy Newes from Kent Being a Relation of the great Fight at *Rochester* and *Maidstone*, betwixt the Parliaments army under the command of the Lord General *Fairfax* and the Kentish Forces commanded by Generall *Hales* . . . London, Printed for R.W. MDCXLVIII., pp. 1–3.
[3] British Library, Thomason Tracts E.446.9, Newes from Bowe . . . Also The particular Relation of the whole businesse in Kent . . . London, Printed by E.A. MDCXLVIII., p. 2.

payment of 1s. 6d. to 'two menn for saving the planckes of the draw bridge w*hich* was throwne into the River by soldiers.'[4]

The Civil War and Commonwealth also affected Rochester Bridge in less dramatic but equally significant ways. Like the rest of Kentish landowners, the Wardens and Assistants were subject to unpopular parliamentary taxes. During the thirteen years between 1644 and 1660 for which records survive, the Wardens and Assistants paid £442 10s. 5d. to their tenants in rent rebates for parliamentary taxes.[5] Combined with unusually high rent arrears resulting from the disrupted economy of the late 1640s, these rebates often produced a deficit in the annual accounts. In 1648–49, for example, when the parliamentary tax of 20d. in the pound amounted to £56 7s. 6d. and rent arrears climbed to £60 18s. 4d., the deficit plunged to £42. 14s. 1d.[6] In 1649–50, with the parliamentary tax at 21d. in the pound, rent rebates totaled £68, or 17 per cent of rent income; and in 1651–52 rent rebates, totaling £76 5s. 8d., equaled 19 per cent of rent income. Four times between 1648 and 1654 parliamentary taxes produced an annual deficit before the relatively calmer years of the later Commonwealth brought lower taxes and restored financial prosperity.[7]

In addition to economic disruption the Civil War also disturbed the closely knit community of county families that had administered Rochester Bridge since 1576. Political change in the county, dividing neighbour from neighbour and father from son, was soon reflected in the changing composition of the Wardens and Assistants. In April 1642, for example, when the Kentish gentry petitioned Parliament, bridge warden Sir William Boteler (1637–43) of Barham Court in Teston along with the Cavalier poet Richard Lovelace presented the petition to the House of Commons. For their pains both Boteler and Lovelace were imprisoned, their estates were sequestered, and at the election assembly on 2 May 1644 Boteler was voted out.[8] At the same assembly the royalists Sir Edward Hales, bart. (1621–43) of Tunstall and Sir John Marsham (1637–43) of Whorne Place in Cuxton lost their positions as bridge wardens. Hales had been imprisoned in Dover Castle for his part in the Kentish rebellion of 1643, and Marsham, who joined the king at Oxford, found his estate sequestered by Parliament and was forced to pay £356 for compounding after the surrender of the king in 1646.[9] A year later Robert Barnham (1633–44), whose royalist sympathies clashed with the parliamentarian support of his father Sir Francis Barnham (1629–30) and led to his imprisonment during the 1648 uprising, surrendered his position of bridge warden until his re-election in 1661.[10] Nor were the parliamentarians immune to the changing times. Bridge

[4] RBT, wardens' accounts, ix, f. 300v.

[5] RBT, wardens' accounts, ix, ff. 136v, 161v, 186v, 222r, 274r, 310v, 318v; x, ff. 13v, 21v–22r, 62r, 65r, 99r, 124v, 130v, 163v, 171v, 205v, 207v, 218v, 249v, 257v, 295v, 305v. For the years 1652–53, 1653–54, and 1655–56 wardens' accounts are missing.

[6] Ibid., ix, f. 321v.

[7] Ibid., x, ff. 24r, 106r, 137v,

[8] Everitt, *The Community of Kent*, 103 and *passim*.

[9] *Dictionary of National Biography*, s.v. 'Hales, Sir Edward' and 'Marsham, Sir John.'

[10] Ibid., s.v. 'Barnham, Sir Francis.'

warden Sir William Brooke (1625–43), who served under Colonel Sandys in 1642 and helped to break the altar rails in Rochester Cathedral, died of battle wounds received at Oxford in 1643.[11]

As royalists retired or were removed from the court of Wardens and Assistants, they were replaced by parliamentarians, due in large part to the political influence of Sir Anthony Weldon (1644–48), chairman of the parliamentarian Committee of Kent, and Augustin Skinner (1644–60) of East Farleigh, MP for Kent during the Long Parliament from 1640 to 1653. Sir Mildmay Fane, Earl of Westmorland (1626–49), for example, imprisoned for his part in the 1648 rebellion and his lands sequestered, was succeeded by Charles Bowles (1649–60), receiver-general for the county committee. Other new wardens and assistants, like George Newman (1640–48), Sir John Sedley, bart. (1642–48), and William James (1644–60), also served actively on the Committee of Kent. Many of the new wardens and assistants sat in Parliament during the 1650s. William James (1644–60), Richard Beale (1659–60), Augustin Skinner (1644–60), and Ralph Weldon (1649–60) all represented Kent in the parliament of 1654; William James (1644–60) and Thomas Style (1652–60) represented Kent in 1658 and 1659. Two of the older bridge wardens, Sir Thomas Walsingham (1630–58) and Richard Lee (1621–53) had represented Rochester in the Long Parliament before being replaced by militia commissioner John Parker (1649–60), who represented the city in the parliaments of 1654 and 1656. Still other bridge wardens and assistants – like Colonel Ralph Weldon who succeeded his father Sir Anthony Weldon in 1649, Colonel John Twisleton (1656–60), Major Thomas Broadnax (1656–60), and Colonel Richard Beale (1659–60) – served in the parliamentarian army.[12] So complete was the political shift during the two turbulent decades that only one bridge warden elected before the outbreak of civil war – George Duke (1638–60) – was still serving at the end of the Commonwealth in 1660. Even though members of the Duke family had served continuously as bridge wardens since 1587, however, not even George Duke survived the first election assembly after the restoration of the monarchy when on 26 April 1661 all fourteen parliamentarian wardens and assistants were replaced by royalists to usher in a new era in the history of Rochester Bridge.

11 Frederick Francis Smith, *Rochester in Parliament 1295–1933*, London 1933, 111–12.
12 Ibid., 112–15; *Dictionary of National Biography*, s.v. 'Weldon, Sir Anthony'; J. Cave-Browne, 'Knights of the Shire for Kent from AD 1275 to AD 1831,' *Archaeologia Cantiana*, xxi (1895), 234–37; Everitt, *Community of Kent*, 149–51, 153, 158–59, passim.

ROCHESTER BRIDGE
1660–1825

The Trade and Navigation of the Medway Valley

In 1802, Rochester Bridge was described as being 'situated in a populous district of a populous County and forming part of the direct communication between the Metropolis and the greater part of Europe'.[1] Seventeenth- and eighteenth-century travellers marvelled at the size and proportions of the bridge. Fiennes and Defoe had little to say about the antiquities of Rochester, but the Medway and its traffic, Rochester Bridge and Chatham Dockyard, then 'the chief arsenal of the royal navy', impressed them enormously. Defoe regarded the bridge as 'the largest, highest and the strongest built of all the bridges in England' with the exception of London Bridge, and the river and its dockyards as 'the most considerable of the kind in the world'.[2] Behind these eulogies lay the simple fact that the port of Rochester – which included the quays and dockyards of Chatham and Sheerness, and wharves in the Isle of Grain and the Hoo peninsula, as well as Rochester's town quay – was the deepest and most sheltered harbour in Kent and Sussex.[3]

The economy of the Medway towns was boosted in the later seventeenth century by the expansion of Chatham dockyard, which had risen in prominence as a result of the Anglo-Dutch wars. Economic growth in the late seventeenth and eighteenth centuries was inseparable from the growth of towns and rural-urban exchange, and in the expanding economy of the Medway towns and the Medway valley, the dominating influence developing from within the region was the expansion of Chatham and its developing naval-industrial complex.[4] The dockyard labour force grew steadily during the century after 1660, from 324 men in 1664 to 797 in 1712, reaching 1,720 in 1758.[5] Maidstone, Tonbridge and the villages of the Medway valley benefitted by the growth of the Medway towns, which provided local markets for food and raw materials, but the economic vitality of the region as a whole

---

1 RBT 520, 'Case and Brief For the Wardens and Commonalty of Rochester Bridge in support of a Bill to enable them to compleat the repairs and Improvement of that Bridge', [1802], 13.
2 C. Morris (ed.), *The Journeys of Celia Fiennes* [c.1685–1703], 1947, 122; D. Defoe, *A Tour through the Whole Island of Great Britain* [1724–6], 1974, 105.
3 J.H. Andrews, 'Geographical Aspects of the Maritime Trade of Kent and Sussex, 1650–1750', London Ph.D., 1954, 124. The normal tidal range was 18 feet and the largest merchant ships could reach Chatham on ordinary tides; vessels employed in the south-east coasting trade could be accommodated at all states of the tide (ibid., 127).
4 J. Ehrman, *The Navy in the War of William III, 1689–1697*, Cambridge 1953, 83–90; D.C. Coleman, 'Naval Dockyards under the Later Stuarts', *Economic History Review*, second series, vi (1953), 134–55; J. Presnail, *Chatham. The Story of a Dockyard Town*, Chatham 1952, passim.; A.J.F. Dulley, 'People and Homes in the Medway Towns, 1687–1783', *Archaeologia Cantiana*, lxxvii (1962), 160–176.
5 J.M. Preston, *Industrial Medway: an historical survey*, Rochester 1977, 20.

was determined largely by forces operating outside it, namely the massive pull of the London market for food, agricultural products, manufactured goods and labour.[6] During the early seventeenth century, coastwise grain imports into London amounted to around 60,000 quarters per year, of which over half normally came from Kent. Although the capital city's dependence on Kentish supplies declined during the seventeenth century, the overall size of the trade continued to grow. By 1680, London's coastwise imports amounted to 192,000 quarters at a time when Kentish ports were contributing about 60,000 quarters per year.[7] London's rate of growth slackened during the eighteenth century as provincial centres of population expanded, but it seems that the economy of Kent became even more closely integrated with that of the metropolis, reflected especially in the narrowing of wage differentials.[8]

Table 22

Population of the Medway Towns, 1676 and 1801

	1676	1801
Rochester	3,332	5,645
Chatham	3,005	10,505
Gillingham	1,500 (estimate)	4,135
Strood	767	1,172
TOTAL	8,604	21,457
Maidstone	5,000	8,027
Tonbridge	1,957	4,371
Total Kent population	150,000	307,624
of which the Medway towns comprised	5.7%	7.0%

Sources: C.W. Chalklin, 'The Compton Census of 1676', *Kent Records*, xvii (1960), 153–74; BPP, 1802, vii, 146–59. Total population for 1676 is adjusted to include children under 16, assumed to comprise 40% of the total (idem, 172).

---

[6] F.J. Fisher, 'London as an "Engine of Economic Growth" ', in J.S. Bromley, *Britain and the Netherlands*, IV, The Hague 1971, 3–16; E.A. Wrigley, 'A simple model of London's importance in changing English society and economy, 1650–1750', *Past and Present*, xxxvii (1967), 44–70; A.L. Beier, 'Engine of manufacture: the trades of London', in A.L. Beier and R. Finlay, *London 1500–1700. The making of the metropolis*, 142.

[7] F.J. Fisher, 'The Development of the London Food Market, 1540–1640', *Economic History Review*, x (1940), reprinted in E.M. Carus-Wilson, *Essays in Economic History*, London 1954, i, 136–9; J.A. Chartres, 'Food consumption and internal trade', in Beier & Finlay, op. cit., 179; Andrews, op. cit., Table 21 (unpaginated).

[8] P.J. Corfield, *The Impact of English Towns, 1700–1800*, Oxford 1982, 67; E. Gilboy, *Wages in Eighteenth Century England*, Cambridge (Mass.) 1934, 41. The inconclusive character of the evidence is emphasised by P.L. Garside, 'London and the Home Counties', in F.M.L. Thompson, *The Cambridge Social History of Britain, 1750–1950*, vol. i, *Regions and Communities*, Cambridge 1990, 473–80.

By the early eighteenth century, the Medway towns had already become a continuous urban area, connected by what contemporaries described as 'large suburbs' to the east, west and south sides of Rochester.[9] The parish registers of Chatham suggest that population grew rapidly from the 1670s to about 1710, after which it remained steady until 1750, judging from the rising level of baptisms.[10] Rochester's population seems to have been comparatively stagnant, and was probably falling during the 1730s, a period when the bridge wardens found it difficult to find tenants for urban properties and when rents were consequently declining. At the same time, local citizens also expressed concern about the extent of poverty and a major scheme was proposed to set up a rope manufactory to employ the poor, supplementing the efforts of the previous decade.[11] It was in 1726 that a new building was erected for the poor of the parish of Chatham 'who are grown numerous'.[12]

The later 1740s seem to have witnessed a recovery, when labourers' wage rates in the area rose perceptibly after a long period of stagnation. Population growth must have been rapid from the late 1780s which saw a substantial increase in the number of marriages, and of course the Medway towns benefitted substantially from the great surge of naval expenditure during the wars against France from 1792–1815.[13] There can be little doubt that this regional growth generated a sizable increase in local land traffic, including the movement of cattle and animals;[14] but it must also be remembered that national population growth produced an enormous increase in the volume of long-distance road transport in the late eighteenth and early nineteenth centuries. As Dr Chartres and Dr Turnbull have shown, the rapid expansion of passenger travel and freight haulage began well before the advent of the railway system, and passenger links between London and the south-east improved markedly between the early 1770s and the end of the century.[15] It was thus the combined growth of local and long-distance road traffic which necessitated the

---

9 *Magna Britannia Antiqua & Nova*, 6 vols, London 1738, ii, p. 1095.

10 Dulley, op. cit., 161.

11 Society of Antiquaries (Thorpe MSS), vol. 186, f. 288r. (undated, c.1734). The proposal put the annual expenditure of the existing Chatham workhouse at £383, whilst the labours of its 42 adults and 32 children raised only £35.

12 Presnail, op. cit., 156.

13 BPP 1801–02, vi, p. 138; Presnail, op. cit., 165–193; Preston, op. cit., 19.

14 The Gravesend-Rochester road was turnpiked as early as 1712, and improved in 1737. An act of 1769 laid the basis for the work of the Pavement Commissioners in Rochester and for the building of the 'New Road' from Star Lane to Chatham Hill. R. Marsh, *Rochester. The evolution of a city and its government*, Rochester 1974, 48–9; F.F. Smith, *A History of Rochester*, Rochester 1928, 424–7.

15 J.A. Chartres and G.L. Turnbull, 'Road Transport', in D. Aldcroft and M. Freeman, *Transport in the Industrial Revolution*, 64–99. Dorian Gerhold has suggested that Chartres and Turnbull have seriously exaggerated the rate of growth of road carrying services in general during this period, and that water transport came to occupy a relatively more important place than road haulage in linking the metropolis with the provinces. But Gerhold's new estimates show that the carrying trade between London and the southeast grew more rapidly than that with any other region during the eighteenth and early nineteenth centuries ('The growth of the London carrying trade, 1681–1838', *Economic History Review*, 2nd series, xli (1988), 392–410).

widening of Rochester Bridge in the late eighteenth century. In 1802, the bridge foreman Thomas Slater claimed that he had witnessed much inconvenience to passengers and many accidents during the previous decade, arising chiefly from the narrowness of the bridge.[16] The growth of river traffic, of course, created problems of a different and more complex kind, the resolution of which was to stretch the ingenuity of a succession of bridge architects and engineers.

The trade of Maidstone and the Medway valley with the Medway towns developed apace during the eighteenth century and was characterised by a complementarity of activity and function. As Defoe noticed, northeast Kent, from the Swale and Sheerness to the Medway towns, was 'embarass'd with business, and inhabited chiefly by men of business, such as ship-builders, fisher-men, seafaring-men and husband-men, or such as depend on them'. The fertile, well-wooded and well-watered Medway valley, however, was 'spangled with populous villages' and farms.[17] It was, of course, cheap water transport which permitted the integration of the coastal maritime economy with the riverborne agrarian-manufacturing economy. An estimate of 1660 compared the capital outlays involved in land and water carriage in the Medway valley thus: the annual charge for a cart and oxen, including servants' wages to maintain them, amounted to £49 16s.; for a boat and implements, £1 12s. 4d., or a proportion of around 30:1.[18] Such estimates were no doubt prone to exaggeration and special pleading, but most contemporaries were well aware of the benefits of good water communications.

The century after 1650 saw a concerted effort to improve the navigable rivers of England, when rivers were recognised as 'the cherishing veines of the body of every Countrey, Kingdome, and Nation'.[19] Dr Chalklin has described in detail how efforts were made during the seventeenth century to extend the navigation of the Medway beyond its upper limit at Maidstone as far as Penshurst.[20] The primary objective was to facilitate the carriage of timber, iron and ordnance from the Weald to Chatham Dockyard. Government support could therefore be relied upon, yet the earliest schemes of 1600 and 1627, promoted by the landowners of the Weald, failed to produce permanent results. A private Act of Parliament in 1665 fared little better, owing to a shortage of capital. Not until the establishment of the Medway Navigation Company in 1739 was work begun to make the river navigable up to Tonbridge. The lower and tidal reaches of the Medway were at this stage still controlled by the Commissioners of Sewers. In 1802, however, a second company was created, known as the Medway Lower Navigation Company, and this dual arrangement continued throughout the nineteenth century.[21] The construction of

---

[16] RBT 289, Proof in support of the Rochester Bridge Bill, [1802], 1.
[17] Defoe, op. cit., 114.
[18] T. S. Willan, *River Navigation in England, 1600–1750*, Oxford 1936, 103–4.
[19] Ibid., 3, quoting the seventeenth-century pamphleteer, John Taylor.
[20] C.W. Chalklin, 'Navigation schemes on the upper Medway, 1600–1665', *Journal of Transport History*, v (1961–2), 105–115; C.W. Chalklin, *Seventeenth Century Kent*, London 1965, 166.
[21] Medway Archives Office, Strood. Inventory of the Medway Navigation Company (S/MN), introductory notes.

locks and weirs by both companies brought immediate improvements to navigation but in the long run exacerbated the growing problem of shoals by restricting the tidal flow.[22]

Of course it was riverborne trade which fed the coasting trade, and in the context of inland navigation, as Professor Willan put it, 'the sea becomes merely a river around England, a river with peculiar dangers, peculiar conditions, and peculiar advantages.'[23] The coasting trade and the river trade met just below Rochester Bridge at the town quay, where incoming bulk cargoes were transferred from ships of 100–400 tons into hoys and lighters of forty tons or less for carriage upriver. In the 1720s, Defoe claimed that large hoys of fifty and sixty tons were able to reach Maidstone. The exports of the Medway valley, on the other hand, were carried by hoys through Rochester bridge either to the port of Rochester, or directly to London and the outports without transshipment.[24] The coasting trade of Kent was a vigorous one, and Rochester-owned or registered vessels were more numerous than those of any other Kentish port in the eighteenth century. By mid-century, half the shipping of the Kentish ports was registered at Rochester, as Table 23 shows. The modest growth of Kent-owned shipping during the third quarter of the eighteenth century was accounted for principally by an increase in the number of Rochester-owned vessels, followed by those registered at Faversham and Sandwich.

The chief imports into the Medway were bulk shipments of coal, malt and barley, and coasting vessels from the Northeast and Kentish ports unloaded these cargoes at Rochester where they were either consumed in the Medway towns or sent upriver to Maidstone. In either case, the town authorities at Rochester collected a local duty which enables the historian to indicate the size of these trades, shown in Table 24. It was the expansion of the brewing and distilling industries at Maidstone and Chatham, developed by the Saunders, Cripps, Bishop and Best families, which substantially explains the remarkable growth of grain and coal imports into the region.[25] Other imports included salt, pipe-clay and deals. Grain was also exported from the Medway valley, particularly oats for the London market; in 1683–4 for example, 4,836 quarters of oats and 713 quarters of wheat were shipped from Rochester, almost all for London.[26] But during years of dearth, cereal imports might flow inwards as in 1727–8 when 20,000 quarters of foreign oats were received, mostly from Danzig. Although sizable quantities of grain were exported from Rochester, contemporary comments give the clear impression that Maidstone remained the commercial centre of the corn trade. The latter was indeed the natural focus of trade for a wide area of the Weald, whereas 'for the district

22 BPP 1820 (267), iii. 29, Report of the Select Committee on the Present State of Rochester Bridge, 11 July 1820, 31 (evidence of John Rennie), and 51 (evidence of Samuel Nicholson, Mayor of Rochester).
23 Willan, op. cit., 5.
24 Defoe, op. cit., 113; R. Marsh, *The Conservancy of the River Medway. 1881–1969*, Rochester 1971, pp. 15–16.
25 J.M. Russell, *History of Maidstone* [1881], Rochester 1978, 325–6.
26 T.S. Willan, *The English Coasting Trade, 1600–1750*, Manchester 1938, 83.

Table 23

Shipping tonnage registered in Kentish ports, 1709–82 (000 tons)

First figure indicates coastal shipping
Second figure indicates total of overseas, coastal and fishing vessels

	1709	1716	1723	1730	1737	1744
Rochester	1.4 | 2.0	1.3 | 2.1	1.3 | 1.9	1.5 | 2.1	1.6 | 2.1	1.5 | 2.1
Faversham*	1.3 | 1.3	1.5 | 1.5	1.9 | 1.9	1.6 | 1.6	1.4 | 1.4	1.4 | 1.4
Sandwich	0.9 | 2.2	0.9 | 2.5	0.7 | 2.1	1.0 | 2.4	1.3 | 2.7	1.3 | 2.3
Deal	0.1 | 0.5	0.2 | 0.5	0.1 | 0.4	0.1 | 0.4	0.1 | 0.3	0.1 | 0.3
Dover	0.7 | 2.1	1.0 | 1.9	0.5 | 1.8	0.4 | 1.5	0.4 | 1.6	0.3 | 1.3
Kentish ports	4.4 | 8.1	4.9 | 8.5	4.5 | 8.0	4.5 | 7.9	4.8 | 8.2	4.6 | 7.4
same as % of Total English Outports	4.5 | 4.5	4.8 | 3.9	4.3 | 3.7	4.1 | 3.4	4.1 | 3.3	3.7 | 3.0

	1751	1758	1765	1772	1779	1782
Rochester	2.3 | 3.1	1.9 | 3.1	2.3 | 3.2	2.5 | 4.3	2.1 | 3.2	2.0 | 3.4
Faversham*	1.5 | 1.5	1.3 | 1.3	2.0 | 2.2	2.2 | 2.3	2.3 | 2.3	1.6 | 1.6
Sandwich	0.8 | 1.9	1.5 | 2.2	2.0 | 3.2	1.1 | 1.9	1.0 | 1.3	0.7 | 0.8
Deal	0.1 | 0.3	– | 0.2	– | 0.2	– | 0.2	– | 0.4	– | 0.4
Dover	0.2 | 1.3	0.3 | 1.0	0.4 | 2.6	0.5 | 2.9	0.6 | 7.1	0.4 | 4.4
Kentish ports	4.9 | 8.1	5.0 | 7.9	6.7 | 11.4	6.3 | 11.6	6.0 | 14.3	4.7 | 10.6
same as % of Total English Outports	3.6 | 2.7	3.0 | 2.4	3.4 | 2.8	2.8 | 2.6	2.4 | 3.1	1.8 | 2.5

Source: BL Add MSS 11,255–6.   * including Milton

north of the Downs there were many quays and creeks from which produce could be shipped as conveniently as from Rochester.'[27]

The export of foodstuffs to London was balanced by coastal imports for domestic consumption: groceries, manufactures, and goods of foreign origin, mainly wine and tobacco. The organisation of the London trade, it seems, lay outside the control of local merchants, whereas the coal trade was invariably handled by collier skippers who acted as merchants as well as carriers of their cargoes.[28] Fullers earth

[27] Dulley, op. cit., 163. During the later seventeenth century, substantially larger quantities of grain were exported coastwise from Faversham, Sandwich and Thanet than was the case from the Medway valley. Whereas Rochester handled cargoes of oats for the London market, Faversham and Milton shipped out wheat and oats, and Sandwich and Thanet shipped a large volume of malt together with smaller quantities of wheat (Andrews, thesis, Table 21).

[28] Ibid., 164.

Table 24

The trade of the Medway: bulk cargoes imported into the port of Rochester,
annual averages, 1694–1825

	Coal	Malt & Barley	Oats	Fuller's earth	Number of annual returns
	'000 (chaldrons)	'000 (quarters)	'000 (quarters)	(tons)	
1690s	3.35	1.26		—	3
1700s	2.59	1.32		—	3
1710s	6.34	—		—	2
1720s	9.28	4.80		153.0	8
1727–8			20.2		1
1730s	9.38	6.45		172.5	8
1740s	12.03	8.64		109.3	9
1750s	16.05	7.97		79.4	10
1760s	17.70	9.98		—	9
1770s	23.04	5.72		—	10
1780s					0
1790s					0
1800s					0
1819–20	37.63	—		—	1
1820–25	82.71	—		—	5

Source: Medway Archives Office, Strood. Rochester City Archives, RCA/N.2, Water Bailiff's Accounts.

was also exported from the Medway, especially to Colchester and the textile centres of eastern England, together with oysters and wool. The bulk of the region's maritime trade thus depended upon coastal traffic, but the oyster fishery provided the basis for a modest overseas export trade, and a high proportion of the wool illegally exported from England was shipped from the Kent coast.[29] A desire to avoid payment of local duties at Rochester, or possibly considerations of convenience, may explain the tendency for some traders to import and export cargoes informally at creeks below Rochester Bridge. In 1737, for example, the bridge wardens were concerned that their tenant at Quarry Farm, Frindsbury, frequently permitted the loading and unloading of corn at Quarry Wharf and that 'others brought and laid timber on the land there, in order for water carriage, without the knowledge or permission of the Wardens'.[30]

As we have already noted, the majority of exports from the Medway valley were not transshipped at Rochester, but passed through the bridge directly on to London and the outports; and since they paid no duties, we cannot measure them. The

[29] Andrews, thesis, 175.
[30] RBT 1617, Minutes of the Committee of Assistants, vol. I, 27 May 1737.

composition of this trade, however, was described in detail by Defoe in 1724 and by William Newton in 1741. Maidstone and its hinterland, according to the former, supplied London 'with more particulars than from any single market town in England.'[31] Newton, less verbose than Defoe, provided an admirable brief account:

> There are besides on the river very many large corn-mills, which grind for the dock and navy at Chatham, and in a good measure furnish the city of Rochester and town of Chatham, with meal and flower, besides great quantities which are sent from hence [Maidstone] to London. Here are also several large paper mills and fulling mills; and from hence are sent to Rochester, Chatham and other places, great quantities of gardners ware. By the hoys going from hence is London likewise supplied with corn, fruit, paving stone, which is exceeding durable, fullers earth, and a fine white sand for the glass-houses, which is reckoned the best in England for melting into flint glass and looking glass plates, and much used for what is called writing-sand. From hence is also conveyed to Chatham for the supply of the King's dock and yards there, great quantities of the largest oak and elm timber, most of which is brought out of the Weald, or Wood of Kent and other places adjacent, by land-carriage, and hence put on board vessels, which carry it up the river. By these means there is good encouragement for the having here several pretty large hoys, which are constantly passing betwixt this place and London, Rochester, Chatham, &c which is a great advantage to this town and neighbourhood, as well as to the owners and persons employed in them.[32]

Although we cannot measure the total volume of the trade of the Medway valley, literary evidence, together with the available local customs material, suggests that the first half of the eighteenth century saw considerable growth. Rochester Bridge however was a serious impediment to river navigation, and the growth of water-borne trade in the eighteenth century increased the likelihood of damage. Hoymasters frequently attempted to pass through the bridge before there was sufficient water, causing vessels to jam between the starlings just below the surface, thus loosening and breaking the piles. By 1728, this had become such a common occurrence that the wardens issued printed notices warning that prosecutions for damages would be laid.[33] The bridge in fact acted like a great dam across the river, restricting the inflow of the tide and holding back the ebb. The considerable size of the starlings and the narrowness and number of the arches produced a large fall of water at the bridge, of around 42 inches, causing danger and delay to navigation. Only vessels of forty tons or less could pass through and 'none of any burthen can pass at all but thro' one particular arch, and that at particular times of tide.'[34] This was the St Mary's lock next to the draw lock, with the widest and deepest channel. It was here, at the Strood end of the bridge, that the strongest currents flowed, and over many centuries the waters had scoured out a deep channel, approaching 32 feet at low

[31] Defoe, op. cit., 113.
[32] W. Newton, *History and Antiquities of Maidstone*, Maidstone 1741, 103.
[33] RBT 1540, Orders of Wardens and Assistants, vol. I, 3 May 1728, 145.
[34] RBT 289, 1.

water in the early eighteenth century.[35] In 1705, the maximum width of hoys permitted to pass through was 17½ feet.[36] At the end of the century, the Bridge Architect wrote:

> the delays, inconveniences, and accidents suffered by the barges which navigate through the bridge are considerable. They can only pass at low or high water; frequently an hour lost loses a tide; and on the falling off of the tides, a tide frequently is followed with the loss of the whole tides till the next springs; whereby barges going to Maidstone, Tunbridge &c are kept on their way a fortnight without the power of getting up. This circumstance sometimes induces bargemen to attempt the passage at improper times, whereby frequent accidents arise. And in point of dimension the barges are now confined to the width of the St Mary Lock, when with a wider opening, their width and tonnage would be unlimited.[37]

Improvement to the passage under the bridge, he concluded, forms '. . . the key stone of future improvements on the River Medway'.

---

[35] RBT 1540, 5 June 1718, 117.
[36] Ibid., 20 April 1705, 92.
[37] RBT 146, Report by Daniel Alexander to the Bridge Wardens and Assistants, 20 April 1798.

The Management and Control of Bridge Affairs

The responsibilities and powers of the bridge wardens remained unchanged throughout this period, resting on the Elizabethan legislation of 1576 and 1585. Only minor adjustments were made in a statute of 1702 when the time appointed for electing bridge wardens and assistants was changed. In the early nineteenth century, when the preservation of the moorings at Chatham Dockyard became an object of national importance, two periods of parliamentary activity raised the possibility of major changes. The Rochester Bridge Bill of 1802, if successful, would have conferred the right to charge tolls; and in 1818, discussions with the Admiralty Board raised the possibility of transferring the wardens' responsibilities and property to the state, a suggestion which was however resisted. Lord Romney expressed the feelings of the bridge wardens at that time when he suggested,

> It will . . . generally be found, that when conducted by a body of proper individuals resident near the place, unless there is suspicion of a view to private advantage or influence, neither of which I am confident can be imported in the present case, or unless there is a disposition to be inattentive to their duty, which there is little reason to impute, a work of this nature is concluded on at least as economical & as sound principles as it can be, if included in the great national mass of public works, where the same minute attention cannot be given.[1]

In the event, the existing arrangements were maintained and management remained 'in the hands of those who have conducted it gratuitously'.

The reform of local corporations was of course a major political issue in 1815–32, and those great landowners such as the Earls of Romney, Darnley, Aylesford and Westmorland who dominated county society must have grown increasingly sensitive to the mounting attack on oligarchy and 'old corruption' in the shires.[2] In fact the affairs of Rochester Bridge seem to have been conducted with reasonable propriety from the later 1730s and 40s, in the manner later outlined by Romney. But there is evidence that the favouritism and mismanagement which had characterised the sixteenth century, noted by Sir Roger Manwood in 1586, continued into the late seventeenth and early eighteenth centuries.[3] An enquiry made by the Committee of Assistants in 1749 had concluded that for many

[1]   RTB 1540, Orders of Wardens and Assistants, vol. I, 24 April 1818, 633.
[2]   See especially W.D. Rubinstein, 'The End of "Old Corruption" in Britain', *Past & Present*, 101 (1983), 55–86.
[3]   Supra., 'The Elizabethan Commissions', 113–14.

years, the wardens had not taken the trouble to give bonds to account for the revenues of the bridge nor to make oath of the allowances demanded by them in their accounts. More seriously, it was claimed that the bridge estates had been leased out 'very much under their true and real values' and that leases were frequently signed by only one of the wardens and a minority of assistants. It was indeed the case that from time to time, wardens and assistants themselves took up leases on individual bridge properties. The Earl of Westmorland, for example, held leases on bridge lands at Little Delce during the 1730s and 40s, as did members of the Boghurst family in 1772–1808 whilst Philip Boghurst was warden. The bridge wardens, continued the enquiry of 1749, 'expended large sumes of money in Gifts or Payments made to the Electors, and in Entertainments for themselves and friends. Most of which Irregularities have been rectifyed within a few years p[ast].'[4]

After the high taxation and uncertainties of the civil war and interregnum, the financial situation facing the bridge wardens was reasonably favourable for the next century and a half, enabling them at least to discharge their responsibility for basic maintenance with little difficulty and, after 1750, to invest substantially in government stock. It appeared highly unlikely that the contributory lands would ever be taxed and enthusiasm for attending the election of wardens was low. In the late sixteenth and early seventeenth centuries, up to 42 separate parishes had provided electors although some of these, it was later realised, lay beyond the seven-mile limit defining the area of the contributory lands. By 1655, representatives of 33 parishes attended elections, and from 1660 to 1731, the figure stabilised at 31. Each parish was required to send two representatives (householders or owners of land lying within the parish) to the annual bridge elections, for which an attendance allowance was provided. Payments were made to between 40 and 62 individuals per annum during these years, though it is clear that some electors voted without the inducement of an allowance. In the election of 1744, for example, as many as 130 voted. The great majority of the electors were apparently ordinary parishioners and householders. Only a relatively small number of the owners of contributory lands bothered to vote, and by no means all the wardens and assistants were owners of such lands. There is nothing to suggest that the wardens and assistants endeavoured to 'represent' the electors of the contributory lands.[5]

It was in 1737 that the bridge administration was substantially improved with the establishment of the Committee of Assistants, which met weekly when business was heavy, otherwise fortnightly or monthly meetings were held to supplement the two annual meetings of the wardens and assistants. From the start, the new committee promoted a much tighter conception of time and work discipline amongst the bridge workforce. One of its early decisions was to appoint the architect

---

4 RBT 1617, Minutes of the Committee of Assistants, vol. I, 27 January 1749, 163–5.
5 Ibid., 155–64. The attendance allowance was paid at the rate of 1s. 6d. in 1660, and 2s. in 1665–1731.

Charles Sloane as Surveyor of Works and Director of the Workmen of the Bridge.[6] This last task, the day-to-day supervision of work, had hitherto fallen to the Bridge Clerk who was expected to check the workmen's attendance as well as to act as Paymaster of Works, Clerk of the Cheque, Receiver of Rents, and Woodreeve. As the repair programme expanded, a new post of Overseer of Workmen was created to relieve the Surveyor of Works of his supervisory role. The Overseer was required to note, 'what work every workman is imployed in, whether unemployed or absent, every hour and part of the day; and if any one of them is negligent in his business, or works in any other work than for the use of the Bridge, he shall give immediate notice of it . . . He shall have a minute watch, that he may observe the time with more exactness; and shall be present with and attend the workmen the whole time of their working; and shall likewise work himself at such times as he is not imployed in making his Book and keeping the Accounts.'[7] The initial appointment to the post was John Rose, the bridge's first mason. In 1740, his authority was extended to encompass the levying of fines for negligence – a quarter of a day's pay in addition to a deduction for loss of time – and in the case of 'persistent neglect', dismissal.[8] He was required to 'ring the bell in the Tower of the Bridge-Chapell, at the times appointed for them to begin and leave off work'.[9]

In the late seventeenth and early eighteenth centuries, the team of day-labourers and craftsmen generally consisted of around ten workmen: a master mason and his mate, two carpenters and their labourer, and perhaps five general labourers whose main task was to dig and carry chalk from the quarry to the starlings. Supervision was light. It was the responsibility of the bridge clerk to consult the carpenters and masons early in June as to the work needed for the ensuing year, and to keep an attendance record of the labour force.[10] It was the clerk who paid the wages, usually weekly, although in the late 1780s and early 90s, monthly payment was the rule until a somewhat restrained collective protest was made. In July 1793, it was 'represented to the Committee [of Assistants] that the workmen of the Bridge are subjected to great inconvenience by being paid only monthly instead of weekly as is the general custom when they work for others'.[11] The craftsmen were kept in 'constant pay': that is, they were retained from year to year although paid a daily rate, with an allowance of 30s for the winter quarter, which was withdrawn in 1680.[12] Thereafter, they were provided with winter work as available, preparing materials, repairing the workshops and the bridge properties in Rochester; but no distinction was made between summer and winter rates of pay until 1760.[13] A single rate was maintained from 1680 through to 1760, although of course there

6 Ibid., 28 July 1738, 17.
7 Ibid., 19 January 1739, 21.
8 Ibid., 4 March, 45.
9 Society of Antiquaries (Thorpe MSS), vol. 198, f. 327r. (undated, c.1738–40).
10 RBT 1540, 3 June 1680, 25.
11 RBT 1618, Minutes of the committee of Assistants, vol. II, 20 July 1793, 243 (ii) [pp. 219–248 are duplicated].
12 RBT 2130, Wardens' Accounts, vol. XIII, 1680.
13 RBT 2141, Wardens' Accounts, vol. XXIV, 1760.

Plate 9. John Thorpe, MD (1682–1750). Engraving by J. Bayley from a portrait by Wollaston published in *Registrum Roffense*, 1769.

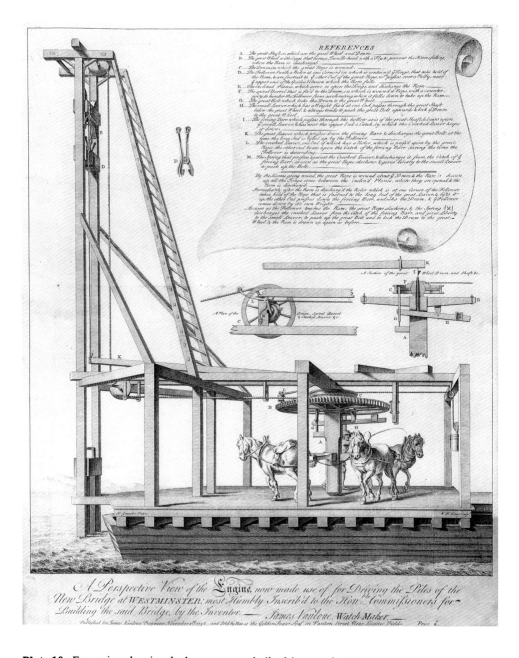

Plate 10. Engraving showing the horse-powered pile-driver used at Westminster Bridge in 1738 (reproduced by kind permission from an original in the British Library).

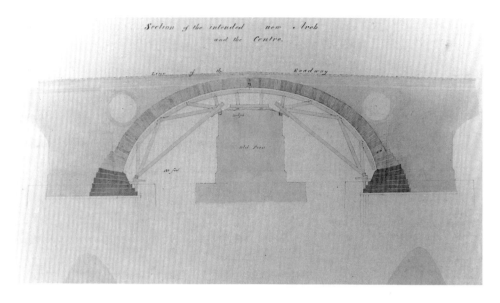

Plate 11(a). Daniel Alexander's plan for the construction of the great central arch, 1817.

Plate 11(b). Nineteenth-century painting of Rochester Bridge showing the enlarged central arch.

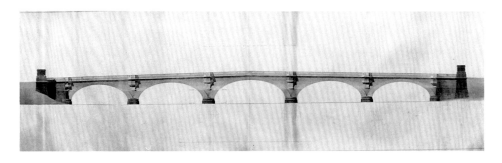

Plate 12(a). Daniel Alexander's design for a new stone bridge of five arches, 1818.

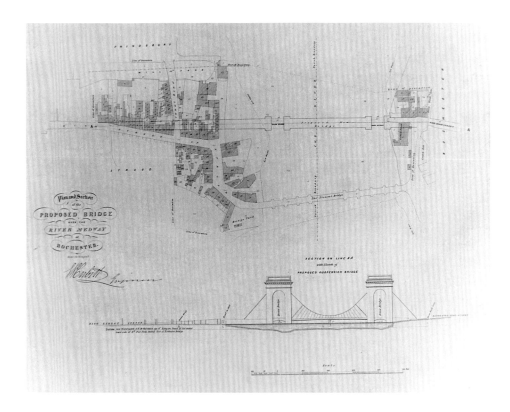

Plate 12(b). William Cubitt's design for the proposed suspension bridge, 1844.

were periods when no work was available. As far as craftsmen were concerned, the principle applied that all should enjoy 'equal Trust, Pay and share of Labour', but that if redundancy were unavoidable, 'he or they that were last enter'd shall be first dismissed.'[14]

It was undoubtedly the series of major repairs to the bridge, undertaken in 1736–41, which underlay the need for serious reorganisation of the management structure, including a tighter supervision of an expanded labour force. But administrative improvements also depended on the energy and commitment of the wardens, and the main driving force during these years was undoubtedly Dr John Thorpe, the celebrated Kent antiquarian. Thorpe, a Fellow of the Royal Society and friend of Sir Hans Sloane, became a bridge warden in 1733. He compiled the earliest surviving list of the bridge archives and instigated publication of lists of the contributory lands and other documents. His interest in the history of the bridge and the responsibilities of the wardens, however, had a practical aspect. His obituary of 1750 suggested that, 'By his enquiries, industry, and labour, that Corporation hath been brought into a much more regular and laudable way of acting than formerly; and as he was very instrumental in redressing the many abuses and irregularities that had inadvertently and insensibly crept into the affairs of that Corporation, so he strenuously opposed the corrupt practice of making a private advantage of a public charity.'[15]

The most conspicuous 'private advantage' in the gift of the bridge wardens lay in the terms and level of rents on which bridge lands might be leased, rather than any lavish hospitality and entertainments provided. In the early 1740s, Thorpe suggested that the bridge rents were very unequal, some being let at 'near their full, some at two-thirds, some at half, and others at one third, or less, of their improved value.'[16] Steps were taken, as we shall see, to tighten up the administration of the bridge estates through the implementation of a series of 'Orders concerning Leases.' By the late seventeenth century, hospitality and entertainment were restricted to the annual Audit Dinner, the total cost of which amounted to roughly £10 in the early 1660s rising to £24 in 1670. Interestingly, the wardens made no effort to economise in this area as expenditure on bridge repairs rose: if anything, the reverse was true. A peak of extravagance was reached in 1677 when £29 was spent on the annual dinner, suggesting that hospitality was used to improve public relations at the time when a new bridge wharf was under construction in

---

14 Society of Antiquaries (Thorpe MSS), vol. 198, f. 331v. (undated, c.1738–40.

15 *Dictionary of National Biography*, s.v. Thorpe, John (1682–1750). J. Nichols, *Literary Anecdotes*, 3 vols., London 1812, III, pp. 509–14. Although Thorpe presides over a major reorganisation of bridge affairs, he was keen to establish a sense of continuity and historic obligation attaching to wardenship. He provided a splendid set of chairs for the bridge chamber; staves for the junior and senior wardens; had the accounts bound in leather; and devised the bridge's coat of arms. Invented tradition seldom demands authenticity, however, and Thorpe unwittingly incorporated the arms of the 'wrong' Knolles into his Knolles and Cobham design. I owe this information to Dr Gibson.

16 Society of Antiquaries (Thorpe MSS), vol. 198, 'Considerations of the Leases of Land and Tenements belonging to Rochester Bridge', ff. 147r–153v, undated, placed next to an item dated 1741, f. 148v.

1672–5. Periods of stable expenditure on hospitality seem to have been followed by short bursts of drastic economies, such as the years 1682–5 when roughly £4 was spent on the Audit Dinner following a decision to exclude guests.[17] During the 1710s and 20s, the cost averaged £19 and £13 respectively, before disappearing from the accounts in 1736. Subsidised hospitality presumably ended at this point. The cost of horse hire was met when the clerk or wardens went about bridge business, bread and beer might be provided for the carpenters, labourers and waggoners on special occasions, and Spanish and Virginia tobacco was supplied 'for the gentlemen and servants' during business meetings in the early eighteenth century.

There is little doubt that service to the court of Wardens and Assistants conferred prestige and the opportunity to exercise influence over local affairs, but the quantity of each seems to have varied from one period to another. An earlier chapter has shown how, in the early sixteenth century, wardenship became associated with men of considerably higher social status than before, with control resting in the hands of the county nobility. During the course of the seventeenth century, the involvement of a closely-knit group of gentry families displaced that of the aristocracy, although the Earls of Westmorland, seated at Mereworth, displayed a continuing interest in bridge affairs which was still evident in the eighteenth century. After the Restoration, it was common for Rochester's member of Parliament to serve as a bridge warden, but fewer did so as the eighteenth century wore on.

John Thorpe distinguished his fellow wardens from their sixteenth- and seventeenth-century predecessors who, he felt, had seen wardenship as 'Places of Reputation [rather] than Places of Trust'.[18] The social background of wardens and assistants seems to have broadened out in the eighteenth century as a more workmanlike approach developed with the reforms of the 1730s and 40s. Alongside members of well-established landowning gentry families such as Twisdens, Culpepers, Dykes, and Polhills, there sat *parvenu* industrialists such as the Bests, brewers of Chatham, and there were also lawyers and professional men such as the Barrells of Rochester, as well as increasing numbers of 'townsmen'.[19] By the 1790s, as Hasted noted, the wardens and assistants were usually chosen 'one half of gentlemen who live in the adjacent country, and the other of the same in

---

[17] RBT 1540, 26 May 1681, 25.

[18] Society of Antiquaries (Thorpe MSS), vol. 198, f. 148v. The whole passage reads, '[after the reign of Queen Elizabeth] the Wardens and Assistances being generally persons of eminent Families and large Estates, living at a distance from the Bridge, taking themselves to be more in Places of Reputation than Places of Trust, and meeting not oftener at most than Twice in the Year, and then not having time sufficient for the Due performance of the Business of the Bridge, but leaving in great measure the whole management as well of the Estates as of the Works of it to their Clerks and Workmen, it has gradually and insensibly come to pass in a Number of Years, that many of the Abuses, which this Act [of 1576] was intended to prevent, have crept in again and prevailed'.

[19] G.E. Mingay, *English Landed Society in the Eighteenth Century*, London 1963, 215–16; F.F. Smith, *Rochester in Parliament, 1295–1933*, Rochester 1933, 123–4, 145–6; R.A. Keen, 'Messrs. Best, Brewers of Chatham', *Archaeologia Cantiana*, lxxii (1958), 172–181.

Chatham and Rochester.'[20] It was only the latter, he continued, who could be relied upon to attend weekly meetings in the bridge chamber. Nevertheless, an association with the county nobility remained, through the Finch, Bligh, Fane and Marsham families, and in the later eighteenth century, the bridge wardens preferred to describe themselves as the 'noblemen and gentlemen of Rochester Bridge'.

Table 25

MPs sitting for Rochester who also served as Bridge Wardens

	MP	Warden
Sir John Marsham	1660	1664, 1671, 1678
Sir Francis Clerke	1661, 1681	1661, 1669, 1676, 1683
Sir John Banks	1679, 1681, 1685, 1688	1680, 1687, 1694
Francis Barrell (d.1679)	1679	1678
Francis Barrell (d.1724)	1701	1692, 1699, 1706, 1720
Caleb Banks	1691	1693
Sir Joseph Williamson	1689, 1696, 1698, 1701	1686, 1693, 1700
Sir Edward Knatchbull	1702	1703, 1710, 1717, 1724
William Cage	1702, 1710, 1713	1702, 1709, 1716, 1723, 1730
Sir Thomas Palmer	1715, 1722	1707, 1714, 1721
David Polhill	1727, 1734, 1743, 1747	1701, 1708, 1715, 1722, 1729, 1736
John Calcraft	1768	1770
George Best	1790	1787, 1792, 1798, 1806, 1814

Sources: RBT, Wardens' Accounts; F.F. Smith, Rochester in Parliament, 1295–1933, Rochester 1933.

A summary of the changing financial background to the work of the bridge wardens is shown below, taken from their accounts which exist in a virtually unbroken series from 1576. Until 1754–5, the accounts were cast on a medieval 'charge' and 'discharge' basis and contain the usual anomalies associated with that 'venerable and idiosyncratic' system.[21] A large accumulation of rent arrears was carried over from one year to the next, the bulk of which was totally beyond recovery, producing the impression of substantial but quite fictional surpluses. In the mid 1750s, the system was modernised so that rents actually received were clearly distinguished, as well as recent arrears. In Table 26 below, written-off arrears have been deducted from income so as to ensure comparability between the years before and after 1754–5. The flow of income shown includes the proceeds of timber sales, redundant materials and other items.

If the bridge wardens were 'tottering on the brink of defecit spending' during the period 1576 to 1650, the financial situation during the following century can be

---

[20] E. Hasted, The History and Topographical Survey of the County of Kent, 12 vols., Canterbury 1797–1800, IV, 82.

[21] Mingay, English Landed Society, 174–5.

Table 26

Rochester Bridge accounts, 1660–1825

	Income	Expenditure	Investment		Borrowing	Loan
			Purchase	Sale		Repayment
	(annual average)		(decadal)		(decadal)	(decadal)
	£	£	£	£	£	£
1661–1671	445	392				
1671–1681	466	564				
1681–1691	457	419				
1691–1701	466	456				
1701–1711	471	475				
1711–1721	489	431				
1721–1731	599	530	827			
1731–1741	665	726	—	390		
1741–1751	664	738	—	335		
1751–1761	958	708	3,464	—		
1761–1771	1,074	1,221	172	1,917		
1771–1781	1,207	1,063	779	—		
1781–1791	1,353	1,005	3,043	—		
1791–1801	1,790	2,762	927	4,588	5,750	384
1801–1811	2,370	1,566	—	—	750	8,942
1811–1821	3,530	2,297	11,143	—	—	—
1821–1825	4,101	6,769	—	12,656	—	—

Source: RBT 2128–2146, Wardens' Accounts, vols XI–XXXI.

described as stable and 'generally even-handed'.[22] The building of a new bridge wharf during the early 1670s put some strain on the bridge finances, but the additional cost seems to have been largely absorbed by substantial cash balances which had been allowed to accumulate. The 1710s and 20s were characterised by an uninterrupted build-up of surplus income, and a limited amount of investment was undertaken, albeit unsuccessfully. In June 1723, the wardens succumbed to the lure of South Sea stock and laid out £200, to which a further £200 was added in the following year. Prior to this, cash balances were held by the bridge clerk, who in future was to be allowed an additional salary of £15 per annum in lieu of 'the advantage he made by the moneys'.[23] By 1733, at the time of the general reduction in the South Sea Company's trading capital, the wardens had built up stocks with a nominal value of £800; as a result of the refinancing operation, this was converted into a new stockholding of £700.[24] When the increasing cost of bridge repairs

---

[22] The description is that of Daniel Alexander (Table 27 and note 32).

[23] RBT 1540, 28 May 1724, 131.

[24] For the reorganisation of the affairs of the South Sea Company at this time, see P.G.M. Dickson,

forced the wardens to sell in 1739–42, the whole realised £725. Although disappointing, this initial foray into the stock market was by no means as disastrous as it might have been.

The late 1730s and early 1740s, however, saw a minor financial crisis in the affairs of Rochester Bridge. Urgent repairs to the bridge could be delayed no longer, and although increased rents on the bridge estates had generated an increased flow of income during the 1720s, the farming community encountered serious difficulties during the 1730s and 40s as grain prices fell.[25] Rent arrears shot up and many tenants were unable to meet the continuing demand for increased rents during the 1740s (shown in figs 12 and 13). Thomas Newman, for example, tenant at Nutts Farm, Leysdown, was eight years in arrears by 1742, at a time when the bridge clerk was writing circular letters to those whose rents were in arrears for more than three years. The problems of the bridge estates were, of course, common to those facing farmers and landowners in many other parts of England; but it seems that the bridge wardens compounded their difficulties by demanding unrealistic rent increases in 1746 and 1747. New high rents imposed on farms in the Isle of Grain, for example, were readjusted at mid-century and the wardens were forced to write off huge arrears amounting to £882 in 1748–53.

The large scale writing-off of arrears provided an opportunity to take a more realistic approach to estate management from the early 1750s. The accounting system was modernised, so that income was seen in terms of rents actually received, rather than merely due; at the same time, the bridge wardens extended their role beyond that of passive rentier, when a concerted effort was made to improve and develop the estates. As early as 1739, the new Committee of Assistants turned its attention to the terms and rent levels on which leases might be renewed, encouraged by its discovery of the 1670 Act for the Maintenance of Bridges which empowered corporate bodies to let lands held in trust at 'improved' rents, backed by the authority of the local justices.[26] John Thorpe, as we have already noticed, repeatedly drew attention to the fact that several bridge properties were let well below their full value, by renewing leases 'some years before the expiry of their respective terms (to prevent, as may be presumed, Competitors).'[27] From 1741 to 1744, a series of new *Orders* was drawn up requiring estimates of the full and most improved annual rents of lands and tenements before any lease could be granted. By the early 1750s, the cumulative impact of the increases was considerable, especially that derived from rural estates in Kent (see fig. 13).

Increased rents, of course, implied new responsibilities on the part of the wardens and assistants, especially in relation to repairs. The new *Orders* required their

---

The Financial Revolution in England. A Study in the Development of Public Credit, 1967, 208; and J. Carswell, *The South Sea Bubble*, 1960, 40–59.

[25] G.E. Mingay, 'The Agricultural Depression, 1730–1750', *Economic History Review*, second series, VIII (1956), repr. in E.M. Carus-Wilson, *Essays in Economic History*, 3 vols., London 1962, II, 309–326.

[26] 22 Cha. II, c. 12.

[27] Society of Antiquaries (Thorpe MSS), vol. 198, f. 148v.

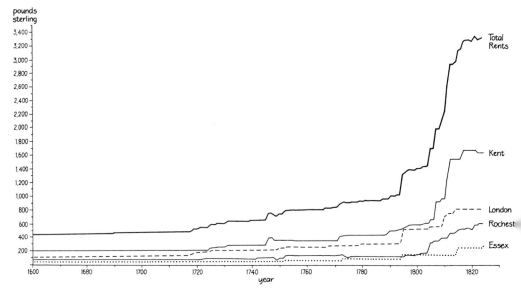

Figure 12. Rochester Bridge estates: rental income, 1660–1825.

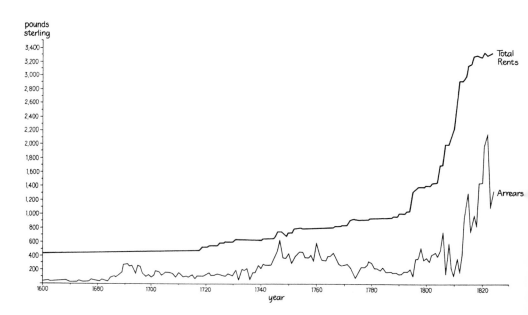

Figure 13. Rochester Bridge estates: rents and arrears, 1660–1825.

successors to put lands and premises into a good state of repair before the granting of leases, and the minutes of the Committee of Assistants show that major efforts were indeed made in this direction.[28] Care was also taken to ensure a modicum of good farming practice, and occasionally one of the wardens might accompany the bridge surveyor or land agents on periodic visits to farms and other properties. Excessive felling of timber and the ploughing up of marshland were discouraged during the depressed conditions of the 1740s. In late June 1743, for example, as a result of such a visit to the Isle of Grain, the surveyors noted that the tenant of seventeen acres of fresh marsh had ploughed up the greater part, and,

> That before it was ploughed it was one of the best pieces of fresh Marsh in that Level, but that it cannot recover itself again for pasture so as to be of the same value p. Acre as before, in many years, unless laid down in a proper manner. That the best way to lay it down and convert it again into pasture, will . . . be by making a Summer Fallow, ploughed three times at least and sowed in proper Season with Clover seed and Rye grass seed, three quarts of Clover seed at the least to one Bushell of Rye-Grass seed.[29]

In 1772, the historian of Rochester was able to note the improvements made to the bridge estates which, under the 'excellent management of the present and late wardens, have proved sufficient for its [the bridge's] repair, without any assistance from the contributory lands'.[30] Revision of leases proceeded apace in the 1750s, and in 1753, three hundred acres of woodland at Nashenden were taken back into the direct ownership and management of the wardens. A part-time woodreeve was soon appointed at a salary of £10 per annum and sales of underwood and timber, mainly oak, provided a new and increasingly valuable source of income.[31] Some elm timber was supplied directly for bridge use, but most of the piles used in bridge repairs were bought in, as before.

Estate improvement and the moderate raising of rents led to a much more secure financial situation: between the 1710s and the 1750s estate income doubled. The accounts show a mounting surplus during the 1750s, which permitted the purchase of £3,600 worth of stocks in 1753–9, most of which were sold (at a 10 per cent loss) during the early 1760s to finance major repairs. The 1770s and 80s saw rental income and timber sales advance further whilst expenditure on repairs fell markedly. Purchase of stocks was resumed. It was the gradual accumulation of income based on estate improvement, rather than income generated from investment in stocks, which provided the basis for the major bridge widening project of the 1790s. In fact heavy losses amounting to 37 per cent were sustained on the sale of stock during the closing years of the century. The results of these changes were

---

[28] During the 1740s, major repairs were carried out to bridge properties at Rochester, Nashenden, Little Delce, Langdon, the Isle of Grain, and Dartford.

[29] RBT 1617, 3 June 1743, 87.

[30] S. Denne, *The History and Antiquities of Rochester and its Environs*, Rochester 1772, 56.

[31] John Siburn succeeded his father Benjamin Siburn as woodreeve in 1781 (RBT 1671, 27 October 1781, 148).

summarised in 1812 by Daniel Alexander, the bridge architect, in an analysis of the state of the bridge funds. Although this exaggerates the extent of the wardens' investments by quoting par values, the report shows the main outlines of the financial situation clearly enough and thus establishes a rough chronology for the more important repairs and improvements of the period.

Table 27

Daniel Alexander's report on the state of the Bridge funds, 1812

Up to 1750–51, the income and expenditure were generally even handed, that is, there was no debt, and until then, there was no saving. In 1751, the Corporation began to purchase savings into the public funds.

	Annual Average:			Total
	Income	Expenditure		Savings
	£	£		£
1751–1761	960 [958]	708 [708]	in 10 years funded	3,600
1761–1771	975 [1,074]	1,221 [1,221]	herein, the sum saved was broken in upon and diminished to	1,400
1771–1781	1,145 [1,207]	1,063 [1,063]	herein the fund increased to	2,400
1781–1792	1,175 [1,369]	1,013 [1,014]	herein the fund accumulated to	6,400
1792–1802	1,760 [1,890]	2,951 [2,952]	herein the savings were spent and a Debt of £6,500 incurred, making a gross expenditure of £12,900 and then it was resolved to save & pay off the Debt	
1802–1811	2,296 [2, 352]	1,366 [1,407]	herein 9 years the debt was paid off and the fund is left. Thus:	
1812	2,628 [2,910]	1,744 [2,016]	leaving a Surplus of £844 [894].	

Source: RBT 201, Report of Daniel Alexander, 8 April 1812. Corrected figures are shown in square brackets.

Maintenance, Repairs and Projects

INTRODUCTION

In the history of building and technology, the years which lie between the Great Fire of London and the Great Exhibition of 1851 are distinguished by the emergence of architecture and civil engineering as two separate professions with distinct spheres of expertise. It was in France during the 1670s that a division between military engineering and architecture was first recognised with the formation of Vauban's *Corps du Génie*. In 1715, the *Directeur-Général des Ponts et Chaussées* took charge of the roads and bridges of France, and for much of the eighteenth century the developing science and vocabulary of bridge building were dominated by the French through the work of men such as Gautier, de Belidor, La Hire and Navier. Precise terms such as voussoir, caisson and battardeau entered the vocabulary of British architects and bridge-builders alongside the more ambiguous medieval vernacular, with its staddles, toggles, sumers and binders – which the bridge architect at Rochester felt compelled to define or redefine in the 1790s.[1]

Without doubt, the British lagged behind the French. It was in 1772 that Charles Hutton of Newcastle produced the first English textbook on bridge building, which combined French theory with English empirical observation. The *Principles of Bridges* followed La Hire, via Emerson, on the form and properties of the arch. As Hutton explained, the book was prompted by a disastrous flood on the Tyne in November 1771, when the river rose about nine feet higher at Newcastle than usual. Newcastle Bridge and others on the Tyne collapsed, and the event provided him with 'many opportunities of hearing and seeing very absurd things advanced . . .' and led him to develop the ideas of Thomas Wright of Auckland, Co. Durham, on the design and siting of piers. Until the appearance of Samuel Ware's *Tracts on Vaults and Bridges* in 1822, Hutton's book was the only text available in English for bridge engineers, and further editions appeared in 1801 and 1812.[2]

The Society of Engineers, in which John Smeaton was the leading figure, was formed in 1771, followed by the Institution of Civil Engineers in 1818. But in spite of these developments, most early nineteenth-century writers still regarded bridge

---

1 S.B. Hamilton, 'Bridges', chapter 16 in C. Singer, E.J. Holmyard, A.R. Hall, and T.I. Williams (eds.), *A History of Technology*, III, *From the Renaissance to the Industrial Revolution*, Oxford 1957, 417–37; S.B. Hamilton, 'Building and Civil Engineering Construction', chapter 15 in ibid., IV, *The Industrial Revolution*, Oxford 1958, 442–64; T. Ruddock, *Arch Bridges and their Builders, 1735–1835*, Cambridge 1979, passim.
2 C. Hutton, *The Principles of Bridges, Containing the Mathematical Demonstration of the Properties of the Arches, the Thickness of the Piers, the Force of the Water against them &c. together with Practical Observations and Directions drawn from the whole*, Newcastle 1772, iii–iv.

building as a species of architecture. In 1829, for instance, the architect James Elwes described bridge engineering as 'Aquatic Architecture', taking as his starting point Palladio's observation that 'bridges ought to have the same qualities that are judged necessary in all other buildings, namely that they should be convenient, beautiful and lasting. The perfection of a bridge consists in its having a good foundation, which makes it lasting; an easy ascent to the crown of its central arch, which makes it convenient; and just proportion in its several parts, which renders it beautiful.' As an opening gambit, such remarks were no doubt unexceptionable, yet more seriously, Hutton was condemned by Elwes as 'too theoretical, although he is a profound mathematician'.[3]

It was at the end of the eighteenth century that a more scientific approach to bridge building became discernible at Rochester, with the appointment of Daniel Alexander as bridge architect. Earlier in the century, the Wardens and Assistants might consult the chief mason at London Bridge and were prepared to pay for the best advice available, and the relatively short journey to London or Greenwich meant that access to specialists was no obstacle. Before the advent of the trained civil engineer, however, sound advice was difficult to come by. Significantly, in the 1730s, when the first and second arches of Rochester Bridge were in danger of collapse, the most detailed and reliable assessment of the problem came from two naval engineers at nearby Chatham dockyard.

The two most notable British civil engineers after Smeaton – Rennie and Telford – provided the wardens of Rochester Bridge with reports and advice on projects for reconstruction in the early years of the nineteenth century, as did the distinguished Swiss architect and engineer Labelye, who had first used a caisson to build the piers of Westminster Bridge in 1738.[4] The possibility of constructing a great arch of cast iron was considered as early as 1792 when the well-known prototype by Abraham Darby at Coalbrookdale was suggested as the basis, with appropriate modifications, for a structure linking the fifth and seventh piers. This was to be a 28-foot-wide arch with a span of 86 feet, formed from seven sets of ribs connected by cross ties and braces 'so as perfectly to connect them into a solid body'.[5] Financial constraints alone might have encouraged this move, since a saving of 55 per cent was expected from the use of cast iron in place of stone. The years from 1770 to 1830 have been described as a 'tentative period' in the use of cast-iron for building construction, and the bridge architect at the time commented, significantly, that 'what animadversions are made herein on the Br. of Coalbrook Dale will I hope appear as no detraction from the very great merit of the person who designed and built it, the first and largest of its kind'.[6]

---

[3] J. Elwes, 'Architecture', in *The London Encyclopaedia or Universal Dictionary*, 22 vols., London 1829, II, 624, 626.

[4] For details of Labelye's career, see R.J.B. Walker, *Old Westminster Bridge*, London 1979, especially pp. 77–86, 217–221; H.M. Colvin, *Biographical Dictionary of British Architects, 1660–1840*, London 1954, 351–2; and Ruddock, op. cit., 3–59.

[5] RBT 134, Letter from Daniel Alexander, Southwark, 26 July 1792, 4. The Coalbrookdale Bridge, completed in 1781, had a span of 100 feet.

[6] Ibid., 8. Although the Coalbrookdale arch produced a mania for iron bridge design in France, it

In the event, a somewhat conservative approach by the bridge wardens and a complicated political context delayed the introduction of new techniques and designs at Rochester at precisely the time when these were becoming more available. The Admiralty strongly urged the building of an entirely new stone bridge of five elliptical arches in 1818. It was unfortunately never built. This elegant and magnificent structure, designed by Alexander, would have greatly eased the congestion of river traffic on the Medway in the early nineteenth century. Instead, a programme of piecemeal repair proceeded from the late seventeenth century through to the 1790s, followed by a period of gradual modernisation and improvement completed in 1825. It was not until 1856 that an entirely new cast-iron bridge of three arches was built 400 yards downstream on the site of the earlier pre-1390s bridge.

In an earlier chapter, Dr Britnell suggests that from the 1390s to the 1530s, the violence of the tides in the Medway combined with an inadequate technology meant that it was impossible to 'build a bridge which would not fail every twenty years or so.'[7] Certainly, the strength of the currents at Rochester and the uneven nature of the chalk riverbed must have discouraged any thoughts of using caissons or mobile cofferdams to construct deep stone foundations. These techniques were relatively new in the England of the mid-eighteenth century, being first introduced at Westminster Bridge in 1738, for which caissons were used, followed by Blackfriars Bridge (1759) and Stockton Bridge (1765) where cofferdams were used.[8]

Improvements in bridge building technique at Rochester were indeed few in number before the 1790s, but the introduction of hydraulic or semi-hydraulic cement must have enabled seventeenth- and eighteenth-century masons to obtain more lasting results than their medieval predecessors. Hydraulic or waterproof cement was used by the ancient Romans, but seems to have been unknown in medieval England. In the early fifteenth century, the masons at Rochester Bridge were using a cement made from lime and pitch with powdered Flemish tiles added to improve the adhesion.[9] By the later seventeenth century, however, the use of tarras was firmly established to produce cement with the required water-resistant quality. Tarras, or 'terrace', was a volcanic rock found in Sweden and Germany which from the 1690s (and possibly earlier) was imported via Holland and hence became known as 'Dutch tarras'. The material, containing particles of spar and quartz, was pulverised and mixed in a trough with lime to form the cement; when other ingredients, such as sand, stone splinters and cinders were added, 'the mass becomes so hard as not to be separated without a pick-axe.'[10] The stonework of the starlings and piers was 'laid in tarras' well into the nineteenth century, even after

had proved 'far more troublesome and costly to build than was expected and the hoped-for flood of new orders did not materialise' in England: J.G. James, 'Some Steps in the Evolution of Early Iron Arched Bridge Designs', *Transactions of the Newcomen Society*, 59 (1987–8), 154.

7   Supra., ['Maintenance and Rebuilding', 47].

8   Singer, op. cit., III, 420–27; Ruddock, op. cit., 3–18.

9   J. Becker, *Rochester Bridge: 1387–1856. A history of its early years*, London 1930, 85; Singer, op. cit., 447.

10 *London Encyclopaedia*, XXI, 666, 755; A. Titley (ed.), *John Smeaton's Diary of his Journey to*

the invention of 'Roman Cement' by James Parker of Northfleet in 1796.[11] The relative strength of the eighteenth-century bridge may therefore owe something to this remarkable material.

Equally important, however, were the thoroughness, organisation and regularity of the bridge works themselves. Here, it is important to distinguish between three kinds of activity, common in their essentials to most kinds of building work. First, there was a programme of regular maintenance, chiefly of the starlings and bridge masonry, the intensity and timing of which could be adjusted according to the flow of income. Second, there was an intermittent need for major repairs, involving items such as the rebuilding of individual piers or arches, or substantial repiling of the staddles. Such work, if neglected for more than a few years, might have disastrous consequences, and occasionally might be needed as a matter of urgency. These two kinds of work were of course interconnected: neglect of regular maintenance would increase the likelihood of dilapidation and collapse, whilst a sound structure would require less intensive maintenance than a defective one. Thirdly, general modernisation and improvements might be undertaken such as widening, reshaping the bridge approaches, and redesign of the archivolts (the curve of the arches).

The timing and extent of these three kinds of building work emerge clearly from the wardens' accounts relating to annual expenditure on labour and materials. These are shown opposite in Fig. 14, which depicts total expenditure on building and maintenance work and breaks this down further into wage payments to craftsmen and labourers ('day labour') and sums expended on materials together with extraordinary labour costs and services (customarily described as 'provision'). The first point to notice about the graph is the steady annual rhythm of maintenance expenditure, varying little from one year to the next and most clearly apparent in the data relating to day wages. From 1660 to 1740 especially, when prices in general were stable, but also from the early 1760s through to the early 1790s when they were steadily rising, this kind of expenditure remained quite stable. The annual cycle of maintenance work was of course determined by the rhythm of the seasons, with intensive periods of work from May to October. Next, we may compare the level of 'provision' with expenditure on day wages, and here, divergence between these two variables reflects certain periods of abnormally high activity. These movements, of course, indicate those years when major repairs were undertaken. Finally, years of abnormally high expenditure on day labour together with conspicuous peaks in total expenditure indicate those periods when improvement projects and modernisation were carried out.

A number of sub-periods can thus he identified during which the following phases of high expenditure and construction work may be examined:

the Low Countries [1755], Newcomen Society, Leamington Spa 1938, 52–3. See also W.H. Chaloner, People and Industries, London 1963, 120–4.

[11] For the early history of 'Roman' and Portland cement manufacture in the Medway valley, see J.M. Preston, Industrial Medway: an historical survey, Rochester 1977, 68–87.

1. 1672–1675, the building of a new bridge wharf;
2. 1736–1741, the rebuilding of first pier and arches;
3. 1759–1765, a general overhaul;
4. 1793–1804, a major improvement and widening programme;
5. 1818 and 1821–3, the 'great arch' project.

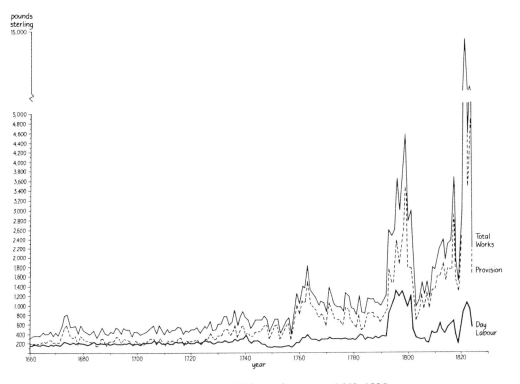

Figure 14. Rochester Bridge maintenance, 1660–1825.

1660–1726

Compared with the preceding century, the late seventeenth and early eighteenth centuries were a time of low and stable prices, both for labour and bridge materials. Unlike many private landowners, the bridge wardens had retained their estates intact throughout the civil wars and interregnum, and were free from problems arising from fines, debt repayments and other encumbrances. During these years and indeed throughout the period 1660–1825, the income of the bridge estates was sufficient to ensure a reasonably adequate programme of continuous maintenance by a team of bridge masons, carpenters and day-labourers as well as tidesmen. During this sub-period, a team of ten or eleven workmen was normally employed except for the years 1673–5 when teams of seventeen and fourteen were engaged in the rebuilding of the bridge wharf and yard at the southwest corner of the bridge at Strood.[12] Separate accounts were kept for this project, indicating a total expenditure of £1,513.

Although the organisation and regularity of maintenance had improved since the medieval period, the basic work routine – repiling the staddles and starlings, packing in chalk, and renewing the horizontal planking across the starlings – remained unchanged. In 1666 for instance, 'The stone-work of the first peer next Rochester was taken down, and 24 piles were there driven with the Ringing Gin and the six-man Beetle. Upon the heads of these piles were trunnelled down 100 ft. of 5-inch [thick] elm plank; and then the stone work was wrought up again upon it . . . the core of the peer was filled up with 4 tun of stones.'[13] The inventory of stores for 1661 shows that the bridge then possessed three pile-driving engines: the six-man beetle, the great ginne and the wheel ginne.[14]

During the seventeenth and early eighteenth centuries, the lack of sufficient work meant that civil engineering in Britain was carried out either by part-time engineers or by undertaker-engineers. Not until the post-1760 period did a clear distinction emerge between the consultant engineer and the contractor.[15] The kind of work described above was undertaken with no overall control other than that of the bridge clerk. In 1704, however, the mason and carpenter of London Bridge were consulted about the state of the first pier, and in 1705, when it had been 'laid open', a surveyor came from London to inspect it and advise on the rebuilding. This unnamed individual may have been George Sorocold of Westminster, who in the previous year had obtained a licence from the bridge wardens to build a sawmill between the starlings under the fifth arch of the bridge, for the cutting of stone and timber.[16] It is at any rate certain that Sorocold, regarded nowadays as the most eminent British engineer of his time, reported in 1712 on the faulty pipework which carried fresh water supplies across the bridge from Rochester to Strood, laid in 1706 by John Wright. During the 1690s and 1700s, Sorocold had been responsible for installing water supply systems at Derby, Leeds, Westminster, Norwich and elsewhere, and plans for the Rochester Bridge sawmills were based on his earlier scheme of 1701–2 at London Bridge.[17] His limited employment at Rochester marks the beginning of a tendency for the wardens to approach undertaker-engineers and others for specialist advice.

---

[12] These are maximum figures and include all individuals employed during the course of the year, with the exception of sawyers.

[13] Society of Antiquaries (Thorpe MSS), vol. 159, f. 9v–10r (undated; the description of bridge repairs ends in 1722).

[14] RBT 2128, Wardens' Accounts, 1661, 'Inventory of Stores belonging to Rochester Bridge'.

[15] A.W. Skempton, 'The Engineers of the English River Navigations, 1620–1760', *Transactions of the Newcomen Society*, xxix (1953), 25–53.

[16] RBT 65, Counterpart Licence, bridge wardens to George Sorocold, to erect his newly invented sawing engine on the starlings of the fifth arch of the bridge, 20 July, 1704. The latter paid an annual rent of £20 per annum.

[17] RBT 66, Letter from George Sorocold to bridge warden Alderman Head, 12 May 1712. Sorocold's pre-eminence is attested by Professor T.C. Barker, amongst others; see, idem., 'The Beginnings of the Canal Age in the British Isles', in L.S. Pressnell (ed.), *Studies in the Industrial Revolution*, London 1960, 4). For a brief summary of Sorocold's career, see A.W. Skempton, op. cit., 43–4.

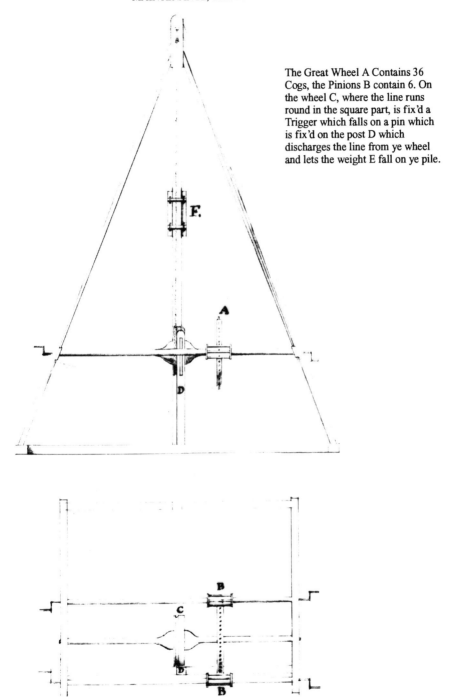

The Great Wheel A Contains 36 Cogs, the Pinions B contain 6. On the wheel C, where the line runs round in the square part, is fix'd a Trigger which falls on a pin which is fix'd on the post D which discharges the line from ye wheel and lets the weight E fall on ye pile.

Figure 15. Drawing of a pile-driver used at Rochester Bridge in the early eighteenth century.

Charles Hutton described traditional bridge work, in his Principles of Bridges, 1772, pp. 103–4 as follows. A set of piles, known as stilts, is 'driven into the space intended for the pier, whose tops being sawed off about low-water mark, the pier is then raised on them. This method was formerly used, when the bottom of the river could not be laid dry; and these stilts were surrounded, at a few feet distance, by a row of piles and planks, &c, close to them like a coffer dam, and called a sterling or jettee; after which, loose stones, &c, are thrown or poured dowm into the space, till it be filled up to the top, by that means forming a kind of pier of rubble or loose work, which is kept together by the sides of the sterlings: this is then paved level at the top, and the arches turned upon it. This method was formerly much used, most of the large old bridges in England being erected in that way, such as London bridge, Newcastle bridge, Rochester bridge, &c. But the inconveniences attending to it are so great, that it is now exploded and disused: for, because of the loose composition of the piers, they must be made very large or broad, or else the arch would push them over, and rush down, as soon as the centre should be drawn; which great breadth of piers and sterlings so much contracts the passage of the water'

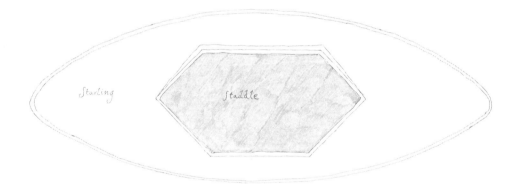

Figure 16. Plan showing a staddle or dense mass of piles upon which each pier was raised, surrounded by a starling for protection.

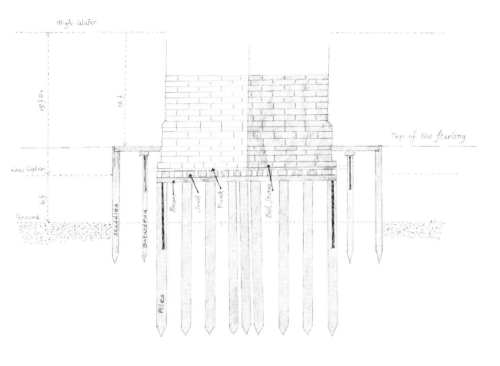

Figure 17. Cross-section of pier and staddle, with plan of staddle and pile heads below, showing the sides of the staddles and starlings enclosed by rows of interlocking piles known as stoppers and binders.

Apart from the building of the new bridge wharf in 1673–5, the reconstruction of the first pier in 1705–7 constituted the only major piece of bridge work in this sub-period. The foundations of the pier and the stonework were entirely rebuilt, as was much of the second arch and spandrells; in total, 112 new piles were driven. The bridge clerk noted that the work was done 'by night as well as by day (or else it might have been another yeare a doing) and was in great danger of falling'. As well as enhanced daily payments, the workmen were given occasional sums for drink, 'they working in great danger of their lives, in the water' and 'all hours, in the night'. The existing team of ten men was increased to thirteen for the duration of the project, and the bridge clerk was paid £50 for his 'great care' of the additional work.[18]

During these years, it seems that the maintenance programme was adequate, but subsequent experience indicates that major structural problems were approached with insufficient specialist expertise and inadequate supervision and control. Night-time working may have speeded up the rebuilding, but it is less clear that proper standards of workmanship were maintained. In 1722, it proved necessary to renew two further ribs of the second arch, yet two years later, it was still considered unstable. Problems were stored up for the future at a time when the volume of traffic on the river was growing rapidly.

1726–1792

Although the rate of growth of river traffic was less rapid than in the previous sub-period, an already substantial traffic doubled in size during these years, increasing the risk of damage to the bridge. By the late 1720s, in spite of the works carried out twenty years earlier, the condition of the first pier and the second arch was again dangerous. It was doubtless this problem, combined with his historical and antiquarian interests, which prompted Dr. John Thorpe to make a detailed examination of the entire pattern of repairs during the previous three centuries. The report was probably compiled around the time of his election to the office of bridge warden in 1733, or slightly earlier. The investigation showed plainly that the recurring problem of the first pier was the symptom of a fundamental structural fault in the 'new bridge', described by Thorpe as 'the great weakness of it, even from the time of its first being built.' The 'great weakness' evidently lay in the manner in which the bridge was anchored to the east bank at Rochester. However Thorpe was unclear whether the fault lay in the design and construction of the abutments and the first pier or to changing ground conditions:

> whether the same [weakness] is owing to its being placed on a loose, moorish, or marshy ground, and just on the edge of the Castle-Ditch; or, on a soil subject to springs and quick sands, as many places of the river are; or to any neglect or errour of the first builders, in not making the foundation sufficiently firm and durable, imagining that a slighter basis than ordinary might serve here (there being probably at that time but little depth and current of water thro' this arch);

---

[18] RBT 2136, Wardens' Accounts, vol. XVII, 1706.

or to the great disproportion between this arch and peer and the others (the arch being between 6 and 7ft. wider than any other arch, and the peer that helps to support it 5ft. less in diameter than its opposite peer); or to several of these causes concurring together, or to any others, I shall leave to better judges, and such as are more experienced in works of this nature, to determine.[19]

In 1737, the distinguished architect and Clerk of Works at Greenwich Hospital, John James, ascribed the sinking of the first pier as 'certainly owing to some, if not all the causes which Dr Thorpe has very judiciously hit upon and enumerated at the end of that useful Abstract he has made of what relates to the Bridge'.[20]

Like other medieval bridges, Rochester Bridge had been designed with a flat roadway approached by fairly steep inclines, particularly at the east end, which doubtless placed a special strain on the first pier. An unsigned memorandum of 1730 shows clearly that the eastern ribs of the second arch were sagging by eleven inches, whilst the parapets were collapsing outwards – both symptoms of the instability of the first pier, which had become 'very much cracked, decayed and out of repair'.[21] During the 1730s, no fewer than nine separate reports were commissioned by the wardens on this perennial problem, excluding Thorpe's own abstract and observations. The source of these reports provides an interesting conspectus of the state and accessibility of professional opinion on civil engineering problems at the time; their number perhaps reflects the difficulty of obtaining reliable technical advice. At least two were provided by stonemasons, William Lerow of London Bridge and William Fellows, mason to the Earl of Burlington; John Price of Richmond, John James of Greenwich and Charles Sloane of Gravesend were all well-known architects, the first of whom had published designs for Westminster and Putney Bridges; Golding and Hammond were probably surveyors, whilst Ward and Holland, based at Chatham Dockyard, were presumably engineers to the Navy Board.

No consensus emerged from the earliest reports of 1730–33 which variously suggested infilling the first arch, resiting the first pier midway between the two arches, and merely rebuilding the sagging section of the second arch in a manner 'well-turned and bonded'. John Montgomery and Charles Sloane, however, recommended the installation of a strong timber frame to prevent sudden collapse, a precaution which was duly carried out, prior to opening up the pier in 1734. Although the final decision to entirely repile and rebuild the first pier and second arch was deferred until 1737 pending further investigation, Charles Sloane acted as consultant to the bridge wardens from 1733 onwards; in July 1738, he was appointed Surveyor and Director of Works until 1745 when the work was finally

---

19　Society of Antiquaries (Thorpe MSS), vol. 159, f. 12r (undated; the description of bridge repairs ends in 1722).

20　RBT 76, Letter from John James to bridge warden John Marsh, Greenwich Hospital, 18 April 1737. James became successor to Nicholas Hawksmoor as Clerk of Works at Greenwich following the latter's death in 1736; at that moment, he was engaged in the controversy over the design of Westminster Bridge as a critic of Hawksmoor, John Price, and Batty Langley (Colvin, op. cit., 314–16).

21　RBT 67, Memorandum on the defects of the second arch, 1730.

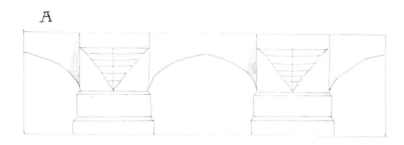

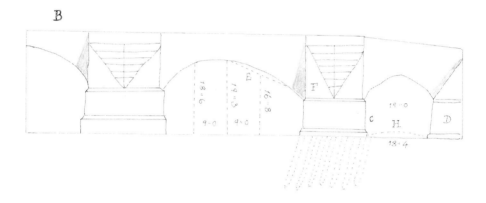

How is it posable that the Arch E can thrust the Peer D into the land without pushing the Peer F the same way – but the Arch E has thrust the Peer F towards the Peer D and the Pile heads with it as is Evident from the bending or rising of those strong peaces of Elm timber laid cross the soak H

Figure 18. Sagging arches: sketch by John Price illustrating problems created by the defective arch, c.1730.

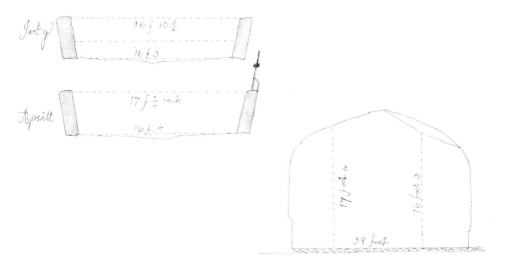

Figure 19. Collapsing parapets: sketch from an unsigned memorandum of 1730 in the Thorpe Mss in the Society of Antiquaries' Library.

completed on the basis of his estimate of £2,361. Sloane believed that the force of
the current had undermined the staddle work, since the pile heads were strongly
inclined eastwards, causing the pier to sink yet remain perpendicular, a view which
accorded with that of two Navy Board engineers, Ward and Holland.[22] Charles
Labelye, in the early stages of his great project to build a new bridge at Westminster, visited Rochester in 1739 to provide an opinion on the work in progess; he
approved it, two years before the foundations for the new pier were laid.[23]

The scale of the repairs undertaken during the years 1737–45, the intractable
nature of the building problems and their diagnosis, and the inadequacy of existing
practices in supervising work combined at this point to encourage the adoption of a
tighter management structure as we have already seen.[24] It was in April 1737 that
the Committee of Assistants was formed, meeting much more frequently than the
court of Wardens and Assistants. Within a matter of weeks, however, as the new
committee began to reform the practice for making tide payments, a fatal accident
occurred, one of the most serious in the entire history of the bridge. As the
labourers were preparing to dismantle the second arch of the bridge, 'it dropt down
of a sudden, without giving any notice', and the first mason and two labourers
were drowned; the accident would not have occurred, it was said, if they had used
the scaffolding provided.[25] This unfortunate episode no doubt increased the new
committee's determination to reform existing methods of labour management,
alongside its main objectives of improved bridge maintenance and estate management. During their first two years of activity, the assistants appointed an overseer
of workmen and a surveyor and director of works, and approved an increase in
labourers' pay from 14d. to 16d. per day.[26]

The work of reconstruction was completed in 1745, after delays resulting from
bad weather and damage caused by ice during the winter of 1739–40. Over the
next fifteen years, between 1746 and 61, the previously large teams of fourteen to
nineteen workmen were reduced to an abnormally small size of between four and

---

[22] Reports were submitted as follows, by: 1, William Lerow, stonemason of London Bridge, 3 June
    1730, recommending the simple rebuilding of a half section of the arch, with a 'true sweep'
    (RBT 68); 2. John Price, Richmond Green, 1 June 1730, with similar recommendations to
    Lerow, but noting the small bulk of pier in relation to the great span of the arch (RBT 69); 3.
    William Fellows, mason to the Earl of Burlington, 14 May 1733, suggested infilling the first
    arch (RBT 70); 4. John Carpenter, 27 May 1730 (mason?), suggested 'squaring' the arch (RBT
    71); 5. John Montgomery and Charles Sloane, 17 May 1733 argued that immediate installation
    of a timber frame was needed to prevent collapse (RBT 72); 6. John Golding and Edward
    Hammond, 14 May 1736, recommended rebuilding the pier and arches on either side, with the
    pier resited in the middle (RBT 73); 7. Ward and Holland of Chatham Dockyard, 12 June 1736,
    recommended rebuilding the pier on a firm new foundation, and reconstruction of both arches in
    a more regular fashion (RBT 74); 8. Charles Sloane, 8 and 22 April 1737, suggested that the
    earth between the piles of the first pier had been washed away, which required the entire
    rebuilding of the pier and both arches (RBT 75 and 78); and 9. John James, Greenwich Hospital,
    18 April 1737, confirmed Thorpe's diagnosis, together with that of Ward and Holland (RBT 76).
[23] RBT 1617, Minutes of the Committee of Assistants, vol. I, 20 July 1739, 34.
[24] Supra., chapter 2, 4.
[25] RBT 1617, 4 June, 4.
[26] RBT 1617, 19 January 1739, 21; 12 June 1739, 32.

seven men. (Between nine and twelve men were usually employed during years of normal maintenance work over the period 1660–1792 as a whole.) The shortfall in day labour, it seems, was compensated for by increased use of tide labour – possibly a false economy – which in effect represented a partial reversion to the medieval system. The change in practice was evidently brought about by pressure to reduce costs, arising from several problems: expenditure on reconstruction work had been substantial over the previous thirteen years, and bank stock purchased for £800 had been sold; labourers' wage rates had risen since 1739; and although rents on the bridge estates had been increased by 17 per cent during the 1740s, low farm prices produced a serious build-up of rent arrears.[27] So in spite of the wardens' efforts to improve management of the repair and maintenance programme after 1737, it is not surprising to find evidence of mounting neglect in the late 1740s and throughout the 50s. During these years, it seems, the bridge wardens gave more attention to estate repairs and improvements.

In 1751, the fifth pier was described as being 'in a dangerous condition'; two years later, the eastern land starling was 'very much out of repair', and by 1759, the assistants noted that 'the sterlings, wharfes and other works of the Bridge being greatly out of repair, it is thought necessary that some person skilled in the making and repairing of such sterlings, wharfes and proper foundations should be employed to survey and direct such work'.[28] Clearly, a general overhaul was necessary together with the reinstatement of an adequate labour force, and it was agreed to employ Thomas Rapley, a master house carpenter, as surveyor and director of bridge works.[29] By about 1753, the cumulative effect of earlier economies was beginning to produce an improvement in the bridge finances, strengthened by increasing timber sales arising from the direct management of Nashenden Woods from that date. Almost £3,500 was invested in bank stock over the next seven years, and in 1761 the wardens were in a position to mount a major programme of repairs. A full team of day labourers, carpenters and masons was established, and by 1765 the overhaul was complete, including the building of a new drawbridge and repairs to the wharves in Strood. These were years marked by rising costs and wages, particularly for masons, and it proved necessary to liquidate the entire capital stock in 1762–6.[30]

Throughout the 1770s and 80s, it appears that the wardens were able to implement a more than adequate programme of maintenance with a team of around nine or ten workmen, whilst at the same time accumulating a sizeable capital stock. From 1770, with the appointment of John Southerden as surveyor and director of works, an exact daily record was kept of all materials used and the work performed

---

27 Supra., 179.
28 RBT 1617, 24 May 1751, 181; 23 March 1759, 300; January 1749, 164–5; RBT 1540, Orders of Wardens and Assistants, vol. I, 29 June 1753, 227.
29 RBT 1617, 23 March 1759, 300. Rapley was paid 6s. per week for his 'Advice, Trouble and Service'.
30 RBT 1540, 26 May 1763, 267, authorised the sale of up to £200 of capital stock 'at any one time occasionally as the expenses of the said bridge and wharves may require at the discretion of the Committee of Assistants.'

by each member of the team, which seems to have achieved a new level of efficiency. 'The keeping of such accounts is of great use', it was agreed, 'as therby more work is done and more care taken of the materials to the great benefit of the bridge & the saving much money to the commonalty thereof'.[31]

It was no doubt the buoyant state of the bridge finances together with the increase in land and river traffic which caused the bridge wardens to consider the question of substantial modernisation in the 1780s. John Gorham, surveyor of the Inner Temple, was appointed in June 1780 to report on the practicability of widening the bridge. The chief problem, he pointed out, lay in the piecemeal nature of repairs over several centuries. London Bridge, 'at its first building' was no wider than Rochester Bridge, but had been continuously demolished and rebuilt; the same was true of the latter, which explained the oblique direction of the several different faces of the arches and parapets (omitted from the simplified drawing by Bingle). Gorham's description of the work required for widening is worth quoting in full, as it was substantially this plan which was finally adopted in 1792.

> the lines of the parapet lye oblique to each other, therefore that if the Bridge was widened the parapet and great part of the face of the pier must be taken down and in order to bring the parapet and footway in a straight line, the bevele part of the piers must be brought up square and new faced & cramped with proper iron tighs, and the arches to be sprung from the first offset or water-table. The arch stones not less than two feet six inches on the face in depth and to be properly secured by iron bars to the old work with room for settling, also secured by pavement laid in terrace [tarras] upon the arches to prevent the water penetrating between the old and the new work.[32]

Much additional piling was needed, and the estimated cost was finally put at £9,400.[33] The wardens decided that it would be imprudent to go ahead with the plan. Public dissatisfaction with the bridge was mounting, however, and some suggested that far from modernising the existing structure, the only solution was complete demolition and replacement with a new bridge. Early in 1787, the *Times* described the bridge as an 'infernal nuisance': 'The river is so choked up with its piers that the fall on the ebb tide is tremendous. Should not Parliament examine into this property and pass a bill to rebuild it in the most complete manner?'. This was to anticipate the view of the authorities at Chatham Dockyard after the end of the Napoleonic Wars. For the moment, the ideas of the Wardens and Assistants were fixed on modernisation.[34]

---

[31] RBT 1618, Minutes of the Committee of Assistants, vol. II, 29 June 1770, 14; 14 August 1772, 40.

[32] Ibid., 23 June 1780, 133; undated (July–August 1780), quoted from a letter dated 24 July 1780, 136.

[33] Ibid., 137.

[34] *The Times*, 26 January 1787; see also ibid., 30 March 1787: 'The bridge at Rochester built so long back as the reign of Henry the Fourth, has ruined the Medway as effectually as London Bridge has the Thames. It is high time they were both demolished, being great national nuisances.'

1792–1815

The years occupied by the French Revolutionary and Napoleonic Wars coincided with the determination of the bridge wardens to embark on the major project of modernisation outlined by John Gorham in 1780. The timing could hardly have been more unfortunate. The period was one in which the extension of naval dockyards, barracks and fortifications, coupled with the housing requirements of a growing population, led to increased competition for building materials. Wartime labour shortages and the disruption of the import trade, together with the increased risk and cost of carrying bulk cargoes coastwise, necessarily produced a sharp rise in building costs. The construction industry was buoyant but unstable, plagued by unpredictable changes in costs and sources of supply. The 1790s experienced exceptionally severe economic fluctuations, as the transition from boom to slump was accelerated by political forces. The years 1796–7 saw a major financial crisis at precisely the time when the bridge wardens most needed to liquidate their investments to meet the costs of the last and vital phase of the improvements.[35]

Into this difficult and unpredictable environment stepped the wardens' first salaried architect and engineer, Daniel Asher Alexander. In April 1792, the wardens again resolved to invite proposals for widening and improving the bridge, offering a premium of fifty guineas for the best scheme. At the time there seemed no reason to doubt Pitt's recent assurance to Parliament that fifteen years of peace had never seemed more likely, and the wardens proceeded with confidence.[36] Alexander's designs and estimates were selected in preference to those of Francis Carter and Charles Beasley. A former student of the Royal Academy, he was then aged 24 and at an early stage of what was to be a long and distinguished career.[37] The following year, he was made surveyor to the London Dock Company and went on to design the most successful and monumental complex of docks and warehouses in the port of London, finer, arguably, than those of Rennie.[38] Significantly, he became architect to Lord Romney, Senior Warden in 1795–6, commencing work on the rebuilding of Mote Park, Maidstone in 1794. He designed Maidstone and Dartmoor gaols, and was publicly commended by Sir John Soane for his restoration work on two buildings by Inigo Jones, the Royal Hospital at Greenwich and Coleshill House, Berkshire. He became surveyor to Trinity House, but continued to be involved with bridge works at Rochester until 1818. His buildings were functional but innovative, displaying 'a characteristic fitness of purpose . . . in his hands the architecture,

---

35 T.S. Ashton, *Economic Fluctuations in England, 1700–1800*, Oxford 1959, 168; J. Parry Lewis, *Building Cycles and Britain's Growth*, London 1965, 23–28; A.D. Gayer, W.W. Rostow and A.J. Schwartz, *The Growth and Fluctuation of the British Economy, 1790–1850*, 2 vols., Oxford 1953, I, 44–54.

36 A. Briggs, *The Age of Improvement, 1783–1867*, London 1959, 135; RBT 1618, 27 April 1792, 242 (i) [pp. 219–248 are duplicated].

37 *Dictionary of National Biography*, s.v. Alexander, Daniel Asher (1768–1846); Colvin, op. cit., 38–9.

38 N. Taylor, *Monuments of Commerce*, London 1968, 5.

whatever it was, was ever made to grow out of and to form an inherent necessity of the structure.'[39]

Alexander's functional approach evidently agreed with the taste and practical requirements of the Wardens and Assistants. Priority, they suggested, should be given to the security of the structure and the accommodation of the public, both by land and water; only slightly less in importance was 'Moderation in expense. The Bridge being a plain ancient building, it is not conceived to be susceptible of ornament'.[40] The main object was to widen the bridge from 14 to 26 feet, including the provision of a footway on both sides. The sixth pier and the arch and draw-bridge on either side were to be removed and the two openings thrown into a single stone arch, along the lines suggested in John Gorham's survey of 1780. Initially, Alexander had been enthusiastic about constructing the proposed new arch from cast iron following the prototype at Coalbrookdale, but finally opted for stone. The cost for the whole project was then estimated at £19,700.[41]

In mid-September 1792, Alexander's plans were accepted and preliminary repair work began on the starlings and piers. The work of widening the first arch and its piers began late in April 1793. At this stage, the wardens appear to have specified no overall completion date, as the relatively modest flow of revenue from the bridge estates and a limited capital stock, then valued at £6,321, permitted the improvement work to progress only gradually alongside the somewhat variable programme of maintenance required for the starlings. The maximum annual rate of expenditure agreed for the new work was to be £2,000 together with the surplus of income over and above the sums normally spent on basic maintenance and repairs. As Daniel Alexander's analysis of expenditure during the first four years of the improvements was to show, the average annual outlay of £2,567 compared with £1,023 spent in the years immediately before the project began (shown in Table 28).[42] Obviously, repair work on the old piers, averaged at £184, formed no part of the improvement programme but savings here were roughly counterbalanced by enhanced management charges, including the architect's salary of £100 per annum. Income from rents and timber sales during the period 1793–1800 averaged £1,700, so that an annual surplus of around £700 was available to supplement withdrawals from capital resources. At this level of funding, completion of the original im-provement programme might be expected to extend over nearly two decades. Whether the wardens envisaged taking up loans at this stage is impossible to say. In the event they did so; nevertheless, thirty years elapsed, and two abortive efforts were made to secure parliamentary support before Daniel Alexander's scheme was finally completed. The delays, of course, resulted primarily from the uncertainties of war which necessitated the frequent rescheduling of works.

It was during the interval between Alexander's appointment and the approval of

[39] *Gentleman's Magazine*, cxix (1846 ii), 211.
[40] RBT 1618, 27 April, 244 (i).
[41] RBT 133, Letter from Daniel Alexander to bridge clerk William Twopeny, Southwark, 19 June 1792, with attached 1 Estimate according to 4 Statements of the Repairs to Rochester Bridge'.
[42] RBT 1540, 12 April 1793, 396; RBT 145, Report by Daniel Alexander to the bridge wardens and assistants, 28 April 1797, London.

Table 28

Daniel Alexander's analysis of bridge maintenance, 1788–1796   (£s)

	1788–1789	1789–1790	1790–1791	1791–1792	1792–1793	Total 5 years	Annual Average
Carpenters' work repairing starlings:	367	436	390	520	502	2215	443 (43.3%)
Smiths' work repairing starlings:	121	129	136	105	116	598	120 (11.7%)
Masons' work repairing old piers:	220	166	145	140	250	921	184 (18.0%)
Management, clerks, wood reeves, &c:	317	262	266	277	261	1383	276 (27.0%)
TOTAL:	1025	984	937	1042	1129	5117	1023

	1793–1794	1794–1795	1795–1796	1796–1797		Total 4 years	Annual Average
Carpenters' work on starlings, scaffolds & centre arches:	672	600	374	630		2276	569 (22.2%)
Smiths' work on cramps & bolts for starlings:	148	170	184	248		750	187 (7.3%)
Masons' work on new arches, piers, & balustrades:	1164	1174	1543	1680		5561	1390 (54.1%)
Management, clerks, architect, woods & general charges:	386	498	416	383		1683	421 (16.4%)
TOTAL:	2370	2442	2517	2941		10270	2567

Note: The percentage figures shown in brackets, which are not given in Daniel Alexander's report, indicate annual average expenditure on each item as a percentage of the total.

the initial improvement plans that hostilities with France broke out, in February 1793. The effects of the war on the building programme soon became apparent when early in May the bridge labourers petitioned for an increase in wages. John Franks, the bridge foreman, reported to the assistants' meeting that the common labourers were dissatisfied with their pay of 20d. per day, and in view of the 'difficulty in providing labourers', it was agreed to raise this to two shillings.[43] The war likewise made an immediate impact on the price of materials. Since Kentish ragstone from the quarries above the bridge was deemed unsuitable, Alexander visited possible suppliers at Purbeck and Portland to examine stone for the arches,

[43] RBT 1618, 4 May 1793, 234 (ii).

and selected Messrs Warrin & Bonfield of Swanage. Within a matter of weeks, peacetime freight rates had risen from 6s. 6d. to 8s. 6d. per ton, which for arch stones involved an increase in price from 1s. 2½d. to 1s. 4¼d. per cubic foot.[44]

Faced by a 20 per cent wage increase and a 12 per cent increase in the cost of materials, the wardens were forced to consider economies. In August 1793, it was agreed that instead of completing the widening of one entire side of the bridge as originally planned, it be widened arch by arch on each side. This enabled the masons to reuse the timber centre on which each new arch was constructed by applying it to the opposite face, and also facilitated the working of stone at the quarries.[45] The job of centring the arches was the most skilled and expensive part of the bridge building process, and the resulting savings were presumably judged to outweigh the obvious disadvantages facing passengers through this alternative procedure. At the same time, it enabled the wardens to delay commencing work on the proposed 'great arch', the most ambitious part of the entire project. In spite of these economies, Alexander's original estimate had risen from £19,700 to £21,309 by June 1794, including additional provision for a stone balustrade at £530. Unavoidably, the wardens decided to abandon the great arch project which accounted for £8,400, leaving a total of £12,900 for the remaining improvements, chiefly widening. It is significant, however, that they justified their decision on technical rather than financial grounds, accepting Alexander's recommendation that the great arch 'cannot with safety be put into execution.'[46]

The volatile financial and economic conditions of the 1790s, combined with a series of challenging technical problems, clearly placed Daniel Alexander in an extremely demanding and difficult situation. He was of course required to provide periodic progress reports which occasionally involved the retrospective analysis of expenditure such as that summarised in Table 28, and a more detailed enquiry of 1818 which was to take him back through the accounts to 1750.[47] He clearly displayed a good grasp of the bridge finances, yet an unwillingess to revise his cost estimates in line with inflation must be seen as a major weakness. The overall figure of £12,909 for the improvements was maintained, even defended, throughout the years 1794–7, and this can hardly be regarded as realistic. And when hard decisions had to be taken, financial and economic realities were disguised with a technical rationale. As we have seen, the decision to abandon the great arch was taken on Alexander's recommendation as an engineer that it could not be safely executed, set out in his report of June 1794. Here, it was suggested that since the

[44] Ibid., 234–6 (ii).

[45] RBT 137, Report by Daniel Alexander to the Bridge Wardens and Assistants, 10 August 1793, London; RBT 1540, 10 August 1793, 404.

[46] RBT 143, Report by Daniel Alexander to the Bridge Wardens and Assistants, 12 June 1794, London; RBT 1540, 12 June 1794, 407.

[47] RBT 201, Report of Daniel Alexander to the Bridge Wardens and Assistants reviewing the Bridge funds from 1751–1812, 8 April 1812, London; RBT 210, Report of Daniel Alexander to the bridge wardens and assistants on bridge expenditure and cost of improvements, 1789–1817, 3 April 1818, Rochester. The latter distinguishes between expenditure on work, taxes, management, investment, and interest payments.

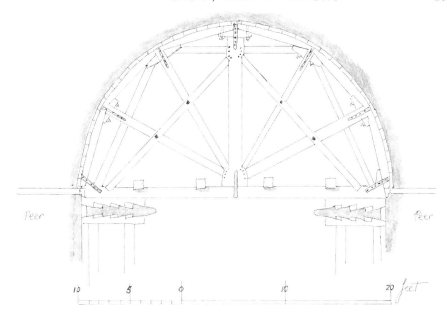

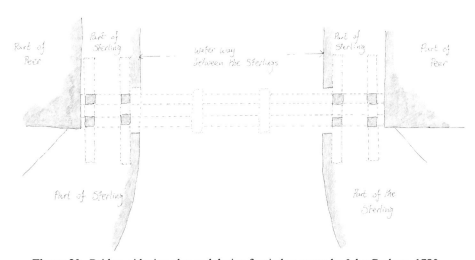

Figure 20. Bridge widening plan and design for timber centre by John Gorham, 1780.

ELM,
OR OTHER TIMBER.

WANTED,

BY THE

Wardens and Commonalty of Rochester Bridge

ABOUT THIRTY-FIVE

Loads of Elm,

OR OTHER

TIMBER,

And Ten Loads more conditionally, if required.

The ELM Timber to be long, slender, and straight Timber, such as is fit for the Bridge use, in Piles from 25 feet long, and upwards. It is to be of two kinds of Trees, that will either equal 9 inches square, or else 15 inches square and upwards, so that one tree, by a cut down the middle, shall make two Piles. The Elm to be measured and paid for in the usual way, as in the round, taking one quarter of the girth as the square, and an inch deducted for rind.

Any Tender for BEECH Timber will be received, if persons are disposed to offer the same ; or they may tender other Timber, if disposed to do so ; in which cases, the Timber is to be of the scantling that shall make one Pile not more than 8 inches square ; or else of the scantlings that shall saw into Piles of any width upon the face, by about 7 inches thick, and straight, and no wain more than 3 inches wide upon the bevel face. It is to be prime, sound Timber, and to be measured by taking the actual square of it, deducting for the wainey edges, so as to produce net Timber.

The Timber is to be entirely subject to the approbation of the Foreman of the Bridge Works in regard to quality, scantling, &c.: the tops that are cut off by his direction not to be measured : the Timber to be delivered in such quantities, and at such times as shall be required by the Wardens and Assistants, or the Foreman: the first quantity will be wanted in February next, and the whole in 1812.

Proposals to be delivered in at the Meeting of the Committee of Assistants, on Saturday the Eighth day of February next, at Twelve o'Clock at Noon, at the Bridge Audit Room, (inst' of the First of February, as mentioned in a former Advertisement.)

For further Particulars inquire at our Office, or of Mr. Slater, Foreman of the Bridge Worl

Rochester,   HUSSEY AND LEWIS,
30th January, 1812.   Clerk of the Bridge.

Caddel, Printer & Stationer, Rochester.

Figure 21. Advertisement for timber to repair the starlings in 1812.

depth and extent of the old foundations appeared to rule out the possibility of driving sufficient piles for new staddle work, there was no alternative but to raise a new arch on the old staddles, and this was considered unsafe or, at best, risky. But it seems likely that Alexander arrived at this conclusion on largely financial grounds because four years later, in April 1798, he was to reverse that advice at a time when local commercial interests were demanding improvements to the Medway navigation and when there seemed to be some prospect that they might provide the necessary finance. This time, he judged that the strength of the old staddles was in fact sufficient to bear the weight of a new 84-foot arch, the interval of four years having provided him with 'many opportunities of investigating and collecting facts which have been proper to be obtained before decision; whereby designs and plans may be reduced to greater maturity and certainty'.[48]

The decision of 1798 to reinstate the great arch project no doubt owed something to Alexander's undoubted success in maintaining a steady rate of progress and in holding costs down in some degree. Great efforts had been made, he claimed, to achieve savings in several areas: by purchasing materials at first hand; by employing workmen under the immediate direction of the architect and foreman without the intervention of master workmen; by the prompt discharge of accounts; and by making use of 'various Mechanical means to shorten labour', including two new piling engines. Prudence and self-interest no doubt prompted him to draw attention to the 'vigilence and exactness' of the Committee of Wardens and Assistants in directing the works and in the confidence placed by them in the architect.[49] Yet good management must play some part in explaining the success with which the bridge wardens and their architect were able to cope with an unprecedented rate of wartime inflation. In 1795, a further increase in labourers' wages had been agreed, from 24d. to 27d. per day, and masons' and carpenters' pay was increased from 42d. to 45d. The price of lime rose at the same time from 9s. to 11s. per load 'from the high price of coals, the advance of wages, and other similar causes'. 'Extraordinary expenses have been incurred', wrote Alexander, 'from the high price of labour; the rise in the freights of stone and timber, the high additional duties theron, and the advance on iron; which have amounted to nearly 1000£, and which nothing but a regular and systematic plan both of management, promptness & oeconomy could have counteracted'.[50] The possibility remains, however, that a proportion of the real cost of the new works was shifted in the accounts to the sums allocated for regular maintenance work on the starlings.

The widening of the bridge was nonetheless accomplished by Easter 1798 with the exception of the two middle arches, and the decision was approved to proceed with the great arch plan provided that the necessary funds could be raised. The cost of widening the sixth arch and throwing a stone arch over the drawlock was

---

[48] RBT 146, Report by Daniel Alexander to the Bridge Wardens and Assistants, 20 April 1798, 2–3.
[49] RBT 145, Report by Daniel Alexander to the Bridge Wardens and Assistants, 28 April 1797, London, 3–4.
[50] Ibid., 4.

estimated at £1,394, which compared with a figure of £5,251 to remove the centre pier and construct a great arch in its place.[51] But the bridge finances were by now at a low ebb: the surplus of revenue available for improvements amounted to a few hundred pounds, cash balances had been run down during 1793–4, and most of the capital stock had been sold with heavy losses at the bottom of the financial crisis of 1796–7. After the remaining holdings were disposed of in May 1798, it was clear that stock valued at £6,321 in the early 1790s had raised only £4,588. In order to proceed with the great arch, a loan of £5,000 would be required.[52]

At this point, the hoymen, barge-owners and other users of the river petitioned the wardens, urging them to press ahead with the great arch in view of what they described as 'the present very dangerous situation through the Bridge from the confined state of the arches.'[53] The hoymen had so far received no benefit whatever from the extensive improvement works, and the deteriorating state of the Medway navigation was becoming increasingly apparent. In his 1798 report on the feasibility of the proposed arch, Daniel Alexander gave much more attention to these problems than he had done four years earlier, conveying the impression that the 'gentlemen hoymen and bargemasters' had already familiarised him with their difficulties.[54] At any rate, the wardens found them ready to provide the required loan of £5,000 and by January 1799, 37 individuals had subscribed, including Lord Romney and a number of Maidstone gentlemen. Fifty bonds of £100 each were issued at an interest rate of 5 per cent. By April 1800, it was apparent that a further £2,500 was required to complete the project but this time, it proved impossible to raise more than £1,500.[55]

The chief difficulty at this final stage was said to have been the weather. During the severe winter of 1799, a mass of ice built up around the starlings between twelve and fifteen feet thick and 'carried to sea [a] great part of the scaffolds erected for the work, and so disabled the exterior level of the old pile work of many of the starlings as to break away large parts of them between wind and water, which otherwise would have lasted many years longer.'[56] In addition however, it appears that ordinary repairs to the starlings had been neglected after 1794 so as to enlarge the fund available for improvements, a fact suggested by Alexander's comment that the starlings had developed 'considerable decays all over them, which appear to have been accumulating for a vast number of years'.[57] A further problem arose when Alexander again modified his plans for the construction of the great arch,

[51] RBT 1540, 20 April 1798, 431.

[52] Loc. cit.; RBT 2147, Wardens' Accounts, vol. XXX, 1798–9.

[53] RBT 520, 'Case and Brief for the Wardens and Commonalty of Rochester Bridge in support of a Bill to enable them to compleat the repairs and Improvement of that Bridge', [1802], 5; RBT 1540, 20 April 1798, 431, 434; see also RBT 148 and 149 for the wardens' response to the petition.

[54] RBT 146, 3.

[55] RBT 1618, 29 December 1798, 12 January 1799, 22 June 1799 (unpaginated from December 1793); RBT 1540, 25 April 1800, 448, and 5 June 1800, 452.

[56] RBT 520, 6.

[57] RBT 183, Report by Daniel Alexander on the state of the repairs and funds of the bridge, 17 April 1801, 1.

deciding that substantial support for the foundations was after all both necessary and feasible.[58] In April 1801, it was clear that these contingencies had absorbed at least an additional £5,000, and Alexander had to admit that it was impossible to estimate the exact extent of further repairs needed to put the starlings in good order. To make matters worse, labourers' wages had advanced by 4d. per day and those of carpenters and masons by 3d. Subscribers to the loans were requested to forgo repayment of part of the principal, receiving only interest until the great arch could be completed, the original loan agreement having provided for repayment at the rate of £500 per year.[59] Their collective reply is not recorded, but evidently it was negative.

The wardens now found themselves rapidly approaching a state of financial embarrassment. Three-fifths of the expenditure to complete the great arch had been committed but much of this was not visible, consisting of stocks of materials and work on the foundations. Considerations of obligation and economy suggested that the momentum of new work should continue, and be seen to continue, whilst the subscribers were demanding repayment on the agreed terms; but at the same time, essential repairs to the starlings were needed.[26] Matters came to a head in May 1801. Alexander reported that a further £3,600 was required to complete the new works and put the starlings back in repair, and reminded the wardens of their debt of £6,500. It was resolved to apply to the government for a loan of £10,000 to secure the repayment of the Maidstone creditors and the continuation of the bridge works.[60]

A meeting followed with the Chancellor of the Exchequer, Henry Addington, but the wardens' request was turned down, awkward though it was for the former to refuse 'so respectable a body'.[61] The obvious solution was a private act of Parliament. Accordingly, a bill was prepared to enable the wardens to erect a turnpike and charge a bridge toll levied on carriages, cattle and horse traffic, and to authorise borrowing on the security of the bridge estates and the tolls collected. The first draft was ready in October 1801.[62] In the initial stages it was proposed only to levy a land toll, but a petition from the Mayor and citizens of Rochester persuaded the wardens to insert a clause adding a river toll, or pontage, in order to reduce the land toll. Other petitions then followed raising objections to the proposed pontage: from the Medway Navigation Company, the hoymen and barge-masters using the river from Tonbridge to Rochester, and the proprietors of the Thames and Medway Canal, on the grounds that a general river toll was already in existence and that a further toll had been authorised to maintain the new canal.[63]

---

[58] Ibid., 2–3.
[59] RBT 1540, 453.
[60] Ibid., 8 May 1801, 456.
[61] Addington met with Lord Darnley, and the latter's reply of 26 August 1801 was copied into the Warden's Order Book: RBT 1540, 31 August 1801, 461–2.
[62] RBT 182, A Bill to Enable the Wardens and Commonalty of the New Bridge of Rochester, in the County of Kent, to complete the Improvements and Repairs of the said Bridge, and to raise Money for the Purpose (draft, 41 Geo. III, 1801).
[63] RBT 187, Copies of petitions against the Rochester Bridge Bill by the Mayor and Citizens of

The pontage clause was withdrawn. But the prospect of a land toll was equally unpopular and a number of private citizens objected to the 'multiplicity' of tolls and turnpike gates in the vicinity, at Strood, Chatham and the New Road at Rochester. There was evidently some feeling amongst the objectors that the bridge estates had been mismanaged, and even that owners of the contributory lands ought now to be called upon to meet their ancient obligations. The wardens rightly pointed out that their responsibilities and those of the owners covered only the repair of the bridge, not its improvement or rebuilding.[64]

In the event, the objectors won the day and the bill was withdrawn at the committee stage in May 1802. After a decade of intensive improvement work, during which more than 130 individual labourers and craftsmen had been employed, the wardens had come tantalisingly close to realising the complete scheme of 1792–3. The minutes, however, record nothing more than their resolve to 'form a plan to reduce the bridge expenses to the lowest scale.'[65]

Although the bridge had been substantially modernised at a cost of more than £20,000, its basic weaknesses still remained: the foundations required constant attention, and the incurably defective first pier at the east end continued to present problems. Before the outcome of the parliamentary proceedings was known, Robert Mylne and George Dance, in consultation with Alexander, had been asked to report on the latter. A perforation was made into the pier and it was discovered that the timber platform upon which it rested had been placed 30 inches above the true level at which it should have been laid during the reconstruction work of the 1740s. The only solution was to replace the defective timber with solid masonry; in addition, they suggested, the abutment arch next to Rochester should be walled up, and the solid starling under the second arch be removed to improve the navigation. Mylne and Dance added their own tailpiece, complimenting Alexander on the great skill and attention with which the new work had been executed. The construction of the great arch, they considered, would be facilitated by supporting the voussoirs (or arch-stones) on cast-iron ribs, which would both make for a lighter construction and save the expense of using timber centres. Finally, the 'enormous extent and magnitude' of the starlings should be reduced so as to improve the navigation and reduce maintenance costs.[66] Leaving aside the great arch project, this was a substantial catalogue of repairs which the wardens could hardly ignore in the

Rochester, the Inhabitants of the City of Rochester, and the hoymen, barge masters, and others interested in the navigation of the Medway, 24 November 1801; RBT 190, Copy of petition to Parliament by the proprietors of the Thames Medway Canal, opposing the Rochester Bridge Bill for fear that the proposed bridge toll will lead to a water toll for passage under the Bridge, 1802; RBT 191, Copy of petition to Parliament by the Company of Proprietors of the Navigation of the River Medway, opposing the Rochester Bridge Bill on the grounds that the proposed bridge toll might lead to a water toll that would discourage navigation, 1802.

[64] RBT 520, 'Case and Brief for the Wardens and Commonalty of Rochester Bridge in support of a Bill to enable them to compleat the repairs and improvement of that Bridge' [1802], 12.

[65] RBT 1540, 22 May 1802.

[66] Ibid., 27 March 1802, 467; RBT 189, Report by Robert Mylne, George Dance and Daniel Alexander to the Bridge Wardens and Assistants, 22 March 1802.

aftermath of the Rochester Bridge Bill espisode. On the other hand, they could afford only a minimal maintenance programme.

It was Daniel Alexander's generosity at this juncture which enabled the work of the bridge wardens to continue satisfactorily. In early June 1802, the wardens declared that they were 'entirely satisfied with the conduct of Mr Alexander, their architect', but because of the necessity of curtailing expenditure they must discontinue his salary which since May 1799 had been increased from 100 to 200 guineas.[67] Alexander, nevertheless, continued to provide his services without payment: two years later, it was reported that he was still very attentive to bridge business and that he should at least receive reimbursement for travelling expenses.[68] Under his direction, the defective first pier was underpinned with stone; repiling of the second was completed prior to opening up the lock under the second arch; and the arch of the St Mary lock, the main channel, was repaired. All work on the great arch was of course suspended. During 1802–4, expenditure on bridge works was reduced from £3,000 to £1,750 falling to £965; timber for constructing the temporary bridge was sold off as were 350 tons of Portland stone intended for the great arch; even the bridge yard in Rochester was rented to a local stonemason.[69] From 1804 onwards, only minimal repairs were carried out on the starlings. These various economies enabled the trust to repay the whole of the £6,500 debt by May 1811.

The war years, of course, had seen substantial increases in costs and money wages, but it seems that rental income rose roughly in line with the general level of inflation. The 1790s and the 1800s in fact saw rent increases of 45 per cent and 50 per cent respectively. The years after 1813, however, were marked by falling prices at a time when the bridge estates were continuing to increase in value: during the 1810s, rental income rose by as much as 57 per cent. At almost exactly the moment when their debts were cleared therefore, the wardens found themselves carried along by a tide of rising real income. From 1812 to 1818, an annual average of £900 was invested whilst an enhanced maintenance programme put the starlings back into a state of complete repair. Two additional piling engines and gangs of men were employed for this purpose costing an additional £500–£600 per year. At the same time, the size of the starlings was reduced with the aid of a mechanical underwater saw, following the earlier recommendations of Mylne and Dance.[70] Periodical payments were now made to Daniel Alexander, and in May 1815, his salary was established at £63 per year 'until the conversion of the two centre arches into one shall be entered upon.'[71]

[67] RBT 1540, 10 June 1802, 477.
[68] Ibid., 13 April 1804, 488.
[69] Loc. cit.
[70] RBT 194, Report by Daniel Alexander to the Bridge Wardens and Assistants, 21 May 1812; RBT 1540, 21 May 1812, 547.
[71] RBT 1540, 18 May 1815, 571.

1815–1825

The problems encountered in implementing the programme of works envisaged in 1792 suggest that it was one thing to reface a medieval bridge with new masonry but quite another to effect radical changes in its structure and design. Nevertheless, the bridge wardens and their architect remained optimistic. In May 1817, co-incidentally the moment at which it was agreed that Daniel Alexander Jnr be associated with his father as architect and engineer of the bridge, it was resolved that father and son prepare working plans and contract specifications for the new arch. The agreed timetable involved the completion of contracts for stone by Whitsun 1818, the turning of the great arch in the same year, with the roadway finished in 1819.[72] The stone was to be prepared and marked in the quarries forthwith, so as to have a summer and a winter seasoning, 'a matter of as much moment in stone almost, as in timber'. Daniel Alexander Jnr was dispatched to the quarries of Derbyshire, Yorkshire and Leith to obtain specimens and tenders, which confirmed his father's preference for Bramley Fall, a hard brownish Yorkshire grit 'procured from a Navigation opened a short time since near Leeds', and hence two-thirds the price of Matlock or Craig Leith stone. The form of the arch was to be elliptical, not a segment of a circle as originally proposed; and the expense of a great timber centre would be saved by laying small centres, part wood and part iron, on the remaining bulk of the old pier.[73]

In mid January 1818, the temporary bridge was completed and pile gauges were set up to establish the state of the tides prior to the commencement of work on the great arch. At this critical moment Sir Robert Barlow, Commissioner at Chatham Dockyard, fired the first of a series of salvoes which were to delay completion of the arch by a further four years. At a specially-convened meeting on 20 January, attended by Barlow, the wardens heard his considered opinion that 'the river Medway, like the Thames, is in a gradual state of decay, and that in time, Chatham will be less valuable as a naval station than it now is' and, furthermore, that he had taken steps to inform the government of his view that a new bridge should be built under the authority of Parliament.[74] Barlow's reasoning was set out in a written statement which relied heavily on a report of 1807 relating to the silting of the Medway prepared by John Rennie for the Navy Commissioners. Barlow quoted Rennie's observation that,

> If Rochester Bridge had been pulled down some years since, and a new one built in the line of the streets through Strood and Rochester, with piers of suitable dimensions, instead of repairing the old one, the large starlings of

---

[72] RBT 1540, 29 May 1817, 586; 2 July 1817, 590.

[73] RBT 195, Report by Daniel Alexander to the Bridge Wardens and Assistants, London Docks, 28 May 1817.

[74] RBT 214, 'Copy of correspondence, reports &c. relating to the negociation with the Admiralty for building a New Bridge', 1818–20, 2–6: Sir Robert Barlow's written statement, Chatham Dock, 20 January 1818.

which act as a dam, and prevent the tide from flowing up to the extent it otherwise would do, the depth of water in front of Chatham, Rochester, and in Cockham Wood Reach, would have been greatly improved. But the trustees having unfortunately determined on repairing the old bridge, this nuisance still remains, and no advantage whatever has been gained; unless, therefore, something is done to preserve at least, if not to improve the navigation of the Medway, the soundings will go on diminishing in depth, and the Dock Yard will become less useful. In its present state, vessels of large draught of water must have all their guns and stores taken out before they can come up the Dock Yard, and be dismantled before they can be taken into dock.[75]

Barlow also relied heavily on Rennie's comparison of soundings taken at various points below Rochester Bridge in 1724 and 1803 which unfortunately proved somewhat ambiguous: although the measurements pointed to a deterioration of high water moorings by four feet in Chatham Reach and two feet in West Gillingham reach at low water, there appeared to be very little change between the bridge and Chatham quay. In the Parliamentary enquiry which followed, much reliable evidence of shoaling was indeed produced, especially by hoymen and bargemasters in relation to the stretch between Maidstone and Rochester. The fact was that the navy itself was responsible for much of the shoaling in the lower reaches of the river, and at this stage, Barlow doubtless felt constrained to present his evidence selectively by relying on Admiralty sources.[76]

The problem of shoaling had hitherto been given little attention by the bridge wardens. Their primary consideration was to keep the existing bridge in good repair and to ensure a 'commodious passage' for travellers and local people; next came the interests of the bargemasters and hoymen, served by maintaining the bridge locks in good order. Apart from repairs to the starlings, this involved ballasting the channel and those parts of the riverbed close to the locks where the current had scoured out rocks and alluvium. Of course the continuous action of tipping chalk and other ballast into the locks greatly exacerbated the problem of shoaling, and over a long period of time, a broad 'rock' of chalk had built up on either side of the bridge.[77] This slow acccumulation of displaced ballast and the general effect of the starlings in encouraging the build-up of shoals were doubtless matters over which the wardens felt they had little or no control. The Admiralty,

---

[75] Ibid., 4.

[76] BPP 1820 (267), Report of the Select Committee on the Present State of Rochester Bridge, 11 July 1820. Rennie, however, pointed out that a major cause of shoaling was the erection of 'jetties and other obstructions in the river, by which the current of the flood tide is impeded, and its direction changed; the bottom, therefore, becomes irregular, and mud accumulates in the sheltered places; this is strongly exemplified by the ordnance bridge at the lower end of the Dock Yard, and by the irregular projection of the Dock Yard wall itself; the jetty where the new Dock is building, has had no small share in contributing to the rapid accumulation of mud in front of the Dock Yard between this jetty and the ordnance bridge' (loc. cit., 31). Rennie's earlier observations on the state of the Medway, contained in his 1807 report to the Navy Board, were also published in the 1820 Select Committee Report, loc. cit., 29.

[77] Evidence of William Benstead, Hoyman, of Maidstone, and George Craddock, bargemaster, of Maidstone, 6 May 1818, 15–16, loc. cit.

however, was well aware of the problem and faced the considerable annual expense of dredging and clearing away the mud at Chatham. For the years 1815–17, the average annual cost was £628 rising to £1,910 in 1818–21.[78] A major programme of dockyard expansion was underway at this time which naturally increased the Admiralty's resolve to prevent any further silting up. The building of a new bridge at Rochester was, therefore, regarded as 'an object of great national importance'.[79]

The bridge wardens appear to have been entirely sympathetic to the Admiralty's concern, not least perhaps because Lord Melville, First Lord of the Admiralty, had suggested that the wardens might obtain the resources for a new bridge by applying to the parliamentary commissioners for a public works loan backed by the issue of exchequer bills.[80] At any rate, they signified their willingness to proceed with the work of a new bridge and to suspend all work on the improvements. A series of complicated negotiations was set in motion between Lord Melville and Sir Byam Martin, Comptroller of the Navy, for the government and Admiralty, and a sub-committee of wardens and assistants consisting of Senior Warden George Smith, Senior Warden-elect Lord Romney and Bridge Clerk William Twopeny. The Admiralty relied throughout on the advice of John Rennie who, since the start of the Napoleonic Wars, had provided innumerable plans for defensive works, docks, harbours, and other engineering projects. A formal meeting between the two parties took place at the Admiralty on 17 April 1818 at which Melville, following Rennie's advice, expressed his preference for a cast-iron bridge on the grounds of economy. The bridge wardens, on the other hand, pressed the case for a stone bridge, and suggested removing alternate piers from the existing bridge so as to remodel it as a bridge of five arches. The estimated cost of the latter was £80,000, and the benefits to the public would accrue as the work progressed. It seemed to the sub-committee that Melville considered this plan the most prudent, and he agreed to discuss it with Lord Liverpool and the Chancellor of the Exchequer, Nicholas Vansittart.[81]

It transpired, however, that the government's preference was for a new cast-iron bridge of three arches, built and maintained at government expense, following the transfer of the trust's estates and other property.[82] As soon as this became known, Romney politely informed Melville that 'an adequate grant to the present corporation would be the most proper way of effecting the object', which the latter appeared to accept.[83] The two men met at Sir Robert Barlow's office at Chatham

---

[78] RBT Eng. C. 12/13, 'A Return of the Annual Expence attending the clearing the Harbour of Chatham of Mud . . . since 1814', Navy Office, 21 July 1828; see also BPP 1820, ibid., 9.

[79] RBT 214, 5.

[80] Under the enabling powers provided by 57 Geo. III, c.34 (1817), which authorised the issue of Exchequer bills and loans, to the extent of £1,750,000, for the implementation of public works programmes.

[81] RBT 214, 25–28 (copy of Romney's account of the sub-committee's meeting with Melville, as reported 14 May 1818).

[82] Ibid., 18 (copy of Melville's letter to Romney, 22 April 1818).

[83] Ibid., 20 (copy of Romney's reply to Melville, 24 April 1818).

Dockyard on 12 May. Two days later, the proposals negotiated by Romney were laid before the Wardens and Assistants and involved the building of a new stone bridge of five arches 'to connect in a direct line the High Streets of Rochester and Strood under the direction of the Corporation of Wardens and Assistants whose powers and funds should be transferred from the existing to the proposed bridge'. Enabling powers would be provided by a public act of Parliament which would require the wardens to mortgage their estates to raise the necessary finance but at the same time would guarantee public funds as required. The estimated expense was £120,000 excluding purchase of property, and the Admiralty Board would approve the plan of works and provide checks against any 'improvident expenditure of the public money'. The necessary surveys and plans together with the execution of works would fall under the sole direction of the wardens. The proposals were accepted.[84]

Daniel Alexander immediately started work on designs for the new bridge. Preliminary plans and estimates were presented to, and approved by, the wardens and assistants a fortnight later, consisting of two elevations, one with a headway of twelve feet in the middle arch at high water and the other with fifteen feet, at an estimated cost of £122,545 and £130,632 respectively. At the same meeting, the bridge clerk's draft bill was approved which together with the plans and estimates were submitted to Lord Melville. Alexander was instructed to complete a series of borings in the riverbed at the intended sites of the four piers.[85] Clearly, the wardens and their officers were totally committed to the project and were moving ahead at maximun speed, hoping perhaps that the bill might be approved before the current session ended. In fact this proved impossible, and during August the Admiralty solicitors raised doubts as to whether the bill should proceed as a public bill. It was at most, they argued, a public *local* act and as such should proceed as a private bill, as was the case when new roads were made at the naval and ordnance departments at Woolwich.[86] Romney remained adamant that it proceed as a public bill, since the proposal had a public purpose in which the wardens were consenting, not soliciting parties. The argument surfaced again in 1820 during the final stage of negotiations.

A second obstacle appeared when John Rennie, as the Admiralty's consultant engineer, was asked to comment on Alexander's detailed plans drawn up in late December 1818. The final plans incorporated the results of the trial borings into the riverbed, and included estimates for compensation and purchase of properties affected by the repositioning of the bridge. The total cost was now put at £159,502, consisting of £136,714 for construction of the bridge, £2,013 for the approaches and £20,775 for compensation payments and purchases. The four piers were to be built directly into the bed of the river within coffer dams, and at low water would occupy a width of only 68 feet, leaving a horizontal waterway of 492 feet. At the old bridge, the massive size of the starlings meant that the equivalent waterway was

---

84 Ibid., 25–33 (report of a meeting of the Wardens and Assistants, 14 May 1818).
85 Ibid., 35–6 (report of a meeting of the Wardens and Assistants, 2 June 1818).
86 Ibid., 39–45 (copies of correspondence between Charles Bicknell, for the Admiralty solicitors, Twopeny and Lewis, bridge clerks, and Lord Romney, 1–30 August 1818).

only 136 feet, rising to 328 feet above the starlings, although it is true that the river at this point was thirty feet narrower than at the proposed new site.[87]

Rennie reported on Alexander's plans at the end of March 1819, and was impressed by the 492-foot waterway which represented an improvement on his own calculations. The sum set aside for the approaches, he felt, was too little; but for the overall construction, Rennie considered that a sum of £120,000 would be sufficient for a stone bridge of the same dimensions, whilst an iron bridge with a slightly narrower waterway could be built for £100,000 (excluding the purchase of property in both cases).[88] Rennie's comments make it clear that the Admiralty had insisted on reopening the question of iron versus stone in spite of earlier agreement favouring the latter; and in the negotiations which followed, Melville's concern to accommodate the preferences of the bridge wardens was rapidly overtaken by his determination to strike a hard bargain. On 13 April, Melville wrote to Romney putting the case bluntly: either the bridge be constructed under the authority of the Admiralty and Navy Boards, under the supervision of their engineer with an appropriate contribution from the bridge wardens; or the wardens undertake the work with a fixed and limited contribution from public funds. Since contractors had offered to undertake either of Rennie's schemes for the specified sums, he added, there was no reason to embark on Alexander's plans, and 'I should hope that the Corporation would give the preference to an Iron Bridge'.[89]

The wardens responded by requesting to see the Admiralty's alternative plans and, if possible, to discuss them with Rennie himself. It transpired that Rennie had produced no detailed estimates or 'regular designs', merely rough sketches. The Admiralty refused to indicate the level of subsidy which it was prepared to provide, and there can be little doubt that Melville was attempting to manoeuvre the wardens into accepting the project as falling entirely within the Admiralty's control.[90] With the implementation of Alexander's proposals looking increasingly doubtful, the wardens resolved at their June meeting to pay him a sum of £300 for producing the estimates and plans.[91] From this point, it is difficult to reconstruct the precise objectives of the wardens, if indeed such existed. Either it was intended to bring Rennie and Alexander together at their August meeting where a

---

[87] Ibid., 53–73 ('Report upon the building a New Bridge at Rochester of Five Arches of Stone' by Daniel Alexander, London, 16 December 1818); for another copy, see RBT 215. The breakdown of total costs for Alexander's design, which involved the use of new and re-used coffer dams, was as follows (RBT 214, 57, 65): 4 piers, 23%; 2 abutments, 14% 5 arches, 21%; centering, 8%; coffer dams, 20%; purchase of property and compensation, 13%.

[88] Ibid., 81–5 (report by John Rennie on Daniel Alexander's plans for a new bridge, submitted by J.W. Croker, for the Admiralty, London, 27 March 1819).

[89] Ibid., 85–7 (copy of Melville's letter to Romney, Admiralty, 13 April 1819).

[90] Ibid., 87–100 (report of two meetings of the wardens and assistants, 23 April and 13 May 1819; copies of correspondence from Rennie to Melville, London, 27 April 1819, and Melville to Romney, Admiralty, 3 May 1819; and report by Daniel Alexander to the Bridge Wardens and Assistants, Blackheath, 8 May 1819).

[91] RBT 1541, Orders of Wardens and Assistants, vol. II, 1819–1846, 3 June 1819, 22. Significantly, the decisions leading to Alexander's dismissal by the wardens were excluded from the volume containing copies of correspondence and reports to the 'new bridge' (RBT 214).

compromise scheme, agreeable to the Admiralty, would be worked out; or the aim was simply to substitute Rennie for Alexander as bridge engineer and thereby satisfy the Admiralty's requirements in relation to design, estimates and execution, whilst the wardens would retain overall control of the project. In fact, events followed the latter course. On 10 August 1819, Daniel Alexander and his son were dismissed and Rennie appointed in their place. The former's generosity in working gratuitously for the trust for almost a decade was apparently overlooked.[92] In the following year, Daniel Alexander Jnr. abandoned civil engineering for the Church of England, ending up as vicar of a Devonshire parish.[93]

It now seemed to the bridge wardens, and evidently to Rennie, that the politics of the project had been neatly settled. On 4 November, Rennie reported Melville's assurance that Lord Liverpool had personally agreed to the building of a stone bridge at Rochester and that 'the necessary steps will be taken in the ensuing session of Parliament to obtain an Act to authorize Government to advance the necessary funds in addition to those of the Wardens and Assistants'.[94] The year 1819, however, had been a particularly difficult one for the Liverpool government and party management at the time, especially under Liverpool's leadership, was extremely weak. All he demanded from his supporters in Parliament, it was said, was 'a generally favourable disposition'.[95] The form in which the bill was presented was therefore of some importance, yet the wardens, urged on by Lord Romney, continued to insist that it came forward as a public bill against Melville's and Rennie's inclinations and against the best advice of the Admiralty solicitors. Possibly the wardens were haunted by the memory of 1802 when their private bill failed. The deadlock was finally broken in February 1820 when the Admiralty Board agreed to refer the question to a Commons Select Committee to enquire into the Medway Navigation and the state of Rochester Bridge which, the wardens hoped, would confirm the necessity of a new bridge on public grounds and recommend a grant of public funds.[96]

The Committee sat from 22 June to 4 July 1820 and produced a sixty-five-page report which included minutes of evidence taken from eleven witnesses, a copy of

---

[92] RBT 1541, 10 August 1819, 24. Alexander was ordered to return all plans and papers 'belonging to the trust' and his son was requested to offer his resignation. A lengthy dispute followed, and the wardens attempted, unsuccessfully, to mount a prosecution against the former (RBT 290, Case for possible criminal proceedings against Daniel Alexander for a fraudulent bill authorising overpayment for a tidal survey of the river, with legal opinion of John Adolphus, Temple, 10 March 1821). There can be little doubt that the wardens were prepared to exploit Daniel Alexander's generosity, and almost four years passed before he was compensated for abortive work on the 'new bridge', following the advice of the distinguished architect, Sir Robert Smirke. (RBT 228, 'Opinion of Sir Robert Smirke on the architectural fees charges by Daniel Alexander', 8 April 1823).

[93] Colvin, op. cit., 39; Gentleman's Magazine, CXIX (1846 ii), 212.

[94] RBT 214, 108–09, (letter from Rennie to the bridge clerks, London, 4 November 1819).

[95] Briggs, op. cit., 188. Liverpool added that he would never attempt 'to interfere with the individual member's right to vote as he may think consistent with his duty upon any particular question.'

[96] RBT 214, 127–8 (report of a special meeting of the Wardens and Assistants, 10 February 1820).

the report issuing from the Navy Board's own enquiry into the state of the Medway, and a series of observations from Rennie on the causes of shoaling which were by far the most wide-ranging and perceptive brought before the committee.[97] The first cause mentioned by Rennie was agrarian improvement and better land drainage, followed by the growth of towns and villages together with 'the improved state of cleanliness' which carried greater deposits into the river. The embankment of lands along the Medway, the natural settlement of alluvium brought down from creeks, the construction of locks immediately above and below Maidstone, and the jetties, dockyard walls and ordnance bridge at Chatham all contributed to the silting up of the river. Lastly, Rochester Bridge greatly impeded the tidal flow, and its removal would be 'a most valuable improvement'. But, he added crucially, in relation to the future of the royal dockyard, 'it would by no means of itself, as a single work, be of the service that the scheme I have proposed would be', namely, the building of a wet dock at Chatham.[98]

Rennie's observations reduced the scale of the 'bridge problem' by introducing broader perspectives. On 11 July, on the edge of a financial crisis, the committee reported its view that 'it does not appear . . . that the water below bridge has decreased, or is decreasing so rapidly as to require of them to recommend to the House a grant, under the existing circumstances of the Country, so large a sum of public money, at least £100,000, as would be required for the immediate removal of this Bridge'.[99] The previous eighteen months had indeed seen a transition from boom to slump conditions, and by summer 1819, the economy was in the grip of a severe depression, the low point of the decade. The Treasury and the Bank of England were preparing to return to the gold standard at pre-war parity, and there was a sharp contraction of the volume of money and credit in order to resume cash payments. Government spending was rigorously curtailed.[100]

The committee went on to recommend that an accurate survey be made of the Medway, to be repeated in five years' time when the question might be 'more

[97] BPP 1820 (267), Report of the Select committee on the Present State of Rochester Bridge, 11 July 1820. The report also included copies of the correspondence between the Commissioner at Chatham, Sir Robert Barlow, and the Navy Board; accounts of the revenues of the bridge estates from 1797 to 1819, and of expenditure on bridge maintenance from 1789 to 1820.

[98] Ibid., 30–4. On Rennie's wet dock proposal of 1814, see J. Presnail, *Chatham: the Story of a Dockyard Town*, Chatham 1952, 219 ff. The proposal consisted of the construction of a 300-foot-wide ship canal between Gillingham and Upnor, and the formation of 'a new channel for the River Medway, by cutting through the peninsula between Upnor and Bridge Reaches . . . in a south-westerly direction, towards Rochester Bridge.' Chatham and Limehouse Reaches would thus become a vast wet dock, by means of dams across the river, enclosing an area of 243 acres.

[99] Ibid., 3.

[100] An Act of May 1818 had scheduled the resumption of gold payments for 5 July 1819, originally suspended by Pitt in 1797. But the price of gold was 6% above the mint price by the time 'resumption day' arrived, and the exchanges were unfavourable. A gradual return to gold was therefore implemented, and a severe contraction of credit was unavoidable. A.D. Gayer, W.W. Rostow and A.J. Schwartz, *The Growth and Fluctuation of the British Economy, 1790–1850*, I, 164; see also B. Hilton, *Corn, Cash, Commerce: the Economic Policies of the Tory Governments, 1815–1830*, Oxford 1977, 69–97.

properly decided' in view of the expense involved. It seems likely that this was little more than a face-saving exercise, as nothing more was heard of the survey programme. Rennie's ambitious proposal to build a wet-dock at Chatham, which would have eased the problem of shoaling, likewise disappeared from view. It was at this critical moment, when the bridge wardens needed to maintain close and continuing relations with the Admiralty, that Rennie's untimely death occurred, after a short and unexpected illness.[101] Thomas Telford was appointed in his place. Although the wardens had found a highly distinguished successor to occupy the position of Bridge Engineer, the latter could hardly be expected to encompass Rennie's detailed knowledge of the river Medway and the work and politics of the Navy Board.[102] Telford's involvement with bridge affairs was to be considerably more remote than that of Rennie, and did little to advance the prospect of a new bridge.

After the failure of their second approach to Parliament for public funds, the bridge wardens returned to the great arch project in the closing months of 1820. Just before his death in October 1821, Rennie had re-opened the question of constructing a great arch of cast-iron at Rochester, and produced plans and estimates for both Bramley Fall stone and cast-iron arches.[103] But the wardens maintained their original preference for a stone arch, even to the extent of using the same Yorkshire quarrymasters with whom Daniel Alexander had dealt. Tenders were invited in January 1821, and a local contractor, Hugh McIntosh, was appointed. At this stage, it was expected that the arch would be completed by the end of the year. The temporary bridge, erected in 1818, was still in place and detailed plans had already been drawn up by Alexander, with Rennie's modification completed in December 1820.[104] The wardens now had ample funds on which to draw, and the Committee of Assistants was empowered to sell annuities to the value of £11,000 to finance the first year's work as it proceeded. The size of the day-labour force was increased from 10 to 21 between 1819/20 and 1821/2, and reliance on tide labour was particularly heavy during the 1821 when much of the new work was indeed completed, at a cost of almost £15,000.[105]

It is difficult to estimate the impact of Rennie's death on the progress of the great arch project. However the minutes of the Committee of Assistants record that Telford's appointment was supplemented by that of a new foreman of works, John Armstrong, who was employed for two years to 'superintend the work of throwing the two centre arches into one.' Armstrong was paid a fee of £50 together with a

---

[101] Rennie died at the age of sixty-one on 4 October 1821, apparently from a disease of the kidneys and liver (*Autobiography of Sir John Rennie, F.R.S.*, London 1875, 154–5).

[102] The work of the Rennies, father and son, on harbours and dockyards in Kent is described in Sir John Rennie's *Autobiography*, chapter III, passim.

[103] RBT 221, letter from John Rennie to the Wardens and Assistants, London, 5 December 1820. The drawings are now in the Samuel Ware collection in the British Library, 1802 c.17, ff. 35–6, 18 December 1820.

[104] RBT 1541, Orders of Wardens and Assistants, 6 December 1820, 67.

[105] RBT 2148, Wardens' Accounts, vol. xxxi; RBT 1986, 1994, 1995, Bills and receipts.

weekly salary of 40s., and was provided with 'a house and premises' plus his removal expenses from Bristol.[106] A major part of his task presumably included the supervision of large numbers of tide-labourers. This final stage of modernisation involved not only the construction of the great arch but also repairs to the adjacent piers and wharves, and removal of numerous piles where the centre pier had previously stood. By April 1824, Telford was able to report on the completion of the work programme and the sound state of the superstructure. A number of redundant piles still remained, consistent with the stability of the adjacent piers, but, as Telford noted, 'loaded barges have a free and safe passage' through the bridge 'excepting for a very short time once a fortnight'.[107]

The project to modernise Rochester Bridge, first mooted in 1780, was thus brought to completion thirty-two years after the commencement of works in 1792, after innumerable delays caused by wartime inflation and rising costs, labour shortages, financial crises and unforseen technical difficulties. The resulting modifications undoubtedly facilitated the movement of increased land and river traffic, but did little to rectify the serious long-term problems associated with the shoaling of the Medway. Nor did the improvements reduce the need for, and the expence of, annual maintenance work on the piers and starlings. The modernisation programme was barely completed when Telford announced that urgent repairs, were needed to the fourth starling, the inner parts of which were 'very much decayed, the outer piles and walepieces are nearly worn out [and] the chalk filling is falling out.' The initial cost was estimated at £500.[108]

The exertions of the previous three decades had served merely to carry an outdated medieval technology into the nineteenth century, while elsewhere, the hesitant advances of the mid-eighteenth century, borrowed from France, were overtaken by a steady stream of home-grown innovations in construction methods and design. Great improvements on the Coalbrookdale model were achieved in two notable cast-iron bridges completed in the mid-1790s: Telford's at Buildwas on the Severn, and Burdon's Wear bridge connecting Sunderland and Monkwearmouth. In 1819, Rennie bridged the Thames at Southwark with three cast-iron spans, though his most successful design, that of London Bridge, was a masonry structure of five arches similar to that planned for the Medway. Suspension bridges were first developed in the United States, but the 1820s saw the completion of a number of British examples, notably Telford's bridge across the Menai Straits.[109]

It was, therefore, precisely during the long period of modernisation at Rochester that some of the most notable advances in bridge-building technique were made. The quickening pace of innovation promised long term economies in maintenance, as well as the possibility of accomodating much larger flows of traffic. Although

---

[106] RBT 1541, 30 May 1822, 96–7.

[107] RBT 224, 27 June 1823; RBT 1541, 30 April 1824, 119.

[108] RBT 1541, 30 April 1824, 120.

[109] C. Singer, E.J. Holmyard, A.R. Hall, T.I. Williams (eds.), *A History of Technology, vol. IV, The Industrial Revolution, c.1750–c.1850*, Oxford 1958, 446–64.

the Parliamentary initiative of 1819–20 had failed, the wardens hardly doubted that the construction of a new bridge was a serious proposition, to be re-examined as soon as the financial climate permitted. Within three years of the completion of the great arch, in fact, the wardens were to approach Thomas Telford, Robert Smirke, W.C. Mylne and George Rennie to advise how this might best be done 'without the pecuniary aid of Parliament, or any additional charge to the public'.[110]

110 RBT 238, Reports and Documents relating to Rochester Bridge, 27 February 1832, 11.

Rochester Bridge

1825–1950

Planning the New Bridge

The repair of the bridge was a constant cause of expense to the wardens. Thomas Telford's 1825 report, for instance, stated that between April 1824 and March 1825 £1,287 0s. 3d. had been expended, including £555 5s. 0d. on elm timber and £515 on labour. The works entailed the second pier from the large arch on the Rochester side having its starling thoroughly repaired; the starling of the third pier being planked on top, partly on the sides and new joists being fitted as required; the second starling from the Strood side being repaired; the wharfage at the back of the carpenter's shop having a considerable portion of new piling and planking, still leaving other portions imperfect but not in need of urgent repair. There remained urgent repairs needed to two starlings on the Rochester side. Telford recommended the second from the shore be completed over the summer and autumn of 1825 at an estimated further cost of £987 15s. 0d. and that £150 should be budgeted for other contingencies.[1] In fact the work was carried out for £1,068 including some small repairs to the third and fourth starlings on the Strood side, but urgent repairs to the first starling on the Rochester side cost a further £232 12s. 0d.

In 1826 Telford reported that the starlings were now in good condition apart from the extensive one on the Rochester side. However, the wharfs at the timber yard and the coping stones of the pier points needed attention and two piers on the Rochester side needed pointing, the estimated cost being £1,117 10s. 0d. in the current season. Further, as a result of requests from the inhabitants of Rochester the roadway over the bridge was to be relaid with small broken stone on the approaches and forty tons of granite pavement sets in lime mortar on the crown of arches. Apart from improving the road surface this would stop water filtering through to decay the arch stones.[2]

In view of this heavy ongoing expenditure and of the continued shoaling in the river, a special court was called for 22 June 1827 to consider the future policy of permanently repairing the old bridge. The meeting resolved that George Rennie, Robert Smirke, W.C. Mylne, and Thomas Telford survey the bridge, report upon its state, and give an estimate of the cost of its annual upkeep until a new bridge could be constructed from the wardens' own sources without parliamentary aid or additional charges to the public.[3]

On 21 March 1828 Smirke, Mylne and Rennie reported that the superstructure and masonry of the bridge were in a good state of repair and would 'probably

---

1   RBT 226, Annual Report, Thomas Telford, 15 April 1825.
2   RBT 227, Annual Report, Thomas Telford, 17 May 1826.
3   RBT 1541, Orders of the Wardens and Assistants (hereafter referred to as Orders), vol. II, 157, 163.

require little expenditure for their preservation and repair for many years'. However, the starlings were 'of a far less permanent nature'. They estimated that in the previous 40 years expenditure on repairs and improvement had amounted to about £80,000, but it had proved difficult to tell how much on repairs alone. This probably totalled £40,000, at an average of £1,000 per annum, mostly on the starlings. In the last five years £8,000 had been spent on the starlings but repairs were still needed. The annual report of 5 January 1828, for example, had listed worm-eaten piles, piles hanging on the fourth starling from Rochester and chalk washed away from the fifth. The action of the current had excavated the riverbed above and below the bridge so that the piers stood on elevated points leaving the feet of the piles at the ends of the starlings above ground and hanging from the rest of the framing. This allowed the chalk and stone fill to be washed away. The bases of the piers were in some instances 20 feet above the bed of the river. The Engineers thought that the upper surface of the starlings could be lowered to allow more water to pass through the bridge, and reduce the scour, although the piles were too decayed to drive in further. They considered that with one exception the starlings were 'safe' for the next five to six years, but iron piles should be used at the next repair. The sum of £400 per year would be sufficient for repairs to the bridge which could last twenty to thirty years. To economise further it would only be necessary to employ a foreman to report on the bridge and to take on proper labour for the duration of repairs. They concluded that a new bridge was desirable due both to the damage being done to the river and to the misalignment of the roads. They estimated that the wardens could accumulate in 25 years sufficient funds to build a new bridge if rentals remained the same as in the previous ten years and the current levels of investment were maintained.[4] The wardens had bought £2,200 3% Consols in 1825, £3,300 in 1826 and £2,500 in 1827.[5]

As a result of this report and also bearing in mind the evidence given by Rennie to a committee of the House of Commons on 22 June 1820 that the starlings were the main cause of shoaling by hindering the tides, a series of important decisions was taken on 18 April 1828: firstly, there was the need to remove the impediment to navigation as soon as possible which meant a new bridge; secondly, a committee was to be appointed to look at income from estates and at where rentals could be raised; thirdly, 'an intelligent person be employed to superintend the general state of the old bridge and more especially the starlings thereof' and to report when repairs were necessary with a view to temporary patching, with as little expense as possible, so as not to exhaust funds; fourthly, to let the bridge yard and sell the timber stock; and, fifthly, that the wardens to have 'some conference with the Government' when documents were available.[6]

These actions were confirmed on 29 May 1828, whereupon Robert Smirke was appointed to be architect of the bridge with a fee of £50 per annum. All the bridge

[4] RBT 230, Report on the State of the Bridge, Smirke, Milne and Rennie, 21 March 1828; annual report, Smirke, 5 January 1828, as quoted in Orders, vol. II, 175–7.
[5] Orders, vol. II, 142, 149, 157.
[6] Ibid., 167–8.

workmen were dismissed apart from David Anderson, the foreman, who would carry out repairs under Smirke's direction.[7] That spending was immediately reduced is illustrated in Smirke's 1829 report which showed only £150 expended since June 1828, including the foreman's wage and repairs to the carriageway. Recommended work included the removal of several piles from the fourth pier from the Rochester side plus some other planking at an estimated cost of £100.[8] In practice less than £200 was spent to 23 April 1830, but the fourth starling remained in bad repair.[9] As a further economising measure it was also decided to apply for a reduction in the sum paid for lighting the gas lamps on the bridge,[10] gas lighting having come in 1825 after the Act for incorporation of the Rochester Gas Company allowed mains to be carried over the bridge.[11] As a precaution it was resolved that in future all leases of premises near the bridge would have a clause providing for reversion on three months' notice if required for rebuilding the approaches to the bridge.

The support and approval of the Admiralty for the wardens' plans would be crucial in any dealing with the government. The intention was to gain government assistance in procuring an Act of Parliament, and to obtain a loan of £100,000 in Exchequer bills at the Exchequer Bill rate of interest which would facilitate construction without any other material advance. The evidence deployed to support their case included extracts from a report made by Rennie on 14 May 1807 which stated that the bridge was the principal obstruction to improving the waterway for warships from Chatham Dockyard to Sheerness and 'that building a new bridge, and taking down the old one is an object of great national importance.' A document produced by the Navy Office dated 21 July 1828 showed that £25,182 7s. 8d. had been expended in removing mud from the waterway by the dockyard between 1814 and 1828. The wardens stated they had disposable funds of £25,000 and a net income of upwards of £3,000 per annum from freehold property which would allow them to redeem the principal and interest on the loan within 35 years. A statement to this effect was approved at a special meeting on 23 December 1831 and forwarded to Mr Barrow, Secretary to the Admiralty.[12]

The response was letters from the Admiralty and the Lords Commissioners of the Treasury requesting as a preliminary step a plan and estimate for a new bridge and verification of the available income and resources. Smirke was ordered to prepare plans for a five-arched bridge of Bramley Fall stone together with an estimate which would include the approaches and the cost of injury to property on a direct line between Strood and Rochester High Streets.[13] The eventual reply from the Treasury dated 3 August 1832 stated the 'only grounds which would make it just or expedient to consider the rebuilding of Rochester Bridge on any peculiar

7 Ibid., 179.
8 RBT 232, Annual Report, Robert Smirke, 30 April 1829.
9 RBT 233, Annual Report, Smirke, 23 April 1830.
10 Orders, vol. II, 11 June 1829, 195.
11 Ibid., 133.
12 Ibid., 220–26.
13 Ibid., 227.

principle of favour would be the saving to the Public, or the improvement of the Naval Station in the Medway that might result from such an improvement. But that the statements received from the Admiralty do not afford such evidence of public advantage as would warrant them in complying with the application made on this subject'.[14]

The measures taken by the sitting Court in preparation for the construction of a new bridge led to a rare event, the 1832 contested election for a place among the Wardens and Assistants. On normal occasions few turned out for the annual election meeting at Castle Hill at which an annual report and accounts were presented, but 1832 was to be different. With the electorate already excited by the struggle for the Reform Bill a split emerged between the Tories and the Reformers. However, a more parochial cause of controversy was fear over the impact of the cost of reconstruction on the contributory parishes. Handbills of the time demonstrate these themes. A meeting was convened for 17 February 1832 at the Sun Tavern, Chatham, of those wanting to protect property from charges for the new bridge.[15] A further gathering of deputations from Chatham and Gillingham put up a scheme whereby finance for the bridge could be found by investing rental and interest over 18 years with no cost to the property holders.[16]

A meeting of deputies of parishes at the Star Inn, Maidstone, on 25 April 1832 produced a recommended list for the election on 4 May, which included Lord Darnley and James Best as wardens and Messrs John Bell of Canterbury, John Mercer of Maidstone, John Dudlow of Malling, William Smith of Meopham, Maximilian Dalison of Mereworth, Jeremiah Rosher of Northfleet, Sir William Geary of Oxenheath, Ald. Lucas of Wateringbury, John Golding of Ditton Place, William Browne of Chalk, D. James of Ightham and T. Poynder of Snodland.[17] A handbill of 27 April 1832 signed Justus 'To freeholders and friends of reform in the parishes of Chatham and Gillingham' saw the election list as an attempt by the Tories to resurrect their power. 'Should this Nomination List be adopted, you will achieve a triumph to your opponents and afford an opportunity to their Graces of Wellington and Buckingham, again to raise the oft repeated cry of reaction.' He recommended a liberal slate.[18] Equally it was seen by 'A Staunch Reformer' as part of an attempt to get Sir William Geary elected to the West Kent seat for the Tories.[19] 'A Freeholder of Frindsbury and Higham' in a handbill of 28 April 1832 deplored the fact that the deputy from his parish had without authority supported the list which made the election 'a party matter'.[20] 'Veritas' replying on 30 April in support of the nominated list stated 'Are not these Persons the most likely to avoid bringing any charge upon the Contributory Parishes – who would themselves have

---

14 Letter, Treasury, 3 August 1832, as quoted in ibid., 245.
15 RBT 716, handbill, 11 February 1832.
16 RBT 721, handbill, 23 March 1832.
17 RBT 723, handbill, meeting 25 April 1832.
18 RBT 726, handbill, 27 April 1832.
19 RBT 728, handbill, 30 April 1832.
20 RBT 727, handbill, 28 April 1832.

AT A VERY SLENDER

Tory Meeting

OF

Holders of Land Contributory

TO

Rochester Bridge,

Held at **MAIDSTONE** this 25th day of April, 1832:

A thorough-paced Anti-Reform Reverend, in the Chair.

A List of the present Wardens and Assistants was laid on the Table.

Resolved unanimously,

That nearly the whole of the above Gentlemen have proved themselves the determined opposers of our present *glorious system* as established in Church and State, and supporters of that vile Reform Bill now in progress through Parliament, and which is calculated to deprive Gentlemen like ourselves of that Power and Patronage, the exercise of which has brought the Country to its present state of *happiness* and *prosperity.*

Resolved unanimously,

That Rochester Bridge wants no more improving than the Constitution of the House of Commons, which these Reformers are now so basely vilifying; and that the economy observed for the last six years by the present Wardens and Assistants in the expenditure of the Bridge Funds, was no more required than the economy that has been practised by the present *ungentleman-like Administration.*

Resolved unanimously,

That it is expedient that nearly all the present Radical set should be turned out on the next day of Election, which will be Friday the 4th day of May, and the following Gentlemen be substituted, who have never supported the vulgar measure of Reform; and for that purpose, good Antis are requested to muster on that day, as the success of our exertions will enable our Noble Eastwell Earl to declare to the House of Lords that glorious truth (so much doubted) that a re-action has taken place in OUR LOYAL COUNTY.

RESOLVED, That the following change is necessary:

	OLD LIST.		NEW LIST.	
All Reformers !!! and supporters of Hodges & Rider.	FOR Mr. Charles Larkin, William Lomas, } Rochester, Thomas Bentley, *Higham,* Samuel Baker, *Chatham and* } *Gillingham,* D. H. Day, *Shorne,* Edward Boys, *Rochester,* Jacob Bryant, *Chatham,* D. J. Day, *Rochester,* Capt. Thomas Baker, *Rochester,* Dr. J. W. Smith, *Rochester,*	TAKE Mr.	James Best, *Chatham,* John Bell, *Canterbury.* William Smith, *Meopham.* John Dudlow, *Malling.* John Mercer, *Maidstone.* M. D. D. Dalison, *Mereworth.* John Golding, *Ditton.* Sir William Geary, *Oxon Hoath.* Mr. Ald. Lucas, *Wateringbury.* D. James, *Ightham.*	All Friends of Church and State!

It was then moved by a Member present, that (as this List might be considered rather too Torified) Lord Darnley be elected to fill the vacancy occasioned by the death of the late Lord Torrington. This motion was reluctantly acceded to.

Rally, then, and your success in this instance will ensure a Church and State Candidate at the next General Election for our County; one of the right sort, Brother Tories, is preparing to start---namely, Sir William Geary !!!

Caddel, Printer, Gazette-Office, Rochester.

Figure 22. Handbill opposing the construction of a new bridge circulated during the contested election of 1832.

to pay the largest share?'[21] 'Playfair' warned of charges likely to be levied on property. 'Do not be led astray by the cry that it is a party or political question – elect such men as will neither mortgage your Estates or put your property to hazard.'[22]

In the event upwards of one thousand persons were present at Castle Hill on 4 May, when the whole of the existing court were removed from office. The *Rochester Gazette* commented upon the result that in 'their desire to commence at an early period the building of a new bridge, [the Wardens and Assistants] furnished their adversaries with the means of creating an opposition to them, by instilling into the minds of the constituency the apprehension of being taxed for its erection', this notwithstanding the fact that the wardens had expressed their intention of applying for an Act 'by which the Contributory Lands were to be forever exonerated from all responsibility,' and 'yet it appeared that few had taken the trouble to inform themselves on the subject'.[23] As a postscript a handbill, entitled 'Triumph of Truth and Plain Dealing over Falsehood, Malevolence and Humbug' and signed 'Anti Envy, Hatred and Malice,' set out to show that the new wardens in fact took very much the same line on a new bridge as their predecessors.[24]

The Tory wardens had in practice little scope for a different policy as it was evident that the bridge would have to be replaced in the foreseeable future. Their only recourse was to limit expenditure to the trifling works recommended by Smirke while accumulating funds. In pursuance of this policy the bridge clerk, William Twopenny, was able to report at the 22 May 1834 meeting that the wardens had invested and at their disposal £16,000 3% Consolidated Bank Annuities and £16,000 3% Reduced Bank Annuities.[25] Property in the line of the proposed new bridge was purchased when the opportunity arose. For instance a wharf near Easton House, Rochester with two houses upon it was bought at auction for £1,190 on 28 August 1835 and the freehold house wharf and premises in Strood formerly occupied by Henry Horsnaill were bought in June 1839 for £2,000.[26]

By April 1839 Robert Smirke was writing to the wardens that 'it will probably soon become necessary either to make some arrangements for rebuilding the Bridge or to adopt some extensive measures of repair for the better security of it.' He also stated his wish to resign due to ill health,[27] resulting in the appointment on 23 May 1839 of William Cubitt as architect and engineer. Under his supervision the policy was to continue that 'only such repairs be done as are indispensably requisite.'[28]

When the bridge clerk, William Twopenny, resigned in May 1840, the accumulated reserve had reached £27,500 3% Consols and £26,000 3% Reduced Bank

---

[21] RBT 730, handbill, 30 April 1832.
[22] RBT 734, handbill, 2 May 1832
[23] *Rochester Gazette and Weekly Advertiser*, 8 May 1832.
[24] RBT 736, handbill, 25 July 1832.
[25] Orders, vol. II, 260.
[26] Ibid., 289, 328.
[27] Letter, Robert Smirke, April 1839, as quoted in Orders, vol. II, 322.
[28] Orders, vol. II, 327, 337.

Annuities. His successor, George Essell, was ordered to purchase £500 stock each time the balance of cash reached £1,000 without awaiting instructions from the Wardens and Assistants. By 1842 the sum invested had increased to £35,000 3% Consols and £31,000 3% Reduced Bank Annuities.[29]

In April 1842 William Cubitt was asked to report his proposals for the erection of the new bridge, and it was on 8 June 1843 further resolved 'that it is the opinion of this court that the time has arrived when this Corporation ought to take into serious consideration the means of erecting a new Bridge,' and a special meeting called for 7 July 1843 'to take into consideration Mr. Cubitt's report and make orders thereon'.[30] Cubitt had drawn up three alternative outline plans. Plan No. 1, a stone bridge of five arches similar to Smirke's plan of 1832, Cubitt thought architecturally 'most beautiful', but it needed four piers in the river and would cost approximately £200,000. Plan No. 2, a bridge of three arches with cast iron ribs, was less aesthetically pleasing but less obstructive of the river and costing only £130,000. Plan No. 3, an iron suspension bridge with a wooden roadway giving 500 feet clear water in one opening, could be elegant in design, was best for the waterway and would only cost £100,000. Cubitt favoured Plan No. 3 for an iron suspension bridge, especially as he recognised the wardens' problem was mainly financial. He was, however, instructed to prepare an estimate of the whole cost of plans No. 1 and No. 3 including the approaches, being allowed professional assistance in drawing up the estimate for the iron bridge and for the probable annual cost of maintenance. Meanwhile the Solicitor General's opinion was also sought on the power of the wardens to erect the bridge. Cubitt called upon the assistance of James Rendel who had 'much experience as a Civil Engineer in general, and with Suspension Bridges in particular' and who had been involved at Montrose in Scotland. Rendel supported the case for a suspension bridge as the most suitable for a 'rapid tideway' which would be left 'free from impediment to tide and flood' as well as being less expensive. His estimate for the cost of a bridge giving 450 feet clear water and a roadway sixteen to twenty feet above the water was £90,000 to £100,000. He advocated a tarred surface for the timber on the roadway to protect it from the weather, thus limiting maintenance to painting for the ironwork. On 30 May 1844 it was resolved that 'it is expedient that a bridge be built of iron according to Messrs Cubitt and Rendel's suggestions if sufficient assistance can be obtained from the Government,' and a committee was formed 'to communicate with the proper officers of the Government', to ascertain what aid they could afford and to prepare a Bill for Parliament to give the necessary powers.[31]

[29] Ibid., 332, 351.
[30] Ibid., 353, 357.
[31] Ibid., 358–9, 362, 364–5; RBT 269, Report, William Cubitt, 30 May 1844; Report, James Rendel to Cubitt, 27 May 1844; RBT 264, Cubitt's Report, 7 June 1843. James Meadows Rendel (1799–1856) had worked as a surveyor under Telford, and was particularly involved in bridge building. His bridge across the Catwater, Plymouth was the second largest iron structure in existence in 1827. He introduced chain ferries to the Dart in 1831, was an expert in hydraulic engineering and worked on New Haven, Littlehampton, Grimsby, Leith and Garston docks. In

ROCHESTER BRIDGE.

ELECTION OF
Wardens and Assistants.

To the Landowners, Inhabitants and House-holders of the Parishes and Places contributory to the maintenance of Rochester Bridge.

At a Meeting of Gentlemen interested in the above Election, held at the Bull Inn, in Rochester, on Saturday, the 18th day of April, 1846, Captain Baker having been called to the Chair, it was—

RESOLVED UNANIMOUSLY,

THAT this Meeting disapproves of that portion of the Bill *prepared under the sanction of the present Bridge Wardens and* now before Parliament, having for its object the construction of a SWING BRIDGE in the proposed new Bridge across the River Medway at Rochester.

RESOLVED UNANIMOUSLY,

THAT this District is inadequately represented in the present Bridge Corporation, and that therefore we use our most strenuous exertions to secure the Election of the following Gentlemen as the Wardens and Assistants of Rochester Bridge for the year ensuing :—

WARDENS.

ROBT CLEMENTS, Esq. *Mayor of Rochester.*   WM. GLADDISH, Esq.

ASSISTANTS.

J. BRENCHLEY, Esq. *(Northfleet).*	W. GOLDING, Esq.	THOS. RIDER, Esq.
J. G. BRYANT, Esq.	C. W. MARTIN, Esq. M.P.	J. W. STRATFORD, Esq.
CAPTAIN BAKER	W. H. NICHOLSON, Esq.	J. STUNT, Esq.
COLONEL BEST	J. NIGHTINGALE, Esq.	E. WICKHAM, Esq.

RESOLVED UNANIMOUSLY,

THAT in order to protect the public against the serious inconvenience, and the contributory property against the enormous expenses which must result from the erection of a Swing Bridge as proposed, and other measures contemplated by the said Bill, the several Land-owners and Inhabitant Householders resident in the Contributory Parishes and Places be requested to assist in securing the Election of the above-named Gentlemen.

Thos. BAKER, *Chairman,*
At the request and on the behalf of the Meeting.

N. B. THE ELECTION will take place near the Castle, at Rochester, on **FRIDAY** next, the **24th** day of April, **1846**, at **10** o'Clock in the Forenoon, and the early attendance of Electors is earnestly requested.

☞ *All Landholders and Householders inhabiting within the Contributory Parishes and Places are qualified to vote.*

JAMES BURRILL, PRINTER, HIGH-STREET, CHATHAM.

Figure 23. Rival slate of wardens and assistants proposed by the Rochester faction of the Commonalty opposed to the swing bridge during the contested election of 1846.

At this juncture the wardens received notice of two projected railway lines, both of which planned to cross the Medway at Rochester. The discussions which followed were of crucial importance in the abandonment of the suspension bridge project and in the definition of the specifications of the new bridge. Committees from the North Kent Company, whose engineer was Charles Vignoles, and the South Eastern Company, whose engineer was George R. Stephenson, attended a meeting on 22 February 1845 and produced plans and elevations of the bridges they proposed to build and the adjacent highway and railway approaches. The court considered 'it desirable to enter into arrangements with any Railway Company intending to cross the Medway at Rochester, so as to have only one Bridge and that to combine the Public Highway and the Railway on the same arches'. The meeting also laid down basic conditions which would have to be met to satisfy the requirements of both the wardens and the Admiralty: the approval of the Admiralty and other government departments be obtained; the design was satisfactory to the Wardens; headway above high water spring tides to be 18 feet at the centre; the bridge be built to allow a ship's passage and drawbridge at the Strood side to allow navigation by masted vessels; the proportion to be paid by the wardens be stated; the bridge to be kept in repair by the railway company, the wardens paying an annual sum; the investment of a sufficient guarantee fund for repairs; the bridge and approaches to be completed before any portion was opened to the public.[32]

The conditions were accepted by both companies, but progress depended upon Parliament passing the railway bills. On balance the wardens favoured the North Kent proposals and Vignoles' plans. However, since both railway companies were promoting bills containing provisions which were thought to infringe the wardens' rights, the wardens resolved to ensure the inclusion in any railway bill of a clause or clauses 'saving the rights and immunities of the wardens and assistants as Conservators and Trustees of the Bridge and Estates thereof, and to prevent such company taking to their separate or exclusive use or purposes or otherwise interfering with any land houses wharfs quays riverway or other property of the wardens and Commonalty.'[33] Sir Walter Riddell was also retained to act as counsel before parliamentary committees. In the event, both bills were rejected in the 1845 session, although the South Eastern Railway Company was allowed the Gravesend-Strood line which could not operate south of the Watermill public house, Strood, where it might have threatened the approaches to the new bridge and possibly the swing bridge.

Meanwhile, one result of the discussions with the railway companies was reported in May 1845 by the committee looking into government aid. The Chancellor of the Exchequer, who had insisted on receiving the case for a new bridge, the resources available to the wardens and Cubitt's estimates for Bridge No. 3 and its approaches, had decided not to proceed further leaving the Trust to its own

1855 he completed a suspension bridge across the Ness at Inverness. He was President of the ICE in 1852–3 and a close professional associate of William Cubitt.

[32] Orders, vol. II, 367–9.
[33] Ibid., 377.

financial resources. The Wardens and Assistants still had no power to act, and with both bills to be reintroduced in the following session,[34] the wardens demanded further conditions from the railway companies: a bridge not exceeding five arches with a clear waterway of five hundred feet, a clear roadway and footpaths of 36 feet width excluding parapets, and a ship's passage at the Strood end built at the same or future time. Designs were to be presented at a meeting on 10 December 1845, with the wardens reserving the right to oppose bills if the designs were not approved.[35]

Progress on the back of railway bills was an uncertain way forward, and as a precaution the bridge clerk was in the meantime directed to prepare notices, plans, sections, estimates and carry into effect all other proceedings requisite to obtain a bill during the 1846 session of Parliament empowering the Trust to build a new bridge, to enter into an agreement with any company to build a bridge with a railway and to raise money.[36] At the court held on 10 December 1845 it was reported that notices of intention to apply for powers to construct a bridge had been posted in the contributory parishes and placed three times in county newspapers and that the clerk together with Cubitt had prepared plans of the site, approaches, and property to be interfered with, together with design plans and sections of the new bridge and swing bridge and a reference book to the plan. Two copies had been deposited with the Clerk of the Peace for the County of Kent on 29 November 1845.[37]

Building a bridge in conjunction with a railway company would limit the wardens' contribution to the capital cost, as illustrated by the designs then presented – one by the North Kent Company, and three by the South Eastern Company. The wardens wanted both companies to agree to their selection, a condition which would produce equality in the bills currently before Parliament.[38] The North Kent design by Vignoles was to be an iron superstructure on stone piers costing £150,000 of which the wardens would contribute £60,000. The South Eastern design No. 1 was for a stone bridge of three arches, the wardens' contribution being £90,000; No. 2 was a three-arched iron bridge on stone piers, contribution £60,000, and No. 3 a stone bridge of five arches, contribution £50,000. On 10 December 1845 the Court favoured the SER design No. 1 which led to disagreement between the companies over costings, both accusing the other of underestimating the costs.[39] Stephenson advised the South Eastern Board not to build to Vignoles' design, preferring a stone bridge. The wardens finally accepted design No. 3 for the stone bridge and sought Admiralty approval so that evidence could be

---

34 Ibid., 384–5; bridge clerk's report, 6 September 1845, as quoted in ibid., 392–9.

35 Ibid., 409–11.

36 Ibid., 406–7.

37 Ibid., 418–20.

38 Ibid., 424.

39 Mr Stephens, solicitor to the North Kent Line, thought design No. 1 would cost £240,000, while Stephenson thought Vignoles' design would cost £185,000 without the approaches.

presented to the committee of the House of Commons dealing with the petition for the Bridge Bill.[40]

The South Eastern Railway design No. 3 was effectively scuttled when the Admiralty then clarified the design specification for any new bridge by requiring only three piers in the river, headway of 18 feet above high water, and a 'draw-bridge' of 50 feet on the Strood side. They gave qualified approval to the North Kent design.[41] Further Admiralty conditions required that there should be 500 feet of clear water, that all arches should spring above high water level, and that additional masonry piers be built for the drawbridge.[42]

Controversy then arose over certain clauses in the Rochester Bridge Bill relating to the swing bridge: Clause 7 requiring Admiralty consent and eighteen feet headroom, Clause 8 requiring the inclusion of a swing bridge, Clause 9 allowing the Admiralty to fix rules for the opening of the swing bridge, and Clause 27 binding owners of contributory lands to maintain and repair the bridge.[43] Petitions against the bill were presented by Rochester and Strood Pavement Commissioners and Rochester Corporation who wanted unobstructed passage across the bridge at all times. On the other hand, support came from the Mayor and Corporation of Maidstone, who favoured the swing bridge which opened the potential for sea-going vessels to penetrate the interior of Kent, especially if Aylesford bridge could be avoided by means of a canal. They also argued that the rights of all contributory lands should receive consideration. The Medway Lower Navigation Company supported the new bridge including the swing bridge for much the same reasons as Maidstone. The South Eastern Railway Company reluctantly agreed to support the North Kent design.[44] In view of the opposition to the bill the wardens again retained Sir Walter Riddell as counsel to appear in support of the bill.

Particularly strong opposition in Rochester and Strood ensured a contested election in 1846, the first since 1832. A meeting held on 18 April 1846 at the Bull Inn, Rochester to disapprove of the bill including a swing bridge put forward a new list of candidates for election as wardens including as prospective wardens Robert Clements, Mayor of Rochester, and William Gladdish and as assistant wardens Captain Baker, Colonel Best, and Messrs. Brenchley, Bryant, Golding, Martin, Nicholson, Nightingale, Rider, Stratford, Stunt and Wickham, who would 'protect the public against serious inconvenience' and 'the enormous expenses which must result from the erection of a swing bridge'.[45] Some of those named did not agree. A handbill issued by James Best, John Stunt, Thomas Rider, Charles Martin, John Stratford and William Golding, all existing assistant wardens, disassociated themselves from the new list as they did not want to oppose their former colleagues.[46] The new list was seen by 'A Freeholder and Elector who will not support the new

40 RBT 1542, Orders, vol. III, 3–10.
41 Ibid., 11.
42 Letter, Trust Secretary to the Admiralty, 3 March 1846, as quoted in ibid., 13.
43 RBT 1281, handbill.
44 Orders, vol. III, 12–22.
45 RBT 1285, Notice of meeting of 18 April 1846.
46 RBT 1294, handbill, 22 April 1846.

list' as an attempt to pack the Trust with Rochester nominees.[47] Stories in the *Rochester Gazette* conjured up fears of what would happen if the swing bridge were to be opened. Rochester market would be hindered and cattle and perhaps four to five hundred sheep be left waiting to cross. Perhaps five or six omnibuses, carts, carriages and hundreds of people waiting would make Strood High Street impassable. The new direct railway link from London to Dover would be held up and express traffic disrupted.[48]

In contrast, support for the swing bridge came strongly from Maidstone. A report of a meeting at Maidstone Town Hall on 7 March 1846 outlines the reasons as expressed by Mr C. Ellis. The swing bridge would allow fixed mast vessels of 400–500 tons access to Maidstone and would avoid trans-shipment into barges below Rochester Bridge, a time consuming and costly operation. The swing bridge would mean for Maidstone more trade and lower prices.[49]

In the event at the election on Tuesday, 28 April 1846, the old list in favour of the swing bridge was returned. The list recommended to 'freeholders desirous of extending the benefits of an improved navigation . . . . and of guarding against the risk of additional burthens on the contributory parishes' was W. Masters Smith, John Mercer, Lord Romney, Thomas Hodges, John Dudlow, William Golding, Thomas Best, Charles Martin, Thomas Rider, Robert Tassell, John Stratford, John Stunt, Michael Lock and Col. Best.[50] Some analysis of the voting showed, as could be expected, that Maidstone supported the old list to get better navigation, while Chatham and Milton had voted against.[51]

The result was not without controversy as a large number of those presenting themselves at Castle Hill for the poll were excluded. Edward Wickham and others protested about the conduct of the poll which they maintained was illegally confined to freeholders. It was a matter of complaint that the poll had been closed on the day without allowing all entitled time to vote.[52] These complaints were ignored, however, and the succcess of the old list in the election meant that the Rochester Bridge Bill including the contentious clauses would remain before Parliament.

Despite the fact that Lord Shaftesbury, Chairman of Committees of the House of Lords, initially objected to a joint bridge with a railway company on grounds of safety of passengers, no supplementary clauses were attached to the Rochester Bridge Bill. The bill received its third reading in the House of Commons on 17 April 1846, when Rochester withdrew its opposition. It was passed by the Lords, despite renewed opposition from Rochester, and received Royal Assent on 14 May. The Rochester Bridge Act 1846 conferred powers for the compulsory taking of land required within three years of the passing of the Act, the construction of a bridge to be completed within seven years, the removal of the old bridge, the

[47] RBT 1287, handbill, [April 1846].
[48] *Rochester Gazette and Weekly Advertiser*, 17 February 1846.
[49] *Maidstone and South Eastern Gazette*, 20 March 1846.
[50] RBT 1295, handbill.
[51] *Maidstone and South Eastern Gazette*, 28 April 1846.
[52] RBT 1301, Letter, E. Wickham and others, 24 April 1846.

borrowing on mortgage of a sum not exceeding £60,000, the repayment of portions of the loan by ballot when surplus revenue amounted to £5,000 or more on six months notice, and the granting of building and repairing leases. But the Act also included the necessity for a swing bridge, conferred on the Admiralty power to regulate the opening of such a bridge, prohibited any deviation from the line of the bridge by more than 10 yards from that shown on the plans and maintained the liability of owners of contributory lands for repairs to the bridge. Both railway schemes were rejected, rendering plans for a joint bridge inoperative, despite South Eastern Railway Company's attempts to renew their bill in 1847.[53] This left the bridge wardens to construct a bridge from their own resources.

However, complications arose. During 1846 and 1847 time had been lost in dealing with the railway bills, and by May 1848 it became obvious that the wardens could not meet the stipulations of the Rochester Bridge Act 1846, which required the purchase of land before 14 May 1849 and completion of the bridge by 14 May 1853. Sir Charles Wood, the Chancellor of the Exchequer, would not include the Rochester Bridge Act within the scope of the Railway Extension of Times Act which granted extensions of time to railway companies to meet the stipulated deadlines of the railway acts. It was also necessary in 1848 to exempt the Bridge from the effects of the Public Health Bill which might have placed the pavements and surface under a Local Board of Health thus dividing authority and responsibility for maintenance.[54] To expedite the purchase of lands required, a committee consisting of Messrs Hodges, Smith and the Earl of Romney was set up which, with the assistance of George Essell and William Cubitt, commenced work immediately to negotiate with owners. Statutory notices were issued by September 1848 and contracts entered into by most on valuations made by Mr Sidden, the Trust's surveyor. A few owners, notably Henry Hulkes and the representatives of Thomas William Hulkes (brewers), Charles and Mary Thompson, Sir Henry Meux and Henry Smith (brewers), Mrs Elizabeth Lash and Messrs John and Alfred Lash and the South Eastern Railway company went to arbitration. Only one owner, Samuel Turner, went to 'enquiry by jury' where he was awarded compensation of £575. Altogether the compensation amounted to £22,947, plus the cost of surveyors, solicitors and stamp duty at £2,728 18s. 11d. and £37 for fixtures. These costs were financed by the sale of stocks realising £28,257 and leaving in hand £62,392 14s. In April 1849, just one month before the parliamentary deadline, the purchases had been completed.[55]

Meanwhile the old bridge still needed to be maintained. That it remained in a 'fair' state of repair Cubitt attributed to the policy of immediate repair. The starlings needed planking in most years and the wharfs also required attention at a cost in 1846 of under £500. In 1847, 40 loads of timber suitable for planking and joists were required, while in 1848 the carpenter was allowed to continue with the starlings in most want of repair and do little for the wharfs except to keep them up,

[53] Rochester Bridge Act 1846; Orders, vol. III, 26–7, 29–30, 35.
[54] Orders, vol. III, 68–9; RBT 576.
[55] Ibid., 75, 90, 93–6,99.

the cost being £463 1s. 7d. The work in 1849 was estimated at £500, needing 40 loads of timber.[56]

Finally, at the Court on 31 May 1849 Cubitt was requested to prepare an outline plan for the bridge. Although Cubitt had not completely abandoned the idea of a suspension bridge, a fixed bridge in three arches with an opening ship's passage was approved by the Trust at a special court on 13 July 1849.[57]

---

[56] RBT 277, Annual Report, William Cubitt, 1846; RBT 278, Annual Report 1848; RBT 677, Annual Report 1849.
[57] Orders, vol. III, 114.

Building the New Bridge

William Cubitt outlined his proposals for the new bridge to the Lords of the Admiralty and Harbour Commissioners in June 1849. The bridge was to be of

> Cast Iron, with Stone Piers, and abutments, having three main arches of 140, 170 & 140 feet span respectively, together with a fourth opening of 50 feet wide intended for a Swing or Opening Bridge for the passage of Masted Vessels making in the whole 500 feet of waterway or thereabouts, with the highest part of the largest, or middle, arch 18 feet above the high water of average Spring Tides, & the lowest part of the Invert of the 50 feet Navigable opening 6 feet below the low water surface of the lowest Spring Tide. The clear width of the Bridge is intended to be 40 feet between the Parapets, or fences, for Carriageway & footpaths.

Cubitt's intention was to

> found the Bridge upon cast Iron hollow Piles 5 to 6 feet in diameter sunk down to the solid Chalk, or to such a Stratum as is sufficient to leave the structure quite safe even if the River should deepen to 20 feet in depth below low water. The Piles would be surmounted with Cast Iron Plates as planking at the level of neap tide low water, on which would be built the Stone Piers. The River, I judge, would maintain a depth of at least six feet under the Middle Arch of the Bridge; but everything relating to the Foundations must be determined by circumstances; possibly recourse may ultimately be had to Coffer Damming and bringing up Stone foundations from the bottom; but this, if found on trial to be necessary, would retard the commencement of the Bridge for some years to come.[1]

The Admiralty approved, subject to the swing bridge being built,[2] and to the Captain Superintendent of Chatham Dockyard being permitted to inspect the official plan during the progress of the works.[3]

Cubitt had discovered a method for forcing piles, 6 feet in diameter, through the loose bottom to the hard chalk at depths from 25 to 50 feet below mean high water without coffer dams. The method, known as Dr Potts' patent process using 'atmospheric' pressure, was supported by the contractors.[4] On this basis Cubitt estimated the following cost of the bridge:

---

[1] Letter, William Cubitt to Lords of the Admiralty, 19 June 1849, as quoted in Orders, vol. III, 119–20.
[2] Letter, J. Parker, Secretary to Lords of the Admiralty, 20 June 1849, as quoted in ibid., 121.
[3] Letter, Capt. Washington, Harbour Commissioner, 21 June 1849, as quoted in ibid., 121.
[4] RBT 1542, Orders, vol. III, 125–7.

For Foundations of Cast Iron Piles, six feet in diameter, sunk down to hard chalk, filled in with best brickwork and Hydraulic Lime Mortar, and covered with Cast Iron Platforms and curtain plates	£25,000
Cast Iron Bridge in three Arches, according to the design approved by the Admiralty, paved, painted, and finished complete	£50,000
Bascule Bridge, Abutments, and Invert Ship passage complete, between main bridge and shore	£15,000
Bascule Bridge complete	£5,000
Approaches, Accommodation Bridge, retaining Walls, Road making &c &c on both sides the river	£10,000
Commission for Plans, Management & professional time and expences, cost of Resident Engineer & Assistants together with a sum to meet contingencies of about Eight per cent	£15,000

TOTAL   £120,000[5]

This was considered to be within the means of the Wardens, and it only remained to decide when to commence construction.

It was decided on 14 January 1850 to contract Messrs Fox Henderson & Co. to sink the foundation piles, to fill them, and to attach the cast iron curtains and platforms; and while this was in progress separate tenders would be sought for the piers and superstructure and for the foundations and masonry of the bascule bridge, and for the approaches.[6] Terms of contract were agreed with Fox Henderson & Co. and notices to quit sent to tenants in Strood. By April 1850 the contractors had set up headquarters at the Old Custom House,[7] and by May materials from demolished tenements in Strood were being sold.[8] Cubitt had secured the services of John Wright as resident engineer to conduct and supervise all matters in the engineering department, for which he was to receive an annual salary of £500, together with an office provided by the Trust, an office keeper, and running costs.

The early days of construction were not without their problems. Although progress was made in preparation and in casting the piles, difficulty had been encountered in driving the timber piles for the guide and scaffold frames. Stone and timber foundations had been hit in the river bed,[9] holding up work, and making it impossible to employ the Potts method of forcing down the piles.

How the problem was overcome was described by John Hughes, the engineer in charge.[10] It was intended that each pier would

5 Ibid., 128.
6 Ibid., 129–30.
7 Ibid., 136, 138, 140.
8 Ibid., 146, 152.
9 Report, William Cubitt, 21 May 1850, as quoted in ibid., 147.
10 John Hughes gave details in a paper entitled 'On the pneumatic method adopted in constructing the foundations of the new bridge across the Medway at Rochester', *Proceedings of the Institute of Civil Engineers*, x (1850/1), 355–7.

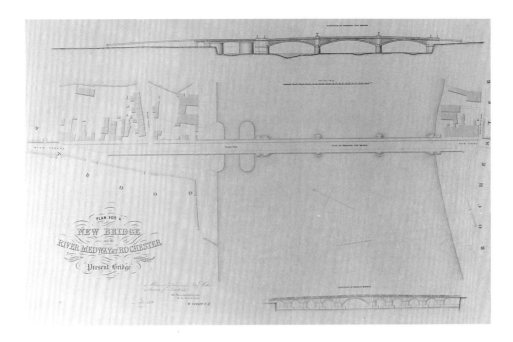

Plate 13(a). Plan and elevation of William Cubitt's cast iron bridge showing its position downstream from the old bridge.

THE EXPLOSION OF OLD ROCHESTER BRIDGE BY THE ROYAL ENGINEERS.—(SEE PAGE 59.)

Plate 13(b). Demolition of the medieval stone bridge by the Royal Engineers from the *Illustrated Times*, 24 January 1857.

Plate 14(a). The Bridge Chamber (right) built in 1879 and Chapel (left) restored in 1937.

Plate 14(b). Damage to the central arch of Rochester Bridge by the lighter *Diamond* in 1896.

Plate 15(a). Slow-moving traffic across the River Medway during the reconstruction of the cast iron bridge in 1912.

Plate 15(b). Removing the arches after the reconstruction of Rochester Bridge in 1913.

Plate 16(a). Aerial view of traffic crossing the duplicated Rochester Bridge in 1977.

Plate 16(b). Aerial view of Rochester Bridge (upper left) and the Frindsbury peninsula before the latter's development by the Wardens and Assistants as an industrial estate.

occupy an area of 1,118 square feet, having a width of 17 feet 8 inches, and a length between the cut waters of 70 feet; and they will stand upon a series of cast-iron cylindrical piles, 7 feet in diameter. . . . The fourteen piles in each of the river piers are at central distances of 9 feet longitudinally, and of 10 feet transversely. The piles in the abutments are 6 feet in diameter: the Strood abutment requiring thirty and the Rochester abutment, twelve. The Rochester abutment would sit on solid chalk rock while the Strood abutment would sit on gravel and require a stronger foundation as discovered by Rendel when investigating the proposed suspension bridge in 1844. Each pile is composed of two, three or more cylinders, 9 feet long, bolted together through stout flanges; the bottom length has its lower edge bevelled so as to facilitate the penetration of the ground.

A substantial timber stage had been erected over the whole site of the pier, chiefly to ensure accuracy in pitching the piles and to hold the piles in position, as well as to provide working space for workmen and machinery.

When the workmen struck the remains of the Roman bridge in the riverbed, making it impossible to induce a semi-vacuum and use atmospheric pressure to drive the piles, Cubitt decided to reverse the process so as to give each pile the nature of a diving bell. This was achieved by bolting a cast iron cover on one of the cylinders. Two cast-iron chambers approximating to air locks were placed through the cover, the top of each having a circular opening 2 feet in diameter with a flap that could be hermetically sealed. At the bottom was a vertical communicating door 2 feet by 3 feet 4 inches again able to close hermetically. Two light cranes were fixed inside the cylinders to empty spoil via buckets. This contrivance when filled with compressed air to hold back water allowed for the manual excavation of each pile. Mr Charles Fox of Fox Henderson & Co. later estimated that the piers were constructed by this method at a cost of £23,000 as against a cost of £53,000 for putting in coffer dams alone, if that method had been adopted.[11]

A further distraction, as pointed out by the merchants of Maidstone in July 1850, was the danger to barge traffic created by the works. As a consequence temporary booms were constructed to prevent accidents. The extra cost was borne by the Trust, but the contractors agreed to allow for the materials.[12] The booms did not prove adequate, for on 17 March 1851 the barge 'Joseph' struck and fractured piling around the western pier, toppling the air pump and two cylinders from the staging, damaging the barge and killing the pilot Edward Hawkins. The coroner's jury recommended that the booms should be extended to provide an adequate safeguard to both works and barges, and the wardens authorised £1,838 for construction of booms. After a second accident to the barge 'Albion' on 21 April 1851, however, Fox Henderson sought compensation from Masters and Sons, Maidstone for the 'ignorance, want of skill and wilfulness' on the part of the crew.[13]

[11] Ibid., 366.
[12] RBT 1542, Orders, vol. III, 153.
[13] Ibid., 153–5.

In spite of these difficulties and setbacks, the building works gradually made progress. Plans and specifications for the Strood approaches were completed so that the wardens could grant building leases for land not required on the north side.[14] The contract for building the arches, retaining walls and earthworks for the Strood approach was awarded to Foord & Son of Rochester on 22 August 1851 with work starting almost immediately.[15] Samuel Sidden of Rochester was awarded the contract to construct the foundations of the opening bridge, which included building a coffer dam, against a tender price of £4,767, and also the contract for the superstructure of the piers and abutments to the springing line of the arches.[16]

By June 1852, however, it had become obvious that the works could not be completed in 1853, and the Bridge Clerk was ordered to take measures to obtain a bill in the next Parliamentary session to extend the Rochester Bridge Act 1846. The Extension Bill provoked six hostile petitions from the South Eastern Railway, the Company of Proprietors of the Navigation of the River Medway, bargemen interested in navigation, John Nightingale and others from whom land was bought under the Rochester Bridge Act 1846, and local inhabitants who thought non-completion was injurious to their interests and that the bridge could be completed in 12 months, which, in the circumstances was completely unrealistic. The case had to be argued in committee and counsel retained, but the resultant Rochester Bridge Amendment Act 1853 extended the time limit for the completion of the bridge to 1 July 1858. It did, however, include a clause to meet South Eastern Railway Company objections, forbidding the Wardens and Assistants 'to obstruct or interfere with the approach to the present or any future station of the South Eastern Railway Company in the parishes of Frindsbury or Strood, or in any manner impede the free and uninterrupted passage of traffic to and from any such station.'[17]

By March 1853 Cubitt had produced plans and specifications for the superstructure of the bridge and plans for the ship's passage, which he proposed should be constructed prior to further work on the superstructure so as to avoid further accidents to barges. In his report of 10 March 1853, Cubitt put on record his reasons for this change of procedure in building the ship's passage during the erection of the piers: firstly, the great length of time consumed in procuring the land for and making the approach on the Strood side; secondly, the difficulty in getting down the foundations for the piers; and thirdly, the protection of barges when the supports for the erection of ironwork were put between the piers. Land required, Cubitt recommended, should be purchased forthwith and tenders advertised.[18] The Lords of the Admiralty preempted any debate, however, by demanding work on the ship passage be carried out 'without delay,' and a further communication

[14] Ibid., 156, 159.
[15] RBT 314; Orders, 174.
[16] RBT 323; Orders, 189, 195
[17] Ibid., 194, 200; The Rochester Bridge Amendment Act 1853.
[18] Orders, vol. III, 198–9.

from the Admiralty in April 1853 commanded the wardens to proceed with the opening bridge immediately.[19]

Just as the wardens began to build the ship's passage, however, the East Kent Railway Company gave notice of intent to build a line through St Nicholas, Rochester, over the Medway to join the North Kent Line in Strood, and that it was seeking powers for building a bridge which might entail altering the Acts relating to Rochester Bridge. The Trust wished to cooperate, yet while not obstructing the East Kent Railway Bill, needed to preserve the integrity of the works in progress. At the 19 May 1853 Court the Bridge Clerk was instructed to take steps to get clauses inserted in the East Kent Railway Bill to ensure that the company completed foundations for the invert arch and abutments of the drawbridge within nine months and foundations and abutments of the main bridge to low water within fifteen months of Royal Assent. In January 1854 the company issued notices of intent to obtain possession of land required for the approaches with a view to an immediate commencement of construction of the piers.[20] The separate railway bridge, also designed by William Cubitt, mirroring the spans of the road bridge and of iron construction on masonry piers, was in operation by the time of the opening of the road bridge in 1857.[21]

The urgency to progress the road bridge scheme led to the establishment on 10 March 1853 of a Committee of Works, consisting of the wardens, the Earl of Darnley, the Earl of Romney, William Smith, Thomas Hodges, George Baker and John Mercer, to undertake the purchase of land and advertise tenders for the superstructure and ship's passage. By early April terms had been agreed with the occupiers of premises which included Alexander Ring's boat-building workshop and the Strood Exchange of the Rochester Oyster Fishery. Tenders for the ship's passage and a temporary timber bridge were advertised nationally in the *Times*, *Builder*, *Railway Times* and *Herapath's Journal*, to be received by 2 May. The result was the award of the contract to Samuel Sidden of Rochester against a tender price of £5,909 19s. 6d.[22] The committee also initially accepted a tender of £47,405 from Mr J.W. Hoby of Renfrew, ironfounder and shipbuilder, for the superstructure of the bridge, but withdrew their offer upon finding his references unsatisfactory and awarded the contract in May 1854 to Cochrane & Company whose tender price was £52,780 8s. 2d. In April 1855 Cochrane & Company were subsequently awarded the contract for the swing bridge on the same price schedule as applied to the superstructure.[23]

A further setback occurred in November and December 1855 when 140 feet of wharf walling between the old bridge and the invert arch of the swing bridge on the Strood side showed signs of bulging and collapse at a point where a temporary bridge had been thrown over the ship's passage to give access to the old bridge. The

---

19 Ibid., 209–10; Letter, Trust Secretary to the Lords of the Admiralty, 2 April 1853, as quoted in ibid., 217–18.
20 Orders, vol. III, 201, 225, 227.
21 *Illustrated London News*, 16 August 1856, 171.
22 Orders, vol. III, 206, 216, 223.
23 Ibid., 234, 239, 242, 257.

wall rested on clay 6 feet below low water, was 26 feet 6 inches high, 9 feet 6 inches thick at the base and 3 feet 6 inches at the top including 18 inches of brick lining. The girders of the temporary bridge rested on a wooden frame on the coping. Settlement had taken place, when traffic had started to cross, and was thought by Wright, the Resident Engineer, to be due to the concrete not having time to set properly. Wright drove piles on the upstream side of the temporary bridge which stopped the bulging.[24]

In April 1856 Cubitt was instructed to draw up plans for the removal of the old bridge and for embanking the Rochester side for which materials would be appropriated from the old bridge. Plans were agreed on 12 June. Although contracts were advertised, no tenders were forthcoming, probably because the original scheme called for the construction of a coffer dam with all the difficulty that it entailed and also because this was a difficult area with drains emptying into the river and springs occurring. Plans were then altered at Cubitt's suggestion to make it unnecessary to build a coffer dam to construct the Esplanade embankment. Cubitt was empowered to try to make a private arrangement to carry out the work.

Work on the new bridge was sufficiently near completion for the Court held on 24 July 1856 to set plans for the opening of the new bridge scheduled to take place on 13 August. The mayors and corporations of Rochester and Maidstone were invited to meet the Wardens and Assistants at the Bridge Chamber at three o'clock from which they would process accompanied by a Royal Marine band across the old bridge via the Strood approach to the centre of the new bridge where it was 'ordered that the Bridge and its Approaches and Stairs thereto be and the same are this day and from henceforth for ever opened and dedicated to and for the free passage and thoroughfare of all Her Majesty's Subjects and all others entitled to pass over and along the Highways of the Realm' and the ancient bridge was ordered closed, after which the procession returned to the Corn Exchange for a public dinner at four o'clock. A firework display was held from the old bridge at nine o'clock. Thus the new bridge came into use.[25]

The Committee on Works still had considerable works to supervise before the whole scheme was completed. These included the removal of the old bridge, the removal of obstructions to navigation, building the esplanade, lighting the new bridge, and fencing stairs to the Strood landing place and from the bridge to Strood High Street. To accomplish these remaining works, Cubitt[26] continued as Engineer-in-Chief at 10 guineas per day and out of pocket expenses for travel, and Wright remained Resident Engineer during the removal of the old bridge and building of wharfs at an annual salary of £500 plus 30 shillings per week for a superintendent

---

[24] Ibid., 268–77.

[25] Ibid., 282, 299, 303, 305.

[26] Cubitt's agreement with the Trust of May 1851 was specifically related to the design and building of the new bridge, and provided remuneration of 3% on all contracts settled plus professional charges and expenses, in all not to exceed £4,500. Demolition of the old bridge and supervision of the works were excluded from his duties.

of works. Wright had the use of the Bridge Chamber for official duties. Mr Anderson, the Bridge Foreman, was to act as office keeper.[27]

Demolition of the old bridge proceeded, until by November 1856 the second and third arches of the old bridge on the Strood side had been entirely removed and the intermediate portion cleared away to 8 feet 6 inches of the starlings. Messrs. Foord supplied the labour, but work was suspended while workmen were transferred to excavate the foundations for the Rochester esplanade. This delay allowed Colonel Sandham, Commanding Officer, Royal Engineers, to try a demolition experiment under water to remove a pier and starling.[28] Colonel Sandham then decided to assist in the demolition while experimenting further with mining and blasting techniques,[29] the wardens commitment being only £200 for powder. Blasting loosened materials which enabled Wright's labourers to easily remove balustrades and masonry required for the esplanade,[30] and surplus stone and material were removed by barge for use at Chatham Dockyard at the expense of the Admiralty.[31] A graphic description of these operations appeared in the *Illustrated Times*:

Old Rochester Bridge . . . has at length fallen; not, however, by time, but by 'villainous saltpetre'. The pier, a solid mass of masonry 45 feet long, 21 feet in depth, and 13 in width, was first mined; 300 lbs of powder were fired, and the huge blocks of masonry were by this small quantity so shaken from their position as to be easily removable. The pier was built on piles driven into the bed of the river, and it is evident that the force of the gunpowder has had as great an effect in loosening the foundations as upon the superstructure. This was as much the object of the engineers as to loosen the constituents of the pier, so that the materials might be readily detached without filling up the bed of the river – a result which was most successfully accomplished.

On Thursday week another and a larger portion of the bridge was destroyed. It consisted of the pier and abutment on which the large arch on the Strood side rested, and was calculated to contain several thousand tons of masonry. The weight of powder used in the explosions was nearly 1,000lbs., and was divided into six charges, as in the previous experiments. Since November last the Sappers and Miners have been engaged in sinking two shafts in this portion of the bridge, which were excavated to the respective depths of twenty-four and twenty-one feet; one shaft having been sunk in the pier, and the other in the abutment. At the base of each shaft sprang two galleries, each nine feet in length, and in these were deposited the charges of powder. They were contained in tin waterproof cases, which were enclosed in wooden boxes; 500 lbs. being required for blowing up the pier, and arch, and 300 lbs. in destroying the abutment. The keystones of the arch were removed by smaller blasts.

. . .

As soon as the arrangements had been completed Colonel Sandham ordered the bugle to be sounded, as a warning to those present to remove out of danger,

27 Ibid., 306, 294.
28 RBT 376, Report, William Cubitt, 27 November 1856.
29 RBT 377, Letter, Col. Sandham, 21 January 1857.
30 RBT, Report, John Wright, 30 January 1857.
31 RBT 378, Letter from Admiralty, 21 March 1857.

and immediately afterwards the bugler sounded 'to fire'. The charges in the arch were first exploded, followed by those in the pier. The effect was very striking, the ground for some distance reverberating as if from the effects of an earthquake, while the pier crumbled in pieces and disappeared. The charges in the galleries on the pier abutment were afterwards fired, and that portion of the bridge was also destroyed. The large arch of the bridge was blown into the river, and the abutment on the Strood side entirely removed. Nearly one-half of the bridge was thus destroyed, and the remaining portion will be demolished as speedily as possible.

The proceedings were watched by a large number of Royal Engineers officers, including General Sir Charles Pasley, General Sir Harry Jones, General T. Blanshard and General P. Yule.[32]

Cubitt's final report in April 1857[33] set out details of a contract with Foords by which they would receive £8,500 for the removal of the superstructure to the level of the starlings, including staging and centring (£2,230), the removal of the large starling on the Rochester side (£600) and seven other starlings (at £461 each) and the building of the Esplanade (£2,377).[34] Still more delays occurred in the removal of the starlings due to Rochester Corporation's failing to decide quickly on the line of the Esplanade. This meant stone was stored on the starlings, preventing removal of the piles which could only be drawn for a few hours at a time during favourable tides. Foords claimed to have removed with difficulty upward of 10,000 piles, representing 250,000 cubic feet of timber, by the time the task was completed in autumn 1859.[35]

The final major task was the removal of the island formed by the digging of the ship's passage; the removal of booms, staging, and piles from the river; and the construction of a landing stage on the Strood side. A sub-committee of the Senior Warden Edward Betts, Junior Warden Robert Tassell, and Mr Baker had been set up at the May 1858 meeting to receive and accept tenders. Wright supervised the works for a fee of £100. The contract was taken by John Ball of Frindsbury who was to make painfully slow progress. As late as April 1863 Wright reported that there were still 100 piles to be removed, for which a new machine was available, and that the guide booms in the river were soon to be removed. In May 1864 Wright accepted Ball's proposal to cut off any remaining piles in an attempt to finally complete the contract.[36]

A few further matters of detail were settled to complete the layout of the area which then remained largely unchanged for the next hundred years. In response to a request of April 1861 from Rochester Corporation for assistance in making a landing place, quay and fishermen's assembly building below the bridge, a piece of

[32] *The Illustrated Times*, 24 January 1857, 59.

[33] Cubitt resigned as Bridge Engineer in May 1858 due to ill health.

[34] Report, Cubitt, 20 April 1857, as quoted in Orders, vol. III, 332–7; RBT 397, contract with Messrs Foord & Sons, 27 May 1857.

[35] Orders, vol. III, 358; *Archaeologia Cantiana*, xxxv (1921), 134.

[36] Orders, vol. III, 352, 359; RBT 425, report, Wright, 16 April 1863; RBT 432, report, Wright, May 1864.

land forty feet wide bounded by Watson's Warehouse and Clements Lane was provided in place of the Town Quay taken for the bridge.[37] A request received also in April 1861 from the inhabitants of Strood for a vessel hard, stone landing steps and the fencing of the river frontage was refused. But Wright's report of 28 March 1864 included the building of stone steps at the upstream end of Strood wharf where a natural sloping hard could be made to accommodate boats. A further Rochester Corporation proposal to use the riverfront land at Strood for a promenade was agreed at the May 1864 Court provided the City placed a fence on the riverside, the Trust retaining a portion for the storage of stone and materials for the repair of the bridge.[38] A final detail was the provision at the suggestion of Rochester Corporation of a urinal 'for the accommodation of the public' at the Rochester end of the bridge under the corner of the wall at the end of the Esplanade, the Corporation and Paving Commissioners being prepared to provide light, water and cleansing. Messrs Foord were contracted to construct at a price of £71 in April 1865.[39]

[37] Orders, vol. III, 391, 397.
[38] Ibid., 390; RBT 1543, Orders, vol. IV, 23, 32; RBT 426, report, Wright, 28 March 1864.
[39] Orders, vol. IV, 37, 49.

Maintaining and Modifying the New Bridge

For forty years after the completion of the new bridge, the main bridge business related to routine maintenance, minor repairs, and requests from companies wishing to carry their services across the Medway. In the first category the ironwork of the bridge required regular painting. Wright[1] in April 1860 was instructed to report on the comparative costs of painting the bridge with Carson's Anti-Corrosion paint, black mineral paint, or common oil paint. A decision was taken to use Carson's, and the first repainting contract went to Foords who had tendered £630.[2] The paintwork required replacing again by 1866, and tenders were advertised for the application of two coats of Carson's Anti-Corrosion paint. Once again Foord's tender of £198 was accepted, and painting was nearly complete by August 1867, although three coats were needed in parts and the cost increased to £220 3s. 4d.[3] The reduced price resulted from the body of paint by now built up upon the structure. Subsequently repainting was required on average once every six years.

When complaints were received in December 1866 over the state of the pavements and the failure to clear early snow, it was found that bridge foreman Daniel Anderson was no longer able to perform his duties and that those actually performing the cleansing of the Bridge had no contract or specification of duties. The Wardens and Assistants approached the Rochester Paving Commisssioners with a view to their contracting to clean and water the bridge, the approaches, and steps from 9 July 1867, and also asked them to present terms for repairing the approaches to the bridge. In anticipation of a contract James Appleton, the acting bridge foreman, was given notice of the termination of his employment from 22 October 1867. In the event the Paving Commission, having taken counsel's opinion as to their powers under their parliamentary acts, declined to take any contract. The cleansing contract was advertised and taken by James Appleton for the annual sum of £150, which was increased to £170 in August 1880.[4]

Rochester Corporation made known, in 1889, its willingness under its powers as

---

[1] After Cubitt's resignation the position of Bridge Engineer was not filled although Wright continued, in effect, in that capacity. Wright asked for an official position as engineer at a nominal salary which would allow him authority to give orders to the bridge foreman as required. As a result he was offered the position of Resident Engineer on 13 June 1867 with a brief to report on repairs and works necessary, to superintend contracts, and supervise the watering, cleansing, repairing and painting of the bridge, approaches and steps, all for a salary of £50 per annum. Orders, vol. IV, 112; Letter, Wright, 17 September 1866.

[2] Orders, vol. III, 381, 383, 385.

[3] Orders, vol. IV, 97, 114, 126.

[4] Ibid., 96–7, 113, 116, 124–5; Orders, vol. V, 48.

an urban sanitary authority to take over the cleansing and watering of the bridge from June of that year. It was arranged for Appleton's contract to end on 21 October. In the half year October 1889 to March 1890 the cost to the Trust of repairing the approaches was £82 16s. 0d. and for cleansing £24 10s. 9d. As the service provided proved satisfactory in May 1890, an agreement was reached with the Corporation to make the arrangement permanent. The wardens could give instructions to the city surveyor over details of work, and would pay for services quarterly. The cost for the first complete year of cleansing was £121.[5]

Under the heading of repairs it was the swing bridge that proved the most troublesome. Although well designed and balanced in some respects, and having an ingeniously simple manual operating mechanism through shafts and gears, the swing bridge did have some weak points. For instance, the surface of the swing bridge was initially planking which was already deteriorating by 1864, necessitating repair by John Ball.[6] Further repair was required in 1874 at a cost of £500 as a result of rot in the planking.[7] In 1881 the rotten wooden cap of the swing bridge parapet railing needed replacing in iron. Rotten wooden footways were replaced with corrugated wrought iron plates covered with concrete and asphalt.[8]

A more permanent solution to the swing bridge problem resulted from the actions of the South Eastern Railway Company who in 1881 introduced a bill in Parliament for powers to construct a railway from Strood to Chatham with a bridge adjacent to the two existing bridges. The wardens entered a petition against the bill, and made representations to the Admiralty to insert clauses requiring a swing bridge which were duly written into the Act.[9] In practice, however, the swing bridge had never been used by the Admiralty, nor had they replied to requests from the Medway Lower Navigation Company for the bridge to be opened for fixed mast vessels on passage to Maidstone. Contrary to the provisions of their Act, the South Eastern Railway Company proceeded to build a bridge without an opening. Consequently, Sir Joseph Bazalgette[10] proposed obtaining powers to fix permanently the opening section of the road bridge, and at the 1 June 1882 court a proposal by Mr Belsey was carried that 'it would be desirable to obtain powers to permanently fix the opening portion of the bridge'.[11] It was not until November 1886, however, that application was made to the Admiralty to relieve the Trust of the duty to maintain the swing bridge, an action partly precipitated by the constant repairs to the wooden pavements. The Admiralty offered no objection to the swing bridge being discontinued, and they contacted the London, Chatham and Dover Railway Company so that in their next parliamentary bill they could insert a clause

5   Orders, vol. VI, 4, 14, 27, 36, 58.
6   Orders, vol. IV, 14, 32.
7   Orders, vol. IV, 202, 236, 255; report, John Wright, 10 April 1874.
8   RBT 603, report, Joseph Bazalgette, 6 June 1881.
9   Orders, vol. V, 70.
10 After the sudden death of John Wright, Sir Joseph Bazalgette was engaged in April 1881 to report on the state of the bridge, and also on other potential crossing places on the Medway. Orders, vol. V, 69.
11 Orders, vol. V, 122.

repealing the obligation to maintain a swing bridge. A clause was duly inserted in the London, Chatham and Dover Railway Bill of 1888, but on 12 March the Chairman of Committees declined to allow a clause relating to the Trust to be brought in a bill relating to another public body. A separate bill would need to be promoted in Parliament.

The Bridge Engineer, Mr V. de Michele,[12] estimated the cost of permanent closure at £2,120. As the wooden surface was in urgent need of replacement, de Michele was instructed to prepare a plan for a false arch across the channel in harmony with the rest of the bridge and for making a permanent roadway of pavement and stone.[13] The cost, however, would have been £5,000 against an average annual cost for repairs of £50. In July 1889, de Michele made a thorough examination of the planking of the swing bridge and found the ends of the upper planking in bad condition but the lower planking generally sound and as a result recommended making the surface uniform with the rest of the bridge at an estimated cost of £450. This course of action was adopted at the court held on 20 November. The lowest tender came from Ball and Gammon at £780. Work did not start until January 1890 due to difficulty in obtaining steel base plates, and extra work found necessary increased the cost by £200.[14] In effect the swing bridge had been closed without further legislation.

Other minor matters occasionally needed attention. Some kerbs on the bridge were worn due to the skidding of carriages, while others on the Strood approach had sunk, partly due to Aveling & Porter traction engines turning on them going in and out of the Strood works. To prevent water from collecting, the kerb and channel required raising from Canal Road to the end of the approach.[15] In 1881 the twenty-foot opening under the Strood approach required strengthening by inserting wrought iron between existing cast iron girders. The design had not foreseen the weight of traffic which would use the bridge in the age of the traction engine. Sir Joseph Bazalgette was delegated 'to take all steps necessary to carry out the works'.[16] Most maintenance and repairs were routine, however, and apart from one or two exceptional years the annual cost of cleansing and repairing the new bridge varied little. From 1860 to 1866 it averaged £267 6s. 7¼d. per annum,[17] while comparable expenditure for the year 1892–3 was £277 1s. 5d.

It was inevitable that as new amenities became available attempts would be

---

[12] A permanent engineer, Mr V. de Michele of Higham, was appointed in April 1883.

[13] Orders, vol. V, 338–9, 352, 406, 416, 443; Orders, vol. IV, 152; RBT 603, report, Sir Joseph Bazalgette, April 1882; RBT 306, letter, Admiralty, 20 December 1886; RBT 571, report, V. de Michele, 13 May 1888.

[14] Orders, vol. VI, 12–14; RBT 604, reports, de Michele, 30 May 1889, 26 July 1889, 26 October 1889. Rochester police regulated traffic during the 1890 works, and took a census of traffic on one Saturday and on one Tuesday in April. On the Saturday the bridge was crossed by 17,139 pedestrians and 1565 vehicles, and on the Tuesday by 12,776 pedestrians and 1824 vehicles.

[15] RBT 430, report, John Wright, 14 January 1867; RBT 603, report, Sir Joseph Bazalgette, 6 June 1881.

[16] RBT 603, report, Sir Joseph Bazalgette, 6 June 1881.

[17] Report, Bridge Clerk, 31 January 1866, as quoted in Orders, vol. IV, 69; Orders, vol. VI, meeting of 14 April 1893.

made to carry the services across the bridge to Strood. In April 1860 notice was given by two water companies – the Brompton, Chatham, Gillingham, Rochester and Strood Waterworks Company and the Maidstone, Rochester and Chatham District Waterworks Company – of their intent to apply to Parliament for powers to supply water and carry their mains over the approaches and the bridge. To protect its rights, the Trust had a clause inserted in the bills that any works on the bridge would be under the inspection and control of the Bridge Engineer.[18] A gas main on the downstream side of the bridge, with means for disconnection to prevent the impeding of the opening of the swing bridge, was approved in 1871.[19] In 1888 the new Chatham Electric Lighting Company wished to carry their wires to Strood. Before committing themselves the Trust took the opinion of an expert electrical engineer, Major General Webber RE, who was able to support the company's application.[20] In 1902 Rochester Corporation gave notice of their intent to run a tramway over the bridge. Much discussion took place over liability for repair of the road surface before agreement was reached providing for the Corporation to repair only the space between the rails and eighteen inches on either side.[21] The laying of the tramway necessitated replacing wood on the swing bridge with steel plates, which Bridge Engineer John Robson thought would be an improvement. The tramline when laid left 12 feet 6 inches clear in the centre of the roadway for other traffic.[22] In 1905 an approach was made to allow the sewer for the proposed Medway Towns main drainage scheme to cross the bridge, but a decision was deferred for further consideration. In practice work on the joint scheme was not to commence until 1925. The Kent Electric Power Company and the National Telephone Company also wanted to cross the bridge jointly with wires in cast iron pipes on the bridge and in concrete conduits on the approaches.[23] The use of the bridge to carry these important services contributed considerably to the economic and social well being of the area.

Maintenance problems far more serious than routine repairs or requests from service companies confronted the Wardens and Assistants around the turn of the century. In 1896 a series of accidents necessitated more expensive repairs, prompting eventually a complete remodelling of the bridge. The first accident happened on 20 February 1896, when the lighter 'Diamond' which was being towed upriver on a high tide struck girders of the central arch, carrying away portions of two. This affected the stability of the bridge and caused some depression. Traction engines were banned, and carriages could cross only at walking pace to prevent vibration. De Michele sent for William Ball who had appropriate plant to provide support for the damaged section until repairs were carried out. Ball completed placing support girders under the damaged section by 1 April, when, once more,

[18] Orders, vol. III, 377–8.
[19] Orders, vol. IV, 193, 202–3.
[20] Orders, vol. V, 431–2; RBT 2607, report, Maj. Gen. Webber, 14 August 1888.
[21] Orders, vol. VI, meetings of 22 May 1902 and 24 April 1903.
[22] Ibid., meeting of 12 April 1907.
[23] Ibid., meeting of 5 May 1905.

traction engines under 20 tons were allowed to cross. Vessels were prevented from using the centre arch, and the Harbour Master was instructed to lay buoys and booms to prevent barges ramming into the damaged arch. John Cochrane & Sons' bid to carry out the repair at a charge giving ten per cent profit on the actual net cost of the repair including all necessary staging, plant and dolphins above and below the bridge, to a maximum of £6,000. In a further slight accident on 16 March William Cory & Sons' lighters *Ruby* and *Turquoise* struck iron plates on the Strood arch but did little damage.[24] Work on the bridge was completed on 18 December 1896 at a cost of £6,310 17s. 11d. including the engineer's fees.[25] A claim for compensation against William Cory & Sons Ltd led to an investigation into the condition of the bridge, revealing 'certain old cracks' in the ironwork of the bridge which had resulted from many previous unreported collisions. As a result compensation was lowered to £5,500.[26]

In addition to highlighting the problem of insufficient clearance under the bridge, the collision also influenced the way in which the bridge was inspected, revealing other hitherto undetected problems. Bridge Engineer de Michele was ordered to make an immediate and thorough inspection of the bridge. Further weekly inspections were to be undertaken by the foreman who would report to the Bridge Engineer. In turn de Michele[27] would make subsequent examinations of the bridge every fifth year, or more often as thought fit, for a special fee of £26 5s.[28] When the first of these quinquennial inspections took place in May 1903, de Michele reported that the general condition of the bridge was 'satisfactory', but listed numerous necessary repairs: repointing brickwork and masonry, tightening and replacing bolts, relaying patches of the approaches, and, the biggest item, repainting. In addition, the scour of the river had exposed the swing bridge pier, and bags of concrete had to be laid at the base of the pier to provide protection. The total cost of this maintenance was £996.[29]

John Robson, de Michele's successor as Bridge Engineer,[30] finally solved the problem of protecting the foundations of the piers and the Strood abutment. He placed close sheet piling filled with concrete bags around the piers, while the existing piling on the Strood abutment was filled with fine concrete and two timber walings were attached for extra protection at a cost of £755 9s. 0d.[31]

In July 1907 a further accident occurred when the lighter 'Spurn' belonging to

---

[24] Ibid., meetings of 6 March 1896 and 17 April 1896.

[25] Ibid., meeting of 30 April 1897.

[26] Ibid., meeting of 1 December 1897.

[27] De Michele's terms of office as permanent engineer were defined in June 1898. In return for a salary of £31 10s. 0d. per annum he would attend courts, prepare reports, prepare specifications for repairs and superintend works. Out of pocket expenses were not to exceed £50, but there would be a 5% commission on works exceeding £500. Orders, vol. VI, meeting of 2 June 1898.

[28] Orders, vol. VI, meeting of 2 June 1898.

[29] Report, de Michele, 22 May 1903, as quoted in Orders, vol. VI, meeting of 4 June 1903.

[30] De Michele died suddenly on 21 March 1906. His assistant H.E. Newton carried on temporarily until the appointment of Mr John Robson M.Inst. CE of High Holborn and Gravesend. Orders, vol. VI, meeting of 27 April 1906.

[31] Orders, vol. VI, meeting of 5 December 1906.

Associated Portland Cement Manufacturers (APCM) collided with the bridge and damaged a girder. APCM disputed liability, offering £500 'without prejudice'. The collision brought to the fore the whole question of headway under the bridge. Vessels up to 340 tons burthen and steam tugs with six lighters two abreast used the bridge, with daily traffic up to 120 movements. The railway bridges had a clearance of 20 feet 5 inches, while in contrast the bases of the arches of the road bridge were awash at high tide. The set of the tide made navigation upstream particularly difficult under these bridges. Robson recommended that the minimum headway under the centre span of the bridge should be 21 feet above the high water spring tide. Three alternative plans were commissioned from Sir John Wolfe Barry and Partners, and were to be put to Mr A.C. Hurtzig of Baker & Hurtzig, consulting engineers, for expert consideration after the 'Spurn' case had been settled.[32] These plans increased the headway marginally by substituting wrought iron for cast iron ribs, but still retained the supporting arches. The result would be a clearance of 23 feet in the middle of the central arch but only 6 feet beside the piers for a cost of £35,000. Robson considered the advantage gained to be scarcely commensurate with the cost and argued that to increase materially the headway, the centre arch must be removed and a new one substituted. This had to be accomplished without affecting the stability of the bridge. His solution was a plan to suspend the ribs of the roadway of the centre span by placing the arch above the bridge. The five new ribs required could be placed in position between existing internal ribs before the old ones were removed. The plan entailed strengthening the hollow piers by filling them with steel reinforced concrete. Although the arch would be no heavier, the total weight of the bridge would be increased but would still be within the capacity of the foundations. Cross bracing would be at least 17 feet above the roadway and provision made for all services to run under the footpaths. This was the basis of plan No. 4 which was also forwarded to Baker & Hurtzig.[33]

In the meantime only work of immediate concern was carried out, including the bolting of a specially designed patch over the rib fractured by the 'Spurn', and preparations to lay steel troughing over the swing bridge to accommodate the tramway at a cost of £1,087. No further steps were taken over the headway, pending the passage of the Rochester Bridge Act 1908, as the Trust did not want to incur heavy expenditure. Even painting the bridge was postponed in view of likely rebuilding.[34]

By June 1908 Robson had extended his proposal to all three arches, and had produced a plan for the 'most economic design for three new steel arches'. The specification was for 'three new steel spans, each supported by two girders of the cambered or hog-backed type, carrying the roadway 25 feet wide between the girders and footpaths, 7 feet wide on cantilevers outside the girders. Under each footpath a hollow subway will be formed for electric cables, mains, etc., the large gas main being carried under the footpath to the east side by the cantilever

---

[32] Letter, Medway Conservancy, 9 October 1907, and reports, Robson, November 1907, as quoted in Orders, vol. VI, meeting of 4 December 1907.

[33] Report, John Robson, 27 April 1908, as quoted in Orders, vol. VI, meeting of 1 May 1908.

[34] Orders, vol. VI, meetings of 4 December 1907 and 1 May 1908.

brackets' to allow a roadway two feet wider than the existing one. 'Distributing girders will be placed under the bearings of the main girders to distribute the weight on the piers and abutments'. The roadway would be paved in wood block and the footpaths in concrete; slight alterations would be made to the masonry of the piers and abutments to accommodate the increased width of the bridge; and the swing bridge would be removed and a new fixed steel span substituted. The proposal allowed for one half of the bridge to be constructed at a time over existing cast iron ribs so that no staging or piling would be necessary in the river. 'Traffic would be diverted over one half the bridge. . . . The temporary footpath would be supported on cantalivers outside the present parapet. The parapets, cornice paving, etc. would be cleared away down onto the floor plates on which the new spans would be erected. When the first half of the bridge is completed traffic would be diverted over it whilst the second half of the bridge is being constructed. After the three new spans are completed the old iron ribs and floor plates would be removed from underneath.' Robson estimated the cost at £48,662, but Joseph Westwood & Company estimated that the design could be carried out for £46,345 (subject to detailed drawings) plus £1,000 for moving electric cables, gas mains and other services.[35]

The report of the quinquennial inspection of 5 April 1909 made further delay impossible. Floor plates of the bridge had cracked in places and needed replacement. A rib was fractured on the Strood arch and Westwoods were patching it. Bolts were defective or missing in 916 places. One cross brace was fractured, and all needed replacing with steel, about 15 feet apart. The total cost would be about £9,886, which sum was not justified if the bridge were to be rebuilt, but absolutely necessary if the present bridge were to be retained.[36]

On 7 July 1909, therefore, the Trust set up a committee to interview Baker & Hurtzig, to consider Robson's design No. 4, and to ascertain who would act as consulting engineers. The result was an agreement whereby Baker & Hurtzig would become chief engineers and act jointly with Robson. Baker & Hurtzig would take a commission of 2½ per cent, Robson 2 per cent with an extra 1½ per cent for taking out bills of quantities. The Charity Commission agreed to sell consols in the Bridge Reserve Fund and India stock from accumulated surplus income to finance the rebuilding, but required tenders from contractors with an indication of which the wardens wanted to accept.[37]

Plans were approved on 8 April 1910 and tenders invited from bridge builders Head, Wrightson & Company Ltd, Andrew Handyside & Company, Sir William Arrol & Company Ltd and Joseph Westwood & Company Ltd, but after objections from Baker & Hurtzig, the contractors S. Pearson & Son Ltd, John Aird & Company,

---

[35] Letter, John Robson, 10 June 1908, as quoted in Orders, vol. VI, meeting of 11 June 1908; Letter, Joseph Westwood & Company Ltd., 28 April 1908, and report, John Robson, 27 April 1908, as quoted in ibid., meeting of 1 May 1908.

[36] Report, John Robson, 5 April 1909, as quoted in Orders, vol. VI, meeting of 23 April 1909, 11–13; Orders, vol. VII, meeting of 3 June 1909, 6.

[37] RBT 1546, Orders, vol. VII, meeting of 7 July 1909, 1–2; ibid., meeting of 26 July 1909, 2–4; Letter, Charity Commission, 22 July 1909, as quoted in ibid., meeting of 26 July 1909, 4.

John Cochrane & Sons, and Price Willis and Reeves were also allowed to tender. The lowest tender was Cochrane's at £64,041, and in ascending order Westwood's £64,184, Handyside's £66,000, Arrol's £75,317, Head, Wrightson's £78,000, Aird's £88,756 and Pearson's £91,942. Agreements were also negotiated with owners of statutory wayleaves for the Trust to contribute half the cost of disturbance.[38] Baker & Hurtzig were instructed to confer with John Cochrane & Sons and their subcontractor Joseph Westwood & Company to see whether they had made full provision to carry out the specification and, if not satisfied, to approach Andrew Handyside & Company. Objections were found to both Cochrane's and Handyside's tenders because they had neglected to provide support for the weight of temporary works during reconstruction. The Trust resolved to accept Arrol's tender, despite Robson having made a good case for accepting John Cochrane & Sons' bid[39] on the grounds that his scheme of not removing the old arches and ribs until after the fixing of the new made supports superfluous. Baker & Hurtzig did not accept his stress calculations, and when the Charity Commission asked Baker & Hurtzig if they would change their opinion, they again declined. As a result on 1 November 1910 the Charity Commission nominated an independent engineer Mr R. Elliott-Cooper, vice president of the Institute of Civil Engineers to report on the bids. He supported the Cochrane bid, and Baker & Hurtzig agreed to remain chief engineers if supporting 'false work' at an extra cost of £3150 were included in the contract.[40] A contract was finally signed on 14 February 1911 for a tender price of £71,392 18s. 3d. but allowing price increases for steel, cement and bricks.[41] Further costs included a reluctantly agreed payment of two-thirds of the cost of any extra policing of traffic on the bridge, not exceeding £500 after an approach from the Rochester Watch Committee.[42] After arbitration the full cost of £2,667 for moving the Kent Electric Power Company cables also fell on the Trust.

The schedule for the progress of the contract was worked out in December 1911 with Messrs. Joseph Westwood & Company as the main subcontractor. By this date the downstream end of the trestles on the piles was virtually completed, and the downstream end of the abutment girders was being lowered into place. The downstream end of the masonry on the piers and abutments would be completed by the end of December 1911. The bedstones for the girders on the fifty-foot opening would be in place by 31 January 1912, and the girders in place by 29 February. The downstream end of the main cross girders would be in place by the end of April 1912, and the downstream main girders by July 1912. Traffic would be diverted from the upstream side to the downstream side by the end of September, and the roadway on the upstream side completed by the end of March 1913. It would then

38 Orders, vol. VII, meeting of 8 April 1910; ibid., meeting of 19 May 1910.
39 Ibid., meeting of 2 June 1910 and 14 June 1910; Report, John Robson, 11 June 1910, as quoted in ibid.
40 Orders, vol. VII, meeting of 10 December 1910; Letters, Charity Commission, 17 August, 23 August, 7 December 1910, as quoted in ibid., meeting of 17 December 1910, 15–16.
41 Orders, vol. VII, meeting of 28 April 1911; Contract with Cochrane and Company, 14 February 1911.
42 Orders, vol. VII, meeting of 1 June 1911, 3.

be possible to remove the existing bridge, and while this was being accomplished the upstream masonry would be completed by the end of May. The porticoes and ornamental masonry could be attached by the end of July 1913. Traffic could use the whole bridge from May 1913 under this plan, but pedestrians would be able to use only one footpath at a time until masonry was completed.[43] To improve the appearance of the bridge, stone work could be recovered from the old bridge and used to face the rebuilt Strood and Rochester abutments. This was more in harmony with the ornate design of the bridge than the planned brickwork, and cost only an extra £250.[44]

Progress remained fairly well on schedule with the downstream main girders for the Strood and Rochester spans erected by May 1912, and the downstream swing bridge girders having been fixed and floored over with steel troughing. The Rochester approach had been raised to its new levels, and work was progressing on the Strood approach.[45] The downstream side was opened to traffic on 11 November 1912 by which time the services of the Tramway Company, Rochester Gas Company and the Kent Electric Power Company had been removed to their permanent positions. The upstream masonry, footpath and road material were being removed and steelwork was being erected at the Strood end.[46] The work was sufficiently advanced to allow the removal of the existing arches between 13 July and 13 October 1913, with one arch at a time being closed to river traffic.[47] Some consideration was given to cosmetics with light grey paint to match the stonework being adopted, along with a copper coating for lamp pillars and lamps.[48] Completion of the whole project, including lavatories on Rochester Esplanade, was held up as John Cochrane & Son could not obtain granite from their supplier United Stone who had gone into liquidation. They had been unable to switch to other quarries to obtain supplies as order books were full. The liquidator managed to extract £300 above contract price to expedite delivery,[49] and the bridge was finally completed at the end of April 1914. A formal opening was performed on 14 May 1914 by Lady Darnley with a parade across the bridge of the civic leaders from Rochester, Maidstone, Chatham and Gillingham, followed by a luncheon at the Corn Exchange for 92 people.[50] The cost of the whole enterprise totalled £95,857.

---

[43] Letter, A.H. Cochrane to A.C. Hurtzig, 5 December 1911, as quoted in ibid., meeting of 11 December 1911, 2.

[44] Letter, Baker & Hurtzig and Robson, 22 September 1911, as quoted in ibid., 3.

[45] Report, Baker & Hurtzig and Robson, 23 May 1912, as quoted in ibid., meeting of 6 June 1912, 13–14.

[46] Report, Baker & Hurtzig and Robson, 18 November 1912, as quoted in ibid., meeting of 2 December 1912, 14–15. The opportunity of reconstruction was taken to plan the laying of a new 14-inch gas main on the downstream side of the bridge and the laying of the main drain. This entailed minor alterations to the design including the addition of a gangway for inspection and the strengthening of support girders.

[47] Report, Baker & Hurtzig and Robson, 21 November 1913, as quoted in ibid., meeting of 1 December 1913, 14–15.

[48] Orders, vol. VII, meeting of 3 March 1913, 8.

[49] Orders, vol. VII, meeting of 1 December 1913, 2–3; letter, John Cochrane & Sons to Baker & Hurtzig and Robson, 20 November 1913, as quoted in ibid., 15.

[50] Ibid., meeting of 4 June 1914, 3.

After the major modification of the bridge, maintenance once again reverted to routine repairs apart from defense precautions taken by the Wardens and Assistants during the two world wars. At the outbreak of war in 1914 the bridge was put under military guard, with guard rooms on the Rochester and Strood esplanades. The downstream footpath was closed, and gas lighting was reduced to avoid possible damage by bombs from airships. Barbed wire was fixed to the bridge in 1916 as added protection.[51]

The main wartime problems, however, were hangovers from the construction of the bridge. In February 1917 the Harbour Master wrote that he had seen 49 piles on a very low spring tide. Most of these were from staging used during the construction work, but some were very old dating from a previous bridge. These were duly cut off by West Bros on 22 to 25 February. Robson observed that surrounding material had been washed away by the scour of the river. The piers of the bridges influenced the flow, as did the large quantities of stone deposited around the piers and abutments. The scour on the Strood side had removed up to three feet, but silting had occurred on the Rochester side.[52]

Another problem stemmed from a fault in the bridge design. The bridge committee met on 16 July 1917 to consider the leakage of rainwater through the main girders and footpaths. An expert, Mr Basil Mott, was called in and modifications recommended requiring drainage points to be inserted. Because the uncertainty due to the war made getting a fixed tender impossible, G.E. Wallis & Sons Ltd of Maidstone were approached to carry out the work for an estimated £892. This work was facilitated by part of the bridge being closed by the military.[53]

By 1920 it was time to complete some outstanding maintenance. Joseph Westwood & Company were awarded two contracts, one to paint the bridge for £3,536, the other to replace woodwork over the bottom booms of the main girders with chequered steel plates.[54] Thereafter triennial painting and repointing were the usual forms of maintenance. Superficial cracking which appeared in the late 1920s was found to be caused by vibration from the growing volume of traffic using the bridge with the rise of private motoring. A traffic census in 1925 had shown 57,364 vehicles crossing the bridge in one week. By 1928 this had increased to 72,743 and showed every prospect of increasing, reaching 77,613 by 1931. Other cracks appeared in the swing bridge pier in 1928 due to subsidence caused by changing loads when the bridge was modified. The solution involved strengthening support for the roadway and stiffening with tie rods.[55]

---

[51] Reports, Robson, August and September 1914, as quoted in ibid., meeting of 12 October 1914, 12–14; report, Robson, 24 May 1916, as quoted in ibid., meeting of 1 June 1916, 8.

[52] Letter, Medway Conservancy, 13 February 1917, as quoted in ibid., meeting of 5 March 1917, 2; Reports, John Robson, 19 February and 25 February 1917, as quoted in ibid., 9–10; and June 1917, as quoted in meeting of 7 June 1917, 10–13.

[53] Reports, Basil Mott, Robson, in Orders, vol. VII, meeting of 10 December 1917, 9–10.

[54] Orders, vol. VII, meeting of 1 March 1920, 1.

[55] RBT 1547, Orders, vol. VIII, meeting of 7 June 1928, 3, 12; meeting of 5 June 1930, 7; City of Rochester Society, *Rochester from Old Photographs*, Rainham 1985; Report, Robson, 27 November 1931, as quoted in Orders, vol. VIII, meeting of 7 December 1931, 13.

A potential solution to the question of traffic overload came with the first intimation that the old iron railway bridge might be available as a second road bridge. The South Eastern Railway Company and the London, Chatham and Dover Railway Company had amalgamated in 1899, and subsequently in 1927 the London, Chatham and Dover Railway bridge had gone out of use, the track and stations in the area being rationalised using the newer South Eastern bridge and equipment. In 1937 the Southern Railway Company had contacted Rochester Corporation who referred the matter to the Trust. Mr C.L. Howard Humphreys, Bridge Engineer, proposed using the piers of the bridge to support the superstructure of a road bridge, but the Trust took no action at that time.[56]

The Second World War virtually brought the proposal to fruition when plans were made for using the railway bridge in emergency. This entailed the removal of the bronze lions and associated masonry which were stored for subsequent replacement, and the building of ramps. However, the ramps interfered with the roadway and were finally removed in 1946 after a delay caused by a shortage of labour.[57]

In the atmosphere of austerity and shortages of the postwar years it would not have been possible to undertake any major improvement scheme. Urgent repairs to the expansion joints which were jammed due to the gradual movement of the Strood abutment were carried out in 1946 by Messrs Wallis & Sons. However, repainting the bridge, which had last occurred in 1941 and had been continually deferred due to shortages of labour and suitable paint, finally happened in 1948. Resurfacing of the bridge had also been deferred. The wood paving, patched and worn, was in urgent need of replacement. When this occurred in 1949, asphalt was laid with some reluctance due to its added weight on the structure, wood blocks being unobtainable.[58]

The Trust adopted a more modern approach to the supervision of engineering matters after June 1950, when Mr G. Howard Humphreys was given six months notice of termination of his appointment as engineer owing to his ill health. It was resolved to appoint a firm of consulting engineers instead of an individual in future. Subsequently the firm of Mott, Hay and Anderson were appointed engineers.[59] This era ends with another point of modernity with provision being made for the fitting of new lamps for the electrical lighting of the bridge.[60]

---

[56] Orders, vol. VIII, meeting of 2 March 1936, 7; Report, C.L. Howard Humphreys, 19 November 1937, as quoted in ibid., meeting of 6 December 1937, 12. John Robson died on 19 October 1931. He was replaced by Mr C.L. Howard Humphreys of 17 Victoria Street, Westminster. He felt the condition of the bridge in 1931, which had been maintained at a cost of only £22,000 since its opening in 1914 reflected great credit on Robson. Report, Howard Humphreys, 22 February 1933, as quoted in Orders, vol. VIII, meeting of 6 March 1933, 11.

[57] Orders, vol. VII, meeting of 2 March 1942, 5.

[58] RBT 1552, Orders, meeting of 6 June 1946, 5; meeting of 1 March 1948, 6; meeting of 5 December 1949, 6-7.

[59] Ibid., meeting of 1 June 1950, 2; meeting of 20 September 1950; meeting of 4 December 1950, 1.

[60] Ibid., meeting of 4 December 1950, 8.

Supporting the Bridge: Finance and the Estate

The Bridge estate provided the essential income to maintain Rochester Bridge. In the years before the construction of the new bridge funds had accumulated in government consols, reduced annuities, and exchequer bills, reaching an aggregate value of £87,000 by 1847. By July 1856 these stocks had been sold to meet the £157,633 costs of construction, the balance being met from surplus income in the region of £2,000 per annum between 1846 and 1860 and £43,000 raised by mortgage loans on the estate. On 24 July 1856 the sum of £10,000 was borrowed from the Kent Fire Office at 4¼ per cent interest. This loan was followed on 18 August by a further £10,000 from the Rev John White. When Cubitt issued a certificate for the completion of their contract, John Cochrane and Sons proposed a 5 per cent discount for early payment of outstanding sums of £9,926 and £6,617, prompting the wardens to take a loan of £18,000 from the Clergy Mutual Society. A final loan of £5,000 was raised via the Kent Fire Office in May 1858.[1] This debt was gradually reduced from 1862 as surplus funds allowed.

Prior to 1867 the Wardens and Assistants were not restricted in any way in the use of funds not required for the maintenance of the bridge or as a reserve, nor were they subject to any external supervision. This situation changed after they resolved to sell the Bridge Woods, which were no longer needed to supply piles for the bridge and which no longer provided any significant return. The Trust did not think it had powers to sell and in June 1867 determined to promote a bill in the next parliamentary session which would allow the sale of any part of the estate. In 1868 the Rochester Bridge Estates Bill was introduced and had a second reading in the House of Lords unopposed. The bill was referred to Lord Redesdale, Chairman of Committees, who argued that powers should not extend to all the estates but only to such portions as could be more advantageously sold than let, these properties to be set out in a schedule. On this basis the bill passed its committee stage. On 2 April 1868, however, notice was given by the Attorney General to the Chairman of Committees claiming 'an ex officio jurisdiction on the ground that the estates proper constituted and were to be administered as Estates held for charitable purposes,' and therefore fell within the scope of the Charitable Trusts Acts. In effect, the powers sought by the Wardens and Assistants might be exercised, if proved beneficial to the Trust, with the sanction of the Charity Commissioners and needed no special Act of Parliament. The wardens took legal advice from Sir

1 Orders, vol. III, 301, 305, 308, 352.

Roundell Palmer and Mr Speed, who advised that the Attorney General's view was correct. As a result they withdrew the Rochester Bridge Estates Bill.[2]

One immediate result of the decision was a claim to the Special Commissioners of Income Tax for exemption of rents on the ground that Sir J.B. Karslake, the Attorney General, held that the estates were 'charitable trusts' and thus, argued the wardens, exempt under the Act 5 and 6 Vict: chapter 38, section 60, clause C. The Commissioner's reply of 5 March refused the application. Counsel's opinion from Mr Mellish and Mr Barrow was taken that the case could not be sustained under the Act.[3]

In pursuance of the new found jurisdiction over the Bridge Trust on 25 June 1869 Mr F.C. Martin, Inspector of Charities, held a public enquiry at the Guildhall into the endowment and administration of the funds of the Bridge Corporation with no direct result as to the conduct of the Trust as he concluded that he 'thought it hardly necessary to hold another public meeting on the Bridge Trust'.[4]

Meanwhile the mortgage debt of £43,000 was being steadily reduced by the application of surplus revenue and of proceeds from compulsory purchases and other sales of property. Between 1854 and 1856, for example, land to the value of £8,925 was taken by the East Kent Railway Company for the construction of their line through Rochester and for approaches to Rochester Bridge. Consequent upon the 'war scare' with France in 1859 Palmerston's government strengthened fortifications around London and the naval depots. In early 1861 the War Department acquired land at Tilbury and Grain for £4,199, and at Nashenden Farm in the parish of St Margaret, Rochester for £5,939.[5] The other signifcant sale was the Rochester Guildhall to the Rochester Corporation in 1864, the purchase price of £4,000 being allotted towards the redemption of Land Tax upon the whole estate.[6]

Paying off the debt opened the prospect of the Trust's having a large surplus income which was not required for the immediate maintenance of the relatively new bridge, and opened the question of what should be the purpose of the Trust vis-à-vis the surplus. Matters were moved on by Maidstone Local Board who in May 1874 sent a deputation to ascertain whether property held by the Bridge Corporation could be appropriated towards the improvement of the bridge at Maidstone. At this prompting the Trust resolved to take measures 'to determine to what purposes the surplus revenues and property of this Corporation should be applied', and on 28 May 1874 a committee consisting of the Junior and Senior Wardens and Messrs. Lee, Coles, Arkcoll and Wigan was set up to consider this question. Further impetus was given by an application from the freeholders of Wateringbury and surrounding district for a new bridge over the Medway at or near Wateringbury to be paid for out of funds or surplus revenues.[7]

2   Orders, vol. IV, 111, 119–120; Letter, A.A. Arnold, 4 June 1903.
3   Orders, vol. IV, 164.
4   Ibid., 178–9; *Rochester & Chatham Journal and Mid Kent Advertiser*, 26 June 1869.
5   Land agent's reports, as quoted in RBT 1542, Orders, vol. III, 227–30, 240–5, 294–5, 349, 368, 376, 398, 425.
6   Land agent's report, as quoted in RBT 1543, Orders, vol. IV, meeting of 8 April 1864.
7   Ibid., 266, meeting of 28 May 1874.

The committee reported back on 18 March 1875. They considered it desirable to furnish funds for Maidstone Bridge, as the Exchequer Loan Commissioners were unable to grant a loan to Maidstone Corporation. They had ascertained that the Metropolitan Life Office would offer a loan of £30,000 on the mortgage of estates at 4¼ per cent repayable in 30 instalments of £1,780. The Charity Commission had been approached in August 1874 as to whether they would authorise the mortgage of £30,000 to pay off £10,000 of existing debt and provide £20,000 to Maidstone Bridge. They requested a formal application for a scheme, and a proposal was presented in October 1874. The Mayor and Corporation of Rochester, however, opposed the scheme. The Charity Commission wanted Rochester and Maidstone interests 'harmonised' to prevent costly disputes. Conferences were held with the mayor on 26 February and 18 March 1875, but Rochester maintained its objections to the proposed scheme for 'the grant from these funds in relief of the rates of Maidstone'. Rochester Corporation proposed that 'a comprehensive scheme' for the appropriation of the surplus funds of the Rochester Bridge Trust should now be settled and submitted to the Charity Commission. Apart from funds for the maintenance of Rochester Bridge and approaches, funds should be provided for a bridge from Wouldham to Halling, and £10,000 be put 'for the benefit of the City of Rochester'.[8]

Feelings were sufficiently strong that for the first time since 1846 a contested election was likely, and preparations made for a poll on 9 April 1875. As it had been so long since the previous contested election, questions arose over the correct procedure to be followed and especially as to the power of the wardens to postpone a contested election. Legal opinion was taken from Mr Meadows White who advised that new statutory powers were required to change procedure. Although, in the event, the election was not contested the Bridge Clerk was instructed to draw up a scheme for an application to Parliament to alter and improve the procedure at elections, to define the qualifications of electors, and to establish the limits of the contributory lands. The resultant parliamentary bill originally called for the appointment of a commissioner to define the limits of the contributory lands, and for male freeholders of contributory lands only to enjoy a vote. Mr Wykeham Martin, MP for Rochester and the County MPs were prepared to introduce such a bill. After the bill had been read a first time in the House of Lords, the Charity Commission persuaded the Attorney General that the proposal to define contributory lands would be both expensive and unnecessary. The Commissioners further suggested that the list of electors for county elections should be adopted in the election of the bridge wardens, even though the electoral districts and the contributory lands did not coincide. A clause was inserted saving the right of any peer being the owner of contributory land to vote at the election. The Mayor and Corporation of Rochester opposed the bill, but were declared to have no locus standi as petitioners. After evidence from Lord Darnley and the Bridge Clerk, the bill proceeded through the Committee of the House of Lords, met no opposition in the Commons and received Royal Assent. The Rochester Bridge Act 1876 allowed

8   Ibid., 268–74.

the wardens to adjourn any poll demanded and to arrange for the poll to be taken at Maidstone for adjacent parishes as well as at Rochester. It set out the names of all parishes supposed to contain contributory lands, including those used in 1846 and given in Sir David Pollock's opinion of 1827. The Act did not limit voting power to males, female landowners also being eligible.[9]

A contested election in 1875 had been prevented when the Charity Commission acceded to the Rochester proposal. The Charity Commission then proposed to appoint Mr Hawkesley as consulting engineer to advise on the application of surplus funds. The application for a bridge from Wateringbury was deferred by the Wardens and Assistants, but requests from Burham and Snodland, and Wouldham and Halling were accordingly forwarded to the Charity Commissioners. When Hawkesley was unable to take up the assignment, he proposed Sir Joseph Bazalgette in his stead. Bazalgette expressed the opinion that at Maidstone means of transit were 'more urgently required' and considered a new stone bridge should be constructed at a cost of £32,000. He also favoured an intermediate bridge between Rochester and Maidstone, detailed consideration of which had to be postponed due to lack of funds.

While Bazalgette was surveying the river, the Charity Commission was considering the financial position of the Trust. Gross income from estates in 1874 amounted to £4,556 9s. 6d. exclusive of an annual average income of £350 from the woodlands. On renewal London leases would increase by about £1,000 per annum. Average annual expenditure on painting, cleansing and lighting the bridge and on salaries amounted to about £1,000. Debt in 1874 was £9,000. These figures all pointed to a considerable future surplus. It appeared to the Charity Commission that the proper purpose of the Trust was to improve transit of the river above Rochester or between Rochester and Maidstone. The Commission was able to authorise the expenditure of a portion for improving approaches, the erection of new bridges, or improvement of existing bridges 'where the works were of a nature too costly to be undertaken out of the ordinary rates of the places benefited' if advised by Bazalgette. It would favourably consider raising a loan to be repaid within 30 years to fund new projects.[10]

The resulting scheme benefited both the inhabitants of Rochester and Maidstone. In March 1876 the inhabitants of Strood had petitioned for the appropriation of a sum not exceeding £7,500 to pay off the debt of the late Rochester Pavement Commission and so abolish tolls and remove the turnpike gate at Strood. The Trust agreed, but decided to apply to the Charity Commission to raise a loan to pay off the balance of £7,000 mortgage debt remaining from the 1846 Act and to raise funds for a share of Maidstone Bridge and remove the Strood toll gate. The Charity Commission gave notice on 13 May of its intention to issue an order by way of a scheme authorising the loan not to exceed £33,000 at not more than 4 per

[9] Ibid., 269, 277, 296, 310, 322, 346, 354; Letter, Charity Commission, 25 February 1876; RBT 39, Rochester Bridge Act 1876.
[10] RBT 1543, Orders, vol. IV, 285, 287, 296, 326–7; RBT 2187, Letters, Charity Commission, 20 May 1875, 17 February 1876 and Report, Bazalgette, 1 March 1876.

cent repayable over 25 years, which was made on 9 August 1876. Charles Arkcoll negotiated a loan of £31,000 with the Kent Fire Office on mortgage of lands in Delce, Nashenden, Grain and East Tilbury repayable in twenty-five annual instalments of £1,240. The bondholders of the Pavement Commissioners were paid off – the total involved being £7,322 16s. 3d. – and the toll gate was abolished on 30 November 1876. The removal of the toll gate was widely supported, and on 2 December 1876 was described in the local press as being 'a boon . . . upon the whole community of this part of the country'.[11] By April 1877 Maidstone Local Board had inserted into the Maidstone Bridge Bill clauses regulating the payment of instalments of the £16,000 committed.[12] However, by May 1880 the total cost of Maidstone Bridge had increased to £48,000, and the Wardens and Assistants proposed to allocate an additional £8,000 towards the extra cost. After a public enquiry by Mr Good, their Inspector, the Charity Commission would allow only £4,000 towards the bridge, which was completed in July 1880.[13]

Bazalgette's other proposal for an intermediate bridge between Rochester and Maidstone met with less success. Although in 1880 the Wardens and Assistants agreed in principle to support a bridge at Snodland, provided some competent body would undertake to maintain it, and, although plans were produced in 1881 by Law and Chatterton, engineers, there was always opposition from the Medway Lower Navigation, Burham Brick Company and other users of the river who feared navigation of the river would be obstructed.[14] The problem was never to be resolved.

Three further small projects were of local benefit. Firstly there was the construction of a pier at Rochester at an estimated cost in 1880 of £2,500, towards which the Trust agreed to contribute £1,200, with work proceeding in 1884.[15] The second proposal came from Chatham Local Board who requested assistance towards the new Sun Pier at Chatham. This was agreed and a grant of £3,500 sanctioned by the Charity Commission in July 1883, with payment made from surplus income.[16] Thirdly, in May 1883 assistance towards the strengthening the embankment of the Medway at Strood to prevent recurrent inundations was requested. The Trust was favourable, and resolved to contribute £3,000 towards the cost in July 1883. The Charity Commission initially questioned the grant as not being within the objects of the Trust, but after consultations with Bazalgette and the Town Clerk, the Trust decided to persist with the scheme. The Commission finally agreed in May 1884.[17]

In April 1887 the Trust responded to a proposal from the Clerk of the Peace for Kent for the improvement of Tonbridge Bridge with an offer to contribute £1,750. The Charity Commission declined to sanction a grant to Tonbridge Bridge as

---

11 Orders, vol. IV, 330–1, 344; RBT 1483, Charity Commission scheme; *Rochester and Chatham Journal*, 11 March 1876, 2 December 1876.
12 Orders, vol. IV, 362–3, 377.
13 RBT 1544, Orders, vol. V, 61.
14 Ibid., 37–8, 55–6, 62, 75–6.
15 Report, Bazalgette, 6 June 1881, as quoted in ibid., 85–8; ibid., 230.
16 Orders, vol. V, 120, 150, 178.
17 Ibid., 154–5, 168–9, 196–7, 271–2; RBT 2427, Draft Scheme, 22 May 1884.

beyond the scope of the Trust. However, the Trust reiterated their desire to make a contribution and asked to be allowed to pay out of current income with the result that the Commission withdrew their opposition.[18]

A completely different use of funds resulted from a deputation of governors of Sir Joseph Williamson's Mathematical School, Rochester – including the Mayor of Rochester, the Dean of Rochester Cathedral, and Mr J. Ross Foord – who requested in April 1882 a grant toward school funds. Application was made to the Charity Commission for sanction to grant £7,000 to the school. The Charity Commission saw this request as 'an opportune time to establish a scheme for provisions for administering the surplus' under the Endowed Schools Act 1868, which allowed any charity with surpluses beyond its needs to divert part to educational purposes. The Charity Commission, however, also wanted funds to endow a new middle class school for girls in Rochester. Subsequently on 4 April 1883 the Trust set up a committee to consider the best mode of appropriating the increased sum of £20,000 for education.[19] The Committee proposed that the sum should be split between Rochester and Maidstone. The Trust agreed in July 1883, as it would allow the establishment of girls grammar schools in Rochester and in Maidstone, as well as providing funds for the Mathematical School and the Maidstone Grammar School. One acre of land on the Maidstone Road was conveyed as the site for the Rochester Girls Grammar School. The scheme was financed partly through the sale of consols, and partly through a loan of £10,000 from the Kent Fire Office on a mortgage of the 'Ship and Turtle' and adjoining London property, the bulk of the sum being paid over to the Commission on 13 July 1886. The scheme provided for the wardens to be represented by two governors on each of the school's governing bodies.[20]

In addition to endowing grammar schools and financing other river crossings, the Wardens and Assistants directed their increasing surplus income toward re-building the Bridge Chamber. Since the seventeenth century the Wardens and Assistants had conducted their business in the first floor room above the western entrance to the Crown Inn. In December 1875, when the Rochester Corporation proposed to pull down the 'Queens Arms' which was adjacent to the Bridge Chamber, their decision opened the prospect of providing additional accommodation and better access to the Bridge Chamber.[21] Mr Bulmer, the bridge surveyor, prepared plans, and a contract for the works was awarded to Foords. When they started work, however, Foords discovered interesting remains of the 'ancient chapel' behind the record room constructed at the west end of the chapel in the eighteenth century, and operations were suspended pending a decision by the wardens at a special meeting on 2 September 1876. It was resolved that the chapel be restored without using any portion of the space for a staircase to the Bridge

---

[18] Orders, vol. V, 344, 379, 386, 425.

[19] Orders, vol. V, 104, 127–9, 140.

[20] Orders, vol. V, 177–8, 182–3, 306–8, 328–9. Report of the Committee on Surplus Funds, 23 April 1883, as quoted in ibid., 162–5.

[21] Orders, vol. IV, meeting of 26 January 1876, 314–15.

Chamber. When in 1877 an adjoining plot was purchased for £300, Mr Bulmer produced a fresh plan with the Bridge Chamber extending some ten feet to the south, incorporating a strong room on the ground floor, a double flight staircase, and the clerk's room, waiting room and lavatory on the first floor. Windows would be in Tudor style. Foords put forward a separate estimate of £1,466 for the restoration of the chapel, but after a private enquiry the Charity Commission stated that although they sanctioned buying the adjoining property and expenditure on the Bridge Chamber, only funds to prevent further deterioration could be spent on the chapel. The Commission wanted to know why the Trust had deviated from the initial plans to repair the Chamber and refused to sanction any larger expenditure than £1,067. The Trust had to argue strenuously the case that for an expenditure of £3,000 they would get a far better building which would serve all their needs economically. The argument was eventually accepted by the Commission, and Foords' estimate of £2,900 was accepted for the rebuilding.

The Bridge Chamber was completed in July 1879, and the first court held there on 9 April 1880. The Junior and Senior Wardens had presented the stained glass window over the entrance staircase. To finish the scheme, Mr Ruck, the acting architect, produced plans for a wall and fence around the Chamber, and for the removal of the old strong room from the front of the chapel.[22] In September 1880 the Charity Commission accepted the plans and gave authority to accept Foords' tender of £568. They would allow no deviation from the plan, however, and were not disposed to allow any further expense.[23] The interior of the Bridge Chapel, therefore, was cleansed and laid with gravel. The exterior was cleaned and rubbish removed.[24] No further work on the chapel, however, was carried out until 1898 when it was noticed that the old oak gallery screen in the Bridge Chapel was exposed to the weather and a galvanised iron roof was erected at a cost of £10.[25]

Once the Bridge Chamber was built and the schemes for education had been passed, the Charity Commission wanted to make a general scheme regulating the Rochester Bridge Trust under the Charitable Trusts Act. In July and August 1886 they collected information from the Bridge Clerk about the estates and the contributory parishes. In May 1887 the Charity Commission submitted a draft scheme which included provisions for the management of the Trust, a definition of its purposes which widened its scope beyond maintaining Rochester Bridge, and provision for setting up building repair and bridge reserve funds. The Estate Repair and Improvement Fund was to receive an annual investment of £200 until a reserve of £5,000 had been built up. The paramount purpose of maintaining Rochester Bridge, its approaches, bank and channel was to be financed by a Bridge Reserve Fund of £50,000 to be built up by annual contributions of £600 from 1888 to 1894,

---

22 Orders, vol. IV, meeting of 22 March 1876, 332–3; meeting of 2 September 1876, 357–9; meeting of 2 March 1877, 366–7; meeting of 23 January 1878, 415–16; and RBT 1544, Orders, vol. V, meeting of 2 April 1880, 20–2. Extra works at this time cost £600, the architect's fee was £120, and furniture and fittings from Messrs Thomas and Homan cost a further sum of £233.

23 Orders, vol. V, meeting of 30 September 1880, 52–3.

24 Ibid., meeting of 21 April 1882, 114.

25 Orders, vol. VI, meeting of 2 June 1898.

£1,000 from 1895 to 1900 and £1,500 from 1900. The Trust would be able to make 'contributions to the execution or maintenance of works tending to facilitate the passage over under or across the Medway' and 'to works of approach to and to the maintenance of banks and channels of the Medway tending to facilitate the passage over under or across the Medway'. The new scheme was sealed by the Commission on 2 March 1888, and by 1 May the scheme was 'legally complete'.[26]

The first beneficiary under the new scheme in November 1891 was the Medway Lower Navigation Company for a minor project to improve Allington Locks which included putting a foot swing bridge over the river at a cost of £195. The Trust decided that the bridge came within its scope and granted £200 to defray the cost.[27]

By the end of the century the gross revenues from the estate were over £7,000 per annum added to which there was a growing investment income from consols. The latter had been purchased from surplus income and from the proceeds of sales of parcels of land from the estates.[28] The debt burden on the Trust was removed in 1900, when the loan to the Kent Fire Office was paid off. The Trust set up a committee to consider the surplus income, the directions in which expenditure was likely to be called for, and whether the Trust could depart from its policy of contributing not more than 50 per cent towards new works.[29] The committee circulated local authorities, asking if there were any projects for which they would seek contributions from the Trust.[30] Apart from requests for bridges at Snodland and Aylesford, where problems had so far been insuperable, requests came from Chatham Borough Council for help in improving Sun Pier, to which the Charity Commission would allow the Trust to contribute not more than £2,000.[31] A request also came from the county surveyor over the rebuilding of Hempstead Bridge, Yalding, towards which £1,000 was voted in 1902.[32] One scheme which did not come to fruition as proposed by Gillingham Urban District Council was a plan for a new pier at Commodore Hard, Gillingham to cost £6,500. The Trust approved a grant not exceeding £2,500, but owing to difficulties in negotiating with the Medway Conservancy and the Admiralty there was no action on this scheme.[33]

Early in 1904 the Bridges and Roads Committee of the Kent County Council proposed a scheme for the reconstruction of the Branbridges, East Peckham. At an estimated cost of £12,500, this entailed the replacement of Great Torbay bridge with a wide single opening bridge, the widening of Little Torbay bridge, and the raising of the roadway between the Medway and the Great Torbay bridges above the flood level and widening to twenty feet with a four-foot six-inch path. The Trust allotted £6,250 towards the scheme. A supplementary grant was requested by

[26] Letter, Charity Commission, 26 May 1887, as quoted in Orders, vol. V, 368–71; RBT 1527, Scheme, Charity Commission, 2 March 1888; Orders, vol. V, 414.
[27] Orders, vol. VI, meeting of 18 November 1891.
[28] Orders, vol. V, 275, 298, 429; Orders, vol. VI, meeting of 18 November 1891.
[29] Orders, vol. VI, meeting of 17 April 1900.
[30] Ibid., meeting of 7 June 1900.
[31] Ibid., meeting of 30 May 1901.
[32] Ibid., meetings of 11 April 1902, 22 May 1902, and 4 June 1903.
[33] Ibid., meeting of 3 December 1902; RBT 2547, letter, Clerk to Gillingham UDC, 10 June 1902.

the clerk of the Kent County Council in April 1905 towards the cost of £3,400 for raising and widening 70 yards of road where the Branbridges improvements had terminated. A sum not exceeding £1,700 was granted.[34]

By 1905 the Trust had built up investments of £13,000 consols and £12,000 India 3% stock. The Charity Commission insisted that all investments be transferred to the Official Trustees of Charitable Funds under clause 8 of the 1888 scheme. The Bridge Clerk was informed that sanction was not required for grants for objects under the scheme of 1888, but before the Official Trustees could sell any part of the stock, the Commission would have to be satisfied that it came within the scope of the scheme. No question would be raised about the amount of a grant. More could be kept on deposit from current surplus income to meet payment of sums voted to objects authorised by the scheme.[35]

This relatively large pool of disposable funds provoked rivalry between the Maidstone and Medway interests, as each manoeuvred to ensure influence over the funds. The new boroughs of Chatham and Gillingham also wished to obtain influence. In 1897, for example, the town clerk of Chatham had written asking that the mayor of Chatham be recognised at the annual bridge elections and take part equally with the mayors of Rochester and Maidstone. Rivalry came to a head in 1907, when thirteen candidates presented themselves for the twelve seats as assistant wardens. A poll was demanded by the mayor of Maidstone when one of the three candidates favoured by the Maidstone lobby, Herbert Monckton, failed to be elected on a show of hands. The Rochester local paper reported that 'men of both political parties joined in the effort to frustrate Maidstone's effort to get further representation . . . at the expense of Chatham and district'. Monckton, however, was elected in the ensuing poll.[36]

A committee was subsequently set up to consider the method of electing members of the Trust. It was found that in the recent election people who lived outside the contributory parishes had voted, and numerous of those eligible to vote probably did not know it. Also the urban parishes with 1,152 votes were gaining a preponderance of influence over the rural with 251 votes. Therefore, because of the difficulty in maintaining a balance and defining right to vote, the committee recommended a bill in the 1908 session of Parliament to change the constitution. As the Trust now had an annual surplus of at least £5,000, it proposed the termination of the notion of contributory lands, and with it the right to elect wardens. In its place they recommended a governing body of fourteen: one being the Lord Lieutenant of Kent, three nominated by Kent County Council, one each by Maidstone, Rochester, Chatham and Gillingham councils, four by the Justices of the Western Division and two co-opted members. This proposal was adopted by the Trust on 29 July 1907. The Charity Commission objected both to the proposal to give county justices the right to nominate, as recent legislation had relieved them

34 Orders, vol. VI, meetings of 15 April 1904, 5 May 1905, and 27 April 1906.
35 Ibid., meeting of 5 May 1905.
36 Ibid., meeting of 25 April 1907; *Maidstone and Kentish Journal*, 18 April 1907; *Rochester and Chatham Journal and Mid Kent Advertizer*, 28 April 1907.

of all but judicial functions, and also to the co-opting power, suggesting instead extra representation for the district councils. Under pressure clause 5 of the draft bill was altered so that, apart from the Lord Lieutenant, Kent County Council would nominate five members, Rochester and Maidstone councils, Chatham and Gillingham councils, the Medway Conservancy and the Medway Lower Navigation Company one each. Further the Trust persisted in allotting the nomination of two members to the county justices. Alteration was also made to clause 11 deleting all wording in the draft giving power to contribute to any charity object in Kent, other than £100 per annum to New College, Cobham.[37]

Presented in January 1908, the bill attracted hostile petitions from Rochester, Maidstone, Chatham and Gillingham councils on the grounds that they received insufficient representation. The Town Clerk of Chatham had attempted to organise a common approach to opposing the bill, but his proposal for a conference of the four authorities came to nothing as there was insufficient agreement between them. A meeting between the town clerk of Rochester and the Conservators on 14 February ended in an agreement not to meet, but to co-operate in lodging separate petitions. As a result a conference was held on 17 March 1908 at the invitation of the Trust. The conference failed to agree a solution. Further Chatham opposed a clause proposed by the Charity Commission giving it power to establish schemes for altering the provisions of the bill. The councils at Gillingham and Chatham wanted equal representation with Rochester and Maidstone. The four councils held a further conference on 28 March when the following resolution was carried:

> That the composition of the Court of Wardens and Assistants should be submitted to each council of the above towns and if accepted that a joint letter containing such suggestion should be forwarded to the Bridge wardens for their acceptance as a means of avoiding litigation viz. the number allotted to the West Kent Justices to be struck out, and that the Court of Wardens and Assistants be constituted as follows: Lord Lieutenant one, Kent County Council three, Rochester, Chatham, Gillingham, and Maidstone Borough Councils two, Medway Conservancy one, Medway Lower Navigation Company one, total fourteen. and if the wardens wanted fifteen the Conservators to have the same number of representatives as the towns. That each Council be asked to make arrangements for the election if no settlement is arrived at, each town to nominate three candidates.

As this was thought to be too far reaching to be accepted by the wardens a further alternative was suggested by Chatham and accepted:

> the representatives of the Justices be struck out and the number of the Court raised to fifteen: Lord Lieutenant one, Kent County Council five, Rochester and Maidstone two each, Chatham and Gillingham one each, Medway

---

[37] Report of Committee on the Election of wardens, 16 July 1907, as quoted in Orders, vol. VI, meeting of 29 July 1907; E.L. Baker, 'Memorandum as to interview between the Deputation of Wardens and Assistants and the Chief Charity Commissioner on the 7th August 1907', 8 August 1907, as quoted in ibid., meeting of 4 December 1907.

Conservancy two, and the Medway Lower Navigation Company one. This on the understanding that of the five members allotted to Kent County Council one of such members shall be a representative from Chatham on the Kent County Council and a representative from Gillingham on Kent County Council thus practically giving the boroughs two members each.

To avoid a contested election in 1908 and the possible withdrawal of the bill due to the petitions lodged against it, the Wardens and Assistants altered the proposed representation once again so that Kent County Council would nominate six, the borough councils of Maidstone, Rochester, Chatham, and Gillingham and the Medway Conservancy each two, and the Medway Lower Navigation Company one. With this final configuration the Rochester Bridge Act 1908 received Royal Assent on 1 August, and the first nominated court met on 3 June 1909, being in the first instance elected for one year.[38]

The reconstituted Trust undertook two major projects and a number of trivial schemes in the years before the Second World War. The first major project concerned the dereliction of the Upper Medway as a result of the Medway Upper Navigation Company having no funds. The Trust was represented by George Marsham on a joint committee which dealt with the subject. The Kent County Council promoted a bill in Parliament to take control of, and restore, the river, at an estimated cost of £30,000. The Trust proposed to contribute two-thirds, not exceeding £20,000. By June 1911 the bill had passed all its stages, the Trust having inserted clauses that the wardens would not be liable for any contribution unless plans were passed by the Bridge Engineer and works certified completed.[39]

By December 1913 the £30,000 initial capital had been exhausted, and a further bill to obtain powers to raise an additional £30,000 to complete the works was promoted, the Trust's share being £5,000. The Upper Medway Navigation and Conservancy Act received Royal Assent on 31 July 1914. The £5,000 was

---

38 *Chatham News*, 11 January 1908, 15 February 1908, 21 March 1908, 11 April 1908; Letter, Marquis of Camden, 21 April 1908, as quoted in Orders, vol. VI, meeting of 1 May 1908; RBT 2679, Rochester Bridge Act, 1908. To overcome the refusal of the Charity Commission to sanction a grant to Cobham College requested in 1904 after the agricultural depression had reduced the College's income to a point where it was insufficient to cover maintenance and had forced a reduction in the pensions paid to the 20 inmates, a clause was included in the Rochester Bridge Bill 1908 which gave powers to contribute £100 per annum to Cobham College. Letter, Charity Commission, 30 November 1904, as quoted in Orders, vol. VI, meeting of 4 December 1904; Orders, vol. VI, meeting of 26 May 1904. The first meeting of the new Trust on 3 June 1909 fixed conventions for the conduct of business. These included a cycle of three meetings per annum being the AGM in June, the Friday following Easter week and the first Wednesday in December. The senior warden present would chair meetings. Funds were in the control of the two wardens who would present an account at the AGM, a Finance Committee of four members would also report to the AGM. Mr Duncan Mackie was confirmed as auditor, while Edward Baker remained as Clerk having taken the office in 1903, John Robson as Engineer, Herbert Cobb as Land Surveyor and Ernest Hammond as House Surveyor.

39 RBT 1546, Orders, vol. VII, meetings of 8 April 1910, 2 June 1910, 3 August 1910, 28 April 1911, 11 June 1911; Letters, Clerk to Maidstone UDC, 7 April 1910, as quoted in ibid., meeting of 8 April 1910, and 29 April 1910, as quoted in meeting of 2 June 1910.

eventually paid over by December 1915, the completion of the works in dredging to seven feet having been held up by labour shortages due to the war.[40]

The second major project arose in 1924 when Maidstone Corporation wanted to widen Maidstone Bridge from 40 to 60 feet at an estimated cost of £48,590. A third of the cost was to be contributed by the Ministry of Transport. The Trust resolved to contribute £17,000, £5,000 before June 1926 and thereafter £1,200 per annum for 10 years. This grant led the Charity Commission to question the powers under which the grant had been made, for the annual surplus, in view of the sinking fund after the sale of Leadenhall Street and the need to pay into the Bridge Reserve Fund, was inadequate to meet commitments. The Commission proposed the suspension of payments to the Bridge Reserve Fund for 15 years on condition that thereafter £3,000 per annum would be paid in until the sum of £160,000 had been reached.[41]

Smaller projects included a grant for a new bridge at Hartlake, Hadlow, which, although the original bridge belonged to the Medway Upper Navigation Company, the Council would maintain. The sum of £850 was agreed in April 1909 towards a ferro concrete bridge, which was completed in 1910.[42] Two commitments made in December 1912 gave half the construction cost to a maximum of £4,000 to renew Bow Bridge, Wateringbury, which connected Nettlestead with Yalding and West Farleigh, and a grant of £1,000 towards the remodelling of the Great Bridge, Tonbridge.[43] Further grants were allowed by the Charity Commission in 1922 towards the restoration of College Hall, Cobham College, and in 1924 £800 for structural repairs, and £250 for internal renovation. The Charity Commission allowed an expenditure in 1936 of not more than £600 for the restoration of the roof and flooring of Cobham College Hall which was ravaged by deathwatch beetle. In the post war years funds were once more used to modernise the accommodation at Cobham College. A maximum of £25 per house was allocated for water and other amenities to bring the houses 'up to standard' as they fell vacant, to an overall total of £536 10s. 6d.[44]

It was in 1922 that the Charity Commission finally clamped down on minor donations, and stated that it would refuse to sanction any future grants outside the scope of the Trust.[45] The wardens had started a practice from the late 1840s to make donations to 'pet' projects or 'worthy' causes in parishes in which they held land. One of the first such donations had occurred in June 1848, when a site of one acre was provided at East Tilbury for the erection of a National School.[46] Many of

---

[40] Orders, vol. VII, meeting of 1 December 1913, 6; 12 October 1914, 4; 3 June 1915, 4; 13 December 1915, 3.

[41] RBT 1547, Orders vol. VIII, meeting of 7 March 1927, 5–6.

[42] Orders, vol. VI, meeting of 23 April 1909, 2–3; Orders, vol. VII, meeting of 2 June 1910; Letter, Clerk to Tonbridge UDC, 21 November 1908, as quoted in Orders, vol. VI, meeting of 2 December 1908.

[43] Orders, vol. VII, meeting of 2 December 1912, 4; meeting of 3 June 1915, 5.

[44] Orders VIII, meeting of 13 January 1936, 2, 4; RBT 1553, Minutes 1943–53, meeting of 1 December 1947, 6.

[45] Orders, vol. VII, meeting of 1 June 1922, 6.

[46] Orders, vol. III, 81.

the donations went towards the building or repair of schools, such as £100 towards the building of a national school at St James, Grain in 1862, the sum of £100 contributed to the church school at Borstal in April 1869, £25 in April 1870 to schools in St Mary's, Strood, or £10 in April 1876 towards schools in St Johns, Chatham. The size of the donations reflected the amount of land held in each parish.[47] One motivation for the donations, especially after the Elementary Education Act 1870, was to obviate the need for a school board and, therefore, to reduce the incidence of rates upon the estate. There was a similar motivation behind the grant in 1872 of £10 to the Frindsbury Churchyard Extension Fund, and a further sum of £25 in 1892, as this would prevent a burial board having to be set up.[48]

These rather mean donations compare badly with the sums received by the other main recipient, churches. For instance, 1865 saw £100 going to the Bishop of Rochester's Diocesan Fund for the Augmentation of Small Livings. The biggest donation was £250 to Rochester Cathedral Restoration Fund in April 1874, the Cathedral receiving a further £250 in April 1875. In 1876, £200 was given towards a new church at Borstal, and in July 1877 £100 was promised to Dartford Church Restoration Fund. These donations prompted the Charity Commission to question the authority of the Wardens and Assistants to pay £250 to Rochester Cathedral. The reply was that they relied on the practice of many years, but although the donations to that date were allowed, thereafter the approval of the Charity Commission was sought for all donations.[49]

Donations continued, but the Charity Commission reduced donations, as in 1881 when the grant to the new Burham Church was cut from £50 to £10 and the donation to Wilmington Church disallowed.[50] Again in 1888 the Charity Commission thought the whole question of making grants of this nature should receive consideration before further applications were made. Ignoring the criticism, the Trust continued to make similar donations, giving in 1890 £10 to St Mary's, Strood National School and £25 to the St James, Grain school enlargement. In November 1891 the Trust proposed to give £20 for the restoration of Dartford Church and £25 towards a dwelling for the curate in charge of Borstal. This the Commission would not approve, but was ready to reconsider if the Trust could show how a grant was beneficial to the estate. Notwithstanding the criticism and the disproportionate amount of time taken on these matters, donations of a similar nature to churches and schools continued to be made regularly until the Charity Commission's decision of 1922 restricted the Trust to financing crossings over or under the River Medway.[51]

The only other significant departure from strict adherence to its scheme was the Trust's restoration of the Bridge Chapel, finally sanctioned by the Charity Commission in 1935. Interest in restoring the chapel had been revived in 1912, when

[47] Ibid., 428, 435; Orders, vol. IV, 156, 182.
[48] Orders, vol. VI, meeting of 9 June 1892.
[49] Orders, vol. IV, 256, 407, 434.
[50] Orders, vol. V, 82–3.
[51] Orders, vol. VI, meeting of 18 November 1891.

Mr Harold Brakspear was employed to give architectural advice on the cheapest way to prevent further deterioration. West Bros. produced an estimate based on his report amounting to £400, a sum which the Trust was unwilling to spend. The level of expenditure they had contemplated for anything of an historical nature was £20 for a tablet placed on the Bridge Chamber marking the site of crossing of the old stone bridge, and £80 for some minor repairs to the east and north walls of the Chapel.[52]

Interest was revived again in 1927 when the Trust requested from William Weir of Letchworth a preliminary report on the chapel with an estimate for roofing, flooring and glazing windows. He estimated the probable cost of making good the structure, and inserting doors and windows at £1,000.[53] The work was not pursued, but a fresh survey was made in 1935 by Herbert Baker of Marsham Street, Westminster. His report advocated an entrance from the vestibule of the Bridge Chamber. The walls should be made good with Portland stone and the windows provided with stone mullions. The roof timbers might be in deal and asphalt covered and the floor covered in red quarry tiles. Estimated cost was £1,670. A higher quality restoration could have been done at a higher price. The Charity Commission approved expenditure of not more than £2,000 for restoration work, which sum they subsequently agreed to raise to £2,500 to allow for oak panelling if the chapel were to be used as a boardroom. One detail of the work which Sir Herbert Baker considered most desirable was that the east window contained stained glass with the arms of the founders, Sir Robert Knolles and Sir John de Cobham. The court of 3 June 1937 was the first to sit in the new boardroom in the chapel.[54]

In order to finance their activities in the years before the First World War, the Wardens and Assistants gradually turned from mortgaging their estate to the sale and purchase of property. Some charitable donations were financed by the sale of building plots on the Delce farms in Rochester, where the land was worth more for its urban development potential than for agriculture, the soil being indifferent. Good prices could be obtained in the Maidstone Road and Mount Road areas, where over £200 per acre could be obtained.[55] One significant pre-war sale was the disposal of the East Tilbury farm land. The proposed sale was at first refused by the Charity Commission, as they could see no advantage to the Trust, but they agreed after hearing an explanation from Herbert Cobb about the costs of maintaining the foreshore and other difficulties. The auction on 21 June 1912 did not

---

52 Orders, vol. VII, meeting of 2 June 1912, 11–12; meeting of 3 March 1913, 8–9; meeting of 5 June 1913, 9–10; meeting of 1 December 1913, 11–13; report of Harold Brakspear, 8 November 1912, as quoted in ibid., meeting of 2 December 1912, 21–3.

53 Ibid., meeting of 7 March 1927, 6; Report on Chapel, William Weir, 14 May 1927, as quoted in ibid., meeting of 2 June 1927, 16–17.

54 Orders, vol. VIII, meeting of 2 December 1935, 12–13; meeting of 13 January 1936, 2, 4; meeting of 2 March 1936, 5–6; meeting of 7 December 1936, 2; meeting of 3 June 1937, 2; Letter, Charity Commission, 16 December 1935, as quoted in ibid., meeting of 13 January 1936, 4.

55 Land Agent's Report, as quoted in Orders, vol. VII, meeting of 1 June 1911, 17; ibid., meeting of 11 December 1911, 7–8.

reach the reserve price, but the farm was subsequently sold for £2,400 to a Mr Mott of Stanford le Hope.[56] Any purchases made prior to the First World War were limited to small parcels adjoining the existing estate. For instance, a further fifteen acres were purchased in 1912 adjoining Marsh Gate Farm for £250.[57] Prices had risen by 1916, when £100 per acre was paid for 5 acres 20 perches of Lord Tredegar's land at Dartford Marshes.

The First World War had some detrimental effect on the estate. The BRH Coal Exploration Syndicate abandoned their scheme to bore for coal on the northern extremity of the Kent coalfield at Langdon Farm, Faversham, as the boring staff were either German or Belgian. A part of Rose Court Farm marshes at Grain was taken by the navy under the Defence of the Realm Act for aircraft bombing practice, and a large part of Nashenden Farm was also in the hands of the military for use for rifle ranges and firing points.[58] A more damaging effect of the war was the depreciation of the Estate Repairs and Improvement Fund which had been paid up in 1909. The investment in consols had been converted to War Stock 5% but these were worth only £3,860 by the end of 1917. The Charity Commission now required a resumption of payments of at least £200 per annum.[59]

The most significant property sale occurred in 1919 after offers were made for the Leadenhall Street properties. The properties were valued by David Watney & Co. at £56,000 for the 'Ship and Turtle' and £78,000 for the Rochester Buildings. The Charity Commission agreed the sale to St Helen's Estates and New Zealand Shipping Co. Ltd. The proceeds of the sale were used to pay off the loans from Royal Insurance which stood at £37,623. This sum the Charity Commission insisted should be replaced by means of a sinking fund. £41,820 would need to be placed in War Loan 5%, which at compound interest would eventually realise £65,623.[60]

During the 1920s there were further sales for industrial and residential purposes, including 36 acres of Dartford marsh to Burroughs Wellcome for £5,507 and 25 acres along the Rochester to Maidstone Road to Rochester Corporation for £5,500 to be used for council housing. In 1921 the War Department compulsorily purchased 344 acres of marshland at Grain for the gun testing site for £7,000, and after protracted negotiations the sale was made of part of the South Level marshes at Grain to the Britannic Oil Storage Co. for £2,100.[61] With the prospect of further residential development in Rochester a major purchase was made in 1924, when

---

56 Land Agent's Report, as quoted in ibid., meeting of 4 March 1912, 18–20; Letter, Charity Commission, 21 February 1912, as quoted in ibid., meeting of 4 March 1912, 8.
57 Land Agent's Report, as quoted in ibid., meeting of 2 December 1912, 20.
58 Land Agent's Reports, as quoted in ibid., meeting of 5 June 1913, 18; meeting of 4 June 1914, 13–14; meeting of 7 December 1914, 14; meeting of 4 March 1918, 9.
59 Letter, Charity Commission, 14 December 1917, as quoted in ibid., meeting of 4 March 1918, 5.
60 Land Agent's Reports, as quoted in ibid., meeting of 5 June 1919, 17–18; meeting of 1 December 1919, 7–9; meeting of 1 March 1920, 6–7.
61 Land Agent's Reports, as quoted in ibid., meeting of 3 June 1920, 14–17; meeting of 6 December 1920, 15–16; meeting of 30 November 1925, 16–18.

the Trust acquired Great Delce Farm for £10,225. Although somewhat rundown, it was considered to have potential for building.[62]

In the 1930s sales for private housing accelerated, particularly in 1934–5 with the sale of land to the west side of City Way, land to the west of the Rochester to Maidstone Road, and a proposal to sell the whole of Great Delce Farm for £160 per acre. The Mathematical School gave £260 per acre for 30 acres of Upper Delce Farm as a site for a new school, and a further 26¾ acres of the farm to the south of the school were sold to become the Valley View estate.[63] In addition, 67 acres of land between the Rochester and Chatham to Maidstone Roads was sold to Rochester Corporation for the creation of an aerodrome and the erection of an aircraft factory by Short Bros 'with a view to finding employment in the district.' The sale price of £75 per acre was recommended by Mr Cobb, the Trust's land agent, as it would accelerate demand for further housing in the area.[64]

As a result of these sales, the financial position of the Trust continued to improve. By May 1937 the sinking fund for the Leadenhall Street Property had been completed, after which an annual contribution of £3,000 to the Bridge Reserve Fund was payable. Dividends on the fund amounted to £4,477. Stocks represented in the fund were £105,108 19s. 0d. Local Loans 3% and £37,828 9s. 7d. 3 1/2% Conversion and amalgamated with £61,881 6s. 4d. Local Loans 3% and £74,088 17s. 3d. 3½% Conversion Stock already credited to the Trust's account. The annual surplus amounted to between £5,000 and £7,000.[65]

Further profitable land deals occurred in the early 1940s. The Trust purchased Great Clayne Farm, Chalk, for £9,000 in 1942, and Cooling Castle Farm, adjoining Marsh Gate Farm in Cooling, was acquired for £1,300. After the war an additional 28 acres of land adjoining Cooling Castle Farm were purchased from the War Department for £1,600.[66] Sales included part of Marsh Gate Farm marshes to the Associated Portland Cement Manufacturers for mud digging for £3,150 and 40 acres of Great Clayne Farm to Essex Aero for £6,000 for the development of an aircraft factory in 1947. Land on Great Delce Farm and at Warren Wood was required by Rochester Corporation for council housing, the price agreed being £25,000 for 175 acres, and 25 acres of Rose Court Farm, Grain were sold to the Anglo Iranian Oil Co. for £2,000 for the proposed oil refinery.[67]

After the war the Trust received advice on investment from Sir Frank Newson-Smith, who recommended a shift in the balance of investment from one-third held in land to one-half. This would help guard against inflationary tendencies while

[62] Land Agent's Report, as quoted in ibid., meeting of 1 December 1924, 12–14.

[63] Land Agent's Report, as quoted in Orders, vol. VIII, meeting of 19 February 1935, 1–2; meeting of 11 March 1935, 3; meeting of 2 December 1935, 3–4.

[64] Land Agent's Report, 21 February 1933 and Letter, Town Clerk of Rochester, 6 February 1933, as quoted in ibid., meeting of 6 March 1933, 7–8.

[65] RBT 1547, Orders, vol. VIII, meeting of 3 June 1937, 11; meeting of 6 December 1937, 2.

[66] Ibid., meeting of 4 June 1942, 2; RBT 1552, Minutes 1943–1953, meeting of 3 March 1947, 2; meeting of 1 March 1948, 4.

[67] Orders, vol. VIII, meeting of 7 December 1942, 2; Minutes 1943– 1953, meeting of 4 March 1946, 6–7.

maintaining income.[68] The result was an active search for suitable farm and commercial land for investment. Eventually in 1947 Boarley Farm, Boxley was purchased for £15,000, and Castle Chambers, Rochester was also purchased for £5,000. The largest purchases came in 1948, when the Canon Frome Estate extending to 2,300 acres in Herefordshire was purchased for £185,000, and in 1949 when the Homend Estate, Castle Frome was acquired for £42,000. On 20 October 1950 Abbey and Street Farms, Boxley were successfully bought at auction for £35,000, taking the balance of investment above 50 per cent in quality property holdings.[69]

With no new projects in hand and relatively small outgoings in the form of grants, the assets of the Trust grew apace. A new scheme was being mooted in 1950, however, a new Medway towns by-pass with a bridge above Rochester. An approach was made by Kent County Council in March 1950, outlining the scheme and requesting a substantial contribution.[70] Although in the end the Trust did not contribute to the M2 motorway bridge, it was soon to direct its resources toward a second river crossing in Rochester.

[68] Minutes 1943–1953, meeting of 6 June 1946, 9.
[69] Ibid., meeting of 1 December 1947, 3; meeting of 1 March 1948, 2; meeting of 6 December 1948, 2; meeting of 5 December 1949, 3; meeting of 4 December 1950, 1.
[70] Letter, Clerk to Kent County Council, 10 March 1950, as quoted in ibid., meeting of 1 June 1950, 4.

Rochester Bridge

1950–1993

An Epilogue

An Epilogue

During the 1939–45 War Rochester Bridge once again proved vital to the national interest. The road and rail bridges carried the greater part of all traffic to and from the Channel ports, and the road bridge also carried all major services to East Kent together with telephone lines to the Continent. Temporary arrangements had been made for the adjacent disused railway bridge to be used for road or rail traffic should either of the bridges be damaged, and a temporary Bailey bridge had been constructed by the Royal Engineers upstream at Cuxton to ensure that lines of communication were maintained. Fortunately, both road and rail bridges escaped almost unscathed from the conflict.

After the war, the end of petrol rationing in the early 1950s saw a considerable increase in traffic, particularly holiday vehicles at weekends and bank holidays. Towards the end of the decade, residents close to the A2 sat on the roadside on Sunday evenings to watch the never-ending stream of homegoing holidaymakers, often stationary from Rochester to Rainham Mark. The Trust maintained that the bridge at Rochester did not cause the hold-ups, which appeared to be due mainly to the road pattern on the Strood side when traffic had to slow down or stop causing a concertina effect when the flow of traffic was heavy. As far back as the 1930s, however, the Court had considered building a new bridge over the Medway to relieve the ever-increasing trunk road traffic through the Medway Towns. These proposals included a high-level bridge at either Borstal or Chatham, but the out-break of war had put an end to any such proposals.

In 1957 the Bridge Engineer suggested that the disused railway bridge could be reconstructed to form a second carriageway across the river. The construction of a duplicate bridge upstream of the present bridges would have meant the additional cost of new foundation works and increased obstruction to the river flow. In contrast, the use of the existing railway bridge would provide suitable piers and abutment foundations, and the old girders could be used as temporary staging. The Court approached the Chief Engineer of British Railways Southern Region, who considered that there would be no serious objection to the Trust acquiring the unused railway bridge.

About the same time, a new major road from Faversham to Strood with a crossing upstream of Cuxton, now known as the M2, was designed and approved by the Ministry of Transport. Feeling that this road would be of little assistance to the internally-generated traffic, the Court were still keen to proceed with their own scheme. However the Ministry of Transport, who would be responsible for the approach roads, assumed that the new M2 bypass would take much of the present traffic and advised that they had no plans or money to relieve traffic over the river at Rochester. They suggested that the Trust should wait and see how the new by-pass affected local traffic. The Charity Commissioners were also concerned and ruled that any adaptation of the old railway bridge must not so deplete funds that the present bridge could not be properly maintained. These discussions and negotiations took several years during a period of high inflation, and the Court became concerned that the cost of the new bridge would be beyond their reach if building were further delayed. In March 1961, Mr Kenneth Anderson, Bridge Engineer, produced a plan and elevation of a new bridge which the Court accepted in principle, but the Ministry of Transport still maintained that there was no urgency.

Meanwhile, cracks began to appear in the Strood abutment of the road bridge. Stones, thought to have been ballast from passing lorries, had entered the expansion joints, reducing their effectiveness; in consequence, inadequately-relieved thermal expansion of the bridge caused the brickwork to crack. Measurement of the movement of these fractures was sent fortnightly for several years to the National Physical Laboratory at Teddington for its opinion as to the effect on the bridge's stability. In a two-month period between August and September 1962 the movement was just over half an inch, but fortunately when the bridge contracted in the winter, the abutment brickwork returned to its original position. Eventually, the problem was eliminated by the construction of an additional expansion joint on the Strood side, which although costly was highly effective.

As for the new bridge, it was not until 1964 that the Trust was able to promote a bill in Parliament, which received royal assent on 5 August 1965. Even then there were difficulties, for at the same time a government bill was promulgated controlling civil engineering and building works over £100,000. Having become quite exasperated with the Ministry of Transport's delays in undertaking any commitment to the construction of the required approach roads, the Court wrote to the Ministry confirming that the Trust would build the new bridge extending to 20 feet from the base of the abutments on either side of the river, and at the same time offered to help by loan or grant so as to limit the cost of the approach roads to £100,000, the maximum the Ministry were prepared to spend. This strong action by the Court forced the hand of a reluctant government department. The Bridge Engineer had proposed underpasses on both Strood and Rochester sides to convey traffic under the main highway, but the Ministry of Transport would not agree to accommodate this facility and regrettably, as events have proved, these underpasses were deleted.

The use of the old railway bridge foundations put restrictions upon the type of bridge which could be constructed. A pre-stressed concrete bridge would weigh 1,500 tons more than the new type of box girder construction, and on a full load the foundations would have been up to 40 per cent overloaded. The Court approved the box girder construction, but toward the end of the construction of the bridge the integrity of the structure was brought into question when three other bridges using a box girder formula collapsed during erection. These doubts were heightened by the televised destruction of an American bridge some years before, when a very gradual movement during high winds had developed into a wave effect and the bridge had broken apart. One of the universities developed special techniques, known as the Morrison Rules, to enable tests and calculations to be made; it is indicative of their complexity that eventually the testing cost £16,000, of which the labour content was £5,000 and calculation by the university £10,000. The work required to strengthen the box girders cost only £1,700 after the extensive examination.

By June 1966 the contract drawings and tender procedure had been agreed, but it was still necessary to obtain consent from the Royal Fine Arts Commission, planning consents under the Town and Country Planning Acts from the Kent County Council, approval by the Kent Rivers Authority and Board of Trade, and consents under the building control legislation. Then there were difficulties in obtaining access to various sites, as certain tenants went to law in defence of their rights. Not until February 1967 was the tender of £288,112 2s. 6d. by A.E. Farr Limited accepted and the starting date of 1 July 1967 agreed. A separate tender for the construction of the services bridge in the sum of £69,007 11s. 3d. was accepted, and the Court agreed that all available revenue, including the Bridge Reserve Fund and surplus income, was to be used in defraying the costs. It was a year later before the Ministry of Transport finally accepted tenders for the approach road construction. Unfortunately, they appointed a different contractor which caused subsequent difficulties in the co-ordination of work in the very limited working and storage areas, with considerably increased costs and claims by the Trust upon the Ministry of Transport. The Department of the Environment indicated that they might be willing to pay for the lighting of the new bridge, but the Court preferred to continue to pay all costs arising from the construction and maintenance of the Bridges, thus maintaining their independence and autonomy. The final cost of the new bridge was £352,000 while the services bridge cost £73,000, paid for by the various utility authorities. Eventually, rather later than originally anticipated, the new bridge was opened on 15 April 1970 by Her Royal Highness the Princess Margaret, Countess of Snowdon. Twenty-six members of the Court and honoured guests were entertained to lunch in the boardroom of the Bridge Chamber with an overflow in the Rochester Corn Exchange, where a lunch for 233 people was hosted by the Junior Warden. The subsequent tea party was attended by 100 members of the Court and guests.

To ensure continuity during the preliminary negotiations and construction of the new bridge, the same two Wardens, Moreton Thorpe Knight and Maurice Owen Gill, had been retained throughout. While they were busy with the legal and engineering preliminaries, some of the Assistants focused their attention upon the Trust's income, recognising that there would be not only a need for considerable capital outlay, but also the responsibility in future for maintaining and subsequently rebuilding two bridges rather than one. The 1946 Trunk Roads Act had left only three charitable trusts responsible for their main-road bridges, and within a very few years Barnstaple and Bideford were unable, for financial reasons, to continue the maintenance and repair they had carried out since medieval times. The Rochester Bridge Trust's continued financial stability had been built mainly upon land and property, the former being available and suitably situated to take advantage of development opportunities just when finances would otherwise have been dangerously low. In line with experience after the heavy expenditure in 1856 and

1914, when the Trust's finances were repaired through owning land in the right place for development, the Court found that the expenditure on the 1970 bridge, which extinguished the Bridge Reserve and Accumulated Income Funds, could be recouped from land and property developed in a buoyant economy.

In 1961 most of the Canon Frome Estate in Herefordshire was sold, and the Court turned its attention to the ancient Quarry Estate at Frindsbury, which was under lease to the Associated Portland Cement Company Limited (known less affectionately as 'A Perfect Curse to the Medway' because the company bought and then closed almost all the numerous cement works along the whole length of the river). The eighty-year lease expired in 1964, and although the company was interested in renewal, the cement-making process, which had pre-war extended along the length of the western frontage, had long since ceased. After demolition of chimneys and buildings, the Frindsbury site presented a derelict appearance. Planning policies at the time did not favour industrial development in close proximity to residential areas, so this isolated tongue of land with river frontage along three sides seemed very suitable for industrial and commercial developers, particularly those requiring delivery or export by water.

The appointment of leading national consultants and advisers proved greatly advantageous. Further land was acquired for access, and a new alternative road agreed. Protracted negotiations were held with an adjoining landowner, Whitewall Investments Limited, who expressed an interest in developing the whole of the peninsula, and at least two leases were prepared to the stage when all clauses were agreed, but the company eventually did not have the finance available for such a project. In retrospect, this failure to complete was good fortune in disguise, as the proposed lease was for 99 years from 1965 at a commencing rent of only £21,000 per annum, reviewable only every 21 years, terms which would have been disastrous in the face of the imminent period of high inflation.

The more successful and important negotiations took place with John Howard & Company Limited, a large engineering and construction company who, having sold their plant depot west of London, desired a new site where they would not conflict with neighbouring activities and eventually acquired 24 acres of saltings on the peninsula for £85,000. Needing hardcore, the company agreed to remove the 'hill', the only elevated area on the peninsula on which several houses and a public house, long-since empty, were situated. This was a very significant development, for the levelling of this area left the Trust with a consolidated site with water frontage, while Howards had the experience and equipment to carry out reclamation work and to pile and construct wharfage and deep water facilities. Unfortunately, the ultimate development of the major part of the Estate was delayed by recession. As a shared venture by the Trust with Arlington Development Company Limited and John Howard and Company Limited, an access road and drainage connecting with the Wainscott Bypass were constructed in 1978, the original quotation of £400,000 being allocated according to acreage within each ownership. This access road was an act of faith at the time, the expenditure being criticised in some quarters, but it opened up some 206 acres on the peninsula, of which the Trust owned 73. By the late 1980s this land was being sold for around £500,000 per acre or leased for commensurate return, yet it had nearly been sold in 1920 for £150 per acre and in 1931 for £10 per acre. Here was part of the original endowment, the source of chalk for the ancient bridge foundations, more recently useless marshland, under water at high tide, which had become the source of significant capital from freehold sales and also revenue from the areas leased.

Coincidentally, a smaller area alongside the River Darent at Dartford, also part of the original endowment, had become derelict in the 1960s, some of the buildings on-site having been developed under lease a hundred years earlier for industrial purposes by men who subsequently became world-famous in their respective spheres. Here Mr Albert Reed, the 'father' of the paper group now Reed International Limited, had built large machine shops and warehouses for papermaking purposes. The London Paper Mills at Dartford had prospered for 75 years until use of the site ceased on 31 March 1968, but unfortunately their long-term lease provided for only one rent review. However, the Trust, after considerable negotiations, were able to buy the reversion of the lease for £120,000 in 1970. A Mr Burroughs and a Mr Wellcome had also leased land immediately adjacent to that let to Mr Reed, where they developed the world-wide pharmaceutical company now the Wellcome Foundation Limited. This company then leased a part of the site previously used by Mr Reed, after much renovation work and some redevelopment which made this ultimately a highly remunerative venture. At both Dartford and Frindsbury, two original endowment sites, having provided revenue from grazing in their time, had thus been turned into valuable industrial sites, producing substantial income.

About the same time another original endowment played its own small part, for in March 1973 one of the large gravel-extracting firms expressed an interest in the gravel deposits under Rose Court Farm on the Isle of Grain. An area was leased to them accordingly, with provision for ultimate reinstatement for agricultural use, probably to a higher standard than before, when it was so low-grade that it had not provided a reasonable living for tenant farmers for some years. Once again good fortune and good management had secured the financial stability of the Trust for the foreseeable future.

During the 1980s, in fact, annual income rose considerably above the annual expenditure on maintaining the estate, maintaining the bridges and providing for future replacements. In 1983 the Court obtained a variation Scheme from the Charity Commission enabling them to make grants for charitable purposes out of surplus income, although until 1992 these grants had to be approved individually by the Commissioners. A Grants Fund was established, small at first, and several small grants were made, as well as two substantial loans on concessionary terms.

The sound financial base thus established enabled close involvement of the Trust in another Medway crossing. The pressing need to secure large-scale redevelopment of the former Chatham Dockyard, coupled with the steady increase in traffic through Rochester since the opening of the second bridge in 1970, have resulted in the Medway Tunnel project for crossing the Medway downstream of the Rochester Bridges. Once the Medway Towns Northern Relief Road has been completed to join the tunnel to the A2/M2 junction at Strood, and to the A2/A278 in Gillingham, there will be a route around the north of the Towns never previously available,

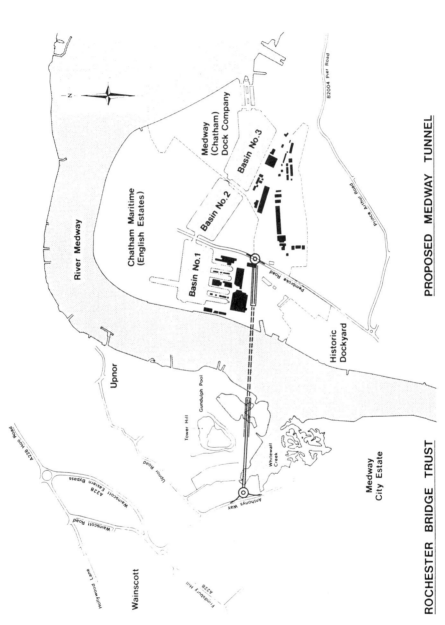

ROCHESTER BRIDGE TRUST   PROPOSED MEDWAY TUNNEL

Figure 24. Plan of the Medway Tunnel downstream from Rochester Bridge.

servicing the developing northern areas of the Towns and reducing the traffic pressures on the central through route across Rochester Bridges. This ambitious scheme, with enormous potential for the future of the Medway Towns, had its origin with the officers of Gillingham Borough Council in their consideration of the development prospects for the Royal Dockyard following the announcement in 1981 of the Government's decision to close the Naval Base in 1984, and by the winter of 1986 the concept of a third Medway crossing had been argued through local government channels into County Council policy.

The involvement of the Trust began in July 1987 with an approach by the Kent County Council for support. The Court readily agreed to contribute substantially towards the cost, the basis being paragraph 9 of the Charity Commission's Scheme of Administration dated 29 November 1976, re-enacting a similar Scheme of 1888, under which contributions can be made out of surplus income towards the execution and maintenance of works tending to facilitate passage over, under or across the River Medway. Public consultation that summer showed a decided preference for a tunnel rather than either a low-level lifting bridge or a high-level bridge. A tunnel would be more expensive, but would not have the disadvantages of a low-level lifting bridge in delaying traffic, nor those of a high-level bridge in taking up valuable land in the long approaches, both forms of bridge being far more obtrusive than a tunnel in environmental terms. Following further discussions with the Kent County Council, the Court agreed in December 1987 to sponsor a Private Bill for a tunnel under the River Medway, linking Pembroke Road in Chatham Maritime to Anthony's Way in Frindsbury. They also agreed to take on the freehold ownership of the tunnel and to consider substantial annual contributions towards cost, but were not in favour of charging tolls. At that stage, in view of the Government's restrictions on local authority capital expenditure, the participants planned to fund the scheme by way of leasing finance, with annual repayments over thirty years, the Trust's share being £½m annually over that period.

Financial, legal and engineering advisers were duly appointed, and detailed planning began in close consultation with the County Council via a Steering Group chaired by the Senior Warden. The geology of the river bed being unsuitable for the usual bored tunnel, it was agreed to use 'immersed tube' construction, essentially a series of pre-formed concrete sections floated out and sunk in a trench excavated in the river bed, which would then be filled back to the original level. This relatively shallow depth would also reduce the approach gradients. Rochester upon Medway City Council and Gillingham Borough Council agreed to make contributions towards the cost; English Estates, the developers of Chatham Maritime on the site of the former Dockyard, made land available without charge at the eastern end of the tunnel, besides agreeing to make a large capital contribution. Application for town planning permission was made in July 1988 and the Parliamentary Bill was lodged in the House of Lords in November. Negotiations for land acquisition were begun, notably with the Ministry of Defence, since the western end of the tunnel would take up land in the Royal Engineers' training area around the southern part of Gundulph Pool. In March 1989 the preliminary agreements between the participants were completed, and English Estates handed over a contribution of £10m to be held jointly by the Trust and themselves on interest-bearing deposit, pending execution of a construction contract. Planning permission was received. In July the Bill completed its passage through the House of Lords, and tenders were invited from financial institutions for the supply of the finance required for the scheme.

So far, all had progressed without serious difficulties, but then problems arose. The scope of the Trust's exemption from VAT, originally granted as a concession in 1973, came under question, notification being eventually received that the concession was to be withdrawn from January 1991, rendering it disadvantageous for the Trust to be responsible for placing the construction contract. Although leasing finance was common commercial practice, adaptation of the concept to the special provisions of charity and local government law, while still retaining the tax advantages, became more and more complex, requiring the formation of subsidiary companies. Negotiations with the Ministry of Defence revolved round the need for expensive accommodation works, and made little progress. Worst of all, the Parliamentary Bill, along with all other Private Bills, failed to go forward in the House of Commons through a series of backbench blocking objections designed to force consideration of proposed changes in the general procedure. Indeed, in December 1989, the usual carry-over motion into the next session was voted down, and all the Bills had to be revived by a special motion in January, the Trust joining in the intense lobbying at political level. The four outstanding petitions against the Bill by local amenity societies were then cleared in Committee, but the Bill was again blocked in the House in spite of the efforts of the three local Members of Parliament in support. It was a great relief when a relaxation of the blocking enabled Third Reading and Royal Assent to be given to the Bill in July 1990, well behind the original timetable. Ironically, the project had been accorded favourable reception at Government level throughout, such figures as Sir Geoffrey Howe (then Deputy Prime Minister), Mr Cecil Parkinson (then Secretary of State for Transport), Mr Michael Portillo (then Minister for Public Transport) and Mr Christopher Chope (then Minister for Roads) all paying visits and expressing support.

With renewed optimism, advertisements were issued inviting construction firms to put their names forward for selection as tenderers, five being selected for this purpose in January 1991. However, the economic climate had changed for the worse by then. The chosen financial partner withdrew, and although another was selected, the whole scheme for leasing finance proved impossible to operate in face of the coming into force of section 48 of the Local Government Act 1989 and the various supporting regulations, under which the annual contributions of the County Council, even though made out of revenue, would have counted as capital, needing to be accommodated within the County Council's centrally-permitted capital programme. This put the whole project in danger, but the political support was now very strong. The structure of the project was totally re-cast. The Trust in effect delegated to the County Council the powers to execute works contained in the Medway Tunnel Act 1990, enabling the construction contract to be let by the County Council without incurring VAT, and also granted to the County Council, for a period of thirty years, the necessary interests in the land acquired to enable the County Council to operate the tunnel. The County Council agreed to vary their capital programme to give priority to the tunnel as a highway scheme, in spite of the claims of other schemes, and with vigorous support from the Department of Trade and Industry on behalf of English Estates, the County Council obtained Transport Supplementary Grant approval from the Government on 19 December 1991. On 20 December 1991 tenders were opened from the selected tenderers and referred to the consultant engineers Messrs. Travers Morgan, for evaluation. The County Council finally accepted a tender of £67.7m from a consortium headed by Tarmac Construction Limited and a Dutch firm HBM Civil Engineering Limited, a separate contract being necessary for the re-designed grade-separated junction with Pembroke Road at the eastern end.

The revised basis of the project having received Government approval, it was necessary to conclude as quickly as possible the outstanding negotiations for land acquisition and also the final documentation between the three main participants, the Trust, the County Council and English Estates. The Medway Tunnel Act had contained powers of compulsory acquisition of land, but these powers did not apply to the acquisition of land from the Crown, including the Ministry of Defence for land at the western end and the Crown Estates Commissioners for half of the riverbed. Agreement with these bodies had not yet been reached. Urged on by the Senior Warden Michael Nightingale of Cromarty, and in an atmosphere more and more heavily charged, these essential negotiations were pressed forward throughout the first half of 1992. In the end most of the cost of the substantial accommodation works for various parties was included in the main construction contract, and the rents of working space were met in the same way. With the inclusion of Transport Supplementary Grant, the Trust's immediate financial contribution was reduced to the £1.8m land costs, another £2m preparatory costs and a £1m direct contribution towards construction. However, a commitment to contribute towards future maintenance, not yet finalised, coupled with the Trust's present intention to determine the County Council's interest at the end of the initial thirty-year period, means that the Trust will remain involved for the foreseeable future.

A ceremony to mark the commencement of the project was held on 22 May 1992, when the Lord Lieutenant of Kent (Mr Robin Leigh Pemberton) dug a large hole with an excavator and the Trust hosted a small reception in the Commissioner's House in the Historic Dockyard. At that time the formal documentation was not complete, but it was in place in June, and the starting date for the construction contract was finally fixed for 13 July, with completion in the winter of 1995/6.

It is perhaps fitting that the Trust should demonstrate its continuing relevance in modern times to the provision of crossings of the River Medway by its close involvement in a form of crossing of such technological modernity. The Trust can safely claim that the project would not have come about at this time, or maybe at all, without the action the Trust took in obtaining the powers of the Medway Tunnel Act, in lobbying so intensively at political level in support of the scheme and in providing, in accordance with the Trust's motto, private resources for public benefit. It remains to be seen what else the future holds in store.

APPENDICES

Appendix A

Wardens and Assistants of Rochester Bridge

INTRODUCTION

The list that follows includes the names of all known wardens and assistants of Rochester Bridge from the late fourteenth century to the present time. Although the statute of Henry V provided for the annual elections of two wardens, in practice elections during the fifteenth and early sixteenth centuries were held only periodically, and once elected the medieval bridge wardens often served for long periods. For some years no record of the wardens survives at all. Where the evidence is available, these early wardens are noted as senior warden (S) and junior warden (J). The Rochester Bridge Act 1576 re-established the annual election of two wardens and added the election of twelve assistant wardens. From this date reliable records of elections begin to be kept. The Rochester Bridge Act 1908 replaced the election of wardens and assistants with their appointment by county and local government bodies and increased the membership of the Court of Wardens and Assistants to seventeen: six from the Kent County Council, two each from Maidstone, Rochester, Chatham, Gillingham, and the Conservators of the River Medway, and one from the Company of the Proprietors of the Lower Navigation of the River Medway, the latter two bodies having subsequently merged to form the Medway Ports Authority.

Between the late fourteenth and the early sixteenth centuries the two wardens were officers of the bridge rather than men of affairs. From the early sixteenth century, however, men of greater local and national importance were appointed wardens, and by the end of the same century one begins to see the growing domination of the Court by local landed families – the Fanes from 1576, Hales from 1596, Twysdens from 1597, Colepeppers from 1599, Dalysons from 1604, Botelers from 1631, Marshams from 1637, and Tuftons from 1661. By the early eighteenth century a number of mercantile families, such as the Bests, also became involved in the affairs of the bridge. The character of the Court changed again from the middle of the nineteenth century when the landed interest began to decline in terms of its membership of the Court, and the number of local politicians on the Court began to increase. Local politicians had become a significant element within the Court by the end of the century, even before the official change to its composition in 1908. From this date the body nominating members to sit on the Court is identified after their names.

A wide range of manuscript and primary printed sources has been consulted to obtain information on the people who served as wardens and assistants. The information given, where this has proved possible to obtain, about wardens and assistants is not designed to be exhaustive but merely to illustrate the background from which members of the Court were drawn and to enable comparisons to be made about the Court's composition at specific dates. Here the compilers have exercised their discretion. This has been particularly the case over the past century where those wardens and assistants nominated by local authorities may have held a number of different positions of authority in those bodies; only those of the greatest significance, such as elections to the mayoralty or chairmanship of the authority, and latterly the title of Leader of the Council, have been included in the list.

The following abbreviations have been used in the list:

Batt	Battalion
Bt	Baronet
Capt	Captain
CB	Commander of the Bath
CBC	Chatham Borough Council
CBE	Commander, Order of the British Empire
Co	County
CPLNM	Company of the Proprietors of the Lower Navigation of the River Medway
cr	created
CRM	Conservators of the River Medway
DL	Deputy Lieutenant
DSC	Distinguished Service Cross
DSO	Distinguished Service Order
FRS	Fellow of the Royal Society
FSA	Fellow of the Society of Antiquaries
GBC	Gillingham Borough Council
Hon	Honorary, Honourable
J	Junior Warden
JP	Justice of the Peace
Jnr	Junior
KB	Knight of the Bath
KBE	Knight Commander, Order of the British Empire
KCC	Kent County Council
KG	Knight of the Garter
Kt	Knighted
MBC	Maidstone Borough Council
MC	Military Cross
MD	Doctor of Medicine
MP	Member of Parliament
MPA	Medway Ports Authority
OBE	Officer, Order of the British Empire
RAEC	Royal Army Education Corps
RAF	Royal Air Force
RASC	Royal Army Supply Corps
RCC	Rochester City Council
Regt	Regiment

Revd	Reverend
RMC	Medway Borough Council (later Rochester Upon Medway City Council)
RN	Royal Navy
S	Senior Warden
Sec	Secretary
succ	succeeded
TD	Territorial Decoration

1383
Robert Rowe (S) 1383–8, 1398–1416

1387
Thomas Godet (J) 1387–8

1398
Peter Cat (J) 1398–9

1399
John Wolsey (J) 1399–1416

1422
John Beaufitz 1422
　　Founded a Chantry to St John the
　　Baptist in Twydall

1423
John Marchaunt (J) 1423–7
　　MP for Rochester 1417, 1421
Henry Rowe (S) 1423–31

1427
William Thorpe (J) 1427
William Champeneys (J) 1427–31

1435
John Huchon (J) 1435–6
Robert Reynolds (S) 1435–6

1438
Henry Baker alias Henry Hunt (J) 1438–
　　40, 1447–57
　　MP for Rochester 1450
Thomas Glover (S) 1438–40, 1442–3

1442
Thomas Teneacre (J) 1442–3

1443
John Custe (J) 1443–6
Richard Smith (S) 1443–6

1447
William Saunder (S) 1447–52

1457
Nicholas Champeneys (J) 1457–65
Thomas Cobham de Hoo (S) 1457–65

1466
William Testewoode (S) 1466–7, 1469–76

1467
William Barker (J) 1467–9
John Looke (S) 1467–9

1469
John Cardon (J) 1469–76

1476
Joan Testewoode 1476–8

1478
John Soneman 1478–81
　　MP for Rochester 1447

1494
John Hawkyns (J) 1494–7
Thomas Pympe (S) 1494–7

1500
Richard Symondes 1500–2

1502
Henry Dene 1502–3
　　Archbishop of Canterbury 1501–3

1506
Richard Chetham alias Richard Reynham
　　1506–30
　　Prior of Leeds
Sir George Neville 1506–35
　　5th Lord Bergavenny succ 1492,
　　KB 1483, KG 1513, Lord Warden of the
　　Cinque Ports 1513

1528
Sir Christopher Hales 1528–41
　　MP for Canterbury 1523, Solicitor
　　General 1525, Attorney General 1529,
　　Assize Judge 1532, Master of the Rolls
　　1540–1

1535
Sir George Brooke 1535–58
　　9th Lord Cobham succ 1529, KG 1549,
　　Lord Deputy of Calais. Arrested for

alleged complicity in Wyatt's rebellion but released 1554.

1541

Sir Thomas Moyle 1541–60
MP for Kent 1542, for Rochester 1545, 1547, 1553, 1554, Speaker of the House of Commons 1542

1558

Sir William Brooke KG 1558–96
J – 1578
MP for Hythe 1547, 1552, Rochester 1555, 10th Lord Cobham succ 1558, Lord Warden of the Cinque Ports 1558, Constable of Dover Castle 1558, Lord Lieutenant of Kent 1559, Lord Chamberlain of the Queen's Household 1596, Founder of Cobham New College

1560

Henry Neville 1560–86
S – 1578
6th Lord Abergavenny succ 1536

1576

Nicholas Barham 1576–7
S – 1577
MP for Maidstone 1562, Serjeant at Law 1567, Town Clerk and Recorder of Maidstone 1562–83
Henry Brokhull 1576–96
J – 1581, 1583, 1591, 1592
George Catelyn 1576–87
J – 1582
MP for Rochester 1571
Sir Thomas Fane 1576–88
J – 1576
Deputy Commissioner in Kent for increasing number and breed of horses
Thomas Fane 1576–93
S – 1582
MP for Dover 1588, 1592, 1597, Deputy Warden of the Cinque Ports 1603, Lieutenant of Dover Castle 1588
Sir James FitzJames 1576–7
S – 1576
Thomas Fludd 1576–1607, 1611–12
J – 1580
S – 1589, 1594, 1600, 1604
Kt 1589, MP for Maidstone 1592, 1596, 1600
Thomas Lovelace 1576–7
Sir William Lovelace 1576
MP for Canterbury 1562, 1571, 1572

Sir Warham St Leger 1576
Sheriff of Kent 1560, Provost Marshall of Munster 1579
Thomas Watton 1576–7
Thomas Wotton JP 1576–86
J – 1577
S – 1583
Sheriff of Kent 1558 and 1578, Custos Rotulorum 1562–87

1577

Thomas Copinger 1577–9
J – 1579
William Painter 1577–85
J – 1584
Clerk of the Ordnance at the Tower of London 1560

1578

William Cromer 1578–98
S – 1580, 1584
MP for Hythe 1571, Sheriff of Kent 1577
Thomas Hendlye 1578–85
Sir Roger Manwood 1578–92
S – 1579, 1585, 1592
MP for Hastings 1555, and for Sandwich 1557, 1558, 1562, 1571, 1572, Serjeant at Law 1567, Puisne Judge of the Common Pleas 1572, Lord Chief Baron of the Exchequer 1578, Member of Star Chamber 1581, Recorder of Sandwich 1555
John Somer 1578–85
S – 1581

1580

Levin Buffkyn 1580–5, 1593
MP for Maidstone 1592

1585

William Lambarde JP 1585–1601
J – 1585, 1589, 1598
S – 1594
Master in Chancery 1592, Keeper of the Records at the Rolls Chapel 1597, Keeper of the Records of the Tower of London 1601, author of *The Perambulation of Kent*, First President of Cobham New College

1586

Edward Becher 1586–92
S – 1587
Henry Cutte 1586–92
J – 1586

John Leveson 1586–1615
  J – 1610, 1614
  S – 1586, 1593, 1598, 1603
  Kt 1589, KB 1603, MP for Bossiney
  1584, for Maidstone 1596, 1600 and
  for Kent 1604, First President of Cobham
  New College
1587
Thomas Duke 1587–1605
  J – 1587, 1596
William Sidley 1587–1618
  J – 1588, 1599, 1605
  S – 1591, 1592, 1613
  Bt cr 1611, Sheriff of Kent 1589
1588
Edward Nevill 1588–92
  S – 1588
  MP for New Windsor 1588
1589
Martin Barnham 1589–95
  J – 1590
  Kt 1603, Sheriff of London and of Kent
  1598
1593
William Beinham 1593–7
  S – 1597
William Lewyn 1593–7
  J – 1593
  MP for Rochester 1586, 1589, 1593,
  Judge of the Prerogative Court of
  Canterbury 1576, Master in Chancery,
  Chancellor of Diocese of Rochester
Thomas Pagett 1593
1594
Robert Bing JP 1594–5
  J – 1595
  MP for Steyning 1555 and for Abingdon
  1558, Sheriff of Kent 1592
William Burrough 1594–8
  S – 1595
  2nd Lord Burgh succ 1550
John Richers 1594–1603
  S – 1596, 1601
  Commissioner of Sewers for Kent 1600
1596
George Bing 1596–1616
  J – 1597, 1608
  S – 1602
  MP for Rochester 1584, Burgess of
  Dover 1604

Sir Percivall Harte JP 1596–8, 1617–37
  S – 1618, 1625, 1632
  MP for Kent 1597 and for Lewes 1601
1597
Henry Brooke JP 1597–1603
  11th Lord Cobham succ 1597, KG 1599,
  MP for Kent 1588 and for Hedon 1593,
  Lord Warden of the Cinque Ports,
  Constable of Dover Castle, Lord
  Lieutenant of Kent 1597–1603. Attainted
  for complicity in the Raleigh conspiracy
  and imprisoned in the Tower of London
  1603
Roger Twysden 1597–1600
  Sheriff of Kent 1599, 1600, Capt. of a
  troop at Tilbury 1588
1598
Thomas Kempe 1598–1600
Peter Manwood 1598–1621
  S – 1599, 1609, 1615
  Kt 1603, MP for Sandwich 1588, 1589,
  for Saltash 1603 and for New Romney
  1620, Sheriff of Kent 1602,
  Commissioner of Sewers for Kent
1599
Sir Thomas Colpepper 1599–1600
Ralph Coppinger 1599–1620
  J – 1600, 1606, 1613, 1620
William Page 1599–1625
  J – 1601, 1616, 1623
  S – 1608
1601
Francis Fane 1601–28
  J – 1603
  S – 1610, 1617, 1624
  KB 1603, Baron Burghersh, 1st Earl of
  Westmorland succ 1624, MP for Kent
  1601 and for Maidstone 1603, 1614, 1620
Richard Lee 1601–18
  J – 1602, 1609
  MP for Canterbury 1593
Thomas Pennestone 1601
1602
Sir Peter Bucke JP 1602–24
  J – 1604, 1611
  S – 1619
  Built and resided at Eastgate House,
  Rochester
Sampson Lennard 1602–3
  Sheriff of Kent 1591, MP for Dunheved
  1571, for Bramber 1584, for St Mawes

1586, for Christchurch 1588, for St
Germans 1592, for Rye 1597, for
Liskeard 1601 and for Sussex 1614,
Rougemont Pursuivant Extraordinary at
College of Arms 1615, Bluemantle
Pursuivant 1616

1604
Sir Maximilian Dalyson 1604–31
    J – 1618, 1625 1631
    S – 1605, 1611
    MP for Rochester 1624, Sheriff of Kent
    1611
Sir John Scott 1604–16
    S – 1607, 1612
    MP for Kent 1604 and for Maidstone
    1614, Member of the Council of Virginia
    1607
Sir Alexander Temple 1604–14
    J – 1612
    S – 1606

1606
Edward Duke 1606–37
    J – 1607, 1615, 1621
    S – 1628, 1636

1608
Sir William Steed 1608–10
    Sheriff of Kent 1613

1613
Sir George Fane JP 1613–40
    J – 1627
    S – 1614, 1635
    MP for Kent 1621 and for Maidstone
    1623, 1626, 1627, Sheriff of Kent 1622

1615
Sir Thomas Walsingham 1615–30
    J – 1629
    S – 1616, 1622
    MP for Rochester 1597, 1601, 1604 and
    for Kent 1614

1616
Sir Robert Brett 1616–20
    J – 1617

1617
Sir Anthony Weldon 1617–28, 1644–8
    J – 1619, 1626
    Clerk of the Kitchen 1604, Clerk of the
    Green Cloth 1609, Member of
    Parliamentary Committee for Kent

1619
George Bing 1619–26

    S – 1620
    MP for Dover 1603
Sir John Sedley Bt, JP 1619–30
    S – 1621, 1629
    Sheriff of Kent 1621

1621
Sir Edward Hales Bt, JP 1621–43
    S – 1623, 1631, 1638
    MP for Kent 1625, Sheriff of Kent 1609
Richard Lee 1621–52
    J – 1622, 1630, 1636
    S – 1642, 1646
    MP for Rochester 1640

1622
Richard Leveson 1622–36
    J – 1624
    KB 1625

1625
Sir William Brooke 1625–43
    S – 1626, 1633, 1640
    MP for Rochester 1628

1626
Sir Mildmay Fane 1626–49, 1661–5
    S – 1627, 1634, 1641, 1647, 1663
    Lord LeDespenser 1626, 2nd Earl of
    Westmorland succ 1628, MP for
    Kent 1625

1627
Peter Bucke 1627–54
    J – 1628, 1637, 1644, 1653

1629
Sir Francis Barnham 1629–30
    MP for Grampound 1603, 1614 and for
    Maidstone 1621, 1624, 1626, 1628, 1640
Sir William Colepepper Bt 1629–51
    S – 1630, 1637, 1644, 1650
    Sheriff of Kent 1637

1631
Sir Oliver Boteler Bt, JP – 1631–2,
    1661–78
    J – 1663, 1670, 1677
Sir Thomas Colepepper 1631–6
    J – 1633
    MP for Tewkesbury 1628
Sir Thomas Walsingham 1631–59
    J – 1631
    S – 1639, 1645, 1651
    MP for Poole 1614 and for Rochester
    1621, 1624, 1625, 1626, 1628, 1640,

Member of Sequestrations Committee
for Kent

1632
Sir John Hales 1632–9
    J – 1634

1633
Robert Barnham 1633–44, 1661–4
    J – 1635, 1643
    Bt cr 1663, MP for Maidstone 1660

1637
William Boteler 1637–43
    J – 1638
    Bt succ 1641, Gentleman Pensioner of
    the King
John Marsham 1637–43, 1661–85
    J – 1639
    S – 1664, 1671, 1678, 1685
    Kt 1660, Bt cr 1663, MP for Rochester
    1660, Clerk in Chancery 1638–48

1638
George Duke JP 1638–60
    J – 1640
    S – 1648, 1653, 1660
Sir Thomas Swan 1638

1639
Henry Clarke 1639–40
    MP for Rochester 1621, 1625, 1626,
    Recorder of Rochester 1629

1640
George Newman JP 1640–8, 1661–77
    J – 1641, 1664, 1671

1641
Edward Lennard 1641
William Paynter 1641–52
    J – 1642, 1649

1642
Sir John Sedley Bt. 1642–8
    J – 1647
    S – 1643

1644
William James 1644–60
    J – 1645
    S – 1652, 1658
    MP for Kent 1654, 1658
Reginald Peckham JP 1644–51
    J – 1646
Augustine Skinner 1644–60
    J – 1648
    S – 1654

MP for Kent 1640, 1654, Chairman of
Parliamentary Committee for Kent

1645
Sir Nicholas Miller JP 1645–59
    S – 1649, 1655
    Sheriff of Kent 1633

1649
Sir Cheyney Colepepper 1649–60
    J – 1650
    S – 1656
    Chairman of the Sequestrations
    Committee for Kent
John Parker 1649–60
    J – 1652
    S – 1657
    MP for Rochester 1653, 1656, Serjeant at
    Law and Registrar of the Prerogative
    Court of Canterbury 1648, Member of
    High Court 1649, Baron of the Exchequer
    1655, Military Commissioner for Kent,
    Recorder of Rochester 1652–5
Ralph Weldon 1649–60
    J – 1651
    S – 1659
    MP for Kent 1654, Colonel 1644,
    Governor of Plymouth 1645

1650
Charles Bowles JP 1650–60
    J – 1654
    Sheriff of Kent 1658, Commissary of the
    County of Kent 1643

1652
Sir Thomas Style Bt 1652–60
    J – 1655
    MP for Kent 1659, 1660, Sheriff of Kent
    1634
Henry Wyatt JP 1652–3

1653
Henry Jellies 1653–5

1654
Sir Robert Honywood 1654–60
    J – 1656
    Colonel (Palatinate Wars), Steward to the
    Queen of Bohemia, Ambassador to
    Sweden 1659–60, Member of Council of
    State 1659
Richard Wilkinson 1654–60
    J – 1657

1655
Sir William Sedley Bt 1655

1656
Major Thomas Broadnax JP 1656–60
    J – 1659
Sir John Twisleton JP 1656–60
    J – 1658
    Colonel (Parliamentary Army)

1659
John Banks 1659–60, 1680–99
    J – 1680, 1687
    S – 1694
    Bt cr 1661, MP for Maidstone 1654, 1695
    and for Rochester 1679, 1681, 1685,
    1688, Governor of the East India
    Company 1683
Richard Beale JP 1659–60
    J – 1660

1660
Robert Watson JP 1660

1661
Sir Edward Hales, Bt, JP 1661–80
    S – 1661, 1668, 1675
Sir Francis Clarke 1661–85
    J – 1661, 1683
    S – 1669, 1676
    MP for Rochester 1661, 1681
Thomas, Lord Colepepper 1661–73
    S – 1667
    Governor of Virginia
Thomas Cripps 1661–3
    S – 1662
Maximilian Dalyson JP 1661–71
    S – 1666
Thomas Flood JP 1661–70
    J – 1665
Allington Paynter 1661–79
    J – 1666
    S – 1673
Sir William Swan Bt, JP 1661–80
    J – 1667
    S – 1674
Sir John Tufton Bt 1661–85
    S – 1662, 1670, 1677, 1684
    MP for Maidstone 1678, 1679, 1681 and
    for Kent 1660, 1661, Sheriff of
    Kent 1654

1663
James Cripps 1663–77
    J – 1668, 1675

1665
Sir Phillip Warwick 1665–77
    S – 1665, 1672
    MP for Radnor 1640 and for Westminster
    1661, Secretary to the Treasury 1661–7

1666
James Fortroy JP 1666–74
    J – 1669

1671
Richard Manley JP 1671–84
    J – 1672, 1679
Sir Vere Fane 1672–93
    J – 1673
    S – 1680, 1687
    4th Earl of Westmorland succ 1691, MP
    for Kent 1678, 1681, 1688, 1690, Lord
    Lieutenant of Kent 1692

1674
Roger Twisden 1674–1701
    J – 1674, 1681, 1688, 1695
    MP for Rochester 1688

1675
Sir Charles Sedley Bt 1675–1701
    J – 1676
    S – 1683, 1690, 1697
    MP for New Romney 1678, 1679, 1681,
    1690, 1696, 1698, 1701

1678
Francis Barrell 1678–9
    J – 1678
    MP for Rochester 1679, Serjeant at Law,
    Recorder of Rochester
James Crispe 1678
Henry, Lord O'Brien 1678

1679
Sir Richard Head Bt 1679–87
    S – 1679, 1686
    MP for Rochester 1667, 1679, Mayor of
    Rochester 1683
John Marsham 1679–91
    J – 1684
    S – 1691
    2nd Bt succ 1685, Sheriff of Kent 1692

1680
Thomas Manley 1680–90
    J – 1685
    Member of King's Council 1672
Sir William Twisden 1680–97
    S – 1681, 1688, 1695

1681
John Cropely 1681–7
    J – 1682

Sir Thomas Stile 1681–1702
    S – 1682, 1689, 1696

1685
Sir Joseph Williamson 1685–1701
    J – 1686
    S – 1693, 1700
    MP for Thetford 1669, for Rochester
    1689, 1696, 1698, 1701 and for Clare
    1692 and Limerick 1695 in the Irish
    Parliament, Under Sec. of State 1665,
    Sec. of State 1674–9, Ambassador to
    Holland 1697–8, President of the Royal
    Society 1678, Recorder of Thetford 1682,
    Founder of the Sir Joseph Williamson
    Mathematical School for Boys in
    Rochester

1686
Sir Thomas Colepepper Bt 1686–1723
    J – 1690, 1697, 1704, 1711, 1718
    MP for Maidstone 1705, 1708, 1710,
    1714, Sheriff of Kent 1702
Thomas Dalison 1686–1736
    J – 1691, 1698, 1705, 1712, 1719, 1726,
    1733
Sir Henry Selby 1686–91

1688
Francis Clarke 1688–91
    MP for Rochester 1685, 1689
Sir Thomas Taylor Bt 1688–95
    J – 1689
    MP for Maidstone 1688, 1690, 1695

1691
Francis Barrell 1691–1724
    J – 1692, 1699, 1706, 1713, 1720
    MP for Rochester 1701

1692
Caleb Banks 1692–6
    J – 1693
    MP for Queenborough 1685, 1695, for
    Maidstone 1689 and for Rochester 1691
John Cromp 1692–1717
    S – 1698, 1705, 1712
Sir Francis Head Bt 1692–1716
    S – 1692, 1699, 1706, 1713

1694
Robert Minor 1694
    J – 1694

1695
Sir Phillip Boteler Bt 1695–1714

    J – 1701, 1708

1696
William Woodyear 1696–1732
    J – 1696, 1703, 1710, 1717, 1724, 1731

1697
Sir Robert Marsham Bt 1697–1703
    J – 1700
    MP for Maidstone 1698, 1700
    Clerk of the Court of Chancery 1698

1698
William Cage 1698–1736
    S – 1702, 1709, 1716, 1723, 1730
    MP for Rochester 1702, 1710, 1713
    Sheriff of Kent 1695

1700
David Polhill 1700–40
    J – 1715
    S – 1701, 1708, 1722, 1729, 1736
    MP for Kent 1708, for Bramber 1723 and
    for Rochester 1727, 1734, 1743, 1747
    Keeper of the Tower of London 1730
    Sheriff of Kent 1715

1702
Richard Etkins 1702–23
    S – 1704, 1711, 1718
Thomas Palmer 1702–23
    J – 1721
    S – 1707, 1714
    Bt cr 1706
    MP for Kent 1708 and for Rochester
    1715, 1722, Comptroller of the Navy,
    Commissioner for stating debts of the army
Richard Somer 1702–36
    J – 1702, 1709, 1716, 1723, 1730
    Commissioner of Customs for Scotland

1703
Edward Knatchbull 1703–29
    S – 1703, 1710, 1717, 1724
    4th Bt succ 1711, MP for Rochester
    1702, for Kent 1713, 1722 and for
    Lostwithiel 1728

1704
Robert Marsham 1704–24
    J – 1707, 1714
    S – 1721
    1st Baron Romney cr. 1716
    MP for Maidstone 1708, 1710 1713,
    1714, Governor of Dover Castle 1717

1715
Sir Thomas Twisden JP 1715–28
    J – 1722
    S – 17i5
1717
Thomas Chiffinch 1717–27
    S – 1720, 1727
    Searcher in Port of Gravesend
1718
Walker Weldon 1718–30
    S – 1719, 1726
    Owner of Rochester Castle
1724
Percivall Hart 1724–38
    S – 1728, 1735
    MP for Kent 1710, 1713, Sheriff of Kent
    1707
Thomas Kempthorn 1724–36
    J – 1725, 1732
William Walter 1724–45
    S – 1725, 1732, 1739, 1744
1725
Phillip Bartholomew 1725–9
    J – 1728
Thomas Best 1725–36
    J – 1727, 1734
1728
Robert Weller 1728–41
    S – 1734
    Sheriff of Kent 1728, Alderman of
    Rochester 1714
1729
John Marsh 1729–37
    J – 1729, 1736
1730
John Finch 1730–8
    S – 1731
    MP for Maidstone 1714, 1722, 1727, 1734
Thomas Pearce 1730–42
    J – 1735
    Commissioner of the Navy
1731
John Thorpe, MD, FRS 1731–50
    J – 1746
    S – 1733, 1742
    Author of *Registrum Roffense*
1733
Heneage Finch 1733–73

S – 1737, 1761
    3rd Earl of Aylesford succ 1757
1737
Mawdistly Best 1737–43
    J – 1738, 1742
    Sheriff of Kent 1730
John Cage 1737–45
    J – 1741
Thomas Dalison Jnr 1737–8
John Fane 1737–57
    S – 1738, 1748, 1755
    Lord Catherlough 1733, 7th Earl of
    Westmorland succ 1736
Robert Marsham FRS 1737–65
    J – 1737
    S – 1746, 1753, 1765
    2nd Lord Romney succ 1724
1738
Joseph Brooke 1738–48
    J – 1739
1739
Francis Barrell 1739–60
    J – 1740
    S – 1750, 1757
Thomas Chiffinch 1739–51, 1772–4
    S – 1741, 1773
    Barrister at Law
Sir Roger Twisden, Bt 1739–64
    S – 1740, 1751, 1758
    MP for Kent 1741, 1747; Officer, King's
    own regiment of horse
1741
Edward Bligh 1741–7
    S – 1743
    Lord Clifton 1722, 2nd Earl of Darnley
    succ 1728, Lord in Waiting to the Prince
    of Wales 1742
1742
John Page 1742–3
    J – 1743
1743
Francis Brooke 1743–8
    J – 1744
1744
James Best 1744–81
    J – 1745, 1748, 1754, 1766, 1771
    S – 1760, 1777
    Sheriff of Kent 1751

Charles Brown 1744–5
S – 1745
1746
Thomas Best 1746–57
S – 1747, 1754
MP for Canterbury 1741, 1761
Lt Governor of Dover Castle
Thomas Fletcher 1746–7, 1752–63
J – 1747, 1753
S – 1759
John Page 1746–68
J – 1751, 1757, 1763
1748
Sir Thomas Dyke, Bt, JP 1748–56
S – 1749, 1756
John Longley 1748–73
J – 1749, 1755, 1761, 1767
1749
John Bligh 1749–50
3rd Earl of Darnley succ 1747
MP for Athboy 1739 and for Maidstone
1741
Robert Williams 1749–70
J – 1750, 1756, 1768
S – 1762
1751
The Hon Robert Fairfax 1751–68, 1772–93
S – 1752, 1763, 1774, 1781, 1790
7th Lord Fairfax succ 1789, MP for
Maidstone 1747 and for Kent 1754, 1761,
Major, 1st Life Guards
George Hinde 1751–56
J – 1752
1756
Charles Whitworth 1756–67
Kt 1768
MP for Minehead 1747, 1768, for
Bletchingley 1761 and for Saltash 1775
Lt Governor of Gravesend and Tilbury
Fort 1758
1757
Isaac Wildash 1757–92
J – 1758, 1768, 1776, 1783, 1790
S – 1764
Member of the Corporation of Rochester
1757
1758
Francis Child 1758–63
J – 1759

Thomas Faunce JP 1758–69
J – 1760
S – 1768
1761
Edward Hasted FRS, FSA 1761–71
J – 1762
Chairman of the Quarter Sessions at
Canterbury, Author of *The History and
Topographical Survey of the County of
Kent.*
1764
John Charlton 1764–70
J – 1764
William Gordon 1764–70
J – 1765
MP for Rochester 1768, Sheriff of Kent
1763, Mayor of Rochester 1775
1765
Roger Twisden 1765–79
S – 1766, 1772
6th Bt succ 1772
1766
Sir John Dyke, Bt 1766–1810
S – 1767, 1778, 1786, 1797, 1805
1768
The Hon Charles Marsham 1768–1809
S – 1769, 1780, 1795, 1803
3rd Lord Romney succ 1793 and 1st Earl
of Romney cr 1801, MP for Maidstone
1768 and for Kent 1774, 1780, 1784,
Lord Lieutenant of Kent
1769
John Calcraft 1769–72
J – 1770
MP for Calne 1766 and for Rochester 1768
Thomas Hanway 1769–71
S – 1770
1770
Benjamin Hateley-Foot 1770–91
S – 1771, 1779, 1788
1771
John Amherst 1771–87
J – 1772, 1778, 1784
Phillip Boghurst 1771–91
J – 1773, 1779, 1785, 1791
William Parry 1771
Admiral RN

1772
Joseph Brooke 1772–91
    J – 1774, 1780, 1786
    Recorder of Rochester
1773
Sir Thomas Rider 1773–85
    S – 1775, 1782
    Sheriff of Kent 1754
1774
Heneage Finch 1774–1812
    S – 1776, 1784, 1791, 1799, 1808
    4th Earl of Aylesford succ 1777, MP for
    Maidstone 1774, Lord Steward of the
    Household
John Longley Jnr 1774–1805
    J – 1775, 1782, 1788, 1794, 1801
    Recorder of Rochester
1775
Leonard Bartholomew 1775–1800
    J – 1777
    S – 1785, 1792, 1799
    Sheriff of Kent 1790
1780
Edward Pilcher 1780–1800
    J – 1781, 1787, 1800
    S – 1793
1782
Sir John Papillon Twisden 1782–6
    S –1783
1786
George Best JP, DL 1786–1816
    J – 1792, 1798, 1806, 1814
    S – 1787
    MP for Rochester 1790
1787
William Geary 1787–1823
    S – 1789, 1798, 1806, 1813, 1820
    Bt cr 1795, MP for Kent 1796
1788
George Gunning 1788–1820
    J – 1789, 1797, 1805, 1813
1792
John Bligh 1792–1827
    S – 1794, 1801, 1809, 1816, 1822
    4th Earl of Darnley succ 1781
Henry Hawley 1792–1808
    J – 1793, 1808
    S – 1800
    Bt cr 1795, Sheriff of Kent 1783,

Chairman of Kent Quarter Sessions
James Roper-Head 1792–1810
    J – 1795, 1803
1793
George Smith 1793–1827
    S – 1796, 1804, 1810, 1817, 1823
    Capt of Lord Darnley's troop of
    Gentleman and Yeomanry Cavalry
1794
Thomas Elliot 1794–1818
    J – 1796, 1804, 1811
1801
William Dann 1801–7
    S – 1802
George T. Hateley-Foot 1801–5
    J – 1802
1806
Thomas Dalton 1806–20
    J – 1807, 1815
Charles Milner 1806–27
    S – 1807, 1815, 1821
1808
Philip Boghurst 1808–21
    J – 1809, 1816
1809
Samuel Tuffnell Barrett 1809–15
    J – 1810
    Sheriff of Kent, Capt 37th Regt
1810
Charles Marsham 1810–26
    S – 1811, 1818, 1825
    2nd Earl of Romney succ 1811
1811
Sir Thomas Dyke, Bt 1811–27
    S – 1812, 1819
    Colonel West Kent Militia
The Hon. John Wingfield Stratford
    1811–27
    J – 1812, 1819
    S – 1827
1813
Heneage Finch FSA 1813–25
    S – 1814, 1821
    5th Earl of Aylesford succ 1813
1816
William Twopenny 1816–26
    J – 1817
    S – 1824

Bridge Clerk 1790–1810

1817

Thomas Fairfax Best, JP, DL 1817, 1844–9
S – 1848
Officer, Grenadier Guards (present at
Corunna)

Robert Turbeville Bingham 1817–27
J – 1818
S – 1826

1818

Francis Hubble Douce 1818
Capt Militia 1801

1819

James Best, JP 1819–49
J – 1820, 1832, 1839
Lt Colonel West Kent Militia

1821

Thomas Augustus Douce 1821–6
J – 1823

Henry Hawley 1821–5
J – 1822

1822

Thomas Rider 1822–7, 1832–47
J – 1824
S – 1832, 1840
Sheriff of Kent 1829

1824

Maximilian D.D. Dalison, JP, DL 1824–7,
1832–44
J – 1825, 1835
S – 1842
Major West Kent Militia

1826

Samuel Baker 1826–36
J – 1826, 1828
Mayor of Rochester 1797, 1802, Member
of Rochester Common Council 1787

David Hermitage Day 1826–31
J – 1827

1827

Edward Boys 1827–31
S – 1830
Member of Rochester Common Council
1810, Mayor of Rochester 1823,
Alderman of Rochester 1820

George Byng 1827–31
S – 1828
6th Viscount Torrington succ 1813, Vice
Admiral of the Blue

William Lomas 1827–31
J – 1831

George Gunning 1827–8

1828

Thomas Bentley 1828–31
J – 1829

The Hon John Bligh 1828–9
Brother of 5th Earl of Darnley

Jacob George Bryant 1828–31
J – 1830

Michael Comfort 1828

David John Day 1828–31

Revd William Edmeades 1828, 1832

Charles Larkin 1828–31
S – 1831

Thomas Poynder 1828–31
S – 1829

1829

Samuel Baker Jnr 1829

William Brown 1829–31

John William Smith, MD 1829–31

1830

Thomas Baker 1830–1

Jeremiah Rosher 1830–1

1832

Edward Bligh 1832–4
S – 1834
5th Earl of Darnley succ 1831, MP for
Canterbury 1818, Lord Lieutenant of
County Meath

John Dudlow 1832–46
J – 1844
S – 1839
Deputy Sheriff of Kent 1807

John Dunkald 1832–40
J – 1833

Sir William Geary, Bt, 1832–42
J – 1842
S – 1836
MP for West Kent 1835

John Golding 1832–43
J – 1836

William Golding 1832–56
J – 1837, 1843

Demetrius Grevis James, JP, DL 1832–3
Sheriff of Kent 1833, Capt Royal Marines

John Mercer, JP 1832–55
J – 1840, 1845
S – 1833, 1846, 1853
Mayor of Maidstone 1839, 1848

John Miller 1832–3

1833
Charles Marsham 1833–74
 J – 1834
 S – 1841, 1847, 1851, 1856, 1861, 1867, 1872
 3rd Earl of Romney succ 1845

1834
John Stunt 1834–56
 J – 1838, 1844
Robert Tassell 1834–61
 J – 1858
 S – 1837, 1843, 1853
 Member of Maidstone Common Council 1815, Jurat 1820

1835
Thomas Law Hodges, JP, DL 1835–57
 J – 1841
 S – 1835, 1850
 MP for Kent 1830, 1847, Major West Kent Militia

1837
William Brown 1837–43
 J – 1838

1841
William Masters Smith, JP, DL 1841–61
 J – 1846
 S – 1845, 1854, 1860
 Sheriff of Kent 1849, MP for Kent 1852

1843
John Wingfield Stratford 1843–9
 J – 1849

1844
Michael Lock 1844–8

1845
Charles Wykeham-Martin, JP 1845–70
 J – 1848, 1854, 1865
 S – 1859
 MP for West Kent 1857 and for Newport 1841, 1865, DL (Kent and Hants), Major 3rd Batt of Kent Volunteers

1847
Edward Twopenny, JP 1847–65
 J – 1856, 1861
 S – 1849
 Bridge Clerk 1818–40

1848
John Stuart Bligh 1848–96
 J – 1851
 S – 1857, 1863, 1869, 1874, 1875,
1881, 1888, 1895
 6th Earl of Darnley succ 1835, County Alderman of Kent 1889–96, Lt Colonel West Kent Yeomanry Cavalry

1849
George Baker 1849–58
 J – 1850
 S – 1855
 Councillor MBC 1873

1850
Edward Ladd Betts 1850–66
 S – 1852, 1858, 1864
 Sheriff of Kent 1858
John Lock 1850–2
William Moore, JP 1850–93
 J – 1857, 1863, 1869, 1881
 S – 1852, 1876, 1889
 Sheriff of Kent 1867

1853
Matthew Bell, JP, DL 1853–90
 J – 1855, 1859, 1871
 S – 1866, 1879, 1885
 Sheriff of Kent 1850

1856
William Lee 1856–81
 J – 1860, 1866, 1872
 S – 1880
 MP for Maidstone 1859, 1865, 1868

1857
Thomas Hermitage Day 1857–69
 J – 1868
 S – 1862
John Savage, JP 1857–68
 J – 1862
 Sheriff of Kent 1857

1858
James Whatman, JP, DL, FRS, FSA 1858–86
 J – 1864, 1870
 S – 1878, 1883
 MP for Maidstone 1852, 1865, 1868 and for West Kent 1857, Councillor MBC 1842, Capt West Kent Militia

1859
Sir Edmund Filmer, Bt, JP 1859–86
 S – 1865, 1870, 1877, 1882
 MP for West Kent 1838, Sheriff of Kent 1870

1862
Maudistly Gaussen Best, JP 1862–1906
  J – 1880
  S – 1868, 1873, 1886, 1892, 1900
  Sheriff of Kent 1881, Major 34th Regt
  (Crimea)
Alexander Randall, JP 1862–9
  J – 1867
  Alderman MBC 1853

1866
William Manclark 1866–86
  J – 1879, 1885
  S – 1871
  Mayor of Rochester 1853, 1856, 1858

1867
Edward Robert Coles 1867–78
  J – 1873
  Mayor of Rochester 1861, 1866,
  Alderman of Rochester 1868

1869
Edward Winch 1869–84
  J – 1874, 1875, 1882

1870
Charles Arkcoll 1870–9
  J – 1877
  Councillor MBC 1856, Mayor of
  Maidstone 1858, 1868, Alderman MBC
  1859
Lewis Davis Wigan 1870–85
  J – 1878, 1883

1871
William Henry Nicholson, JP 1871–80
  J – 1876

1875
Philip Wykeham-Martin, JP 1875–8
  MP for Rochester 1856, DL (Kent &
  Warwick)

1879
Sir Francis Flint Belsey, JP 1879–1908
  J – 1884
  S – 1891, 1899, 1907
  Councillor RCC 1870, Alderman RCC
  1884, Mayor of Rochester 1878, 1890
Charles Ellis JP 1879–1900
  S – 1884, 1890, 1896
  Councillor MBC 1858, Mayor of
  Maidstone 1860, 1864, 1872, 1878,
  Alderman MBC 1868, Councillor KCC
  1892

1880
William Laurence 1880–99
  J – 1886
  S – 1893
  Mayor of Maidstone 1853, 1865

1881
General George William Powlett Bingham,
  CB, JP 1881–98
  S – 1887, 1894

1882
Henry Arthur Brassey, JP, DL 1882–91
  J – 1887
  MP for Sandwich 1868, Sheriff of Kent
  1890, Officer 7th Dragoon Guards,
  Major West Kent Militia

1885
George Winch 1885–1908
  J – 1888, 1896
  S – 1904
  County Alderman of Kent 1889–1901

1886
George Marsham, JP 1886–1920 (KCC
  from 1908)
  J – 1889
  S – 1897, 1905, 1911, 1915
  DL (Kent & Co. Leitrim), Sheriff of
  County Leitrim 1878, Councillor KCC
  1889, Alderman KCC 1892

1887
The Hon Evelyn E.T. Boscawen, CB, JP
  1887–1908
  J – 1890
  S – 1898, 1906
  7th Viscount Falmouth succ 1889, Baron
  Le Despencer succ 1891, DL (Kent &
  Cornwall), Colonel Coldstream Guards
Fiennes Stanley Wykeham Cornwallis, JP,
  DL 1887–1934 (KCC from 1908)
  J – 1891, 1899, 1907, 1931
  S – 1912, 1917, 1932
  1st Baron Cornwallis cr 1927, MP for
  Maidstone 1888, 1898, President of the
  Royal Agricultural Society, Chairman of
  KCC 1910–30, County Alderman of
  Kent 1895–1935
William Allan Smith-Masters, JP
  1887–1936 (KCC from 1908)
  J – 1892, 1930
  S – 1901, 1908, 1909, 1910, 1916, 1931
  Councillor KCC 1918–22

1891
Henry Edmeades, JP, DL 1891–1908
  J – 1893
  S – 1902
  Major General, Royal Artillary
1892
Albert Frederick Style 1892–5
  J – 1894
  Councillor KCC 1889–95
1894
Henry Leonard Campbell Brassey, JP
  1894–1904
  J – 1895
  S – 1903
1896
George Montague Style 1896–1906
  J – 1897, 1905
  Councillor KCC 1897 and MBC 1898
1897
Sir William Webb Hayward, JP 1897–8
  J – 1898
  Mayor of Rochester 1896
1899
Austin Frederick Budden, JP 1899–1901
  J – 1901
Thomas Colyer-Fergusson, Bt, JP
  1899–1939 (KCC from 1908)
  J – 1900, 1926
  S – 1927
  Sheriff of Kent 1906
1900
John Arkcoll 1900–35 (CPLNM from
  1908)
  J – 1902
  S – 1914
1901
George Youngman 1901–13 (MBC from
  1908)
  J – 1903
  Councillor MBC 1868, Mayor of
  Maidstone 1876
1902
Percy John Neate, JP 1902
  Councillor RCC 1895, Mayor of
  Rochester 1899, Councillor KCC 1904
1903
Ivo Francis Walter Bligh, JP 1903–27
  (KCC from 1908)
  J – 1904

  S – 1913, 1918
  8th Earl of Darnley succ 1900
  Alderman KCC 1906–25
1905
Frederick F. Smith 1905–41 (RCC from
  1908)
  J – 1906
  S – 1913, 1920
  Councillor RCC 1890, Mayor of
  Rochester 1892, 1903, 1904, Alderman
  RCC 1904
1907
Richard David Batchelor, JP 1907–36
  (CBC from 1908)
  J – 1908, 1909, 1910
  S – 1919
  Councillor CBC 1891, Mayor of Chatham
  1906
Sir Robert Marcus Filmer, Bt, JP, MC
  1907–15 (KCC from 1908)
  Capt Grenadier Guards 1898–1904,
  Officer in East Kent Yeomanry
Herbert Monckton 1907–21 (MBC from
  1908)
  J – 1916
  Recorder of Maidstone 1874, Town Clerk
  of Maidstone
1909
William Ball, JP 1909–13 (CRM)
  Councillor KCC 1895–1904
George Henry De La Cour 1909–14 (CBC)
  J – 1914
  Councillor CBC 1891, Alderman CBC
  1896, Mayor of Chatham 1897
Francis Edward East, JP 1909–16 (KCC)
  Councillor KCC 1889–1910, Alderman
  KCC 1910–16
John Robert Featherby JP 1909–22 (GBC)
  J – 1912
  S – 1922
William King 1909 (GBC)
Samuel Lee Smith, JP 1909–18 (CRM)
  Councillor KCC 1889–1914, Alderman
  KCC 1914–23
Charles Willis, JP, 1909–43 (RCC)
  J – 1911
  S – 1921
  Councillor RCC 1900, Mayor of
  Rochester 1906, 1907, 1908, 1909,
  Alderman RCC 1907

1910
Richard Sheepwash 1910–12 (GBC)

1913
Thomas Lake Aveling, JP 1913–30 (CRM)
    J – 1915
    S – 1923
James Davis, JP 1913–30 (GBC)
    J – 1917
Edmund Ward Vaughan 1913–21 (MBC)
    J – 1918
    Councillor MBC 1895, Auditor MBC
    1899, Mayor of Maidstone 1899, 1906,
    Alderman MBC 1908
    Councillor KCC 1900

1915
William Paine 1915–29 (CBC)
    J – 1919
    S – 1924
    Councillor CBC 1900, Mayor of Chatham
    1912–18, Alderman CBC 1914

1916
Osmond E. D'Avigdor Goldsmid, JP, DL
    1916–40 (KCC)
    J – 1921
    S – 1926
    Bt cr 1934, Sheriff of Kent 1912,
    Councillor KCC 1910–17, Alderman
    KCC 1917–36, Lt Colonel RASC
Charles Tuff, JP 1916–29 (CRM)
    J – 1920
    S – 1925
    MP for Rochester 1903, Mayor of
    Rochester 1900, 1901

1920
William Lee Henry Roberts 1920–8 (KCC)
    J – 1922, 1927
    S – 1928
    Councillor KCC 1898–1909, Alderman
    KCC 1909–19, Sheriff of Kent 1920

1921
William Day 1921–45 (MBC)
    J – 1923, 1928
    S – 1929
    Councillor MBC 1890, Mayor of
    Maidstone 1902, 1920, 1933, Alderman
    MBC 1895, Councillor KCC 1921,
    Alderman KCC 1937

1922
John James Knight 1922–45 (GBC)
    J – 1925, 1939

S – 1940
    Councillor GBC 1914, Mayor of
    Gillingham 1920, 1922, 1923, 1924,
    Alderman GBC 1922, Freeman of the
    Borough of Gillingham 1926, Councillor
    KCC 1943
Frank G. Lawrence, JP 1922–31 (MBC)
    J – 1924, 1929
    S – 1930
    Councillor MBC 1892, Alderman MBC
    1907

1927
Esme Ivo Bligh 1927–54 (KCC)
    J – 1932
    S – 1933
    9th Earl of Darnley succ 1927, 18th
    Baron Clifton succ 1937, Major RAF

1928
Charles Tuff Jnr 1928–63 (KCC)
    J – 1933
    S – 1934
    Kt 1953, Councillor KCC 1922,
    Alderman KCC 1934, Councillor RCC
    1900, Mayor of Rochester 1900

1929
Arthur Lambert Oswald 1929–42 (CRM)
    J – 1934
    S – 1935
Herbert Francis Whyman 1929–36 (CBC)
    Councillor CBC 1904, Mayor of
    Chatham 1905, 1920, 1921, 1922, 1929,
    1930, Alderman CBC 1908, Councillor
    KCC 1913–19, 1930–46, Freeman of the
    Borough of Chatham 1936

1931
Alfred Mark Davenport 1931–45 (GBC)
    J – 1936
    S – 1937
    Councillor GBC 1906, Alderman GBC
    1919, Mayor of Gillingham 1929, 1930,
    1931
Ernest Albert Gill 1931–53 (CRM, KCC)
    J – 1942
    S – 1943
    Councillor KCC 1936–49, Alderman
    KCC 1949–53

1934
Arthur Charles Davis, JP, DL 1934–45
    (CRM)
    Kt 1943, Bt 1946, Sheriff of Kent 1934,

Lord Mayor of London 1945, Hon
Colonel Royal Engineers (Territorial)
Hugh Garrard Tyrwhitt-Drake, JP, DL
1934–63 (MBC)
    J – 1937
    S – 1938
    Kt 1939, Sheriff of Kent 1956, Councillor
    MBC 1912, Mayor of Maidstone 1915,
    1923–4, 1928, 1930, 1934, 1939–43,
    1949, Alderman MBC 1934, Hon
    Freeman of the Borough of Maidstone,
    Councillor KCC 1933

1935
The Hon Wykeham Stanley Cornwallis, JP,
MC, KBE 1935–51 (KCC)
    J – 1948
    2nd Lord Cornwallis succ 1935, Lord
    Lieutenant of Kent 1944, Councillor
    KCC 1928–33, Alderman KCC 1933–38,
    Chairman of KCC 1935–36, Capt Royal
    Scots Greys

1936
Leslie Caldecott 1936–45 (CPLNM)
    J – 1938
    S – 1939

1937
Percy Ansell 1937–9 (CBC)
    Councillor CBC 1922, Mayor of Chatham
    1934
Richard Frederick Brain 1937–45 (CBC)
    J – 1941
    S – 1942
    Councillor CBC 1891, Alderman CBC
    1891, Councillor KCC 1938
Richard Mansfield Wakely 1937–43 (KCC)
    J – 1940
    S – 1941
    Councillor KCC 1910–29, Alderman
    KCC 1929–43

1940
William Rolfe Nottidge 1940–66 (KCC)
    J – 1944, 1951
    S – 1945, 1952
    Kt 1948, Councillor KCC 1928–34,
    Alderman KCC 1934–58, Chairman of
    KCC 1952–8
William James Webb, JP 1940–5 (CBC)
    J – 1943
    S – 1944
    Councillor CBC 1920, Alderman CBC
    1920, Mayor of Chatham 1919, Freeman

of the Borough of Chatham 1945,
Councillor KCC 1919

1941
Isaac Granville Winch, JP 1941–2 (RCC)
    Councillor RCC 1911, Alderman RCC
    1935, Mayor of Rochester 1919, 1920,
    1936

1942
William Edward R. Randall 1942–5 (RCC)
    Councillor RCC 1930, Councillor KCC
    1937

1943
Alfred Hinge 1943–51 (KCC)
    J – 1946
    S – 1947
    Councillor KCC 1929–41, Alderman
    KCC 1941–50
Frederick Charles A. Matthews 1943–5
(RCC)
    Councillor RCC 1920, Mayor of
    Rochester 1927
Sidney John Shippick 1943–51 (CRM)
    J – 1945
    S – 1946

1945
Moreton Thorpe Knight 1945–78 (CRM)
    J – 1947, 1963
    S – 1948–9, 1964–9

1946
Thomas Armstrong, JP 1946–8 (MBC)
    Councillor MBC 1921, Mayor of
    Maidstone 1929, 1953, Alderman MBC
    1938
Gerald Bensted 1946–57 (CPLNM)
    J – 1950
    S – 1951
Walter Blackmore 1946–8 (CBC)
    Councillor CBC 1933, Alderman CBC
    1945
Herbert James Clinch 1946–8 (RCC)
    Councillor RCC 1938, Alderman RCC
    1946
Bert Harker Dalton 1946–8 (GBC)
    Councillor GBC 1945–8
Edwin James 1946–9 (GBC)
    Councillor GBC 1945–9
Henry James Stearne 1946–51 (CBC)
    J – 1949
    S – 1950
    Councillor CBC 1926, Mayor of Chatham
    1935–7, 1946–7, Alderman CBC 1945,

Councillor KCC 1946
William George Weller 1946–8 (RCC)
  Councillor RCC 1945
1949
George Vernon C. Darley 1949–57,
  1963–73 (GBC, KCC)
  J – 1954
  S – 1954, 1955
  Councillor GBC 1947–50
  Councillor KCC 1952–64, Alderman
  KCC 1964–73
William Day Jnr 1949–54 (MBC)
  J – 1953
  Councillor MBC 1898, Mayor of
  Maidstone 1905, 1945, 1947, Alderman
  MBC 1945
Cyril Sherwin Knight, JP 1949–63,
  1967–72 (RCC, KCC)
  J – 1952
  S – 1953, 1954
  Councillor RCC 1937, Mayor of
  Rochester 1938–44, Alderman RCC 1949
James Presnail 1949–54 (CBC)
  Councillor CBC 1905, Alderman CBC
  1950
Charlie Henry R. Skipper 1949–63 (RCC)
  J – 1955
  S – 1956
  Councillor RCC 1946, Mayor of
  Rochester 1953, 1954, Alderman RCC
  1955, Councillor KCC 1949–58, 1967–70
Alfred John Andrew Woodcock 1949–63
  (GBC)
  J – 1956
  S – 1957
  Councillor GBC 1947–52, Alderman
  GBC 1952–7, Mayor of Gillingham
  1955–6, Councillor KCC 1951–2
1952
Frank Harold Lawrence 1952–4, 1957–60
  (CBC)
  Councillor CBC 1927, Alderman CBC
  1942, Mayor of Chatham 1947–53
Rupert Pratt 1952–60 (CRM)
George St Vincent Harris, CBE, MC, JP,
  DL 1952–75 (KCC)
  J – 1957
  S – 1958
  5th Baron Harris succ 1932, Vice-
  Lieutenant of Kent 1948–72, Capt
  late Royal East Kent Imperial Yeomanry

Sir Henry Joseph D'Avigdor Goldsmid,
  Bt, DL, JP, MC, DSO 1952–66 (KCC)
  J – 1958
  S – 1959
  MP for Walsall South 1955, Sheriff of
  Kent 1953, Councillor KCC 1946–51,
  Alderman KCC 1951–4, Major 4th Batt
  Queen's Own Royal West Kent Regiment
1953
Maurice Owen Gill 1953–4, 1961–75
  (KCC, CRM)
  J – 1964–9
  S – 1970
  Councillor RCC 1951
  Councillor KCC 1952
1954
Charles Gordon Larking 1954–60 (MBC)
  Councillor MBC 1922, Mayor of
  Maidstone 1931, 1944, 1950, Alderman
  MBC 1944, Councillor KCC 1937
1955
Leslie Doubleday, JP 1955–75 (KCC)
  J – 1959
  S – 1960
  Kt 1957, Sheriff of Kent 1942, 1951,
  Councillor KCC 1925–40, Alderman
  KCC 1940–74
William Newman 1955–7 (KCC)
Arthur Stanley Price 1955–7 (CBC)
  Councillor CBC 1944, Alderman CBC
  1951, Mayor of Chatham 1954–5
Frank Burdett Semple 1955–69 (CBC)
  J – 1960
  S – 1961
  Councillor CBC 1945, Alderman CBC
  1954, Mayor of Chatham 1957–8
1957
John Hanks Day, JP 1957–69 (CPLNM)
  J – 1961
  S – 1962
  Chairman of the Medway Lower
  Navigation Company, Lt 2nd Batt Royal
  West Kent Regiment 1914–19
1958
Henry Hobart M. Cuthbert 1958–63 (GBC)
  J – 1962
  S – 1963
  Councillor GBC 1947, Alderman GBC
  1952, Mayor of Gillingham 1953
George Wickham Pagett 1958–60 (KCC)
  Councillor KCC 1949–6

1961
Arthur Henry Clark 1961–8 (MBC)
    Councillor MBC 1940, Alderman MBC
    1952, Mayor of Maidstone 1954, 1960
Mary Turnbull Cox 1961–3 (CBC)
    Councillor CBC 1952
Edwin Henry H. Rhodes 1961–6 (KCC)
    Councillor KCC 1958–65

1964
Louis George T. Birch 1964–80 (GBC)
    J – 1970
    S – 1971
    Councillor GBC 1949–58, Alderman
    GBC 1958–73, Deputy Mayor of
    Gillingham 1959, 1965
Albert George C. Brown, JP 1964–78
    (CBC)
    S – 1974
    Councillor CBC 1949, Alderman CBC
    1954, Mayor of Chatham 1967, Freeman
    of Borough of Chatham 1974
Philip Frederick Cooper 1964–74 (GBC)
    J – 1971
    S – 1972, 1973
    Councillor GBC 1951–60, Alderman
    GBC 1960–7, Mayor of Gillingham
    1962, Bridge Clerk 1974–80
John Edward Evans 1964–74 (MBC)
    J – 1972, 1973
    Councillor MBC 1957, Mayor of
    Maidstone 1963, 1965, Capt RAEC
Albert Tawning 1964–6 (RCC)
    Councillor RCC 1962
Henry Wilson 1964–6 (RCC)
    Councillor RCC 1945, Alderman RCC
    1958, Mayor of Rochester 1959

1967
Maurice Huntley Cole 1967–75 (RCC)
    J – 1975
    Councillor RCC 1951, Mayor of
    Rochester 1966, Alderman RCC 1967
Robert Harold Cooper 1967–75 (KCC)
    Councillor KCC 1965–74
Ivor John Phillips, JP 1967–75 (RCC)
    Councillor RCC 1952, Mayor of
    Rochester 1960, 1961, Alderman RCC
    1967
Charles George Todd 1967–75 (KCC)
    J – 1974
    S – 1975
    Councillor KCC 1958–70, Alderman

KCC 1970–4, Chairman Kent Police
    Authority
1968
Percy Albert Barden 1968–75 (MBC)
    Councillor MBC 1960, Alderman MBC
    1965, Mayor of Maidstone 1966,
    Councillor KCC 1967
1970
Norman Staff, JP 1970–7 (MPA)
    S – 1976
John Samuel Thomas 1970–2 (CBC)
    Councillor CBC 1951, Alderman CBC
    1958, Mayor of Chatham 1959
1973
Robert Ernest Bean 1973–84 (CBC, RMC)
    Councillor CBC 1958, MP for Rochester
    and Chatham 1974–9, Councillor KCC
    1973
Maurice Fuller 1973–90 (KCC)
    J – 1976
    S – 1977–9
    Councillor KCC 1961–70, Alderman
    KCC 1970–4
Major Allan Wyndham Green, DL
    1973–81 (KCC)
    J – 1977–8
    Councillor KCC 1961–70
1974
Martin William J.G. Corps 1974–8 (MBC)
    Councillor MBC 1973–76, Mayor of
    Maidstone 1974–5
Michael Lewis 1974– (GBC)
    J – 1979
    S – 1980
    Councillor GBC 1960–91 (Leader
    1968–74, 1976–90)
1975
Stuart James Cox, JP, MD, 1975– (KCC)
    J – 1982
    S – 1983
    Councillor KCC 1970– , (Deputy Leader
    1989–92)
1976
Horace Hamilton Ashton 1976–7 (MBC)
    Councillor MBC 1973–7, Mayor of
    Maidstone 1975–6
The Right Hon Gavin, Lord Astor of Hever
    1976–8 (KCC) DL (Sussex), Sheriff of
    Sussex 1955, Lord Lieutenant of Kent,
    Capt Life Guards

Guy Stewart C. Clarabut, JP, DL, DSO, DSC 1976– (MPA)
    J – 1981
    S – 1982
    Commander RN
Stuart Fry 1976–8 (RMC)
    Councillor RCC 1956, Mayor 1965–6
Robert Haydon Goldsborough 1976–8 (KCC)
    Councillor KCC 1973–7
Trevor William Kemsley 1976– (KCC)
    J – 1980
    S – 1981
    Councillor KCC 1970–81
Gordon John Priestman 1976–8 (RMC)
    Councillor RMC 1974–87 (Leader 1974–6)

1977
Peter Waite 1977–8 (MBC)
    Councillor MBC 1976–9

1978
John Warren Bedson 1978–87 (MBC)
    J – 1983
    S – 1984
    Councillor MBC 1976–88

1979
Edward St John Brice, DL 1979–81 (KCC)
    Sheriff of Kent 1980, Lt Royal East Kents, Hon Colonel 39th (City of London) Signal Regiment (Special Committee) Volunteers 1991–
Reginald David Cox 1979–91 (RMC)
    J – 1985
    S – 1986
    Councillor KCC 1967–73
    Councillor RMC 1974–, Mayor 1981–2, 1993
Horace Waterton Lee, OBE, DL 1979–87 (KCC)
    J – 1984
    S – 1985
    Councillor KCC 1958–87
Thomas George Mason 1979–91 (RMC)
    J – 1986
    S – 1987
    Councillor KCC 1977–89
    Councillor RMC 1974–, Mayor 1984–5
Clive John Morman 1979–80 (RMC)
    Councillor RMC 1974–81 (Leader 1976–81)
Arthur Geoffrey Robinson, CBE,

1979–80, 1985–9 (MPA)
    Chairman Medway Ports Authority 1978–87
    Chairman British Ports Association
Gareth William M. Thomas 1979–84 (MBC)
    Councillor MBC 1976–84

1980
Kenneth Cooper, OBE 1980–4, 1988– (MPA)
    J – 1992–3
    Chief Executive Medway Ports Authority 1964–88, Marine Pilotage Commission 1980–5, Chairman National Association of Ports Employers 1985–9, Chairman European Association of Port Employers 1985–8, Chairman Medway Ports Authority 1988–92
Robert Filmer 1980–4 (RMC)
    Councillor RMC 1976–83 (Leader 1981–2)
Paul Edward J. Harriott 1980– (GBC)
    J – 1988
    S – 1989
    Councillor GBC 1962–, Mayor 1974

1982
Anthony Harry Hart, CBE, 1982–7 (KCC)
    Councillor KCC 1975–93 (Leader 1984–92)
Edward Moore, OBE, DL 1982– (KCC)
    J – 1987
    S – 1988
    Councillor KCC 1945–, Alderman KCC 1970–74, Chairman KCC 1981–3

1985
Gerald Chalker 1985–91 (RMC)
    Councillor RMC 1976–
Douglas McColl MacInnes, CBE 1985–91 (RMC)
    J – 1990
    Councillor RMC 1976–91 (Leader 1982–91)
Michael David Nightingale of Cromarty, OBE, FSA 1985– (MBC)
    J – 1989
    S – 1990–1
    Councillor Hollingbourne RDC 1961–74, Councillor MBC 1973– (Leader 1976–7), Mayor 1984–5, Councillor KCC 1973–7

1987
Ronald Foster 1987– (KCC)
    Mayor of Chatham 1965, Mayor of

Medway 1974, Councillor KCC 1979–93
John Alexander Spence 1987– (KCC)
  J – 1991
  S – 1992–3
  Councillor GBC 1961–72, Councillor
  KCC 1973–93

1988
Peter Victor Vincent 1988–90 (MPA)
Paula Gülen Yates 1988– (MBC)
  Councillor MBC 1984–92 (Leader
  1987–92)

1991
James Taylor Armstrong 1991– (RMC)
  Councillor RMC 1987–

Leslie Walter Brown 1991– (MPA)
Vernon Allan Hull 1991– (RMC)
  Councillor RMC 1983–
Ann Deborah Marsh 1991– (RMC)
  Councillor RMC 1987–
Sir Idris Pearce, CBE, TD, DL 1991–
  (KCC)
  Chairman English Estates
John Christopher Shaw 1991– (RMC)
  Councillor RMC 1983–7, 1988– (Leader
  1991–)

Appendix B

Rochester Bridge Accounts, 1398–1914

From the late fourteenth to the early sixteenth century the bridge wardens kept their annual accounts on parchment or paper rolls. Eighty such rolls survive for the years 1391–1508. For the next sixty-eight years there are only sporadic accounts of the bridge officers – clerk, surveyor, paymaster, and receiver – and accounts of the collection of tax and tolls in the 1550s and 1560s. Many of these rolls and pamphlets are incomplete rough accounts, from which the wardens' accounts presumably would have been compiled. For example, only incomplete expense accounts of paymaster John Burwell and receiver John Fowle, bound haphazardly in a volume of miscellaneous accounts, survive for the years 1547 to 1549, making totals for these years impossible to establish. Revised wardens' accounts resume following the Rochester Bridge Act 1576 and continue to the present day in a series broken only by three missing accounts during the Civil War.

Until 1754 the bridge wardens used the charge and discharge accounting method. In this accounting system, instead of recording actual monies received, the wardens for each year charged themselves for all rents due including rent arrears, any surplus balance carried forward from the previous year, and any miscellaneous income from fines, sales, or other proceeds. Against the total charge was set the discharge, all monies paid out month by month by the paymaster for labour and provisions. After subtracting the discharge from the charge to arrive at an initial balance, the wardens then asked that allowances be made for any rent arrears or debts unpaid. After the subtraction of allowances, any surplus in the final balance was then carried forward to the next year's charge. A deficit balance was not subtracted from the next year's charge; rather it was repaid as part of the provisions in the next year's discharge. In the tables which follow, figures in italics represent adjusted totals reflecting payment of parliamentary tax, repayment of debt to the accountant, or discrepancies discussed in the footnotes. In 1754 the bridge wardens adopted the income and expenditure accounting method.

As a result of these changes in accounting method and the inconsistencies and gaps in the early accounts, it has been impossible to present over 500 years of accounts in a consistent format. In the record of income and expenditure which follows in the first section of this appendix, then, there are three major groups: the medieval accounts from 1398 to 1558 with considerable gaps, the early modern accounts from 1576 to 1754 following the charge and discharge method, and the later modern accounts from 1754 to 1914 following the income and expenditure method. In the early accounts exact classification of receipts and expenditure is not always possible; thus the medieval figures should be regarded as close approximations. Moreover, as historical circumstances changed, so also did the subcategories of income and expenditure – receipts from alms and pardons giving way to interest on investments and expenses for the chapel and chaplains yielding to parliamentary taxes and loan repayments. Thus from time to time the subheadings for income and expenditure vary to reflect the changing interests of the Wardens and Assistants. Following the record of income and expenditure, the second section of this appendix lists the rental income from the bridge estate from 1576 to 1914 subdivided by location, and the third section of the appendix gives a further breakdown of expenditure on bridge repair and estate maintenance for the same period.

Receipts

	Land			Lease of boats and fishing			Custom of carts			Sales			Ferry			Alms and pardons			Other		
	£	s	d	£	s	d	£	s	d	£	s	d	£	s	d	£	s	d	£	s	d
1398–9	18	13	4	–	–	–	–	–	–		15	8	–	–	–	25	11	4½	–	–	–
1399–1400	75	19	7	–	–	–	–	–	–	–	–	–	–	–	–	14	2	11	–	–	–
1400–1	114	0	3½	–	–	–	–	–	–	–	–	–	–	–	–	–	–	–	–	–	–
1401–2	96	3	1	–	–	–	–	–	–	–	–	–	–	–	–	–	–	–	–	–	–
1402–3	116	9	2	–	–	–	–	–	–	–	–	–	–	–	–	–	–	–	–	–	–
1403–4	70	1	10	–	–	–	–	–	–	–	–	–	–	–	–	–	–	–	–	–	–
1404–5	63	4	4	–	–	–	–	–	–	–	–	–	–	–	–	–	–	–	–	–	–
1405–6	63	4	4	–	–	–	–	–	–	–	–	–	–	–	–	–	–	–	–	–	–
1406–7	63	4	4	–	–	–	–	–	–	–	–	–	–	–	–	–	–	–	–	–	–
1407–8	63	4	4	–	–	–	–	–	–	–	–	–	–	–	–	–	–	–	–	–	–
1409–10	57	10	2	–	–	–	–	–	–	–	–	–	–	–	–	109	18	7¾	60	3	4[1]
1410–11	67	0	4	–	–	–	–	–	–		1	0	–	–	–	43	15	5¼	14	6	8[2]
1411–12	89	17	8		17	3	–	–	–	–	–	–	–	–	–	35	0	4	–	–	–
1412–13	90	9	2	1	12	9	–	–	–	–	–	–	–	–	–	1	9	5	–	–	–
1413–14	90	1	8½	1	0	8	–	–	–	–	–	–	–	–	–	–	–	–	–	–	–
1414–15	88	4	9	2	7	8	–	–	–	–	–	–	–	–	–	60	1	11	–	–	–
1415–16	88	0	10	1	7	4	–	–	–	–	–	–	–	–	–	62	13	4	–	–	–
1423–4	96	10	11	1	0	0	–	–	–	–	–	–	–	–	–	111	12	0	–	–	–
1425–6	98	3	11	1	0	0	–	–	–	–	–	–	–	–	–	200	9	6	–	–	–
1426–7	73	3	0		15	0	–	–	–	–	–	–	–	–	–	12	0	6½	1	6	8[3]
1428–9	113	4	6	1	5	4	–	–	–	3	6	8	–	–	–	8	0	0	–	–	–
1429–30	101	0	8	1	1	0	–	–	–	–	–	–	–	–	–	17	0	0	–	–	–

[1] from money borrowed
[2] £14 of money borrowed, 6s. 8d. 'ressu de un maroner pur damage que il ffit a le pount'
[3] from the former farmer of Nashenden in lieu of repairs

Expenditure

	Bridgework £ s d	Wardens' salaries £ s d	Costs of administration[4] £ s d	Upkeep and improvement of property £ s d	Rents and taxes £ s d	Chapel and chaplains £ s d	Other £ s d
1398–9	42 9 3½	11 13 4	1 8	– – –	– – –	– – –	– – –
1399–1400	22 16 6	8 13 4	– – –	– – –	13 5½	39 6 2	– – –
1400–1	10 8 11	8 13 4	4 7 11	19 3½	21 0 4½	18 0 0	14 1 7½
1401–2	20 18 4	8 13 4	17 8	8 13 3¾	18 0 5¾	17 11 7½	16 19 6
1402–3	18 15 9	8 13 4	– – –	24 9 3	18 12 0	17 6 11	2 14 0
1403–4	11 4 5	8 13 4	6 2 6	– – –	19 10 5	16 14 0	3 15 5
1404–5	19 19 10¾	8 13 4	3 8	12 19 6	19 0 6¼	18 0 0	2 5 4
1405–6	30 7 3½	10 0 0	4 17 0	2 13 7	18 2 7	18 15 10½	2 12 0
1406–7	36 10 7	10 0 0	1 0	– – –	17 18 6	18 15 10	2 12 0
1407–8	40 6 10¾	10 0 0	3 4 8	– – –	18 19 4	18 15 10	2 12 0
1409–10	155 19 5¼	10 0 0	24 5 7½	4 1 4	17 12 7	12 10 7½	– – –
1410–11	87 14 3	10 0 0	20 4 5	1 7 8	17 12 7	12 16 6	3 5 4
1411–12	60 6 4½	14 0 0	10 18 9	12 13 11	4 11 7	12 19 1	18 0
1412–13	54 4 0¼	10 0 0	14 16 2	10 16 5¾	4 5 11	12 13 0½	– – –
1413–14	70 0 8¼	10 0 0	8 7 7	2 0 10	4 5 11	18 12 10	– – –
1414–15	100 10 6	10 0 0	12 19 9	5 14 1	4 5 11	18 13 1½	– – –
1415–16	117 19 4¾	10 0 0	8 5 2½	5 0 9	4 5 11	23 8 11	– – –
1423–4	132 18 5¼	10 0 0	14 6 2½	17 16 1	1 1 6	18 13 5	– – –
1424–5	40 16 3	10 0 0	14 3 7½	109 16 5½	1 1 6	19 0 2½	8 0 0
1425–6	252 2 6¼	10 0 0	12 12 4	31 0 6	1 7 6	18 16 6½	– – –
1426–7	50 11 3½	7 0 10	11 12 8	6 9 6	1 2 5	10 0 4	2 3 4
1428–9	58 13 3	10 0 0	12 12 10½	20 16 2	1 17 10	12 6 11	– – –

---

[4] including clerical and legal costs

	Land			Lease of boats and fishing			Custom of carts			Sales			Ferry			Alms and pardons			Other	
	£	s	d	£	s	d	£	s	d	£	s	d	£	s	d	£	s	d	£	s
1430–1	100	1	4½	1	1	0	–	–	–	–	–	–	–	–	–	12	6	8	7	3⁵
1435–6	114	18	9	10	0		–	–	–	4	4	10	–	–	–	15	7	8	–	– –
1438–9	123	3	3	10	0		–	–	–	2	4	0	–	–	–	33	6	8	–	– –
1439–40	123	15	2½	10	0		–	–	–	1	0	0	–	–	–	32	1	4	–	– –
1443–4	134	6	5	–	–	–	–	–	–		4	0	–	–	–	18	6	8	–	– –
1444–5	129	14	3		3	0	–	–	–	–	–	–	53	10	1	171	19	4	46	0 8⁶
1445–6	122	17	8	10	0			1	0	–	–	–	8	19	0	26	15	0	–	– –
1447–8	127	2	2	1	5	7	–	–	–	3	16	3	–	–	–	33	6	8	2	6 8⁶
1449–50	109	7	3	16	0		2	0	0	–	–	–	–	–	–	–	–	–		6 8⁷
1450–1	113	17	8	16	0		1	13	4	–	–	–	–	–	–	13	6	8		6 8⁷
1451–2	116	6	3	12	0		2	1	8	1	13	4	–	–	–	10	13	4		6 8⁷
1456–7	102	4	8	12	0		2	8	0	3	18	9	–	–	–	6	6	8		6 8⁷
1457–8	108	6	8		6	8	4	11	0	5	1	10	–	–	–	15	8	4		6 8⁷
1458–9	110	13	7½	13	4		1	18	10	3	13	4	–	–	–	17	0	0	–	– –
1460–1	101	9	4	–	–	–		?		4	16	0	–	–	–		6	8		6 8⁷
1463–4	97	6	11	13	4		6	0	0		2	8	–	–	–	–	–	–	–	– –
1466–7	94	3	6		6	8		18	6		9	5	–	–	–	–	–	–	–	– –
1467–8	100	4	0	13	4			9	10	4	13	2	–	–	–	4	11	8	–	– –
1469–70	112	13	3	10	0		2	1	5	1	6	10	–	–	–	–	–	–	–	– –
1471–2	98	18	0½	13	4			15	8	2	1	0	–	–	–	–	–	–	–	– –
1472–3	99	16	0½	11	4			14	4	–	–	–	–	–	–	12	3	11	1	8⁸
1473–4	106	1	9	14	8			8	0		3	10	–	–	–	1	16	5	–	1 0⁸
1475–6	101	14	0		3	0			8	–	–	–	–	–	–	–	–	–	–	– –
1476–7	99	19	9½		2	0		1	4	–	–	–	–	–	–	–	–	–	–	– –
1478–9	102	12	7	10	0			7	0	–	–	–	–	–	–		6	8	–	– –
1500	95	2	0¾	–	–	–	–	–	–	1	2	0	67	17	4	–	–	–	–	– –
1507–8	71	11	3	–	–	–	–	–	–		15	10	35	6	0	–	–	–	48	6 8⁹
1522–3¹⁰	96	13	9	inc. in sales			–	–	–		5	4¼	–	–	–	–	–	–	–	– –
1523–4¹⁰	96	13	9	inc. in sales			–	–	–		5	4¼	–	–	–	–	–	–	–	– –

5 'de tolnetis pro passagio diuersarum rerum venalium cariatarum per et subtus pontem licencia regia inde acquesita'
6 from repayment of debt received on a letter of obligation
7 from payment of arrears
8 'pro stacionibus erga le fflourdelice'
9 received from the prior of Leeds (one of the wardens). Perhaps part of this sum was from rents.
10 The account covers two years, and the figures shown are annual averages.

	Bridgework £ s d	Wardens' salaries £ s d	Costs of administration £ s d	Upkeep and improvement of property £ s d	Rents and taxes £ s d	Chapel and chaplains £ s d	Other £ s d
1430–1	55 9 9	10 0 0	9 13 0	– – –	4 0	13 5 0	– – –
1435–6	68 0 4	10 0 0	11 14 0	38 9 3½	1 5 6	11 13 10	– – –
1438–9	57 6 2½	6 13 4	12 17 0	7 16 0½	10 9 2¾	14 12 6½	– – –
1439–40	70 11 0½	6 13 4	13 5 6½	13 8 4½	10 9 2¾	13 9 3	– – –
1443–4	66 18 3	7 10 0	10 10 1	10 17 9½	13 3 3¾	20 1 5	– – –
1444–5	288 7 11½	10 0 0	22 4 2	33 16 1	13 3 3¼	18 10 5½	– – –
1445–6	182 9 1¼	10 0 0	11 9 0	12 4 1	12 11 4½	14 6 5	– – –
1447–8	48 3 0	10 0 0	7 5 6	15 8 4	9 8 8¾	17 2 10	– – –
1449–50	35 19 4½	10 0 0	8 7 8½	32 7 5	2 15 1	18 15 7	8
1450–1	49 0 2½	10 0 0	6 12 11½	22 0 1	2 15 1	19 0 1	1 0
1451–2	60 17 0½	10 0 0	6 11 7½	26 17 2	2 15 1	16 3 2½	1 0
1456–7	86 6 0½	10 0 0	12 3 11½	15 5 2	1 7 7	16 7 2	7 9 8
1457–8	58 0 11	7 10 0	5 11 3	23 9 4¾	1 13 0	12 16 11	1 0
1458–9	69 0 11¼	10 0 0	14 6 11	27 10 10	1 13 0	12 6 7	1 0
1460–1	35 3 4¾	10 0 0	9 8 7	26 16 0	?	12 4 5[11]	1 0
1463–4	46 17 11	10 0 0	7 6 8½	40 14 2½	1 13 0	18 0 5½	4 4
1466–7	57 8 8½	10 2 3¾	16 9 5½	14 19 10½	11 5 7	7 18 7½	– – –
1467–8	31 2 4½	10 0 0	6 10 1½	30 18 9¼	7 10 8	9 11 10	– – –
1469–70	45 5 8¼	10 0 0	6 13 4	33 13 5½	2 7 4	12 14 10½	– – –
1471–2	27 15 7	10 0 0	7 19 3	28 18 1¼	2 4 9	13 2 10	34 0 0
1472–3	26 3 3½	10 0 0	8 0 4	21 11 7½	2 14 11	12 17 3½	1 0 0
1473–4	32 15 1½	10 0 0	8 3 4	9 19 5½	3 10 3	12 11 0	– – –
1475–6	44 14 7½	8 6 8	6 6 0	15 10 3	2 8 1	12 14 10½	– – –
1476–7	75 8 2¾	6 13 4	5 11 0	13 13 0	2 4 3	15 10 7	– – –
1478–9	71 8 5½	16 16 8	8 12 6½	15 11 6¼	3 2 10	17 12 6	– – –
1500	394 0 6½	– – –	6 12 3	7 11 10	3 2 4	12 8 4½	– – –
1507–8	159 11 2	– – –	27 13 0[12]	11 3 8[13]	10 1	10 0 0	– – –
1522–3[14]	39 5 5¾	– – –	17 2 11	12 2 8	1 19 3¼	18 18 6	1 1
1523–4[14]	39 5 5¾	– – –	17 2 11	12 2 8	1 19 3¼	18 18 6	1 1

[11] excluding sacramental wine
[12] £19 19s. 5d. of 'necessary expenses' (unspecified) and £7 13s. 7d. of expenses 'in the lawe'
[13] £10 14s. 1d. of 'reparaciones' (unspecified) and 9s. 7d. for 'laborers at Tilbur(y) wall'
[14] average of two years' expenses

	Land £ s d	Lease of boats and fishing £ s d	Custom of carts £ s d	Sales £ s d	Ferry £ s d	Alms and pardons £ s d	Other £ s d
1544[15]	45 19 8	– – –	– – –	– – –	– – –	– – –	– – –
1544–45	54 6 4	– – –	– – –	– – –	– – –	– – –	– – –
1545–46	79 2 2	– – –	– – –	– – –	– – –	– – –	– – –
1546–47	96 8 8	– – –	– – –	– – –	– – –	– – –	– – –
1547–48	96 8 8	– – –	– – –	– – –	– – –	–– –	38 0 0
1549–50	78 6 8	– – –	– – –	9 4	– – –	– – –	– – –
1550–51	38 12 4	– – –	– – –	– – –	– – –	– – –	– – –
1555–56	92 12 7	– – –	– – –	– – –	– – –	2 10 0	– – –

Charge

CHARGE	Fine arrears £	Rent arrears £	Rent due £	Previous surplus £	Tolls, tax, fines, gifts, & sales £	TOTAL £
1576–77	–	–	87.2	–	316	403.2
1577–78[16]	–	27.4	272.9	–	178.5	478.8
1578–79	–	–	211.9	201.0	–	412.9
1579–80	–	–	213.0	228.6	–	441.6
1580–81	–	–	213.1	220.0	–	433.1
1581–82	–	–	214.4	180.8	4.0	399.2
1582–83	–	–	214.5	76.7	25.0	316.2
1583–84	–	–	215.8	28.1	56.7	300.6
1584–85	–	–	215.8	19.5	80.5	315.8
1585–86	–	–	215.8	71.4	6.8	294.0
1586–87	–	–	217.6	–	6.3	223.9
1587–88	–	–	217.6	6.8	5.0	229.4

[15] This account of paymaster John Burwell runs only from Midsummer to Michaelmas 1544.

[16] During 1577–78 the due date for rents was moved from Michaelmas to the Feast of the Annunciation. The rent arrears figure represents rents unpaid at Michaelmas 1576; the rents due figure represents eighteen months' rent from Michaelmas 1576 to the Annunciation 1578. Thereafter rents continue to be collected annually on Lady Day.

	Bridgework £ s d	Wardens' salaries £ s d	Costs of admini-stration £ s d	Mainten-ance £ s d	Rents and taxes £ s d	Chapel and chaplains £ s d	Other £ s d
1542–44[17]	20 17 5	— — —	2 6 8	6 4 9	3 4	7 11 1	40 2 9[18]
1544[19]	9 15 8	3 10 0	15 0	— — —	2 0 6	4 15 4	— — —
1544–45	61 8 5	— — —	3 18 6	2 5 5	4 6 1	19 1 2	— — —
1545–46	54 2 7	— — —	4 11 8	3 16 4	3 12 4	11 14 9	12 12 10[20]
1546–47	31 11 6	— — —	8 17 8	1 11 6	4 8 10	8 2 6	— — —
1549–50	73 5 1	— — —	3 0 4	— — —	1 1 1	— — —	— — —
1550–51[21]	40 17 11	— — —	30 0	— — —	— — —	— — —	— — —
1555–56	78 7 3	— — —	18 13 6	— — —	1 9 5	— — —	— — —
1557–58[22]	113 5 7	— — —	1 2 0	— — —	— — —	— — —	— — —

Discharge

DISCHARGE	Fine arrears £	Rent arrears £	Bridge and estate works £	Parliamentary tax rebates £	Deficit repaid £	Total £	BALANCE £
1576–77	–	27.4	458.4	–	–	485.8	(5.3)
1577–78	–	–	272.6	–	5.3	277.9	201.0
1578–79	–	–	184.3	–	–	184.3	228.6
1579–80	–	–	221.6	–	–	221.6	220.0
1580–81	–	–	252.3	–	–	252.3	180.8
1581–82	–	–	322.5	–	–	322.5	76.7
1582–83	–	–	288.1	–	–	288.1	28.1
1583–84	–	–	281.1	–	–	281.1	19.5
1584–85	–	–	244.4	–	–	244.4	71.4
1585–86	–	–	352.8	–	–	352.8	(58.8)
1586–87	5.0	2.0	150.3	–	58.8	216.1	6.8
1587–88	–	4.0	160.3	–	–	164.3	65.1

17 This account of surveyor John Turke runs from Michaelmas 1542 until Lady Day 1544 and contains expenses only.
18 arrears from last account.
19 This account of paymaster John Burwell runs from Midsummer to Michaelmas 1544.
20 arrears from last account.
21 According to the heading this account should run from 18 May 1550 to 18 May 1551. The end of the account, however, is missing, the last payment being dated Michaelmas 1550.
22 These accounts of paymaster Nicholas Brydges record only expenses from 4 March 1557 to 29 September 1558.

CHARGE	Fine arrears £	Rent arrears £	Rent due £	Previous surplus £	Tolls, tax, fines, gifts, & sales £	TOTAL £
1588–89	–	–	220.6	65.1	4.0	289.7
1589–90	–	1.0	226.6	79.6	1.5	308.8
1590–91	–	–	227.5	65.1	5.0	297.5
1591–92	–	–	227.5	71.4	–	298.9
1592–93	–	12.0[23]	227.5	96.5	26.7	362.7
1593–94	5.5[24]	23.8[24]	228.1	69.6	13.3	340.3
1594–95	9.0	25.6	228.1[25]	–	5.5	268.2
1595–96	14.5	26.8	242.7	34.2	4.7	322.9
1596–97	18.5	8.0	242.7	12.3	5.0	286.5
1597–98	23.5	12.3	244.7	70.1	3.5	354.1
1598–99	27.0	14.3	248.3	2.7	2.0	294.3
1599–1600	29.0	14.3	249.3	36.3	2.0	330.9
1600–01	31.0	15.3	249.3	57.8	–	353.4
1601–02	34.5	18.3[26]	250.1	89.6	2.0	394.5
1602–03	–[27]	14.0	251.3	76.0	–	341.3
1603–04	–	15.0	251.8	105.9	3.0	375.7
1604–05	–	16.0	252.2	214.2	1.5	483.9
1605–06	–	17.0	262.7	189.4	2.0	471.1
1606–07	–	19.6	262.7	116.9	2.5	401.7
1607–08	–	19.0	262.7	109.3	–	391.0
1608–09	–	20.0	263.0	138.0	–	421.0
1609–10	–	21.0	266.3	149.4	2.5	439.2
1610–11	–	22.0	266.8	155.8	1.0	445.6
1611–12	–	23.0	271.8	222.4	2.5	519.7
1612–13	–	24.0	276.0	253.5	–	553.5
1613–14	–	25.0	276.0	131.7	3.5	436.2

[23] This figure represents six years of rent arrears for land in Sheppey which did not appear in the charge between 1586 and 1592.

[24] These arrears are first accounted for this year by the new paymaster Philip Symonson.

[25] The rental for 1594–95 totals £239.2; however, that figure has been crossed out in the charge and the previous year's rental of £228.1 inserted.

[26] The charge includes the following note writing off arrears amounting to £5 6s.8d. owed by the late Bridge Clerk William Beane: 'The said Beane died so poore that this debt cannot be paid, so it is forgiven and is to be omytted in all future Accompts.'

[27] The charge includes the following note writing off £38 in unpaid fines for parishes not appearing at the election: 'This some of xxxviij^li is omitted out of this accompt and to be left out of any future Accompt bycause by the negligence of the Collectors it doth not appear who hath paid and who not.'

DISCHARGE	Fine arrears £	Rent arrears £	Bridge and estate works £	Parliamentary tax rebates £	Deficit repaid £	Total £	BALANCE £
1588–89	–	2.0	208.1	–	–	210.1	79.6
1589–90	–	2.0	241.7	–	–	243.7	65.1
1590–91	–	2.0	224.1	–	–	226.1	71.4
1591–92	–	2.0	200.4	–	–	202.4	96.5
1592–93	–	12.5	280.5	–	–	293.0	69.7
1593–94	9.0	24.8	326.4	–	–	360.2	(19.9)
1594–95	14.5	25.6	193.9	–	–	234.0	34.2
1595–96	18.5	10.3	261.9	–	19.9	310.6	12.3
1596–97	23.5	12.3	180.6	–	–	216.4	70.1
1597–98	20.0	14.3	317.1	–	–	351.4	2.7
1598–99	31.0	16.3	210.7	–	–	258.0	36.3
1599–1600	31.0	14.3	227.8	–	–	273.1	57.8
1600–01	26.0	15.3	222.5	–	–	263.8	89.6
1601–02	36.5	22.3	259.7	–	–	318.5	76.0
1602–03	–	15.0	220.4	–	–	235.4	105.9
1603–04	–	16.0	145.5	–	–	161.5	214.2
1604–05	–	17.0	277.5	–	–	294.5	189.4
1605–06	–	18.0	336.2	–	–	354.2	116.9
1606–07	–	19.0	273.4	–	–	292.4	109.3
1607–08	–	20.0	232.7	–	–	252.7	138.3[28]
1608–09	–	21.0	250.6	–	–	271.6	149.4
1609–10	–	22.0	261.4	–	–	283.4	155.8
1610–11	–	23.0	200.2	–	–	223.2	222.4
1611–12	–	24.0	242.2	–	–	266.2	253.5
1612–13	–	29.0	259.9	–	–	288.9	264.6[29]
1613–14	3.5	26.0	313.9	–	–	343.4	92.8

[28] The balance of £138 0s.7d. instead of £138 7s.7d. is incorrectly entered at the foot of the 1607–08 accounts and carried forward to the 1608–09 accounts.

[29] Unpaid election fines amounting to £14 5s.0d. are written off, and repayment of debts owed by Bridge Clerk Hugh Southerne amounting to £118 12s.6d. are rescheduled this year, reducing the balance carried forward to £131 14s.4d. Over the next twelve years the debt is repaid in installments, making the rent arrears received each year £13 6s.8d. higher than that allowed in the discharge.

CHARGE	Fine arrears £	Rent arrears £	Rent due £	Previous surplus £	Tolls, tax, fines, gifts, & sales £	TOTAL £
1614–15	–	44.6	276.0	92.8	–	413.4
1615–16	–	42.3	276.9	71.6	–	390.8
1616–17	–	46.0	277.0	187.1	–	510.1
1617–18	–	44.3	277.0	98.1	–	419.4
1618–19	–	39.6	277.0[30]	198.9	–	515.5
1619–20	–	27.6	289.7	235.7	0.5	553.5
1620–21	–	28.7	290.5	–	–	319.2
1621–22	–	35.4	292.3	19.4	20.2	367.3
1622–23	–	22.0	294.9	36.4	–	553.3
1623–24	–	22.6	294.9	31.7	–	349.2
1624–25	–	22.9	295.8	92.5	–	411.2
1625–26	–	2.6	301.5	138.5	–	442.6
1626–27	–	7.1	305.0	187.2	–	499.3
1627–28	–	23.0	305.4	261.9	–	590.3
1628–29	–	2.7	307.6	93.0	–	403.3
1629–30	–	4.9	310.4	112.5	–	427.8
1630–31	–	2.7	310.4	108.7	–	421.8
1631–32	–	–	311.0	84.7	–	395.7
1632–33	–	3.7	319.6	91.3	–	414.6
1633–34	–	9.7	333.8	42.0	–	385.5
1634–35	–	2.0	334.4	104.9	–	441.3
1635–36	–	2.0	334.6	192.6	–	529.3
1636–37	–	2.0	335.3	168.0	–	505.3
1637–38	–	2.0	340.3	161.3	13.5	517.1
1638–39	–	2.0	340.8	175.2	3.5	521.5
1639–40	–	18.7	345.4	130.4	–	494.5
1640–41	–	2.0	345.4	193.0	–	540.4
1641–42	–	5.3	357.2	213.4	–	575.9
1642–43	–	11.3	364.6	224.9	–	600.8
1643–44	–	15.3	364.7	178.0	–	558.0
1644–45	–	–[31]	380.1	230.1	–	610.2
1645–46	–	16.3	383.8	220.3	–	620.4

[30] The 1618–19 rental totals £278 9s.3d., but the charge records rent receipts of only £276 19s.3d as in the three previous years.

[31] The £4.1 allowed for rent arrears in 1643–44 does not appear in the charge for 1644–45.

DISCHARGE	Fine arrears £	Rent arrears £	Bridge and estate works £	Parliamentary tax rebates £	Deficit repaid £	Total £	BALANCE £
1614–15	–	27.5	314.3	–	–	341.8	71.6
1615–16	–	31.3	172.4	–	–	203.7	187.1
1616–17	–	30.0	382.0	–	–	412.0	98.1
1617–18	–	32.0	188.5	–	–	220.5	198.9
1618–19	–	14.4	265.4	–	–	279.8	235.7
1619–20	–	15.3	555.5	–	–	570.8	(17.3)
1620–21	–	16.9	*265.6*	–	17.3	299.8	19.4
1621–22	–	20.0	310.9	–	–	330.9	36.4
1622–23	–	22.7	298.9	–	–	321.6	31.7
1623–24	–	22.9	233.8	–	–	256.7	92.5
1624–25	–	2.5	270.2	–	–	272.7	138.5
1625–26	–	7.1	248.3	–	–	255.4	187.2
1626–27	–	23.0	214.4	–	–	237.4	261.9
1627–28	–	3.0	494.3	–	–	497.3	93.0
1628–29	–	4.9	285.9	–	–	290.8	112.5
1629–30	–	2.7	316.4	–	–	319.1	108.7
1630–31	–	0.2	336.9	–	–	337.1	84.7
1631–32	–	3.7	300.7	–	–	304.4	91.3
1632–33	–	9.7	342.9	–	–	352.6	62.0
1633–34	–	2.0	278.6	–	–	280.6	104.9
1634–35	–	2.0	246.7	–	–	248.7	192.6
1635–36	–	2.0	359.3	–	–	361.3	168.0
1636–37	–	2.0	342.0	–	–	344.0	161.3
1637–38	–	2.0	339.9	–	–	341.9	175.2
1638–39	–	18.7	372.4	–	–	391.1	130.4
1639–40	–	2.0	299.5	–	–	301.5	193.0
1640–41	–	5.3	321.7	–	–	327.0	213.4
1641–42	–	11.3	339.7	–	–	351.0	224.9
1642–43	–	15.3	407.5	–	–	422.8	178.0
1643–44	–	4.1	323.7	–	–	327.8	230.2
1644–45	–	16.3	347.8	25.8	–	389.9	220.3
1645–46	–	25.7	*383.3*	31.8	–	440.8	179.6

CHARGE	Fine arrears £	Rent arrears £	Rent due £	Previous surplus £	Tolls, tax, fines, gifts, & sales £	TOTAL £
1646–47	–	34.0[32]	385.2	179.6	–	598.8
1647–48	–	42.9	385.2	189.0	–	617.1
1648–49	–	60.9	393.1	73.3	–	527.3
1649–50	–	45.9	393.2	–	24.1	463.2
1650–51	16.0	25.3	398.0[33]	19.1	–	458.4
1651–52	–	18.9	403.9	82.5	–	505.3
1652–53[34]						
1653–54						
1654–55	–	39.7	412.6	–	–	452.3
1655–56[35]						
1656–57	–	20.7	412.9	–	1.0	434.6
1657–58	–	9.8	415.4	–	–	425.2
1658–59	–	66.1	415.8	92.0	–	573.9
1659–60	–	45.4	427.4	239.9	–	712.7

CHARGE	Rent arrears £	Rent due £	Previous balance £	Interest, sales & proceeds £	TOTAL £
1660–61	44.2	434.2	330.2	–	808.6
1661–62	37.1	437.9	469.3	–	944.3
1662–63	35.8	441.9	559.6	–	1037.3
1663–64	36.3	442.0	631.9	–	1110.2
1664–65	29.2	442.0	720.1	–	1191.3
1665–66	32.2.	442.0	797.3	5.3	1276.8

[32] The arrears in this year's charge include £10 still owed by Peter Bucke, who was warden in 1644–45.

[33] The total rents this year should equal £399 3s.8d., but both the rental and the charge have an incorrect total of £398 0s.4d.

[34] Accounts for 1652–53 and 1653–54 are missing.

[35] Accounts for 1655–56 are missing.

DISCHARGE	Fine arrears £	Rent arrears £	Bridge and estate works £	Parliamentary tax rebates £	Deficit repaid £	Total £	BALANCE £
1646–47[36]	–	28.8	*361.8*	19.2	–	*409.8*	*189.0*
1647–48	–	42.9	*474.5*	26.8	–	543.8	73.3
1648–49	–	60.9	*454.2*	54.9	–	570.0	(42.7)
1649–50	–	45.9	*377.1*	67.0	–	490.0	(26.8)[37]
1650–51	–	25.3	*293.5*	57.1	–	375.9	82.5
1651–52	–	18.9	*443.9*	76.3	–	539.1	(33.8)
1652–53							
1653–54	(46.4)						
1654–55	–	39.7	*352.6*	26.4	46.4	465.1	(12.8)
1655–56	(17.1)						
1656–57	–	8.7	*343.7*	30.9	17.1	400.4	34.2[38]
1657–58	–	10.1	*305.3*	17.8	–	333.2	92.0
1658–59	–	45.4	*277.0*	11.6	–	334.0	239.9
1659–60	–	44.2	*318.3*	20.0	–	382.5	330.2

DISCHARGE	Rent arrears £	Bridge and estate works £	Unspecified payments £	Total £	BALANCE £
1660–61	37.1	302.2	–	339.3	469.3
1661–62	35.8	348.9	–	384.7	559.6
1662–63	36.3	369.1	–	405.4	631.9
1663–64	29.2	360.9	–	390.1	720.1
1664–65	32.2	361.8	–	394.0	797.3
1665–66	35.2	433.4	–	468.6	808.2

36 The accounts and rental for 1646–47 are bound out of order. In addition, there were two paymasters that year: John Atkins who returned accounts for months 1–3 and 7–9 and Philip Ward who returned accounts for months 4–6 and 10–12. In his accounts for provisions Atkins made four payments to Ward totalling £209 16s.5d., out of which Ward made his payments for labour and provisions. Both paymasters claimed the full paymaster's fee of £20 18s.4d., but Ward's claim was disallowed by the auditors. Both paymasters show their total discharge and balance. The adjusted figures for this year's discharge subtract the £209 16s.5d. from Atkins account and divide it between labour and provisions according to Ward's account. The balance carried forward is the sum of both paymaster's balances plus the £20 18s.4d. disallowed by the auditors and subtracted from Ward's discharge.

37 The 1648–49 deficit of £42 14s.1d. was not repaid this year, nor was the 1649–50 deficit of £26 16s.1d. repaid in 1650–51. Instead, a surplus of £19 2s.3d. before allowances for rent arrears was carried forward to the 1650–51 charge.

38 Following the death of paymaster John Atkins, this balance was not carried forward to the next year's accounts but appears in the arrears for 1658–59.

CHARGE	Rent arrears £	Rent due £	Previous balance £	Interest, sales & proceeds £	TOTAL £
1666–67	35.2	442.3	808.2	4.9	1290.6
1667–68	38.3	442.6	856.0	4.0	1340.9
1668–69	41.2	443.8	905.0	13.0	1403.0
1669–70	*23.8*	444.0	898.6	5.2	1371.6
1670–71	26.9	445.0	983.2	5.0	1460.1
1671–72	*18.9*	446.4	1017.1	5.2	1487.6
1672–73	*20.9*	446.9	1099.6	3.8	1571.2
1673–74	17.9	446.9	1012.2	27.6	1504.6
1674–75	36.8	447.1	705.1	20.0	1209.0
1675–76	24.4	447.5	381.5	15.3	868.7
1676–77	19.4	447.9	295.8	15.0	778.1
1677–78	16.5	447.8	216.2	10.0	690.5
1678–79	19.5	447.8	114.3	6.5	588.1
1679–80	*24.7*	448.0	135.8	38.2	646.7
1680–81	13.1	449.0	25.7	50.5	538.3
1681–82	35.0	449.0	21.5	18.3	523.8
1682–83	32.8	450.2	46.5	–	529.5
1683–84	55.5	452.5	48.9	–	556.97
1684–85	40.0	453.7	118.4	–	612.1
1685–86	33.5	454.5	116.5	–	604.5
1686–87	75.5	456.0	211.2	–	742.7
1687–88	100.1	456.7	239.2	–	796.0
1688–89	85.3	457.3	187.1	–	729.7
1689–90	124.5	457.5	203.6	–	785.6
1690–91	163.5	461.4	242.8	–	868.7
1691–92	270.7	461.4	162.5	–	894.6
1692–93	279.7	461.8	196.3	2.0	939.8
1693–94	243.1	462.5	166.6	18.2	890.4
1694–95	246.6	462.7	136.8	–	846.1
1695–96	153.0	463.0	283.7	–	899.7
1696–97	251.0	464.5	134.8	–	850.3
1697–98	222.3	464.7	142.5	–	829.5
1698–99	147.6	464.7	204.1	–	816.4
1699–1700	104.5	465.4	365.0	2.0	936.9
1700–01	123.2	466.7	369.8	–	959.7
1701–02	84.1	466.7	442.4	–	993.2

DISCHARGE	Rent arrears £	Bridge and estate works £	Unspecified payments £	Total £	BALANCE £
1666–67	38.3	396.3	–	434.6	856.0
1667–68	41.2	394.7	–	435.9	905.0
1668–69	39.4	465.0	–	504.4	898.6
1669–70	26.9	361.5	–	388.4	983.2
1670–71	17.5	425.5	–	443.0	1017.1
1671–72	20.5	367.5	–	388.0	1099.6
1672–73	17.9	541.1	–	559.0	1012.2
1673–74	36.8	762.7	–	799.5	705.1
1674–75	24.4	803.1	–	827.5	381.5
1675–76	19.4	553.5	–	572.9	295.8
1676–77	16.5	545.4	–	561.9	216.2
1677–78	19.5	556.7	–	576.2	114.3
1678–79	30.3	392.0	30.0	452.3	135.8
1679–80	13.1	577.7	30.2	621.0	25.7
1680–81	35.0	481.8	–	516.8	21.5
1681–82	32.8	444.5	–	477.3	46.5
1682–83	55.5	418.7	6.4	480.6	48.9
1683–84	40.0	398.5	–	438.5	118.4
1684–85	33.5	462.1	–	495.6	116.5
1685–86	75.5	317.8	–	393.3	211.2
1686–87	100.1	403.4	–	503.5	239.2
1687–88	85.3	523.6	–	608.9	187.1
1688–89	124.5	401.6	–	526.1	203.6
1689–90	163.5	379.3	–	542.8	242.8
1690–91	270.7	435.5	–	706.2	162.5
1691–92	279.7	418.6	–	698.3	196.3
1692–93	243.1	530.1	–	773.2	166.6
1693–94	246.6	507.0	–	753.6	136.8.
1694–95	153.0	409.4	–	562.4	283.7
1695–96	251.0	513.9	–	765.0	134.8
1696–97	222.3	485.5	–	707.8	142.5
1697–98	147.6	477.8	–	625.4	204.1
1698–99	104.5	346.9	–	451.4	365.0
1699–1700	123.2	443.9	–	567.1	369.8
1700–01	84.1	433.2	–	517.3	442.4
1701–02	108.9	386.5	–	495.4	497.8

CHARGE	Rent arrears £	Rent due £	Previous balance £	Interest, sales & proceeds £	TOTAL £
1702–03	108.9	467.6	497.8	1.3	1075.6
1703–04	172.4	469.3	486.3	–	1128.0
1704–05	160.9	469.7	526.3	–	1156.9
1705–06	126.8	469.7	537.3	0.3	1134.1
1706–07	161.5	471.2	420.3	–	1053.0
1707–08	160.7	472.0	311.8	–	944.5
1708–09	147.7	472.9	399.0	–	1019.6
1709–10	127.8	474.3	295.2	–	897.3
1710–11	81.0	474.4	322.8	–	878.2
1711–12	153.0	475.4	329.1	–	957.5
1712–13	112.5	475.8	345.3	0.1	933.7
1713–14	92.4	476.4	399.5	–	968.3
1714–15	98.1	476.5	395.4	–	970.0
1715–16	89.1	476.5	391.4	0.6	957.6
1716–17	132.1	476.5	266.2	–	874.8
1717–18	70.8	479.2	257.0	–	807.0
1718–19	102.6	502.6	289.1	–	894.3
1719–20	102.5	522.5	318.5	–	943.5

CHARGE	Rent arrears £	Rent due £	Previous balance £	Sales & proceeds £	Interest £	TOTAL £
1720–21	109.5	525.5	389.3	–	–	1024.3
1721–22	128.6	539.5	403.6	–	–	1071.7
1722–23	154.3	546.5	417.7	–	–	1118.5
1723–24	116.4	547.1	464.8	–	–	1128.3
1724–25	117.9	554.1	392.0	–	33.8	1097.8
1725–26	130.1	589.4	276.2	–	21.0	1016.7
1726–27	130.2	589.4	310.0	–	33.0	1062.6
1727–28	*104.5*	601.4	217.5	–	28.5	951.9
1728–29	114.3	601.4	166.7	–	24.0	906.4
1729–30	138.5	601.5	279.9	–	32.0	1051.9
1730–31	120.3	611.3	222.7	–	49.6	1003.9
1731–32	114.6	637.1	280.7	–	60.7	1093.1
1732–33	190.0	637.1	300.5	–	29.7	1157.3

DISCHARGE	Rent arrears £	Bridge and estate works £	Unspecified payments £	Total £	BALANCE £
1702–03	172.4	416.9	–	589.3	486.3
1703–04	160.9	440.8	–	601.7	526.3
1704–05	126.8	492.8	–	619.6	537.3
1705–06	161.5	552.3	–	713.8	420.3
1706–07	160.7	580.5	–	741.2	311.8
1707–08	147.7	397.8	–	545.5	399.0
1708–09	127.8	596.6	–	724.4	295.2
1709–10	81.0	493.5	–	574.5	322.8
1710–11	153.0	396.1	–	549.1	329.1
1711–12	112.5	499.7	–	612.2	345.3
1712–13	92.4	441.8	–	534.2	399.5
1713–14	98.1	474.8	–	572.9	395.4
1714–15	89.1	489.5	–	578.6	391.4
1715–16	132.1	559.3	–	691.4	266.2
1716–17	70.8	547.0	–	617.8	257.0
1717–18	102.6	415.3	–	517.9	289.1
1718–19	102.5	473.3	–	575.8	318.5
1719–20	109.5	444.7	–	554.2	389.3

DISCHARGE	Rent arrears £	Bridge and estate works £	Investments £	Total £	BALANCE £
1720–21	128.6	492.1	–	620.7	403.6
1721–22	154.3	499.7	–	654.0	417.7
1722–23	116.4	537.3	–	653.7	464.8
1723–24	117.9	416.2	202.2	736.3	392.0
1724–25	130.1	482.8	208.7	821.6	276.2
1725–26	130.2	576.5	–	706.7	310.0
1726–27	121.3	516.4	207.4	845.1	217.5
1727–28	114.3	670.9	–	785.2	166.7
1728–29	138.5	488.0	–	626.5	279.9
1729–30	120.3	500.2	208.7	829.2	222.7
1730–31	114.6	608.6	–	723.2	280.7
1731–32	190.0	602.6	–	792.6	300.5
1732–33	54.2	770.5	–	824.7	332.6

CHARGE	Rent arrears £	Rent due £	Previous balance £	Sales & proceeds £	Interest £	TOTAL £
1733–34	54.2	637.8	332.6	–	58.3	1082.9
1734–35	*207.5*	632.6	99.3	–	27.5	966.9
1735–36	185.9	632.6	183.4	–	28.0	1029.9
1736–37	233.6	629.9	137.6	6.8	28.0	1035.9
1737–38	53.0	630.7	72.5	–	27.0	783.2
1738–39	155.4	628.2	72.5[39]	–	26.1	930.0
1739–40	158.7	628.2	13.0	389.5	26.1	1215.5
1740–41	*250.3*	628.2	81.8	1.7	12.0	974.0
1741–42	221.0	640.9	(1.1)	357.8	–	1218.6
1742–43	283.1	642.4	263.3	8.5	–	1197.3
1743–44	269.6	642.4	391.3	7.6	–	1310.9
1744–45	264.9	648.9	429.3	14.7	–	1357.8
1745–46	270.4	648.9	385.4	12.2	–	1316.9.
1746–47	373.4	754.4	243.8	47.5	–	1419.1
1747–48	458.7	752.4	261.4	48.0	–	1520.5.
1748–49	638.9[40]	725.9	106.8	41.7	–	1513.3
1749–50	*313.7*	704.2	103.8	30.5	–	1152.2
1750–51	*357.1*	737.7	345.8	8.8	–	1449.4
1751–52	*364.9*	737.7	448.6	119.1	7.0	1677.3
1752–53	*304.8*	794.5	656.2	67.2	14.0	1836.7
1753–54	*299.5*	800.3	747.6	152.1	423.0[41]	2422.5

INCOME	Rents received + Sales £	of which Rent due £	Previous balance £	Interest £	Sale of investments £	TOTAL £
1754–55	1091.0	[801.3]	964.0	42.0	–	2097.0
1755–56	966.8	[792.3]	736.3	63.0	–	1766.1
1756–57	998.4	[795.8]	719.2	77.0	–	1794.6
1757–58	894.1	[793.8]	704.2	45.5	–	1643.8
1758–59	961.0	[801.4]	910.6	90.2	–	1961.8
1759–60	1092.6	[801.4]	622.8	156.0	–	1871.4

[39] Incorrect balance of £72.5 entered instead of £74.7.
[40] From 1748–53, rent arrears of £881.9 were written off.
[41] Capital value of the previous year's purchase of Bank Stock included in the Charge.

DISCHARGE	Rent arrears £	Bridge and estate works £	Investments £	Total £	BALANCE £
1733–34	212.6	771.0	–	983.6	99.3
1734–35	185.9	597.6	–	783.5	183.4
1735–36	233.6	658.7	–	892.3	137.6
1736–37	53.0	910.3	–	963.4	72.5
1737–38	155.4	553.1	–	708.5	74.7
1738–39	158.7	758.3	–	917.0	13.0
1739–40	252.3	881.4	–	1133.7	81.8
1740–41	221.0	754.1	–	975.1	(1.1)
1741–42	283.1	672.2	–	955.3	263.3
1742–43	269.6	536.4	–	806.0	391.3
1743–44	264.9	616.7	–	881.6	429.3
1744–45	270.4	702.0	–	972.4	385.4
1745–46	373.4	699.7	–	1073.1	243.8
1746–47	458.7	699.0	–	1157.7	261.4
1747–48	638.9	774.8	–	1413.7	106.8
1748–49	711.4	698.1	–	1409.5	103.8
1749–50	376.4	430.0	–	806.4	345.8
1750–51	452.1	548.7	–	1000.8	448.6
1751–52	305.6	715.5	–	1021.1	656.2
1752–53	376.9	712.2	–	1089.1	747.6
1753–54	424.7	398.5	635.3	1458.5	964.0

EXPENDITURE	Bridge and estate works £	Investments £	Total £	BALANCE £	Rent arrears £
1754–55	525.0	835.7	1360.7	736.3	464.8
1755–56	651.4	395.5	1046.9	719.2	467.2
1756–57	735.4	355.0	1090.4	704.2	381.3
1757–58	372.7	360.5	733.2	910.6	376.3
1758–59	775.0	564.0	1339.0	622.8	421.0
1759–60	1221.0	318.0	1539.0	332.4	351.9

INCOME	Rents received + Sales £	of which Rent due £	Previous balance £	Interest £	Sale of investments £	TOTAL £
1760–61	683.3	[801.4]	332.4	108.0	–	1123.7
1761–62	1231.2	[805.4]	147.2	108.0	–	1486.4
1762–63	1019.8	[803.9]	82.4	99.0	360.3	1561.5
1763–64	941.1	[803.9]	226.0	81.0	1037.0	2285.1
1764–65	847.8	[805.5]	417.3	57.0	165.5	1487.6
1765–66	833.9	[805.5]	203.5	45.0	354.7	1437.1
1766–67	969.0	[811.1]	222.2	42.0	–	1233.2
1767–68	1102.6	[827.0]	112.5	42.0	–	1257.1
1768–69	1052.3	[823.8]	267.4	42.0	–	1361.7
1769–70	1151.0	[825.3]	260.2	42.0	–	1453.2
1770–71	987.2	[836.0]	406.1	48.0		1441.3
1771–72	1043.2	[840.6]	419.7	48.0		1510.9
1772–73	986.3	[897.0]	143.6	48.0		1177.9
1773–74	1269.9	[922.0]	36.9	48.0		1354.8
1774–75	1258.8	[914.0]	341.5	48.0		1647.8
1775–76	1002.0	[914.5]	682.6	48.0		1732.6
1776–77	1067.5	[925.8]	772.7	55.5		1895.7
1777–78	1132.3	[925.8]	621.6	63.0		1816.9
1778–79	1356.1	[925.8]	550.7	63.0		1969.8
1779–80	1154.1	[937.5]	776.7	81.0		2011.8
1780–81	1221.3	[937.5]	682.7	81.0		1985.0
1781–82	1241.2	[946.0]	1080.5	110.0		2432.7
1782–83	1055.4	[946.0]	1074.7	141.0		2271.1
1783–84	1065.5	[946.0]	541.0	141.0		1747.5
1784–85	942.8	[946.5]	893.7	156.0		1992.5
1785–86	1154.2	[946.7]	874.2	177.0		2205.4
1786–87	1150.4	[947.7]	671.6	177.0		1999.0
1787–88	1307.9	[947.7]	876.0	177.0		2360.9
1788–89	1282.9	[962.4]	1231.0	193.0		2706.9
1789–90	1253.8	[966.4]	1245.8	208.0		2707.6

EXPENDITURE	Bridge and estate works £	Investments £	Total £	BALANCE £	Rent arrears £
1760–61	976.5	–	976.5	147.2	589.6
1761–62	1404.0	–	1404.0	82.4	433.1
1762–63	1335.5	–	1335.5	226.0	348.5
1763–64	1867.8	–	1867.8	417.3	334.3
1764–65	1284.1	–	1284.1	203.5	391.6
1765–66	1214.9	–	1214.9	222.2	409.1
1766–67	1120.7	–	1120.7	112.5	447.1
1767–68	989.7	–	989.7	267.4	391.2
1768–69	1101.5	–	1101.5	260.2	295.5
1769–70	1047.1	–	1047.1	406.1	265.7
1770–71	849.3	172.3	1021.6	419.7	277.8
1771–72	1367.3	–	1367.3	143.6	286.0
1772–73	1141.0	–	1141.0	36.9	260.7
1773–74	1013.3	–	1013.3	341.5	197.0
1774–75	965.2	–	965.2	682.6	77.6
1775–76	959.9	–	959.9	772.7	167.5
1776–77	866.6	407.5	1274.1	621.6	227.0
1777–78	1266.2	–	1266.2	550.7	233.3
1778–79	1193.1	–	1193.1	776.7	262.6
1779–80	957.9	371.2	1329.1	682.7	318.8
1780–81	904.5	–	904.5	1080.5	284.0
1781–82	775.5	582.5	1358.0	1074.7	226.0
1782–83	1141.5	588.6	1730.1	541.0	217.3
1783–84	854.8	–	854.8	893.7	191.4
1784–85	827.1	291.2	1118.3	874.2	235.8
1785–86	1136.5	397.3	1533.8	671.6	178.5
1786–87	1123.0	–	1123.0	876.0	169.6
1787–88	1129.9	–	1129.9	1231.0	171.8
1788–89	1061.8	399.3	1461.1	1245.8	151.5
1789–90	1033.8	393.5	1427.3	1280.3	156.1

INCOME	Rents received + Sales £	of which Rent due £	Previous balance £	Interest & Loans £	Sale of investments £	TOTAL £
1790–91	1369.1	[1013.4]	1280.3	223.0	–	2872.4
1791–92	1297.3	[1010.9]	1512.4	238.0	–	3047.7
1792–93	1365.7	[1010.9]	1023.5	253.0	–	2642.2
1793–94	1340.7	[1035.3]	1447.9	253.0	–	3041.6
1794–95	2085.6	[1035.3]	480.7	253.0	–	2819.3
1795–96	1765.9	[1329.7]	394.5	232.0	676.0	3068.4
1796–97	1671.6	[1378.0]	475.6	163.0	2186.2	4496.4
1797–98	1557.1	[1398.0]	846.4	43.0	1045.0	3491.5
1798–99	1432.3	[1397.0]	485.1	2500.0	680.7	5098.1
1799–1800	1930.6	[1397.0]	1343.7	2500.0	–	5774.3
1800–01	2023.0	[1413.0]	1031.7	750.0	–	3804.7
1801–02	2532.4	[1418.2]	826.8	750.0	–	4109.2
1802–03	2238.3	[1438.5]	814.4	–	–	3052.7
1803–04	1932.8	[1448.6]	538.7	–	–	2471.5
1804–05	2408.1	[1458.9]	651.4	–	–	3059.5
1805–06	1918.3	[1709.2]	963.0	–	–	2881.3
1806–07	1496.9	[1709.2]	358.9	–	–	1855.8
1807–08	2844.4	[1998.3]	103.4	–	–	2947.8
1808–09	2347.3	[1999.5]	898.0	–	–	3245.3
1809–10	2861.5	[2089.7]	1585.6	–	–	4447.1
1810–11	3119.4	[2228.3]	1968.3	–	–	5087.7
1811–12	2910.5	[2651.1]	671.8	–	–	3582.3
1812–13	3599.5	[2936.1]	721.0	44.8	–	4365.3
1813–14	2825.7	[2936.1]	1088.0	90.4	–	4004.2
1814–15	2675.4	[2990.8]	777.2	124.2	–	3576.8
1815–16	3261.9	[3137.8]	560.9	172.8	–	3995.6
1816–17	3923.7	[3174.6]	565.2	246.0	–	4734.9
1817–18	2955.6	[3277.4]	1757.2	306.0	–	5018.8
1818–19	4096.3	[3292.4]	635.3	306.0	–	5037.6
1819–20	3327.2	[3287.4]	3018.9	426.0	–	6772.1
1820–21	3534.9	[3266.4]	2503.0	471.0	–	6508.9
1821–22	3192.6	[3338.3]	1770.6	396.0	9757.6	15116.8
1822–23	3936.9	[3298.4]	342.1	138.0	930.0	5347.0
1823–24	4959.3	[3318.4]	818.4	66.0	1968.0	7811.7
1824–25	3746.1	[3333.3]	2127.5	30.0	–	5903.6

EXPENDITURE	Bridge and estate works £	Investments £	Interest & Loan repayment £	Total £	BALANCE £	Rent arrears £
1790–91	969.4	390.6	–	1360.0	1512.4	136.2
1791–92	1097.1	927.5	–	2024.6	1023.5	143.8
1792–93	1194.3	–	–	1194.3	1447.9	165.2
1793–94	2560.9	–	–	2560.9	480.7	162.5
1794–95	2424.8	–	–	2424.8	394.5	212.4
1795–96	2592.8	–	–	2592.8	475.6	109.7
1796–97	3650.0	–	–	3650.0	846.4	352.6
1797–98	3006.4	–	–	3006.4	485.1	358.4
1798–99	3754.4	–	–	3754.4	1343.7	517.8
1799–1800	4583.9	–	158.7	4742.6	1031.7	341.1
1800–01	2752.7	–	225.2	2977.9	826.8	384.0
1801–02	2999.0	–	295.8	3294.8	814.4	318.9
1802–03	1749.4	–	764.6	2514.0	538.7	426.7
1803–04	965.7	–	854.4	1820.1	651.4	459.6
1804–05	1115.2	–	981.3	2096.5	963.0	391.8
1805–06	1481.2	–	1041.2	2522.4	358.9	476.2
1806–07	1215.5	–	536.9	1742.4	103.3	734.9
1807–08	1509.5	–	540.3	2049.8	898.0	116.8
1808–09	1090.1	–	569.6	1659.7	1585.6	601.8
1809–10	1792.5	–	686.3	2478.8	1968.3	222.3
1810–11	1744.1	–	2671.8	4415.9	671.8	112.5
1811–12	2015.9	845.4	–	2861.3	721.0	381.6
1812–13	2232.4	1044.8	–	3277.2	1088.1	144.0
1813–14	2378.6	848.4	–	3227.0	777.2	434.2
1814–15	1928.4	1087.5	–	3015.9	560.9	1008.9
1815–16	2291.9	1138.5	–	3430.4	565.2	1316.7
1816–17	2345.2	632.5	–	2977.7	1757.2	722.8
1817–18	3651.0	732.5	–	4383.5	635.3	1020.3
1818–19	1928.7	–	–	1928.7	3108.9	824.9
1819–20	1479.1	2790.0	–	4269.1	2503.0	1444.5
1820–21	2714.5	2023.8	–	4738.3	1770.6	1452.7
1821–22	14774.7	–	–	14774.7	342.1	1982.6
1822–23	4528.6	–	–	4528.6	818.4	2187.5
1823–24	5684.5	–	–	5684.7	2127.0	1072.9
1824–25	2087.4	–	–	2087.4	3816.2	1317.2

INCOME	Rents received + sales £	of which Rent due £	Previous balance £	Interest £	Sale of investments £	TOTAL £
1825–26	4428.3	[3383.3]	3816.2	79.5	–	8324.0
1826–27	3742.2	[3383.3]	3945.6	195.0	–	7882.8
1827–28	3688.3	[3419.3]	2817.7	195.0	–	6701.0
1828–29	3268.9	[3582.5]	2815.8	446.4	–	6531.1
1829–30	3769.4	[3582.5]	2182.6	450.0	–	6402.0
1830–31	4392.5	[3602.5]	2274.8	555.0	–	7222.3
1831–32	3951.6	[3633.5]	2665.5	705.0	–	7322.1
1832–33	3389.9	[3620.5]	1326.7	780.0	–	5496.6
1833–34	4185.8	[3620.5]	1939.8	915.0	–	7040.6
1834–35	4869.7	[3507.4]	1590.7	1027.5	–	7487.9
1835–36	3853.9	[3749.4]	352.6	1155.0	–	5361.5
1836–37	3856.4	[3749.4]	623.1	1237.5	–	5717.0
1837–38	4633.8	[3769.4]	790.3	1365.0	–	6789.1
1838–39	3970.7	[3720.4]	594.7	1492.5	–	6057.9
1839–40	4232.1	[3817.4]	618.1	1567.5	1353.8	7771.5
1840–41	4610.0	[3817.4]	252.9	1642.5	–	6505.4
1841–42	4351.7	[3871.4]	45.6	1777.5	–	6174.8
1842–43	4200.4	[4017.2]	269.1	1839.3	548.2	6857.0
1843–44	4261.0	[4073.6]	483.3	1970.3	–	6714.6
1844–45	4302.7	[3952.3]	243.4	2086.8	–	6566.3
1845–46	4186.1	[4051.3]	595.8	2212.0	–	7110.5
1846–47	4294.1	[4071.3]	221.0	2300.9	–	6816.0

INCOME	Rents received + sales £	of which Rent due £	Loans £	Previous balance £	Interest £	Sales of investments £	TOTAL £
1847–48	4703.3	[3983.5]	–	256.8	2499.6	–	7459.7
1848–49	4061.7	[4038.9]	–	467.1	2655.7	25712.9	32897.4

EXPENDITURE	Estate & bridge works £	Investments £	Interest £	Total £	BALANCE £	Rent arrears £
1825–26	2397.0	1981.4	–	4378.4	3945.6	349.9
1826–27	2481.7	2583.4	–	5065.1	2817.7	621.5
1827–28	1385.1	2500.0	–	3885.1	2815.8	468.9
1828–29	1409.2	2939.3	–	4348.5	2182.6	782.5
1829–30	1357.1	2770.1	–	4127.2	2274.8	817.0
1830–31	1100.6	3456.2	–	4556.8	2665.5	567.2
1831–32	1787.9	4207.5	–	5995.4	1326.7	512.4
1832–33	974.3	2582.5	–	3556.8	1939.8	761.8
1833–34	1174.8	4275.1[42]	–	5449.9	1590.7	811.2
1834–35	1181.6	5953.7	–	7135.3	352.6	940.0
1835–36	1710.4	3028.0[43]	–	4738.4	623.1	990.5
1836–37	1314.8	3611.9	–	4926.7	790.3	1286.3
1837–38	2014.4	4180.0	–	6194.4	594.7	799.8
1838–39	1709.7	3730.1	–	5439.8	618.1	841.0
1839–40	3287.5	4231.1[44]	–	7518.6	252.9	962.9
1840–41	2427.9	4031.9	–	6459.8	45.6	629.3
1841–42	1830.7	4075.0	–	5905.7	269.1	702.5
1842–43	1765.5	4608.2[45]	–	6373.7	483.3	813.3
1843–44	1821.9	4649.3[46]	–	6471.2	243.4	795.9
1844–45	1995.5	3975.0	–	5970.5	595.8	502.8
1845–46	4397.4	2492.0	–	6889.5	221.1	542.2
1846–47	2329.0	4230.2	–	6559.2	256.8	457.1

EXPENDITURE	Estate & bridge works £	Rates and Taxes £	Investments £	Loans repaid £	Interest £	Total £	BALANCE £	Rent arrears £
1847–48	1789.0	549.9	4653.7[47]	–	–	6992.6	467.1	299.3
1848–49	1966.9	569.6	26543.9[48]	–	–	29080.4	3817.2	789.1

[42] This figure includes £695 2s. 4d. for the purchase of land at Frindsbury.
[43] This figure includes £1195 10s. 10d. for purchase of land in Rochester needed for the new bridge approach.
[44] This figure includes £1950 for the purchase of land in Strood.
[45] This figure includes £803 15s. 1d. for purchase of land in Strood and Rochester needed for the new bridge approach.
[46] This figure includes £228 13s. for purchase of land in Strood.
[47] This expense includes £390 10s. for the purchase of woodland at Burham.
[48] This figure includes £22,267 7s. 7d. for land purchased for the new bridge approaches.

INCOME	Rents received + sales £	of which Rent due £	Loans £	Previous balance £	Interest £	Sales of investments £	TOTAL £
1849–50	4964.8	[4066.4]	–	3817.2	1649.9	28837.5	39269.4
1850–51	5115.8	[4020.4]	–	228.5	1759.3	8923.4	16027.0
1851–52	4290.2	[3829.4]	–	81.1	1712.6	11372.4	17456.3
1852–53	3835.6	[3846.1]	–	1325.8	1544.7	–	6706.1
1853–54	4639.8	[3722.0]	–	375.7	1530.6	5062.7	11608.8
1854–55	4985.2	[3722.0]	–	563.5	1383.0	5596.1[49]	12401.8
1855–56	3968.4	[3704.0]	–	207.2	1124.2	32585.7	37885.5
1856–57	4582.7	[3945.5]	38000	660.6	–	9304.9	52548.2
1857–58	4524.7	[4029.3]	–	6798.1	–	–	11322.8
1858–59	4256.8	[4056.0]	5000	216.8	–	4751.2[50]	14224.8
1859–60	4865.0	[4080.5]	–	3961.2	–	–	8826.2
1860–61	4696.8	[4116.8]	–	2776.3	–	–	7473.1
1861–62	4587.4	[4059.2]	–	3045.2	–	6362.1[51]	13994.7
1862–63	4520.8	[3950.4]	–	8298.2	197.7	14203.9[52]	27220.6
1863–64	4231.3	[3818.7]	–	3674.9	51.4	1305.0[53]	9262.6
1864–65	4176.4	[3874.2]	–	3171.4	10.5	–	7358.3
1865–66	4084.6	[3952.1]	–	1380.6	–	–	5465.2
1866–67	4419.1	[4014.4]	–	1260.4	–	–	5679.5
1867–68	4582.6	[4083.9]	–	1429.7	39.0	–	6051.3
1868–69	4460.4	[4101.7]	–	1323.1	–	–	5783.5
1869–70	4483.1	[4115.6]	–	3248.5	5.1	–	7736.7

[49] This figure includes £2523 6s. 3d. from sale of land at Strood to the East Kent Railway Company.

[50] This figure includes £4751 1s. 5d. from compulsory purchase of land at Rochester and Langdon Manor Farm by the East Kent Railway Company.

[51] This sum represents a £2050 compulsory purchase by the London Chatham and Dover Railway Company at Strood and a further £4312 1s. 7d. compulsory purchase by the War Department in Grain and East Tilbury.

[52] This figure includes £6125 9s. 7d. received from the War Department for compulsory purchase of lands at Nashenden.

[53] This sum represents sales of land in the parishes of East Tilbury and St. Margaret's, Rochester.

EXPENDITURE	Estate & bridge works	Rates and Taxes	Investments	Loans repaid	Interest	Total	BALANCE	Rent arrears
	£	£	£	£	£	£	£	£
1849–50	2046.1	512.0	42486.5[54]	–	–	39040.9	228.5	1110.4
1850–51	11171.3	512.5	4181.0	–	–	15945.9	81.1	1098.4
1851–52	13214.3	477.5	2438.7	–	–	16130.5	1325.8	945.9
1852–53	4718.4	592.0	1020.0	–	–	6330.4	375.7	1219.6
1853–54	10426.2	619.1	–	–	–	11045.3	563.5	917.7
1854–55	11447.6	747.0	–	–	–	12194.6	207.2	367.7
1855–56	36545.2	679.7	–	–	–	37224.9	660.6	619.5
1856–57	44961.8	788.3	–	–	–	45750.1	6798.1	491.5
1857–58	9007.4	488.9	–	–	1609.7	11106.0	216.8	360.3
1858–59	8089.8	444.6	–	–	1729.2	10263.6	3961.2	539.9
1859–60	3714.6	528.2	–	–	1807.1	6049.9	2776.3	282.0
1860–61	2100.5	522.7	–	–	1804.7	4427.9	3045.2	151.1
1861–62	3397.5	492.9	–	–	1806.1	5696.5	8298.2	131.8
1862–63	1195.0	456.9	8207.5	12000	1686.3	23545.7	3674.9	12.4
1863–64	1870.7	432.9	–	2500	1287.6	6091.2	3171.4	3.6
1864–65	2509.5	297.5	–	2000	1170.7	5977.7	1380.6	8.2
1865–66	1785.4	280.2	–	1000	1139.2	4204.8	1260.4	1.7
1866–67	1071.5	269.4	–	1800	1108.9	4249.8	1429.7	–
1867–68	1987.2	279.9	145.5	1300	1015.6	4728.2	1323.1	–
1868–69	1182.5	300.6	–	100	951.9	2535.0	3248.5	17.7
1869–70	1269.1	286.2	–	3500	918.6	5973.9	1762.8	1.3

[54] This expense includes £3,445 11s. 5d. for land purchased for the new bridge approaches.

INCOME	Rents received + sales £	of which Rent due £	Loans £	Previous balance £	Interest £	Sales of investments £	TOTAL £
1870–71	4463.7	[4179.2]	–	1762.8	–	–	6226.5
1871–72	4410.6	[4187.2]	–	1087.1	–	–	5497.7
1872–73	4902.0	[4472.9]	–	1353.6	7.9	–	6263.5
1873–74	5133.3	[4556.5]	–	2217.0	16.6	–	7366.9
1874–75	5264.0	[4586.0]	–	854.0	–	–	6118.0
1875–76	5229.5	[5738.1]	–	2690.6	10.9	–	7931.0
1876–77	6619.6	[5777.7]	15000	2897.6	–	–	24517.2
1877–78	6351.7	[5874.6]	–	3371.1	–	–	9722.8
1878–79	6079.1	[5983.3]	13900	4451.0	–	–	24430.1
1879–80	5914.5	[5989.1]	–	4439.9	–	–	10354.4
1880–81	5487.8	[6060.1]	6100	4303.5	–	–	15891.3
1881–82	6568.6	[7839.3]	–	4045.9	–	–	10614.5
1882–83	6262.2	[7837.3]	–	4469.2	–	–	10731.4
1883–84	6979.9	[7905.5]	–	6697.1	–	–	13677.0
1884–85	8023.7	[7802.3]	–	9360.2	278.9	–	17662.8
1885–86	9892.0	[8144.3]	–	9333.3	228.5	1610.7	21064.5
1886–87	8085.0	[7738.7]	10000	6294.4	134.8	5054.7	29568.9
1887–88	8880.2	[7870.8]	–	4507.1	251.8	9009.8[55]	22648.9
1888–89	7475.8	[7814.5]	–	4974.1	163.5	700.0[56]	13313.4
1889–90	8271.9	[7335.4]	–	3251.0	240.2	–	11763.1
1890–91	6610.5	[7743.9]	–	3639.6	251.7	6541.3	17043.1
1891–92	8636.6	[7729.8]	–	1808.2	72.5	1488.9	12006.2
1892–93	7515.6	[7802.9]	–	4536.5	184.7	600.0	12836.8
1893–94	7127.8	[7512.3]	–	3688.0	280.9	–	11096.7
1894–95	7762.6	[7302.2]	–	2739.3	169.9	6000.0	16671.8
1895–96	6929.2	[7478.3]	–	3335.2	349.2	1650.0	12263.6
1896–97	8280.7	[7398.8]	–	2373.2	264.1	4000.0	14918.0
1897–98	14692.6[57]	[7577.0]	–	2345.3	281.8	–	17319.7
1898–99	7272.0	[7592.4]	–	4466.1	441.3	700.0	12879.4
1899–1900	7743.6	[7634.8]	–	3212.0	479.8	–	11435.4

[55] This figure includes £6819 purchase money from the South Eastern Railway Company for lands in Grain and £1690 5s. 6d. from sale of land on the Maidstone Road in the parish of St Margaret's, Rochester.

[56] This figure represents sale of surplus land in Strood.

[57] Income this year includes £5,500 received from Cory & Son for damage to the bridge by the lighter Diamond.

EXPENDITURE	Estate & bridge works £	Rates and Taxes £	Donations £	Investments £	Loans repaid £	Interest £	Total £	BALANCE £	Rent arrears £
1870–71	766.1	276.6	–	–	3300	796.7	5139.4	1087.1	3.4
1871–72	1498.2	305.6	190.0	–	1500	650.3	4144.1	1353.6	–
1872–73	2157.3	261.1	40.0	–	1000	588.1	4046.5	2217.0	8.0
1873–74	2333.9	268.0	280.0	–	3100	531.0	6512.9	854.0	–
1874–75	2110.6	244.5	250.0	–	400	422.3	3427.4	2690.6	–
1875–76	1890.9	233.9	35.0	–	2500	373.6	5033.4	2897.6	399.0
1876–77	5863.3	278.7	7220.0	406.8	7000	377.3	21146.1	3371.1	–
1877–78	3131.8	281.3	105.0	–	1240	513.7	5271.8	4451.0	–
1878–79	3663.1	343.0	14100.0	–	1240	644.1	19990.2	4439.9	263.3
1879–80	3282.6	463.8	100.0	–	1240	964.5	6050.9	4303.5	474.9
1880–81	2922.4	478.4	6210.0	–	1240	994.6	11845.4	4045.9	1225.5
1881–82	3165.3	418.6	10.0	–	1440	1111.4	6145.3	4469.2	1309.6
1882–83	1066.2	431.3	10.0	–	1440	1086.8	4034.3	6697.1	1415.5
1883–84	1378.9	416.9	47.1	–	1440	1033.9	4316.8	9360.2	1403.7
1884–85	5368.1	486.1	59.2	–	1440	976.1	8329.5	9333.3	1444.3
1885–86	1192.2	503.6	3967.0	6754.3	1440	913.0	14770.1	6294.4	513.0
1886–87	2684.5	471.6	19466.8	143.6	1440	855.3	25061.8	4507.1	426.4
1887–88	2222.7	401.4	2560.3	6112.6	5040	1337.8	17674.8	4974.1	502.0
1888–89	1410.3	367.7	922.1	4689.3	1740	993.0	10062.4	3251.0	1119.2
1889–90	1591.5	360.8	62.5	3442.4	1740	926.3	8123.5	3639.6	474.4
1890–91	3123.0	306.3	37.1	9170.1	1740	858.4	15234.9	1808.2	1229.4
1891–92	1601.3	395.5	–	2942.4	1740	790.5	7469.7	4536.5	467.1
1892–93	1468.9	447.7	227.1	4542.4	1740	722.7	9148.8	3688.0	759.9
1893–94	1607.8	510.4	32.1	3814.3	1740	652.8	8357.4	2739.3	1476.3
1894–95	1916.9	669.7	106.5	2947.3	7240	456.2	13336.6	3335.2	1323.4
1895–96	2658.1	685.2	5.3	4990.1	1240	311.7	9890.4	2373.2	1848.7
1896–97	9091.6	772.4	5.0	1200.0	1240	263.7	2572.7	2345.3	1949.2
1897–98	2287.2	885.4	25.2	8200.0	1240	215.8	12853.6	4466.1	470.3
1898–99	4527.6	829.9	2.1	2900.0	1240	167.8	9667.4	3212.0	845.1
1899–1900	2658.9	899.2	62.4	3460.3	1240	119.9	8440.7	2994.7	876.1

INCOME	Rents received + sales £	of which Rent due £	Loans £	Previous balance £	Interest £	Sales of investments £	TOTAL £
1900–01	9485.6	[7515.1]	–	2994.7	568.5	7000.0	20048.8
1901–02	7285.3	[7514.8]	–	2526.8	830.3	–	10642.4
1902–03	7941.1	[7629.3]	–	3667.0	904.6	1188.0	13700.7
1903–04	7497.4	[7412.5]	–	2659.6	877.1	–	11034.1
1904–05	6804.3	[7423.9]	–	3160.4	907.1	–	10871.8
1905–06	7528.6	[7399.8]	–	750.8	968.3	37.5	9285.2
1906–07	8648.0	[7283.5]	–	1305.6	969.1	–	10922.7
1907–08	8751.9	[7588.3]	–	2390.1	969.1	–	12111.1
1908–09	8688.1	[7594.2]	–	1296.6	284.1	–	10268.8
1909–10	7780.8	[7590.0]	–	3982.9	430.6	–	12194.3
1910–11	8213.4	[7623.7]	–	5515.9	430.6	–	14159.9
1911–12	8996.0	[7628.1]	–	3991.7	1302.5	25370.0	39660.2
1912–13	7616.4	[7433.9]	13000	3584.2	932.3	31802.5	56935.4
1913–14	8150.7	[7431.9]	22000	2876.1	512.1	225.0	33763.9

EXPENDITURE	Estate & bridge works £	Rates and Taxes £	Donations £	Investments £	Loans repaid £	Interest £	Total £	BALANCE £	Rent arrears £
1900–01	2894.4	903.3	100.3	11084.7	2480	59.3	17522.0	2526.8	292.9
1901–02	1535.2	947.7	7.1	4485.4	–	–	6975.4	3667.0	589.2
1902–03	3814.1	1015.6	29.2	6182.2	–	–	11041.1	2659.6	449.1
1903–04	2936.2	887.5	2350.0	1700.0	–	–	7873.7	3160.4	613.6
1904–05	2251.8	825.9	3061.6	3981.7	–	–	10121.0	750.8	2118.3
1905–06	2315.4	866.7	3060.0	1737.5	–	–	7979.6	1305.6	1292.9
1906–07	4188.7	998.9	1645.0	1700.0	–	–	8532.6	2390.1	832.6
1907–08	2227.7	912.4	1974.4	5700.0	–	–	10814.5	1296.6	645.8
1908–09	3113.7	972.2	200.0	2000.0	–	–	6285.9	3982.9	575.7
1909–10	3738.9	939.6	200.0	1800.0	–	–	6678.4	5515.9	794.0
1910–11	6266.6	998.6	1103.1	1800.0	–	–	10168.2	3991.7	533.4
1911–12	27256.6	1041.0	5278.4	2500.0	–	–	36076.0	3584.2	445.2
1912–13	37711.4	1065.3	12232.6	3050.0	–	–	54059.3	2876.1	457.3
1913–14	27342.5	976.8	3099.5	525.0	–	743.8	32687.6	1076.3	505.3

Rochester Bridge Estates: Rental Income

	Kent £	Rochester £	London £	Essex £	TOTAL £	Arrears £
1576–77	58.8	9.3	19.1	–	87.2	–
1577–78	137.1	42.1	64.8	51.3	295.3	–
1578–79	117.4	26.2	43.3	25	211.9	–
1579–80	117.5	27.2	43.3	25	213.0	–
1580–81	117.5	27.2	43.4	25	213.1	–
1581–82	119.0	27.0	43.4	25	214.4	–
1582–83	118.5	27.6	43.4	25	214.5	–
1583–84	118.5	28.9	43.4	25	215.8	–
1584–85	118.5	28.9	43.4	25	215.8	–
1585–86	117.5	29.9	43.4	25	215.8	–
1586–87	118.3	30.9	43.4	25	217.6	2.0
1587–88	118.3	30.9	43.4	25	217.6	4.0
1588–89	121.3	30.9	43.4	25	220.6	2.0
1589–90	127.3	30.9	43.4	25	226.6	2.0
1590–91	127.4	30.9	44.2	25	227.5	2.0
1591–92	127.4	30.9	44.2	25	227.5	2.0
1592–93	127.4	30.9	44.2	25	227.5	12.5
1593–94	127.4	31.5	44.2	25	228.1	24.8
1594–95	127.4	33.3	48.5	30	239.2	25.6
1595–96	127.6	34.1	51.0	30	242.7	10.3
1596–97	127.6	34.1	51.0	30	242.7	12.3
1597–98	129.6	34.1	51.0	30	244.7	14.3
1598–99	133.0	34.1	51.0	30.2	248.3	16.3
1599–1600	134.0	34.1	51.0	30.2	249.3	14.3
1600–01	134.0	34.1	51.0	30.2	249.3	15.3
1601–02	134.0	34.8	51.0	30.3	250.1	22.3
1602–03	133.9	36.1	51.0	30.3	251.3	15.0
1603–04	133.9	36.6	51.0	30.3	251.8	16.0
1604–05	133.9	36.7	51.3	30.3	252.2	17.0
1605–06	144.0	36.7	51.5	30.5	262.7	18.0
1606–07	144.0	36.7	51.5	30.5	262.7	19.0
1607–08	144.0	36.7	51.5	30.5	262.7	20.0
1608–09	144.0	37.0	51.5	30.5	263.0	21.0
1609–10	144.0	37.0	54.8	30.5	266.3	22.0
1610–11	144.1	37.0	55.2	30.5	266.8	23.0

	Kent £	Rochester £	London £	Essex £	TOTAL £	Arrears £
1611–12	144.1	41.0	56.2	30.5	271.8	24.0
1612–13	144.6	41.0	59.9	30.5	276.0	29.0
1613–14	144.6	41.0	59.9	30.5	276.0	26.0
1614–15	144.6	41.0	59.9	30.5	276.0	27.5
1615–16	145.0	41.5	59.9	30.5	276.9	31.3
1616–17	145.0	41.6	59.9	30.5	277.0	30.0
1617–18	145.0	41.6	59.9	30.5	277.0	32.0[58]
1618–19	146.5	41.6	59.9	30.5	278.5[59]	14.4
1619–20	146.7	41.6	59.9	41.5	289.7	15.3
1620–21	146.7	42.0	60.3	41.5	290.5	16.9
1621–22	145.2	43.7	61.9	41.5	292.3	20.0
1622–23	145.2	44.5	63.7	41.5	294.9	22.7
1623–24	145.2	44.5	63.7	41.5	294.9	22.9
1624–25	145.2	44.5	63.7	42.4	295.8	2.5
1625–26	148.2	44.5	66.3	42.5	301.5	7.1
1626–27	149.9	46.3	66.3	42.5	305.0	23.0
1627–28	149.9	46.7	66.3	42.5	305.4	3.0
1628–29	152.1	46.7	66.3	42.5	307.6	4.9
1629–30	154.2	46.9	66.3	43.0	310.4	2.7
1630–31	154.2	46.9	66.3	43.0	310.4	0.2
1631–32	151.1	49.9	67.0	43.0	311.0	3.7
1632–33	159.5	50.1	67.0	43.0	319.6	9.7
1633–34	159.5	50.8	80.5	43.0	333.8	2.0
1634–35	160.2	50.8	80.5	43.0	334.4	2.0
1635–36	160.2	51.0	80.5	43.0	334.6	2.0
1636–37	160.2	51.6	80.5	43.0	335.3	2.0
1637–38	165.2	51.6	85.5	43.0	340.3	2.0
1638–39	165.7	51.6	85.5	43.0	340.8	18.7
1639–40	161.2	55.7	85.5	43.0	345.4	2.0
1640–41	161.2	55.7	85.5	43.0	345.4	5.3
1641–42	167.5	61.2	85.5	43.0	357.2	11.3
1642–43	173.4	61.4	86.8	43.0	364.6	15.3
1643–44	173.5	61.4	86.8	43.0	364.7	4.1

[58] Memoranda this year record the cancelling in future accounts of £30 of rent arrears.
[59] The 1618–19 rental totals £278 9s. 3d., but the charge records rent receipts of only £276 19s. 3d. as in the three previous years.

	Kent	Rochester	London	Essex	TOTAL	Arrears
	£	£	£	£	£	£
1644–45[60]					380.1	16.3
1645–46	173.4	61.6	102.3	46.5	383.8	25.7
1646–47	174.4	62.0	102.3	46.5	385.2	28.8
1647–48	174.4	62.0	102.3	46.5	385.2	42.9
1648–49	174.4	63.4	108.8	46.5	393.1	60.9
1649–50	174.4	63.5	108.8	46.5	393.2	45.9
1650–51	178.4	64.1	110.2	46.5	399.2[61]	25.3
1651–52	183.1	64.1	110.2	46.5	403.9	18.9
1654–55	186.1	64.4	115.6	46.5	412.6	39.7
1656–57	186.1	64.4	115.9	46.5	412.9	8.7
1657–58	186.1	66.9	115.9	46.5	415.4	10.1
1658–59	186.1	67.3	115.9	46.5	415.8	45.4
1659–60	197.7	67.3	115.9	46.5	427.4	44.2
1660–61	203.0	64.3	116.4	50.0	434.2	37.1
1661–62	203.9	67.1	116.4	50.5	437.9	35.8
1662–63	204.4	68.1	119.0	50.5	441.9	36.3
1663–64	204.4	68.1	119.1	50.5	442.1	29.2
1664–65	204.4	68.1	119.1	50.5	442.1	32.2
1665–66	204.4	68.1	119.1	50.5	442.1	35.2
1666–67	204.5	68.2	119.1	50.5	442.3	38.2
1667–68	204.5	68.2	119.4	50.5	442.6	41.2
1668–69	205.0	68.2	120.1	50.5	443.8	39.4
1669–70	205.0	68.4	120.1	50.5	444.0	26.9
1670–71	205.0	68.4	121.1	50.5	445.0	17.5
1671–72	205.2	68.4	122.4	50.5	446.4	20.5
1672–73	205.7	68.4	122.4	50.5	446.9	17.9
1673–74	205.7	68.4	122.4	50.5	446.9	36.8
1674–75	205.8	68.5	122.4	50.5	447.1	24.4
1675–76	205.8	68.6	122.6	50.5	447.5	19.4
1676–77	205.8	68.8	122.6	50.7	447.9	16.5
1677–78	205.8	68.8	122.6	50.7	447.9	19.5
1678–79	205.8	68.8	122.6	50.7	447.9	60.3
1679–80	205.9	68.8	122.6	50.7	448.0	43.2
1680–81	206.6	68.8	122.9	50.7	449.0	35.0

[60] The rental for 1644–45 is missing.
[61] The total rents this year should equal £399 3s. 8d., but both the rental and the charge have an incorrect total of £398 0s. 4d.

	Kent	Rochester	London	Essex	TOTAL	Arrears
	£	£	£	£	£	£
1681–82	206.6	68.8	122.9	50.7	449.0	32.8
1682–83	206.6	69.8	123.1	50.7	450.2	55.5
1683–84	206.6	71.8	123.1	51.0	452.5	40.0
1684–85	207.3	71.9	123.6	51.0	453.8	33.4
1685–86	207.3	72.0	124.2	51.0	454.5	75.5
1686–87	207.3	72.0	125.7	51.0	456.0	100.1
1687–88	207.5	72.5	125.7	51.0	456.7	85.2
1688–89	207.6	72.8	125.9	51.0	457.3	124.5
1689–90	207.6	72.9	125.9	51.0	457.4	163.5
1690–91	208.6	75.9	125.9	51.0	461.4	270.7
1691–92	208.6	75.9	125.9	51.0	461.4	279.7
1692–93	208.6	75.9	126.3	51.0	461.8	243.1
1693–94	208.9	76.0	126.6	51.0	462.5	246.6
1694–95	208.9	76.2	126.6	51.0	462.7	153.0
1695–96	209.2	76.2	126.6	51.0	463.0	251.0
1696–97	210.1	76.4	127.1	51.0	464.6	222.3
1697–98	210.1	76.4	127.3	51.0	464.8	147.6
1698–99	210.1	76.4	127.3	51.0	464.8	104.5
1699–1700	210.4	76.6	127.3	51.1	465.4	123.2
1700–01	210.4	76.6	128.6	51.1	466.7	84.1
1701–02	210.4	76.6	128.6	51.1	466.7	108.9
1702–03	210.5	76.9	129.1	51.1	467.6	172.4
1703–04	211.1	77.7	129.4	51.1	469.3	160.9
1704–05	211.1	78.1	129.4	51.1	469.7	126.8
1705–06	211.1	78.1	129.4	51.1	469.7	161.5
1706–07	211.1	78.1	130.9	51.1	471.2	160.7
1707–08	211.1	78.2	131.6	51.1	472.0	147.7
1708–09	211.6	78.4	131.8	51.1	472.9	127.8
1709–10	211.9	78.4	132.7	51.1	474.3	81.0
1710–11	212.0	78.4	132.7	51.1	474.4	153.1
1711–12	213.1	78.5	132.7	51.1	475.4	112.5
1712–13	213.1	78.6	132.9	51.2	475.8	92.4
1713–14	213.5	78.8	132.9	51.2	476.4	98.1
1714–15	213.5	78.9	132.9	51.2	476.5	89.1
1715–16	213.5	78.9	132.9	51.2	476.5	132.1
1716–17	213.5	78.9	132.9	51.2	476.5	70.8
1717–18	216.0	79.1	132.9	51.2	479.2	102.6

| | Kent | Rochester | London | Essex | TOTAL | Arrears |
	£	£	£	£	£	£
1718–19	216.0	79.1	156.3	51.2	502.6	102.5
1719–20	216.0	79.9	175.4	51.2	522.5	109.5
1720–21	216.0	79.9	178.4	51.2	525.5	128.6
1721–22	216.0	82.4	189.9	51.2	539.5	154.3
1722–23	216.9	87.4	191.0	51.2	546.5	116.5
1723–24	216.9	87.5	191.5	51.2	547.1	117.9
1724–25	219.4	87.5	196.0	51.2	554.1	130.1
1725–26	244.5	88.2	205.5	51.2	589.4	130.2
1726–27	244.5	88.2	205.5	51.2	589.4	121.3
1727–28	259.3	85.4	205.5	51.2	601.4	114.3
1728–29	259.3	85.4	205.5	51.2	601.4	138.5
1729–30	259.3	85.5	205.5	51.2	601.5	120.3
1730–31	262.1	85.5	212.5	51.2	611.3	114.6
1731–32	284.8	88.6	212.5	51.2	637.1	190.0
1732–33	284.8	88.6	212.5	51.2	637.1	54.2
1733–34	285.0	88.6	212.5	51.7	637.8	212.6
1734–35	285.0	83.4	212.5	51.7	632.6	185.9
1735–36	285.0	83.4	212.5	51.7	632.6	233.6
1736–37	285.1	79.5	213.6	51.7	629.9	53.0
1737–38	285.1	79.5	214.4	51.7	630.7	155.4
1738–39	285.1	77.0	214.4	51.7	628.2	158.7
1739–40	285.1	77.0	214.4	51.7	628.2	252.3
1740–41	285.1	77.0	214.4	51.7	628.2	221.0
1741–42	285.1	89.7	214.4	51.7	640.9	283.0
1742–43	286.6	89.7	214.4	51.7	642.4	269.5
1743–44	286.6	92.7	214.4	51.7	645.4	264.9
1744–45	286.6	96.2	214.4	51.7	648.9	270.4
1745–46	286.6	96.2	214.4	51.7	648.9	373.4
1746–47	389.8	98.5	214.4	51.7	754.4	458.7
1747–48	387.8	98.5	214.4	51.7	752.4	638.9
1748–49	362.6	97.2	214.4	51.7	725.9	379.6
1749–50	362.6	75.5	214.4	51.7	704.2	376.4
1750–51	365.6	88.0	232.4	51.7	737.7	452.1
1751–52	365.6	88.0	232.4	51.7	737.7	304.6
1752–53	353.1	126.5	254.4	60.5	794.5	376.8
1753–54	354.5	130.9	254.4	60.5	800.3	424.7
1754–55	354.5	128.9	257.4	60.5	801.3	464.8

	Kent	Rochester	London	Essex	TOTAL	Arrears
	£	£	£	£	£	£
1755–56	354.5	123.2	254.1	60.5	792.3	467.2
1756–57	354.5	126.7	254.1	60.5	795.8	381.3
1757–58	354.5	124.2	254.6	60.5	793.8	376.3
1758–59	354.5	127.8	258.6	60.5	801.4	421.0
1759–60	354.5	127.8	258.6	60.5	801.4	351.9
1760–61	354.5	127.8	258.6	60.5	801.4	589.6
1761–62	358.5	127.8	258.6	60.5	805.4	433.1
1762–63	357.0	127.8	258.6	60.5	803.9	348.5
1763–64	357.0	127.8	258.6	60.5	803.9	334.3
1764–65	357.1	129.3	258.6	60.5	805.5	391.6
1765–66	357.1	129.3	258.6	60.5	805.5	409.1
1766–67	357.1	133.3	260.2	60.5	811.1	447.1
1767–68	358.6	133.9	274.0	60.5	827.0	391.2
1768–69	358.6	130.7	274.0	60.5	823.8	295.5
1769–70	362.5	128.3	274.0	60.5	825.3	265.7
1770–71	369.8	130.7	275.0	60.5	836.0	277.8
1771–72	369.8	134.8	275.5	60.5	840.6	286.0
1772–73	418.9	142.2	275.5	60.5	897.0	260.7
1773–74	418.9	137.2	275.5	90.4	922.0	197.0
1774–75	429.4	118.7	275.5	90.4	914.0	77.6
1775–76	431.4	108.2	284.5	90.4	914.5	167.5
1776–77	434.4	116.5	284.5	90.4	925.8	227.0
1777–78	434.4	116.5	284.5	90.4	925.8	233.3
1778–79	434.4	116.5	284.5	90.4	925.8	262.6
1779–80	434.4	116.9	295.8	90.4	937.5	318.8
1780–81	434.4	116.9	295.8	90.4	937.5	284.0
1781–82	434.4	116.9	304.3	90.4	946.0	226.0
1782–83	434.4	116.9	304.3	90.4	946.0	217.3
1783–84	434.4	116.9	304.3	90.4	946.0	191.4
1784–85	434.4	117.4	304.3	90.4	946.5	235.8
1785–86	434.4	117.4	304.5	90.4	946.7	178.5
1786–87	435.4	117.4	304.5	90.4	947.7	169.6
1787–88	435.4	117.4	304.5	90.4	947.7	171.8
1788–89	448.7	118.8	304.5	90.4	962.4	151.5
1789–90	452.7	118.8	304.5	90.4	966.4	156.1
1790–91	497.7	118.8	306.5	90.4	1013.4	136.2
1791–92	497.7	116.3	306.5	90.4	1010.9	143.8

	Kent £	Rochester £	London £	Essex £	TOTAL £	Arrears £
1792–93	497.7	116.3	306.5	90.4	1010.9	165.2
1793–94	517.7	120.7	306.5	90.4	1035.3	162.5
1794–95	517.7	120.7	306.5	90.4	1035.3	212.4
1795–96	542.1	120.7	516.5	150.5	1329.7	109.7
1796–97	573.1	137.9	516.5	150.5	1378.0	352.6
1797–98	593.1	137.9	516.5	150.5	1398.0	358.4
1798–99	593.1	136.9	516.5	150.5	1397.0	517.8
1799–1800	593.1	136.9	516.5	150.5	1397.0	341.1
1800–01	593.1	152.9	516.5	150.5	1413.0	384.0
1801–02	593.1	158.1	516.5	150.5	1418.2	318.9
1802–03	598.4	173.1	516.5	150.5	1438.5	426.7
1803–04	608.5	173.1	516.5	150.5	1448.6	459.6
1804–05	618.8	173.1	516.5	150.5	1458.9	391.8
1805–06	668.8	334.6	555.2	150.5	1709.1	476.2
1806–07	668.8	334.6	555.2	150.5	1709.1	734.9
1807–08	932.3	360.2	555.2	150.5	1998.2	116.8
1808–09	933.6	360.2	555.2	150.5	1999.5	601.8
1809–10	973.5	399.2	566.5	150.5	2089.7	222.3
1810–11	973.5	399.2	705.0	150.5	2228.2	112.5
1811–12	1346.3	399.2	755.0	150.5	2651.0	381.6
1812–13	1563.3	467.2	755.0	150.5	2936.0	144.0
1813–14	1563.3	467.2	755.0	150.5	2936.0	434.2
1814–15	1558.0	467.2	815.0	150.5	2990.7	1008.9
1815–16	1558.0	514.2	815.0	250.5	3137.7	1316.7
1816–17	1583.8	525.2	815.0	250.5	3174.5	722.8
1817–18	1686.6	525.2	815.0	250.5	3277.3	1020.3
1818–19	1686.6	540.2	815.0	250.5	3292.3	824.9
1819–20	1686.6	535.2	815.0	250.5	3287.3	1444.5
1820–21	1686.6	514.2	815.0	250.5	3266.3	1452.7
1821–22	1686.6	586.2	815.0	250.5	3338.3	1982.6
1822–23	1646.6	586.2	815.0	250.5	3298.3	2187.5
1823–24	1646.6	606.2	815.0	250.5	3318.3	1072.9
1824–25	1646.6	606.2	815.0	265.5	3333.3	1317.2
1825–26	1101.1	1201.8[62]	815.0	265.5	3383.3	349.9
1826–27	1101.1	1201.8	815.0	265.5	3383.3	621.5

[62] From this year Rochester rents include properties in both St Nicholas and St Margaret's parishes and from 1839–40 also property in Strood.

	Kent £	Rochester £	London £	Essex £	TOTAL £	Arrears £
1827–28	1137.1	1201.8	815.0	265.5	3419.3	468.9
1828–29	1372.3	1129.8	815.0	265.5	3582.5	782.5
1829–30	1372.3	1129.8	815.0	265.5	3582.5	817.0
1830–31	1392.3	1129.8	815.0	265.5	3602.5	567.2
1831–32	1423.3	1129.8	815.0	265.5	3633.5	512.4
1832–33	1410.3	1129.8	815.0	265.5	3620.5	761.8
1833–34	1410.3	1129.8	815.0	265.5	3620.5	811.2
1834–35	1377.2	1049.8	815.0	265.5	3507.4	940.0
1835–36	1292.2	1088.8	1103.0	265.5	3749.4	990.5
1836–37	1292.2	1088.8	1103.0	265.5	3749.4	1286.3
1837–38	1292.2	1108.8	1103.0	265.5	3769.4	799.8
1838–39	1292.2	1070.8	1092.0	265.5	3720.4	841.0
1839–40	1299.2	1120.8	1132.0	265.5	3817.4	962.9
1840–41	1299.2	1120.8	1132.0	265.5	3817.4	629.3
1841–42	1358.2	1115.8	1132.0	265.5	3871.4	702.5
1842–43	1353.8	1265.9	1132.0	265.5	4017.2	813.3
1843–44	1363.8	1312.3	1132.0	265.5	4073.6	795.9
1844–45	1374.9	1249.9	1062.0	265.5	3952.3	502.8
1845–46	1374.9	1348.9	1062.0	265.5	4051.3	542.2
1846–47	1394.9	1348.9	1062.0	265.5	4071.3	457.1
1847–48	1379.9	1276.1	1062.0	265.5	3983.5	299.3
1848–49	1412.8	1301.1	1059.5	265.5	4038.9	789.1
1849–50	1412.8	1271.1	1117.0	265.5	4066.4	1110.4
1850–51	1413.8	1224.1	1117.0	265.5	4020.4	1098.4
1851–52	1267.8	1204.1	1117.0	240.5	3829.4	945.9
1852–53	1265.8	1222.8	1117.0	240.5	3846.1	1219.6
1853–54	1263.8	1100.7	1117.0	240.5	3722.0	917.7
1854–55	1263.8	1100.7	1117.0	240.5	3722.0	367.7
1855–56	1263.8	1082.7	1117.0	240.5	3704.0	619.5
1856–57	1283.8	1121.7	1299.5	240.5	3945.5	491.5
1857–58	1292.8	1014.0	1482.0	240.5	4029.3	360.3
1858–59	1325.3	995.3	1482.0	258.5	4056.0	539.9
1859–60	1331.8	990.2	1482.0	276.5	4080.5	282.0
1860–61	1131.8	1026.6	1482.0	276.5	4116.8	151.1
1861–62	1308.3	1016.5	1482.0	252.5	4059.2	131.8
1862–63	1289.8	950.1	1482.0	228.5	3950.4	12.8
1863–64	1354.8	753.5	1482.0	228.5	3818.7	3.6

	Kent £	Rochester £	London £	Essex £	TOTAL £	Arrears £
1864–65	1362.5	769.6	1497.4	244.7	3874.2	8.2
1865–66	1442.4	758.6	1497.4	253.7	3952.1	1.7
1866–67	1492.4	770.9	1497.4	253.7	4014.4	–
1867–68	1536.4	796.4	1497.4	253.7	4083.9	–
1868–69	1543.4	789.1	1515.5	253.7	4101.7	17.7
1869–70	1534.8	811.6	1515.5	253.7	4115.6	1.3
1870–71	1541.8	868.2	1515.5	253.7	4179.2	3.4
1871–72	1549.8	868.2	1515.5	253.7	4187.2	–
1872–73	1793.8	903.1	1515.5	260.5	4472.9	8.0
1873–74	1860.3	907.2	1528.5	260.5	4556.5	–
1874–75	1897.3	899.7	1528.5	260.5	4586.0	–
1875–76	1825.3	973.8	2678.5	260.5	5738.1	399.0
1876–77	1822.4	1016.3	2678.5	260.5	5777.7	–
1877–78	1822.4	1113.2	2678.5	260.5	5874.6	–
1878–79	1854.4	1189.9	2678.5	260.5	5983.3	263.3
1879–80	1823.8	1226.3	2678.5	260.5	5989.1	474.9
1880–81	1846.8	1274.3	2678.5	260.5	6060.1	1225.5
1881–82	1842.8	1289.5	4446.5	260.5	7839.3	1309.6
1882–83	1842.8	1287.5	4446.5	260.5	7837.3	1415.5
1883–84	1910.9	1287.6	4446.5	260.5	7905.5	1403.7
1884–85	2099.4	995.9	4446.5	260.5	7802.3	1444.3
1885–86	2101.4	1335.9	4446.5	260.5	8144.3	513.0
1886–87	1785.3	1306.4	4446.5	200.5	7738.7	426.4
1887–88	2013.8	1210.0	4446.5	200.5	7870.8	502.0
1888–89	1880.4	1287.1	4446.5	200.5	7814.5	1119.2
1889–90	1941.4	1002.0	4191.5	200.5	7335.4	474.4
1890–91	2298.9	1053.0	4191.5	200.5	7743.9	1229.4
1891–92	2298.9	1038.9	4191.5	200.5	7729.8	467.1
1892–93	2351.0	1059.9	4191.5	200.5	7802.9	759.9
1893–94	2107.6	1012.6	4191.5	200.6	7512.3	1476.3
1894–95	1916.1	994.1	4191.5	200.5	7302.2	1323.4
1895–96	1984.0	847.3	4446.5	200.5	7478.3	1848.7
1896–97	1912.1	1094.7	4191.5	200.5	7398.8	1949.2
1897–98	1832.1	1097.9	4446.5	200.5	7577.0	470.3
1898–99	1895.5	1097.9	4446.5	200.5	7592.4	845.1
1899–1900	1889.9	1097.9	4446.5	200.5	7634.8	876.1
1900–01	1808.9	1059.2	4446.5	200.5	7515.1	292.9

	Kent	Rochester	London	Essex	TOTAL	Arrears
	£	£	£	£	£	£
1901–02	1808.6	1059.2	4446.5	200.5	7514.8	589.1
1902–03	1866.2	1166.1	4446.5	200.5	7629.3	449.1
1903–04	1644.6	1120.9	4446.5	200.5	7412.5	613.6
1904–05	1640.6	1136.3	4446.5	200.5	7423.9	1367.5
1905–06	1646.5	1106.3	4446.5	200.5	7399.8	1292.3
1906–07	1594.8	1041.7	4446.5	200.5	7283.5	832.6
1907–08	1594.6	1046.7	4746.5	200.5	7588.3	645.8
1908–09	1594.9	1052.3	4746.5	200.5	7594.2	575.7
1909–10	1594.6	1048.4	4746.5	200.5	7590.0	794.0
1910–11	1628.3	1048.4	4746.5	200.5	7623.7	533.4
1911–12	1640.4	1040.7	4746.5	200.5[63]	7628.1	445.3
1912–13	1646.7	1040.7	4746.5	–	7433.9	457.3
1913–14	1656.7	1028.7	4746.5	–	7431.9	505.3

[63] The farm at East Tilbury was sold on 11 November 1912.

Expenditure on Bridge Works and Estate Maintenance

	Total expenditure £	Day labour £	Provision £
1576–77	458	214	244
1577–78	273	53	190
1578–79	184	76	108
1579–80	222	82	140
1580–81	252	100	152
1581–82	322	146	176
1582–83	288	119	169
1583–84	281	115	166
1584–85	244[64]	72	172
1585–86	353	152	201
1586–87	150	63	87
1587–88	160	77	83
1588–89	209	95	114
1589–90	242	74	168
1590–91	218	82	136
1591–92	200	59	141
1592–93	280	114	166
1593–94	326	147	179
1594–95	194	62	132
1595–96	262	120	142
1596–97	181	82	91
1597–98	317	125	192
1598–99	211	89	122
1599–1600	228	106	122
1600–01	222	146	76
1601–02	260	109	151
1602–03	220	114	106
1603–04	145	98	47
1604–05	277	113	164
1605–06	336	199	137
1606–07	273	151	122
1607–08	233	128	105

[64] Expenditure this year includes £33 for the audit chamber and £10 for a new lighter.

	Total expenditure	Day labour	Provision
	£	£	£
1608–09	251	164	87
1609–10	261	134	127
1610–11	220	139	61
1611–12	242	141	101
1612–13	260	158	102
1613–14	314	146	168
1614–15	314	148	166
1615–16	172	97	75
1616–17	382	258	124
1617–18	188	117	71
1618–19	265	87	178
1619–20	555	255	300
1620–21	265	140	125
1621–22	311	163	148
1622–23	299	138	161
1623–24	234	114	120
1624–25	270	151	119
1625–26	248	136	112
1626–27	214	119	95
1627–28	494[65]	173	321
1628–29	286	146	140
1629–30	316	178	138
1630–31	337	187	150
1631–32	301	177	124
1632–33	343	196	147
1633–34	278	137	141
1634–35	246	144	102
1635–36	359	184	175
1636–37	342	164	178
1637–38	340	183	157
1638–39	372	197	175
1639–40	299	170	129
1640–41	322	184	138
1641–42	339	177	162

[65] Expenditure this year includes £54 for a new lighter and £101 for the new bridge chamber.

	Total expenditure £	Day labour £	Provision £
1642–43	407	200	207
1643–44	324	187	137
1644–45	348	171	177
1645–46	*383*	191	*192*
1646–47	*362*	209	*153*
1647–48	*475*	189	*286*
1648–49	*454*	207	*247*
1649–50	*377*	207	*170*
1650–51	*293*	176	*117*
1651–52	*444*	202	*242*
1654–55	*399*	212	*187*
1656–57	*344*	189	*155*
1657–58	*305* [66]	187	*118*
1658–59	*277*	128	*149*
1659–60	*318*	187	*131*
1660–61	302	147	155
1661–62	349	160	189
1662–63	369	180	189
1663–64	361	176	185
1664–65	362	166	194
1665–66	433	194	233
1666–67	396	177	219
1667–68	395	156	239
1668–69	465	188	277
1669–70	361	153	208
1670–71	425	195	230
1671–72	367	159	208
1672–73	521	167	355
1673–74	763	259	504
1674–75	803	221	582
1675–76	554	194	360

[66] From 16 May 1657 until 3 October 1657 rough accounts of the monthly pay for labour and provisions were recorded by paymaster John Atkins who died during October. Revised wardens accounts, dating from 5 September 1657 to 29 May 1658, record under provisions during the last month a lump repayment to Atkins's widow for the first four months' pay laid out by Atkins. This figure has been divided between labour and provisions as in the rough accounts to produce the adjusted figures for this year.

	Total expenditure £	Day labour £	Provision £
1676–77	545	226	319
1677–78	557	195	362
1678–79	392	221	171
1679–80	578	213	365
1680–81	482	199	283
1681–82	445	178	267
1682–83	419	178	241
1683–84	399	198	201
1684–85	462	229	233
1685–86	318	189	129
1686–87	403	201	202
1687–88	524	207	317
1688–89	402	205	197
1689–90	379	215	164
1690–91	435	187	248
1691–92	419	195	224
1692–93	530	199	331
1693–94	507	180	327
1694–95	409	189	220
1695–96	514	211	303
1696–97	485	205	280
1697–98	478	230	248
1698–99	347	190	157
1699–1700	444	197	247
1700–01	433	208	225
1701–02	387	181	296
1702–03	417	233	184
1703–04	441	211	230
1704–05	493	212	281
1705–06	552	224	328
1706–07	581	289	292
1707–08	398	230	168
1708–09	597	269	328
1709–10	494	216	278
1710–11	396	211	185
1711–12	500	235	265

	Total expenditure £	Day labour £	Provision £
1712–13	442	199	243
1713–14	475	204	271
1714–15	489	246	243
1715–16	559	233	326
1716–17	547	236	311
1717–18	415	218	197
1718–19	473	203	270
1719–20	445	240	205
1720–21	492	207	285
1721–22	500	226	274
1722–23	537	254	283
1723–24	416	225	191
1724–25	483	240	243
1725–26	577	270	307
1726–27	518	248	270
1727–28	671	252	419
1728–29	488	194	294
1729–30	501	209	292
1730–31	609	240	369
1731–32	603	239	364
1732–33	771	280	491
1733–34	771	248	523
1734–35	598	222	376
1735–36	659	233	426
1736–37	910	301	609
1737–38	553	249	304
1738–39	758	277	481
1739–40	881	291	590
1740–41	754	379	375
1741–42	672	246	426
1742–43	536	202	334
1743–44	617	244	373
1744–45	702	253	449
1745–46	700	241	459
1746–47	699	207	492
1747–48	775	191	584

	Total expenditure £	Day labour £	Provision £
1748–49	698	117	581
1749–50	430	124	306
1750–51	549	111	438
1751–52	715	129	586
1752–53	712	123	589
1753–54	398	116	282
1754–55	525	111	414
1755–56	651	122	529
1756–57	735	137	598
1757–58	373	112	261
1758–59	775	139	636
1759–60	1221	189	1032
1760–61	977	217	760
1761–62	1404	311	1093
1762–63	1336	294	1042
1763–64	1868	379	1489
1764–65	1284	281	1003
1765–66	1215	271	944
1766–67	1121	267	854
1767–68	990	248	742
1768–69	1101	291	810
1769–70	1047	293	754
1770–71	849	283	566
1771–72	1367	328	1039
1772–73	1141	303	838
1773–74	1013	291	722
1774–75	965	293	672
1775–76	960	287	673
1776–77	867	303	564
1777–78	1266	322	944
1778–79	1193	281	912
1779–80	958	274	684
1780–81	904	302	602
1781–82	775	259	516
1782–83	1141	398	743
1783–84	854	366	488

	Total expenditure £	Day labour £	Provision £
1784–85	827	286	541
1785–86	1137	325	812
1786–87	1123	305	818
1787–88	1130	297	833
1788–89	1061	334	727
1789–90	1034	303	731
1790–91	969	329	640
1791–92	1096	351	745
1792–93	1194	343	851
1793–94	2561	814	1747
1794–95	2425	975	1450
1795–96	2593	1099	2362
1796–97	3650	1288	2362
1797–98	3006	1186	1820
1798–99	3754	1284	2470
1799–1800	4583	1110	3473
1800–01	2753	970	1783
1801–02	2999	1193	1806
1802–03	1749	495	1254
1803–04	966	333	633
1804–05	1115	307	808
1805–06	1481	294	1187
1806–07	1215	303	912
1807–08	1509	229	1280
1808–09	1090	211	879
1809–10	1792	449	1343
1810–11	1744	414	1330
1811–12	2016	411	1605
1812–13	2232	621	1611
1813–14	2379	489	1890
1814–15	1928	411	1517
1815–16	2292	543	1749
1816–17	2345	606	1739
1817–18	3651	689	2962
1818–19	1929	407	1522
1819–20	1479	197	1282

	Total expenditure £	Day labour £	Provision £
1820–21	2715	519	2196
1821–22	14775	875	13900
1822–23	4529	1039	3490
1823–24	5685	931	4754
1824–25	2087	508	1579
1825–26	2397	482	1915
1826–27	2482	525	1957
1827–28	1385	394	991
1828–29	1409	180	1229
1829–30	1357	165	1192
1830–31	1101	158	943
1831–32	1788	171	1617
1832–33	974	155	819
1833–34	1175	181	994
1834–35	1182	194	988
1835–36	1710	155	1555
1836–37	1315	195	1120
1837–38	2014	217	1797
1838–39	1710	227	1483
1839–40	3288	383	2905
1840–41	2428	270	2158
1841–42	1831	234	1597
1842–43	1765	224	1541
1843–44	1822	169	1653
1844–45	1996	175	1821
1845–46	4397	196	4201
1846–47	2329	181	2148
1847–48	1789	176	1613
1848–49	1967	190	1777
1849–50	2046	198	1848

	Total expenditure £	Day labour £	Provision £	Bridge work by contract £
1850–51	11171	198	1143	9830
1851–52	13214	206	993	12015
1852–53	4718	202	880	3636

	Total expenditure £	Day labour £	Provision £	Bridge work by contract £
1853–54	10426	138	737	9551
1854–55	11448	114	736	10598
1855–56	36545	129	782	35634
1856–57	44962	124	1864	42974
1857–58	9007	119	1143	7745
1858–59	8090	68	867	7115
1859–60	3715	60	1114	2541
1860–61	2100	66	733	1301
1861–62	3397	67	996	2334
1862–63	1195	63	763	369
1863–64	1871	58	741	1072
1864–65	2510	60	1128	1322
1865–66	1785	136	1617	32
1866–67	1072	140	932	–
1867–68	1987	89	1678	220
1868–69	1182	211	971	–
1869–70	1269	166	817	286
1870–71	766	150	616	–
1871–72	1498	155	1334	9
1872–73	2157	162	1950	45
1873–74	2334	156	2119	59
1874–75	2111	176	1119	816
1875–76	1891	163	1629	99
1876–77	5863	162	5523	178
1877–78	3132	150	2822	160
1878–79	3663	164	3428	71
1879–80	3283	173	3054	56
1880–81	2922	185	2655	82
1881–82	3165	170	1723	1272
1882–83	1066	165	714	187
1883–84	1379	170	1000	209
1884–85	5368	170	5298	–
1885–86	1192	170	1000	22
1886–87	2684	170	2506	8
1887–88	2223	170	1685	368
1888–89	1410	170	1201	39

	Total expenditure	Day labour	Provision	Bridge work by contract
	£	£	£	£
1889–90	1591	127	1340	124
1890–91	3123	–	2191	932
1891–92	1601	–	1399	202
1892–93	1469	–	1065	404
1893–94	1608	–	1394	214
1894–95	1917	–	1541	376
1895–96	2658	–	1324	1334[67]
1896–97	9092	–	2953	6139[67]
1897–98	2287	–	1447	840[67]
1898–99	4528	–	1189	3339
1899–1900	2659	–	2465	194
1900–01	2894	–	2704	190
1901–02	1535	–	1389	146
1902–03	3814	–	3550	264
1903–04	2936	–	1790	1146
1904–05	2252	–	1942	310
1905–06	2315	–	1318	997
1906–07	4189	–	2935	1254
1907–08	2228	–	1724	504
1908–09	3114	–	2176	938
1909–10	3739	–	1448	2291
1910–11	6267	–	2041	4226
1911–12	27257	–	1880	25377
1912–13	37711	–	1516	36195
1913–14	27342	–	2447	24895

[67] Bridge work during these years includes repair of damage caused by the lighter Diamond.

Appendix C

An Edition of the Rochester Bridgework List

[*Note on editorial conventions.* The spelling is that of the manuscripts, save that abbreviations have been extended (except where there is doubt or where repetition makes extension unnecessary), the initial letters of place-names have been capitalized and a small number of errors have been corrected in the text but noted in the apparatus. The punctuation of the OE is that of the manuscript except that some omitted *punctus* have been supplied; that of the Latin has been modernised.]

   I   The Old English Text
  II   The Latin Text
 III The Canterbury Version

I

The Old English Text

Manuscripts

B Maidstone, C[entre for] K[entish] S[tudies], DRc/R1 (*Textus Roffensis*), ff. 166v–167: copy (f. 166v a supplied leaf of s.xii/xiii, f. 167 in the main hand of the cartulary of s.xii¹).

Edited

   a. W. Lambarde, *Perambulation of Kent*, London, 1576, 307–11.
   b. W. de G.Birch, *Cartularium Saxonicum*, 3 vols, London, 1885–93, [Hereafter cited as BCS] no.1322.
   c. A.J. Robertson, *Anglo-Saxon Charters*, Cambridge, 1939, no. 52.

Facsimile

Textus Roffensis, part 2, ed. P.H. Sawyer, Early English Manuscripts in Facsimile, xi, Copenhagen, 1962.

Printed from B.

Þis is þære bricce geweorc on Hrouecæstre

Her syndon genamad þa land þe man hi of scæl weorcan.
Ærest þære burge biscop fehð on þone earm[a] to wercene þa land peran. 7 þreo

---

[a] *The Latin versions (II, III) suggest that the word* east *or* easterne *may have been omitted from the OE text here.*

gyrda to þillianæ. 7 ·iii· sylla to lycanne. Þæt is of Borcstealle. 7 of Cucclestane. 7 of Frinondesbyrig. 7 of Stoce.

Þanne seo oðer per gebyrað to Gyllingeham. 7 to Cætham. 7 an gyrd to þillanne. 7 ·iii· sylla to leccenne.

Þonne seo þridde per gebyrað eft þam biscope. 7 þridde healf gyrd to þillianne. 7 ·iii· sylla to lecenne. of Heallingan. 7 of Trotescliue. 7 of Meallingan. 7 of Fliote. 7 of Stane. 7 of Pinindene. 7 of Falchenham.

þonne is se feorðe per[b] þæs cinges. 7 fiorðe healf gyrd to þillanne. 7 sylla ·iii· to leccanne. of Ægelesforda. 7 of ellan þam læþe þe þær to liþ. 7 of Ufanhylle. 7 of Aclea. 7 of þam smalanlande. 7 of Cusintune. 7 of Dudeslande. 7 of Gisleardeslande. 7 of Wuldeham. 7 of Burhham. 7 of Æcclesse. ....[c] 7 of Horstede. 7 of Fearnlege. 7 of Tærstane.[d] 7 of Cealce. 7 of Hennhyrste.[e] 7 of Ædune.

Þonne is sy fifte per þæs arcebiscopes[f]. to[g] Wroteham.[h] 7 to Mægþanstane. 7 to Woþringabyran. 7 to Netlestede. 7 to þam twam Peccham. 7 to Hæselholte. 7 to Mæranwyrþe. 7 to Lillanburnan. 7 to Swanatune. 7 to Offaham. 7 to Dictune. 7 to Westerham. 7 ·iiii· gyrda to þyllanne. 7 ·iii· selle to leccanne;

Þonne is syo syoxte per to Holinganburnan. 7 to eallan þam læþe. 7 ·iiii· gyrda to þelliene. 7 ·iii· sylla to lecenne.

Þonne is syo syoueþe 7 syo eahteþe per to Howaran lande to wyrcenne. 7 fifte healf gyrd to þillanne. 7 ·vi· sylla to lycanne.

Þonne is syo nigaþa per þæs arcebiscopes. þæt is syo land per æt þæm west ende. to Flyote. 7 to his Cliue. 7 to Hehham. 7 to Denetune. 7 to Melantune. 7 to Hludesdune. 7 to Meapeham. 7 to Snodilande. 7 to Berlingan. 7 to Peadeleswyrþe. 7 ealla þa dænewaru. 7 ·iiii· gyrdu to þilianne. 7 þryo sylle to leccanne.

DATE. The document is undated, and neither the rubric nor the opening explains its origin. Earlier attempts to date the document to s.x² on the basis of what is known of the history of the estates assigned to the piers of the bishop, the archbishop or the king were based on two erroneous assumptions: that all the estates so allocated had belonged to those lords when the document was compiled and that the present form of the document preserves the original text accurately. See above, pp. 18–20.

The earliest manuscript, the *Textus Roffensis*, preserves the first half of the text on a replacement leaf of s.xii/xiii while the second half was written by the main scribe of the *Textus* of c.1120. It is likely that the replacement leaf was written in order to hide alterations to the estates assigned to the bishop of Rochester's piers. Both scribes seem to have rendered their exemplar with care. Mr P.R. Kitson suggests (*personal communication*) that the language is very largely consistent throughout and was composed

---

b   *B has* se *in error.*
c   *Erasure in B. For the four names that have been deleted see III.*
d   *c erroneously reads* Cærstane.
e   *B reads* Hennhyste.
f   *B reads* arcebiscope.
g   *Fol. 166v, the supplied leaf ends here.*
h   Wroteham *is the first word on f. 167, and is written by the main scribe of the Textus Roffensis.*

in s.xi[1] or s.xi med. He draws attention to the following features which point to s.xi[1] rather than to the classical OE of s.x[2]: the occasional monopthongization (*ellan*) and/or smoothing (*scæl*, *Hehham*), dative plurals in *-an* never *-um*, weak genitive plurals having lost their final vowel (*Holingan-* and perhaps *Falchen-*), occasional *-ene* beside *-anne* and *-enne* in inflected infinitives, declension of the loanword *per* ('pier' from Latin *pera*) with its nominative singular endingless and accusative singular in *-an*, and with variable gender. In the second half of the text somewhat more Kentish forms appear than in the first (*sy(o)* against *se(o)*, *ænde* and *dænewaru*), but are unlikely to have been introduced by the scribe of the replacement leaf. He may have been responsible for the redundant first *n* in *Frinondesbyrig* and for *Cucclestane* where the second *c* should have been a vowel, but otherwise he succeeded in copying older forms faithfully.

II

The Latin Text

Manuscripts

B Maidstone, CKS, DRc/R1 (*Textus Roffensis*), ff. 164v–5: copy. (f. 164v a supplied leaf in a hand of s.xii/xiii, f. 165 in the main hand of the cartulary of s.xii[1].)
C Maidstone, CKS, DRc/R2 (*Custumale Roffense*), ff. 63v–64v: copy, s.xiii.
D Maidstone, CKS, Drb/Ar2 (*Registrum temporalium*), ff. 140v–141: copy, s.xiv[med].
E London, P[ublic] R[ecord] O[ffice], SC8/85 Ancient Petitions 4234: copy of 1391–2.
F London, PRO, SC8/86 Ancient Petitions 4256: copy of c.1395.

Edited

    a. W. Lambarde, *Perambulation of Kent*, London, 1576, 311–12, from B.
    b. BCS 1321, from B.

Facsimile

Textus Roffensis, part 2, ed. P.H. Sawyer, Early English Manuscripts in Facsimile, xi, 1962.

Printed from B, with principal variants in C, D, E and F.

Hec descriptio demonstrat aperte unde debeat pons de Rouecestra restaurari quotiens fuerit fractus:[a]

Primum eiusdem ciuitatis episcopus incipit operari in orientali brachio primam peram de terra, deinde tres uirgatas plancas ponere, & tres suliuas, id est tres

---

[a] *Rubric in B only*; De ponte C; De hiis qui debent facere pontem Roffensem D; Domesday pour le pount de Roucestre salonc lescheqer E.

magnas trabes, supponere. Et hoc faciat de Borcstealla[b], & de Cuclestana[c], & de Freondesberia[d], & de Stoche[e].

Postea secunda pera pertinet ad Gillingeham[f] & de Cætham[g]; & unam uirgatam plancas ponere, & ·iii· suliuas supponere.

Deinde tertia pera pertinet iterum ad episcopum ciuitatis eiusdem; & duas uirgatas & dimidiam plancas ponere, & tres[h] suliuas supponere; & hoc fiet de Hallingis[i], & de Trotescliua[j], & de Meallingis[k], & de Fleotes[l], & de Stanes, & de Pinindene[m], & de Falceham[n].

Postea quarta pera pertinet ad regem; & tres et dimidiam uirgatam plancas ponere, & tres suliuas supponere; & hoc debet fieri de Æilesforda[o], & de toto illo lesto quod ad illud manerium pertinet, & de super montaneis `quod est et de Ufen-hylle´[p], & de Aclea[q], & de Smalalande[r], & de Cusintonæ[s], & de Dudeslande[t], &[u] de Gisleardeslande[v], & de Wldeham[w], & de Burhham[x], & de Æclesse[y], ...[z] & de Horstede[a2], & de Fearnlega[b2], & de Terstane[c2], & de Cealca[d2], & de Hænhersta[e2], & de Hathdune[f2].

Deinde quinta pera est archiepiscopi; quattuor[g2] uirgatas plancas ponere, & tres suliuas summittere; & hoc debet fieri de Wroteham[h2], & de Mæidesstana[i2], & de Oteringaberiga[j2], & de Netlasteda[k2], & de duobus Peccham[l2], & de Hæselholte[m2],

---

[b] Borcstalla C; Borstalle D, E, F.

[c] Cukelstane D; Cokilstane E, F.

[d] Frendesberia C; Frendesber' D; Frendisbery E, F.

[e] Stoke E, F.

[f] Gillyngham D, E, F.

[g] Chetham C, D, E; Chatham F.

[h] *B here and subsequently writes* tres *as* ·iii· *with the letters* es *written superscript.*

[i] Hallinges C; Hallynges D; Hallyng' E, F.

[j] Trottescliue C; Trottesclyu' D; Trottisclyue E, F.

[k] Meallinges C; Mallynges D, E, F.

[l] Southflete E, F.

[m] Pinyngdenne D; Pynynden' E, F.

[n] Falcesham F.

[o] Eylesfordia C; Eylesford' D, E, F.

[p] quod ... Ufenhylle *is a marginal note by the scribe of this leaf in B, which is wrongly marked for insertion after* de Aclea. De Hufenhille *(C),* de Ovenhulle *(D, E)* and de Ufenhulle *(F) all accordingly follow* Aclea.

[q] Acleia D.

[r] Smalalanda C; Smalelande D, E, F.

[s] Cusintone C; Cusyntone D; Cosynton' E, F.

[t] Dudeslonde F.

[u] *Fol. 164v of B ends here. From* de Gisleardeslande *the text is written by the main scribe of the Textus Roffensis.*

[v] Gisleadeslonde C; Gislardeslande D; Gisleadislande E; Gisleadislonde F.

[w] Woldeham D; Woldham E, F.

[x] Burgham C, D, F.

[y] Aclesse C, D; Acclesse E, F.

[z] *1½ lines of text erased here in B. For the missing names, see III.*

[a2] Horsteda C; Herstede E, F.

[b2] Farnlega C; Farnlegha D; Farlegh' E, F.

[c2] Thorstane C.

[d2] Chealka C; Chealcha D; Chalke E, F.

[e2] Henhersta C, D; Henhurst E, F.

[f2] Hathduna C; Hathdenne E, F.

[g2] *Here and subsequently* quattuor *is written in B as* ·iiii· *with* or *superscript.*

[h2] Wrotham D, E, F.

[i2] Meidestane C; Maydestane D; Maidestan' E, F.

[j2] Woteringeberge C; Oteryngberga D; Otteryngbery E, F.

[k2] Netlesteda C, D; Netelsted' E, F.

[l2] Pecham D; Pekham E, F.

[m2] Heselholte C, E, F; Haselholte D.

& de Mæreuurtha[n2], & de Lilleburna[o2], & de Suuanatuna[p2], & de Offeham, & de Dictune[q2], & de Westerham.

Postea sexta pera debet fieri de Holingeburna[r2] & de tota illo lesto quę ad hoc pertinet; quattuor uirgatas plancas ponere, & tres suliuas supponere.

Septimam & octauam peram debent facere homines de Hou[s2]; & quattuor et dimidium uirgatas plancas ponere, et sex suliuas supponere.

Deinde nona pera, quę ultima est in occidentali brachio, est iterum archiepiscopi, quattuor uirgatas plancas ponere, & tres suliuas summittere; & hęc debe<n>t fieri de Northfleta[t2], & de Cliua[u2], & de Heahham[v2], & de Denituna[w2], & de Meletuna[x2], & de Hludesduna[y2], & de Meapeham[z2], & de Snodilanda[a3], & de Berlingæs[b3], & de Pedlesuurthe[c3], & de omnibus illis hominibus qui manent in illa ualle. Et sciendum est quod omnes illę suliuę quę in ponte illo ponantur tantę grossitudinis debent esse, ut bene possint sustinere omnia grauia pondera superiacentium plancarum & omnium desuper pertranseuntium rerum.

DATE. The Latin text precedes the Old English in the *Textus Roffensis*, an order which reflects the cartularist's perception of the status of the two languages. Nonetheless the Latin was clearly composed later and translated from a version of the OE text. Thus the OE term *sylle* ('beams') is rendered *suliuas*, which has to be translated *id est tres magnas trabes* on first occurrence; the OE *of Ufanhylle* is mistranslated *de super montaneis* and a later interlineation explains *quod est de Ufenhylle*; and OE *ealla þa dænewaru* is woodenly rendered *de omnibus illis hominibus qui manent in illa ualle*. Miss A.J. Robertson (*ASCharters*, 351) hesitated to accept the priority of the OE text, because it used the loanword *per* 'pier' (from Latin *pera*), which is not otherwise recorded before the fourteenth century but which could derive from the Latin text. But in the absence of other early documents in English describing bridges the non-appearance of the word has no significance. Mr P.R. Kitson has kindly pointed out to me that the number of estate-names which have a weak first element ending in *-an* or *-a* in the OE, but in *-a* or *-e* in the Latin, also strongly supports the priority of the OE text. Nonetheless the Latin version was produced by someone with a living knowledge of OE, who, for example, recognized *of Heallingan* and *of Meallingan* as English dative plurals and rendered them as *de Hallingis* and *de Mallingis*. It could therefore be the work of an English monk of Rochester who was a boy at the time of the Conquest, but who lived on into the twelfth century.

There is, moreover, one place where the Latin text may have rendered its original

[n2] Merewurtha C; Mereworth D, E, F.

[o2] Lilleburne D; Lillebourna E, F.

[p2] Swanatune C; Swaneton' D, Swanatuna E, F.

[q2] Dittune C; Dittone D; Dytton' E, F.

[r2] Holyngburna D; Holyngbourn' E, F.

[s2] Ho C; Hoo D.

[t2] Northflete D, E, F.

[u2] Clyue D, E, F.

[v2] Hecham D; Hegham E, F.

[w2] Denintuna C; Denytone D.

[x2] Meltona D; Meltuna E, F.

[y2] Ludesduna C; Luddesduna D; Lodesdona E, F.

[z2] Mepeham C, D, E, F.

[a3] Snodilande C; Snodelande D; Snodelonde E, F.

[b3] Berlinges C; Berlynges D; Bierlyng' E, F.

[c3] Pedlesworthe C, D; Padelesworth E, F.

more faithfully than the extant OE text (here the replacement leaf of *s.xii/xiii*): *in orientali brachio* where the OE only has *on þone earm* (above, p. 17 n. 31, though this could just be an explanatory addition by the translator). In general the OE and Latin texts convey identical information, but the Latin rubric is fuller than the brief OE heading, and the final sentence of the Latin text about the need for the beams to be of sufficient size to bear the weight both of the planking and of traffic on the bridge has no parallel at all in the OE. It may have been added to meet a particular post-Conquest need, when a repair had proved inadequate.

III

The Canterbury Latin Version

Manuscripts

G London, British Library, Cotton Galba E. iv, f. 20: copy, s.xiv[1].
H Canterbury, D & C, Reg. K, f. 77r: copy of E, s.xiv[1].
I London, British Library, Harley MS 1757, f. 178: copy of G, s.xvii.

Edited

    a. W. Lambarde, *Perambulation of Kent*, London, 1576, 304–6, from Nicholas Wotton's copy of H or its exemplar.

Printed from G, with principal variants from H.

De Assisa pontis Roffensis[a]

Episcopus Roffensis debet facere primam peram de ponte Roffensi, 7 debet inuenire tres sulliues, 7 debet plancare iii uirgatas super pontem; 7 hoc debent facere Borstalle, Cuculestan, Frendesbery[b], Stoke.

Secunda pera debet habere iii sulliues, 7 debet plancare unam uirgatam; 7 hoc debent homines de Gylingham[c], 7 de Chetham.

Episcopus Roffensis debet facere tertiam peram, 7 debet iii sulliues, 7 plancare ii uirgatas 7 dimidium; 7 hoc debetur[d] de Halling', Trokescliue[e], Malling', Suthflete, Stane, Pynindene[f], Falcham.

Quarta pera debet iii sulliues, 7 plancare iii uirgatas; 7 hoc debent homines de Borgham de ·vi· sullingis, 7 de Woldeham cum Roberto Biset 7 sociis suis 7 cum Roberto Neue de iii sullingis, de Acle[g] una sullinga, de Henherste dimidium sullinga, de Hondene quartam partem unius sullingae, de Cusintone dimidium

---

a *In H the rubric reads*: Memorandum de ponte Roffensi
b Frendebery H.
c Gillingeham H.

d debet H.
e Trockescliue H.
f Pinindene H.
g Athle H.

sullinga, de Boueheld dimidium sullinga, de Echles xxv acr', de Therstane i sulling', de Farlegh[h] una sulling', de Lose una sulling', de Lillintone ii sulling', de Stokebere ii sulling', de Glislardelande[i], de Sinelonde, de Dudelonde, de Lichebundelonde, de Horsted, de Chelke.

Quinta pera pertinet ad archiepiscopum, 7 debet iii sulliues, 7 plancare iiii uirgatas. Et hoc debet de Wroteham, Meydestane, Woteringebery, Nethelestede, Pecham 7 altera Pecham, Heselholte, Mereworthe, Leyburn, Swaneton[j], Offeham, Dicton[k], Westerham.

Sexta pera pertinet ad hundredum de Heyhorne, 7 debet iii sulliues, 7 plancare iiii uirgatas; 7 hoc debent homines de Boxele, scilicet de vii sulling' et dimidium sed contradicunt dimidium sulling', de Detling unam sulling' 7 dimidium 7 quartam partem unius, <de> Thornham ii sulling' 7 tertiam quam contradicunt, de Aldintone unam sulling' 7 aliam quam contradicunt, de Stokeberi[l] duas sulling', de Ethnothinton[m] ii sulling', de Bikenore ·i· sulling', de Wedneselle ·i· sull', de Holingeburne ·vi· sull', de quibus Godintone debet ii sull', 7 Boctone archiepiscopi dimidium sull', de Herebertone cum Frensted[n] ·j· sull', de Lhedes iii sull', de Heriettesham cum Little Wrotham[o] ·ii· sull', de Wrenstede dimidium sull', de Withelinge cum Eastselue ·j· sull', de Lenham iiij sull' 7 dimidium, de Langele[p] cum Oteringdenn'[q] ·ij· sull' 7 dimidium, de Eastlenham ·ij· sull', de Bocton[r] Bauelingham ·j· sull', de Hulecumbe ·ij· sull' 7 dimidium quam contradicunt, de Farburne di' sull' 7 dimid' quam contradicunt, de Suthone ·vij· sull' 7 dimid', 7 de Otteham ·j· sull', de Wyherintone[s] dimidium sull'.
Notandum quod ad vj sull' de Holingeburne debet Bocton dimidium sull', Godinton ij sull', Rucherste dimidium jugum, Wilmidene 7 Hokebere dimidium iugum, Witthiherste ·j· iugum, Herindene dimidium iugum, Hallerebroc 7 Herberteste di' iug', Bresing[t] di' iug', Beaurepeyr di' iug', Stanburne 7 Thrumsted di' iug', Ripple di' iug' Bradestrete di' iug', Brechedene quartem partem unius iugi, Symon de Porta v acras, Gilebertus de Thrumstede ·xv· acras, terra Ospeck v acras, Thomas supra montem ·x· acras, Sara de Dene, Robertus de Swaneden' cum sociis xlv acras, Bradherst[u] ·iiij· iug', Huking di' iug', Wodetone ·j· iug', ...[v] Herste ·j· iug', Heyhorne di' iug', La Reye di' iug', Greneweye ·j· iug', Suthgreneweye ·j· iug', Gerin cum sociis di' iug', terra Jacobi de Hamme[w] di' iug', Cotmanni di' iug', Nutmannestone 7 terra Bellardi di' iug', Sheldesburn di' iug', Suade quartem

---

[h] Farlege H.	[p] Longele H.
[i] Gliselardelond H.	[q] Oteringedenn H.
[j] Swanetone H.	[r] Bostone H.
[k] Dictone H.	[s] Wiherintone H.
[l] Stokebery H.	[t] Breping H.
[m] Eilnothintone H.	[u] Bradherste H.
[n] Frenstede H.	[v] *Gap in G and H, apparently of one property.*
[o] Litle Wroteham H.	[w] Hannye H.

partem <iugi>, Worham v acras, Rode v acras, Symon Cockel xxv acras, heredes Thome de la Dane v acras, Walter Larson[x] ·v· acras, Willelmus Clyve ·x· acras.
Septima 7 octaua pertinent ad homines de Ho; 7 debent ·vi· sulliues, 7 plancare ·iiij· uirgatas 7 dimid'.
Nona pera pertinet ad archiepiscopum; 7 debet ·iij· sulliues, 7 ·iiij· uirgatas plancare; 7 hoc debetur de ....[y] 7 Clyue[z], Hegham, Dennintone, Meltone, Ludesdone, Mepeham, Snodeslonde, ... [a2], Pedelesworthe[b2], 7 et de omnibus hominibus in eadem uilla.

DATE. There is no indication in either of the principal manuscripts (G, H) about when this 'assize' or memorandum was produced. In both cartularies it came in a section comprising legal and financial documents copied from the royal exchequer or chancery. It is clearly a product of a judicial enquiry, since the objections of the tenants of Boxley, of Aldington (in Thornham) and of Fairbourne to the assessments of their holdings are recorded (*sed contradicunt dimidium/unam sullingam*). The 'assize' belongs to a time when the fourth and sixth piers had both needed repair, since the document provides very much fuller details of the obligations of the estates assigned to those two piers in terms of their assessment in sulungs (and in some instances even of yokes and acres). Since Cotton Galba E iv dates from the last decade of Henry of Eastry's office as prior of Christ Church (1270–1328), it is possible that the assize belongs to one of the inquisitions of the reign of Edward I of whose objective we are uncertain, namely to that of 1277 or that of 1280. (See above, 38–9.) It may, however, be a copy of an earlier inquest. More precise dating will depend upon the identification of the named tenants. It is instructive that the royal chancery in the thirteenth century was evidently using a text of the Bridgework List that contained the four estates whose names had been erased from the list for the fourth pier in the Latin and OE versions of the document in the *Textus Roffensis* [and which are therefore missing from all texts that descend therefrom]. It is also of interest that the chancery was no longer declaring the king's responsibility for the fourth pier.

---

[x] Larsone H.
[y] *Erasure in G, presumably of the estate of Northfleet; gap in H.*
[z] Cliue H.

[a2] *Erasure in G; gap in H; The missing estate is Birling, and Lambarde reads* Bearlinges.
[b2] Medelesworthe G, H.

Index

Abergavenny, Lords *see* Neville
Abington, Sir John, 112
Act . . . for Changing the Day of Election
  (1702), 131, 172
Act for the Maintenance of Bridges (1670), 179
Acts of Parliament *see also* Chantries Act;
  Medway Tunnel Act; Rochester Bridge
  Acts; Upper Medway Navigation and
  Conservancy Act
Addington, Henry, 1st Viscount Sidmouth, 207
Addington (Kent), 27
Admiralty, and Rochester Bridge
  (1660–1825), 185, 211, 212–15, 217
  (1825–1950), 225–6, 231, 232–3, 235, 237,
    240–1, 243, 247, 264
Adolphus, John, 215n
'Advertisements of good Order', 142–3, 146
Æthelberht I, King of Kent, 14, 15
Æthelberht II, King of Kent, 13–14
Æthelnoth Cild, 29
Aird, John, & Co., 252, 253
Albertson, Richard, 111
Albini, William de, 37
Alcock, Robert, 126
Aldington, 135
Alexander, Daniel, Jnr, 210, 215
Alexander, Daniel Asher, 182, 184, 185,
  199–210, 213–15, 217, Plates 11–12
Allhallows (Hoo), 52, 57, 133
Allington, 29, 35, 61, 264
alms and pardons, income from, 14th–16th
  cent., 52, 57, 72, 77, 85–91, 312, 314, 316
Amherst, John, 299
Anderson *see also* Mott, Hay and Anderson
Anderson, Daniel, 243, 246
Anderson, David, 225
Anderson, Kenneth, 278
Anglo Iranian Oil Co., 272
Ansell, Percy, 306
Ansfrid, lord of Allington, and family, 35
Appleton, James, 246–7
architects to Rochester Bridge *see* Alexander;
  Cubitt; Rennie; Smirke; Telford
Arkcoll, Charles, 258, 261, 303
Arkcoll, John, 304
Arlington Development Company, 280
Armstrong, James Taylor, 310
Armstrong, John, 217–18
Armstrong, Thomas, 306
Arnold, A.A., 258n
Arrol, Sir William, & Co., 252, 253

Arundel, Thomas, Archbishop of Canterbury,
  86, 88
Ashton, Horace Hamilton, 308
Associated Portland Cement Manufacturers,
  251, 272, 280
Astor, Gavin, Lord Astor of Hever, 308
Atkins, John, 133, 135
attorney, office of *see* bridge attorney
audit chamber *see* Bridge Chamber
audit dinners *see* entertainments
auditor, office of, 53, 98, 103–4, 105, 113, 122,
  134, 135
Augustine, Saint, 14
Aveling, Thomas Lake, 305
Aveling & Porter, 248
Aylesford, 3, 58, 61, 62, 89, 132
  bridges at, 233, 264
  property of Rochester Bridge, 55, 56
  in Rochester bridgework list, 17, 20, 33, 39
  see also Preston; Rowe Place; Tottington
Aylesford, Earls of *see* Finch
Aylesford, lathe of, 17, 26–34

Baddeshill, 135
Bain, Richard, 87
Baker, Captain ———, 230, 233
Baker, Edward L., 266n, 267n
Baker, George, 241, 244, 302
Baker, Henry, alias Hunt(e), 87, 92–3, 94, 98,
  101–2, 105, 291
Baker, Sir Herbert, 270
Baker, Sir Richard, 127
Baker, Samuel, 227, 301
Baker, Samuel, Jnr, 301
Baker, Thomas, 227, 230, 301
Baker & Hurtzig, 251, 252, 253, 254n
Ball, John, 244, 247
Ball, William, 249, 304
Ball and Gammon, 248
Bam, John, 97, 98
Bam, Richard, 98
Bamburgh, John, 95, 98
Banks, Caleb, 177, 297
Banks, Sir John, 177, 296
Barbour, John, 52
Barden, Percy Albert, 308
Barham, Nicholas, 112, 126, 127, 129, 135,
  137–8, 139, 292
Barham Court, 138, 158
Barker, William, 291
Barlow, Sir Robert, 210–11

Barming, East and West, 29
Barnham family, 135, 137
Barnham, Alice, wife of Robert Honywood, 137
Barnham, Sir Francis, 137, 140, 141, 158, 294
Barnham, Sir Martin, 137, 293
Barnham, Sir Robert, 134, 137, 141, 142, 158, 295
Barnstaple (Devon), bridge, 47, 48, 279
Barrell family, 176
Barrell, Francis (fl. 1678–9), 177, 296
Barrell, Francis (fl. 1691–1724), 177, 297
Barrell, Francis (fl. 1739–60), 298
Barrett, Samuel Tuffnell, 300
Barrow, John (fl. 1831), 225
Barrow, Francis (fl. 1868), 258
Barry, Sir John Wolfe, and Partners, 251
Bartholomew, Leonard, 300
Bartholomew, Phillip, 298
Batchelor, Richard David, 304
Bazalgette, Sir Joseph, 247, 248, 260, 261
Beale, Richard, 141, 159, 296
Bean, Robert Ernest, 308
Beane, William, 135
Bearsted, 135
Beasley, Charles, 199
Beaufitz, John, 57, 93, 291
Beaufort, Henry, Cardinal, Bishop of
    Winchester, 86–7, 88, 93
Becher, Edward, 292
Bedgebury, 136
Bedson, John Warren, 309
beech, used in bridge construction, 9
beetles (pile-driving implements), 154, 188
Beinham, William, 293
Beke, Richard, 72
Bell, John, 226, 227
Bell, Matthew, 302
Belsey, Sir Francis Flint, 247, 303
Benstead, William, 211n
Bensted, Gerald, 306
Bentley, Thomas, 227, 301
Bergavenny, Lords see Neville
Bery, William, 102n
Best family, 167, 176, 289
Best, George, 177, 300
Best, James, 298
Best, Colonel James, 226, 227, 230, 233, 234, 301
Best, Maudistly Gaussen, 303
Best, Mawdistly, 298
Best, Thomas (fl. 1725–36), 298
Best, Thomas (fl. 1746–57), 299
Best, Thomas Fairfax, 234, 301
Bettenham, Stephen, 54, 56
Bettes, ———, 132
Betts, Edward Ladd, 244, 302
Betts, William, 143
Beweley, John, 97

Bicknell, Charles, 213n
Bideford (Devon), bridge, 47, 48, 279
Bikerton, John, 105
Bing, George (fl. 1596–1616), 135–6, 137, 139, 293
Bing, George (fl. 1619–24), 133, 136, 140, 294
Bing (Binge), Robert, 127, 135, 139, 293
Bingham, General George William Powlett, 303
Bingham, Robert Turbeville, 301
Bingle, Stephen, 198
Birch, Louis George T., 308
Birling, 17, 27, 61, 63, 94, 109, 135, 136
Bishop family, 167
Bishop of Rochester's Diocesan Fund for the
    Augmentation of Small Livings, 269
Blackett, Elias, 135
Blackmore, Walter, 306
Blanshard, General T., 244
Bligh family, 177
Bligh, Edward, 2nd Earl of Darnley, 298
Bligh, Edward, 5th Earl of Darnley, 226, 227, 301
Bligh, Esme Ivo, 9th Earl of Darnley, 305
Bligh, Florence, Lady Darnley, 254
Bligh, Ivo Francis Walter, 8th Earl of Darnley, 304
Bligh, Hon. John, 301
Bligh, John, 3rd Earl of Darnley, 299
Bligh, John, 4th Earl of Darnley, 172, 207n, 300
Bligh, John Stuart, 6th Earl of Darnley, 241, 259, 302
boats see bridge boats; ferries
Bocher, John, 116
Boghurst family, 173
Boghurst, Philip (fl. 1771–91), 173, 299
Boghurst, Philip (fl. 1808–21), 300
Boleyn, Geoffrey, 89
Bolle, John, 69
Bonfield see Warrin & Bonfield
Borstal, 17, 51, 63, 151, 269, 277
Boscawen, Evelyn E.T., 7th Viscount Falmouth, 303
Boteler family, 135, 136, 289
Boteler, Sir Oliver, 137, 294
Boteler, Sir Phillip, 297
Boteler, Sir William, 158, 295
Botlesham, William, 111n
'Bottylle', 61
Boughton Malherbe, 123, 135
Boughton Monchelsea, 137
Bourgchier, Thomas, Archbishop of
    Canterbury, 96
Bourne, Henry, 86
Bowles, Charles, 159, 295
Boxley, 61, 62, 72, 151
    Abbey Farm, 273
    abbot of, 52
    Boarley Farm, 273

Street Farm, 273
see also Weavering
Boys, Edward, 227, 301
Brain, Richard Frederick, 306
Brakspear, Harold, 270
Bramley Fall stone, 210, 217, 225
Brassey, Henry Arthur, 303
Brassey, Henry Leonard Campbell, 304
Bregge, John, Jnr, 85
Brenchley, J., 230, 233
Brett, Sir Robert, 294
BRH Coal Exploration Syndicate, 271
Brice, Edward St John, 309
bricks, used in bridge maintenance, 15th-16th
    cent., 69, 124
bridge attorney, office of, 102–3, 105, 113
bridge boats, 62, 68, 69, 104, 124, 153
    income from lease of, 84, 143, 312, 314
Bridge Chamber, 118, 142, 150, 242, 243,
    262–3, 270, 279, Plate 14
Bridge Chapel, 85, 174, Plate 14
    foundation (1393), 49–50, 100, 111
    maintenance (1393–1530), 70, 80, 84, 92,
        111, 313, 315, 317
    suppression (1548), 111–12
    restoration, 262–3, 269–70
    see also chaplains
bridge clerk, office of, 101–2, 105, 122, 135,
    174
Bridges (Brydges), Nicholas, 113, 116
bridgework, Anglo-Saxon period, 14–15, 16,
    21–5; see also Rochester bridgework list
Bristol, bridge, 47, 48, 49
Britannic Oil Storage Co., 271
British Railways Southern Region, 277
Broadnax, Major Thomas, 159, 296
Broke, Thomas, 72, 105
Brokhull (Brockehill), Henry, 135, 150, 292
Bromleigh, 52
Brompton, Chatham, Gillingham, Rochester
    and Strood Waterworks Company, 249
Brooke family, 137; see also Broke
Brooke, Francis, 298
Brooke, Sir George, 9th Lord Cobham, 99,
    110, 112, 113, 115, 117, 120, 136, 137,
    291–2, Plate 5
Brooke, Henry, alias Cobham, 127, 144
Brooke, Henry, 11th Lord Cobham, 136, 137,
    138, 139, 140, 293
Brooke, John, 7th Lord Cobham, 97
Brooke, Joseph (fl. 1738–48), 298
Brooke, Joseph (fl. 1772–91), 300
Brooke, Sir William, 136, 139, 141, 159, 294
Brooke, Sir William, 10th Lord Cobham, 117,
    118–19, 120, 122, 126, 127, 135, 136, 137,
    138, 292, Plate 5
broom faggots, used in bridge maintenance,
    124

Broomy, 31
Brown, Major ———, 157
Brown, Albert George C., 308
Brown, Charles, 299
Brown, Leslie Walter, 310
Brown, William (fl. 1829–31), 301
Brown, William (fl. 1837–43), 302
Browne, William, 226
Brun, Hamon le, 30
Bruyn, Richard, 98
Bruyn, William, 102
Bryant, Jacob George, 227, 230, 233, 301
Brydges see Bridges
Bucke, Peter (fl. 1627–54), 136, 294
Bucke, Sir Peter (fl. 1602–24), 136, 293
Buckmore, 57
Budd(e), John, 66, 104
Budden, Austin Frederick, 304
Buffkyn, Levin, 140, 292
Buildwas (Shropshire), bridge, 218
Bulmer, Martin, 262–3
Burdon, ———, 218
Burgh, Lords see Burrough
Burghersh, Lords, 136
Burghley, Lords see Cecil
Burham, 17, 62, 151, 269
    proposed bridge to Snodland see Snodland
Burham Brick Company, 261
Burrough, William, 2nd Lord Burgh, 293
Burroughs, Silas Mainville, 281
Burroughs Wellcome, 271
Burwell, John, 111, 112, 113, 115
Byer, Nicholas, 144
Byng, George, 6th Viscount Torrington, 227, 301

Cæsterware/Cæstersæte, territory of, 34
Cage, John, 298
Cage, William, 177, 297
caissons, used in bridge building, 184, 185
Calcraft, John, 177, 299
Caldecott, Leslie, 306
Calehill, 103
Cambregg, William, 88
Camden, Marquises see Pratt
Canon, Robert, 100
Canon Frome Estate (Hereford and Worcester),
    273, 280
Canterbury, 72, 89, 118, 135, 226
    archbishops of, 19–20, 57, 87, 90, 95–8,
        100, 109
        in Rochester bridgework list, 17, 19–20,
            21, 30, 31
        see also Arundel; Bourgchier; Chichele;
            Courtenay; Cranmer; Dene; Morton;
            Stafford; Warham
    cathedral (Christ Church)
        dean and chapter, and Rochester Bridge,
            119, 126, 127, 150

Canterbury (*continued*)
  cathedral (Christ Church) (*continued*)
    estates, Anglo-Saxon and Norman,
      19–20, 27, 29
    manuscript of Rochester bridgework list,
      16, 38–9, 367–9
    mayor and aldermen, and Rochester Bridge,
      123, 124, 126, 127
    Quarter Sessions (1561), 121, 123
    St Augustine's Priory, 80
Cardon, John, 291
Carmelite Friars, 93, 95
Carpenter, John, 196n
carpenters, employed on bridge maintenance,
  60, 104–6, 153, 154, 174; *see also* master
  carpenter
carriage *see* transport
Carson's Anti-Corrosion paint, 246
Carter, Francis, 199
Cartere, John, 68
carts *see curtene*; custom of carts
Cartwright, Hugh, 126
cast iron bridges, origins of, 184
Castle Frome (Hereford and Worcester),
  Homend Estate, 273
Cat, Peter, 291
Catelyn (Catlyn), George, 135, 139, 292
Catlett, James, 135
Cecil, Robert, Earl of Salisbury, 119
Cecil, William, Lord Burghley, 119, 121, 126,
  127, 128, 129
cement, used in bridge construction and
  maintenance
  15th cent., 70
  17th–19th cent., hydraulic or
    semi-hydraulic, 185–6
Chalk (Kent), 17, 27, 132, 226, 272
chalk, used in bridge construction and
  maintenance
  (1381–1530), 60, 64–7, 70, 71–2, 79
  (1530–1660), 148, 153
  (1660–1825), 188
Chalker, Gerald, 309
Champeneys, John, 105
Champeneys, Nicholas, 291
Champeneys (Champenays, Chaumpenays),
  William, 52, 57, 70, 94, 105, 291
Champion, Richard, 144
chantries *see* Bridge Chapel
Chantries Act (1547), 111–13
chapel *see* Bridge Chapel
chaplains, of Rochester Bridge Chapel, 50, 51,
  109, 111, 313, 315, 317
  role in bridge administration, 86, 89, 92, 98,
    100–1, 102, 105, 109
  stipends diverted to bridge funds after
    suppression of chapel, 111–13, 129
Charing, 137

Charity Commission, and Rochester Bridge,
  252, 253, 257–71, 278, 281, 283
Charles, Richard, Snr and Jnr, 57
Charlton, John, 299
Chartham, 91
Chatham
  brewing and distilling industry, 167, 176
  Chatham Maritime, 283
  dockyard
    (1660–1825), 163, 166, 170, 172, 184,
      193, 198, 210–11, 212–13, 216, 217,
      225
    (1825–1950), 237, 243
    (1950–1993), 281, 283, 285
  and maintenance and rebuilding of
    Rochester Bridge
    (AD 43–1381), 17, 24, 31
    (1381–1530), 51, 52, 62, 63, 69
    (1660–1825), 177
    (1825–1950), 226, 234, 254; right to
      nominate members of Rochester
      Bridge Trust, 265–7, 289; and use of
      Rochester Bridge Trust funds, 265–7
    (1950–1993), 277
  Medway Tunnel access, 283
  population (1660–1825), 164, 165
  St John's, schools, 269
  Sun Pier, 261, 264
  Sun Tavern, 226
  see also Brompton, Chatham, Gillingham,
    Rochester and Strood Waterworks
    Company; Horsted; London, Chatham
    and Dover Railway Company;
    Maidstone, Rochester and Chatham
    District Waterworks Company
Chatham, hundred of, 31
Chatham Electric Lighting Company, 249
Chatterton *see* Law and Chatterton
Chaumpenays *see* Champeneys
Chechele *see* Chichele
Chertsey, Edmund, 98
Chester, Roman bridge, 5
Chesyldenne, William, 52
Chetham, Richard, alias Reynham, Prior of
  Leeds, 90, 99, 105, 106n, 109, 291
Chetham, William de, 66
Chevening, 137
Cheyne, William, 80
Chichele (Chechele), ———, 88
Chichele, Henry, Archbishop of Canterbury, 96
Chichele (Chechele), Robert, 88, 94, 105
Chiffinch, Thomas (fl. 1717–27), 298
Chiffinch, Thomas (fl. 1739–74), 298
Child, Francis, 299
Childs, John, 154
Chope, Christopher, 284
churches, funded by Rochester Bridge Trust,
  269

Clarabut, Guy Stewart C., 309
Clare, Gilbert de, 37
Clark, Arthur Henry, 308
Clarke, Francis, 297
Clarke (Clerke), Sir Francis, 177, 296
Clarke (Clerke), Henry, 138, 140, 141, 295
Clarke, John, 154
clay, used in bridge maintenance, 15th cent., 68
Clements, Robert, 230, 233
Clerc, William, 52
Clergy Mutual Society, 257
clerk, office of *see* bridge clerk
Clerke *see* Clarke
Cleterowe, Richard, 88
Cliffe, 17, 20, 33, 52, 151
Clifford, John, 46
Clinch, Herbert James, 306
Clyfton, John, 79
coal, supplied for bridge maintenance, 15th cent., 69
Coalbrookdale (Shropshire), bridge, 184, 200, 218
Cobb, Herbert, 267n, 270, 272
Cobham family, 54, 135
Cobham, Lords *see* Brooke
Cobham, Henry *see* Brooke
Cobham, John (fl. 1571), 126, 127
Cobham, Sir John de, 44–7, 49–51, 53–8, 70, 75, 111, 144, 270, Plate 1
Cobham, Ralph de, 53
Cobham, Reginald de, 53, 54, 56
Cobham, Thomas, de Hoo, 291
Cobham, William, 113, 115
Cobham (Kent), 27, 44, 45, 52, 61, 62
    Cobham College, 52, 54n, 112, 138, 151, 266, 267n, 268
    Cobham Hall, 113, 118
Cochrane, A.H., 254n
Cochrane, John, & Sons, 250, 253, 254, 257
Cochrane & Co., 241
Cockamhill, 81
coffer-dams, 8–9, 10, 125, 185, 237, 239, 240, 242
Cokerell, John, 111
Colchester (Essex), 169
Cole, Maurice Huntley, 308
Cole, William, 150
Colepepper (Culpeper) family, 135, 136, 176, 289
Colepepper, Sir Cheyney, 295
Colepepper (Culpeper), Peter, 52
Colepepper (Culpepper), Thomas (fl. 1560s), 122, 124, 128, 134, 149
Colepepper (Colpepper), Sir Thomas (fl. 1599–1600), 293
Colepepper (Culpeper), Sir Thomas (fl. 1631–6), 141, 294
Colepepper, Sir Thomas (fl. 1686–1723), 297

Colepepper, Thomas, Lord (fl. 1661–73), 296
Colepepper, Sir William (fl. 1629–51), 294
Coles, Edward Robert, 258, 303
Collins (Colyn), Revd Martin, 122, 125n
Colyer-Fergusson, Thomas, 304
Combes, William, 93
Comfort, Michael, 301
commissions
    to investigate decay of Rochester Bridge
        first commission (appointed 1561), 119–26
        second commission (appointed 1571), 126–7
        third commission (appointed 1574), 127–9
    to survey and enquire into land in Sherinden and Elmley (1589), 144
Committee of Assistants, establishment of (1737), 173, 196
Commonalty of Rochester Bridge *see* contributory parishes
Company of the Proprietors of the Lower Navigation of the River Medway *see* Medway Lower Navigation Company
Company of the Proprietors of the Navigation of the River Medway *see* Medway Navigation Company
Conservators of the River Medway *see* Medway Conservancy
contributory parishes (Commonalty of Rochester Bridge)
    (1381–1530), 56–9, 92, 93–8, 100
        commonalty established (1399), 53
    (1530–1660), 120–1, 125–6, 127, 128–9, 130
        reorganised under Rochester Bridge Act (1576), 130
    (1660–1825), 173
    (1825–1950), 226–8, 235, 259–60
        abolished under Rochester Bridge Act (1908), 265–7
    see also bridgework; wardens and assistants, election of
Cooke, Gilbert, 88
Cooling, 29, 45
    Cooling Castle, 97, 99, 113
    Cooling Castle Farm, 272
    Marsh Gate Farm, 271, 272
Cooper, Cropley Ashley, 6th Earl of Shaftesbury, 234
Cooper, Kenneth, 309
Cooper, Philip Frederick, 308
Cooper, Robert Harold, 308
Coppinger family, 135
Coppinger, Ralph, 293
Coppinger (Copinger), Thomas, 127, 136, 137, 292
Coppyng, Thomas, 72

Cornwall, John, Lord Fanhope, 86, 87, 88
Cornwallis, Fiennes Stanley Wykeham, 1st
    Lord, 303
Cornwallis, Wykeham Stanley, 2nd Lord, 306
Corps, Martin William J.G., 308
Cory, William, & Sons, 250
Cossington see Cozenton
Coste, John, 72
Cosyngton, John de, 52
Coton, John, 105
'Cotoron', 62
counting house, by medieval bridge, 49
Courtenay, William, Archbishop of Canterbury,
    85
Cowdale, Richard, 113, 115
Cox, Mary Turnbull, 308
Cox, Reginald David, 309
Cox, Stuart James, 308
Cozens, Robert, 135, 153
Cozenton (Cossington), 17, 33n
Craddock, George, 211n
Craig Leith (Lothian), stone from, 210
Cranmer, Thomas, Archbishop of Canterbury,
    111
Cripps family, 167
Cripps, James, 296
Cripps, Thomas, 296
Crispe, James, 296
Croker, J.W., 214n
Cromer, William, 126, 127, 137, 139, 144, 292
Cromp, John, 297
Cropely, John, 296
Crouch, John, 90
Croumer, William, 88
Crown Estates Commissioners, and Medway
    Tunnel, 285
Cubitt, William, 228, 229, 231, 232, 235–44,
    257, Plates 12–13
Culpeper see Colepepper
curtene, 72
Cust(e), John, 92, 291
custom of carts, income from, 15th cent., 84,
    96, 143, 314
Cuthbert, Henry Hobart M., 307
Cutte, Henry, 292
Cuxton, 51, 61, 63, 64, 66, 151, 277
    in Rochester bridgework list, 17, 27
    see also Whorne Place

Dalison (Dalyson) family, 289
Dalison (Dalyson), Maximilian, 296
Dalison (Dalyson), Sir Maximilian, 137, 141,
    294
Dalison, Maximilian D.D., 226, 227, 301
Dalison, Thomas, 297
Dalison, Thomas, Jnr, 298
Dalton, Bert Harker, 306
Dalton, Thomas, 300

Dalyson see Dalison
Damsyll, Sir William, 126
Dance, George, 208, 209
Dane, Thomas de la, 39
Dann, William, 300
Danzig, cereal imports from, 18th cent., 167
Darby, Abraham, 184
Darell, John, 80, 88, 93, 98, 103
Darley, George Vernon C., 307
Darnley, Earls of see Bligh
Dartford, 89, 269
    property of Rochester Bridge
        (1381–1530), 55, 57, 77, 93, 94, 101,
            102; rents, 78, 81, 82, 84
        (1530–1660), 110, 144, 145; rents, 114,
            145, 146
        (1660–1825), 181n
        (1825–1950), Dartford Marshes, 271
        (1950–1993), London Paper Mills site,
            281
Dartmoor Gaol (Devon), 199
Davenport, Alfred Mark, 305
Davis, Sir Arthur Charles, 305–6
Davis, James, 305
Day, David Hermitage, 227, 301
Day, David John, 227, 301
Day, John Hanks, 307
Day, Thomas Hermitage, 302
Day, William, 305
Day, William, Jnr, 307
De La Cour, George Henry, 304
de Michele, Victor, 248, 249, 250
Deal, 156, 168
Dean, Robert, 122, 124
Defoe, Daniel, 163, 166, 167, 170
Delce, property of Rochester Bridge
    (1381–1530), Great Delce, 81; Little Delce,
        63, 78, 79–80, 81, 82, 102
        timber for bridge maintenance from, 62,
            63
    (1530–1660), Little Delce, 114, 119, 145,
        146
    (1660–1825), Little Delce, 173, 181n
    (1825–1950), 261, 270; Great Delce, 272;
        Upper Delce Farm, 272
Dene, Henry, Archbishop of Canterbury, 98,
    109, 291
Denney, abbess of, 71
Denton, 17, 19
Department of the Environment, and second
    carriageway for Rochester Bridge, 279
Department of Trade and Industry, and
    Medway Tunnel, 285
Depyng, John, 79, 101
Despencer, Lords, 136
dinners provided by wardens see entertainments
Ditton, 17, 61, 133
    Ditton Place, 226

Dodmere, Thomas, 44
donations to bridge, medieval *see* alms
Doubleday, Sir Leslie, 307
Douce, Francis Hubble, 301
Douce, Thomas Augustus, 301
Dover, 168
  castle, 156, 158
  St Mary's, manuscripts from, 36
  see also London, Chatham and Dover
    Railway Company
Dowdes, 17, 33n
drainage, sewers carried across Rochester
  Bridge, 249
drawbridges
  medieval, 38, 39, 47, 48, 154–5, 156–8
  18th cent., 197
Drewe, Sir John, 46, 47, 88
Dudlow, John, 226, 227, 234, 301
Duke family, 159
Duke, Edward, 136, 294
Duke, George, 134, 136, 159, 295
Duke, Thomas, 136, 293
Dundas, Robert Saunders, 2nd Viscount
  Melville, 212–13, 214
Dunkald, John, 301
Durobrivae, 3, 12, 34
'Dutch tarras', 185
Dyke family, 176
Dyke, Sir John, 299
Dyke, Sir Thomas (fl. 1748–56), 299
Dyke, Sir Thomas (fl. 1811–27), 300

Eadgifu, Queen, 29
East, Francis Edward, 304
East, place names beginning with, *see under
  second element*
East Kent Railway Company, 241, 258
Eastwell, 117
Eastwick Marsh, 55, 56, 78, 81, 82, 145
Eccles, 17
Edmeades, Henry, 304
Edmeades, Revd William, 301
Edwyne, Wulstan, 36
Eldeham, John, 52, 57
elections of wardens and assistants *see* wardens
  and assistants
electricity
  electric lighting on bridge, 256
  services carried across bridge, 249, 253, 254
Elizabeth I, Queen of England, 118–19, 121,
  122, 127, 128, 129, 144
Elliott, Thomas, 300
Elliott-Cooper, R., 253
Ellis, C., 234
Ellis, Charles, 303
elm, used in bridge construction and
  maintenance
  (AD 43–1381), 9

(1381–1530), 49, 60, 62, 63–4, 71, 93
(1530–1660), 148, 153, 154
(1660–1825), 181, 188, 204 (Fig. 21), 223
Elmley, 45, 54, 55, 144
Elwes, James, 184
English Estates, 283–4, 285
entertainments provided by wardens
  (1530–1660), dinners after meetings and
    elections, 133–4
  (1660–1825), 173
  Audit Dinner, 175–6
Ernulf, Bishop of Rochester, 35
Essell, George, 229, 235
Essex Aero, 272
Estfeld, William, 87
Etkins, Richard, 297
Evans, John Edward, 308
Exeter, bridge, 87
Eyhorne, 27, 29, 151
Eyhorne, hundred of, 31

Fairfax, Robert, 7th Lord, 299
Fairfax, General Thomas, 156–7
fairs *see* Maidstone
Falmouth, Viscounts *see* Boscawen
Fane family, 136, 137, 177, 289
  Earls of Westmorland, 176
Fane, Francis, 1st Earl of Westmorland, 136,
  137, 140, 141, 293
Fane, Sir George, 133, 136, 137, 140, 141, 294
Fane, John, 7th Earl of Westmorland, 173, 298
Fane, John, 10th Earl of Westmorland, 172
Fane, Sir Mildmay, 2nd Earl of Westmorland,
  136, 137, 141, 159, 294
Fane, Thomas (of Lynton), 127, 135, 136, 137,
  138, 139, 140, 144, 292
Fane, Sir Thomas (of Baddeshill), 135, 136,
  137, 292
Fane, Sir Vere, 4th Earl of Westmorland, 296
Fanhope, Lord *see* Cornwall
Farall, Thomas, 135
Farleigh, East and West, 17, 20, 27, 156, 159,
  268
Farr, A.E., Limited, 279
Faunce, Thomas, 299
Faversham, 57, 68, 133, 156, 167, 168; *see also*
  Langdon
Fawkham, 17, 19, 30
Featherby, John Robert, 304
Fellows, William, 193, 196n
Ferour, Roger, 79
ferries
  across Medway
    (AD 43–1381), 35, 39, 40
    (1381–1530), 43, 44, 45, 58, 72, 73, 74,
      77, 85, 314
  across Thames at Tilbury, 54, 73, 114
Fevere, John le, 36

Filmer, Sir Edmund, 302
Filmer, Robert, 309
Filmer, Sir Robert Marcus, 304
Finch family, 177; *see also* Fynche
Finch, Heneage, 298
Finch, Heneage, 4th Earl of Aylesford, 300
Finch, Heneage, 5th Earl of Aylesford, 172, 300
Finch, John, 298
fishing, income from lease of, 15th–16th cent.,
    84, 143, 312, 314
fitzGilbert, Richard, lord of Tonbridge, 29
Fitzhugh, Lord, 89
Fitzjames, Sir James, 135, 292
FitzWalter, Robert, 37
Flemyng, John, 55
Fletcher, Thomas, 299
Flood, Thomas, 296
Fludd family, 135
Fludd, Sir Thomas, 127, 135, 140, 143, 150,
    292
Fogg(e), Sir John, 96, 97
Foord, John Ross, 262
Foord & Son, 240, 243, 244, 245, 246, 262–3
Fortroy, James, 296
Foster, Ronald, 309–10
Foule, John, 113, 115
Fox, Charles, 239
Fox Henderson & Co., 238, 239
France, bridge building, 18th cent., 183
Franke, Nathaniel, 135
Franks, John, 201
Freeman-Mitford, John Thomas, 1st Earl of
    Redesdale, 257
Frenyngham, John de, 52, 55, 56, 57, 67, 77
Frere, John, 30
Frindsbury, 51, 226, 240, 244, 269
    chalk for bridge maintenance from
        (1381–1530), 64, 66–7, 71–2, 79
        (1530–1660), 148, 153
    Medway Tunnel access, 283
    property of Rochester Bridge
        (1381–1530), 55, 62, 63; Walshes, 64,
            66–7, 71–2, 79, 81
        (1660–1825), Quarry Farm, 169
        (1950–1993), Quarry Estate, 280–1
    in Rochester bridgework list, 17, 27
    see also Broomy; Islingham
Fry, Stuart, 309
Fuller, Hugh, 104
Fuller, Maurice, 308
Fynche, Sir Thomas, 120
Fynes, Sir Edward, 126
'Fyssheresford', 62

Gammon *see* Ball and Gammon
gas
    gas lighting on bridge, 225, 255
    services carried across bridge, 249, 254

Gawdy(e), Sir Thomas, 112, 126
Geary, Sir William (fl. 1787–1823), 300
Geary, Sir William (fl. 1832–42), 226, 227, 301
Geboun, John, 88
'Gervayssisforstall', 61
Gesling, Isaac, 144
Geste, Edmund, Bishop of Rochester, 120, 127
Gibbons, Major, 156
Gill, Ernest Albert, 305
Gill, Maurice Owen, 279, 307
Gillingham, 36, 62, 63, 96, 164, 254, 265–7,
    289
    Commodore Hard, 264
    as contributory parish, 51, 151, 226
        in Rochester bridgework list, 17, 24, 29,
            31, 34
    and Medway Tunnel, 283
    see also Brompton, Chatham, Gillingham,
        Rochester and Strood Waterworks
        Company
Gillyngton, John, 87
gins, 60, 63, 68, 69, 125, 188
Gisleardesland, 17, 26
Gladdish, William, 233
Glover, Thomas, 88, 291
Goda, 29
Gode, William, 52
Godet, Thomas, 291
Godfrey, William, 96
Godyng, William, 52
Golding, John (fl. 1730s), 193, 196n
Golding, John (fl. 1832–43), 226, 227, 230, 301
Golding, William, 233, 234, 301
Goldsborough, Robert Haydon, 309
Goldsmid, Sir Henry Joseph D'Avigdor, 307
Goldsmid, Sir Osmond E. D'Avigdor, 305
Gonell, John, 71, 72
Good, ——, 261
Gordon, William, 299
Gorham, John, 198, 199, 200, 203 (Fig. 20)
Goring, George, Lord, 157
Grain, Isle of, 27–9, 31, 96, 163, 269
    property of Rochester Bridge
        (1381–1530), 53–4, 56, 57, 64, 101, 102,
            102n; rents, 56, 57, 77, 78, 81, 82
        (1660–1825), 179, 181, 181n
        (1825–1950), 258, 261, 271
    see also Rose Court
granite, used in bridge construction, 254
Gravesend, 27, 52, 138, 156, 157, 231
grease, supplied for bridge maintenance
    14th cent., 69
    16th cent., 154
'great arch' project, 200, 202, 205–7, 208, 209,
    210, 217–18
Green, Major Allan Wyndham, 308
Greenway, 3
Greenwich Hospital, 193

Gryffyn, John, 113
Gunning, George (fl. 1788–1820), 300
Gunning, George (fl. 1827–8), 301
Gunstone, Benjamin, 119

Hackington-next-Canterbury, 136
Hadersham, John, 88
Hadlow, 17, 52, 268
Haggart, John, 153
Hales family, 135, 289
Hales, Sir Christopher, 99, 110, 291
Hales, Sir Edward (fl. 1609–43), 137, 141,
    158, 294
Hales, Sir Edward (fl. 1661–80), 296
Hales, Sir John, 295
Halling, 3, 61, 62, 68, 136, 151
    proposed bridge from Wouldham to Halling
        (1870s), 259, 260
    in Rochester bridgework list, 17, 34
Halstow, 52; see also Eastwick Marsh; High
    Halstow
Hammond, Edward, 193, 196n
Hammond, Ernest, 267n
Hamon, Thomas, 123
Handyside, Andrew, & Company, 252, 253
Hanway, Thomas, 299
Harlowe, Richard, 135
Harper, Thomas, 120, 135
The Harper at Rochester, 36, 39
Harpley (Norfolk), 46
Harriott, Paul Edward J., 309
Harris, George St Vincent, 5th Lord, 307
'Harry, Sir', 86, 101; see also Bourne, Henry
Hart family, 136
Hart, Anthony Harry, 309
Hart, Frances, wife of Sir Peter Manwood, 136
Hart(e), Sir Percival(l) (fl. 1596–1637), 136,
    140, 293
Hart, Percivall (fl. 1724–38), 298
hassock stone, 72
Hassok, John, 72
Hasted, Edward, 299
Hastings, John, Earl of Pembroke, 45
Hateley-Foot, Benjamin, 299
Hateley-Foot, George T., 300
Haven Street, 17
Hawkesley, ———, 260
Hawkins, Edward, 239
Hawkyns, John, 291
Hawley, Henry, 301
Hawley, Sir Henry, 300
Hay see Mott, Hay and Anderson
Hayward, Sir William Webb, 304
Haywoode, William, 135
HBM Civil Engineering, 285
Head, Sir Francis, 188n, 297
Head, Sir Richard, 296
Head, Wrightson & Co., 252, 253

Hendeman, John, 104
Henderson see Fox, Henderson & Co.
Hendlye (Hendley, Henley), Thomas, 119, 126,
    149, 150, 292
Henhurst, 17
Henry (chaplain), 105
Henry I, King of England, 35, 39
Henry III, King of England, 37
Henry IV, King of England, 54
Henry V, King of England, 87–9, 289
Henry VI, King of England, 68, 80, 89
Henry VII, King of England, 74
Henry VIII, King of England, 74
Hert, Simon, 104
Heryng, Nicholas, 58
Heth, Thomas, 103
Hide (Hyde), Gilbert, 127, 134
High Halstow, 29
Higham, 17, 52, 62, 132, 226
Hinde, George, 299
Hinge, Alfred, 306
Hobbe, Nicholas, 52
Hoby, J.W., 241
Hodges, Thomas Law, 227, 234, 235, 241, 302
Hoke, John, 52
Holand, Ralph, 88
Holbeche, Henry, Bishop of Rochester, 111
Holland, ———, 193, 196
Hollingbourne, 17, 27, 33, 34, 39, 137
Holt, William, 88
Holwood, 62, 63
Homan see Thomas and Homan
Honywood family, 137
Honywood, Sir Robert, 137, 295
Hoo, 52, 57, 62, 72, 151
    estate of the Hoo people (Howare), in
        Rochester bridgework list, 17, 21, 24, 29,
        31, 33
    Hoo Street, 62, 63
    see also Allhallows; Halstow; High
        Halstow; St Mary's Hoo
Hopper(e), John, 72, 73
Horsnaill, Henry, 228
Horsted, 17, 62, 63
Howard, John, & Co., 280
Howe, Sir Geoffrey, 284
Huchon, John, 291
Hughes, John, 238–9
Hulkes, Henry, 235
Hulkes, Thomas William, 235
Hull, Vernon Allan, 310
Humphreys, C.L. Howard, 256
Humphreys, G. Howard, 256
Hunt(e) see Baker, Henry
Hunton, 27
Hurtzig see also Baker & Hurtzig
Hurtzig, A.C., 251, 254n
Husbands, Major, 156

Hutton, Charles, *The Principles of Bridges*,
    183, 184, 190
Hyde *see* Hide
hydraulic cement, 185
Hykkes, Henry, 102–3
Hythe, New, 61, 62

Ifield, 27
Ightham, 27, 30n, 226
indulgences, 14th cent., 85
Institution of Civil Engineers, 183, 253
Inwood, Matthew, 135
Irenmonger, John, 69
ironwork
    used in bridge maintenance, 15th–16th
        cent., 68–9, 71, 124, 154
    see also cast iron
Islingham, 62, 63, 79

James, Demetrius Grevis, 226, 227, 301
James, Edwin, 306
James, John (fl. 1520s), 99, 100, 105
James, John (d. 1746), 193, 196n
James, William, 141, 142, 159, 295
Jellies, Henry, 295
Jenkinson, Robert Banks, 2nd Earl of
    Liverpool, 212, 215
John, King of England, 37
Johnson, William, 105
Jones, General Sir Harry, 244
justices of the peace, and bridge tax (1561),
    121–2, 124
Justus, Bishop of Rochester, 13, 14

Karslake, Sir J.B., 258
Kempe, Thomas (fl. 1598–1600), 293
Kempe, Sir Thomas (fl. 1561–75), 120, 126,
    127
Kempthorn, Thomas, 298
Kemsley, Trevor William, 309
Kent, tax on county (1561), 121–5, 149
Kent County Council
    and Medway Tunnel, 283, 284–5
    and proposed Medway towns bypass, 273
    and proposed reconstruction of Branbridges,
        264–5
    right to nominate members of Rochester
        Bridge Trust, 265–7, 289
Kent Electric Power Company, 249, 253, 254
Kent Fire Office, 257, 261, 262, 264
Kentish ragstone, 9, 201
King, William, 304
kings of England
    in Rochester bridgework list, 17, 19, 20, 31,
        39
    see also individual kings by name
Knatchbull, Sir Edward, 177, 297
Knight, Cyril Sherwin, 307

Knight, John James, 305
Knight, Moreton Thorpe, 279, 306
Knole, 97, 119
Knolles, Sir Robert, 45–7, 50–1, 53, 70, 75,
    80n, 111, 270
Knolles, Thomas, 88
Kotys, John, 70

Labelye, Charles, 184, 196
Lambarde, William
    A Perambulation of Kent, 44, 46, 75
    as bridge warden, 137, 138, 142–3, 150, 292
Lamberd, Richard, 36
Landour, Geoffrey, 103
Lane, John, 88
Langdon, John, Bishop of Rochester, 88
Langdon (Kent), property of Rochester Bridge
    (1381–1530), 54–5, 56, 86, 93, 94, 102, 103
        rents, 77, 78, 81, 82
    (1530–1660), 114, 119, 145, 146, Plate 2
    (1660–1825), 181n
    (1825–1950), 271
Langley, Thomas, Bishop of Durham, 78–9, 84
Larkin, Charles, 301
Larking, Charles Gordon, 307
Lash, Mrs Elizabeth, 235
Lash, John and Alfred, 235
Laurence, William, 303
Law and Chatterton, 261
Lawrence, Frank G., 305
Lawrence, Frank Harold, 307
lead, used in bridge maintenance, 16th cent.,
    124
Lee, Horace Waterton, 309
Lee, Richard (fl. 1601–18), 293
Lee, Richard (fl. 1621–52), 141, 159, 294
Lee, Sir Richard (fl.1470s), 89
Lee, William, 258, 302
Leeds
    Leeds Castle, 135
    priory, 90
        priors of *see* Chetham; St Leger
Legh, Robert, 88
Leith (Lothian), stone from, 210
length of Rochester Bridge
    Roman, 5
    late Anglo-Saxon, 21–2
    medieval, 48
Lenham, 151
Lennard family, 135, 137
Lennard, Edward, 295
Lennard, Elizabeth, wife of Francis Barnham,
    137
Lennard, Sampson, 137, 139, 140, 293–4
Lenne, William, 88
Leofwine, Earl, 29
Lerow, William, 193, 196n
Leveson family, 135, 136

Leveson, Sir John, 136, 138, 139, 140, 293
Leveson, Richard, 294
Lewis, David Baxter, 213n
Lewis, Michael, 308
Lewyn (Lewin), William, 138, 139, 140, 144, 150, 293
Leybourne, 17, 133
Leyburn, Roger, 37
Leysdown, 80, 103
    Nutts Farm, 179
Lichebundesland, 17
Lidsing, 29
lime
    income from sale of, 15th cent., 85
    limekiln, property of Rochester Bridge, 78, 81, 82
    used in bridge maintenance, 15th–16th cent., 69, 124, 154
Linton, 17, 30n, 33n
Liverpool, Earls of *see* Jenkinson
Lock, John, 302
Lock, Michael, 234, 302
Lomas, William, 227, 301
Lomb, Ralf, 36
London
    Baynard Castle, 69
    Billingsgate, 70
    Blackfriars Bridge, 185
    Drapers' Company, 93
    inn signs painted at, 70
    London Bridge
        Roman, 5
        medieval, 44, 46, 47, 48, 49, 68, 125
        18th–19th cent., 188, 218
        officers give advice about Rochester Bridge, 117, 120, 124, 135, 184, 188, 193
    money raised for Rochester Bridge, (1381–1530), 72, 85, 86, 87, 88, 89
    port of, docks and warehouse buildings, 199
    property of Rochester Bridge
        (1381–1530), 78, 79, 81, 82, 93, 94, 100, 102, 105; Cornhill, 54, 77
        (1530–1660), 113, 114, 143, 146
        (1825–1950), 260, 262; Leadenhall Street, 262, 268, 271, 272
    office of rent collector, 102, 105, 113
    Rochester Bridge administration, (1381–1530), 102–3, 105
    Rochester Bridge business transacted in, (1381–1530), 93, 94, 96, 97, 101, 103, 105
    St Paul's Cross, 85
    Southwark Bridge, 218
    Tower of London, 69, 143
    as trading centre
        (1381–1530), 69–70

(1660–1825), 164, 167, 168–70
Westminster
    bridge attorneys at, 103, 105
    Westminster Bridge, 184, 185, 196
London, Chatham and Dover Railway Company, 247–8, 256
London Paper Mills, 281
Longley, John, 299
Longley, John, Jnr, 300
Looke, John, 291
Loose, 17, 33n, 72
Lote, Stephen, 70
Lovelace family, 135
Lovelace, Richard, 158
Lovelace, Thomas, 135, 292
Lovelace, Sir William, 119, 120, 122, 123, 125, 126, 127, 129, 135, 138, 139, 292
'Lowyneshole/Lowynyshole/Lowynshole', 62, 68
Lucas, Ald., 226, 227
Luddesdown, 17
Lullingstone, 136
Lynton, 135

M2 motorway, 273, 277
MacInnes, Douglas McColl, 309
McIntosh, Hugh, 217
Mackie, Duncan, 267n
magistrates *see* justices of the peace
Maidstone
    battle of (1648), 156, 157
    bridge, 258–9, 260–1, 268
    fairs, 61, 63, 93, 94
    gaol, 199
    Girls Grammar School, 262
    Maidstone Grammar School, 262
    and maintenance and rebuilding of Rochester Bridge
        (AD 43–1381), 17, 19, 31, 33
        (1381–1530), 68, 72, 87, 93, 94, 96, 97, 101
        (1530–1660), 121, 127, 133
        (1660–1825): bridge loan (1798–9), 206, 207
        (1825–1950), 226, 234, 254, 260; new bridge (1850s), 233, 234, 239, 242; right to nominate members of Rochester Bridge Trust, 265–7, 289; and use of Rochester Bridge Trust funds, 258–9, 265–7
    Mote Park, 199
    population (1676 and 1801), 164
    Star Inn, 226
    trade and economic prosperity, (1660–1825), 163, 166, 167, 170
Maidstone, Rochester and Chatham District Waterworks Company, 249
Makenade, William, 53, 54, 55, 56, 57, 67

Malling, East and West, 61, 97, 126, 133, 135, 226
  in Rochester bridgework list, 17, 19, 30n
Man, John, 85
Manclark, William, 303
Manley, Richard, 296
Manley, Thomas, 296
Manwood family, 136
Manwood, Sir Peter, 136, 139, 140, 293
Manwood, Sir Roger, 112–14, 118, 119, 126, 127–9, 130, 136, 138, 139, 142, 144, 145, 292
Marchall, John, 105
Marchall, Simon, 105
Marchaunt, John, 93, 291
Margaret, H.R.H. Princess, Countess of Snowdon, 279
Marsh, Ann Deborah, 310
Marsh, John, 193n, 298
Marsham family, 177, 289
Marsham, Charles, 3rd Baron Romney and 1st Earl of Romney, 199, 206, 299
Marsham, Charles, 2nd Earl of Romney, 172, 212–13, 214, 215, 300
Marsham, Charles, 3rd Earl of Romney, 234, 235, 241, 302
Marsham, George, 267, 303
Marsham, Sir John (fl. 1637–85), 134, 142, 158, 177, 295
Marsham, Sir John (fl. 1679–91), 296
Marsham, Sir Robert, 297
Marsham, Robert, 1st Lord Romney, 297
Marsham, Robert, 2nd Lord Romney, 298
Martin, Sir Byam, 212
Martin, Charles Wykeham see Wykeham-Martin
Martin, F.C., 258
Martyn, John, 86, 88
Mary I, Queen of England, 115
Mason, Thomas George, 309
masons, employed on bridge maintenance
  (1381–1530), 60, 105
  (1530–1660), 148, 153
  (1660–1825), 174
master of boats, office of, 104, 105
master carpenter, office of, 113, 135, 147
master of the store house, office of, 104, 105
master of the works (surveyor and paymaster), office of, 99–100, 105
Masters and Sons, 239
Matlock (Derbyshire), stone from, 210
Matthews, Frederick Charles A., 306
May, John, 102n
Maydeston (Mayston), William, 86, 88
Medway, river
  schemes to extend navigation, (1660–1825), 166–7
  and site of Rochester Bridge, 3, 4 (Fig. 1)

trade and navigation of Medway valley, (1660–1825), 163–71
transport of materials for bridge maintenance
  (AD 43–1381), 25
  (1381–1530), 61–2, 64, 67, 68
Medway Conservancy, 264, 266–7, 289
Medway Lower Navigation Company, 166–7, 233, 247, 261, 264, 266–7, 289
Medway Navigation Company, 166–7, 207, 240
Medway Ports Authority, 289
Medway Towns Northern Relief Road, 281
Medway Tunnel, 281–5, 282 (Fig. 24)
Medway Tunnel Act (1990), 283–4, 285
Medway Upper Navigation Company, 267, 268
Meller, John, 155
Mellish, George, 258
Melville, Viscounts see Dundas
Menai Straits, bridge across, 218
Meopham, 17, 20, 29n, 226
Mercer, John, 226, 227, 234, 241, 301
Mereworth, 17, 136, 176, 226
Metropolitan Life Office, 259
Meux, Sir Henry, 235
Michell, John, 88
Middilton, William, 89
Mildmay, Sir Walter, 127
Milgate, 135
Miller, John, 301
Miller, Sir Nicholas, 295
Millhall, 61, 63
mills see Northfleet
Milner, Charles, 300
Milton, 17, 27, 132, 168, 234
Ministry of Defence, and Medway Tunnel, 283, 284, 285
Ministry of Transport, and second carriageway for Rochester Bridge, 277–9
Minor, Robert, 297
minster-churches, 33
Mokkyng, John, 88
Monckton, Herbert, 265, 304
Mone, Guy, Bishop of St David's, 86
Mongeham, Edward, 102
Monkdown Wood, 62
Monkwearmouth (Tyne and Wear), Wear bridge, 218
Montfort, Simon de, 37
Montgomery, John, 193, 196n
Moore, Edward, 309
Moore, William, 302
Morgan, Courtenay, 3rd Baron and 1st Viscount Tredegar, 271
Morman, Clive John, 309
Morton, John, Cardinal, Archbishop of Canterbury, 73, 74, 75, 90, 98, 109
Mot, William, 30
Mott, William Edward, 271
Mott, Basil, 255

Mott, Hay and Anderson, 256
Moyle, Sir Thomas, 99, 110, 112, 113, 115, 117, 119, 120, 292
Multon, George, 137
Mylne, Robert, 208, 209
Mylne, W.C., 219, 223
Mymmes, William, 77

nails, used in bridge maintenance, 15th–16th cent., 69, 71, 154
Nashenden, property of Rochester Bridge (1381–1530), 55, 56, 57, 61
  rents, 78, 81, 82
  timber for bridge maintenance from, 62, 63
  (1530–1660), 114, 143, 145, 146
  (1660–1825), 181n
    woods under direct management, 181, 197
  (1825–1950), 258, 261, 271
National Telephone Company, 249
Neate, Percy John, 304
Nethersole, John, 103
Nettlestead, 17, 268
Neubold, Sir William, 78, 89, 101, 102
Neve, William, 100, 105
Neville family, 136, 137
Neville, Dorothy, wife of 10th Lord Cobham, 119, 136, 137
Nevill(e), Edward, 139, 293
Neville, Sir George, 5th Lord Bergavenny, 99, 105, 109, 119, 136, 137, 291
Neville, Henry, 6th Lord Abergavenny, 119, 126, 127, 129, 135, 136, 137, 142, 292
New Hythe, 61, 62
New Zealand Shipping Co., 271
Newcastle upon Tyne, bridge, 5, 47, 48, 183
Newman, George, 159, 295
Newman, Thomas, 179
Newman, William, 307
Newson-Smith, Sir Frank, 272
Newton, Frances, wife of 10th Lord Cobham, 119
Newton, H.E., 250n
Newton, William, History and Antiquities of Maidstone, 170
Nicholson, William Henry, 230, 233, 303
Nightingale, John, 230, 233, 240
Nightingale of Cromarty, Michael David, 285, 309
North Kent Railway Company, 231, 232–3, 241
Northfleet, 17, 19, 20, 29, 33, 132, 151, 186, 226
  mill, 78, 80, 81, 82, 93, 94
Norton, Stephen, 52
Nottidge, Sir William Rolfe, 306
Nurstead, 29
Nycolls, John, 120

oak, used in bridge construction and maintenance, 9, 10, 24, 25, 63, 154
Oakleigh, 17
Oare, Romacres, 61
O'Brien, Henry, Lord, 296
Odo, Bishop of Bayeux, 29
Offham, 17, 133
Olyver, William, 88
Oswald, Arthur Lambert, 305
Otterbury, John, 75
Overhill, 17, 33n
overseer of workmen, office of, 174, 196
Oxenheath, 226
Oxford
  Exeter College, 86
  university, 86

Paddlesworth, 18
Page, John (fl. 1742–3), 298
Page, John (fl. 1746–68), 299
Page, William, 293
Pagett, George Wickham, 307
Pagitt, Marian, 138
Pagitt (Pagett), Thomas, 138, 293
Paine, William, 305
Painter see Paynter
Palladio, Andrea, 184
Palmer, Sir Roundell, 258
Palmer, Sir Thomas, 177, 297
pardon money see alms and pardons
Paris, Roman bridge, 13
Parker, J., 237n
Parker, James, 186
Parker, John, 138, 141, 159, 295
Parkinson, Cecil, 284
Parliament, wardens and assistants in, (1530–1660), 138–42
Parry, William, 299
Pasley, General Sir Charles, 244
Pawlett, Giles, Lord, 144
Pawlett, William, 1st Marquis of Winchester, 75, 121
paymaster, office of, 113, 134, 135, 174; see also surveyor and paymaster
Paynter (Painter) family, 135
Paynter, Allington, 296
Paynter (Painter), William (fl. 1560–85), 292
Paynter, William (fl. 1641–52), 295
Pearce, Sir Idris, 310
Pearce, Thomas, 298
Pearson, S., & Son, 252, 253
Peckham (Pekham), James, 52, 55, 57, 67
Peckham, Reginald, 295
Peckham (Kent), East and West, 17, 20
  Branbridges, 264–5
Pemberton, Robin Leigh, 285
Pembroke, Earls of see Hastings
Penne, John, 88

Pennestone, Thomas, 293
Penshurst, 166
Peron, Thomas, 111
Pett's Court, 137
Phillips, Ivor John, 308
Philpott, John, 134
pier-territories *see* bridgework
Pilcher, Edward, 300
pile-drivers and piling engines, 188, 189 (Fig.
    15), 205, 209, Plate 10; *see also* beetles; gins
pile shoes, iron, 68, 154
Pilgrims' Way, 3
Pinden, 17, 19, 30
pitch, supplied for bridge maintenance
    15th cent., 69, 70
    16th cent., 124
Polhill family, 176
Polhill, David, 177, 297
Pollock, Sir David, 260
Porte, William, 87
Porter *see* Aveling & Porter
Portillo, Michael, 284
Portland (Dorset), stone from, 201, 209
Portlowe, John, 69
Potts, Dr, patent process, 237
Potyn, Alice, 54–5, 84
Potyn, Nicholas, 54–5, 56, 67
Poynder, Thomas, 226, 301
Pratt, John Charles, 4th Marquis Camden, 267n
Pratt, Rupert, 307
Presnail, James, 307
Preston (in Aylesford), 61
Preston (near Faversham), 57
Price, Arthur Stanley, 307
Price, John, 193, 194–5 (Fig. 18), 196n
Price Willis and Reeves, 253
Priestman, Gordon John, 309
Purbeck (Dorset), stone from, 201
purveyor, office of, 122, 134
Purveyour, Richard, 44
Pympe, Reginald, 52
Pympe, Thomas, 291

ragstone, used in bridge construction and
    maintenance, 9, 49, 67–8, 70, 72, 201
railways
    and proposals for new bridge (1840s),
        231–5, 240
    railway bridges at Rochester
        East Kent Railway Company, 241
        London, Chatham and Dover Railway
            Company, 247–8; converted to road
            bridge, 256, 277–9
Rainham, 70
Rainham Mark, 277
ram, used to repair staddles, 60, 68, 69
Randall, Alexander, 303
Randall, William Edward R., 306

Rapley, Thomas, 197
receiver, office of, 100, 105, 113, 122, 134,
    135, 174
Reculver, Hoath chapel, 91
Redesdale, Earls of *see* Freeman-Mitford
Reed, Albert, 281
Reed International, 281
Reeves *see* Price Willis and Reeves
Remsey, ———, 112
Rendel, James Meadows, 229, 239
Rennie, George, 219, 223
Rennie, John, 184, 199, 210–11, 212, 213–17,
    224, 225
rent collector in London, office of, 102, 105,
    113
resin (rosin), used in bridge maintenance,
    15th–16th cent., 69, 73, 124
Reynham, Richard *see* Chetham
Reynold(s), Robert, 101, 291
Rhodes, Edwin Henry H., 308
Richard II, King of England, 46, 53, 54, 61, 67,
    77, 85
Richardson, George, 111
Richers, John, 293
Richmond, Archdeacon of, 87
Rickhill, Sir William, 46, 53, 56, 57, 67
Riddell, Sir Walter, 231, 233
Rider, Thomas, 227, 230, 233, 234, 301
Rider, Sir Thomas, 300
Ridley, 57
Ring, Alexander, 241
Roberts, William Lee Henry, 305
Robinson, Arthur Geoffrey, 309
Robson, John, 249, 250, 251–3, 254n, 255,
    256n, 267n
Rochester
    bishops of, 13, 96, 269
        estates, Anglo-Saxon, 18, 19, 20, 31
        in Rochester bridgework list, 17, 18, 19,
            21, 30, 31
        see also Ernulf; Geste; Holbeche; Justus;
            Langdon; Yong
    Boley Hill, Satis House, 118
    bridge *see* Rochester Bridge
    Bull Inn, 233
    castle, 37, 44, 130, 131, 155
    Castle Hill, 226, 228, 234
    cathedral and priory, and maintenance and
        rebuilding of Rochester Bridge
        (AD 43–1381), 13, 16, 35, 39; *see also*
            Textus Roffensis
        (1381–1530), 52, 70
        (1530–1660), 122, 126, 127, 138, 150
        (1825–1950): use of Rochester Bridge
            Trust funds, 262, 269
    in Civil War, 156, 159
    Corn Exchange, 242, 254, 279
    Durobrivae, 3, 12, 34

Eastgate House, 136
Easton House, wharf near, 228
esplanade, 242, 243, 244, 254
Girls Grammar School, 262
market, 234
mayor and aldermen, and maintenance and
    rebuilding of Rochester Bridge
    (1530–1660), 120, 123, 124, 126, 127
    (1660–1825), 207
    (1825–1950), 254, 259; and new bridge
    (1850s), 233–4, 242; right to
    nominate members of Rochester
    Bridge Trust, 265–7, 289; and use of
    Rochester Bridge Trust funds, 244–5,
    259, 265–7
and Medway Tunnel, 283
Old Custom House, 238
omitted from Rochester bridgework list, 31,
    33
Pavement Commissioners, 233, 246, 260, 261
pier (constructed 1880), 261
population (1660–1825), 164, 165
port (1660–1825), 167, 168, 169
property of Rochester Bridge
    (1381–1530), 55, 56, 64, 77–9, 81, 82,
    84, 104; the Copped Hall, 81; Crown
    Inn, 69–70, 74, 77–9, 82; the
    Fleur-de-lis, 81; the Horseshoe, 81;
    marsh adjoining the Boley, 56, 92; the
    Pewterpot, 77; the Star, 55
    (1530–1660), 146; Crown Inn, 114, 118,
    130, 145, 146
    (1660–1825), 181n, Plate 8
    (1825–1950), 271, 272; Castle
    Chambers, 273; Crown Inn, 262;
    Guildhall, 258
    see also Delce; Nashenden
'Queens Arms', 262
railway bridges, 231–5, 241, 247–8, 251
    disused railway bridge used as basis for
    second carriageway of Rochester
    Bridge, 256, 277–9
Richard Watts Charity, 138
St Margaret's parish, 52; see also Delce;
    Nashenden
Satis House, 118
Sir Joseph Williamson's Mathematical
    School, 262, 272
timber for bridge maintenance from, 15th
    cent., 63
town quay, 163, 167, 245
urinal at end of bridge (1860s), 245
wardens often from (1660–1825), 176–7
Watch Committee, 253
see also Brompton, Chatham, Gillingham,
    Rochester and Strood Waterworks
    Company; Maidstone, Rochester and
    Chatham District Waterworks Company

Rochester Bridge
(AD 43–1381)
    by period
    origins, 3–11; Roman bridge, 3–11, 22,
        25, 43, 67
    sub-Roman and early Anglo-Saxon
        periods, 12–15; maintenance, 12–15
    later Anglo-Saxon period, 16–20;
        maintenance, 16–25; reconstruction
        of bridge, 21–5; territory of bridge,
        26–34
    (1066–1380s), 35–40; maintenance, 38–40
(1381–1530)
    accounts, 46, 312–15
    administration, 92–106
    building of new bridge (1383–91), 43–59
    finance and bridge estates, 51–6, 70,
        76–91
    maintenance and rebuilding, 50–9, 60–75
(1530–1660)
    accounts, 142; expenditure on bridge
        works and estate maintenance, 352–4;
        income and expenditure, 316–23;
        rental income from estates, 342–4
    by period
    (1530–61), 109–17; administration,
        109–13; finance and bridge estates,
        113–17; maintenance and rebuilding,
        115, 117
    (1561–76), 118–29; administration, 122,
        125–9; Elizabethan commissions,
        118–29; finance and bridge estates,
        120–5, 126, 127–9; maintenance and
        rebuilding, 119–26
    (1576–1640s), 130–55; administration,
        130–43; Elizabethan statutes, 130–55;
        finance and bridge estates, 130, 142,
        143–52; maintenance and rebuilding,
        149, 152–5
Civil War and Commonwealth, 156–9
(1660–1825)
    accounts, 177, 178; expenditure on
        bridge works and estate maintenance,
        354–9; income and expenditure,
        322–33; rental income from estates,
        344–8
    administration, 172–82
    finance and bridge estates, 173, 175,
        177–82
    maintenance, repairs and projects,
        183–219; 'great arch' project, 200,
        202, 205–7, 208, 209, 210, 217–18;
        new bridge proposed, 198, 210–17;
        new bridge wharf (1672–5), 175–6,
        178, 187–8, 192; widening, 166, 181,
        198, 199, 200, 202, 203 (Fig. 20), 205
    trade and navigation of Medway valley,
        163–71

Rochester Bridge (*continued*)
(1825–1950)
    accounts: expenditure on bridge works
        and estate maintenance, 359–61;
        income and expenditure, 334–41;
        rental income from estates, 348–51
    finance and bridge estates, 228–9,
        257–73
    new bridge: planning, 223–36; building,
        237–45; opening (1856), 242;
        maintenance and modifications,
        246–56; swing bridge, 233, 234, 235,
        237, 240–1, 247–8, 252, 254, 255
    old bridge: maintenance, 223–4, 235–6;
        removal, 242–4, Plate 13
(1950–93), 277–85
    finance and bridge estates, 279–81
    Medway Tunnel, 281–5
    second carriageway constructed on
        foundations of disused railway bridge
        (1970), 277–9
    see also Bridge Chamber; Bridge Chapel
Rochester Bridge Act (1576), 130–1, 135, 143,
    150, 289
Rochester Bridge Act (1585), 130–2, 133,
    150–1
Rochester Bridge Act (1846), 234–5
Rochester Bridge Act (1876), 131, 259–60
Rochester Bridge Act (1908), 131, 251, 265–7,
    289
Rochester Bridge Act (1965), 278
Rochester Bridge Amendment Act (1853), 240
Rochester Bridge Bill (1801–2), 172, 207–8
Rochester Bridge Estates Bill (1868), 257–8
Rochester Bridge Trust *see* wardens and
    assistants
Rochester bridgework list, 16–20, 35, 38–9, 50,
    362–9
    and reconstruction of late Anglo-Saxon
        bridge, 21–5
    and territory of late Anglo-Saxon bridge,
        26–34
Rochester Gas Company, 225, 254
Rochester Oyster Fishery, 241
Roger Chaplain, 105
Romacres, 61
'Roman Cement', 186
Romney, Barons and Earls of *see* Marsham
Romney Marsh, 123
Roper, Roger, 69
Roper-Head, James, 300
ropery, used in bridge maintenance, 15th–16th
    cent., 69, 124, 154
Rose, John, 174
Rose Court, manor and farm, 54, 114, 115,
    145, 146, 271, 272, 281
Rosher, Jeremiah, 226, 301
rosin *see* resin

Rowe, Henry, 93, 94, 291
Rowe, John, 98
Rowe, Robert, 46, 55, 58, 70, 92, 98, 101, 291
Rowe, Roger, 72
Rowe Place, 58
royal beasts, on drawbridge, 17th cent., 154–5
Royal Engineers, and destruction of old
    Rochester Bridge, 243–4, Plate 13
Royal Insurance, 271
Roydon, Thomas, 100
Ruck, Frederick W., 263
Rudstone, Robert, 119, 123, 126
Russe, Isabel, 88
Ryarsh, 27
Ryxton, Richard, 94

Sackville, Sir Richard, 117n, 119, 121–2, 123,
    125n, 126, 127
St Augustine, lathe of, 123, 124, 149
St Helen's Estates, 271
St Leger (Sentleger), Arthur, Prior of Leeds,
    109
St Leger (Seintleger), Sir Warham, 119, 135,
    136, 137, 292
St Mary's Hoo, 150
Salisbury, Earls of *see* Cecil
sand, used in bridge maintenance, 15th cent., 68
Sandgate, castle, 156
Sandham, Colonel, 243–4
Sandown, castle, 156
Sandwich, 88, 138, 156, 167, 168
Sandys, Sir Thomas, 144
Saunder (Saundre), William, 87, 92, 105, 291
Saunders family, 167
Savage, John, 302
sawmill, built under 5th arch of bridge (1704),
    188
sawyers, employed on bridge maintenance,
    (1530–1660), 148, 153
Scadbury, 135, 136
schools, funded by Rochester Bridge Trust,
    262, 268–9
Scott, Sir John, 140, 294
seals, of Wardens and Commonalty of
    Rochester Bridge, 53, 142
Seathe, Robert, 149
Sedley family, 135
Sedley, Sir Charles, 296
Sedley, John (fl. 1500), 103
Sedley, Sir John (fl. 1619–30), 294
Sedley, Sir John (fl. 1642–8), 159, 295
Sedley, Sir William, 295
Seintleger *see* St Leger
Selby, Sir Henry, 297
Semple, Frank Burdett, 307
Sentleger *see* St Leger
Seprawns, Sir William, 87
Sergant, John, 88

Sevenoaks, 93, 94
Sevenoke, William, 69, 86, 93–5, 105
sewers, carried across Rochester Bridge, 249
Shadworthe, John, 88
Shaftesbury, Earls of see Cooper
Sharnden, manor of, 54, 55
Sharp, Hugh, 102
Shaw, John Christopher, 310
Sheepwash, Richard, 305
Sheerness, 68, 163, 166
Shefeld, Robert, 91
Sheppey, Isle of, 144
    Lidlez, 78, 80, 81, 82
    see also Elmley; Leysdown; Tunstall
Sherinden, manor of, 144
Sherland, William, 135
Shipbourne, 27
Shippick, Sidney John, 306
Shorne, 27, 52, 57
Short, Richard, 99, 100
Short Bros., 272
Shropshire, John, 85
Siburn, John and Benjamin, 181n
Sidden, Samuel, 235, 240, 241
Sidley, Sir William, 293
Sissinghurst, 127
Sittingbourne, 116, 156
Skelton, Richard, 113, 115
Skinner, Augustin(e), 141, 159, 295
Skipper, Charlie Henry R., 307
Skynnere, John, 80
Slater, Thomas, 166
Sloane, Charles, 174, 193–6
Smeaton, John, 183
Smirke, Sir Robert, 215n, 219, 223, 224–5, 228, 229
Smith, Frederick F., 304
Smith, George, 212, 300
Smith, Henry, 235
Smith, John, 69
Smith, John William, 227, 301
Smith (Smyth), Richard, 72, 86, 92, 96, 291
Smith, Samuel Lee, 304
Smith, Thomas, 69
Smith, William, 226, 227
Smith, William Masters, 234, 235, 241, 302
Smith-Masters, William Allan, 303
Snayth, William and Charles, 80
Snodland, 17, 19, 61, 62, 93, 94, 226
    proposed bridge from Snodland to Burham (1870s/80s), 259, 260, 261, 264
Soane, Sir John, 199
Society of Engineers, 183
Somer (Sommer), John, 150, 292
Somer, Richard, 297
Somer, William, 132, 133, 135
Soneman, John, 97, 101–2, 105, 291

Sorocold, George, 188
Soutere, Robert, 72
South Eastern Railway Company, 231, 232–3, 235, 240, 247, 256
South Sea Company, 178
Southcote, Sir John, 112, 126
Southerden, John, 197
Southern Railway Company, 256
Southerne, Hugh, 135
Southfleet, 17, 30, 133
Southwark, donations for Rochester Bridge from residents of, 86, 88
Southwick, Roger of, 30
Speed, William, 258
Spence, John Alexander, 310
Springfeelde, John, 135
Stacye, John, 111
staddles and starlings, construction and maintenance
    (1381–1530), 48–9, 60, 63, 64, 67, 70, 71, 72
    (1530–1660), 120, 125, 153–4
    (1660–1825), 186, 188, 190–1, 197, 200, 201, 204 (Fig. 21), 205, 206, 207, 209, 218, 223
    (1825–1950), 224, 225, 235
Staff, Norman, 308
Stafford, John, Archbishop of Canterbury, 96
Stanstead, 27
Starkey, Humphrey, 103
starlings see staddles and starlings
Stearne, Henry James, 306–7
Steed, Sir William, 294
Stephens, William, 232n
Stephenson, George R., 231, 232
Stile see also Style
Stile, John, 72
Stile, Sir Thomas, 297
Stockton-on-Tees (Cleveland), Stockton Bridge, 185
Stoke, 17, 31, 51, 133
Stokenbury, 17
Stone, Nicholas, 105
Stone (Kent), 17, 30
stone, used in bridge construction
    Roman bridge, 8–11, 21, 22
    medieval bridge, 48–9
    see also Bramley Fall stone; chalk; Craig Leith; granite; hassock stone; Matlock; Portland; Purbeck; ragstone
stonemasons see masons
Stopyndon, John, 88
Stratford, John Wingfield (fl. 1843–9), 230, 233, 234, 302
Stratford, Hon. John Wingfield (fl. 1811–27), 300
Strood, 30, 36, 58, 105
    Aveling & Porter works, 248

Strood (*continued*)
  and maintenance and rebuilding of
      Rochester Bridge
      (AD 43–1381), 27
      (1381–1530), 52, 57, 62
      (1530–1660), 132
      (1825–1950), 233–4
  Medway embankment, 261
  population (1676 and 1801), 164
  promenade and stone steps, 245
  property of Rochester Bridge, 228, 238, 240
  railways at, 231, 240, 241, 247
  Rochester Oyster Fishery, Strood Exchange,
      241
  Rochester and Strood Pavement
      Commissioners, 233
  St Mary's, schools, 269
  St Mary's Hospital, 38, 44, 58, 71
  St Nicholas parish, 115n
  toll gate, 260–1
  see also Brompton, Chatham, Gillingham,
      Rochester and Strood Waterworks
      Company
Stunt, John, 230, 233, 234, 302
Style *see also* Stile
Style, Albert Frederick, 304
Style, George Montague, 304
Style, Sir Thomas, 141, 142, 159, 295
Sunderland (Tyne and Wear), Wear bridge, 218
surveyor and director of works, office of, 174,
      196
surveyor and paymaster (master of the works),
      office of, 99–100, 105
suspension bridges, 218, 229, 231
Swan, Sir Thomas, 295
Swan, Sir William, 296
Swanage (Dorset), 202
Swanton, 17
Sylewode, 57
Symkins (Symkyns), John, 122, 125n
Symmes, William, 88
Symondes, Richard, 90, 98, 101, 109, 291
Symonson, Philip, 135, 145

Tannere, John, 79
tar, supplied for bridge maintenance, 16th
      cent., 124, 154
Tarmac Construction, 285
tarras ('terrace'), 185–6
Tassell, Robert, 234, 244, 302
Tawning, Albert, 308
tax, on county of Kent, for bridge repairs
      (1561), 121–5, 149
Taylor, Sir Thomas, 297
Teddington, National Physical Laboratory, 278
telephone services, carried across Rochester
      Bridge, 249
Telford, Thomas, 184, 217–19, 223

Temple, Sir Alexander, 294
Teneacre, Thomas, 291
'terrace' *see* tarras
Testewoode (Testwode), Joan, 97, 291
Testewoode (Testwode), William, 96–7, 98,
      291
Teston, 17, 136, 158; *see also* Barham Court
Textus Roffensis, Rochester bridgework list,
      16–20, 35, 50, 362–7
Thames and Medway Canal, 207
Thanet, 168n
Thomas, Gareth William M., 309
Thomas, John Samuel, 308
Thomas and Homan, 263n
Thompson, Charles and Mary, 235
Thorpe, John, 18, 26, 175, 176, 179, 192–3,
      298, Plate 9
Thorpe, William, 291
Throgmerton, John, 87, 88
Thurnham, 133; *see also* Aldington
tide labour
      (1381–1530), 60, 104
      (1660–1825), 197, 217, 218
Tilbury, East (Essex)
  ferry across Thames, 54, 73, 114
  National School, 268
  property of Rochester Bridge
      (1381–1530), 54, 56, 64, 73, 92–3, 94,
          101; rents, 78, 81, 82, 84
      (1530–1660), 144, 145, 146; South Hall
          manor, 114
      (1825–1950), 258, 261, 270–1, 351n
tiles, used in bridge maintenance, 15th cent.,
      69, 70
Tilletson, George, 111
timber, used in bridge construction and
      maintenance
      (AD 43–1381), 8, 9, 10, 21–5, 31, 38, 40
      (1381–1530), 49, 60, 61–4, 67, 70, 71, 72,
          93, 94
      (1530–1660), 120, 124, 125, 148, 153–5
      (1660–1825), 188–92, 204 (Fig. 21), 223
      (1825–1950), 235–6
Todd, Charles George, 308
tolls, for crossing Rochester Bridge
      (AD 43–1381), 35, 39
      (1381–1530), 71, 73
      (1530–1660), 115–17
      (1660–1825), 207–8
Tonbridge, 163, 164, 166
      bridge, 261–2, 268
Topcleve, John, 52, 57
Toppe, John, 105
Torrington, Viscounts *see* Byng
Totesham, John, 52
Tottington, 61
tramway, across Rochester Bridge (1902), 249,
      254

transport
  by land
    (1381–1530), 60, 62, 72
    (1530–1660), 148, 153
  by water
    (AD 43–1381), 25
    (1381–1530), 60, 61–2, 64, 67, 68, 72
    (1660–1825), trade and navigation of
      Medway valley, 163–71
Travers Morgan, 285
Tredegar, Lords see Morgan
Trewe, Richard, 30
Trier (Germany), Roman bridge, 7 (Fig. 3),
    8–9, 10, 13
Trottiscliffe, 17, 33, 52, 97, 133
trug see tug
Tudeley, 136
Tuff, Charles, 305
Tuff, Sir Charles, Jnr, 305
Tufton family, 289
Tufton, Sir John, 296
tug (trug), equipment for transporting heavy
    timber, 15th cent., 62, 68, 69, 72
Tunstall, 80, 144, 158
Turke, John, 100, 112
Turner, Samuel, 235
Twisden (Twysden) family, 176, 289
Twisden, Sir John Papillon, 300
Twisden (Twysden), Roger (fl. 1588–1600), 293
Twisden, Roger (fl. 1674–1701), 296
Twisden, Sir Roger (fl. 1739–64), 298
Twisden, Sir Roger (fl. 1765–79), 299
Twisden, Sir Thomas, 298
Twisden, Sir William, 296
Twisleton, Sir John, 159, 296
Twopenny, Edward, 302
Twopenny (Twopeny), William, 200n, 212,
    213n, 228, 300–1
Twysden see Twisden
Tynte, Edmund, 113, 117, 120, 122
Tyrwhitt-Drake, Sir Hugh Garrard, 306

Underwode, John, 52
United Stone, 254
Upnor, castle, 113, 157
Upper Medway Navigation and Conservancy
    Act (1914), 267

Vansittart, Nicholas, 212
Vaughan, Edmund Ward, 305
Vidgeon, John, 154
Vignoles, Charles, 231, 232
Vincent, Peter Victor, 310

Wainscott bypass, 280
Waite, Peter, 309
Wakely, Richard Mansfield, 306
Walderne, William, 88

Wallis, G.E., & Sons, 255, 256
Walmer, castle, 156
Walshe, John, 64n
Walshes see Frindsbury
Walsingham family, 135, 136–7
Walsingham, Sir Thomas (fl. 1615–30), 135,
    137, 138, 140, 294
Walsingham, Sir Thomas (fl. 1631–59), 135,
    136, 140, 141, 159, 294–5
Walter, William, 298
Wangford, William, 54, 77, 102
Ward, ———, 193, 196
Ward, Philip, 155
wardens and assistants, 289–310
  assistant wardens introduced (1576), 130
  Committee of Assistants established (1737),
    173, 196
  duties and powers
    (1381–1530), 46, 51–2, 53, 57–9, 92–106
    (1530–1660), 128–9, 130, 135
    (1660–1825), 172
  election of
    (AD 43–1381), 289
    (1381–1530), 50, 53, 58–9, 96, 97
    (1530–1660), 125, 130, 131–4, 142, 155,
      289
    (1660–1825), 172, 173
    (1825–1950), 226–8, 227 (Fig. 22), 230
      (Fig. 23), 233–4, 259–60, 265–7, 289
  entertainments provided by, 133–4, 173,
    175–6
  salaries, 14th–16th cent., 313, 315, 317
  seal, 53, 142
  social standing, 98–9, 100, 110–11, 135–9,
    158–9, 176–7
Ware, Samuel, Tracts on Vaults and Bridges,
    183
Warenne, John, Earl of, 37
Wareys, Isabelle, 52, 57
Warham, William, Archbishop of Canterbury,
    75, 91, 109
Warner, John, 75, 90, 91
Warren Wood, 272
Warrin & Bonfield, 202
Warwick, Sir Phillip, 296
Washington, Captain, 237n
water services carried across bridge
    18th cent., 188
    19th cent., 249
Wateringbury, 17, 72, 226, 258, 260
    Bow Bridge, 268
Watling Street, 5
Watney, David, & Co., 271
Watson, Robert, 296
Watton, Thomas, 135, 292
Watts, John, 122, 134
Watts, Richard, 113, 118, 120, 122n, 138
Weavering, 61

Webb, William James, 306
Webber, Major General, 249
Weever, John, 'The Mirror of Martyrs', 90–1
Weir, William, 270
Weldon, Sir Anthony, 159, 294
Weldon, Ralph, 141, 159, 295
Weldon, Walker, 298
Wellcome, Henry Solomon, 281; *see also* Burroughs Wellcome
Wellcome Foundation, 281
Weller, Robert, 298
Weller, William George, 307
West, place names beginning with, *see under second element*
West Bros., 255, 270
Westerham, 17, 30, 31
Westminster *see* London
Westmorland, Earls of *see* Fane
Westwood, Joseph, & Co., 252, 253, 255
Weye, William atte, 104–5
Whatman, James, 302
Whetstead, 52
White, Revd John, 257
White, Meadows, 259
Whitewall Investments, 280
Whittington, Richard, 86, 88
Whitworth, Sir Charles, 299
Whorne Place, 158
Whyman, Herbert Francis, 305
Wickham, Edward, 230, 233, 234
Wigan, Lewis David, 258, 303
Wigmore, John, 86
Wildash, Isaac, 299
Wilkins, Elizabeth, 145, 149
Wilkins, John
    lease of Rose Court manor, 115, 145
    as receiver of revenue, 113, 115, 116, 117, 119, 120, 122–4, 128, 134, 135, 149
Wilkinson, Richard, 295
Williams, Robert, 299
Williamson, Sir Joseph, 177, 297
Willis *see also* Price Willis and Reeves
Willis, Charles, 304
Willoughby, Thomas, 127
Wilmington, 269
Wilson, Henry, 308

Winch, Edward, 303
Winch, George, 303
Winch, Isaac Granville, 306
Winchester, Marquises of *see* Pawlett
winding chamber (winding-house), medieval, 47, 48
Winter, William, 119
Wodd, Alan, 113
Wode, Thomas and Bartholomew, 88
Wolsey (Wolcy), John, 58, 92, 101, 291
Wood, Sir Charles, 235
wood *see* timber; woodlands
Woodcock, Alfred John Andrew, 307
woodlands, timber for bridge construction and maintenance from, 61–3, 72, 93, 181, 197, 257
Woodyear, William, 297
Worcester, 36
Wotton, Nicholas, 119, 120, 122, 123, 125, 126
Wotton, Thomas, 112, 119, 123, 126, 127, 135, 137, 149, 150, 292
Wouldham, 17, 19, 20, 63, 151, 259, 260
Wright, John (fl. 1520s), 99
Wright, John (fl. 1706), 188
Wright, John (fl. 1850s), 238, 242–3, 244, 245, 246, 247n
Wright, Thomas, 183
Wrightson *see* Head, Wrightson & Co.
Wrotham, 52, 133, 135, 151
    in Rochester bridgework list, 17, 19, 20, 27, 33, 34
Wyatt, Henry, 295
Wye, 87, 126
Wykeham-Martin, Charles, 230, 233, 234, 302
Wykeham-Martin, Philip, 259, 303
Wymond, Geoffrey, 88

Yalding, 29, 264, 268
Yates, Paula Gülen, 310
Yevele, Henry, 44, 45, 46
Yong, John, Bishop of Rochester, 150
York
    archbishops of, 87
    Roman bridge, 5
Youngman, George, 304
Yule, General P., 244